Library of
Davidson College

The Politics of Defense Contracting

The Politics of Defense Contracting
THE IRON TRIANGLE

GORDON ADAMS

Transaction Books
New Brunswick (U.S.A.) and London (U.K.)

Charts: Lillian Bogeinsky

Transaction edition 1982

Copyright © 1981 by the Council on Economic Priorities, 84 Fifth Avenue, New York, N.Y. 10011

All rights reserved under International and Pan-American Copyright Conventions. No part of this book may be reproduced or transmitted in any form or by any means, electronic or mechanical, including photocopy, recording, or any information storage and retrieval system, without prior permission in writing from the publisher. All inquiries should be addressed to Transaction Books, Rutgers—The State University, New Brunswick, New Jersey 08903.

ISBN: 0-87855-457-2 (cloth), 0-87871-012-4 (paper)
Printed in the United States of America

TABLE OF CONTENTS

Preface 7
Acknowledgments 13

PART I THE IRON TRIANGLE: CONGRESS, THE PENTAGON AND THE DEFENSE CONTRACTORS

1 The Business of Defense 19
2 Research Methods and Data 31
3 Selling Weapons: A Parable 43

PART II THE WEAPONS BUSINESS—INSTITUTIONS, ROLES AND PEOPLE

4 Officers and Members of the Board 57
5 Financial Institutions and Auditors 65
6 Personnel Transfers 77
7 Research and Development 95

PART III THE INFLUENCE BUSINESS—POLITICS AND POWER

8 Backing the Candidates: Political Action Committees 105
9 Control at the Center: Washington Operations 129
10 Strength in Unity: Trade Associations 155
11 A Voice in Policy-Making: Advisory Committees 165
12 Getting Together: Entertainment 175
13 Moving the Public: Advertising and the Grass Roots 185
14 Greasing the Machinery: Questionable Payments 199

PART IV CONCLUSIONS AND RECOMMENDATIONS

15 Penetrating the Iron Triangle 207

PART V PROFILES

Key 223
Boeing 227
General Dynamics 255
Grumman 281
Lockheed 305
McDonnell Douglas 339
Northrop 367
Rockwell International 393
United Technologies 421

Appendix A 445
Appendix B 451
Bibliography 453

PREFACE

The past decade has seen a significant change in the ability of business to obtain information on Federal policy-making, penetrate the councils of Government and move Congress and the public to support its political agenda. In the past decade, most of the *Fortune* 500 companies have established corporate offices in Washington to gather information, participate in public policy-making, and coordinate the firm's overall Government relations effort. At a stunningly rapid pace, corporations have taken advantage of recent legislation to create Political Action Committees, channelling millions of dollars into campaign contributions to Federal candidates.

The Council's interest in corporate political activity combines a tradition of a decade of research on defense contracting with a realization of the widespread and growing political influence of corporations. For decades contractors have had a special stake in public policy—for some, contract dollars provide the bulk of their total business. Not surprisingly, then, defense contractors have pioneered in the development of Government relations tools and policies. Consequently, this study focuses on the political power of the defense industry. We analyzed in detail individual companies choosing eight that are major defense contractors and significant part of whose sales are with the Department of Defense: Boeing, General Dynamics, Grumman, McDonnell Douglas, Northrop, Rockwell International and United Technologies. These eight companies dominated the top 10 contractor list two-thirds of the time between 1970 and 1979, receiving over $100 billion in DoD contracts, 25 percent of all DoD awards. Nearly $25 billion of this was for research and development—37 percent of the DoD total for R & D.

They also received over $11.4 billion in NASA contracts, 36 percent of the NASA total. Fifty percent of the sales of these companies in the past decade have been principally with these two Federal agencies. Grumman was high, with 82 percent, and Boeing low with 30.8 percent.

We have pulled together information from many areas: board/financial networks, political action committees, personnel transfers, grass-roots activities, lobbying, the Washington office, in order to understand the nature and scope of corporate Government relations practices. The resulting study has led to the following findings:

1. Newly released data shows that five companies in our study (Boeing, General Dynamics, Grumman, Lockheed, Rockwell International) spent a total of $16.8 million during a two-year period in the 1970s to operate their offices in Washington. Rockwell International's Washington office, alone, spent $7 million. This amount includes substantial spending on lobbying and Government relations, much of which is subsidized by the taxpayer. These five contractors charged $15.8 million of this amount to the Department of Defense as part of general and administrative expenses, an amount later slightly reduced as a result of audits conducted by the Defense Contract Audit Agency. All eight companies had registered lobbyists in Washington in the late 1970s—Boeing the most (15) and General Dynamics the fewest (1). In terms of disclosed lobbying expenditures, Northrop's lobbyists reported receiving the most funds for lobbying from 1977-79 ($340,000), followed by Lockheed lobbyists ($158,000). General Dynamics was again low ($1,600).

2. The Political Action Committees of the defense industry, according to the most recent available data (1977-78), are the largest corporate PACs, averaging $81,000 a year in total disbursements and $55,000 in contributions to Federal campaigns. The eight PACs in this study, created between April 1976 and February 1978 had spent over $2 million by summer 1980, 60 percent of it ($1.26 million) in contributions to Federal campaigns. General Dynamics had the largest volume of total PAC spending ($510,000 from July 1977 to August 1980) while Northrop had the lowest ($110,416 from February 1978 to July 1980). Measuring Federal campaign contributions alone, Grumman gave the most—$338,000 by June 1980—and Boeing the least, $86,000 by May 1980.

We also aggregated Federal campaign data for the first time according to contributions to members of key committees and the geographic location of the district. We found that the McDonnell Douglas PAC concentrated the highest proportion of its contributions on key committee members and candidates from areas with company plant locations (79 percent), followed by Lockheed (67 percent), with Boeing the lowest (36 percent).

3. These eight PACs concentrated their contributions in Congress on a small number of committee members most central to their business. In the Senate Armed Services Committee, the leading recipients of contributions from the eight PACs (to summer 1980) were:

Sen. Strom Thurmond (R-SC)	$14,300
Sen. John Tower (R-TX)	$13,175
Sen. John Warner (R-VA)	$11,000
Sen. Sam Nunn (D-GA)	$ 9,100
Sen. Barry Goldwater (R-AZ)	$ 7,800

On the Senate Defense Appropriations Subcommittee the leading recipients were:

Sen. Ernest Hollings (D-SC)	$13,000
Sen Warren Magnuson (R-WA)	$10,200
Sen. Jake Garn (R-UT)	$ 5,500
Sen. Edward Brooke (R-MA)	$ 5,300
Sen. Daniel Inouye (D-HI)	$ 5,100

In the House Armed Services Committee the ranking recipients were:

Rep. Charles Wilson (D-CA)	$12,925
Rep. Jim Lloyd (D-CA)	$11,650
Rep. Mendel Davis (D-SC)	$10,100
Rep. Bob Wilson (R-CA)	$ 9,700
Rep. Richard Ichord (D-MO)	$ 9,925

In the House Defense Appropriations Subcommittee, the ranking recipients were:

Rep. Joseph Addabbo (D-NY)	$10,800
Rep. Robert Giaimo (D-CT)	$ 7,700
Rep. Jack Edwards (D-AL)	$ 7,250
Rep. Bill Chappell (D-FL)	$ 6,400
Rep. Bill Burlison (D-MO)	$ 6,200

4. The eight companies have access to the defense policy process through significant movements of personnel between the Government and the firms. Our review of DoD data showed that 1,942 individuals (uniformed and civilian) moved between DoD/NASA and the eight companies between 1970 and 1979. Of these, 1,672 were hired by the companies, while 270 company employees went to work for DoD and NASA. The highest number of such transfers was with Boeing (398), followed by Northrop (360) and Lockheed (321). Grumman (96) and United Technologies (83) had the fewest transferees. Reviewing civilian transfers in particular, Northrop hired the largest number of civilian employees from DoD (50), while Rockwell had the highest number of civilian transfers to DoD (47). Grumman hired the lowest number of civilians from DoD (5), while United Technologies had the lowest civilian flow to DoD (12). We estimate, on the basis of their own descriptions, that one third of all civilian transfers involved personnel in the crucial area of research and development. Grumman had the highest proportion (41 percent), while General Dynamics had the lowest (28 percent). Based on employees' own descriptions, we estimate that 24 percent of civilian transfers (116) placed personnel in positions which constituted an "appearance of potential conflict of interest." (See Chapter 6 for definition.) While these situations do not constitute wrong-doing and

may have been resolved in ways that eliminate any conflict, the high number suggests a need for more adequate reporting requirements, stricter enforcement of conflict of interest legislation, and new legislation to put greater distance between DoD and the industry.

5. The eight companies in this study play a key role in defining future weapons systems, principally through their access to the early definition of research and development policies and projects. Initial contractor R & D activity is funded by the Federal Government through DoD's Independent Research and Development and Bids and Proposals (IR & D and B & P) programs. The Defense Department spends roughly $1 billion each year on these two programs, which have minimal Congressional supervision.

On the basis of data voluntarily supplied by Grumman, we calculate that 78 percent of company R & D investment between 1973 and 1979 was funded through IR & D and B & P, combined. On the basis of data disclosed by DoD in response to a Freedom of Information Act request, we estimate that at the high end 65 percent of Northrop's R & D investment, between 1973 and 1978, and at the low end, 14.5 percent of United Technologies' was funded through DoD's IR & D program.

6. Grass-roots mobilizations are becoming a crucial element in contractor lobbying. At least two of the companies in the study—Rockwell and Grumman—undertook major grass-roots efforts on behalf of their defense programs in the 1970s. Between 1975 and 1976 Rockwell spent $1.35 million, some of it reimbursed by DoD contracts, on efforts aimed at mobilizing employees, stockholders, communities and mass organizations on behalf of the B-1 bomber. Grumman organized a similar campaign for its F-14 program between 1977 and 1978.

7. Members of company boards of directors can provide a useful informational and Government relations resource, though data on their role is limited. Directors of these eight companies have a large number of ties with financial institutions, many of which lend to the companies. Members of Lockheed's board are also directors of 18 financial institutions; Rockwell has 17 such shared memberships; and Boeing 16; while Northrop (10), and McDonnell Douglas (9) were lowest in such shared memberships. Some major banks are lenders to several companies in the study: Chase Manhattan (5), Citicorp (4), Morgan Guaranty (4), and Security Pacific (4). In addition, 41 percent of the directors of these eight companies are directors of other companies which received nearly $2 billion in 1979 contracts from DoD.

8. All eight companies are prominently represented on the key advisory committees of the Department of Defense and NASA, where, at an early stage, they discuss and help formulate projects in which they have a direct corporate interest. Boeing had the highest membership total on such committees—23—followed by Lockheed—20.

9. Lavish entertainment of Federal officials, once a frequent practice in the defense industry, appears to have declined markedly as a result of stricter measures taken by DoD in the late 1970s.

10. Although with the exception of Northrop there is little evidence of illegal political contributions by these firms in the U.S., all eight admit to some involvement in overseas payments about which questions have been raised (see Chapter 14). In some cases, such payments were linked to military sales. The three companies most involved with overseas sales—Boeing, Lockheed and McDonnell Douglas—also have the highest amounts of such overseas payments.

11. The eight companies in the study all refused to disclose information on their Government relations practices, pleading cost, lack of time, proprietary information, and national security. In response to our request that each company review the preliminary draft of its profile, three companies—General Dynamics, McDonnell Douglas and Rockwell—failed to respond in any way. Northrop and Lockheed replied with hostile and totally uninformative communications. We rate all five very poor on disclosure. Boeing and United Technologies provided a small amount of additional information, rating poor in disclosure. Grumman provided an informative review of the profile, making its fair rating the best in the study.

12. Information on Government relations is hard to come by. The secrecy of the contractors is matched by the inadequacy of Federal record keeping and requirements on disclosure. Data on research and development spending is uneven and uninformative. Data on subcontracting is undisclosed, and lobbying data is thin.

A powerful flow of people and money moves between the defense contractors, the Executive branch (DoD and NASA), and Congress, creating an "iron triangle" on defense policy and procurement that excludes outsiders and alternative perspectives. The concluding chapter of this study discusses ways in which the public might penetrate the triangle, reclaiming its right to a voice in this critical area of national policy.

ACKNOWLEDGMENTS

The author is grateful to many individuals and organizations which made this study possible. Over the years of work, a succession of dedicated research assistants and interns gathered and updated the data on the companies, chasing after and invariably locating the most remote pieces of information. This support army included: Stephen Becker, David Bennett, Nigel Collie, Stephen Coye, Alan Draper, Michael Florio, Lisa Friedman, Dennis Gaffney, Carl Goldfischer, Christine Griffin, Jean Hamerman, Sharon Herb, Mona Hochberg, Harriet Kerwin, Stefanie Lenway, Andrew Mason, Janet Natoli, Richard Reice and Tom Van Buren. We owe a special vote of thanks to the early efforts of Fritzie Cohen and the staff of the Military Audit Project in Washington, D.C., who helped us wend our way through the thickets of some of the data sets in Washington.

Many government officials also helped us locate and understand data and legislation discussed in the study. Although individuals must remain unnamed, we had excellent cooperation and assistance from employees of the Department of Defense, NASA, the Federal Election Commission, the U.S. Congress, the Defense Contract Audit Agency, and the Library of Congress. The New York Public Library, as well as the resources of the New School, New York University and Columbia University were invaluable.

A number of typists worked long hours with difficult material to get through the manuscript: Jennifer Blood, George English, Dudley Giehl and Michele Raymond. Robert Zwed deserves special thanks for a dedicated effort on the company profiles. Miranda Beeson and Camille

Taboldio proofed the often difficult galleys, supplying them to Claude Barilleaux, who pushed them through the production process with speed and good humor.

Several individuals, though they did not read the study itself, provided the support and encouragement the author needed at critical moments. Special, personal thanks go to Jerry Aron, Tom Asher, Kai Bird, Dorothy Elliot, Frank Fischer, Susan Herschkowitz, Kare Hornschuch, Tina Simcich, Tim Smith, Cora Weiss and especially Bernard Rivers.

A large contingent of advisors read the draft text, making many useful comments. The author would like, particularly, to thank Nancy Anderson, Peter Barash, Philip Brenner, Amy Bridges, Edwin Epstein, Mary Gardiner Jones, Michael Locker, Michael Mann, Carol O'Cleireacain and Margaret Simms. Alice Tepper Marlin and David Gold at CEP made particularly helpful comments, while Nancy Sokoloff edited the result with the patience and dedication of a saint. Richard Kurnit deserves special mention for his careful reading of the manuscript.

I am deeply grateful for the donations the Institute for World Order, Mr. and Mrs. Philip Lilienthal, Stewart Mott, the New York Community Trust, and the Samuel Rubin Foundation made to CEP for this project and to the many individuals and foundations which provide CEP with general support.

THE POLITICS OF DEFENSE CONTRACTING

PART I
THE IRON TRIANGLE: CONGRESS, THE PENTAGON, AND THE DEFENSE CONTRACTORS

1
The Business of Defense

The defense budget of the United States, which now accounts for roughly one quarter of all Federal spending, will rise rapidly in the 1980s. Many justifications are offered for its dramatic increase: inflation, the high price of increasingly sophisticated weapons, the rivalry between the military services, and the need for an arms build-up to protect United States interests in an unstable world.[1] Rarely mentioned, however, are the pressures that the defense contracting industry exert on the Government, their chief "customer."

In approaching the Government, contractors take advantage of both their opportunities as members of the "big business" community and their unique role and special access as manufacturers of weapons that guarantee "national security." The benefits to the industry of aggressive "Government relations" practices are great. The cost to the country, however, in an inflated budget and a narrowing of the debate on strategic and foreign policy, is high.

Business as Usual

For over a century, private industry has asserted its power in American politics. "Big business" has both sought Government favors and battled Government efforts to control it.[2] Business leaders constantly warn that Government has become too large and exercises too much influence in the private sector. They castigate regulatory agencies as costly, restricive, and inefficient. But alongside this apparent antagonism another, more cooperative set of relations has developed. During World War I business leaders were brought into the Federal Government as wartime production planners for virtually all sectors of U.S. industry. In the 1920s Secretary of Commerce Herbert Hoover organized permanent advisory commissions to the Department composed of business representatives from different sectors of the economy. President Roosevelt attracted a number of businessmen into Government positions first to combat the Depression and later, in World War II, to plan wartime production. As the war ended, many Government commissions and the new Council on Economic Advisors turned to business for staffing and ideas about post-war economic, foreign and military policy.

Members of regulatory commissions are often drawn from the regulated industry; personnel move steadily between the agency, the industry being regulated and its legal support community.[3] In certain areas, regulation—far from being the whipping boy of the business community—is welcomed. Much is gained by industry through regular Federal involvement in price-setting and entry and exit from the markets.

Since 1946, and especially in the sixties and seventies, America's corporations expanded and developed practices and structures to influence Congressional and Executive policy-makers. A growing number of major companies now have a corporate office responsible for "Government relations." Most of the Fortune 500 companies have offices in Washington whose purpose is to gather information and exert political pressure. Government relations is the art of making connections: between the company's needs, its potential support at the grass roots (workers, communities, stockholders), its campaign spending, the key staff and members of Congress, and officials in agencies in the Executive branch.

At a stunningly rapid pace, companies have taken advantage of the Federal Election Reform Act of 1971, as amended in 1974 and 1976, to establish Political Action Committees to channel their campaign contributions. Increasingly, PACs are being used as the corporate forum for determining a company's Government relations strategy. Corporations in America today are more sophisticated, more thorough and more coherent in developing political strategies than ever before. As *Fortune* noted:

> The business community has become the most effective special interest lobby in the city. Suddenly business seems to possess all the primary instruments of power—the leadership, the strategy, the support troops, the campaign money—and a new will to use them.[4]

According to Philip Shabecoff of *The New York Times Magazine*, "These are the days of wine and roses—of champagne, even, and orchids—for business interests in Washington. . . . Quietly, cautiously, but with growing success, the business community has been moving to influence legislation, administrative decision-making and the regulatory process."[5]

A Special Kind of Business

While the defense industry holds many characteristics in common with other members of the "big business" community, contractors play a unique role in American society. As manufacturers of strategic weapons, they are widely identified as guardians of "national security." The Federal Government not only regulates their activities but serves as one of their best customers. The weapons they manufacture follow the specifications of their Federal client; the procurement process is initiated and sustained by members of both the industry and the Government. This close interdependence has made them pacesetters in developing Government relations practices that safeguard their interests.

This intimacy developed early. Dependence on Government procurement began during World War I; many firms disappeared between the wars when procurement declined. In response, defense industry leaders, the financial community, and Government officials made vigorous efforts in the 1920s to establish national policies—air mail subsidies, Federal regulation, and consistent defense procurement—that would help the industry survive. After World War II, industry pressure and Government decisions led to Federal support for a private defense capacity, in effect subsidizing industry to keep critical personnel in working teams and production facilities open.

The decision to maintain a large, privately-owned defense manufacturing capacity has led to a bewildering variety of Federal procurement policies, many of which foster a high degree of intimacy between the Pentagon and its contractors and inhibit cost control.[6] Contractors expect that the Federal Government will not force them to do business at a loss; they assume that their productive capacity will be maintained and that profit margins will be ensured as their costs are reimbursed. DoD practices perpetuate these expectations: most defense contracts are negotiated rather than competitive. There are, in fact, 17 exceptions to the procurement requirement for competitive bidding and they cover important areas:

—Public exigency
—Supplies or services for which it is impractical to secure competition by formal advertising
—Experimental, developmental, or research work
—Technical equipment requiring standardization and interchangeability of parts
—Technical or specialized supplies requiring substantial initial investment or extended period of preparation for manufacture
—Negotiation after advertising
—Purchases in the interest of national defense or industrial mobilization.[7]

Through frequent contract changes initiated by both sides of the relationship, most DoD contracts turn into cost-plus. In addition to a visible profit, the contractors are the recipients of indirect benefits. Federal procurement policies provide defense contractors with a large amount of rent-free procuction space and equipment,[8] offer interest-free loans for "progress" on work completed by contractors, and rotate contracts among firms to ensure that no major contractor is without a contract for too long a period of time.[9]

Some see this interdependence as a form of Government control. The Department of Defense now maintains a bureaucracy of three million people, one million of whom are civilians, to design, produce, use, and repair weapons. Some critics of the DoD such as Seymour Melman and John Galbraith describe this "military-industrial complex" as a corporation that is dominated by a Government that saddles it with the frustrating task of producing non-commercial goods at high prices, using inefficient methods that reduce profits, sap management capabilities, hinder their commercial effectiveness and drain the productivity of the American economy as a whole.[10]

Analysts of defense spending also note bureaucratic pressures to expand military programs. Like all bureaucracies, the DoD and the services need to justify and perpetuate their existence. Defense budget-making is riddled with tales of bureaucratic policies in which the military have redefined the policy to fit a particular program. The Strategic Air Command (SAC) fought hard to keep manned bombers alive, despite Secretary of Defense Robert MacNamara's effort to kill them in the early 1960s. Without the B-1, SAC had no airborne role, a function that they wanted to maintain. The Navy argued for submarine-based weapons partly because they wished to keep a strategic function under their control.

The interdependence of supplier and purchaser in this highly political market creates special problems. Richard Kaufman, counsel to the Congressional Joint Economic Committee, lists some of them:

> padded costs, the use of government-owned equipment for commercial activities, the cash flow advantages of progress payments, the privilege of making late delivery of products that do not meet original specifications, bail-outs and get-well devices for contractors with cost overruns, executive salaries and fringe benefits and the personal career opportunities for those who oscillate between the Pentagon and the defense industry and who operate within those two powerful publicly-supported institutions.[11]

In spite of—and often because of—inefficiency and red tape, weapons manufacturers have received steady income from doing business with DoD. There is evidence that, contrary to the denial of contractors, profits for defense firms have run higher than the general manufacturing average, when one measures income as a proportion of capital investment rather than of sales.[12] For some aerospace companies a significant proportion of profits, for others corporate survival itself, depends on Federal contracts. Between 1972 and 1976, 36 firms on the DoD top contractors' list received contract awards that totalled over 10 percent of company sales.[13]

Their dependency on Federal procurement places the contractors and their constituents in a special position. As contractors are quick to point out, more than company profits are at stake. The net of defense spreads outwards from the contractor to the labor force and the community. In the absence of alternatives, defense contracting provides careers and jobs for scientists, engineers, technicians and production workers, a group who numbered 1,170,000 in 1980, according to the Aerospace Industries Association.[14] Defense firms are major employers and sources of revenue in the areas where their production facilities are located. Union leaders know that contracts mean strengthened membership for the aerospace divisions of such unions as the United Auto Workers (UAW) and the International Association of Machinists (IAM). Local officials in San Jose, Los Angeles, Seattle, Dallas, Fort Worth, Hartford, Groton, St. Louis, Cincinnati, and Long Island—politicians from heavily defense-dependent states such as California, Connecticut, Missouri, Washington, Texas, Ohio, and New York—all know that there are few real alternatives to the work from defense contracting. To succeed in the weapons business, they must succeed in the "influence business." Accordingly, they have created "Government relations practices," a variety of tools and relationships that has taken them far beyond the classic model of the free enterprise system.

Government Relations

Contractors' Government relations, like those of other corporations, trade in two commodities: information and influence. A contractor seeks information from Congress and the Executive in answer to many questions: what programs are forthcoming and where and how are they being defined; what are Federal procurement plans and regulations going to look like, where do bureaucrats and members of Congress stand on particular systems, when will legislation be considered and what form will it take? The company reworks this information, which flows in vast quantities, to focus on company needs and possibilities. In other words, it becomes intelligence.[15] The need for such intelligence is virtually endless, and contractors' Government relations officers and Washington staff spend a substantial portion of their time talking on the phone, visiting Pentagon and Congressional offices, reading documents, and deciphering information useful to the company. In addition, Government relations specialists play a key role in providing information in the other direction—from the company to the Government—on company plans and needs.

This flow of information facilitates the other principal task of Government relations—the exerting of influence. Corporate officers for Government relations advise their company on how to gain access and manipulate the Government to serve their needs, often recommending changes in policy.[16] They manage the most important direction of communication: that towards the Government, becoming expert at neutralizing opposition in Congress, selling a company plan in the Executive branch, reversing unfavorable decisions and regulations, directing campaign contributions, focusing grass-roots lobbying efforts, and even taking a hand in drafting proposed legislation.

Government relations efforts also aim towards defending the industry and its views on policy from outsiders, critics and alternative perspectives. The industry makes the most of its unique role: as manufacturer of weapons it assumes a major role in defining national and global security. Industry spokesmen guard the terms of debate, challenging the legitimacy of alternative views and scoring participants who are not members of the fraternity. Even unlikely targets face criticism. The top defense planners of the Reagan Administration, until recently considered outsiders, were described by pro-industry spokesmen, columnists Roland Evans and Robert Novak, as follows:

> Casper Weinberger: Weinberger's nearly total ignorance on defense questions... was fully revealed in his Senate confirmation hearings.
>
> Frank Carlucci, Deputy Secretary of Defense: a civil servant with no Defense Department background.
>
> William Howard Taft, III, adviser to Weinberger: a Washington lawyer who knows even less about defense than Weinberger and Carlucci.
>
> Richard Stubbing, adviser to Taft: a Carter administration anti-defense expert at the Office of Management and Budget whose views generally coincide with Sen. George McGovern's.[17]

The Iron Triangle

Over the years the defense industry has become a *de facto* participant in the policy-making process. As in other areas dominated by powerful corporate interests, a policy sub-government or "iron triangle" has emerged.

Political scientists describe an "iron triangle" as a political relationship that brings together three key participants in a clearly delineated area of policy-making: the Federal bureaucracy, the key committees and members of Congress, and the private interest.[18] In defense, the participants are the Defense Department (plus NASA and the nuclear weapons branch of the Department of Energy); the House and Senate Armed Services Committees and Defense Appropriations Subcommittee, as well as Congressional members from defense-related districts and states; and the firms, labs, research institutes, trade associations and trade unions in the industry itself.

The special interests and the Federal bureaucracy interpenetrate each other. Policy-makers and administrators move freely between the two arenas and policy issues are discussed and resolved among participants who share common values, interests, and perceptions. As

Senator Aiken has put it, "Agencies and their clientele tend to develop coincident values and perceptions to the point where neither needs to manipulate the other overtly. The confident relationships that develop uniquely favor the interest groups involved."[19] The distinction between public and private starts to disappear as a sector of industry begins to "appropriate" Government authority.[20]

The creation of an "iron triangle" takes time and active efforts of its participants. All three sides work to maintain it as economic circumstances change. There is continuous communication between the Executive, Congress and the industry, creating a community of interest in which it becomes difficult to answer the question, "Who controls whom?". Once molded, the triangle sets with the rigidity of iron. The three participants exert strenuous efforts to keep it isolated and protected from outside points of view. In time they become unwitting victims of their own isolation, convinced that they are acting not only in their own but in the public interest.

> In the day-to-day performance of their tasks, administrators see very little of the more general public support which accompanied the establishment of the agency. The only people who are likely to come to the attention of administrators are those whose problems are uniquely a part of the administrative environment... Under such circumstance it is not surprising that the administrator's perception of the public interest is in reality defined by the interests of the regulated parties.[21]

In Congress, defense-related committees and their members jealously guard their sovereignty over defense legislation and appropriations and other committees and members tend to follow their leadership.[22] Other Congressional forums for debating defense policy have little legislative power and almost no influence over policy debates. The Joint Committee on Defense Production, the Joint Economic Committee, and Government Operations committees in both houses have regularly debated defense policy and procurement issues, but have had little access to actual legislation and appropriations bills. The Joint Committee on Defense Production was abolished in 1978 as part of committee reforms in Congress, and its functions were absorbed by the banking committees, eliminating one significant forum for public discussion of alternative approaches to defense procurement policy.

Even in the Executive branch, there is little opposition to the defense "iron triangle." DoD's Office of Economic Adjustment, founded to help communities adjust to base closings and contract terminations, has limited authority and almost no influence over procurement policy planning.[23] The Arms Control and Disarmament Agency, which seeks to reduce defense spending through arms control, has little say in policy-making.

The power to exclude is the mirror image of special access. Because of its entrenchment and paramount role in defining national security, the "iron triangle" of defense has acquired a special clout and protection from criticism. This is especially apparent at the Executive level. The Office of Management and Budget (OMB) has virtual final say over the budget requests of all agencies with one exception—the Defense Department. The Department has wide-ranging power to appeal to the President, who often overrules the OMB. As former Budget Bureau Deputy Director Philip Hughes put it:

> The most relevant consideration is, in blunt terms, sheer power—where the muscle is—and this is a very power-conscious town, and the Secretary of Defense and the defense establishment are a different group to deal with, whether the Congress is dealing with them or whether the Budget Bureau is dealing with them.[24]

The development of the "iron triangle" has put an end to those brave days described by political theory when, in the "separation of powers," Congress legislated, the Executive administered, and corporations did business with the government at arms' length. Instead, according to economist Murray Weidenbaum:

> The close, continuing relationship between the Department of Defense and its major suppliers is resulting in convergence between the two, which is blurring and reducing much of the distinction between public and private activities in an important branch of the American economy.[25]

This study examines the "iron triangle" in defense, extracting the role played by eight contractors and describing the techniques they have developed to strengthen their side of the triangle. It presents profiles of individual companies and examines in some depth the Government relations practices common to the industry, analyzing current issues, detailing current disclosure and reporting requirements, discussing brief cases of corporate practice in each area, and evaluating the available data for each of the eight companies. While the limitations of data prevent us from offering a definitive analysis, we hope that these portraits will serve as a starting point for further work by scholars, journalists, activists, members of Congress, corporate officials, and the general public.

FOOTNOTES

1. There is a wide range of literature debating these various explanations for the growth and contents of the defense budget. Inflation and other elements of cost growth in weapons spending are discussed, for example, in A. Ernest Fitzgerald, *The High Priests of Waste* (New York: Norton, 1972); Jacques S. Gansler, *The Defense Industry* (Cambridge: MIT Press, 1980); and Richard F. Kaufman, *The War Profiteers* (Garden City, NY: Doubleday,

Anchor Books, 1972). Cost increases of specific weapons systems are discussed in Gordon Adams, *The B-1 Bomber, An Analysis of Its Strategic Utility, Cost, Constituency and Economic Impact* (New York: Council on Economic Priorities, 1976); the space shuttle in *Aerospace Daily*, 11 Feb. 1980, p. 217; and the F-18 fighter in "Options on F-18 Cancellation Weighed," *Aviation Week and Space Technology*, 20 June 1980. The weapons procurement process and the bureaucratic politics of the Pentagon are discussed in Morton J. Peck and Frederick M. Scherer, *The Weapons Acquisition Process: An Economic Analysis* (Boston: Harvard Graduate School of Business Administration, Division of Research, 1962), pp. 98-99; J. Ronald Fox, *Arming America: How the U.S. Buys Weapons* (Boston, Harvard Graduate School of Business Administration, 1974), Chap. 4; Harvey M. Sapolsky, *The Polaris System Development: Bureaucratic and Programmatic Success in Government* (Boston: Harvard University Press, 1972), pp. 77-78; Fitzgerald, *The High Priests of Waste* pp. 59-61; and Kaufman, *The War Profiteers*, p. xvi. Economic aspects of defense spending are covered by Paul Baran and Paul M. Sweezey in *Monopoly Capital* (New York: Monthly Review Press, 1968), Chap. 7; United Nations Centre for Disarmament, *Economic and Social Consequences of the Arms Race and Military Expenditures*, Updated Report of the Secretary-General (New York: United Nations, 1978), and United Nations Centre for Disarmament, Research reports commissioned by United Nations Group of Governmental Experts on the relations between disarmament and development, submitted to U.N. Secretariat, 1980; Seymour Melman, *The Permanent War Economy* (New York: Simon and Schuster, Touchstone Books, 1964); Lloyd Dumas, "Economic Conversion, Productive Efficiency and Social Welfare," *Journal of Sociology and Social Welfare*, 4, nos. 3 and 4, Jan./March 1977; David Gold and Gordon Adams, "The Military Budget, Politics and the American Economy," *URPE Newsletter* of the Union for Radical Political Economics, 12, no. 4, July/Aug. 1980; and Michael Edelstein, *The Economic Impact of Military Spending* (New York: Council on Economic Priorities, 1977). International developments and U.S./Soviet military balance issues are discussed in Franklyn D. Holzman, "Are the Soviets Really Outspending the U.S. on Defense?" *International Security*, Spring 1980; Les Aspin, "Judge not by numbers alone," *The Bulletin of Atomic Scientists*, June 1980; U.S., C.I.A., *A Dollar Cost Comparison of Soviet and U.S. Defense Activities, 1968-78*, Jan. 1979; and John Collins, *U.S.-Soviet Military Balance: Concepts and Capabilities, 1960-1980* (New York: McGraw-Hill, 1980). Weapons technologies are discussed in Richard Burt, *New Weapons Technologies, Debate and Directions*, International Institute for Strategic Studies, Adelphi Paper no. 126 (London: International Institute for Strategic Studies, 1976); and Daniel Goure and Gordon McCormick, "PGM: No Panacea," *Survival* (International Institute for Strategic Studies), 22, no. 1, Jan./Feb. 1980.
2. Arthur Bentley, *The Process of Government: A Study of Social Pressure*, 2nd ed. (Evanston, IL: Principia Press of Illinois, 1945); E.E. Schattschneider, *The Semi-Sovereign People*, 2nd ed. (Hinsdale, IL: Dryden Press, 1975); David Truman, *The Governmental Process: Political Interests and Public Opinion* (New York: Knopf, 1975); and Edward Pendleton Herring, *Group Representation Before Congress* (Baltimore, MD: Johns Hopkins Press, 1929).
3. Marver Bernstein, *Regulating Business by Independent Commissions* (Princeton, NJ: Princeton University Press, 1955); Grant McConnell, *Private Power and American Democracy* (New York: Knopf, Inc., 1967); and Common Cause, *Serving Two Masters, A Common Cause Study of Conflicts of Interest in the Executive Branch* (Washington, DC: Common Cause, 1976).
4. "Business is Learning How to Win in Washington," *Fortune*, 27 March 1978.
5. Philip Shabecoff, "Big Business Is on the Offensive," *The New York Times*

Magazine, 9 Dec. 1979. See also Steven Rattner, "Big Industry Gun Aims at the Hill," *The New York Times,* 7 March 1979; "A Threat to Crime-Code Reform," *Business Week,* 28 Jan. 1980; Ann Crittenden, "Study Finds Corporations in Broader Political Role," *The New York Times,* 31 May 1979; and Phyllis S. McGrath, *Redefining Corporate-Federal Relations,* A Report from the Conference Board's Division of Management Research (New York: The Conference Board, 1979).

6. Sen. William Proxmire, *Report From Wasteland* (New York: Praeger Publishers, 1970); Fox, *Arming America;* Kaufman, *The War Profiteers;* Fitzgerald, *High Priests of Waste;* Peck and Scherer, *Weapons Acquisition Process;* Adam Yarmolinsky, *The Military Establishment* (New York: Harper & Row, 1971) and Dumas, "Economic Conversion, Productive Efficiency and Social Welfare."

7. Fox, p. 253.

8. Each company in our study operates plants and equipment which are actually owned by the Federal Government [usually called Government-Owned, Contractor-Operated (GOCO)]. Richard Kaufman gives estimates of Federal investment in GOCO as at least $15 billion (pp. 141-142). This investment is often justified as a necessary subsidy to the industry for doing defense business.

   Using GOCO plants and equipment is a real benefit for the contractors. Instead of borrowing capital or using company funds to invest in productive capacity, these are provided virtually rent free. The relatively lower capital costs of defense contracting may be a factor in the higher rate of return as a proportion of invested capital in this industry. (See Murray Weidenbaum, "Arms and American Economy: A Domestic Convergency Hypothesis," Papers and Proceedings of the 80th Annual Meeting of the American Economic Association, *American Economic Review,* 58, no. 2, May 1968.) Use of GOCO floor space may confer other advantages on the company. Pratt and Whitney division of United Technologies, for example, used GOCO facilities for nine years in the 1950s and 1960s to produce 10,000 jet engines for commercial buyers, paying no rent to the Federal Government and making reductions in contract prices on Government engines as a result of the unit price in savings (Kaufman, p. 174). Grumman has disclosed that it intends to use Government-owned facilities on Long Island to carry out subcontract work for Boeing on the latter's new 767 commercial air transport.

9. Peck and Scherer, pp. 375-76; Kaufman, p. 265; and James R. Kurth, "The Political Economy of Weapons Procurement: The Follow-On Imperative," *American Economic Review,* 62, no. 2, May 1972, pp. 304-311.

10. Seymour Melman, *Pentagon Capitalism* (New York: McGraw-Hill Book Company, 1970) and *The Permanent War Economy;* and John Kenneth Galbraith, *How to Control the Military* (New York: The New American Library, 1969).

11. Kaufman, p. xviii.

12. Weidenbaum, "Arms and the American Economy," p. 434.

13. Council on Economic Priorities, "The Defense Department's Top 100, 1977," *Council on Economic Priorities Newsletter,* CEP Publication N7-5, Aug. 1977.

14. *Aerospace Daily,* 13 Nov. 1980, p. 58.

15. Lewis Anthony Dexter, *How Organizations are Represented in Washington* (Indianapolis: Bobbs-Merrill, 1969).

16. Phyllis McGrath, *Redefining Corporate-Federal Relationships.* The Conference Board.

17. Roland Evans and Robert Novak, *The Washington Post,* 9 Jan. 1981.

18. See Gordon Adams, "Disarming the Military Subgovernment," *Harvard Journal on Legislation,* 14, no. 3, April 1977; Lester V. Salamon and John J. Siegfried, "Economic Power and Political Influence: The Impact of Industry Structure on Public Policy," *American Political Science Review,* 71, no. 3, Sept. 1977; Joel D Auerbach and Burt Rockmen, "Bureaucrats and Clientele

Groups: A View from Capitol Hill," *American Journal of Political Science*, 22, no. 4, Nov. 1978; McConnell, *Private Power and American Democracy*; John Lieper Freeman, *The Political Process* (Garden City, NY: Doubleday, 1955), pp. 7 and 31; Charles Jones, *Introduction to the Study of Public Policy*, 2nd ed. (North Scituate, MA: Duxbury Press, 1977), chap. 2; Stephen Bailey, *Congress in the Seventies*, 2nd ed. (New York: St. Martin's Press, 1970), p. 61; and Douglas Cater, *Power in Washington* (New York: Random House, 1964).
19. Harmon Zeigler and Wayne G. Peak, *Interest Groups in American Society*, 2nd ed. (Englewood Cliffs, NJ: Prentice Hall, 1972), p. 172.
20. McConnell describes this as the "privatization of the state," p. 244; James O'Connor describes it as the "appropriation of a sector of state power by private interest" in *The Fiscal Crisis of the State* (New York: St. Martin's Press, 1973, p. 66). See also, Edward S. Flash, *Economic Advice and Presidential Leadership* (New York: Columbia University Press, 1965), pp. 36-39; and Fred Block, *Origins of International Economic Disorder* (California: University of California Press, Ltd., 1977), pp. 102-108.
21. Michael T. Hayes, "The Semi-Sovereign Pressure Groups: A Critique of Current Theory and Alternative Typology," *The Journal of Politics*, vol. 40, 1978, pp. 134-61; Schattschneider, *Semi-Sovereign People*; and Zeigler and Peak, *Interest Groups in American Society*, p. 172. Auerbach and Rockmen note in their survey study, "Bureaucrats and Clientele Groups," that 84 percent of the members of Congress they polled felt that the influence of interests in the administrative process was at the expense of the public interest.
22. Adams, "Disarming the Military Subgovernment."
23. Confidential interviews, 1979.
24. Kaufman, *War Profiteers*, p. 180.
25. Weidenbaum, "Arms and the American Economy," p. 428.

2
Research Methods and Data

Categories and Sources

Before selecting a sampling of firms that were both major DoD contractors and defense-dependent, we needed to develop a set of data categories that would indicate a company's activities and avenues of access to the Federal policy apparatus. We reviewed numerous studies of the defense procurement process, as well as literature on corporate Government relations[1] and drew up a fairly comprehensive list of the data that we felt we needed. Covering both Government relations and basic corporate data, it read as follows:

- the extent of a company's defense contracting, especially for research and development
- major defense products and work locations
- contractor use of Government-owned plants and equipment
- company use of subcontractors and the locations of subcontracting work
- the role of boards of directors, bank lenders and auditors
- the movement of personnel between the company and the key Federal agencies
- the company's campaign contributions to candidates for Congress
- the structure, size and activity of the Washington office of the company
- company participation in trade associations and advisory committees

— company entertainment of Federal officials
— advertising and grass-roots mobilization
— questionable sales practices

Having developed a reasonably comprehensive list of information that would help identify Government relations activities, we proceeded to gather data from all available public sources: media accounts of corporate activity, company annual reports and disclosures to the Securities and Exchange Commision (SEC), Congressional hearings and investigations, and data provided by a variety of Federal agencies, ranging from the Library of Congress to the Department of Defense. This task proved enormous and difficult in virtually every category.

Information on a company's financial position came from the annual reports to stockholders and filings with the SEC, information on Government contracting from the Department of Defense and NASA. In order to match products with plant locations, we had to combine company, DoD and media data. Information on the support apparatus (accountants, legal counsel, advertising agency, banks) was drawn from the standard business sources, the SEC, and reference works on specific professions. Some data in this category were simply unavailable: company stock ownership is unevenly disclosed, at best, while no company breaks down its annual advertising budget by type of product.[2]

We drew together a contracting history of each company using the above sources, plus extensive clipping files of the standard media and business press. Data on a company's use of Federally-owned plants were obtained from annual documents maintained by each of the armed services. Research and development contracts and data on expenditures depended on DoD contracting information, company *10Ks* and DoD's response to a Freedom of Information Act request filed by *The Nation* magazine at our request in 1979.

Data on the members of the boards of directors came from biographies supplied by some of the companies, company proxy statements, and a detailed survey of biographical registers. Information on the DoD contracts held by companies on whose boards the directors of our eight companies sit was obtained from the DoD.

Data on personnel transfers depended on close scrutiny of reports filed annually by all personnel who move either from DoD or NASA to a defense/NASA contractor or vice versa. These reports are maintained in Washington, a minimal summary is provided annually by DoD, and NASA is sometimes willing to mail its reports to researchers.

Information on Political Action Committees was gathered from the Federal Elections Commission (FEC) in Washington. Some data can be mailed to researchers, while a significant part is not computerized and can only be gathered by a careful examination of microfilm at the FEC. Data on key members of Congress and candidates from areas where the company has plant locations were drawn from *The Congressional Directory* and *The Almanac of American Politics*.

Information on corporate Washington offices came from a variety of sources. Each quarter *The Congressional Record* and *Congressional Quarterly* provide a listing of the filings of lobbyists, including names of clients, receipts and expenditures. The media discuss Washington activities of defense contractors from time to time. *Washington Representatives* provided further data. In 1980, *Armed Forces Journal International* reviewed the Washington offices of several contractors, including the eight in our study. After considerable effort we were able to obtain through Common Cause audits of the Washington office expenditures of five of the eight companies, covering 1974 and 1975. These audits provided virtually the only data available on the cost of operating such an office.

Information on trade association membership was solicited by circulating a questionnaire to 30 defense-related associations. This questionnaire met with uneven response but did provide some basic information on association activities, membership and objectives. Advisory committee data were drawn from three sources: three successive annual reports of membership data prepared by the Subcommittee on Reports, Accounting and Management of the Senate Government Operations Committee (discontinued since 1979), annual reports on advisory committees prepared by the General Services Administration, and annual reports of committees filed with the Library of Congress.

Data on entertainment activities was provided through media accounts and reports and hearings of the Joint Committee on Defense Production. This included a 1976 survey conducted by the Joint Committee which covered four companies as well as several others. The data from this survey, however, were minimal. Information on questionable payments overseas was obtained from press accounts and disclosures by the company to the SEC.

Though grass-roots networks are frequently crucial to a company's Government relations strategy since they spread contract dollars across a wide geographic area, data are hard to obtain. There is no systematic disclosure by contractors and the DoD maintains minimal data.[3] We were, however, able to obtain press accounts of some grass-roots lobbying, as well as disclosures by some firms to the House Subcommittee on Commerce, Consumer and Monetary Affairs, which indicate some of the resources spent on such efforts.

The Companies

After gathering a vast amount of data on 15 companies, we drew up a questionnaire (see Appendix), which we sent by registered mail. This practice, routine in Council studies, met with a deafening near-silence— broken by cries of protest:

> We are asked for information that we consider to be private data.
>
> —B.H. Cook, Lockheed

> A significant amount of the data and information requested in your letter and accompanying questionnaire is considered to be of a proprietary nature, and, therefore, I must respectfully decline our participation in your study.
> —C. MacGregor, United Technologies

> In reviewing the questionnaire... I find that it would be almost impossible for us to respond without violating our policy on several counts. These include both sensitivity and the sheer time and money involved in gathering data which is not collected at Boeing in the manner that your questions seem to envision.... To supply quite a few elements that we consistently have labeled as proprietary to others would be improper.
> —P. Bush, Boeing

> I'm sorry, but we can't agree that the information you're requesting has no competitive significance. I'll be amazed if you get it from any other company.
> —W.B. Jones, Grumman

> Many of the questions are inappropriate and cannot be answered. Others pertain to information that is either highly proprietary to the Corporation or may be confidential from a security classification standpoint. A response thereto is precluded.
> —F.H. Menaker, Jr., Martin Marietta

> In response to your letter of June 1, Raytheon Company will not be participating in the study.
> —T.L. Phillips, Raytheon

> We do not choose to participate.
> —W. Gurnee, Northrop[4]

Having already done a great deal of research, we were then in a position to make a final selection of sample companies, choosing eight that were both defense-dependent and major contractors with the Federal Government.[5] These eight—Boeing, General Dynamics, Grumman, Lockheed, McDonnell Douglas, Northrop, Rockwell International and United Technologies—have a twenty-year history in defense contracting. Together they have received 25 percent of all NASA contracts for the period and 37 percent of all DoD prime contracts for R & D (see Chart I and Table II). Since 1970, they have appeared a total of 68 times out of a possible 100 among the top 10 DoD contractors. Lockheed has been the Pentagon's number one contractor for five of the 10 years, General Dynamics for three, and McDonnell Douglas for two.[6]

Their relationship with the DoD is symbiotic: not only does the DoD depend on them for a significant percentage of contracts but also the contractors themselves depend on DoD and NASA for a large percentage of their business.[7] Ranked by DoD and NASA contracts as a percentage of sales over the 10 years, the scale runs from a high of 93.8 percent (Grumman) to a low of 31.2 percent (Boeing). Ranked

TABLE I
COMPANY SALES AND CONTRACTING
1970-79
($millions)

Company	Total Sales	Contracts DoD	Contracts NASA	% of Total Sales	Govt Sales $	Govt Sales % of Total Sales	Foreign Military Sales Contracts	Foreign Military Sales % of Total Sales	Overseas & Export Sales	Overseas Sales % of Total Sales
Boeing	41,402.6	12,039.1	864.9	31.2%	12,744.4	30.8%	337.9	.82%	17,301.30	41.8%
General Dynamics	24,121.5	17,900.8	666.9	77.0%	11,854.5 (1973 on)	64.1%	2,499.7	10.4%	N.A.	Under 10%
Grumman	12,015.8	10,772.6	492.6	93.8%	8,512.6 (1971, 1973 on)	82.3%	1,008.7	8.4%	820.7 (1977 on)	18.2%
Lockheed	31,356.0	17,473.4	684.8	57.9%	21,214.2	67.7%	1,263.7	4.0%	6,911.4	22.0%
McDonnell Douglas	32,713.6	18,461.1	1,952.6	62.4%	20,237.00	61.9%	3,718.3	11.4%	9,860.6 (1972 on)	34.5%
Northrop	10,593.8	6,175.4	177.1	60.0%	6,741.5 (1972 on)	71.8%	3,701.2	34.9%	4,379.4 (1971-72 1975 on)	46.6%
Rockwell	42,060.3	8,322.0	6,244.2	34.6%	16,785	39.9%	220.5	.52%	7,283 (1973 on)	21.1%
United Technologies	42,002.2	13,734.2	347.6	33.5%	13,690.1	32.6%	986.0	2.3%	13,424.2	32.0%
Total	236,265.8	104,878.6	11,430.7	49.2%	111,779.5	50.0%	13,736.0	5.8%	59,980.6	25.4%

Sources: Company Annual Reports and 10K's; U.S Department of Defense, *100 Companies Receiving the Largest Dollar Volume of Military Prime Contract Awards*; NASA, *Annual Procurement Report*.

NOTE: PERCENTAGES BASED ON DATA WHICH IS NOT AVAILABLE FOR CERTAIN YEARS ARE DERIVED FROM TOTAL SALES FIGURES FOR ONLY THOSE YEARS WITH AVAILABLE DATA.

TABLE II
GOVERNMENT CONTRACTING
1970-79
($millions)

Company	DoD Contracts	% of Total DoD Contracts	DoD R&D Contracts	% of Total DoD R&D	NASA Contracts	% of Total NASA
Boeing	$ 12,039.1	2.9%	$ 4,757.9	7.1%	864.9	2.7%
General Dynamics	17,900.8	4.3%	2,947.5	4.4%	666.9	2.1%
Grumman	10,772.6	2.6%	1,813.4	2.7%	492.6	1.5%
Lockheed	17,473.4	4.2%	4,298.0	6.4%	684.8	2.1%
McDonnell Douglas	18,461.1	4.4%	4,618.8	6.9%	1,952.6	6.1%
Northrop	6,175.4	1.5%	644.6	1.0%	177.1	0.6%
Rockwell	8,322.0	2.0%	3,867.9	5.8%	6,244.2	19.6%
United Technologies	13,734.2	3.3%	1,910.1	2.8%	347.7	1.1%
Total	$104,878.6	25.3%	$24,858.2	37.1%	11,430.8	35.9%

Source: U.S. Department of Defense, *100 Companies Receiving the Largest Dollar Volume of Military Prime Contract Awards; Top 500 Research & Development Contractors*; and NASA *Annual Procurement Report*.

by company disclosed data on Government sales for the same period, the scale ranges from 82.2 percent (Grumman) to 30.9 percent (Boeing). (See Table I.)

Dividing the data provided by the companies into appropriate categories (contracting data, contracting history, research and development, boards of directors, personnel transfers, Political Action Committees, trade association and advisory committee memberships, entertainment practices, and questionable payments), we drew up profiles. Each set of data posed particular problems and each required careful checking and further calculations, described in each chapter below. Once we had completed a draft profile, as is our practice, we circulated it for comment to each company. Once again, the response to our request for factual comments was largely ignored. We received no reply from three companies: General Dynamics, McDonnell Douglas, and Rockwell. Two companies—Boeing and United Technologies—provided us with a little information, most of which we had already used. Two companies—Northrop and Lockheed—responded with uncomplimentary and even threatening letters. Only one company, Grumman, gave a careful reading of the profile, offering additional information which we have incorporated into the final draft.

The main text examines the general background of Government relations and defense contracting and discusses each item in some detail. This text was sent out for review to nine outside readers, whose comments were taken into account in redrafting. In addition to the text we present aggregations of data from the profiles, permitting us to compare corporate practices.

In breaking the data down into categories, it is easy to lose sight of the whole. Each category appears to be discrete, independent of the others. Such is not the case. Grass-roots lobbying is closely tied to PAC contributions; the links with trade associations are often made by personnel who have transferred from one side of the triangle to the other. The effectiveness of the tools in maintaining the company's side of the triangle is regularly reviewed, and company executives spend increasing resources in developing and coordinating the firm's Government relations policies. In presenting profiles of individual companies of importance, the study in effect describes the Government relations practices common to the industry, analyzing current issues, detailing current disclosure and reporting requirements and discussing cases of corporate practice in each area.

Chart Ia

DEPARTMENT OF DEFENSE CONTRACTS, 1970-1979

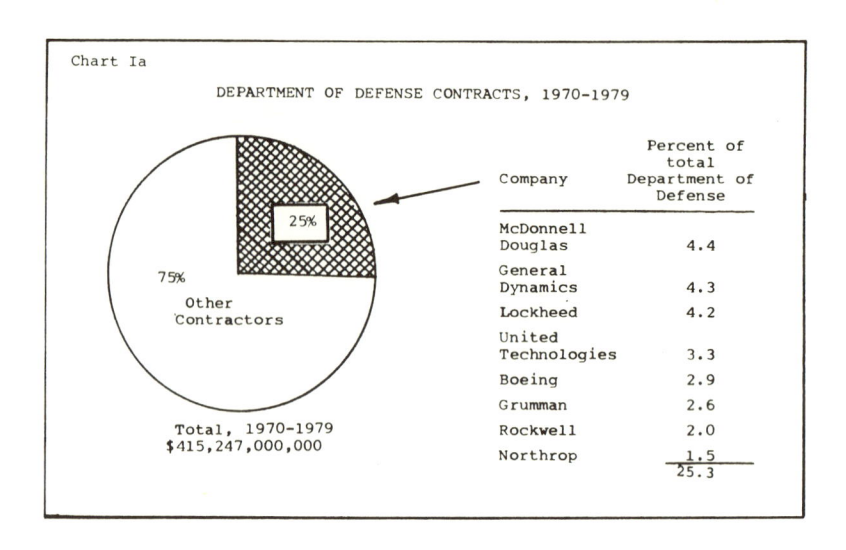

Total, 1970-1979
$415,247,000,000

25%
75% Other Contractors

Company	Percent of total Department of Defense
McDonnell Douglas	4.4
General Dynamics	4.3
Lockheed	4.2
United Technologies	3.3
Boeing	2.9
Grumman	2.6
Rockwell	2.0
Northrop	1.5
	25.3

Chart Ib

**DEPARTMENT OF DEFENSE RESEARCH AND DEVELOPMENT CONTRACTS
1970-1979**

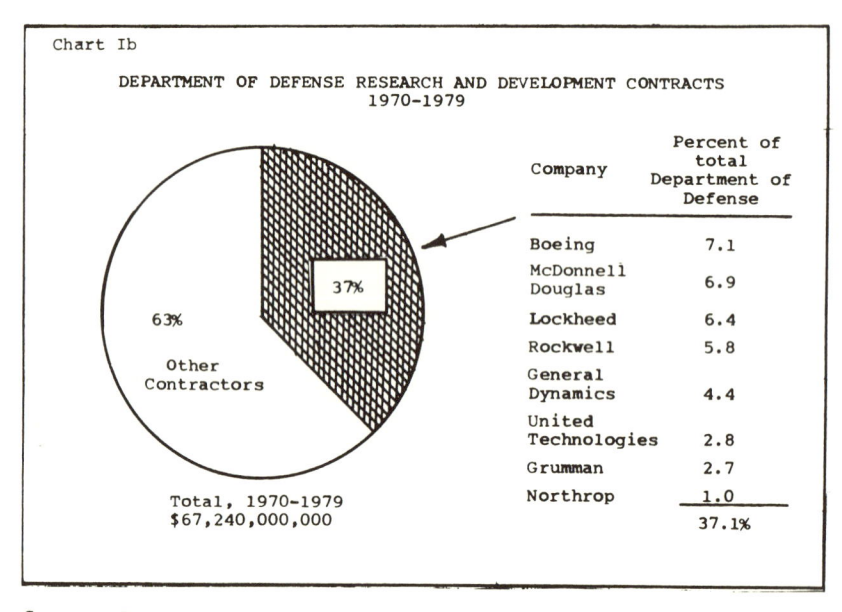

Total, 1970-1979
$67,240,000,000

37%
63% Other Contractors

Company	Percent of total Department of Defense
Boeing	7.1
McDonnell Douglas	6.9
Lockheed	6.4
Rockwell	5.8
General Dynamics	4.4
United Technologies	2.8
Grumman	2.7
Northrop	1.0
	37.1%

Source: Department of Defense <u>500 Research and Development Contractors</u>.

Chart Ic

NASA CONTRACTS, 1970-1979

Total, 1970-1979
$31,864,000,000

64% Other Contractors / 36%

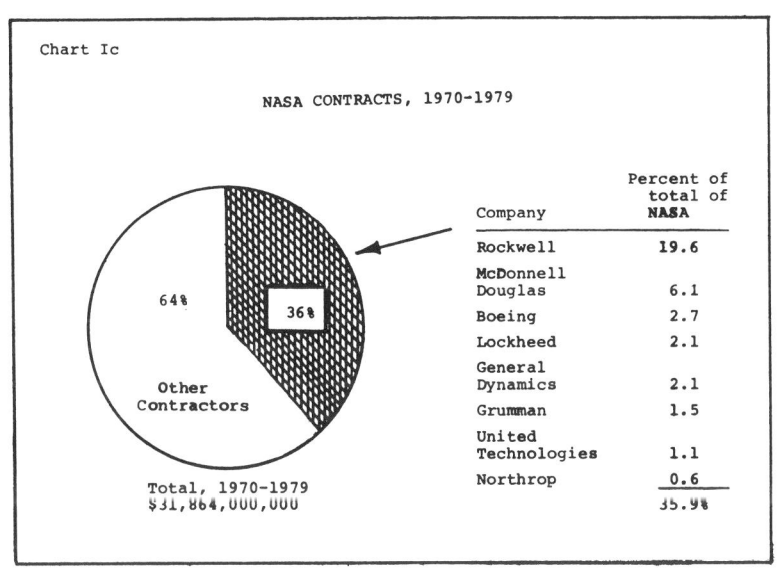

Company	Percent of total of NASA
Rockwell	19.6
McDonnell Douglas	6.1
Boeing	2.7
Lockheed	2.1
General Dynamics	2.1
Grumman	1.5
United Technologies	1.1
Northrop	0.6
	35.9%

Source: NASA Annual Procurement Reports

Chart II

COMPANY DEPENDENCY ON GOVERNMENT AND FOREIGN SALES IN THE SEVENTIES
(Covers years as noted in Table 1)

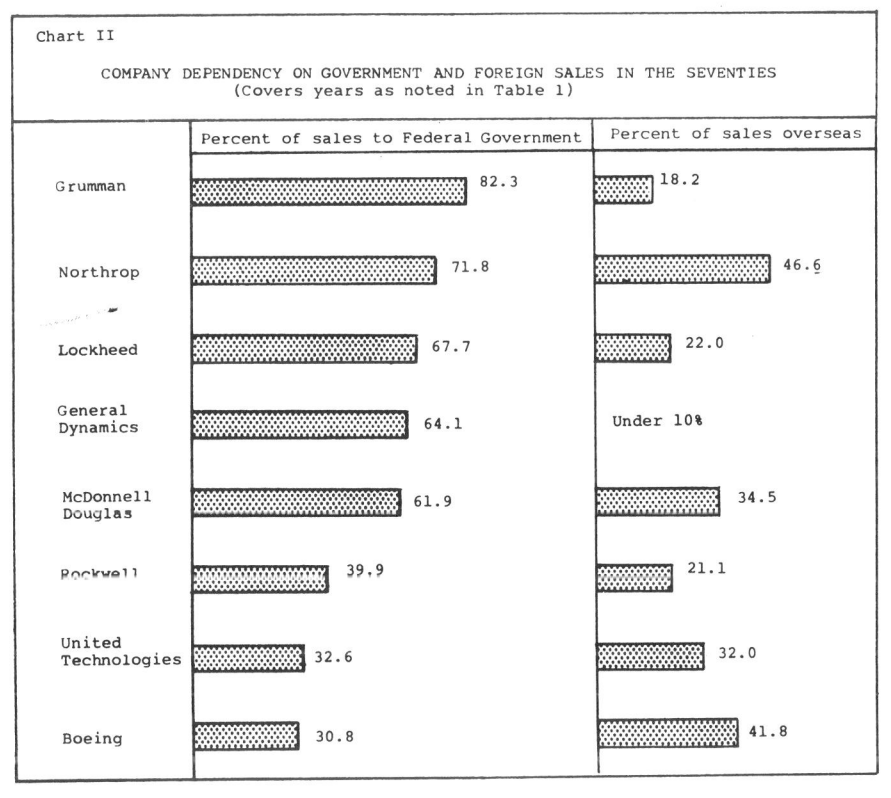

Company	Percent of sales to Federal Government	Percent of sales overseas
Grumman	82.3	18.2
Northrop	71.8	46.6
Lockheed	67.7	22.0
General Dynamics	64.1	Under 10%
McDonnell Douglas	61.9	34.5
Rockwell	39.9	21.1
United Technologies	32.6	32.0
Boeing	30.8	41.8

Research Methods and Data

Chart III

COMPANY EMPLOYMENT
1979

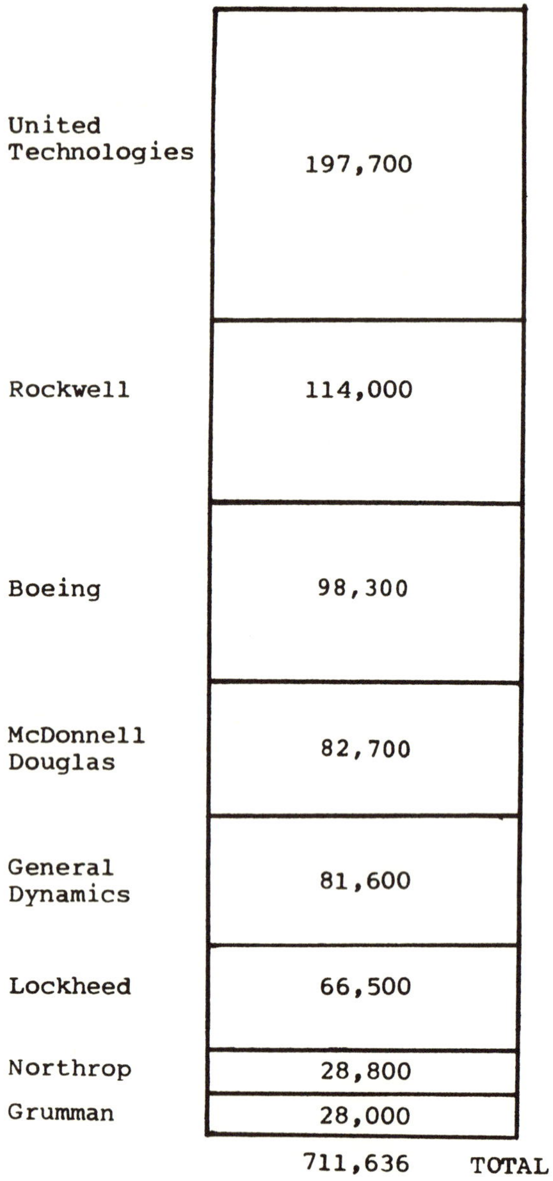

United Technologies	197,700
Rockwell	114,000
Boeing	98,300
McDonnell Douglas	82,700
General Dynamics	81,600
Lockheed	66,500
Northrop	28,800
Grumman	28,000
TOTAL	711,636

Source: Company annual reports

TABLE III

DEPENDENCY ON GOVERNMENT AND FOREIGN CONTRACTS AND SALES

(% of Total Company Sales)

(RANK BY PERCENTAGE OF SALES)

Company	DoD/NASA Contracts*	Government Sales	Foreign Military Sales Contracts	Overseas Sales
Boeing	31.2%	30.0%	.02%	11.0%
General Dynamics	77.0%	64.1%	10.4%	under 10%
Grumman	93.8%	82.3%	8.4%	18.2%
Lockheed	57.9%	67.7%	4.0%	22.0%
McDonnell Douglas	62.4%	61.9%	11.4%	34.5%
Northrop	60.00%	71.8%	34.9%	46.6%
Rockwell	34.6%	39.9%	.52%	21.1%
United Technologies	33.5%	32.6%	2.3%	32.0%

* Data on contracts covers 1970-79; data on sales covers years as noted in Table I.

FOOTNOTES

1. Morton J. Peck and Frederic M. Scherer, *The Weapons Acquisition Process: An Economic Analysis* (Boston: Harvard Graduate School of Business Administration, Division of Research, 1962); J. Ronald Fox, *Arming America: How the U.S. Buys Weapons* (Boston: Harvard Graduate School of Business Administration, 1974); Gordon Adams, "Disarming the Military Subgovernment," *Harvard Journal on Legislation*, 14, No. 3, April 1977; Richard Kaufman, *The War Profiteers* (Garden City, NY: Doubleday, Anchor Books, 1972); Phylis S. McGrath, *Redefining Corporate-Federal Relations*, A Report from the Conference Board's Division of Management Research (New York: The Conference Board, Inc., 1972); Lester Milbrath, *The Washington Lobbyists* (Chicago: Rand-McNally Inc., 1963); David Sims, "Spoon-Feeding the Military How New Weapons Come to Be," in *The Pentagon Watchers*, ed. Leonard Rodberg and Derek Shearer (Garden City, NY: Doubleday, 1970); Harmon Zeigler and Wayne Peak, *Interest Groups in American Society*, 2nd ed. (Englewood Cliffs, NJ: Prentice Hall, 1972); Charles Jones, *Introduction to the Study of Public Policy* (New York: St. Martin's Press, 1970); Paul Cherrington and Ralph Gillen, *The Business Representative in Washington* (Washington: The Brookings Institution, 1962); and Congressional Quarterly, *The Washington Lobby*, 3rd ed. (Washington D.C.: The Congressional Quarterly, 1979).

2. The only partial substitute would be to count advertising pages over a given period of time in specific publications and multiply by the publication's advertising rates. In spite of a vast expenditure of effort, this procedure would have produced only partial and imperfect data. CEP did make a preliminary effort of this kind earlier; see "Advertising to the Military," *Economic Priorities Report* (New York: Council on Economic Priorities, Nov./Dec. 1972).
3. Aggregate data is now reported by DoD in U.S., Dept. of Defense, *Geographic Distribution of Subcontract Awards*, Washington Headquarters Services, Directorate for Information Operations and Reports. For 1979, moreover, DoD maintains a print-out of first and second tier subcontractors for most major prime defense contractors. This data will not continue to be maintained, however. Other researchers have noted this problem: Barry S. Rundquist, "On Testing a Military Industrial Complex Theory," *American Politics Quarterly*, 6, no. 1, Jan. 1978, p. 45. Some journalistic or partial data is available by regular reading of *Aviation Week & Space Technology* and *DMS* (Defense Marketing Service).
4. We received no response at all from eight of the 15 companies: General Dynamics, McDonnell Douglas, Rockwell, E-Systems, Hughes, LTV Corporation, Litton and TRW.
5. Several elements led to the elimination of some firms. Our original list numbered 29, an impossibly large number. We reduced the list to 15, eliminating companies which were very small or specialized, or for which little data on Government relations are available. This latter decision may have left out firms which did considerable Government business, but which felt little need for massive Government relations apparatus. However, we felt that their omission would not affect our findings. We focused instead on major, long-term dependent contractors, whose Government relations practices had higher visibility. Our list of 15 was further reduced to eight, in order to make the volume of data manageable.
6. If one averages the ranking of these companies over the past ten years, Lockheed has averaged 2.0; McDonnell Douglas 3.1; General Dynamics 4.0; United Technologies 5.1; Boeing 6.1; Grumman 7.4; Rockwell 10.0; and Northrop 16.5. The other 32 positions in the top 10 over this period were occupied by General Electric (10); Hughes Aircraft (7); Litton Industries (5); AT&T (4); Raytheon (2); Tenneco (2); LTV (1); and Textron (1). Average rank for these companies was General Electric 4.4; Hughes 9.5; Litton 10.4; AT&T 11.9; Raytheon 12.5; Tenneco 18.4; LTV 20.1; and Textron 16.6.
7. There are several ways to estimate defense dependency of a firm. One is to calculate DoD and NASA contracts as a proportion of annual sales. Since contract awards are paid out over several years, however, and since fiscal years for companies and the Government rarely match, this figure does not reflect actual defense dollar cash flow to the firm in any given year. It does, however, suggest a range of dependency over time. The other method computes total Government sales as a proportion of total corporate sales. This figure, not always disclosed by the company, includes non-defense as well as defense contract dollars. In spite of this limitation, it provides an accurate measure of Government cash flow to the firm over a set period of time. A similar limitation applies to the relation between foreign military sales contracts and company disclosure of overseas sales. In addition, company disclosure of overseas and export sales includes both commercial and military sales, making it difficult to determine company dependency on overseas defense markets.

3
Selling Weapons: A Parable

Description and analysis, the essential tools of the researcher, both reveal and distort reality. They stop the action and transpose many dimensions into a two-dimensional listing of facts and figures. Inevitably, they shift the emphasis from reality as process to reality as-structure.

Yet in this study it is primarily process that interests us. Our focus centers on the practices that contractors have developed to influence Government policy. Description and analysis alone cannot show how these blend together to affect a single DoD decision. This can only be done through narrative. To fill this gap we have invented a case study. It is hypothetical and fictional. No actual events, pesons or corporations are described.[1]

Jack Wilson, sitting at his desk in San Jose, was a company man. He had started his career with General Electronics International in 1947, after war-time service in the Air Force. He had had only two brief stints elsewhere. Once, when GEI lost a major contract, he spent two years in Boston with United Electronics. Later, GEI seconded him for three years to the Air Force at Wright Patterson Air Force Base as a liaison officer on the company's supersonic-swing-wing (RPV) program. Promotions had come steadily—from engineer to production manager, to division chief for missile programs, and now, to corporate vice president for Government relations. With steady raises, increasing corporate perks, and more power, Jack had developed a loyalty, a family feeling about GEI that would never die. He expected to retire, at least as a vice president, or even—who knows . . . .

Samuel T. ("Chuck") Fuller had to go some day, leaving the

president / chief operating officer job open. Chuck, too, had had a full career. In the 1930s, fresh out of Stanford Engineering, he had created a defense electronics firm, ERW, in the suburbs of San Jose— California's famous Silicon Valley. The sudden boom in Pentagon missile spending had made the firm's fortune and Chuck's career. Having engineered ERW's merger with Fargo Electronics, Chuck went to Washington as the second deputy to the Pentagon's Director for Defense Research and Engineering, one of the Pentagon's most powerful jobs. After four years with the Administration, Chuck had returned to California and GEI which had by then absorbed ERW/Fargo as part of a corporate diversification program. Chuck rose rapidly to the top and would retire in two years.

A key to promotion, Jack knew, was the procurement of a major Pentagon contract, which would establish him as the heir apparent for the top job.

Yet Jack knew that there was another strong candidate—and another route. Bruce Collins, the former astronaut and vice president for commercial markets, had tried to diversify GEI by developing commercial markets. His efforts had succeeded. If DoD contracts were slow in coming, GEI could build its future in commercial aviation.

For Jack, however, there was no choice. GEI's defense programs had been run separately from commercial business since the War. Company management had simply closed them off. Jack couldn't re-tool as a commercial man overnight.

Things were at a crucial point for GEI's defense work, moreover. Production on the giant Thunderbird ship defense missile for the Navy was tailing off. Jack had design crews, researchers, engineers, looking for work. The end of the Thunderbird contract might force the company to lay them off. With any luck—for them—they would go to work for Thor Election, or Rubicon, or another industry competitor, making the next contract even harder and more expensive for GEI to bid on. It could be worse though. GEI didn't have to worry about maintaining expensive overhead costs. The Navy owned the building and machinery at Plant 5803 outside San Jose. GEI simply used it at minimal rent. If the Thunderbird contract ended, GEI could always give the plant back to the Navy.

Still Jack needed a better option. With a new contract and a continued flow of defense funds into the company, he wanted to help create a humming production facility.

Jack knew he needed more information. What did the Navy think it wanted? What could the company make? He reached for the phone and set up a meeting with George ("Smiley") Cooper, Director of GEI's advanced research and development office, fondly called the "Junk Works" around GEI because it was located next to San Jose's city dump. He sat down with Cooper and went over the projections. They had to know what the Navy had up its sleeve, what new missile systems they were thinking about. Cooper knew a lot on this score. For the past ten years, about $15 million a year had flowed into the Junk Works from the Pentagon's Independent Research and Development program. GEI scientists used the money to fund new weapons research ideas—ideas they could sell back to the Pentagon. As long as the ideas that came back were promising, the Pentagon kept a loose hand on the money reins.

For the past five years, Cooper had also been a member of the Navy Science Board's Advisory Committee on Ship Defense Systems. This Committee brought together everybody—Navy people, Green Aerospace, Rubicon, the McDavis Group, GEI. Most of the big contractors had a scientist or engineer member of the group, which was designed to pool ideas on ship defense systems. The Navy used it as a sounding board, while the industry people used it to get to know each other and the Navy and to push new ideas.

Several years ago, Cooper had done a concept paper at the request of the Committee chairman. One of his old friends, Deputy Asst. Navy Secretary for R & D, Duffy McNee, had taken a real interest in the proposed system: a new, all-weather missile with a 75-100 mile range, which could carry nuclear or conventional weapons. Just the thing the Navy (and GEI) needed, thought Cooper. For three years he had been using IR&D to develop the concept, and it was near time to move toward real R & D contracts.

There was some risk in pushing this missile, Cooper told Jack. The Navy had to be convinced. GEI's competitors, moreover, had seen Cooper's paper and could be working on their own designs. Rubicon Aerospace was said to be forging ahead. On the other hand, a success in pushing this system would make GEI's Missile Division golden for a decade to come. Cooper and Wilson agreed they needed more information on how to sell the Navy and on the work of competitors. Cooper went off to call Assistant Secretary McNee.

Jack began sounding out some other key contracts. First, he called Buff Johnson, his deputy and Government liaison officer in GEI's Washington office, which had been established ten years ago as a central location to gather information on Pentagon and NASA contracting and to guide GEI's out-of-town staff when they came to Capitol Hill for testimony and meetings with key members of Congress. Buff had many useful sources. Every couple of weeks, he would have lunch (Dutch treat, under the new entertainment guidelines from the Pentagon) with old friends in the Navy's Research Office. It had been seven years since he had retired from the staff there, moving immediately to GEI. But he had kept up his contacts.

He had also spent time on the Hill. While contracting for the Navy, he had met many of the staff of the House and Senate Armed Services Committees who worked on Naval R & D and procurement. He knew that they were important to getting future defense programs funded. His job now was to keep them informed on GEI programs and to keep a close ear to committee attitudes toward the defense budget. Though not officially registered as a lobbyist—the law was very loose—he did a fair amount of lobbyist's work.

Jack asked Buff for information about his Pentagon network. Had he talked recently with McNee or junior civilian and military people? Did he know where future ship missile defense systems were heading? Who was in charge of this work? Were there special advisory groups GEI ought to be in? Buff found the answers—the Navy group working on ship defense was impressed with GEI's progress using IR&D money. But there were other competitors in the field, and he did not know how far along they were, or how interested the Navy was in their work. Jack urged Buff to pin down more detailed information. He also asked him to do some sleuthing in ADPA. GEI, along with other major defense firms, belonged to the American Devense Preparedness Association, a trade group committed to serving "the defense needs of our nation." Jack asked Buff to attend the next meeting of ADPA's Missiles Committee to determine who among GEI's competitors had drawn a bead on the market.

Jack then focused in on Navy Research and Development. What kind of missile designs could they be sold? He made a call to Tony Lakeland at the Naval Weapons Center at China Lake. Lakeland had been with GEI's missile division for five years before moving to China Lake as an R & D Program Director. Jack suggested they meet for lunch when he came to GEI's China Lake office the following week. He knew that if GEI was to get in on the ground floor, he had to have some influence over the missile specifications the Navy would draw up in preparing its request for bids for R & D contract work. The discussion with Tony gave him useful information and even more useful input into Navy thinking.

After these preliminary calls Jack started to plan for a Washington trip. He put Buff to work on the schedule after clearing the trip and the program with an enthusiastic President Fuller. A courtesy visit to Deputy Assistant Secretary McNee was in order, which Cooper arranged. Buff set up detailed discussions with McNee's staff. In addition, there were meetings with the ADPA committee secretary and a friendly visit to the Aerospace Industries Association to discuss forthcoming changes in Federal procurement policy.

Buff also arranged some meetings with Hill staffers, though it was early in the missile program to think about a Congressional focus for GEI's effort. Jack did meet with Congresswoman Claire Sampson from San Jose. GEI had made steady contributions to Sampson's last three campaigns through its Good Government Fund, a Political Action Committee, and Buff had friendly access to Sampson's legislative assistant. As Representative from GEI's district and a member of the Defense Appropriations Subcommittee which would consider the money requests for Navy missile R & D, Sampson was doubly important to GEI. The Defense Subcommittee was famous on the Hill for going through Pentagon requests with a fine-toothed comb. In his visit, Jack explained that he was on a general information gathering trip and described GEI's current R & D projects, including ship defense missiles. He pointed out to her how much GEI's 16,000 employees in San Jose supported her work and how important it was to the economy of the district that they be fully employed.

Jack took along a young employee of GEI's Washington office, Neil Jones to meet with the R & D staff of the House and Senate Armed Services Committees. Jones was a Presidential Interchange Executive with GEI. He knew missiles inside out and was very familiar with GEI's technical work. He was also intimately familiar with Navy thinking, having been on the staff of the Navseasystcom tactical planning group for two years. He talked technical with the R & D staff and made strong arguments for the military need for GEI's missile.

During Jack's visit, the Washington office arranged a reception attended by several top brass and key civilian policy makers, as well as several members of Congress and staffers—a sort of informal, get-acquainted party. It was a quiet, cautious event. Jack could remember the old days before Proxmire had uncovered abuses. GEI used to have a hunting lodge on Wye Island, off the Maryland coast where they had full weekends with top Pentagon and Hill personnel—hunting, playing cards, drinking and generally socializing. Press revelations and hearings on Thor Electron and Bow-Wing Electronics, had changed all that. Now there was only the occasional cocktail party at a trade association meeting, free tickets to a Redskins' game, a lunch here and there, and—a rarity—a plane trip to the coast for a Congressman or bureaucrat. The days of big entertainment and favors were gone, at least for now.

Buff called several weeks after Jack's return from Washington. One of McNee's key staffers was working up a draft Request for Proposals (RFP) for ship defense missiles and GEI had to move fast. Jack called Smiley Cooper and urged him to arrange a meeting between the Navy staffer and a Junk Works expert to go over GEI's ideas. A quick weekend conference in Washington was arranged and GEI got its input into the RFP.

When the RFP came out, a month later, it took a middle line between GEI and Rubicon and implied that more than one contractor might be funded for designs. Both GEI and Rubicon bid and won contracts.

Jack's work, however, was just beginning; the production contract was no sure thing. Rubicon had a lot of missile experience and equally good contracts with the Pentagon and the Hill. As the design work proceeded, Jack picked up the pace, keeping up with advance information and bringing influence to bear in the Pentagon. The two design contracts were followed by two engineering development contracts and, in turn, two contracts for prototype development. The Navy wanted to fly-off the two missiles against each other.

As the competition heated up and the program progressed, it became more visible, more expensive, and more controversial. The

Selling Weapons: A Parable   47

wider the circle of people involved, the more Jack had to do.

There were those both in the defense industry and in Congress who opposed a new missile. Thor Electron, which made the current ship defense missile, met regularly with Hill staffers to encourge Congress to accept a more modest program involving a redesign of the current weapon. Congressman Jerry Friedman of Wisconsin worried about the cost of a new missile. Senator Scott Moran from Pennsylvania warned that the Pentagon budget was eating up social funding.

There was also opposition inside the Pentagon. A Navy missile program was pushing the projected budget upwards. Supporters of existing systems argued that the new expenditure was not needed and updates of current equipment were adequate. Outside the Navy, the other services resisted the threat a growing Navy missile procurement program posed for growth in their own weapons-buying.

Sometimes Jack felt like a duck stamping out a forest fire. Every time he thought he had one brush fire out, another jumped up a few feet, or a few offices away.

Jack mobilized everyone and everything to push through his program. He paid regular visits to Washington, visiting both the Hill and the Pentagon. He brought company specialists with him, who could make convincing technical cases for the GEI design. They met endlessly with Navy people, some of whom had worked for GEI, discussing design changes, problems, cost, etc. Jack had two goals: keep the missile in the DoD budget and encourage GEI's design into the winner's seat. He knew that for this to happen, he had to work both the Pentagon and Hill sides of the street.

Mobilizing the staff of GEI's Washington office, Jack and Buff outlined a campaign of visits to critical members of the House and Senate Committees: the Armed Services and the Defense Appropriations Subcommittee, and their staffs. They sent their technical people to convince the R & D Subcommittee staff of the vital importance of the program. They reviewed campaign contributions from GEI's Good Government Fund, noting key members to whom contributions had been made. They looked at the pattern of GEI's subcontract awards. For some years the company had tried to be attentive to the economic and political impact of its subcontracts through which it farmed out over 40% of its prime contract dollars. The economic argument carried weight in Congress. Several million dollars in subcontracts in a district was hard to argue with. But, GEI couldn't make this argument directly. Its motives would be questioned.

Jack commissioned a study by a private economic consulting firm on the regional impact of the program. District-by-district, GEI could then forecast the results, tailoring individual presentations for specific members of Congress.

Special meetings were held with the two California Senators and the San Mateo/San Jose members, Congressman Mattini and Congresswoman Sampson. The economic impact of the program would be largest in their districts. Past history had shown that Mattini, who generally took a critical stance on defense spending, had always been willing to go to bat for GEI when jobs in the district were at stake. The California delegation moved into action, calling on colleagues, sending staff around to encourage other staffers to support the program, and writing the Pentagon.

Congresswoman Sampson was a major leader of this effort. As a member of the House Defense Appropriations Subcommittee her arguments commanded attention in the Pentagon. The Pentagon and the White House knew that her support was needed for other programs. Trade-off possibilities were endless. With an incumbent President up for reelection, Sampson's arguments about electoral support in her district found receptive listeners among the White House staff.

Turning to the Pentagon, Jack worked on other problems. GEI had to be sure its prototype came within close range of Rubicon in price, performance and schedule. Buff's office and the California staff pursued contacts and discussions with the Navy's technical and contracting people, acquiring up-to-date information on the missile test evaluation. Jack and Buff also marshalled every possible supporter to argue in the Office of the Secretary of Defense that the weapon was necessary. He made several calls to analysts of naval strategy in various universities, one of whom agreed to write an opinion piece on the missile in *The New York Times*, which the policy makers would read.

Jack aimed at other journals, making several phone calls a week to writers for *Aviation Week* and the *U.S. Naval Institute Proceedings*. He offered to provide information on recent developments in GEI's program and arrange visits to the plant for reporters. Several favorable write-ups resulted from these efforts, including a highly detailed, technical piece in *Aviation Week*. Jack mobilized the company's PR people in San Jose who placed GEI's missile in the advertising copy of *Time* and *Business Week*.

Jack moved, too, to bring GEI's local dependents to put pressure on Congress and the Executive branch. A company planning committee, Operation Common Good, had drawn up a plan aimed at mobilizing public opinion in San Jose. OCG prepared films and demonstrations for Fourth of July exhibits and American Legion meetings, provided speakers for men's and women's clubs' meetings on the nation's defense and the importance of a well-defended fleet. It sent press releases to local papers in all the key subcontracting locations and arranged for plant visits for important union and local government officials. It organized delegations of local citizens to visit Congress and the White House with statements of support. A nationwide campaign of ads urged readers to write GEI for an "Owner's Manual" for the missile and Jack drafted a letter from President Chuck Fuller to employees, subcontractors, and stockholders, urging them to write Congress.

Decision time was near. Rubicon Aerospace and GEI kept pushing. White House and Hill pressures won the day over the opposition of the Secretary of Defense: the missile was approved. Now came the question of funding. Jack and Rubicon's lobbyist turned to the Hill, with more visits to key staff, more reminders of campaign contributions and subcontracting benefits. The opponents of the missile lost in the Appropriations Committee, introduced a motion on the floor of the House amending the Defense Appropriations Act, but lost again, 207-142. The arena for the contestants now was moved to the Senate.

Senator Scott Moran from Pennsylvania led an effort in the Senate Appropriations Committee to delay a production decision on the missile until after the Presidential campaign. The amendment barely squeaked through the Committee, which meant a floor fight. Despite door-to-door lobbying and Pentagon phone calls, the amendment was passed.

The competing contractors united in their efforts to support the program. GEI and Rubicon pulled out all stops in the Conference Committee, calling members, orchestrating local employee, stockholder, subcontractor and other grass-roots pressures. Two GEI Board members who formerly worked at high levels in the Pentagon, made personal calls to several key Senators and Congressmen. One of them, the chairman of United Western Bank, also made some calls to former colleagues in the Treasury Department, pointing out the importance of funds to California's industrial sector. In response, Congressional relations staff at Treasury made contact with key Appropriations Committee members. The battle in Conference was won; the amendment was removed; funding was approved.

Jack's attention turned back to the Pentagon and White House. He could not be sure that his missile would win. The two missiles were close in design and performance specifications. GEI had a slight lead in the fast schedule it could promise to the Navy, but inside information from GEI's friends in Navy R & D suggested that Rubicon might come in with a slightly lower price. He would have to move carefully. In an election year, some pressure had to be directed toward the White House. All avenues would have to be carefully worked.

Jack called Dave Brahman, GEI board member, Harvard graduate and partner in Shadly, Todd, Millbrook and Coy, one of Washington's leading law firms. In the 1960s he had served as Deputy Secretary of the Army and later put in two years as Director of the Defense Intelligence Agency. His Washington network was wide, his reputation as an insider was unbeatable. Brahman gave Jack advice on how to approach the Republican National Committee and the White House in this election year and agreed to pay visits to some old friends on the White House staff to make the case for GEI's bid.

Meanwhile, in Washington Buff Johnson had come close to blowing the contract. In his anxiety to obtain information on the progress of the Navy evaluation, he had sent Gene McConnell, former Navy engineer and GEI Washington Technical specialist, to the Navy program office. There, McConnell, who had a high security clearance, examined a memorandum going through the most recent technical discussions of the Navy's missile needs. In it he found some valuable information for GEI's final bid. When Buff saw the notes Gene had taken, he could hardly wait to rush to the Telex and send word back to San Jose. A San Jose employee with lower security clearance, not realizing how sensitive the information was, called the Navy R & D office to double-check some points, inadvertently revealing the disclosure of classified information. The flap led to the suspension of two R & D office employees and the temporary withdrawal of Gene and Buff's security clearances. The bad publicity caused new headaches for Jack, as he fought off press inquiries and tried to dissipate the sense that GEI had special inside information.

From his friends at the Aerospace Industries Association, however, Jack had learned some good news. Rubicon was overloaded with missile work and planners in the Office of the Secretary of the Navy, worried about the state of the Navy Industrial Plant Reserve, wanted to keep GEI's technical work force and operating capacity in missiles alive. When a final contract recommendation reached the Secretary of the Navy's desk, this consideration could weigh in GEI's favor.

Turning back to national politics, Jack helped Dave Brahman set up meetings with finance people from the Republican National Committee to let them know about GEI's Good Government Committee contributions to the President's primary campaign. Brahman impressed on the National Committee staff that an award in Santa Clara County would produce a good turnout for the President, while an award in Boston (site of Rubicon's plant) would not necessarily counter the natural tendency of that area's electorate to support the President's liberal challenger. Bob Sperling of GEI's Washington counsel, Worthington & Sperling, made several phone calls, reminding Republican Party officials of GEI's past services and support.

Once more Jack organized local groups who would send delegations to Washington. The San Jose delegation included the Mayor, two Council members, the head of the local Chamber of Commerce, and the local leader of the metalworkers' union, which organized part of GEI's plant. In Washington, they visited Congresswoman Sampson, Congressman Mattini, the chair of the House and Senate Armed Services Committees, and a staffer from the White House, impressing on each the economic and political benefit of a contract award to San Jose. A local San Francisco banker in the delegation paid a special visit to a friend at Treasury, carefully understating, while making clear, GEI's case.

Mattini, the San Mateo County member of Congress, approached the White House with a joint letter, made calls to friends in the Pentagon, urged other members of Congress to support the effort and inserted pro-GEI material in the *Congressional Record,* which would be reprinted and distributed.

As the pressure built toward a decision and the contract award, Jack received a phone call from an insider in the Navy R & D office, who said Rubicon's missile looked like a winner because of its cost advantages. Jack relayed the bad news to Chuck Fuller, who looked over GEI's cost proposal and then asked Jack how the Navy intended to write the contract—one contract for all of the missiles or one for a purchase in batches. Could GEI bid low for the first batch, take the loss, and make it up by getting a higher price for subsequent batches? Fuller knew this was a risky strategy—GEI could end up eating the loss as other contractors had in the past. Fuller's staff debated the issue and came up with a marginal price. Buff indicated that his Navy sources felt a revised bid could save the day for GEI. The bid was lowered. A week later, to the popping of champagne corks in Washington and San Jose, GEI's Sting-Ray was announced the winner.

After a contract award, there are always a few protests. True to form, columnist Bill Sanderson suggested that political favoritism had won the day: President Hardy, wanting to curry the support of Californians for his campaign, had promised the Congressional delegation the contract. Jack had already planned his strategy. He and Buff called the White House, prepared a statement that denied any such commitments, and discussed a press release with the PR people at the Office of the Secretary of Defense pointing out the favorable evaluation of GEI's missile, its performance in the fly-off and the price competitiveness with Rubicon. Gradually the public furor died down.

Once GEI had the production contract for the new Sting-Ray Missile, Jack's operation became less central. In San Jose, GEI workers worked side-by-side with Navy engineers and contract managers and an auditor from the Defense Contract Audit Agency (DCAA). This working relationship was made easy by the fact that, over the years, GEI had hired several former employees of the Navy and DCAA. They knew the contract guidelines and procurement regulations, knew how to negotiate contract changes, understood the red tape and paperwork, and could help ease the relationship with the Navy.

The calm did not last forever. Two years later, as part of a more general investigation into the relationship between contractors and the Pentagon, the Senate Banking Committee held hearings to examine efforts to stimulate grass-roots support for their defense programs. The Committee was concerned that the expenditures for such grass-roots lobbying had been charged to contract costs. The Pentagon might be indirectly subsidizing lobbying aimed at Congress. A questionnaire to GEI, among others, asked about their grass-roots lobbying. It was sent straight to Jack Wilson, who immediately got on the phone with the Government relations officers of the other companies in the survey to see if they intended to respond. In the end, they all agreed that a failure to respond could lead to a subpoena of data and to negative PR for the companies. As a group, they prepared a general outline for each company to use in its response to the Committee, providing a minimum of information, but trying to appear helpful

Further work remained, though, since the Committee was bound to proceed to hearings. The Committee staff wrote President Fuller asking him to testify. Jack prepared the testimony. He knew that the facts were amply documented by the Defense Contract Audit Agency. He decided, therefore, to come clean and offer to negotiate a payback to the Pentagon. In addition he drafted some possible questions and answers, prepared full data on GEI's many grass-roots efforts for the Sting-Ray, and arranged Fuller's trip to Washington. He made sure that GEI's documentation went in at the last minute limiting the Committee's time for careful perusal. Fuller's testimony went well, and Jack had to respond to only a few followup inquiries the President had thought it unwise to answer on the spot. By and large, Jack knew, the publicity from these kinds of hearings had a short shelf-life; in a few months it would be forgotten.

Jack's most important remaining job on the Sting-Ray Program was to deal with the press about the increasing cost problem the company faced, as materials became more scarce and management cost control proved inadequate. By now, he knew, much of the public was numb to cost overrun problems. As long as the information could be kept fairly quiet, GEI's image was not likely to suffer.

The Sting-Ray was a success. Jack Wilson had played a key role in bringing a new major contract to GEI.

Two years later President Fuller retired. President Jack Wilson, tanned from the Caribbean holiday that his wife had insisted he take, sat down at his new desk. Zestfully, he leafed through the paper outlining his first item of business: plans for a successor missile to the Sting-Ray.

---

1. We make no effort to describe, in depth, Congressional or Defense Department processes, which also have an impact on such decisions. There are many case studies of weapons decisions, many of which focus on bureaucratic and legislative processes. See Michael H. Armacost, *The Politics of Weapon Innovation: the Thor-Jupiter Controversy* (New York: Columbia University Press, 1969); Robert J. Art, *The TFX Decision* (Boston: Little, Brown and Company, 1968); Harvey M. Sapolsky, *The Polaris System Development: Bureaucratic and Programmatic Success in Government* (Massachusetts: Harvard University Press, 1972). Others provide helpful insights into the corporate side as well. See Gordon Adams, *The B-1 Bomber: An Analysis of Its Strategic Utility, Cost Constituency and Economic Impact* (New York: Council on Economic Priorities, 1976); A.F. Fitzgerald, *The High Priests of Waste*

(New York: Norton, 1972); Michael Mann, "Rockwell's B-1 Promotion Blitz," *Business and Society Review*, Fall 1976; Sen. William Proxmire, *Report from Wasteland* (New York: Praeger Publishers, 1970); Berkely Rice, *The C-5A Scandal* (Boston: Houghton Mifflin Co., 1971); Anthony Sampson, *The Arms Bazaar* (New York: Viking Press, 1977); U.S. Congress, Joint Committee on Defense Production, *DoD-Industry Relations: Conflicts of Interest and Standards of Conduct*, 94th Congress, 2nd Session, Feb. 1976; U.S. Congress, Joint Committee on Defense Production, Report by the Subcommittee on Investigations, *Conflict of Interest and the Condor Missile Program*, 94th Congress, 2nd Session, Sept. 1976.

PART II
THE WEAPONS BUSINESS: INSTITUTIONS, ROLES AND PEOPLE

4
Officers and Members of the Board

The defense contracting companies are run by men of experience, much of it acquired through years of service in the industry or the Government. The managers of the eight companies are highly respected—and highly paid—leaders in the contracting business and the corporate world. Five of them—Harry Gray of United Technologies, T.A. Wilson and Malcolm T. Stamper of Boeing, Willard Rockwell, Jr. and Robert Anderson of Rockwell International—ranked among the 15 best paid corporate executives in 1978, each receiving total compensations of over $1 million. Chairman Gray was the most highly paid CEO of 1976 and ranked third in 1978.[1]

Top managers and members of the board bring to their work a wide range of knowledge and impressive networks of ties to positions of influence, giving them a significant role in a contractor's Government relations strategy. Some board members are drawn from management itself and have direct responsibility for this area. Others have ties to financial institutions that handle the company's business. Still others hold membership on boards of other companies which supply goods to them or are themselves defense contractors. Forty-eight out of 116 directors (41 percent) are directors of other companies which, combined, received over $2 billion in DoD contracts in FY 1979. These ties strengthen the cohesiveness of a board, reinforcing their common assumptions and perceptions.

Such interlocks serve the companies well. How well they serve the public may be another matter. A 1977 Senate study comments on the dangers posed by a concentration of power and information in any segment of the economy. "These patterns of director interrelationships imply an overwhelming potential for anti-trust abuse and possible conflicts of interest which could affect prices, supply and competition and impact on the shape and direction of the American economy."[2]

Board members also have knowledge of, and experience with, the Federal Government. Twenty-three percent (28) of the directors of our companies have current advisory connections or have held positions in the Federal Government that could bring them into contact with information and policies of use to the company. A survey shows them serving in a variety of capacities, as Chairman of the Science Board, Assistant Secretary of State for Research and Development, Ambassador to Uganda, member of the U.S. Council on Human Rights, counsel to the Central Intelligence Agency. Clearly, some experiences are more relevant to this study than others. The facts are listed here simply because a board member's employment by the Federal Government is an asset. Like the transfer of personnel at a lower level, it can cement the common perceptions of industry and the Government.

TABLE IV

BOARDS OF DIRECTORS

Company	Number of Directors	Shares Held (%)	Financial Institution Ties
Boeing	13	0.14%	16
General Dynamics	17	24.4%*	13
Grumman	14	1.96%	13
Lockheed	16	1.57%	18
McDonnell Douglas	17	13.78%**	9
Northrop	11	2.08%	10
Rockwell	20	7.54%***	17
United Technologies	16	2.34%	15

* Crown family and co-investors hold 23.6%.

** McDonnell family holds 12.89% and controls employee savings plans with 24.17% and the McDonnell Foundation with 2.17%.

*** Rockwell family holds 5.3% of shares.

The Companies

In addition to a willingness to play an active role, an effective board member must have experience and connections. To discover the qualifications and background of members, we requested information from the companies. Some were willing to provide us with biographies of board members, data that depend on individual self-disclosure and may be incomplete. We have supplemented these data with information available from biographical registers and public sources. Of these the Government sources were the least helpful. The Department of Defense does not gather detailed data, nor does it disclose any biographical information on board members as it made clear to the Senate in 1977:

> *Department of Defense:* (including Army, Navy and Air Force) . . . does not collect detailed or extensive information relating to interlocking officers or directorships of defense contractors. However, in the course of our administration of the Defense Industrial Security Program, we do obtain certain information regarding interlocking directorships, . . . in order to insure that contractors properly safeguard classified information. [This] may not be in a form susceptible to analysis for your purposes. Therefore, we do not believe this information would be meaningful or responsive in the context of your inquiry.[3]

It would have been useful, as well, to obtain full information on who holds stock in these companies, since significant stockholders might be expected to have a stake in the success of a company's defense contracting and an incentive to support Government relations efforts and become a network of influential contacts for the firm. Unfortunately, these data are quite difficult to obtain. We have presented, in each company profile, data on the stock holdings of the boards, where disclosure is required by the SEC.[4] In reporting on inside and outside directors, we have taken the narrow standard that insiders occupy management positions in the firm while outsiders do not.

In describing these positions, stock holdings, and interlocks, we are not necessarily indicating blame or wrong-doing. From the contractor's point of view, such ties are "right-doing" since they provide multiple channels for information and access, thus strengthening the company's position. For the purposes of a study of Government relations, however, such ties suggest "old boy" networks of information and access that reenforce perceptions and interdependencies within the "iron triangle."

Boeing: Boeing President Stamper ranked among the top 15 corporate officers in compensation in 1978.[5] Stamper joined the company in 1962, while Chairman T.A. Wilson started with Boeing in 1943, providing the company with long experience in its business and defense contracting.

Boeing directors include three insiders and 10 outsiders, but the board as a whole has only a small stake (0.14 percent) in the company's stock. Board members do, however, provide a fairly extensive network of connections to financial institutions (see Chapter 5). Moreover, Boeing's directors were board members of other firms receiving $1,034 million in DoD contracts in FY 1979, the highest amount for any company in the study. Most of these companies were suppliers of components and petroleum to the firm. (See **Chart** IV.)

Four Boeing directors have or have had outside ties which would bring them into contact with defense policy-makers in the Government. Harold J. Haynes, CEO of Standard Oil, is also a trustee of California Institute of Technology. Carter Defense Secretary Harold Brown was Cal Tech president while Haynes was a trustee. David Packard, who joined Boeing's board in 1978, was Deputy Secretary of

Chart IV

BOARD OF DIRECTORS DEFENSE INDUSTRY INTERLOCKS

Company	Number of company board members with other defense industry directorships	Other defense firms	
		Principal products	Department of Defense contracts FY 1979
Boeing	7	Communications Electronics Petroleum	$975.8
United Technologies	9	Components Petroleum	$355.5
Lockheed	5	Petroleum Raw Materials	$269.0
General Dynamics	7	Components Petroleum	$251.1
Northrop	7	Components Petroleum Raw Materials	$85.9
Rockwell	7	Components Metal	$34.9
McDonnell Douglas	3	Communications	$11.1
Grumman	3	Components	$3.2

(Dollars in millions)

Source: Department of Defense, *Prime Contractors over $10,000*, 1979

Defense from 1969 to 1971 and is the chief executive officer of a major defense contractor, Hewlett-Packard. William Reed was a member of the President's Council at Cal Tech while Brown was president. George Weyerhaeuser has been a member of the advisory council of the Stanford Research Institute (now SRI International) and of the Rand Corporation, both of which are defense contractors.

General Dynamics: The top leadership of the company provides it with long experience in defense contracting and the defense industry. Company Chairman David Lewis was previously at McDonnell Douglas and joined GD in 1970, while President Oliver Boileau came in 1980 after many years with Boeing.

The company's board of directors has a large stake in the company's growth and development, since directors control 22.4 percent of outstanding shares of common stock. In 1967, Henry Crown became the firm's major stockholder. Several of Crown's colleagues also purchased GD stock at that time. Nathaniel Cummings, an outside director, holds substantial shares, while Lester Crown, an inside manager, is also a major holder.[6] Board members link GD with several major financial institutions (see Chapter 5). GD's directors also held board memberships with companies which received $251.4 million in DoD contracts in FY 1979, ranking fourth in the study. Most of these were suppliers of components and petroleum to DoD.

Three General Dynamics board members have had previous associations with the Federal Government in the defense area, though in two cases these were long ago. Executive Vice President James Beggs spent seven years as a Navy submarine officer after graduating from Annapolis and two years in the late 1960s as associate administrator in the Office of Advanced Research Technology at NASA (followed by five years as Under Secretary of Transportation). Donald Cook was counsel to the House Naval Affairs Committee in the 1940s and counsel to the Senate Armed Services Committee in the 1950s. (He was also commisioner and Chairman of the Securities and Exchange Commission.) Earl D. Johnson spent five years in DoD in the 1950s as Assistant Secretary of the Army for Manpower and Reserve Affairs (1950-52) and Under Secretary of the Army for procurement and R & D (1952-55). More recently he has been a trustee of the Air Force Academy.

Grumman: Grumman Chairman John Bierwirth arrived relatively recently with the firm (1971), with past experience outside the defense industry. Company President Joseph Gavin, however, has been with Grumman since 1946.

The board as a whole has a small stake in the company's stock (1.96 percent). The members have some connections with the financial community (see Chapter 5), but very few with other defense contracting firms; other firms where they are directors received only $8.3 million in DoD contracts in FY 1979.

Four Grumman board members have had working experience with the Federal Government, though only two have had direct experience with Defense Department agencies. John F. Carr, board vice chairman, spent three years in the 1950s in the Navy's office of general counsel, while Ira Hedrick has been a member of advisory boards to the Air Force and NASA. C. Clyde Ferguson and Ellis Phillips, Jr. both have foreign policy experience. Ferguson, a professor of law, was civil rights adviser to Governor Nelson Rockefeller of New York, a member of the U.S. Commission on Human Rights, relief program coordinator for victims of the Nigerian civil war, Ambassador to Uganda, Deputy Assistant Secretary of State for African Affairs and U.S. Representative on the U.N.'s Economic and Social Council. Phillips was Special Assistant to the U.S. Ambassador to Britain in the 1950s.

Lockheed: Lockheed Chairman Roy Anderson has been with the firm since 1956. President Lawrence Kitchen brings substantial Government experience, having been an aeronautical engineer with the Navy from 1946 to 1958, including a tour as staff assistant to the Assistant Chief for the Bureau of Aeronautics (Logistics, Plans and Policy). Kitchen joined Lockheed in 1968. Their predecessors, Dan Haughton and A. Carl Kotchian, had also spent a number of years with the firm.

Lockheed has a very large board, substantially expanded in the 1970s with the addition of outside directors. Board members, however, have only a small stake in the firm, owning 1.57 percent of outstanding common stock. The largest board shareholder is Michael Berberian, a wholesale foods distributor from Fresno, CA (1.23 percent). Lockheed's board has numerous ties with the financial community (see Chapter 5), and five board members hold directorships with other firms that received $269.5 million in FY 1979 DoD contracts (third ranking in the study), mostly in raw materials and petroleum.

In addition to Kitchen, other board members have had a high degree of experience with Federal defense policy-making. Edward Carter, a recent board member (1979), was a Navy Rear Admiral, a staff member with Naval Operations in 1962-64 and 1974-76, and a Deputy Commander of Weapons Systems and Engineering in the Navy's Seas Systems Command (1976-78). Willis Hawkins, recently retired from the firm's management, was Assistant Secretary of the Army for Research and Development from 1963 to 1966, a longstanding member of the Army's Scientific Advisory Panel, and, since 1974, a technical consultant to NASA.

McDonnell Douglas: McDonnell Douglas has been a family-dominated firm since it was founded by the late James S. McDonnell. His nephew Sanford McDonnell is now chairman, while John McDonnell, a son of the founder, is president. The McDonnell family, its foundation, and the employee pension fund on whose board family members sit, owned or controlled 39.23 percent of company stock as of 1979.

Board members have limited ties with the financial community and sit on boards of other firms which received a relatively low amount of DoD contracts in FY 1979—$15.3 million.

Three board members have had advisory or administrative experience with the Government. In the case of Donald S. MacDonald, the Government was Canadian. MacDonald, a lawyer, was a member of the Canadian parliament for 15 years and held posts in the ministries of Justice, Finance, and External Affairs. He was Canadian Minister of National Defense from 1970-1972, Minister of Energy, Mines and Resources from 1972-74, and Minister of Finance from 1975-77. MDC has some plants in Canada and, in 1980, won a Canadian order for its F-18 fighter.

George S. Graff, company vice president, has been a member of several NASA advisory committees from 1951 to the present. Robert L. Johnson, senior vice president of the company and head of its aerospace operations, was Assistant Secretary of the Army from 1969 to 1973 and a scientific consultant to DoD.

Northrop: Northrop Chairman T.V. Jones has been with the firm since 1953. President Thomas O. Paine brings both industry and Government experience to the firm. He was NASA Administrator from 1968 to 1970 and spent the following six years with General Electric before joining Northrop in 1976.

Northrop's board was expanded to include a larger number of outsiders in the 1970s. Board members control a small proportion (2.08 percent) of company stock, and have numerous ties with financial institutions (see Chapter 5). Board members are directors of other firms which received only a relatively small amount of FY 1979 DoD contracts—149.7 million.

In addition to Paine five Northrop board members have had Federal Government experience, four of them with defense and space agencies. William Ballhaus was a member of the Technical Advisory Panel on Aerospace to the Secretary of Defense from 1954 to 1960 and advisor to the National Advisory Committee for Aeronautics (NASA's predecessor) from 1955 to 1957. Ivan Getting was briefly an Assistant to the Air Force Deputy Chief of Staff and had substantial contact with the DoD when he was President of the Aerospace Corporation for 16 years. Richard Horner spent nearly 20 years with the Air Force as an officer (1940-48) and employee, directing field testing at Wright Field until 1955, serving as Deputy Assistant Secretary of the Air Force (1955-57), then as Assistant Secretary of the Air Force for Research and Development (1957-59). He then became NASA Associate Administrator (1959-60). Board member Charles Robinson served as Under Secretary of State for Economic Affairs from 1974 to 1976.

Rockwell: Rockwell Chairman Robert Anderson came from the Chrysler Corporation to Rockwell in 1968. He succeeded Willard Rockwell, Jr. as chairman in 1974. Anderson and Rockwell ranked among the 15 best compensated corporate executives according to the 1978 *Business Week* survey. Company President Donald R. Beall had been with Collins Radio, absorbed by Rockwell in the early 1970s.

Rockwell's board is the largest in the study—20 members, principally outsiders. The board controls 7.54 percent of company stock, principally through Rockwell family members. Board members have a wide network of ties in the financial community (see Chapter 5), but relatively fewer memberships on boards of other defense contractors. Only $34.7 million in FY 1979 DoD contracts went to firms that included Rockwell directors on their boards.

Rockwell Board members reported no direct experience with Federal and defense policy-making.

United Technologies: United Technologies Chairman Harry Gray, with Litton until he joined UT in 1971, was the highest compensated corporate executive in 1976, according to the *Business Week* survey. For several years the firm had no president. In 1979, however, retired General Alexander M. Haig was named president. Haig also had extensive experience with White House policy-making as staff member of the National Security Council and close advisor to President Richard Nixon. Currently Haig is serving as Secretary of State.

FOOTNOTES

1. "Stock Appreciation Rights Come Into Their Own," *Business Week,* 15 May 1978; "Stocks Sweeten Pay at the Top," Ibid., 12 May 1980; "A New High for Pay at the Top," Ibid., 14 May 1979.
2. U.S. Congress, Senate, Committee on Government Affairs, Subcommittee on Reports, Accounting and Management, *Interlocking Directorates Among the Major U.S. Corporations,* Jan. 1978, p. 287 ff.
3. Ibid., p. 990
4. For partial data, detailing mostly financial institution holdings, see U.S. Congress, Senate Committee on Government Operations, Subcommittee on Intergovernmental Relations, Budgeting, Management and Expenditures, *Disclosure of Corporate Ownership,* March 1974; U.S. Congress, Senate Committee on Governmental Affairs, Subcommittee on Reports, Accounting and Management, *Corporate Ownership and Control,* Nov. 1975; Ibid., *Institutional Investors: Common Stock Holdings and Voting Rights,* May 1976; Ibid., *Voting Rights in Major Corporations,* Jan. 1978. For detailed discussion of data problems and sources of data on stock ownership, one can consult the excellent series of directories on stock ownership in transportation, agribusiness, banking and energy of the Corporate Data Exchange, 198 Broadway, New York, NY 10038.
5. "Pay at the Top," *Business Week.*
6. *Business Week,* 27 March 1978; Richard T. Griffin, "Taking Account of Henry Crown," *The New York Times,* 12 Dec. 1976.

5
Financial Institutions and Auditors

Financial institutions and auditors, offering specific technical services, constitute a significant, though relatively less studied element in a corporation's network of relations with the economic and political world around it. Closely involved with company activity, these institutions can be a subtle, often nearly invisible resource in a company's definition of its corporate future and its relationship with the Federal Government.

Banks supply substantial services to the corporation, including loan capital, financial and management advice and such technical activities as stock registration and transfer, handling of stock and bond issues, and management of savings plans and pension funds. Bank trust departments, moreover, may be significant stockholders in a corporation.[1] Auditors regularly review corporate activity through annual audits and management advice and verify the data a company provides to the Federal Government and the public. Both financial institutions and auditors provide networks of connections and information for a company that can be important resources as a firm defines its financial and Government relations strategy.

Financial Institutions

Financial institutions—commercial, investment and savings banks, as well as insurance and finance companies—are tied into a corporation's operations in a wide variety of ways. Though the relationship between the two is often cloaked in confidentiality making specific data difficult to obtain, the decisions of financial institutions can be critical to a company's fate. A decision to approve or deny credit can sometimes mean the difference between survival, merger, or bankruptcy. Bank trust departments, investment houses, insurance companies or mutual funds may control significant amounts of company stock, providing them with access for input into corporate decision-making and influence over a company's stock value. Investment banks can play a major role in defining a company's diversification, acquisition, or merger strategies. Board members of a company may have significant ties with the boards of financial institutions and vice versa, giving each an interest in, and involvement with, the activities of the other. Banks themselves may come to depend to some extent on the fate of the company: "If you owe the bank ten thousand dollars, the bank owns you; if you owe the bank a million dollars, you own the bank."[2]

Financial institutions, then, are sufficiently closely tied to a company's fate to have an interest in the Government relations activity of a firm that is heavily dependent on Federal contracting. In addition, financial institutions are large and powerful lobbies in their own right, with extensive influence at the local, state, and Federal levels. Locally, banks are frequently so critical to the economic fate of communities that bankers become key actors in local political and economic policy-making.[3] Banks have been credited with having played major roles in resolving financial problems of New York and Cleveland and have a hand in shaping Federal policies.[4] The major financial regulatory agencies—the Federal Reserve Board, the Comptroller of the Currency, the Federal Deposit Insurance Corporation—are staffed by personnel who come from or return to the financial industry.

Banking lobbies—the American Banking Association, the Independent Bankers Association, and other more specialized groups—play an important role in Executive branch and Congressional decision-making with regard to banking policy and regulation. Banking Political Action Committees such as Bankpac provide contributions to members of the Banking Committees in the House and Senate. As one lobbyist for a large bank put it: "The bank lobby can almost certainly stop anything it does not want in Congress."[5] Reenforcing the political influence of financial institutions, an informal network links bankers and financial officers to politicians and policy-makers, giving them a major role in national policy-making. As chairman of Chase Manhattan, for example, David Rockefeller's influence and role in international affairs has been widely discussed, particularly during the events surrounding the admission of the Shah of Iran to the U.S. in the fall of 1979.

The network of relations between a company and the financial community, then, may provide important clues to a company's political power and network. Data on these ties, however, are incomplete and often difficult to obtain. Corporations do not disclose regularly or in detail which financial institutions they do business with or that manage large shareholdings of the company.[6] Investment banks and insurance companies do not provide details on their shareholdings, control over shares, or their role in corporate activities.

The Companies

For this study, we have pulled together available Government and journalistic data on the working ties between the financial community and the eight companies. Company disclosure of their links with lending and investment banks varied greatly. Boeing, Lockheed, and United Technologies provided a full list of lenders with the value of the lines of credit, and the latter two also named some of their investment bankers. Other companies—Grumman, McDonnell Douglas, Northrop and Rockwell—disclosed only some of the banks providing credit, with Rockwell and McDonnell Douglas naming some investment house ties. General Dynamics disclosed no lenders or ties with investment banks.

Data disclosed by the companies on long- and short-term debt shows a wide variation in the extent to which a company is drawing on its banking network (see Table V). Grumman, Lockheed, Rockwell, and United Technologies carry significant debt.[7] Grumman's borrowing in the 1970s was tied principally to the requirements of its F-14 production program, while Lockheed funded the research, development and production of the L-1011 commercial air transport (see Profiles). Rockwell's requirements are less clear, though borrowing may be connected to the firm's substantial commercial business. A large amount of United Technologies' long-term debt represents the conversion of short-term debt to assist the company in commercial diversification—principally the purchase of Carrier Corporation.

Lending ties and board memberships connect several financial institutions closely with the firms in this study. Chase Manhattan lends to five of the companies—Boeing, Grumman, Lockheed, Northrop, and United Technologies—and shares a board member with Lockheed (John Swearingen, chairman of Standard of Indiana). Secretary of State and former United Technologies President Alexander M. Haig was also on the Chase board.

Citicorp lends to four of the companies—Boeing, Grumman, Lockheed and United Technologies. It shares directors with three: Boeing (William Batten, chairman of the New York Stock Exchange; Harold J. Haynes, chairman of Standard Oil of California; and Charles Piggott, president of PACCAR, Inc., a transportation equipment company), Lockheed (John Swearingen), and United Technologies (UT Chairman Harry Gray, Citicorp President William Spencer, William Simon, and D. Smith). Citicorp has long had an interest in Boeing and UT. In the late 1920s the bank was instrumental in creating one of the nation's first aviation trusts, United Aircraft. This trust, dismantled in 1934, combined Pratt & Whitney Engines, Sikorsky Helicopters, Hamilton Standard Propellers, United Aircraft, United Airlines and Boeing. Security Pacific lends to Boeing, Lockheed, Northrop and Rockwell and shares directors with Northrop (Richard Flamson, III, president of Security Pacific) and Rockwell (Robert Anderson, chairman of Rockwell, and Frederick Larkin, Jr., chairman of Security Pacific). Morgan Guarantee also lends to four firms—Boeing, Grumman,

Financial Insitutions and Auditors 67

Lockheed, and United Technologies.

Several banks lend to, and are interconnected with, three of the companies. The Bank of New York lends to Boeing, Grumman, and Lockheed. Grumman Treasurer Robert Freese sits on the Bank's advisory board. Bankers Trust is the lead bank in Lockheed's lending consortium (see below) and lends, as well, to Boeing and Grumman. Manufacturers Hanover lends to Boeing, Lockheed, and Northrop. The Mellon Bank lends to Boeing, Grumman, and Lockheed. Wells Fargo in San Francisco lends to three West Coast companies—Boeing, Lockheed, and Northrop. Another 11 banks lend to two companies in the study, Boeing and Lockheed. Still another 34 banks, some regional and many national, lend to the eight companies (see Profiles). These include the Bank of America, Chemical Bank, Continental Illinois, First National of Boston, First National of Chicago, Irving Trust and United California Bank.

TABLE V

COMPANY DEBT

($millions)

Company	Long-Term Debt (1979)	Credit Line
Boeing	$ 80.7	$1250.0
General Dynamics	53.3	95.0
Grumman	169.2	200.0
Lockheed	526.2	675.0
McDonnell Douglas	86.7	100.0
Northrop	15.3	50.0
Rockwell	431.0	428.0
United Technologies	913.5	1250.0

For several companies, notably Boeing, Grumman, and Lockheed, banks have formed into consortia to handle the firm's financial needs. Boeing's 40-bank consortium is the largest though the amount of credit is larger in the case of Lockheed's consortium of 24 banks. In Grumman and Lockheed's consortia, covenants apply to the credit line conferring on the banks the right to review certain company actions such as the development of new lines of business, investment decisions, mergers, and acquisitions.

Further data on the corporate financial network are available by examining the corporate boards and ascertaining which members also serve on the boards of financial institutions. Our data show that the companies are tied to the following institutions through board membership:

Boeing: 16 (12 of 13 board members)
>BanCal Tri-State Corp. (Skinner)
>Bank of Investment and Credit, Switzerland (H.W. Haynes)
>Brown Brothers Corp. (McPherson)
>Citicorp (Batten, H.J. Haynes, Piggott)
>Commercial National Bank (Morgan)
>Crocker National Corp. (Hiller)
>Equitable Life Assurance Society (Weyerhaeuser)
>Federal Reserve Bank of San Francisco (Stamper)
>First Chicago Corp. (Morgan)
>Manufacturers Hanover (McPherson)
>Pacific National Bank (H.W. Haynes)
>Puget Sound National Bank (Weyerhaeuser)
>SAFECO (Piggott, Reed, Skinner, Weyerhaeuser)
>Seattle First National Bank (Piggott, Reed, Wilson)
>Simpson, Reed & Co. (Reed)
>Skinner Corp. (Skinner)

General Dynamics: 13 (10 of 17 board members)
>Bankamericorp (Lewis)
>Bank of Ladue (Canada) (MacDonald)
>City Investing Co. (Stein)
>Continental Illinois National Trust (Reneker)
>Farmers Investment Co. (Falkoff)
>First Chicago Corp. (Ayers)
>General American Life Insurance Co. (Stein)
>Lazard Freres (Cook)
>Lincoln National Corp. (Cook)
>Multibank Financial Corp. (Veliotis)
>Scherck, Stein & Franc (Stein)
>United Bank of America (Jenner)
>Washington Mutual Savings Bank (Boileau)

Grumman: 13 (9 of 14 board members)
>Atlantic Mutual Insurance Co. (Bierwirth)
>Bank of New York (Freese)
>Centennial Insurance Co. (Bierwirth)
>Discount Corp. (Axelson, Dunbar)
>Dreyfus Third Century Fund (Benson)
>Drexel, Burnham, Lambert (Albright)
>Dry Dock Savings Bank (Axelson)
>East River Savings Bank (Dunbar, Sargent)
>European-American Bancorp. (Gavin)
>General Reinsurance Co. (Bierwirth)
>Long Island Trust Co. (Skurla)
>Protection Mutual Insurance Co. (Axelson)
>Tricontinental Corp. (Dunbar)

Financial Insitutions and Auditors

Lockheed: 18 (10 of 16 board members)
>American National Bank and Trust Co. (Swearingen)
Chase Manhattan (Swearingen)
Compagnie Financiere de Suez (Gurash)
Fiduciary Trust Co. (Downer)
First Chicago Corp. (Ellis)
First City Savings & Loan Assn. (Shaw)
Freemont General Corp. (Flournoy)
Gibraltar Financial Corp. (Flournoy)
Great Western Financial Corp. (Shaw)
Household Finance Corp. (Ellis, Gurash)
Insurance Co. of North America (Gurash)
Lloyds Bank of Calif. (Gurash)
MGIC Investment Corp. (Gurash)
Pacific Mutual Life Insurance (Carter, Horton)
Sutro Mortgage Investment Trust (Anderson)
Union Bancorp (Rensch)
United California Bank (Anderson, Carter, Horton)
Western Bancorp (Carter, Horton)

McDonnell Douglas: 9 (8 of 16 board members)
>American International Group (Chetkovich)
Boatmen's National Bank (Capps)
California Life Corp. (McMillan)
Capistrano National Bank (Douglas)
First Union Bancorp (Jones, S. McDonnell)
General American Life Insurance (Capps, Jones)
Mercantile Bancorp (Orthwein)
St. Louis Union Trust Co. (Jones, J.S. McDonnell, III)
VICO Insurance Co. (Capps)

Northrop: 10 (8 of 11 board members)
>Associated South Investment Co. (McDaniel)
Bankamericorp (McDaniel)
California First Bank (Barger)
City Investing Co. (Jorgenson)
First National Bank of Waseca, Minn. (Getting, Horner)
Kaufman & Broad (Barger, Flamson)
Northwestern National Bank (Horner)
Pacific Indemnity Co. (Ballhaus, McDaniel)
Pegasus Income and Capital Fund (Millar)
Security Pacific Corp. (Flamson)

Rockwell: 17 (16 of 20 board members)
>Cleveland Trust Co. (Karch, Toot)
East River Savings Bank (Duke)
European-American Bancorp (DePalma)

First of Michigan (B. Rockwell)
Mellon National Corp. (W.F. Rockwell)
Metropolitan Life Insurance (Sneath)
Old Republic Insurance (Seifert)
Pittsburgh National Corp. (Roesch, Seymour)
Rice-Hall Association (Muchnic)
Security Pacific Corp. (Anderson, Larkin)
Seneca Bank & Trust (Johnson)
United California Bank (Mudd)
Valley Corp. (Muchnic)
Western American Bank, Ltd. (Larkin)
Western Bancorp (Mudd)

United Technologies: 15 (14 of 16 board members)
Advance Investors Corp. (R. Smith)
Aetna Life & Casualty (Gray)
American Fletcher Corp. (Probst)
Asia Pacific Capital Corp. (Spencer)
Banque Rothschild (Faure)
Chase Manhattan (Haig)
Citicorp (Gray, Simon, D. Smith, Spencer)
Detroit Bancorp (O'Malley)
Federal Reserve Bank of Boston (Van Sinderen)
Hartford National Corp. (Ford, Carlson)
Lincoln Financial Corp. (Holm)
Lincoln First Banks (Holm)
Mutual of New York (Holm)
Security Trust Co. (Sproull)
Travelers Corp. (Ford)

Data on the direct involvement of financial institutions in a company's Government relations activities are extremely scarce. Because these companies depend, in varying degrees, on defense contracting, however, it is fair to assume that the lenders have an interest in and discuss company defense business. Lazard Freres, a major investment house, played a key role in 1974 in trying to help Textron purchase a major interest in Lockheed (see Profiles). Presumably the banks that provided loans to United Technologies also approved of the company's efforts to diversify from defense production. President William I. Spencer of Citicorp, who sits on UT's Board and whose bank is a lender, noted that, "There was a lively awareness in 1971 that the only thing United had done was buy Norden, and that wasn't the most riotously successful thing in the world."[8] It is equally likely that Citicorp looked with favor on Chairman Harry Gray's later success at further diversification.

The link between the lending of money and a corporation's Government relations activity is more evident. Grumman sought to revise the contract for its F-14 program in the early 1970s when it encountered cash flow problems (see Profile). Although the Defense Department was willing to provide financial assistance to the firm, Congress rejected a proposed package. In 1974 a banking consortium, joined by the Melli Bank of Iran, stepped in with a $200 million line of credit.

In the case of Lockheed, the banking consortium also was probably aware of the firm's Government relations efforts in the 1970s. In 1971, after the firm had successfully negotiated solutions to several major contract disputes with DoD, the engine supplier for its L-1011 air transport, Rolls-Royce, went into bankruptcy. In order to deal with the delay in delivery and additional cost of the L-1011 program, Lockheed requested a Federal loan guarantee of $250 million. The firm's banks were directly involved in this process, because they desired the guarantee in order to provide further loans to the firm (see Profile).

Lockheed's banks were also involved in the effort to restructure the firm's management in 1976, in the wake of revelations of the company's questionable payments overseas.

With respect to the other firms in the study, most of which are less dependent on defense contracting than Lockheed and Grumman, indications of bank involvement in defense contracting issues are less clear.

The Accounting Business

While accounting firms may play no direct role in marketing and lobbying for their corporate client, their work has implications for a company's relationship with the Federal Government. The accounting profession and its association, the American Institute of Certified Public Accountants (AICPA), play a central role in defining appropriate accounting standards for business. This role is exercised, in large part, through their participation in the Financial Accounting Standards Board (FASB), a private body established to set accounting standards.[9]

There are eight leading firms in the AICPA and the FASB: Arthur Andersen & Co., Arthur Young & Co., Coopers & Lybrand; Deloitte, Haskins & Sells; Ernst & Whinney; Peat, Marwick & Mitchell; Price Waterhouse & Co., and Touche Ross & Co. "These eight firms are so big and influential in relation to other accounting firms that they dominate the practice of accounting in the United States and probably throughout the world."[10]

These firms function as independent auditors reviewing a corporation's financial data and certifying it to the Federal Government, the stockholders, and the general public. They seek to ensure that a company has fully and accurately described its financial situation. The information that they choose to recognize—or ignore—is accordingly of great significance. In addition to setting accounting standards and auditing a company's books, accounting firms increasingly fulfill a third role in relation to the firm—that of management advisor.

In all three of these roles, accounting firms can have an effect on the relationship between defense contractors and the Federal Government. The nature, content, and quality of financial data disclosed by contractors to the Government is an important element in evaluating peformance. Admiral Hyman Rickover has questioned the data:

> Defense contractors cite figures from their annual reports in efforts to negotiate higher profits on new orders, to obtain better claim settlements, or to change defense procurement policy....
>
> Given the importance of corporate annual reports to the economy as a whole, and also to defense procurement, one would expect that the figures in these reports accurately reflect the results of a company's operations and its financial condition. I find that little credence can be placed on these figures. Companies have great latitude in how they can account for costs and profits for financial accounting purposes. As a result the figures are susceptible to manipulation and judgments which can dramatically change reported profits— all within the constraints of the so-called "generally accepted accounting principles."[11]

Although we have not raised questions about the quality of the basic financial data disclosed by the contractors, clearly accounting standards which permit "manipulation and judgments" leave some uncertainty as to how effectively the Government can judge contractor performance and administer contracts.

Accounting firms can also have an important impact on contractor behavior through their auditing function. The eight firms in the study are audited by six of the "Big Eight" firms: Arthur Andersen & Co. (General Dynamics, Grumman); Arthur Young & Co. (Lockheed); Deloitte, Haskins & Sells (Rockwell International); Ernst & Whinney (McDonnell Douglas); Price Waterhouse (United Technologies); and Touche Ross & Co. (Boeing, Northrop). A Senate report on accounting (1976) was highly critical of the extent to which these firms represented the private over the public interest in their function as auditor.

> It appears that the "Big Eight" firms are more concerned with serving the interests of corporate managements who select them and authorize their fees than with protecting the interests of the public, for whose benefit Congress established the position of independent auditor.[12]

Admittedly, an auditor, no matter how "independent," might encounter some serious problems in being tough. Auditors must rely for information, cooperation and future business on the companies they audit. William Gladstone, managing partner with Arthur Young & Co. noted "you can't be an adversary and do an audit of a company."[13] Nevertheless, some firms have been criticized for being too lenient, especially in their handling of data on questionable payments by corporations.[14] The Senate report criticized Arthur Young & Co. for its handling of Lockheed's financial data in the early 1970s:

> As independent auditor for Lockheed, Arthur Young & Co. has approved the use of accounting methods which possibly misrepresent Lockheed's actual financial situation. To the extent that it has approved such accounting methods, Arthur Young & Co. has served the interests of Lockheed's management rather than the public interest.[15]

On the other hand, Arthur Young & Co. may have served the public interest in their later handling of Lockheed's questionable overseas payments. According to the Lockheed board's report on the investigation of these payments, Young's auditors were disturbed by the data on payments in several foreign countries. They attempted to obtain company verification that the payments complied with company policy and did not include payments to foreign government officials, and that company personnel did not know how consultants might have used the money. When Lockheed officers declined to verify these propositions, Young & Co. undertook further investigation leading to the disclosures of June and July 1975.[16]

Auditing firms may also find themselves in a difficult position vis-a-vis defense contractors in their third role, as management consultant. Virtually all of the firms which do business with private contractors do substantial management consulting work for the Federal Government as well. Although the details are not available, the firms which audit the companies in this study disclosed having done work for the following DoD agencies and NASA:

> Arthur Andersen—Navy, NASA
> Arthur Young—Air Force, Army, Navy, OSD
> Deloitte, Haskins & Sells—Navy
> Price Waterhouse—Navy
> Touche Ross—Army[17]

The Senate report is critical of what they describe as the "conflict of interest" which can arise from consulting on both sides of the contractor/Government relationship:

> The "Big Eight" accounting firms provide extensive services to Federal, State, and local governments. They are able to directly influence the course of governmental policies and programs through performance of their services. Conflicts of interest occur when "Big Eight" firms influence governmental authorities on matters which affect their corporate clients. The "Big Eight" firms have been able to spread the scope of their influence across both the public and the private sectors.[18]

In addition to offering advice as Government consultants, accounting firms often provide Congressional and public testimony promoting the views of their corporate clients. The Senate Report notes, for example, that Ernst and Whinney urged the Cost Accounting Standards Board (CASB) to permit defense contractors to include the cost of borrowing as an allowable cost for contract reimbursement purposes.[19] The "Big Eight" could have had considerable impact on CASB standards, since their representatives dominated the AICPA's Cost Accounting Standards Board Committee, which handled liaison between the profession and the CASB.[20]

FOOTNOTES

1. *CDE Handbook: Banking and Finance: The Hidden Cost* (New York: Corporate Data Exchange, 1980).
2. Adam Yarmolinsky, *The Military Establishment* (New York: Harper & Row, 1071), p. 70.

3. See, for instance, Floyd Hunter, *Community Power Structure* (Chapel Hill: University of North Carolina Press, 1953) and Robert Dahl, *Who Governs: Democracy and Power in America* (New Haven: Yale University Press, 1961).
4. "Banks' Influence in Capital Called Strongest of Any Regulated Industry," *The New York Times*, 23 Dec. 1977.
5. Ibid.
6. Corporate filings with the SEC (stock prospectuses and proxies) provide some data. Standard business sources, such as Moody's, often disclose only the banks serving as transfer agents or registrars.
7. Boeing's borrowing may rise as it becomes more involved in the early stages of producing its new 757 and 767 commercial transports.
8. A.F. Ehrbar, "United Technologies' Master Plan," *Fortune*, 22 Sept. 1980, p. 99.
9. See U.S. Senate, Committee on Government Operations, Subcommittee on Reports, Accounting and Management, *The Accounting Establishment: A Staff Study* (Washington, DC: GPO, 1976).
10. Ibid., p. 4.
11. Ibid., Reprint of testimony before the Seapower Subcommittee of the House Armed Services Committee, Sept. 1974, p. 1722.
12. Ibid., p. 58.
13. *Forbes*, 15 May 1976.
14. Price Waterhouse was criticized for its handling of General Tire and Rubber, United Brands and Gulf Oil payments. See *The Wall Street Journal*, 11 April 1975 and 11 May 1976; and Senate report, *Accounting Establishment*, p. 63.
15. Ibid., p. 58; see also pp. 1605-1700 for detailed discussion by Prof. A.J. Briloff, Baruch College.
16. *Report of the Special Review Committee of the Board of Directors of Lockheed Aircraft Corporation*, 16 May 1977, p. 20.
17. See Senate report, *Accounting Establishment*, pp. 225, 253, 320, 375, 395.
18. Ibid., p. 67. The report notes that Coopers and Lybrand did a study for the DoD on the profits of defense contractors. The firm, which has major defense contractors as clients, concluded that defense business was "riskier than commercial business, and that Federal procurement regulations are unnecessarily complex and demanding" (quoted on p. 66).
19. From 1970 to 1980 the CASB operated as a Federal agency defining cost accounting standards for Federal contractors. In 1980, its authority was allowed to lapse by the Congress. The Senate report noted that the CASB had, in general, done an effective job (Ibid., p. 26).
20. Ibid., pp. 60, 186.

6
Personnel Transfers

A flow of personnel—uniformed and civilian—links the Executive with the industry side of the "iron triangle." Defense contractors regularly hire DoD civilian employees and retiring military officers who bring a wealth of professional experience and useful contacts to the company. From its side the Defense Department hires personnel from the companies, providing the Government with skilled executives.

This circular flow creates a community of shared assumptions about policy issues and developments. To the insider, this intimacy seems to foster technical and political knowledge that smooths the contracting process, insuring a more efficient defense of national security and the public good. To the outsider, however, it suggests favoritism, a narrowing of perspective in which the private and Government interests converge in a single vision that excludes a wider perspective.

Past and Present

Public concern over defense/industry personnel transfers is longstanding. In 1959, when it was revealed that over 700 retired Pentagon employees had accepted employment in the defense industry, Representative Alfred E. Santangelo (D-NY) introduced an amendment to the Defense Appropriations Bill that would have denied contracts to any company that employed a former general or admiral who had seen active duty within the preceding five years. In a close vote his amendment was defeated.

Ten years later Senator William Proxmire stated that the top 100 DoD contractors had employed over 2,000 former military personnel, over half of them with 10 companies that included Boeing, General Dynamics, McDonnell Douglas, Lockheed and Rockwell. In the climate of reform that followed, a bill was passed that required recent transferees — civilian and military moving from the DoD to the contractors as well as contractor employees who transferred to DoD — to file an annual report with DoD for three years after the transfer.

In 1975, CEP published the first systematic review of these reports. The Council found that the top 100 contractors had hired 1,400 former DoD civilian and military employees between 1969 and 1973.[1] In addition, CEP found that compliance with the reporting requirement was poor, with a minimum of 1,500 required reports not filed.[2] The study also noted that in the same period 379 reports were filed by former contractor employees who had been hired by the Department of Defense.

In this study we have examined the reports for eight companies which hired 1,672 former military and civilian employees of DoD and NASA between 1970 and 1979. During this period, moreover, 270 company employees who moved to DoD and NASA filed reports. In short, the flow of personnel has continued unabated, bringing the Executive and the industrial sides of the "iron triangle" ever closer.

Chart V

PERSONNEL TRANSFERS
Department of Defense, 1971-1979
NASA, 1974-1979

Company	Military	Civilian	Total personnel transfers
Boeing	316	82	398
Northrop	284	76	360
Lockheed	240	81	321
General Dynamics	189	50	239
Rockwell	150	84	234
McDonnell Douglas	159	52	211
Grumman	67	29	96
United Technologies	50	33	83
	1,455	487	1,942

A Single Point of View

Military retirees provide the industry with a pool of men and women who are knowledgeable in the ways of Government, aerospace technology, and procurement strategies. A former ITT vice president gives this description:

> (Tom Gallagher) was one of a large number of military retirees who became "commercial representatives." They were an unusual lot. Although sales was their function, they were prevented by law from actively selling to the military for three years after discharge or retirement. But, being clever in the methods of Pentagon procurement, they found ways around such awkward regulations. Lunch and cocktail hours were used to maximum advantage, as well as the golf course and private clubs. By and large, they performed their marketing chores without setting foot inside the Pentagon....
>
> It was a lucrative game—for a while. The "representatives" exploited contacts and an intimate knowledge of certain military programs for as long as both lasted. The span was usually two to three years.[3]

The expertise brought by these individuals is not only technical but political: information on and access to policy-making that helps create a closed network in a community of shared assumptions. Political scientists Harman Zeigler and Wayne G. Peak comment:

> Ideally, one sure way for an interest group to guarantee close ties with an agency is to play a part in the selection of its personnel. Generally unsuccessful in their efforts to influence the electoral process interest groups have had more luck in the appointment of administrative personnel. The acknowledgment that the interest group and the government agency will work together in a common area of interest of less concern to a more general public perhaps establishes more credibility.[4]

The contractors obtain many benefits from the movement of personnel: information on current and future DoD and NASA plans, especially in research areas; access to key offices in Federal agencies, technical expertise for weapons development and marketing, skilled personnel with an intimate knowledge of both sides of contracting. The "revolving door" enhances the ability of a contractor to develop a successful Government relations strategy and gives the Government useful insights into the contractors' ways of doing business.

Both sides defend the transfer of personnel, claiming that it serves the national interest. Rockwell's Robert Anderson summarized the company's position:

> It is our policy to consider former Federal officials for positions for which they may be qualified. This policy, I believe, is consistent with the policies of our Government

which do not prohibit the employment by Government contractors of a former Federal official merely because of his prior Government service.... Moreover, a Government contractor might thereby be denied valuable talents in performance of difficult tasks.

There are, of course, statutory provisions relating to the hiring of former Government officials and our personnel people are mindful of them in implementing our employment policy....

Based on my experience at Rockwell, I do not believe such employment has adversely affected the Government. Obviously, our hiring qualified, experienced people improves our products and performance, but it does not give us any improper advantage or influence in our dealings with the Government. There are two factors on which I would like to comment in this connection.

First, for the reasons I mentioned earlier, the procurement process is so highly regulated and controlled that previous associations can have little or no weight.

Second, constant changes in technologies, requirements, policies, and personnel make it likely that the insights that a former official may have into the affairs of an agency for which he worked will be of little relevance within a short time after he leaves Government service. Thus the emphasis in hiring former Government officials has to be on their qualifications to perform duties and responsibilities for the company rather than assuming that information gained in Government service will be of any long-range utility....

Finally, I want to express my concern that industry's performance on the programs for which it has responsibility may be adversely affected if it becomes more difficult to attract able and experienced people from industry to Government. Public service, and particularly public service by capable people willing to do so for the productive periods in their career, should be encouraged and supported. Restrictions beyond those presently in effect that would make employment with a Government contractor more difficult after Government service are not, in my judgment, in the Government's long-term interest.[5]

Government officials also defend the personnel movement as in the national interest:

I believe the interchange of people between NASA and industry is a healthy and extremely important one to the productivity, efficiency and success of our aeronautic and space programs. It is therefore NASA policy to include among its top management members a mix of career civil servants and managers with extensive industry experience.[6]

Representative Samuel Stratton (D-NY) warned against restricting the movement of personnel:

> We are denying to our defense industries... the services and assistance of the very people who have had the most experience in the fields of weapons and related matters to which the government looks to such contractors. If this amendment were to go through in this extreme form, we would actually be jeopardizing our own national defense.[7]

Federal Statutes

Public discussions of the personnel transfer issue have focused less on policy bias and special access to information and Federal offices than on the risk of conflict of interest. According to one Civil Service Commission representative,

> the purpose for conflict of interest legislation in the Federal sector is to protect the impartiality of the Federal Government decision-making processes. This purpose can only be accomplished by insuring that an individual employed in the Federal service and engaged in these processes is not influenced by any private and personal considerations in performance of his duties, such as to attempt to effect any particular Government action which will be advantageous to any of his personal interests.[8]

Several Federal statutes are designed to prevent such conflicts. Provisions of 18 U.S.C. 203, 205 and 209 prohibit a Federal employee from representing any other party before agencies of the Federal Government in which the employee has a job or an interest. They also prohibit an employee from participating in his/her Governmental capacity in any matter in which he/she, a spouse or minor child, or business associate or person with whom he/she is negotiating for employment has a financial interest.[9]

Section 207 of the statute covers the post-employment period. Former Federal employees are barred "from acting as an agent or attorney in a particular matter involving specific parties in which the United States had an interest and in which the individual had substantially and personally participated while at the agency" (Section a). This prohibition has no termination point in time. Section b prohibits former Federal employees for one year "from personally appearing as an agent or attorney for anyone before an agency in a particular matter involving specific parties in which the United States had an interest and over which he/she had had official responsibility within the past year."[10]

In 1978, the Ethics in Government Act (PL 95-521) revised this statute to increase the prohibition in Section b from one year to two and to prohibit some specific aid and assistance activities by former Government employees who were ranked GS-17 and above. This amendment also added Section c which prohibits for one year specified former high level agency officials from "any contacts with their former agencies on behalf of others to influence the outcome of any matter pending before their former agencies."[11]

Two other Federal statutes refer directly to the activities of former military officers, prohibiting them from selling to the Federal Government. The "criminal selling law" (18 USC 281) states: "Nothing herein shall be construed to allow any retired officer to represent any person in the sale of anything to the Government through the department in whose service he holds a retired status."[12]

Civil statute 37 USC 801(c) prohibits for three years any payments to a retired officer "who is engaged for himself or others in selling, or contracting or negotiating to sell, supplies or war materials to any agency of the Department of Defense, the Coast Guard, the Environmental Science Services Administration or the Public Health Services."[13]

Unfortunately, as CEP's earlier study of personnel transfers noted, these statutes have not been firmly enforced. Furthermore, they do not deal with some of the more subtle dangers: "temptation" and "appearance."

"Temptation" and "Appearance": Definitions

Regulation seeks to put some distance between the Government official and the industry with which he/she is dealing, in order to avoid the "temptation" to perform in certain ways while in office because of personal interests he/she has in the future in the industry. As the New York Bar puts it:

> A conflict of interest does not necessarily presuppose that action by the official favoring one of these interests will be prejudicial to the other, nor that the official will in fact resolve the conflict to his own personal advantage rather than the government's. If a man is in a position of conflicting interests, he is subject to temptation, however he resolves the issue. Regulation of conflicts of interest seeks to prevent situations of temptation from arising.[14]

One major form of "temptation," particularly relevant to the "iron triangle" of defense policy, is the lure of future employment in the defense industry. A civilian or military official might be tempted to shave a little on cost control, delivery deadlines, performance specifications or choice of contractor. The data in this study suggest that the possibilities of such employment, hence of "temptation," are real. Former Assistant Secretary of Defense J. Ronald Fox described the situation:

> The availability of jobs in industry can have a subtle, but debilitating effect on an officer's performance during his tour of duty in a procurement management assignment. If he takes too strong a hand in controlling contractor activity, he might be damaging his opportunity for a second career following retirement. Positions are offered to officers who have demonstrated their appreciation for industry's particular problems and commitments.[15]

The New York Bar comments:

> The risk is not bribery through the device of job offers. The risk is that of sapping governmental policy especially regulatory policy, through the nagging and persistent conflicting interests of the Government official who has his eye cocked toward subsequent private employment. To turn the matter around, the greatest public risks arising from post-employment conduct may well occur during the period of Government employment, through the dampening of aggressive administration of Government policies.[16]

A Civil Service Commissioner requested that Federal employees avoid situations

> which might result in or create the appearance of... using public office for private gain;... losing complete independence or impartiality of action;... or affecting adversely the confidence of the public in the integrity of the Federal Government.[17]

Appearances, of course, can be misleading. In an area as critical as defense, however, extra efforts should be expended to avoid even the appearance that a Defense Department official might be involved in decisions affecting the firm with which he was previously employed, or may be employed in the future.

We have focused on the problem of appearances in our review of the reports filed by transferees working for the eight companies in this study. We note transferees[18] who worked in similar areas in policy-making and weapons systems on one side of the triangle before moving to a similar area on the other. For example, an Assistant Secretary of Strategic Planning in the Directorate of Defense Research and Engineering might by virtue of his office have had responsibility involving a specific strategic weapons system. As a company vice president for long-range planning either before or after DoD employment, he might have been involved in defining the contractor's interest in the same system. We have called these situations "appearance of a potential conflict of interest."

We are deliberately cautious in listing these employees. In the first place, the quality of data disclosed varies enormously. Some employees provided some description of their responsibilities, while others noted only their title in the company or Government office. Second, we are not assuming that these people are or were insensitive to the conflict of interest issue. They may well have taken strict measures to ensure that they had no involvement with their former employer. We are not accusing *any* of these individuals, in other words, of wrongdoing. As Michael Kinsley has put it:

> We should do them the courtesy of treating an appearance of a conflict as an *appearance*. We should not automatically impute criminality or immorality and those who have disclosed the facts have a right to be indignant when we do. But we should have the right to question them about the appearance and they should not feel indignant when questioned.[19]

Personnel Transfers

TABLE VI

PERSONNEL TRANSFERS
(DoD 1970-79)
(NASA 1974-79)

Company	Total Flow	Flow to Company DoD Military	Flow to Company DoD Civilian	NASA	Flow to Government To DoD	to NASA
Boeing	398	316	35	3	37	7
General Dynamics	239	189	17	1	32	0
Grumman	96	67	5	1	16	7
Lockheed	321	240	30	6	34	11
McDonnell Douglas	211	159	12	2	29	9
Northrop	360	284	50	9	16	1
Rockwell	234	150	26	6	47	5
United Technologies	83	50	11	3	12	7
Total	1942	1455	186	31	223	47

The Companies

Our review of personnel transfers covered all reports filed by former DoD and NASA employees (civilian and military) as well as all filed by company employees who had come to the company from DoD or NASA.[20] We have reported this data for each of the eight companies in the Profiles and have aggregated it for all eight (see Tables VI, VII, VIII, IX).

During the years covered by the data, the eight companies in the study hired 1,455 former military and 186 former civilian employees of DoD, and 31 former employees of NASA. During the same years, the contractors sent 270 company employees to DoD and NASA. In total, disclosed data show that just over 1,940 individuals transferred between these eight contracting companies and the two Government agencies which provided their principal Federal market between 1970 and 1979. Moreover, due to underreporting this figure probably understates the total traffic (see Table VI).

Boeing ranked highest in total transfers for the decade—398, followed by Northrop (360) and Lockheed (321). General Dynamics, McDonnell Douglas and Rockwell had over 200 transfers each with DoD, while Grumman and United Technologies each had under 100. While such a number of transfers may provide a rough indication of the closeness of the relationship of the corporation with the Federal

Government, it may also indicate that some companies more strongly urge their employees to comply with the reporting requirement than others.

In terms of civilian transfers, particularly from DoD, a slightly different pattern emerges. Northrop hired the largest number (50), while Rockwell was the source of the largest number of civilian employees hired by DoD during the decade (47). (See Table VI.)

Our examination of transfer reports took particular notice of persons employed in the principal research and development activities of the Federal Government: the Directorate of Defense Research and Engineering (Office of Secretary of Defense—OSD), the research and development offices of the Army, Navy, and Air Force, and NASA. The research and development arena is particularly crucial to a company's effort to obtain early information and access to DoD and NASA policies and procurement. Of the 487 total civilian transfers between DoD and NASA and the eight companies, fully 165 or 33.9 percent were to or from these offices. An even higher proportion of transfers with Grumman (41 percent) and United Technologies (39 percent), both of whom had low transfer rates overall, were with these offices (see Table IX).

Looking specifically at civilian transfers, we noted 119 employees whose job descriptions fell into the category of "appearance of potential conflict of interest," as defined above.[21]

These constitute 24 percent of total civilian transfers over the decade. Proportions of such cases were particularly high for Grumman (34.5 percent), General Dynamics (32.0 percent) and Northrop (30.3 percent). (See Table VIII.)

TABLE VII
PERSONNEL TRANSFERS BY AGENCY*
(DoD 1970-79)
(NASA 1974-79)

Company	NASA	USAF	USA	USN	OSD	Other	Total
Boeing	10	271	50	37	25	5	398
General Dynamics	1	111	23	85	10	9	239
Grumman	8	26	4	47	7	4	96
Lockheed	17	175	30	71	9	19	321
McDonnell Douglas	11	127	21	33	8	11	211
Northrop	10	224	22	68	14	22	360
Rockwell	11	117	19	59	15	13	234
United Technologies	10	38	15	8	7	5	83
Total	78	1089	184	408	95	88	1942

* Counting movements in both directions.

Boeing had the highest number of total transfers in the study, reflecting both a close relationship with DoD and, perhaps, a high standard for employee compliance with the reporting requirement. Since the bulk of Boeing's DoD sales are to the Air Force, it is hardly surprising that 68.1 percent of their transferees were with that service. Boeing also had the highest number of transfers in the study with the Army (50) with which its Vertol Division does substantial business. Boeing also ranked first in transfers with the Office of Secretary of Defense (25), the principal policy-making apparatus for the Department. Five Boeing transfers—Edward Ball, Jr., Elliot Harwood, T.K. Jones, Hua Lin and Ben Plymale—worked in the Directorate of Defense Research and Development, an arena of crucial access to information on future DoD weapons planning. All five also fall into the "appearance" category, as defined above (see Profiles for further discussion).

Other Boeing transferees present equally interesting illustrations of the close connection between agency and company. Frank Shrontz, a Boeing employee, became Assistant Secretary of the Air Force in 1973 and subsequently Assistant Secretary of Defense (Installations and Logistics) before returning to Boeing in 1977. Leonard Sullivan, employed by Boeing as a consultant, had previously been an Assistant Secretary of Defense for Program Analysis. Dale Babione, who moved to Boeing's Washington office in 1979, had been with DoD for 29 years, most recently as Deputy Assistant Secretary of Defense for Procurement.

General Dynamics ranked fourth in total transfers. It had only one reported exchange with NASA, for which it is a small contractor. DoD transfers were split between the Air Force (46.4 percent) and Navy (35.6 percent), both of which do substantial contracting with the company (missiles and aircraft for the Air Force, missiles and ships for the Navy).

General Dynamics employee and former employee reports show a fairly high proportion of "appearance of possible conflict of interest" cases, as defined above: 32 percent of civilian transferees.

Grant Hansen went from Assistant Secretary of the Air Force for Research and Development to the post of vice president and general manager of the Convair Division of General Dynamics. Convair Division had responsibility for developing the Air Force version of General Dynamics' Tomahawk cruise missile which competed for (and lost) an Air Force production contract in 1978-80. Kenneth Ray Hinman went from a General Dynamics post on cruise-missile and fighter-attack aircraft programs to a job in the key research and engineering office of OSD, working on air warfare and monitoring advanced R & D on weapons systems and interdiction programs. General Dynamics has a number of missile programs which fulfill this role.

Grumman had a low number of transferees—96, nearly half of whom were with its principal customer, the Navy. Of the eight companies, Grumman had the highest proportion of "appearance of potential conflict of interest" cases (34.5 percent) among civilian transferees. James Erickson left Grumman as a supervisor of production for aerospace systems and joined the Air Force in 1975 as a director for manufacturing operations. Grumman has a significant Air Force contract for conversion of the F-111 to surveillance electronics. John Garafolo left the Navy, Grumman's main customer, as an assistant branch head in the Anti-submarine and Special Mission Air Support group and became Grumman's planning manager for Integrated Logistics Support. William Luckenbill, Navy Program Analyst, moved directly to Grumman's Washington office as a Government liaison representative, a post he has since left. Hugh McCullough moved from being Grumman's director of long-range planning to a position as Special Assistant to the Assistant Secretary of Defense for Installations and Logistics. In 1969 Sidney Singer, former budget analyst with the OSD, became a Grumman staff assistant for liaison with Government agencies.

Lockheed ranked third in total transfers (321) and in number of company transfers to DoD (34). Three-quarters of Lockheed transfers were with the Air Force (54.5 percent) and the Navy (22.1 percent), sources of most of Lockheed's DoD contracts. In addition, Lockheed had the highest number of transfers with NASA (17), with which the company has some important contracts.

Lockheed has had several interesting cases of "appearance of potential conflict of interest," though these rank next to last in the study as a proportion of total civilian transfers (16.0 percent). Leonard Alne, former Director of Sales Negotiations for the Defense Security Assistance Agency (DSAA), became a consultant to Lockheed in January 1977 on the sale of military aircraft to foreign buyers. Lockheed has made a considerable overseas sales effort for its C-130 cargo and P-3C anti-submarine warfare planes, contracts for which pass through the DSAA. Willis Hawkins, Army Assistant Secretary for Research and Development in the mid-1960s, returned to Lockheed in 1966 and became the company's senior vice president. He remained a consultant to the Army Science Board. In the late 1960s, Lockheed received a major R & D contract for the Army's Cheyenne helicopter. The system never went into production. In 1974, Bartley Osborne, Jr., Lockheed's senior engineering advisor on tactical aircraft R & D for the Navy and Air Force moved to a position in the Directorate of Research and Engineering (OSD), reviewing aeronautics programs. In 1978, he returned to Lockheed to manage contract and company sponsored conceptual studies on new military aircraft. James W. Plummer, Chief of Communications and Navigation at the Naval Air Test Center, became a Lockheed vice president in 1955. In 1973 he became Under Secretary of the Air Force. Three years later he returned to Lockheed's Missile and Space Company as executive vice president.

McDonnell Douglas ranked sixth in overall transfers and fourth in the number of company employees who went to DoD and NASA. Over half (60.2 percent) of the company's transfers were with the Air Force, the source of most of its defense business (F-4, F-15). The company had a fairly high rate of "appearance of potential conflict of interest" cases, as defined above—28.8 percent of civilian transfers. Robert L. Johnson was MDC vice president for research and engineering in 1969 when he took a position as Assistant Secretary of the Army for Research and Development. After three years with the Army, Johnson returned to MDC as corporate vice president for engineering and research, became president of the McDonnell Douglas Astronautics Company and in 1980 became a corporate senior vice president with responsibility for the Douglas Aircraft Division. Arthur N. Thomas, Jr. moved from MDC's Astronautics Company to a position as Deputy Assistant Secretary of the Army for Research and Development concerned with air and missile defense. Charles R. Weiser, who worked in the Directorate for Defense Research and Engineering (OSD), became MDC's director for advanced defense systems in 1971. Wayne Winten went from MDC's Astronautics Company where he worked on ballistic missile defense, to a position as program director in the Army's Ballistic Missile Defense Office. MDC is the Pentagon's principal contractor for ballistic missile defense.

Bruce James, program manager for research and development at MDC Astronautics, moved to Defense Advanced Research Projects Agency (DARPA) in 1974 as Deputy Director of the Tactical Technology Office, managing research and development programs. James T. Rose, manager of MDC's space shuttle program support, went to

TABLE VIII
APPEARANCE OF POTENTIAL CONFLICT OF INTEREST
(CIVILIAN TRANSFEREES)

Company	Civilian Transfers	Appearance of Potential Conflict	%
Boeing	82	16	19.5%
General Dynamics	50	16	32.0%
Grumman	29	10	34.5%
Lockheed	81	13	16.0%
McDonnell Douglas	52	15	28.8%
Northrop	76	20	26.3%
Rockwell	84	18	21.4%
United Technologies	33	8	24.2%
Total	487	116	24.4%

NASA in 1974 to direct engineering on the space shuttle program, and then returned to MDC two years later as manager of payload development for research and commercial applications in space. MDC has a NASA contract for shuttle payload work.

Northrop had the second largest number of transfers in the study—360. This represents a rapid increase since CEP's last review, which could reflect both increased hiring and a more active corporate policy on compliance with the reporting requirement.

The largest proportion of Northrop transfers were with the Air Force (62.2 percent). Northrop does much of its contract work with the Air Force, particularly the sales of the F-5 series overseas. In 1976 and 1978, a large number of officials transferred from the Air Force's San Antonio Logistics Center and Wright-Patterson Air Force Base to Northrop, principally to work in aircraft services and foreign military sales. Eleven of Northrop's civilian transferees reported working with Northrop's Worldwide Services subsidiary, which handles logistics, sales, and service for the company's sales, including the massive Peace Hawk program in Saudi Arabia.

In 1976, Northrop CEO Thomas Jones praised the technical knowledge that the retirees had provided:

> [With regard to] our development of airplanes requiring officers or individuals experienced in logistics support, supply and maintenance, we find that the Air Force retirees who have that direct experience had nothing to do with selling. The largest portion of these officers that were hired in the last 3 years, by far the largest portion, were in those areas of technical maintenance, logistics support and product support.[22]

Northrop had a number of cases of "appearance of potential conflict of interest." Robert Alexander left the Air Force Logistics Command as Deputy Director of the Directorate of Mission and Management, to become a field manager for Northrop in Dayton, analyzing information on foreign military sales. Leonard Alne, former Director of Sales Negotiations for DSAA, in 1974 became a consultant to Northrop on the sale of military aircraft to foreign buyers. Rufus Crocket moved from being Deputy Assistant Secretary of the Air Force to Program Director for technical facilities and construction for Northrop's Peace Hawk program in Saudi Arabia in 1975. In 1978, Larry James, director of DARPA's Tactical Technical Office became vice president of Northrop's Ventura Division, which handles a number of advanced research projects. Joe Jones was Deputy Assistant Secretary of the Air Force for Research and Development when he left in 1974 to become assistant to Northrop's chairman for aeronautical systems. Kent Kresa, Deputy Director of DARPA's Strategic Technology Office and later Director of the Tactical Technology Office, became vice president and manager of Northrop's Research Technology Center in 1975 and later corporate vice president and manager of the company's Ventura Division.

TABLE IX
TRANSFEREES IN RESEARCH AND DEVELOPMENT

Company	OSD	DARPA	Air Force	Navy	Army	NASA	Total R & D Trans.	Total Civilian Transfers	%
Boeing	11	2	4	3	—	9	29	82	35%
General Dynamics	7	1	1	3	1	1	14	50	28%
Grumman	1	—	—	2	1	8	12	29	41%
Lockheed	5	—	1	4	2	18	30	81	37%
McDonnell Douglas	1	1	—	—	3	11	16	51	31%
Northrop	1	4	7	2	—	11	25	76	33%
Rockwell	7	1	1	4	2	11	26	84	31%
United Technologies	2	—	1	—	—	10	13	33	39%
Total	35	9	15	18	9	79	165	486	34%

Rockwell ranked fifth in total transfers, but first in transfers of company personnel to DoD (47). Despite being NASA's largest contractor, Rockwell had fewer transfers with NASA (11) than other firms. Most of Rockwell's transfers were with the Air Force (50.0 percent) and a smaller amount with the Navy (25.2 percent). The company does substantial contracting with both agencies. Five transfers were between DoD and Rockwell's Autonetics Marine Systems Division, which has contracts with the Navy. Six transferred between the Naval Elecronics Lab and Rockwell electronics positions. Another five took place between Rockwell and the Defense Communications Agency; Rockwell is a major communications contractor with DoD.

Rockwell had several cases of "appearance of potential conflict of interest"—21.4 percent of civilian transfers. David Anderson, Operations Research analyst for the Air Force, became an executive advisor to Rockwell's B-1 Division in 1970 and later a staff specialist in the Directorate of Defense Research and Engineering. John Brinkman, director of research and development of the Rockwell Autonetics Division and of the company's Science Center became Army Deputy Director for Research, Development and Engineering. Spencer Clapp, manager of Rockwell's Navy/Air Force Laser Program, went to the Army Missile Command as a general engineer associated with the high energy laser project ofice. William Erers also moved from Rockwell laser work to the Army program. Joseph Cruden, Rockwell's planning director, became Deputy Director of the Navy Material Command in 1971.

William Laidlaw, Special Assistant to the Director of Defense Research and Engineering (OSD), became Rockwell's vice president for research and engineering in 1967. Harold Larson, Deputy Director at DSAA became manager for international marketing at Collins Radio in 1973. Dale Myers moved from a NASA position as Associate Administrator for Manned Flight to the post of president of North American Aircraft Operations in 1974. Robert Parker, Rockwell engineer, became Principal Deuputy Director of Defense Research and Engineering in 1973. Thomas Walsh, Rockwell research engineer, also went into the Directorate of Research and Engineering in 1976.

United Technologies had the lowest number of transferees in the study (83), most of whom (50) were retired military employees of DoD. Almost half of these were with the Air Force (38 or 45.8 percent), with which United Technologies does air engine contracting. United Technologies had a fairly high rate of "appearance of potential conflict" cases (24.2 percent among civilian transfers) and the highest rate of transfers in the R & D area in the study. Howard Cantus, former Deputy Assistant Secretary for Legislative Affairs in the Office of Secretary of Defense became, in 1977, the manager of energy programs for the Washington office of the United Technologies Power Systems Division. Hugh Witt, Senior Civilian Assistant to the Assistant Secretary of Defense for Installations and Logistics in the OSD (and then Director of the Office of Federal Procurement Policy), became director of Government liaison in United Technologies' Washington office in 1977. One recent United Technologies transfer, not yet formally reported to DoD, concerns former NATO Commander Alexander M. Haig, who became the president and chief operating officer at United Technologies in 1979 before resigning to become Secretary of State in 1981.

FOOTNOTES

1. Leon S. Reed, *Military Maneuvers: An Analysis of the Interchange of Personnel Between Defense Contractors and the Department of Defense* (New York: Council on Economic Priorities, 1975). Another 499 former employees filed reports in 1974. See "More Military Maneuvers," *CEP Newsletter*, 11 August 1975. The CEP study's criteria for situations of conflict of interest were as follows:
    —a former DoD contract auditor or contract adjustment official was working for a company formerly in his or her jurisdiction (contract adjustment officials allow increases in payments to contractors when a determination of legitimate cost increases has been made, or make a determination of failure to meet contract specifications and reduce payments to the contractor);
    —a former official responsible for evaluating contractor performance, such as a plant representative or a contract administrator, was working for a company he or she formerly evaluated;
    —a former DoD systems project director was working for the producer of that system;
    —a former high official with management responsibility for planning systems development or for making decisions about procurement needs was working for a company producing those same systems;
    —a retired military officer appeared to be violating criminal laws prohibiting his or her selling to the DoD.
2. Many of these were second and third reports for transferees who filed once.
3. Thomas S. Burns, "Inside ITT's Washington Office," *Business and Society Review*, Autumn 1974, p. 23.
4. L. Harmon Zeigler and G. Wayne Peak, *Interest Groups in American Society*, 2nd ed. (Englewood Cliffs, NJ: Prentice Hall, 1972), p. 169.
5. Testimony of Robert Anderson, Chairman, Rockwell International in U.S. Congress, Joint Committee on Defense Production, *Hearings on DoD-Industry Relations: Conflict of Interest and Standards of Conduct*, 2-3 February 1976 (Washington, DC: GPO, 1976), pp. 27-28. (Hereafter referred to as Joint Committee on Defense Production, *DoD-Industry Relations*.) In the same hearings, Northrop Chairman Thomas Jones echoed Anderson's views:

Northrop's policy with respect to hiring men and women is to obtain the services of the most competent and most qualified individuals possible. Military officers alone possess actual operating experience with weapons systems that is unique and is unavailable elsewhere. We employ those people because they have experience in understanding the extremely complex organizational, administrative and operational problems of the Defense Department, and can relate the capabilities and limitations of our company to developing solutions to those problems. It is obvious that this experience is of great value. (Ibid., p. 54.)

6. Testimony of Dr. George Low, NASA Deputy Administrator to Joint Committee on Defense Production, *DoD-Industry Relations*, p. 85.
7. Rep. Samuel Stratton (D-NY), *Congressional Record*, 3 June 1959, p. H9742.
8. Speech by Joan Slous, Office of the General Counsel, U.S. Civil Service Commission, 9 Sept. 1974, reprinted in Joint Committee on Defense Production, *DoD-Industry Relations*, pp. 498-499.
9. Joint Committee on Defense Production, *DoD-Industry Relations*, p. 489.
10. GAO summary in GAO *Employee Standards of Conduct: Improvements Needed in the Army and Air Force Exchange Service and the Navy Resale Systems Office*, FPCD-79-15, 24 April 1979, pp. 11-12.
11. Ibid., p. 11.
12. Ibid.
13. Ibid.
14. Special Committee on the Federal Conflict of Interest Laws of the Association of the Bar of the City of New York, *Conflict of Interest and Federal Service* (Boston: Harvard University Press, 1960), pp. 3-4, cited in Reed, *Military Maneuvers*, p. 10.
15. Ronald J. Fox, *Arming America: How the U.S. Buys Weapons* (Boston: Harvard Graduate School of Business Administration, 1974), p. 61.
16. Thomas Goldwasser, "The Official Flow to Private Industry," *The New York Times*, 3 April 1977.
17. Joan Slous, Civil Service Commission in Joint Committee on Defense Production, *DoD-Industry Relations*, pp. 499-500.
18. In discussing DoD transfers we have chosen to focus on civilians. To include military transferees, the subject of our earlier study, would have enormously lengthened the research.
19. "The Conflict of Interest Craze," *Washington Monthly*, Nov. 1978, p. 47.
20. DoD reports cover the years 1970 to 1979. In some cases, transferees who filed for the first time in 1970, when the reporting requirement came into effect, transferred before 1970. NASA data start in 1974, the first year that NASA had a reporting requirement. The data are subject to two qualifications. First, not all transferees file, though all are legally required to do so for three years after a change of employment. Second, since the filing requirement covers three years, we attempted to eliminate all duplicate filings in our count. The uneven quality of DoD filing made this effort difficult, but errors are likely to be randomly distributed.
21. In several cases below, we note the movement of a transferee from a position in one sector to responsibilities in the other covering a similar area of work. We also note that the individual's corporate employer has contracting interests in weapons systems which fell within the agency with which the employee worked in the Federal Government. We cannot say that the specific individual had personal responsibility for that system or for relations with the contractor. Such information is simply not available on the public record. Moreover, the individual transferee may have done everything possible to remove him/herself from such a situation. We are saying, however, that the positions and systems can be juxtaposed and that the public record leaves what we have called the "appearance of a potential conflict of interest."
22. Joint Committee on Defense Production, *DoD-Industry Relations*, p. 66.

Personnel Transfers

7
Research and Development

Research and development lies at the heart of the defense "iron triangle." Over 60 percent of all Federal funding for R & D is spent on aerospace and defense programs sponsored by DoD, NASA, and the Department of Energy. A study in 1980 by the Battelle Memorial Institute projects a 1981 growth rate in R & D spending of over 14 percent, four percent of which would be real growth after inflation.[1] Defense-related R & D for 1981 of over $20 billion constitutes roughly one-third of the nation's entire private and public investment in R & D. The defense industry employs roughly 40 percent of the nation's scientific and engineering talent. In an era of declining productivity, stiff competition abroad and social and environmental problems of awesome proportions, this focus raises serious questions.

The close collaboration between DoD, NASA and the defense industry in R & D is a significant element in perpetuating this concentration. Long before most members of Congress or the general public become aware of weapons development or changes in strategic policies, new weapons and missions are being defined by the two Federal agencies and the specialists in the industry. Even the Congressional committees given the specific responsibility of watching over defense R & D are forced into a subsidiary and ineffective role. Senator Thomas McIntyre (D-NH, retired) while chairman of the Senate Armed Services Subcommittee on Research and Development, complained that they were simply overwhelmed with material. "We spend an awful lot of time, but we are lucky if we can take a look or have a briefing or hearing on, say, 15 percent of those projects."[2] If the Subcommittee members are stunned by too much disclosure, the public, including other members of Congress, are silenced by too little. The discussion of "stealth" aircraft, for example, came as a surprise in the summer of 1980,[3] even though the technology development, with its profound implications for new weaponry, the defense budget and strategic policy, had been underway for several years. Only the most advanced and expensive R & D items, such as the B-1 bomber or the MX missile receive real scrutiny.

The reluctance of the Defense Department and the industry to divulge their plans is justified on grounds of national security. Clearly, this argument has merit in some cases. Equally clearly, however, the argument serves the purposes of contractors who are bent on designing weapons that they can sell to the Government. Secrecy permits the contractors and the Department to decide the nation's military future without having to deal with dissident or alternative views. In theory, at least, the Department decides what it needs and then shops around for a contractor who can fill those needs. In practice, however, needs and fulfilment, missions and weapons systems are so intertwined that it is almost impossible to tell where one stops and the other starts. Generally, the Department defines a "mission"; it then doles out R & D money to the companies who refine a weapons system over a series of stages and in consultation with the Defense Department. On the other hand, the companies themselves often take the initiative. Once a major weapons system exists, momentum is created within the company, the DoD and Congress to buy it, particularly since the Government has already heavily invested in the company R & D. Technological and economic determinism, in addition to pressure from the corporation and the bureaucracy, creates a powerful momentum towards production.

The Chicken and the Egg: Government Policies and Company Programs

In order to retain their leadership, defense contractors maintain extensive research and development operations, a substantial portion of which are subsidized by the Government (see Table X). As Paul Cherington and Ralph Gillen note in a Brookings Institution study, "In the case of companies primarily in the defense business, the share of time and effort devoted to R & D marketing is very high, since many production contracts have their genesis in R & D contracts."[4] Boeing, Lockheed, and McDonnell Douglas, for example, reportedly employed 6,000 specialists to draw up their proposals for the Air Force C-5A competition in the 1960s.[5] Lockheed's research and development operation, the so-called "Skunk Works," is well known for its crucial role in contributing to the development of high altitude surveillance aircraft for the Air Force and the CIA. As economists Morton Peck and Frederick Scherer noted in the 1960s:

> Defense firms are not only major sources of new weapons program ideas, but they also provide information on the technological feasibility of new concepts and on estimated

development costs and schedules. In addition, by the late 1950s practically every major weapon system prime contractor had an operations analysis group which studies the relative military value of the new weapons possibilities.[6]

TABLE X

DoD INDEPENDENT RESEARCH AND DEVELOPMENT FUNDING

(1973-78)

($millions)

1973-78	DoD and NASA Contracts (R&D)	Co. IR&D Investment**	IR&D Costs Reimbursed ***	% Company IR&D Reimbursed by DoD
Boeing	$3692.6	$1183.6	$206.6	17.5%
General Dynamics	2507.3	159.8	70.1	43.9%
Grumman	704.4	237.7	185.6	78.1%*
Lockheed	3273.5	299.6	151.5	50.1%
McDonnell Douglas	3714.5	812.8	123.2	15.2%
Northrop	569.5	173.1	112.6	65.0%
Rockwell	7115.2	486.3	154.3	31.7%
United Technologies	1224.7	2030.6	294.7	14.5%

* The % reimbursed to Grumman is a more accurate figure than the % for other companies due to Grumman's disclosure to CEP.
** As calculated by CEP.
*** From DoD response to Feedom of Information Act request.
Source: DoD, Top 500 R&D Contractors; Company Annual Reports and 10K's; DoD disclosure to CEP FOIA request.

Contractors want to get in on the R & D process as early as possible, realizing that if they wait until the Defense Department defines its needs they may be too late to compete for contracts. G.A. Busch, Lockheed's director of corporate planning, has noted:

> We recognize it is the Government agency that must prepare the "Mission Element Need Statement," but we feel that industry may be able to provide valuable inputs to the agency as it defines its mission needs. In our company, we tried our hand at drafting MENS ourselves.[7]

Defining the mission can be an important preliminary to defining the weapon itself. This stage long precedes any proposal for an actual weapon, following the logic described by former Assistant Secretary of Defense J. Ronald Fox: "The most important lesson the contractors have learned from their experience with the source selection process is the importance of reaching the customer before submitting a formal proposal."[8]

In designing weapons, contractors implicitly have taken a hand in formulating policy. The practical "possible" often becomes the strategic "desirable." A 1974 study of the R & D proposal sponsored by the National Security Industrial Association, the Electronics Industries Association and the Aerospace Industries Association noted: "On occasion, contractors have recognized Government needs, and have had solutions for a critical deficiency prior to its formal recognition by the Government."[9] Some contractor representatives describe their impact in even blunter terms:

> The day is past when the military requirement for a major weapons system is set up by the military and passed on to industry to build the hardware. Today it is more likely that the military requirement is the result of joint participation of military and industrial personnel, and it is not unusual for industry's contribution to be a key factor. Indeed, there are highly placed military men who sincerely feel that industry currently is setting the pace in the research and development of new weapons systems (Peter Schenck, Raytheon Corp.).
>
> Your ultimate goal is actually to write the RFP, and this happens more often than you might think (North American Official).
>
> We have the technical superiority and are on the offensive. We spoon-feed them. We ultimately try to load them with our own ideas and designs, but in such a way that, when they walk away from the conference table, they are convinced it was their idea all along (Pratt & Whitney/UT Official).[10]

Public Money and Private Gain

To a considerable extent, the Department of Defense subsidizes the efforts contractors make to devise new weapons systems and market them to the Federal Government (see Table X). Through the Independent Research and Development (IR & D) and Bid and Proposal (B & P) programs, DoD funds a proportion of contractor investment in early R & D as well as the costs of preparing and submitting bids to DoD. As a trade association study describes the two programs:

> IR & D is that research and development effort which is not sponsored by a contract, grant or other arrangement. IR & D describes normal in-house or company-initiated R & D programs. It is planned, sponsored and directed internally and is a basic part of any company's effort to generate and provide better products and services for its customers, whether defense, commercial or a mixture of both.[11]

> B & P is a term devised by DoD and used by Federal agencies to describe a contractor's technical and supporting effort directed at preparing and submitting proposals (solicited or unsolicited) to a customer to meet an identified customer requirement. B & P efforts are a part of the process by which companies bring their products to the attention of their customers.[12]

A contractor, in other words, who engages in future-oriented defense research and who incurs expenses for preparing proposals for Government contracts is reimbursed by the Government for part of the costs of this activity. The amount of funding a contractor receives for IR & D and B & P is negotiated by DoD with each contractor in relationship to the percentage the company's total DoD contract work represents of total company business.[13] These funds escape detailed Congressional, let alone public scrutiny, yet they total nearly $1 billion a year. In addition, the weapons which emerge from this process can become major and expensive programs: cruise missiles, high energy lasers, space-based satellite surveillance systems, precision-guided munitions, lightweight fighters, strategic bomber research.[14] According to DoD data, moreover, the IR & D/B & P programs focus on the larger firms, helping maintain a concentrated defense industry. Half of the total spending each year goes to the top 10 DoD contracting companies.[15]

Well aware of the importance of obtaining these funds, the defense industry uses virtually all of the tools of Government relations to ensure a close and sustained intimacy with DoD and NASA at this stage. Northrop Chairman Thomas V. Jones has contrasted this early need for intimacy with the later process of weapons procurement:

> There is, however, a clear and necessary distinction between Government-industry relationships during the procurement phase and those that are required during the conceptual phase, and again, during the service life of the product in the field. The evaluation and source selection process must be conducted in an environment that is sterile and aloof; by contrast, the conceptual phase that begins many years before demands close communication, knowledge, and understanding.[16]

The flow of personnel helps foster this intimacy. Roughly one-third of all personnel transfers between the defense industry and the DoD

Research and Development

and NASA from 1970 to 1979 worked in the R & D area, between them handling $14.8 billion (1980). AS John Finney of *The New York Times* has pointed out, this movement constitutes a "game of corporate musical chairs":

> Today, policy making circles in the Defense Department are largely populated by business executives in mid-career, passing through the Pentagon on the way to bigger and better jobs in industry.... The trend is particularly pronounced in Dr. Currie's research and development office, by far the most important office in the Pentagon for industry because it decides which weapons are to be developed.... The roster of deputy directors is filled with men who used to work for industry and plan to return to it. As in a game of corporate musical chairs, industry executives rotate in and out of what is known in the Pentagon as "the R and D cartel."[17]

The access of the company to R & D funds is achieved not only through the transfer of personnel, but also through corporate membership on Federal advisory committees and trade associations. Company personnel on the advisory committees obtain information and provide input into the definition of weapons and policies. Through trade associations they discuss defense R & D with Government officials—frequently behind closed doors. The newsletter of the American Defense Preparedness Association notes, for example, that the Air Force had recently established offices at two bases, Andrews and Wright-Patterson, and at the Space Missile Systems Organization in Los Angeles in order to make "information available to industry on research and development planning and requirements" and to "deal primarily with planning documents for the development of future Air Force projects."[18] Paul Skrabut, advisor to Senator Harrison William (D-NJ), warns:

> The politics of this are incestuous and the company tends to develop its contracts with the contract award authority.... They, one-on-one, know the colonels that are issuing the contracts and the people who are setting up the specifications, and once the specifications and the policy requirements are done, that's it. From the beginning, whatever checks and balances there are, are in those personal relationships.[19]

The intimacy between the public and the private sector is to some extent inevitable and not always damaging to the public interest. These officials constitute a central bank of talent and knowledge in a highly technical field. Nevertheless, in a republic that has prided itself on the public participation in national policy and the control of military by civilian policy-makers and elected representatives, it raises serious questions.

The Companies

As might be expected from the critical role of early funds in positioning a company for future procurement contracts, each of the companies in the study has received substantial income from R & D contracts. As a group, moreover, these eight companies have received an even larger share of total DoD and NASA contracts for R & D than they have of DoD contracts overall. Of all DoD R & D contracts from 1970 to 1979, 37.1 percent went to these eight companies, while of total NASA contracts for the same period, virtually all of which are R & D work, 43.5 percent went in the same direction. Rockwell was, by far, the largest beneficiary in this period, due to its work on the B-1 bomber and the space shuttle program. McDonnell Douglas, Boeing, and Lockheed also received substantial R & D funds.

As the profiles indicate, these contract funds went for systems which are all central to future procurement programs: cruise missiles, vertical/short takeoff and landing aircraft, anti-ballistic missile systems, export fighters, electronic systems, the MX missile, laser weaponry and space satellites, among many others. Data on such projects are not always easy to obtain, since the DoD does not disclose a full list of R & D contracts and the companies are also selective in their disclosure of R & D. It is equally difficult to establish exactly how much money a company spends on defense-related research and development. The SEC provides no standard definition for this category, leaving each company free to use its own formula. It is usually unclear, as a result, just which funds are being spent on company sponsored (commercial or military) R & D as opposed to company R & D contracts with DoD and NASA.

In addition, it is extremely difficult to obtain clear data on the amount of company-invested R & D spending reimbursed through DoD's programs for IR & D and B & P. For years, the DoD has disclosed to the Congress only the aggregate expenditures under these programs, without any company breakdown.[20] In 1979, *The Nation* at our urging initiated a Freedom of Information Act request for such data. The disclosed data allowed us to make a first estimate of company IR & D receipts as a proportion of total company spending for R & D between 1973 and 1978 (see Table X).

In addition to this disclosure of IR & D funding, one company in the study, Grumman, disclosed directly to us both IR & D and B & P receipts for 1973 to 1979.[21] On the basis of Grumman's data, we estimate that IR & D and B & P receipts of $226.6 million over the seven year period represented 76.3 percent of total company R & D effort. Using only the IR & D data, we also estimate that between 1973 and 1978, Northrop depended on the IR & D program for 65 percent of its R & D funding, while Lockheed (51 percent) and General Dynamics (44 percent) also received substantial subsidies.

1. *Aerospace Daily*, 29 December 1980, p. 277.
2. Quoted in L. Fisher, "Senate Procedures for Authorizing Military Research and Development," in U.S. Congress, Joint Economic Committee, Subcommittee on Priorities and Economy in Government, *Priorities and Efficiency in Federal Research and Development: A Compendium of Papers*, 94th Congress, second session, 1976, p. 26.
3. "U.S. Builds Plane That Foils Radar," *The New York Times*, 21 Aug. 1980; Richard Burt, "Brown Says Radar-Evading Planes Shift Military Balance Toward U.S.," *The New York Times*, 23 Aug. 1980; *Aerospace Daily*, 25 Aug. 1980, pp. 306-308.
4. Paul W. Cherington and Ralph L. Gillen, *The Business Representative in Washington* (Washington: The Brookings Institution, 1962), p. 23.
5. Ronald J. Fox, *Arming America: How the U.S. Buys Weapons* (Boston: Harvard Graduate School of Business Administration, 1974), p. 295.
6. Morton J. Peck and Frederic M. Scherer, *The Weapons Acquisition Process: An Economic Analysis* (Boston: Harvard Graduate School of Business Administration, 1962), p. 242.
7. Christopher Paine and Gordon Adams, "The R & D Slush Fund," *The Nation*, 26 January 1980.
8. Fox, *Arming America*, p. 242. See his Chapter 14 for discussion of this stage. Other industry figures underline the importance of early access. A General Dynamics employee noted, "You have to get in on the ground floor or forget it." (David Sims, "Spoon-Feeding the Military—How New Weapons Come to Be," in Leonard Rodberg and Derek Sherer (eds.), *The Pentagon Watchers* (Garden City, NY: Doubleday, 1970), p. 237. Another defense industry employee noted, "If you wait around until the RFP (Request for Proposals), you're dead." (Ibid., p. 238.)
9. Tri-Association Ad Hoc Committee on IR & D and B & P, *Technical Papers on Independent Research and Development and Bid and Proposal Efforts*, March 1974, p. 74. Also cited in Paine/Adams, "The R & D Slush Fund," p. 75.
10. Sims, "Spoon-Feeding the Military," pp. 248-250. Sapolsky notes that in the Polaris development, "The technical preferences and orientations of the contractors of necessity affected the development process" (Harvey M. Sapolsky, *The Polaris System Development: Bureaucratic and Programatic Success in Government*, Boston: Harvard University Press, 1972, p. 51).
11. Tri-Association, *Technical Papers*, p. 4.
12. Ibid., p. 248.
13. Paine/Adams, "The R & D Slush Fund," and Tri-Association, *Technical Papers*.
14. Ibid.
15. Paine/Adams, "The R & D Slush Fund."
16. U.S. Congress, Joint Committee on Defense Production, *Hearings on DoD-Industry Relations: Conflict of Interest and Standards of Conduct*, 2-3 February 1976 (Washington, DC: GPO, 1976), p. 53.
17. John W. Finney, "The Military-Industrial Complex Grows More So," *The New York Times*, 11 April 1976. J. Ronald Fox notes that "of all senior Pentagon appointees, those assigned to research and development most frequently identify with the point of view of the contractors." (Fox, *Arming America*, p. 77.)
18. American Defense Preparedness Association, *The Common Defense*, 15 October 1976.
19. John O. Membrino, "The MX Contract: It was a case of square shooting," *The Boston Globe*, 17 Feb. 1980.
20. Council on Economic Priorities, "Contingency Costs," *CEP Newsletter*, 30 August 1976.
21. These data were disclosed in response to a specific request following Grumman's review of the profile in November 1980.

PART III
THE INFLUENCE BUSINESS: POLITICS AND POWER

8
BACKING THE CANDIDATES: POLITICAL ACTION COMMITTEES

"No doubt since the beginning of organized society, a number of the people potentially affected have sought to bend government decisions to their advantage. In a money economy, one doesn't have to look far to find a handy means to that end.... There are a lot of ways to skin a cat—or a taxpayer—and a politician's vote can be corruptly influenced by other routes than campaign giving. But campaign giving had become such a wide open and easy game that it was the preferred mode; only old fashioned or stupid people resorted to bribes any longer. Even in those cases in which campaign giving was clearly illegal, it was a reputable illegality."[1]

John Gardner

"More dollars were spent on fireworks last year than all congressional elections combined."[2]

Rep. Guy Vander Jagt

Corporate campaign contributions have always been controversial. Money, bribery, under-the-table hand-outs have been grist for the muckraker's mill since the American republic was created. When Mark Hanna, William McKinley's campaign manager, dragooned corporations into giving regularly to the Republican war chest, the public clucked its collective tongue. Cartoonist Thomas Nast made a career of lampooning members of the Senate whom he caricatured as lackeys of corporate trusts. The 1907 Tillman Act, which prohibited corporate contributions to Federal candidates, either directly or through committees, was aimed at halting such practices. The prohibition, repeated in the 1925 Federal Corrupt Practices Act, was extended to include giving a candidate "anything of value."[3]

Recent History

As a result of these legal prohibitions, corporations rarely created Political Action Committees (PACs) until the 1970s. Trade unions, however, following the dramatic increase in labor's political role in the 1930s set the precedent. With the encouragement of Sidney Hillman of the Amalgamated Clothing Workers, they created PACs which have focused on registration, get-out-the-vote drives, and campaign contributions. In the Smith-Connally Act of 1943 and the Taft-Hartley Act of 1947, unions were prohibited from using union funds as campaign contributions, a restriction which led to a reliance on voluntary donations. When the American Federation of Labor and the Congress of Industrial Organizations merged in 1955, they created the Committee on Political Education (COPE), which became instrumental in labor's voter education activities over the past 25 years. In addition, a number of unions created their own PACs.[4]

Corporations, however, did not follow the labor model for political participation. While labor PACs focused on "getting-out-the-vote," giving less attention to campaign funding, corporations encouraged individual contributions by company directors, managers and other officials.[5]

Before the Federal election law reforms, according to Edwin Epstein, an authority on PACs:

> money from business-related sources could legally enter the electoral arena, almost undetected, in almost unlimited amounts in the form of individual contributions by wealthy persons affiliated with corporations and other business organizations.[6]

W. Clement Stone, a prominent Chicago insurance man, and his wife, for instance, gave the Nixon campaigns of 1968 and 1972 a total of over $5 million. Within a corporation, top management would encourage, even demand campaign contributions from management personnel. In some cases, salaries would be raised and a portion then kicked back, by agreement, into campaign funding. A high volume of corporate campaign funding entered the political arena in these ways.[7]

Industry-wide and trade association contributions were rare. The Chamber of Commerce and the National Association of Manufacturers encouraged their member corporations to stimulate employee involvement in the political process. The Public Affairs Council, formed in 1954 by corporate Government relations specialists, also encouraged voter education and registration. In 1963, a group of corporate officials formed the Business-Industry Political Action Committee (BIPAC), modeled after COPE. At first, merely, "a pale shadow of COPE," as one observer put it,[8] BIPAC has emerged as an important campaign contributor to more conservative Democrat and Republican candidates for the House and Senate.[9]

Federal Election Campaign Act of 1971

As corporate individual giving increased in the late 1960s, reformers joined with trade unions in seeking to create legal guidelines. The Federal Election Campaign Act (FECA) of 1971 was the result.[10] (Ironically, this first step toward the dramatic growth of corporate PACs had almost no corporate support.) This Act permitted both unions and companies to communicate with members and stockholders, respectively, on political subjects; to carry out voter registration and "get-out-the vote" activities; and to create a "separate, segregated fund" for political activity (PAC) with union or corporate funds. The PAC could then solicit its members.[11]

In addition the 1971 FECA required candidates and campaign committees to disclose all campaign contributions over $100. This requirement led to a flurry of campaign fund-raising before the law went into effect on April 7, 1972 and the subsequent disclosure of large contributions by corporate personnel to the Nixon campaign.[12] Watergate followed with revelations that included additional corporate money contributed to the Presidential campaign, much of it, illegal and "laundered."

The 1971 Act also contained a clause that prohibited Government contractors from making campaign contributions. This clause had worried labor leaders and given pause to the business community. Most trade unions were Government contractors, administering Federally-financed training programs. Many corporations in the coal and gas business, commercial banks, construction firms, communications companies, savings and loan associations and transportation were affected by Government regulation. Some had created PACs; most, however, had shied away.

These fears were acerbated by a 1972 lawsuit brought by Common Cause against TRW, Inc., a defense contractor, that questioned whether TRW's PAC was legal and led to its dissolution. Labor Unions joined with Common Cause in pushing for amendments to the 1971 FECA that would repeal the prohibition against the PACs of Government contractors.

Federal Election Campaign Act of 1974

The Federal Election Campaign Act of 1974, the result of their efforts, was comprehensive. It set ceilings on both individual and PAC campaign contributions. Individuals were limited to a contribution of $1,000 per candidate per election (primary, runoff and general) and $5,000 to a party committee, and to an annual ceiling of $25,000 in total contributions to all Federal level candidates. PACs could be created by unions, corporations, associations, or "non-connected" groups, whether or not they were Government contractors. They were restricted to a ceiling in campaign giving of $5,000 per Federal candidate per election. Candidates could create only a single committee to receive contributions.

The Act revolutionized campaign financing by providing for public financing of Presidential primaries and general elections. At the primary stage, a complex structure allowed Presidential candidates to match private funds with public financing. In the general election, only public funds could be used. The law also limited candidates for Federal office in the amount of personal and family money they could contribute: $50,000 for Presidential candidates, $35,000 for Vice Presidential and Senate candidates and $20,000 for House candidates. The Act also placed ceilings on total campaign spending.

Finally, the Act required the disclosure of campaign financing, creating a Federal Elections Commission (FEC) of six members to administer, interpret, and enforce the Act and receive reports. It required that all PACs, candidates, and campaign committees file regular reports with the FEC, disclosing receipts. PACs were required to also list their contributions to Federal candidates and party campaign committees.

Corporations, which originally had been hesitant—less than 150 corporate PACs existed before 1974—began to take advantage of the new opportunities. Observers were quick to note the irony of legislation, backed by the trade unions, that had benefited the corporations. As one put it, "Labor pulled business' chestnuts out of the fire."[13]

Two critical opinions turned the flow into a rush: the 1975 FEC advisory opinion on the SUN-PAC and the 1976 Supreme Court decision in the case of *Buckley v. Valeo*. In 1975 the Sun Oil Company sought an FEC opinion on the activities of its PAC. That opinion permitted SUN-PAC to use general corporate funds to establish and administer the PAC, so long as they were kept separate from other corporate funds. It also permitted PACs to solicit company employees, in addition to stockholders and managers, for contributions. Employees were, thus open to two solicitations, one from a trade union, if the firm was unionized, and one from management. Management was also allowed to establish a withholding system to draw contributions from an employee's paycheck. The SUN-PAC opinion clarified the registration terms, requiring that PACs register with the FEC six months before they begin dispersing funds, receive contributions from more than 50 persons (each limited to $5,000 to the PAC), and contribute to five or more Federal candidates.

The *Buckley v. Valeo* decision (424 U.S. 1-294 1976) provided further clarification, establishing the constitutionality of the key provisions of the 1974 FECA: PACs, individual and PAC contribution ceilings, public financing for Presidential campaigns, and the disclosure requirements. Disclosure, the Court argued, would inhibit electoral corruption:

> First, disclosure provides the electorate with information... in order to aid the voters in evaluating those who seek federal office. It allows voters to place each candidate in the political spectrum more precisely than is often possible solely on the basis of party labels and campaign speeches. The sources of a candidate's financial support also alert the voter to the interests to which a candidate is most likely to be responsible and thus facilitate predictions of future performance in office.
>
> Second, disclosure requirements deter actual corruption and avoid the appearance of corruption by exposing large contributions and expenditures to the light of publicity.[14]

The Court did rule, however, that candidates could not be limited in the amount of personal funds used for their campaigns, nor could the amount of campaign spending be restricted.

> The candidate, no less than any other person, has a First Amendment right to engage in the discussion of public issues and vigorously and tirelessly to advocate his own election and the election of other candidates.[15]

In addition, the Court struck down the appointment procedure for the FEC which had permitted Congressional officials to name four members, as a violation of the separation of powers.[16]

Federal Election Campaign Act of 1976

Labor was concerned about the effect of the SUN-PAC decision, which permitted widespread corporate solicitations (stockholders, management, supervisors, employees) and payroll deductions. Congress responded with further clarifications. The 1976 FECA amended the Campaign Act to restrict management to two solicitations of employees per year. The unions in return were given the right to solicit company stockholders, a right so far not used. Unions would also be permitted a dues check-off for PAC donations.

The 1976 Act also allowed companies and unions to establish an unlimited number of PACs, as long as their campaign contributions were treated as one, closing off the possibility that corporate subsidiaries or union locals might create PACs that could make additional contributions. The amendments also required all PACs to report to the FEC any "independent" campaign expenditures over $100 and confirmed that candidates could spend unlimited amounts of personal funds on their own campaigns. Finally, the Act restructured the FEC so that all its members were appointed by the President with Senate confirmation.

The results of this Act were sweeping. Epstein comments:

> In summary, while the 1976 amendments restored part of what organized labor had lost as a result of SUN-PAC, they gave the business community far greater running room in

the electoral process than heretofore. Ironically, as a consequence of three rounds of election legislation during the 1970s, both labor and especially business are in a position to exert a much more direct and stronger impact upon federal electoral politics than they could at the beginning of the decade, a development neither anticipated nor desired (and, indeed, vigorously opposed) by reformers who have sought to free the electoral process from undue influence by "special interests."[17]

Corporate PACs and Government Relations

Since 1976, the business community has seized the opportunity to increase their campaign contributions. The number of corporate PACs had grown from 89 in 1974 to 1,204 in 1980. Trade association PACs, most of which are linked to business, had risen from 318 to 574, while "non-connected" organization PACs grew from 110 in 1977 to 378. Labor PACs had shown the least growth, rising from 201 to 297 (see Figure VI).

The trends in PAC contributions to candidates (Table XI) shows that the level of contributions of corporate PACs has now drawn even with those of labor, each standing in the neighborhood of $10 million. This data understates business contributions, moreover, since a substantial portion of trade association PAC contributions are linked to business groups. PACs of trade associations, "non-connected" organizations, cooperatives and corporations without stock contributed $7.5 million to the corporate total.[18] It is, however, too soon to judge the effect of PACs on the two-party system. Both business and labor show a general tendency to support incumbents running for reelction, though more recent data suggest that the trend may be changing, with business more willing to support challengers than ever before.[19] Since the Congress during this period was controlled by a Democratic majority, corporate contributions were not devoted exclusively to Republican candidates (see Table XI). Labor contributions, on the other hand, concentrated on the Democratic candidates.

Some observers agree with Congressman Van der Jagt, quoted at the beginning of this chapter, that the power of PACs is overrated. They point out that, through 1978, PAC contributions were not increasing as a share of a candidate's total campaign receipts.[20] It is true that general fund-raising has attracted a high volume of individual contributions to candidates, matching PAC funding in some cases. The PAC phenomenon is so new, however, that it is too early to conclude that they have no impact. Representatives David Obey (D-WI) and Tom Railsback (R-IL) have concluded that PAC growth trends and the ties of PACs with special interests threaten the independence of members of Congress.[21] Epstein points out that data since 1978 suggests a trend toward a greater PAC role in overall campaign finance. Moreover, the role of business PACs could well become overwhelming in the future, since there is clearly more room for their expanding in

Chart VI

POLITICAL ACTION COMMITTEES
1974-1980

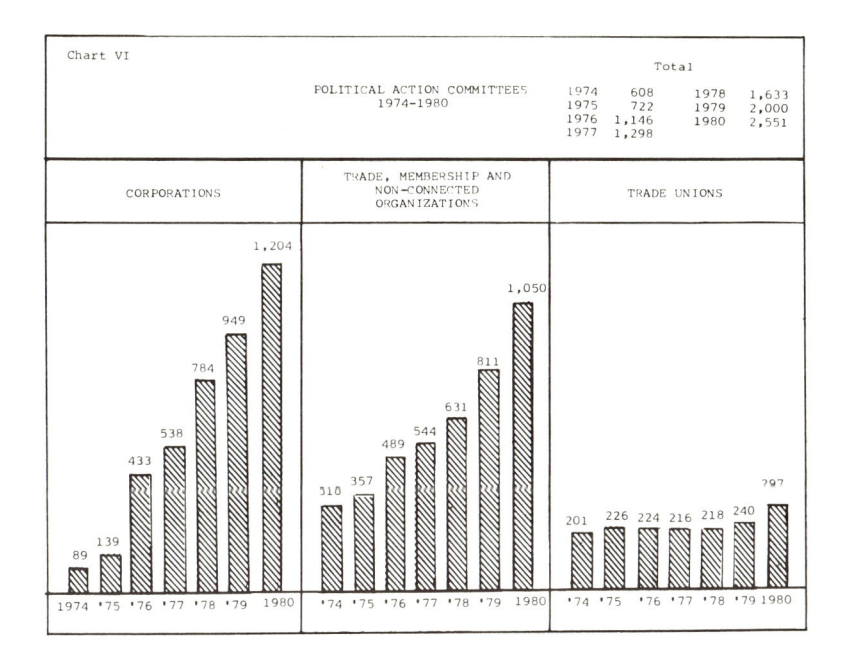

Total
1974	608	1978	1,633
1975	722	1979	2,000
1976	1,146	1980	2,551
1977	1,298		

CORPORATIONS
1974	89
'75	139
'76	433
'77	538
'78	784
'79	949
1980	1,204

TRADE, MEMBERSHIP AND NON-CONNECTED ORGANIZATIONS
'74	318
'75	357
'76	489
'77	544
'78	631
'79	811
1980	1,050

TRADE UNIONS
'74	201
'75	226
'76	224
'77	216
'78	218
'79	240
1980	297

number and funding than there is for trade union PACs.[22]

From the corporate point of view PACs are assuming ever greater significance as an element of a company Government relations strategy. A PAC contribution, in conjunction with other Government relations work can help cement the relationship between the industrial and the Congressional sides of the "iron triangle." PAC committees are becoming involved with internal corporate political education programs for managers, supervisors and employees and help plan grass-roots lobbying.[23] PACs, to quote *The Wall Street Journal*,[24] are now "a fundamental vehicle for the business community's growing political zest." Joseph Fanelli, Director of BIPAC, notes that, with PACs, "Business is on the verge of a political renaissance."[25]

In the Congress there is a growing perception that PAC expenditures are helping shift the political balance towards the right. As one member of the House Ways and Means Committee put it:

> These PACs are influencing a lot of Democrats. You're seeing people from mainstream Democratic districts, elected with labor support, who are now voting with business.[26]

Business Week[27] has suggested that the defeat of labor on such issues as common situs picketing, labor law reform and the Consumer Protection Agency may be linked to corporate PAC giving. An anonymous member of Congress summed up the potential impact on Congress and the party system:

There's a one-liner going around the cloakroom. 'Business already owns one party and now it has a lease, with option to buy, on the other.'[28]

Buying votes, however, is not the only, or even the major purpose. Observers in a variety of fields agree that buying access is more important. According to journalist Steven Roberts:

> Many Congressmen say that taking a contribution creates a feeling of obligation and sympathy, a debt that must eventually be paid. In one sense, power in Washington can be equated with access—the quicker your phone call gets returned, the more influence you have. And when a lobbyist calls a lawmaker who has taken his money, the return time is reduced considerably.[29]

Fred Wertheimer, the vice president of Common Cause, comments:

> It's not a question of buying votes, it's a question of relationships that get built, obligations and dependencies that get established.... It puts PACs at the head of the line as opposed to the great bulk of a Congressman's constituents.[30]

An expert on Government relations states:

> "Purchasing access"—though PAC proponents don't talk publicly about this term—is the motivating force behind what has been described as the "explosive" growth in the number of PACs since 1974.... Many organizations now consider PACs an integral component of their government relations or lobbying program. They complement each other—both provide avenues of access for communicating views to the government.[31]

Individuals close to corporate PAC operations agree that access is the commodity foremost in their minds. The Conference Board quotes one corporate CEO as stating: "The PAC is not designed to influence elections, but to open the doors."[32] A leading consultant to corporate PACs underlines the link between access and PAC assistance:

> One without the other is a half-hearted exercise. You can't ask someone to support your interests and then leave him vulnerable at election time.[33]

Congresswoman Patricia Schroeder (D-CO) goes even further to suggest that corporate donations have become an active part of Congressional deliberations:

> I've had people on my committee ask how many tickets a company bought to a fund-raiser, while we're trying to decide on what planes to buy.[34]

TABLE XI
CORPORATE AND LABOR CAMPAIGN CONTRIBUTIONS

Recipients		1972-1974	1975-1976	1977-1978	1979-1980***
Incumbents	Corp.	$1,898,727	$4,715,950	$5,750,000	$7,500,000
	Labor	2,762,017	5,108,747	6,050,000	7,510,000
Challengers	Corp.	181,535	1,159,568	2,070,000	2,600,000
	Labor	1,657,690	1,676,861	2,240,000	1,530,000
Open Seats	Corp.	316,918	1,057,406	2,000,000	1,200,000
	Labor	1,321,965	1,281,656	2,000,000	1,230,000
Democrats	Corp.	948,961	2,532,946	3,700,000	4,900,000
	Labor	5,368,497	7,788,174	9,800,000	9,620,000
Republicans	Corp.	1,448,219	3,342,572	6,100,000	6,400,000
	Labor	373,175	279,090	600,000	650,000
Total	Corp.	2,506,946*	6,932,924**	9,800,000**	11,300,000
	Labor	6,315,488	8,067,264	10,300,000	10,300,000

*1974 categories do not add up to total because they do not include contributions to primary losers. See Common Cause's *Congressional Campaign Finances, 1974 Vol. J.*
**1975-80 totals include contributions to other candidates not listed in the categories above.
***Does not include last six weeks of 1980.
Source: Federal Election Commission.

Defense Industry PACs: Comparative Findings

Data for the 1977-78 period showed that aerospace PACs were the largest in the corporate world in average size ($81,000) and in average Federal-level campaign contributions ($54,000).[35]

Before the 1970s these contributions were made only by individuals. In 1968 officers and directors of the top 25 DoD, NASA, and nuclear contracting companies made Federal campaign contributions of $1.2 million concentrated primarily on Republican candidates.[36] During 1972 they gave $2.876 million, again mostly to Republicans.[37]

The Nixon campaign staff focused on defense firms, among others, usually suggesting a contribution of $100,000 from the larger firms.[38] They found a sympathetic ear: officers and directors of the top 100 contractors gave $3.2 million before the April 7 disclosure deadline and another $2.2 million afterwards.[39] In addition at least one contractor, Northrop, admitted to making illegal corporate campaign contributions worth $150,000.[40]

Although management personnel were large contributors, defense firms held off creating PACs until after the 1974 FECA, the SUN-PAC opinion and the Supreme Court decision in *Buckley v. Valeo*. Once the road was clear, contractors have shown themselves as eager to move into political action as other corporations. As of 1978, the most recent data available, roughly 60% of the top aerospace firms had formed PACs, a level similar to that of most other industries.[41] Their contributions are split nearly 50/50 between Republicans and Democrats.[42]

Like other aerospace contractors, the eight companies in our study created PACs between April 1976 and February 1978. From the time they were created until 1980, they had total expenditures of $2.1 million (see Chart VII). Of this amount, FEC data shows total Federal-level campaign contributions of $1.26 million (see Table XII). The FEC, which ranks all corporate PACs by receipts, gross disbursements, and contributions to Federal candidates, included several of these companies in the top 10 firms for these categories in the 1977-78 period (the most recent data available). On the list of the top 10 in gross receipts, Grumman ranked ninth ($171,434) and Boeing 10th ($165,155); in gross disbursements (covering all spending—Federal, state, and local candidates; party committees and other), Grumman ranked eighth ($156,435), General Dynamics ninth ($155,956), and Boeing 10th ($135,377). Of the top 10 in contributions to Federal candidates, United Technologies ranked ninth ($198,725).

According to the FEC data for the eight companies,[43] General Dynamics had the largest PAC in gross disbursements, nearly $510,000, followed by Grumman—$391,000, United Technologies—$342,000, and Boeing—$261,000 (see Chart VII). We also examined the Federal-level campaign contributions of the eight firms (combining contributions to candidates with contributions to campaign committees), and ranked the companies.

TABLE XII

POLITICAL ACTION COMMITTEES FEDERAL CAMPAIGN CONTRIBUTIONS

Company	Total Contributions to Federal Campaigns*		Key Geographic Contributions		Key Committee Contributions		Geography & Committee**		Other Candidates***		Party Campaign Committees		Pres. Campaign Committees	
	$		$	%	$	%	%		$	%	$	%	$	%
Boeing	$ 85,655		$ 10,729	12.5%	$ 27,629	33.3%	36.4%		$ 18,215	21.3%	$ 32,416	37.8%	$ 3,925	4.6%
General Dynamics	109,121		33,064	30.3%	33,000	30.2%	51.8%		21,690	19.9%	16,690	15.3%	14,177	13.0%
Grumman	337,990		82,700	24.5%	134,850	39.9%	49.0%		31,350	9.3%	114,440	33.9%	26,500	7.8%
Lockheed	126,510		51,910	41.0%	60,975	48.2%	67.4%		25,275	19.8%	6,900	5.5%	9,525	7.5%
McDonnell Douglas	115,200		63,525	55.1%	67,795	58.8%	77.8%		15,775	13.7%	8,825	7.7%	500	0.4%
Northrop	88,039		21,695	24.6%	41,595	47.2%	57.0%		18,150	20.6%	11,042	12.5%	8,702	9.9%
Rockwell	104,270		23,395	27.2%	39,025	37.4%	52.8%		15,250	14.6%	24,800	23.8%	9,150	8.8%
United Tech.	289,225		34,850	12.0%	89,800	31.0%	38.3%		97,800	33.8%	69,075	23.9%	12,600	4.4%
Total	$1,256,010		$326,868	26.0%	$494,669	39.4%	51.3%		$243,505	19.9%	$284,188	22.6%	$85,079	6.8%

*This figure was calculated by CEP based on the FEC's D index of contributions to federal candidates and FEC listings of contributions to party campaign committees.

**The total represented here eliminates duplicates from recipients who both represent a geographic location and belong to a key committee.

***This category is the sum of contributions to other influential members of Congress and contributions to other (miscellaneous) candidates, as listed in the company profiles.

As a proportion of total PAC spending, six of the eight PACs in the study concentrated over 70% of their funds on contributions to Federal campaigns. McDonnell Douglas had the highest concentration—92%. Two PACs, Boeing (33%) and General Dynamics (21.4%) spent a far smaller proportion.[44] Grumman made by far the largest Federal level campaign contributions: $337,990; followed by United Technologies—$289,225, and Lockheed—$126,510 (see Table XII).

We were particularly interested in examining the intentions of these companies in their PAC contributions at the Federal level. It was our expectation that a sizeable proportion of contributions would be given to candidates for Congress who either represented districts and states where the company had plant locations or who were members of committees in the Congress which considered legislation and appropriations of importance to the company's business.

We matched company plants to Congressional districts, which was not always easy since some metropolitan areas have several House districts and the company's work force is often spread across a wide residential area. We decided to include all House candidates from key states on the assumption that a defense contractor would argue that their contracting benefitted the state economy as a whole. As Table XII indicates, Grumman contributed the largest absolute amount to candidates from key geographic locations ($82,700), though McDonnell Douglas contributed the highest proportion (55.1%). Other company PACs ranged between 13% and 41% of contributions to candidates from key geographic areas, the average being 28.4%.[45]

We also selected eight committees in Congress whose deliberations on legislation and appropriations could affect the fortunes of aerospace companies. The House and Senate Armed Services Committees and the House and Senate Defense Appropriations Subcommittees are obviously crucial. In addition, we selected five other committees or subcommittees which handle scientific and technological issues, NASA oversight and appropriations, and the aviation industry:[46]

    Senate Committee on Commerce, Science and Transportation,
        Subcommittee on Aviation, Subcommittee on Science,
        Technology and Space
    Senate Committee on Environment and Public Works,
        Subcommittee on Transportation
    House Committee on Science and Technology
    House Committee on Public Works and Transportation,
        Subcommittee on Aviation.

As Table XII indicates, the companies gave a substantial proportion of their contributions to members of these key committees. Grumman, again, contributed the highest amount—$134,850, while McDonnell Douglas was again highest in proportion—58.8%. The general range for the other companies in this category was higher than that for key geographic areas—from 30% to 48%, with the average being 41%. In general, key committee contributions focused on members of the Armed

Services and Defense Appropriations committees. Only companies significantly involved in commercial air transport (Lockheed, McDonnell Douglas) or in NASA contracting (Lockheed and Rockwell) made major contributions to aviation, science and technology committee members.

Combining the two categories and eliminating double counting (a key geographic key committee member), we found that the eight companies contributed 59% on average of their PAC funds to these two categories. Two PACs, McDonnell Douglas (78%) and Lockheed (67%), clearly focused their Federal contributions on key geographic locations and key committee members. Northrop (57.0%), Rockwell (53%), and General Dynamics (51.8%) spent over half their Federal funds this way. Two other PACs clearly had different intentions. Boeing contributed over 59% of its Federal PAC funds to political party campaign committees and non-geographic, non-key committee candidates, while United Technologies spent over 58% of its fund in this way.

We also examined contributions for all eight PACs to determine which key committee members were most favored by this segment of the defense industry between 1976 and 1980. Such data might identify the key Congressional actors. The following were the leading recipients of campaign contributions for the House and Senate Armed Services and Defense Appropriations Subcommittees:

Senate Armed Services (NOTE: Year up for election in parenthesis)

Member	$	No. PACs
Thurmond (1980)	$14,300	8
Tower	13,125	7
Warner	11,000	7
Nunn	9,000	5
Goldwater (1980)	7,800	4

Senate Defense Appropriations

Hollings (1980)	$13,000	8
Magnuson (1980)	12,400	6
Garn	5,550	4
Brooke	5,300	5
Inouye	5,100	5

House Armed Services

C. Wilson	$12,925	6
J. Lloyd	11,650	8
Davis	10,100	8
Wilson, B.[47]	9,700	7
Ichord	9,925	8
Dickinson	8,500	8

Price	6,020	3
Daniel, R.	5,900	5
Spence	5,800	7
Mitchell	5,200	7
House Defense Appropriations		
Addabbo	$10,800	6
Giaimo	7,700	7
Edwards	7,250	8
Chappell	6,400	6
Burlison	6,200	6
McFall	5,900	7
Cederberg	5,800	7
Dicks	3,775	6
Kemp	2,100	2
Robinson	1,700	4

The Companies

A brief review of each PAC indicates some specific features of their contributions and some of the key connections of major recipients of funds.[48]

Boeing: The Boeing Civic Pledge Program expended $260,850 through May 1980. Roughly one third ($85,655) was contributed to Federal candidates, 36.4% of which went to candidates from key geographic locations or key committees. Senator Warren Magnuson, Chairman of the Senate Appropriations Committee, had received $3,900 by June 1980. (Magnuson was defeated in November 1980.) Representative Norman Dicks of Tacoma, Washington, and a member of the Defense Appropriations Subcommittee had received $1,175. Representative Mike McCormack of Washington, protege of Senator Henry Jackson (Senate Armed Services) received $800. Representative Allan Swift of Washington, of the Everett district where Boeing recently enlarged its production facilities, received $400. In Kansas, Representative Dan Glickman, of the Wichita district (home of Boeing's plant), who sits on the House Science and Technology Committee, received over $500. Among key committee members, Boeing gave significant sums to Senators Morgan and Thurmond of Senate Armed Services and Senators Magnuson and Hollings of Defense Appropriations. On the House side, large contributions went to Representatives Spence, Ichord, Davis, Dickinson and Byron of the Armed Services Committee, while Representative Dicks was the leading recipient on Defense Appropriations. Boeing also contributed $16,415 to non-key Senate and House candidates, including Representative Al Ullman, Chairman of House Ways and Means and Senator Richard Stone, a Florida conservative Democrat (both defeated in the fall of 1980). The

Company contributed twice as much to Republican Party Campaign Committees, giving over one-third of total contributions, as it did to Democratic Party Committees.

General Dynamics' Voluntary Political Contribution Plan was created in July 1977 and by August 1980 had expended over half a million dollars, the largest amount in the study. Only 21.4% ($109,121) was spent in Federal contributions. A third of this was contributed to candidates from key areas, including Representative Robert Giaimo (D-CN), then Chairman of the House Budget Committee ($2,000); Representative Bob Wilson (R-CA), Chairman, then ranking Republican on House Armed Services ($1,700); Senator John Tower (R-TX), new chairman of the Senate Armed Services Committee and well-supported by the industry ($1,125); and Leo Berman, Republican of Ft. Worth, Texas, losing candidate for the Congressional seat in a district which includes GD's plant. Smaller, though significant amounts went to Representative Martin Frost of Ft. Worth (Berman's victorious opponent); Representative Thomas Loeffler (Republican of San Antonio), a Tower protege; and Representative Richard Ichord of Missouri (also on House Armed Services). GD also gave a substantial sum ($1,500) to William Bronson (R-MA) running against Representative Nick Mavroules, in the district near GD's Quincy, Massachusetts shipyard; and the same amount to Senator Claiborne Pell of Rhode Island where GD's Electric Boat Division has a plant.

Roughly a third was contributed to members of key committees including Tower and Thurmond ($2,000) of Senate Armed Services, Bob Wilson, and James Courter (R-NJ) ($1,500) of House Armed Services. On the Appropriations side, Senator Hollings ($2,000) and Senator Edward Brooke received substantial sums as did Representatives Giaimo, Addabbo and Chappell, who represents a Navy district in Florida. GD also gave to some key conservative candidates, including Leo Thorsness in South Dakota and John Porter (R-IL) who was running against Democratic liberal Abner Mivka, in Illinois.

Grumman created its Political Action Committee in January 1977 and the PAC had spent $390,980 by May 1980, ranking second in the study. Grumman's Federal level contributions ranked first, however, ($337,990), constituting over 85% of total expenditures. Grumman's PAC is clearly part of its Government relations strategy with nearly one quarter of its Federal contributions going to candidates from key geographic areas. Representatives from Long Island were prominent beneficiaries: Addabbo, Ambro, Lent, Downey, Wolff, Wydler, and Carney. Senator Daniel Patrick Moynihan (D-NY) also received a sizeable amount ($5,000). Moynihan was particularly outspoken on Grumman's behalf during the controversy over the production rate for Grumman's F-14.[50]

Grumman also contributed large amounts to two key Georgia members of Congress: Senator Sam Nunn of the Armed Services

Committee, grandnephew of Carl Vinson, with a reputation as a leading defense spokesman in Congress ($5,000); and Representative Billy Lee Evans from Milledgeville, Georgia, where Grumman has its major Georgia production facility ($1,400).

Grumman's contributions to members of key committees in Congress were also high ($134,850) and were a significant proportion of total spending (39.9%). Senators Nunn, Thurmond, Tower and Hollings all received $5,000 from Grumman's PAC, with other significant contributions to Senators Warner, Culver, Garn, Humphrey, Morgan and Jepson—10 Armed Services Committee members in all. In the House, 20 Armed Services Committee members received Grumman money, including Bob Wilson, Charles Wilson, Donald Mitchell, James Lloyd (defeated in 1980), Mendel Davis, Larry McDonald, and Richard White. Another beneficiary, Addabbo, Chairman of Defense Appropriations, will be a key figure for some years.

Grumman funds also went to Appropriations members in the Senate and House, including Elford Cederberg ($1,000), Bill Chappell ($4,000), and Jack Edwards ($3,000). Cederberg, ranking Republican on this committee while in Congress, is now a registered lobbyist for Grumman. Chappell is closely linked to the Navy, Grumman's chief customer, and Edwards is the ranking Republican on the committee. Although only a small proportion of Grumman PAC spending went to other influential members of the Senate and House, the actual amounts were considerable: $5,000 to Senator Howard Baker, the new Senate Majority Leader; and $2,500 to Representative James Wright, the House Majority Leader.

Grumman also contributed a third of its Federal funds to party campaign committees, favoring the Democrats, then in control of both houses of Congress. The intentionality of Grumman's contributions is clear from the fact that decisions on the recipients are made by the firm's chief registered lobbyist in Washington, Gordon Ochenrider. "The decisions on Federal races are reached on the basis of recommendations from Mr. Ochenrider in Washington, who keeps tabs on incumbents' voting records."[51]

Lockheed created its Good Government Program in January 1977. Its expenditures ($172,805 by June 1980) placed it in the middle of our ranking. Lockheed, like Grumman, spent a high proportion of its PAC resources in contributions to Federal candidates and committees ($126,510)—73%).

Lockheed ranked second in the share of contributions going to candidates from key geographic areas (41%). Nearly half of Lockheed's plant-oriented contributions were given to California candidates. Key recipients included Senator Alan Cranston ($1,500); Representative Norman Mineta ($2,050) of Santa Clara, near the company's Missiles and Space Division; Representative Charles Wilson; John Rousselot (prominent conservative); Jim Lloyd (former Navy pilot, highly influential on defense issues); Barry Goldwater, Jr., (son of the Senator);

Chart VII

POLITICAL ACTION COMMITTEE EXPENDITURES

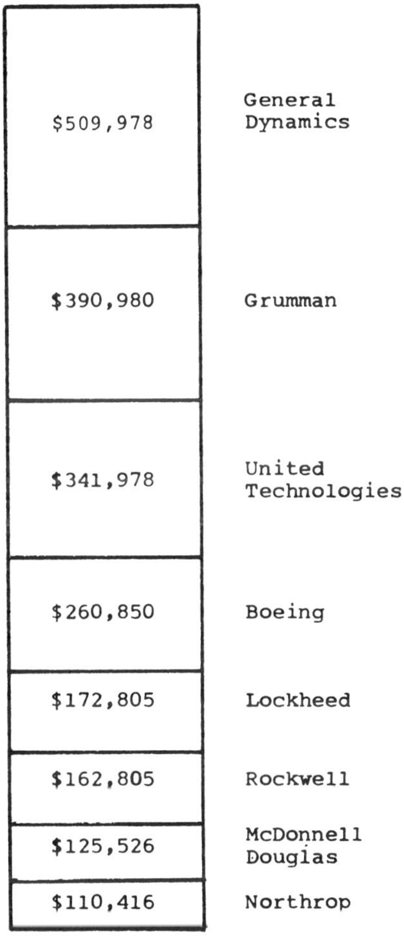

$509,978	General Dynamics
$390,980	Grumman
$341,978	United Technologies
$260,850	Boeing
$172,805	Lockheed
$162,805	Rockwell
$125,526	McDonnell Douglas
$110,416	Northrop

TOTAL $2,075,338

Data through: May 1980-Boeing, Grumman, Rockwell, United Technologies; June 1980-Lockheed; July 1980-McDonnell Douglas, Northrop; August 1980- General Dynamics.

and James Corman (whose district has many aerospace workers). In Washington state, where Lockheed builds ships, Senator Magnuson received $2,000, which may have been related to his key position as Chairman of the Appropriations Committee and Chairman of the Subcommittee on Aviation of the Senate Committee on Commerce, Science and Transportation. (Lockheed has a major commercial air transport program, the L-1011.) Representative Norman Dicks, whose district includes Lockheed's shipbuilding company, received $1,800.

Lockheed has a major electronics facility in Plainfield, New Jersey, the district of Representative Matthew Rinaldo, who received $1,500. Senator Bill Bradley also received a contribution. In Georgia, Representative Larry McDonald (of House Armed Services) received $1,500 and Senator Sam Nunn $2,000.

Lockheed's key committee contributions were also high—48.2%, ranking third. They went to 13 Senate Armed Services Committee members, including $2,500 for Senator Tower, $2,100 for Senator Thurmond, in addition to Senator Nunn. In the House Mendel Davis, Jim Lloyd, Larry McDonald, Bob Wilson and Charles Wilson were supported. Lockheed also funded Appropriations subcommittee members Senators Brooke, Garn, Hollings, Inouye and Stevens and Representatives Addabbo, Cederberg, Flynt, and McFall.

Unlike the other PACs, in the study, Lockheed also made significant contributions to members of committees concerned with science, technology, aviation policy and NASA, including Senators Kassebaum and Griffin, and Representatives Wydler and Gingrich. These contributions may be linked to the importance of those committees for Lockheed's space, satellite and commercial air transport business. In all, two thirds of Lockheed's Federal-level contributions concentrated on key geographic and committee members.

Lockheed's PAC also made significant contributions to a wider range of Members of Congress and candidates, including 15 in the Senate ($1,000 each to Rudy Boschwitz of Minnesota and Charles Percy of Illinois) and 54 in the House.

McDonnell Douglas created its Good Government Fund in April 1976, one of the two earliest in the study. Its total expenditures, $125,526 by July 1980, however, make it one of the smallest in the study. Like Grumman and Lockheed, MDC has concentrated its PAC spending on Federal campaign contributions—roughly 92%. MDC's PAC concentrated these funds on candidates from key areas and those on key committees—77.8% of total Federal giving.

In Missouri, home of the corporation, MDC gave to every incumbent Congressman but one and to two candidates. Large contributions went to E. Thomas Coleman, Richard Ichord (on House Armed Services), Gene Taylor and Robert A. Young. Mel Price, Chairman of the House Armed Services Committee, who received $5,120, represents East St. Louis in Illinois, which sends workers into Missouri to work at MDC. In California where the firm makes transport aircraft,

Senator Cranston received $1,000, while other major contributions went to a long list of key committee and district members: Glenn Anderson (from Long Beach where Douglas Aircraft is located), Robert Badham, Mark Hannaford (also from Long Beach), Jerry Patterson, James Corman, Jim Lloyd, John McFall, Bob Wilson and Charles Wilson. James Jones of Tulsa, site of a MDC production facility, received $1,400.

McDonnell Douglas concentrated a high rate of expenditures (58.8%) on members of key committees: nine from the Senate Armed Services Committee (including Thurmond and Tower) and 29 from House Armed Services (including Badham, Dickinson, Ichord, Lloyd, Price, Bob Wilson and Charles Wilson). Smaller MDC contributions went to Appropriations subcommittee members; but, like Lockheed, the firm put considerable amounts into the campaigns of members of the other aviation and NASA related committees such as Representative Flippo (D-AL) from Huntsville, a major NASA location. McDonnell Douglas manufactures a key air transport plane, the DC-10, in its Long Beach, California, facility.

Northrop created its Employees Political Action Committee in February 1978, the most recent in the study. PAC expenditures of $110,416 by 1980 make it the smallest PAC in the study. Northrop also concentrated its expenditures on Federal-level contributions— $88,039 or nearly 80% of total spending. In addition, Northrop ranked third in the study in the concentration of its Federal spending on candidates from key geographic areas and members sitting on key committees—57% of the total.

• Candidates in key geographic areas received nearly a quarter of PAC federal contributions, including significant amounts to California Representatives Charles Wilson, Bob Wilson and Jim Lloyd.

Twelve members of the Senate Armed Services committee, including Nunn, Thurmond and Tower received Northrop contributions. House Armed Services recipients included Lloyd and the two Wilsons. Smaller amounts went to Defense Appropriations subcommittee members and aviation and NASA-related committee members.

Northrop also gave over 20% of its Federal contributions to other candidates and another 13% to party campaign committees.

Rockwell created its Good Government Committee in May 1976 and had expended $162,805 by 1980, making it a medium-sized PAC in the study. Roughly 64% of total spending went to Federal campaigns, 53% of which was concentrated on candidates in key geographic areas and on key committees. Small amounts were spent in Pennsylvania, where the corporate headquarters are located; equally small in Ohio to, among others, Representative Sam Devine of Columbus, site of the Rockwell aircraft plant, and $1,000 to Senator Taft, then on the Senate Armed Services Committee. Senator Tower of Texas and Representative James Collins (Dallas) received sizeable contributions in the home state of Rockwell's Collins Radio Division.

Some significant contributions were also made in California, where the firm has aerospace facilities. These included donations to Senators Cranston and Hayakawa; Representatives Dornan (a strong B-1 supporter), Jim Lloyd, and John McFall.

A third of Rockwell's contributions went to members of key committees. Senate Armed Services members Taft and Tower received major sums, while 16 House members and candidates also received contributions. Then Senate Appropriations Chairman Magnuson received $2,500, while House Chairman Jamie Whitten received $800. Rockwell also contributed a considerable amount of money to members of NASA-related committees, e.g. Representatives Fuqua (Chairman of a key Science and Technology Subcommittee), Flowers, and Teague. Rockwell is the prime contractor for NASA's space shuttle program.

United Technologies created its Political Action Committee in April 1976, one of the two earliest in the study. With total spending of $341,978 through 1980, UT's PAC was the third largest in the study. Eighty-five percent of that sum was spent in Federal-level contributions. On the other hand, UT had the second lowest (after Boeing) rate of concentrating its spending on candidates from geographic areas and members of key committees.

The 12% contributed to geographic candidates focused on California (Senator Hayakawa; Representatives Mineta from Sunnyvale, where UT's Chemical Division is located; Barry Goldwater Jr., and Bob Wilson) and Connecticut (Senator Weiker; Representatives Cotter, Giaimo, Dodd; and candidates Guidera and Sarasin). Roughly one third of Federal spending went to key committee members, including 14 Senate Armed Services Committee members and 22 House Armed Services members. Defense Appropriations Subcommittee members also received UT contributions: Senators Brooke, Stevens, and Weiker; and Representatives Addabbo, Cederberg, Edwards, Giaimo and Sikes. In addition, major space and aviation-related committee members received UT money: Senators Griffin, Schmitt, Buckley, and Stafford; and Representatives Goldwater, Milford, Pursell, Rudd, Teague, Wydler, and Mineta, among others.

United Technologies ranked first in proportion of contributions to other candidates—nearly 34% of its total federal spending. UT has a wide range of commercial activities and may be seeking access in a correspondingly wide set of Congressional districts. In addition, many of the candidates they chose to fund are politically conservative. Contribubutions went to 26 Senatorial candidates, including significant amounts to Armstrong, Bell, Boschwitz, Chafee, Cochran, Durenberger, Esch, Flowers, Lugar, McCollister, and Moore. Another 125 House candidates received funding, including Devine, Duncan, Ireland, Kelly, Livingston, Lott, McDade, Quayle, Scott, and Shriver.

FOOTNOTES

1. John W. Gardner, "Foreword," in Herbert E. Alexander (ed.) *Campaign Money: Reform and Reality in the States* (N.Y.: The Free Press/Macmillan, 1976), pp. v-vi.
2. Rep. Guy Vander Jagt (R-MI), quoted in Congressional Quarterly, *The Washington Lobby,* 3rd. ed. (Washington, D.C.: Congressional Quarterly, October 1979), p. 79.
3. The Act also prohibited individual contributions of over $5000 to any single national campaign committee, a restriction that the parties evaded by creating numerous committees.
4. See Edwin M. Epstein, "Corporations and Labor Unions in Electoral Politics," *Annals of the American Academy of Political and Social Science,* Vol. 425 (May 1976), pp. 35-58; Epstein, "Business Corporations and Labor Unions in the American Electoral Process: A Policy Analysis of Public Regulation; The Rise of Political Action Committees," Colloquium Paper, Woodrow Wilson Center, Washington, D.C., 15 June 1978, esp. pp. 5-11; Epstein, "The Emergence of Political Action Committees," in Herbert E. Alexander (ed.), *Political Finance, Sage Electoral Studies Yearbook,* Vol. 5 (Beverly Hills: Sage Publications, 1979), pp. 159-197.
5. Edwin M. Epstein, "Business and Labor Under the Federal Election Campaign Act of 1971," in Michael A. Malbin (ed.) *Parties, Interest Groups, and Campaign Finance Laws* (Washington, D.C.: American Enterprise Institute, 1980), p. 111.
6. Ibid.
7. See Alexander Heard, *The Costs of Democracy* (Chapel Hill, N.C.: University of North Carolina Press, 1960) and Herbert E. Alexander, *Money in Politics* (Washington, D.C.: Public Affairs Press, 1972) for discussions of these practices.
8. Epstein in Malbin, p. 111.
9. See Epstein, 1978 Colloquim Paper, pp. 10-24.
10. 18 U.S.C. 610 (1972).
11. See Epstein 1978 Colloquium Paper, p. 27 and Epstein in Malbin, p. 112.
12. The campaign finance director, Maurice Stans, reportedly raised nearly $20 million before the deadline. Following a suit initiated by Common Cause, many of the donors were disclosed. See *The New York Times,* 13 Oct. 1974 and Gardner "Foreword" to Alexander, *Campaign Money,* pp. vii-viii.
13. Congressional Quarterly, *The Washington Lobby,* 3rd. ed., p. 74.
14. Supreme Court Opinion, pp. 66-67.
15. Ibid., p. 52.
16. The Opinion also allowed PACs to make unlimited "independent" campaign expenditures — funds spent in support of or against particular candidates without any coordination with a candidate's campaign. This permitted a major 1979-80 effort by the National Conservative Political Action Committee which was instrumental in the defeat of Senators Frank Church, Birch Bayh, John Culver and George McGovern. It also permitted the creation of several independent campaign committees in support of Ronald Reagan, which spent over $7 million. The public financing ceiling for each of the two major party candidates for President in 1980 was $29 million. See James M. Perry, "Liberal Incumbents Are Main Targets of TV Ads as Political-Action Groups Exploit Court Ruling," *The Wall Street Journal,* 25 Jan. 1980; Bernard Weinraub, "Million-Dollar Drive Aims to Oust 5 Liberal Senators," *The New York Times,* 23 March 1980; Leslie Bennetts, "Conservative and Antiabortion Groups Press Attack Against McGovern," *The New York Times,* 2 June 1980; Larry Light, "Surge in Independent Campaign Spending," *Congressional Quarterly,* 14 June 1980, pp. 1635-39; "A Financing Loophole Helps Reagan," *Business Week,* 23 June 1980; Adam Clymer,

"'Independent' Groups Aim to Give Reagan Financial Edge," *The New York Times*, 23 June 1980. Herbert Alexander described such expenditures as "a good safety valve for people to vent their emotions." (*Congressional Quarterly*, 14 June 1980, p. 1636.) As Lee Ann Elliott, Associate Director of the American Medical Association PAC put it: "The Supreme Court is on our side. The Court has ruled we can spend all the money we want as independent expenditures." (James Perry, "Congress Unlikely to 'Reform' Campaign Finances," *The Wall Street Journal*, 21 Dec. 1978.

17. Epstein in Malbin, pp. 114-115.
18. Ibid., p. 118.
19. Ibid., p. 123.
20. See, for example, Michael Malbin, "The Business PAC Phenomenon: Neither a Mountain Nor a Molehill," *Regulation*, Vol. 3, No. 3 (May-June 1979).
21. Epstein in Malbin, pp. 139-140.
22. Ibid., pp. 143-49. Epstein notes (p. 146):

    Electoral politics, so to speak, has come out of the corporate closet and is now recognized as a legal and appropriate activity for business.... Political legitimacy coupled with the institutionalization of politics within the organizational framework no doubt will lead to increased and more effective corporate political action.

23. See Phyllis McGrath, *Redefining Corporate-Federal Relations* (N.Y.: Conference Board, 1979) and Congressional Quarterly, *The Washington Lobby*, 3rd ed. (Washington, D.C.: Congressional Quarterly, 1979).
24. Robert W. Merry, "Firms' Action Groups are Seen Transforming the Country's Politics," *The Wall Street Journal*, 11 Sept. 1978.
25. Ibid.
26. Ibid.
27. 30 October 1978.
28. *The Wall Street Journal*, 11 Sept. 1978.
29. "Problem of Campaign Funds," *The New York Times*, 19 Oct. 1979.
30. Quoted in Bill Keller and Irwin B. Arieff, "As Campaign Costs Skyrocket, Lobbyists Take Growing Role in Washington Fund-Raisers," *Congressional Quarterly*, 17 May 1980, p. 1333.
31. Quoted in *Political Practices Report*, 19 Feb. 1980, pp. 10-11. Scholarly analysts of PACs agree. "In the largest number of cases, those contributors who seek material rewards, like the policy-oriented givers, expect to be given *access* to decision-makers to press their claims for patronage, preferments or policy. In short, they seek a sympathetic hearing," David Adamany, *Campaign Finance in America* (N. Scituate, MA: Duxbury Press, 1972), p. 172.
32. Phyllis McGrath, *Redefining Corporate-Federal Relations*, p. 50.
33. H. Richard Mayberry, quoted in *Political Practices Report*, 19 Feb. 1980, p. 11.
34. Quoted in Steven V. Roberts, "House Members Pressing to Curb Special Interest Gifts," *The New York Times*, 26 Sept. 1979.
35. Unpublished data supplied to the author, originally presented by Dr. Edwin Epstein at the 1980 convention of the American Political Science Association.
36. "Corporate Chiefs Donate to Parties," *The New York Times*, 20 Sept. 1970.
37. John L. Moore, "Weapons Builders Aid GOP," *The Washington Post*, 13 October 1974. See also Herbert Alexander, *Financing Politics: Money, Elections and Political Reform*, 2nd ed. (Washington, D.C.: Congressional Quarterly Press, 1980).
38. Alexander, p. 77.
39. These included contributions from Northrop personnel of $126,000, from General Dynamics of $92,595, from Lockheed of $50,000 and from

McDonnell Douglas of $84,432. Morton Mintz, "$3.2 Million in Election Gifts Laid to Defense Contractors," *The Washington Post,* 10 Dec. 1973.
40. Alexander, *Financing Politics,* p. 76.
41. Epstein in Malbin, p. 134. Epstein apparently used the *Business Week* classification of firms for this calculation.
42. Data supplied to the author by Dr. Epstein.
43. The Federal Election Commission provides numerous data on receipts, gross disbursements and contributions to Federal candidates, so amply, in fact, that "it takes an expert to extract useful information from the FEC filings." (William J. Lanouette, "Complex Financing Laws Shape Presidential Campaign Strategies," *National Journal,* 4 Aug. 1979, p. 1285.) There is usually a gap between gross disbursements and contributions to Federal candidates. This is explained by the following, only some of which can be quantified. PACs spend certain amounts on administrative costs, internal operations and political communications—amounts which are not disclosed. In addition, contributions are made to state and local candidates (unevenly disclosed), as independent campaign expenditures (reported to FEC), and to political party campaign committees at the local, state and federal level (unevenly disclosed). In addition, PACs are required to disclose only contributions to Federal-level candidates above $250.

Data on Federal contributions can be obtained in two ways: by examining the verified "D Index," covering contributions to individual candidates, and by reviewing each monthly and quarterly report by the PAC for contributions to party campaign committees.

Corporations may also have some access to candidates through contributions by individual corporate employees, limited to $1000 per candidate. Each candidate files regular reports with the FEC disclosing contributions form all sources over $100. It is, unfortunately, usually impossible to trace the corporate connection of the contributors, since the reporting form does not require clear disclosure of employer.

Finally, FEC data on gross disbursements is reported at different points in time from data on Federal contributions, leaving a gap of one or more months between the two sets of data and making comparison difficult.
44. FEC data do not provide information to explain why these figures are so low, though both PACs may concentrate on smaller contributions, on state and local contests and on other, non-contributory activities.
45. It would be interesting to compare the distribution of campaign contributions with the distribution of corporate defense subcontracts. Unfortunately, inadequate data make this impossible.
46. All eight firms in the study are involved in the air transport or general aviation markets, either as aircraft manufacturers, engine suppliers or subcontractors.
47. Bob Wilson (R-CA, ret.) received the 1980 James Forrestal Memorial Award from the National Security Industrial Association "for his long and dedicated Congressional support for effective partnership between government and industry in the interests of national security." (*Aviation Week,* 21 April 1980.)
48. See also the company "Profiles." Comments on the candidates, unless otherwise noted, are drawn from Michael Barone, Grant Ujifusa and Douglas Matthews, *The Almanac of American Politics, 1980* (N.Y.: E.P. Dutton, 1979).
49. The Boeing company's Civic Pledge Program, created in 1971, has a different structure than the other PACs. Employees receive a list of recommended candidates from the Civic Pledge Office and are free to contribute to them, or to candidates of their own choice. Contributions are made by a personal check, sometimes drawn from individual bank accounts set up under a company payroll deduction plan. The company PAC operates as a "conduit" (its official FEC designation) for the individual

checks. Although the PAC retains no funds of its own, it must report a total amount of receipts to the FEC. The amount is based on payroll deductions that go into employee bank accounts, although employees are under no obligation to use these accounts for political contributions. Boeing states the PAC was set up in this manner to allow greater freedom of choice for employees, but it has caused confusion over whether contributions come from individuals or the corporation. From May 1981, the Civic Pledge Program will operate like the other PACs. Our data, which covers the period from 1976, is sketchy because the Civic Pledge Program expenditure reports to the FEC are listed by individual contributors and can not usually be found on computer print-outs. Research on available reports shows that Boeing expended $260,850 through May 1980. Roughly one third ($85,655) was contributed to federal campaigns.
50. Subsequent FEC data show that Grumman contributed $5000 each to Al D'Amato and Jacob Javits and $2000 to Elizabeth Holtzman during the 1980 New York Senate campaign. Holtzman reportedly returned the check, though this is not shown on FEC records. See James Barron, "How Grumman Spends Its Campaign Funds," *The New York Times,* 26 October 1980.
51. Ibid.

9
Control at the Center
Washington Operations

General Activities

The last 20 years have brought great changes in the Federal Government: an increase in spending and regulation, greater Congressional influence on the size and content of the budget, growth in the number of Congressional subcommittees and weakened power of committee chairpersons. Corporations have responded by increasing the importance of their Washington base. Over 500 corporations now have an office in the nation's capital, a five-fold increase over ten years ago.[1] The Business-Government-Relations Council created in 1966, which brings together top Washington office officials, increased its membership in 1979 from 75 to 90.[2] Aerospace firms, which have been closely involved for decades with government procurement policies, have led this trend.[3]

With expansion the role of the Washington office has altered dramatically. Two decades ago a defense contractor's Washington staff gathered information, monitoring procurement developments and legislative activity. Occasionally it applied pressure, lobbying and entertaining friendly members of Congress. Day-to-day interactions between the Government and the contractor, however, were usually handled in conversations between company production staff and Defense Department personnel. Today, in contrast, information and pressure, the two main activities of the Washington office, are closely coordinated. Grouped under the general term "Government relations", they are the key to success.

A contractor's Washington office integrates its activities in two ways that greatly strengthen its side of the "iron triangle." First, "Government relations" makes no distinction between relations with Congress—"lobbying" in the traditional sense—and relations with the Executive branch. The staff follows issues and seeks to shape legislation, procurement and appropriation decisions as they move rapidly between the Executive side of the "iron triangle" and the Congressional. Second, the Washington office plans a company's entire political strategy from grass-roots efforts aimed at employees, stockholders, and local communities; to campaign contributions to members of Congress; to direct contacts with powerful figures in Washington.

The battle between Grumman and McDonnell Douglas/Northrop over aircraft for the Navy that took place in 1977 and 1978 is a telling example of the scope of these activities. In the Navy, procurement funds were insufficient to buy as many of both Grumman's F-14 and McDonnell Douglas/Northrop's F-18 as the Navy and the contractors wished. Which plane should be cut back? The Washington office staffs of the three firms each deployed a vast effort to influence this decision. Grumman retained a new lobbyist, Fred Slatinshek, former counsel to the House Armed Services Committee. Each firm detailed information contrasting the performance and cost of the two fighters—and making the most of the qualifications of its entry. They then enlisted Congressional delegations to pressure the Executive branch decision-makers who would write the budget request for Congress. Grumman pressed Patrick Moynihan, Governor Hugh Carey and the Long Island House delegation into action. McDonnell Douglas/Northrop, whose F-165s were equipped with General Electric engines made in Lynn, Massachusetts, enlisted the aid of Senator Edward Kennedy and Speaker Tip O'Neill. As the pace picked up, company representatives ferried information back and forth between the services and the Hill. Nor did Grumman, the loser, give up easily. Failing in the Executive branch, Grumman continued its battle in the winter and spring of 1978, ultimately obtaining Congressional approval for an increased production of their planes and on the terms that they had originally hoped for.[4]

Information and Pressure

The success of any defense corporation in obtaining contracts for its weapons systems depends upon its effectiveness in trading information and applying pressure.

Washington representatives gather vast amounts of data on Government activity, the status of legislation, the work of key members of Congress, procurement policy decisions in the Executive branch, plans and programs for research and development, emerging regulatory actions and Federal rule-making. This information is sifted, evaluated, and then communicated to appropriate company officials. Some companies distribute a Washington office newsletter to officers and personnel; others simply provide regular written and oral communications to top company officials. This "in-house" reporting is highly valued.

Asked to cite the most important activity they perform, the largest group of Government relations executives talk about their role in communicating political and governmental information to management; an internally directed activity rather than an externally directed one.[5]

In order to gather this information, the staffs pay regular visits to key offices in the Executive branch and Congress, participate in formal and informal advisory committee meetings, meet with trade association groups, and attend hearings. Sometimes the information-gathering function itself becomes controversial. Boeing's Washington representatives, for instance, obtained information about the strategic missile program by reading documents in the Air Force's Office of Research and Development. They telexed that information directly to company officials in Seattle, leading to a Government investigation of a possible breach of security.[6]

Washington office staffers can become so central to the flow of information that they become the medium for communications between the other two sides of the "iron triangle." According to one Pentagon source, "the best thing about corporate lobbyists is that they pass on to us a lot of stuff that they've learned on Capitol Hill. It's usually the quickest way for us to find out what's happening up there."[7]

The line between informing and applying pressure is fine. The two activities complement each other. Information and pressure—getting your views and wishes across and encouraging others to adopt them—is directed at both branches of the Government. A good Washington representative develops and maintains a wide variety of contacts. One, formerly with the Office of the Management of the Budget (OMB) and now with General Dynamics, stated, "It's important for the companies to know they have access to the President's staff." In addition to the White House, corporate staff cultivates the DoD officials who deal with current—or future—company contracts, procurement policy-makers in each service with which the company does business, and policy-making officials in the Office of Secretary of Defense.

The Washington office staff also weaves a network in Congress, starting with the Representatives and Senators on committees that are important to the company—Armed Services, Appropriations, Science and Technology—and from districts and states in which the company has plant locations. In general Washington staffers tend to visit and encourage their friends, rather than try to sway opponents of a program. Yet when a program becomes highly controversial, they will widen their scope to include the uncommitted, or even hostile. In 1975 and 1976 Rockwell International retained extra Washington staff to lobby in Congress for their B-1 bomber.

The most important contacts, however, are often not the members themselves, but their staff and the staffs of key committees. Michael Malbin points out that these now number 23,500.[8] Their role is crucial. "Once a bill is on the agenda, the staff works to assemble a coalition behind it, arranging detailed amendments with other staff members and with interest group representatives to broaden support for the bill without sacrificing the goals the chairman, often at their urging, has adopted."[9] A legislative counsel to a Senator or a key committee plays a major role in developing policies.

The Washington office's direct liaison with the Executive branch and Congress is supplemented by contacts with trade associations, which supply useful information and support the industry's goals, the foreign diplomats often critical to a company's overseas marketing efforts, and others. In addition they coordinate the schedules of company officials who visit Washington either on a political or technical mission.

More central, however, is their role in planning the company's strategy. As politics has become critical to management decision-making, planning the Government relations effort has been more closely tied into overall corporate strategy. This development is reflected in the corporate structure. Once the head of the Washington office was merely an assistant to the chief executive officer or a member of the public affairs staff. Today he or she is a company vice president with formal standing in the hierarchy. In addition, the CEOs have become more personally involved in Government relations. Irving Shapiro of Dupont and Reginald Jones of General Electric, for example, have been active in Washington, Shapiro as head of the Business Roundtable and Jones as head of the Business Council. Northrop CEO Thomas V. Jones testifies regularly in Washington on company and industry issues.[10]

The mix of responsibilities and activities is graphically detailed in a description supplied by Boeing to the Defense Contract Audit Agency in 1975. The Governmental Affairs department of Boeing's Washington office had as its function:

> to prepare and implement congressional strategies on Boeing programs.... Department duties include:
> —Preparing and distributing fact sheets to selected members of Congress to inform them of the effects that pending legislation will have on Boeing.
> —Preparing and disseminating legislative data to Boeing personnel.
> —Following the course of legislation through the Congress and determining when it is appropriate and timely for members of Boeing management to participate directly (testimony) or indirectly (written statements) in hearings on legislation directly affecting the successful management of Boeing.
> —Helping to prepare bills or amendments to existing laws, finding sponsors for such legislation, and helping the bill through the

legislative process by preparing and presenting material to support such legislation. These duties are only performed when Boeing considers the specific piece of legislation essential to its well being.

—Attending hearings and sessions of both houses to report directly and timely the actions being taken on legislation of interest to Boeing.

—Overseeing the preparation of data on members of Congress who are seeking support in elections and making recommendations to the Civic Pledge Committee [Boeing's Political Action Committee].

—Encouraging members of Congress, their staffs, and the staffs of committees to visit Boeing plants. Preparing agendas and coordinating the Congressional visits with the various segments and divisions of the company.

—Recommending visits of top executives to selected members of Congress. Preparing material for such visits and briefing the visitor on subjects to be discussed, the purpose of the visit, the likes and dislikes, special interests, etc., of the Congressional member.

—Providing the focal point for coordinating all contacts between the legislative branch of the Government and Boeing. Assuring that all company contacts "on the Hill" in support of Boeing segments and divisions are coordinated with their representatives in the Washington office.[11]

The Strategic Planning department of the Washington office provided contacts and long-range thinking. Its function was:

to develop and recommend company strategies relative to national issues and trends that could affect Boeing programs and its business environments. Its duties include:

—Being aware of all pertinent developments on key issues and trends that could impact Boeing programs and its business environment.

—Maintaining a repository for management information on national and international plans, events, or trends and activities which may affect corporate objectives or policies.

—Apprising appropriate Boeing managers of significant developments that could affect their programs or areas of responsibility and also informing them of potential new business opportunities.

—Ensuring coordination between Boeing management and key Government personnel concerning national issues and trends.

—Providing analytical research, writing, and dissemination of information on special areas of interest to management.[12]

The Boeing office also maintained departments that worked on behalf of specific corporate divisions. The Boeing Aerospace Company

(BAC) department, for instance,

> obtains information and monitors actions of specific customers, product lines, and programs.... Department duties include:
> —Establishing and maintaining relations with customers in the Washington area.
> —Investigating and developing new business opportunities.
> —Developing an understanding of customer plans.
> —Developing and maintaining significant customer and industry contacts.
> —Providing inputs to assist in developing and implementing Boeing Aerospace Marketing plans in the Washington area.
> —Assisting BAC personnel in contacting important customer laboratories and technical organizations.
> —Arranging visits between BAC field personnel and customer personnel in the Washington area and maintaining surveillance over customer reaction to presentations.
> —Representing Boeing at business and social functions in the area and attending conferences and presentations.[13]

Lobbying

Work aimed at Congress often begins outside Washington. The Washington office knows full well that many of its political activities ultimately aimed at influencing Federal decision-making can only be furthered through grass-roots support.

> A few years ago we began to understand that while Government policies are executed in Washington, their impetus lies elsewhere, at the grass roots. Since then, we have involved more and more plant managers in letter and telegram writing, personal visits, and telephone calls on Governmental policies because their views are more important than those of the Washington lobbyist.[14]

The Washington staff enlists the support of employees, shareholders, and the local communities dependent upon the economic well-being of their plants. They also often allocate the campaign contributions of the company's Political Action Committee, thus reenforcing access to key lawmakers. A member of Grumman's Washington office states: "The decisions on Federal races are reached on the basis of recommendations from Mr. Ochenrider in Washington, who keeps close tabs on incumbents' voting records."[15]

Because of the complexity of the work, corporations like to hire lawyers, public affairs experts, and technicians. Past experience with the Government is a shining asset. Much of the work, however, they give over to outside lobbyists. A firm's legal counsel in Washington also handles what is essentially Government relations work. Cherington and Gillen quote a Washington representative as saying, "In fact, a very substantial part of the law practice in Washington is really representation of the company and its sales, as well as a lot of strictly legal matters."[16] Mark Green describes lobbying as "a primary raison d'etre of capital counsel, who practice in Washington precisely because they try to tilt federal policy to their clients' interests."[17]

Given the growing sophistication and power of the corporate presence in Washington, it is hardly surprising that reformers have attempted to curtail its influence. These attempts have centered on lobbying.

In the 1946 Legislative Reorganization Act, lobbying was defined so as to cover special interest activities aimed at Congress. Lobbying is legal. A lobbyist is required to register with the Clerk of the House of Representatives if he/she:

> directly or indirectly, solicits, collects or receives money or any other thing of value to be used principally to aid, or the principal purpose of which person is to aid, in the accomplishment of any of the following purposes: a) the passage or defeat of any legislation by the Congress of the United States; b) to influence, directly or indirectly, the passage or defeat of any legislation by the Congress of the United States (Title III, Section 30F).[18]

This Act also requires lobbyists to disclose their receipts and expenditures on lobbying activities on a quarterly basis. The definition used in the Act, and consequently the data made available, is woefully inadequate. Because lobbying, under the law, must be a "principal activity," many staff members who work on Congressional matters may avoid registering, while still undertaking activities aimed at influencing Congress. In addition, the law assumes—erroneously—that lobbying is something directed towards Congress.[19] As Lester Milbrath observed, "Most registered lobbyists spend as much time and energy lobbying before the executive branch as before the legislative branch. Most lobbyists try to influence decisions at all stages."[20] Milbrath offers an expanded definition. Lobbying is "the stimulation and transmission of a communication by someone other than a citizen acting on his own behalf, directed to a governmental decision-maker with the hope of influencing his decision."[21] It is clear that many staff persons engage in lobbying in this broader sense, though because of the narrow definition in the legislation, they are not required to register as lobbyists (see Chapter 15).

In view of the inadequacy of the definition—and the overlap implicit in the terms "information-giving," "pressure," and "lobbying"— much of the Washington activity of the companies is not covered by existing legislation and is, accordingly, undisclosed. As a result, an enormous part of Government relations and lobbying activities does not see the light of day, a fact that serves the interests and power of the industry side of the "iron triangle." As a defense lobbyist for General Electric put it: "Visibility is the last thing that I need."[22]

The Companies

Despite the obstacles posed by inadequate registration and disclosure requirements, we were able to obtain useful data on the Washington operations of the eight companies in this study. All eight have maintained a substantial Washington operation for some years. Rockwell International has the largest staff with 85 employees, roughly 40 of whom work on defense issues.[23] In decreasing order of size and staff the other companies rank as follows: United Technologies, Boeing, Northrop, General Dynamics, McDonnell Douglas, Lockheed, and Grumman. A high proportion of Washington staffers work on defense issues for McDonnell Douglas, General Dynamics, and Northrop (see Table XIII), indicating a major Government relations effort by these three companies.

These efforts, obviously, include the lobbying of both staff and outside specialists. Taking advantage of the inadequate definition in the 1946 Act, only some have registered as lobbyists. All eight office directors play an active role in coordinating, directing and carrying out information-gathering and pressure activities[24], but only two have registered: Boeing's Russell Light and Grumman's Gordon Ochenrider.

Counting all persons who registered as lobbyists for the company between 1977 and 1979, Boeing had by far the largest number (15), followed by Northrop (12) and Rockwell (6). All of Boeing's registered lobbyists in this period were company employees, while most of Northrop's (11 of 12) were outside lobbyists. General Dynamics, many of whose Washington staffers work on defense issues, had only one registered lobbyist, an outsider—Fred Slatinshek.

Lobbyists' receipts and expenditures also suggest that Northrop and Grumman maintain a substantial Washington effort.[25] Northrop's lobbyists disclosed being paid nearly $340,000 for lobbying activity between 1977 and 1979, while Grumman's lobbyists reported $249,000 (see Table XIII). Lockheed and United Technologies followed. General Dynamics again fell low, reporting minimal receipts and no expenditures.

In addition to the information on lobbying, some data are available on the Washington office expenditures of five of the eight companies in the study. In 1976 and 1977, the Defense Contract Audit Agency, which reviews contractor claims for costs incurred on defense contract work, undertook special audits of the 1974 and 1975 expenditures of the Washington offices of ten defense contractors, including Boeing, General Dynamics, Grumman, Lockheed and Rockwell International.[26]

These audits reviewed Washington office activities, including overall office costs and costs claimed by the companies against Government contracts. The preliminary versions of these audits, completed in 1976, were made available to the contracting offices of the DoD (the Air Force and Navy) and to the contractors. Once negotiations between the contractors and the DoD were completed, final versions of the

TABLE XIII

WASHINGTON OPERATIONS

Company	Employees*	No. Working on Defense*	Costs** 1974-75** Costs ($thousands)	Questioned by DCAA	Lobbyist*** No.*** Lobbyists (1977-79)	Lobbyist*** Receipts (1977-79) ($thousands)	Expenditures (1977-79) ($thousands)
Boeing	58	26	$3,629	20.2%	15	$ 52.2	$ 40.5
General Dynamics	48	40	2,777	29.8%	1	1.64	N.A.
Grumman	14	7	560	12.2%	3	40	10.2
Lockheed	23	12	2,739	19.8%	3	158.5	11.8
McDonnell Douglas	25	20	N.A.	—	5	15.7	7.6
Northrop	50	40	N.A.	—	12	340.0	183.1
Rockwell	85	40	7,048	31.5%	6	80.4	13.6
United Technologies	60	15	N.A.	—	3	142.7	10.7

* Source: *Armed Forces Journal International*, June & July, 1980.

** Source: Defense Contract Audit Agency, except Grumman, audits of Washington offices, 1974-75. Subsequent revisions of these audits reduced the questioned costs as follows: Boeing-8.2%; General Dynamics-NA; Grumman-12.2%; Lockheed-12.9%; Rockwell-13.7%.

*** Source: Quarterly filings with Clerk of the House of Representatives, as printed in *Congressional Record*.

audits were prepared by DCAA, eliminating as questioned costs items accepted by DoD as allowable against contract costs.

Despite numerous earlier efforts to obtain these audit reports, the preliminary versions of audits for eight companies (including Boeing, General Dynamics, Lockheed and Rockwell International) were only released in January 1981. Common Cause filed a Freedom of Information Act request for the audits in 1977 and received "sanitized" versions, eliminating total office costs, claimed costs and many details on questioned costs, as well as each company's description of its Washington office's activities. Common Cause then sued for the full version of the audits, a suit settled in 1981 when the Air Force released the full text of the preliminary audits for eight companies, including Boeing, General Dynamics, Lockheed and Rockwell International.[27] In addition, while the Common Cause suit was pending, the Defense Department released "sanitized" versions of final audits for six companies, including Boeing, Grumman, Lockheed and Rockwell.[28] These final versions also excluded descriptions of Washington office activities, overall costs and details of questioned costs.

On the basis of the released documents, we can obtain an indication of the magnitude of effort involved in Washington. We concluded that the Washington offices of five companies—Boeing, General Dynamics, Grumman, Lockheed and Rockwell International spent nearly $16.8 million between 1974 and 1975 for their Government relations activities, over $15.8 million of which was initially charged to contracts (see Table XIII). Rockwell International had by far the most extensive operation in this period, with a total expenditure of over $7 million, followed by Boeing ($3.63 m.), General Dynamics ($2.78 m.), and Lockheed ($2.74 m.).[29] Only Grumman, with roughly $568,000 in expenditures for 1974 and 1975, could be said to have a relatively "small" operation.[30]

Both the preliminary and the final versions of these audits indicate that a substantial portion of these expenditures were for lobbying activity, in the sense of seeking to influence legislation and appropriations in Congress. Many of these expenditures were questioned by DCAA as possibly "unallowable costs" against contracts. As DCAA pointed out in every audit:

> We found that generally, the costs incurred by the Washington office were for interface with regulatory agencies; import/export licensing; public relations; and market research, information gathering, and liaison activities. However, based on evaluation of available supporting documentation and employee interviews, we noted that some individuals were engaged in unallowable lobbying (influencing legislation) and entertaining.[31]

While DCAA was not asserting that the contractors had no right to lobby, the agency questioned whether such expenditures ought to be charged to Government contracts:

> We find no recognizable benefit to Government contracts since the Department of Defense and other executive agencies make determinations of policy and program needs, and justify their own requirements for appropriations. Attempts by contractors to influence legislation favoring procurement of their products can be inimical to Department of Defense policies as well as requirements determinations.[32]

DCAA also suggested that, in the agency's view, using contract funds to support lobbying activity may be unallowable under Title 18, U.S. Code Section 1913, which states:

> No part of the money appropriated by any enactment of Congress shall in the absence of express authorization by Congress, be used directly or indirectly to pay for any personal service, advertisement, telegram, telephone, letter, printed or written matter, or other device, intended or designed to influence in any manner a Member of Congress, to favor or oppose, by vote or otherwise, any legislation or appropriation by Congress, whether before or after the introduction of any bill or resolution proposing such legislation or appropriation.[33]

Using the data supplied by the preliminary audits, we calculate that a substantial proportion of Washington office costs were questioned by DCAA as being possibly unallowable for the above reasons. Rockwell again led the list in questioned costs—over $2 million or 31.5 percent of total claimed costs.[34] General Dynamics had nearly the same proportion questioned—30.3 percent of claimed costs. For all five companies over a quarter of claimed costs were questioned by DCAA in the preliminary audits.

Following negotiations between the Air Force and the companies on the basis of the preliminary DCAA audits and new DoD guidance on allowability, these figures on questioned costs were scaled down sharply. Partial data disclosed in the "sanitized" final audits suggests that 13.7 percent of Rockwell's claimed costs were finally questioned, while over 12 percent of the claimed costs of Grumman and Lockheed's Washington offices were deemed "unallowable." The Boeing figure dropped to 8.2 percent.[35]

This decline does not suggest, however, that less lobbying was taking place than originally thought by DCAA. It reflects, instead, the outcome of negotiations and new guidance. The Defense Department has abandoned attempts to define a suitable cost allowability standard for lobbying costs (see below, Chapter 15), and taxpayer funds continue to support some contractor lobbying. DCAA noted in the final "sanitized" version of Rockwell and Boeing's audits that some expenditures related to lobbying may be included in claimed costs, but simply cannot be sorted out:

> There is no assurance that the amounts so determined as lobbying or entertainment constitute the entirety of the employees' efforts spent in these areas. There may be addi-

Control at the Center: Washington Operations

tional amounts of unallowable directly associated costs related to these activities.[36]

There is no assurance that amounts reported as lobbying constitute the entirety of the contractor's lobbying efforts.[37]

Overall, these data on total Washington office costs and the details on questioned costs suggest that at least four of the companies in the study—Boeing, General Dynamics, Lockheed and Rockwell—maintain Washington operations of substantial size, a good part of whose activity is devoted to lobbying and Government relations work. A company-by-company discussion reveals more detail on the size and characteristics of each firm's Washington activity.

Boeing

Boeing's sizable Washington office is headed by Executive Vice President Russell Light. Light is considered one of the most effective industry representatives in Washington. He received a degree in aeronautical engineering from the University of Washington in 1950. At Boeing he worked first as an engineer (bomber and fighter programs), later as a sales representative, then as sales director and finally program manager. In 1970 he joined the staff of the Washington office as Director of Congressional Affairs and has remained for the past decade, becoming vice president in 1977.[38]

In addition to Light, 14 other Boeing employees have registered as lobbyists between January 1977 and December 1979, suggesting both a high rate of compliance with the reporting requirement and an active lobbying effort. Two of these have defense-related backgrounds. Clifford C. LaPlante, who has since moved on to General Electric, is a former Air Force colonel. Dale Babione spent 29 years in the Defense Department, most recently in the key job of Deputy Under Secretary of Defense for Acquisition Policy. As of August 1980, Boeing had 12 registered lobbyists, including nine Washington office employees.

According to the DCAA preliminary audit, Boeing's Washington office spent $3,628,821 from January 1977 through September 1978, claiming $3.35 million as contact costs.[39] The activities of the office are typical of a contractor's Washington operation: information gathering, liaison with the Executive branch, lobbying in Congress, public relations, liaison with foreign diplomats and communications with corporate headquarters. DCAA questioned 20.2 percent of the claimed costs as unallowable in the preliminary audit and 8.2 percent in the final audit, because "some individuals were engaged in unallowable lobbying (influencing legislation) and entertaining."[40] As an indication of the level of activity, the preliminary audit pointed out that in interviews with staffers Light and LaPlante:

> both stated that 100 percent of their work is spent on lobbying, either talking directly to Congressmen or their staffs,

or obtaining information to support Company positions. Mr. Light stated that Mr. Bradley performs the same functions.[41]

One major illustration of staff work grew out of Boeing's interest in the MX missile. Boeing's Washington marketing representative Thomas O'Rourke learned in March 1978 from a former Boeing employee Peter Hughes, then on the staff of the House Armed Services Committee, that a DoD report on MX had recently gone to the White House. According to press reports, O'Rourke approached Air Force contacts and urged them to play a more active role in the DoD discussions on the future of land-based strategic missiles. One of these contacts reportedly received a copy of the memo from his superior for comments. This "bootleg" copy had come from Hua Lin in the Office of the Under Secretary of Defense for Research and Engineering. Lin, according to *The Wall Street Journal*,[42] was "a Boeing employee on leave to work in the Pentagon's Weapons Research and Development Office." Boeing Aerospace Vice President for Marketing Ben Plymale, former Assistant Secretary of Defense for Strategic and Space Systems, learned of the memo and urged O'Rourke to try to obtain a copy. Although O'Rourke was refused a copy, he was allowed to read the memo and take notes. He then transmitted a report by Telex to Plymale in Seattle. When it later became clear that Plymale had read this report he stated, according to the *Journal*, that the information had come from an "unknown source." Pentagon investigators claimed that the telexing of the information violated national security restrictions and might have allowed the information to be intercepted by foreign intelligence agents.[43]

This example nicely illustrates the role of Washington staff and personnel transfers in obtaining early information on a major weapons system. *The Wall Street Journal* underlined its importance:

> Defense officials say the incident underscores some of the problems inherent in the comfortably symbiotic relationships that develop between military planners and major contractors. They must exchange information while designing weapons, and they come to share a commitment to promoting their projects over competing alternatives.
>
> The movement of weaponry experts between industry and Government jobs, frequently on the same project, facilitates the easy flow of information and tends to blur the distinction between national security and corporate goals.
>
> "This type of thing goes on all the time," one defense official says, referring to the Boeing case.[44]

General Dynamics

General Dynamics' Washington office concentrates the work of 40 of its 48 employees on defense issues, though no staff employee is a registered lobbyist. Office head and corporate Vice President Edward

J. LeFevre holds a Business Administration degree from Penn State and joined General Dynamics in 1951 as a product planner in the Convair Division and in 1958 was assigned to the Washington office, becoming a corporate vice president in 1966. LeFevre was especially active in 1978, urging Congress to accept the Navy proposal for a settlement of its claims against Electric Boat Division for shipbuilding cost overruns. Through the office of Congressman Christopher Dodd (D-CT), he worked closely with the Rhode Island and Connecticut Congressional delegations in this effort.[45]

General Dynamics retains an outside firm as its only registered lobbyist—F. Slatinshek & Associates. Slatinshek, former general counsel to the House Armed Services Committee, has unique access to Congress. Representative Sam Stratton, House Armed Services Committee member, says of Slatinshek, "He has maximum entree around here. He's bright and respected, he knows what's going on, and he has moxie."[46]

General Dynamics' Washington office, according to the DCAA, spent $2,777,255 between January 1974 and September 1975, almost all of which was claimed as contract costs. The office conducts activities similar to those of Boeing. According to the preliminary audit, the Government Relations Department handled "liaison with all departments and agencies of the Legislative and Executive branches of the Government for all divisions of the company with Government sales, to facilitate market research and sales planning and provide a climate conducive to the sale of General Dynamics' products and services."[47]

E.J. LeFevre provided DCAA with further details on what this activity entailed:

> Responsibilities include creating and implementing, in conjunction with elements of Corporate and division management and their technical groups, the basic tactics and strategies for pursuing and winning Government business. The Corporate Vice President of Government Relations is assisted by a technical staff of professionals who are experts in the fields of aerospace technology, marine systems and tactical missiles, electronics, and international sales. It is the responsibility of this group to participate in all Corporate and Division planning functions and to provide professional inputs as to the Government's interests and/or concerns relative to General Dynamics' projects, programs and long range plans as related to the company's Government business. These staffs also participate in all proposal preparations by actively working with each Division of the Corporation on all Government business proposals.
>
> The Government Relations Department responds to the requests of Congressional Offices representing the Districts in which General Dynamics facilities are located...[and] provides up-to-date information to these offices on the programs and progress within the General Dynamics family.[48]

DCAA's preliminary audit questioned 29.8 percent of General Dynamics' claimed costs and no final version of the audit has been disclosed. DCAA noted that they found "substantial amounts of questionable cost pertaining to business entertainment, inadequately supported business conferences and lobbying (influencing legislation)."[49] General Dynamics stated in the audit that, in its view, the Armed Services Procurement Regulations "does (sic) not state that lobbying is unallowable. The bulk of this effort consists of responses to Congressmen and their staff, to which General Dynamics is a constituent."[50] The costs questioned by DCAA included over $100,000 in

> expenses in connection with various receptions, banquets, tickets to theatrical and sporting events, refreshment costs, and costs incurred at various country clubs. Items of this nature are considered unallowable pursuant to ASPR 15-205.11. Items of this nature are normally conceded by the contractor.[51]

DCAA also noted that General Dynamics had claimed costs of over $45,000 for retaining one P.W. Kelleher as a consultant, who "was consulted on dealings with Congress. We consider such services lobbying activities (influencing legislation) and have questioned all Mr. Kelleher's fees and expenses."[52]

Grumman

Grumman's Washington office is substantially smaller than the others in the study and their actual lobbying activity was minimal until the late 1970s. They may have felt little need to lobby since they have had close ties for over 30 years with one defense market—the Navy. Office head and Senior Vice President Gordon Ochenrider typifies this relationship. He is an Annapolis graduate, with more than 14 years of Navy flying experience, and has been with Grumman for 25 years, working largely in business development, until he went to Washington in 1974 as head of the recently opened Washington office.[53] Moreover, William Luckenbill, a Grumman Government liaison representative in the 1970s, was formerly a Program Analyst in the Naval Air Systems Command.

Ochenrider is the only company employee registered as a lobbyist. When Grumman expanded its activity in the late 1970s, it retained two outside firms as lobbyists: F. Slatinshek & Associates, and Cederberg Associates. Slatinshek worked closely with Ochenrider in 1978 and 1979 to convince Congress to fund a higher production rate of the F-14. Elford Cederberg, a member of Congress for 26 years and the ranking Republican on the House Defense Appropriations Subcommittee, was also an effective spokesman for Grumman.

Grumman's Washington office, according to our information, expended roughly $560,000 during 1974 and 1975, a measure of its relatively smaller size.[54] According to the sanitized DCAA audit, $68,210 (12.2 percent) of those expenditures were questioned as contract costs, since they related to "contractor personnel engaged in unallowable entertainment and lobbying (influencing legislation) activities."[55]

Grumman's office activities were described in the audit as follows:

> The contractor's personnel stated that the primary functions of the Washington office are to: (i) provide liaison between contractor and Government personnel, (ii) keep abreast of Congressional activities and their effect on company programs, (iii) perform public relations, (iv) gather information, and (v) support foreign marketing and international sales of aircraft.[56]

Lockheed

Lockheed's Washington office of 23 persons is headed by corporate Vice President Richard K. Cook, who holds degrees in international relations and business. Cook's career has been closely linked to Congress. He began as a legislative assistant for the American Trucking Association, and was then an aide to Congressmen Edwin B. Dooly (1961-63) and Oliver P. Bolton (1963-65). He was minority staff assistant on the House Committee on Banking and Currency (1965-69) and Deputy assistant to President Nixon (1969-73). In 1973 he joined Lockheed as vice president in Washington. Cook is rated as one of the more influential defense industry representatives in Washington, though he is not a registered lobbyist.[57] Ricardo R. Alvarado, director of Government affairs and a former Air Force colonel, supplements Cook's efforts and is registered as a lobbyist. Lockheed's Washington law firm, Miller and Chevalier, is also registered as a lobbyist.

Lockheed's Washington office spent $2,739,073 between 1974 and 1975, according to the preliminary DCAA audit, of which over $2,660,000 was claimed as contract costs. According to the description supplied by Lockheed to DCAA, the office's prime function was "technical liaison." In addition, DCAA noted, the Aircraft Corporation's office

> also engages in public relations functions, marketing intelligence activities to determine future Government requirements, lobbying activities, responding to Congressional inquiries, entertainment activities, foreign sales liaison and office administration.[59]

DCAA questioned 19.8 percent of the office's costs as unallowable in the preliminary audit, a figure which dropped to 12.9 percent in the final version. The agency noted that their evaluation of documentation and employee interviews suggested that "some individuals were engaged in unallowable lobbying (influencing legislation) and related legislative liaison which, in our opinion, supports lobbying activities."[60]

DCAA did note that entertainment costs, including "meals, receptions, refreshments, and activities such as golf, costs of tickets to theatres, ball games, etc." had not been charged to contracts.[61] Lobbying activity had been so charged, however, in DCAA's view. The preliminary audit questioned a substantial portion of Ricardo Alvarado's time as being "devoted to lobbying activities (influencing legislation) and to monitoring Congressional actions and answering Congressional inquiries."[62]

McDonnell Douglas

McDonnell Douglas' relatively small Washington office staff (25) mainly handles defense issues. The head of the office is Vice President Gordon Graham, who works with Albert J. Redway, corporate vice president of the Eastern Region of the company. Little data is available on Graham. Redway has a degree in aeronautical engineering (Princeton, 1949) and joined MDC that year. He became vice president for the Washington office in 1966, where he has remained.[63]

Although Redway is not a registered lobbyist, three other members of the Washington office staff are: James E. Wilson, Jr.; John Dierker, administrative assistant to Redway; and Earl J. Morgan, director of legislative liaison, who is considered a leading aerospace lobbyist.[64] Thomas Gunn of St. Louis is also a registered lobbyist for MDC. McDonnell Douglas retains as Washington counsel the prestigious law firm of Covington & Burling. The firm is not registered as a lobbyist, but its access to the Executive branch and Congress is legendary.[65]

MDC's Washington office was not audited by the DCAA. It doubtless carries out the same activities as other firms. The office has been active in the late 1970s, urging favorable DoD and Congressional decisions on funding for the F-18 program, production of the F-15 and for its AV-8B Advance Harrier program. Senator Gary Hart of Colorado attributed Congressional approval of F-18 funds to "swarming" lobbyists on Capitol Hill from MDC and co-producer Northrop.[66]

Northrop

Northrop's Washington office, whose staff also concentrates on defense issues, is headed by Stanley Ebner, corporate vice president and Eastern Regional manager. Ebner has a law degree from Yale (1958) and wide experience in the Federal Government. He was a lawyer in the Army's Judge Advocate General Office and in the Intelligence Corps between 1960 and 1969. He then served as a legislative counsel in the office of the U.S. Deputy Attorney General, as minority counsel to the U.S. Senate Judiciary Committee and legislative assistant to Senator Roman Hruska (R-NE). He was general counsel in the Office of Management and Budget (OMB) from 1973 to 1979 and left to become vice president and chief legal officer at Timmons & Co. He became the manager of Northrop's Washington office in 1979.[67] Ebner works with James V. Holcombe, senior vice president and a former Marine Corps colonel. Holcombe is considered one of the most influential defense industry representatives in Washington.[68]

Northrop's office has mounted a major Government relations effort in the 1970s. Northrop's 12 registered lobbyists between 1977 and 1979 received the largest disclosed amount of money of the eight companies in the study. The array of lobbying talent is striking. Company employees John Pesch and Stanley L. Sommer, both responsible for legislative relations in the D.C. office, accounted for the lion's share of Northrop's lobbying expenditures from 1977 to 1979. In addition, Northrop also retained several outside lobbyists. Timmons & Co. was headed by William Timmons, who was legislative liaison for the Nixon White House and left to form his own firm in 1975.[69] Tom Korologos, Nixon White House legislative liaison, is also a member of the firm. Timmons & Co. worked hard on the sale of Northrop's F-18 to Congress. According to Korologos, "We had our work cut out. We had a good product to sell, which is the most important thing to a lobbyist. But we also had to do some convincing from the constituent angle on the Hill."[70]

Other firms retained by Northrop have had good connections in Washington. The law firm of Manatt, Phelps, Rothenbert & Tunney, registered as a Northrop lobbyist, included John Tunney, former California Senator. Winston Wilson (USAF-ret.) handled much of Northrop's entertaining activities.[71] Northrop also retained as counsel the influential Washington law firm of Wilmer, Cutler & Pickering (now Wilmer & Pickering). Lloyd Cutler, former senior partner, is one of the most powerful lawyers in the Washington scene. Mark Green decribes him as moving "with the deftness of a chameleon between the boardrooms of corporate power and the anterooms of advocacy groups, as each comes to accept him as one of their own."[72] Ben Gordon, staff assistant on the Senate Small Business Committee says, "When I see Lloyd Cutler representing anybody, I know that it is not in the public interest."[73] Yet Cutler, who became special counsel to President Carter in 1979, is also an advocate of campaign finance reform. As of August 1980, Northrop had five registered lobbyists, including Sommer.

No DCAA audit was done of Northrop's Washington office. It appears, however, to have expanded rapidly from 1976 on as the firm began to market its F-5 overseas, competed with the General Dynamics F-16 for the Air Force and European fighter orders, and sold its version (renamed the F-18 and co-produced with McDonnell Douglas) to the Navy.

Rockwell

Of the eight companies, Rockwell has the largest Washington office. Office head William L. Clark, staff vice president of the Washington and Eastern Region, holds a J.D. from Yale (1952) and joined the company's predecessor, North American Aviation, in the late 1950s as assistant general counsel. From 1962 to 1968 he was vice president for contracts before he took his current post.[74]

Clark is not a registered lobbyist for the firm, nor is their counsel Covington and Burling. Rockwell does employ several registered lobbyists, however. Company employee Ralph J. (Doc) Watson is considered their most effective lobbyist and was especially active in Congress on the B-1 program, as were John Torbet and Anne Genevieve Allen. Potter International, a law firm, and Theodore Littman are also registered as Rockwell lobbyists.

According to the DCAA preliminary audit, Rockwell's corporate and Collins Radio division offices in Washington spent $7,048,717 between 1973 and 1975, of which $6.5 million was initially charged to Government contracts.[75] The Agency described Rockwell's Washington functions as including:

— Lobbying support activity — monitoring congressional (legislative) activities that have an impact on various Rockwell International programs (B-1 bomber, Space Shuttle), and making frequent trips to Capitol Hill.
— Support of Mr. R.J. Watson, a registered lobbyist, in attempts to obtain congressional support for on-going Rockwell programs.
— Marketing liaison — maintaining liaison with the military, legislative and executive departments.
— Public relations — making presentations at industrial, trade and military association functions and symposiums on contract management matters.[76]

The Collins audit divided office tasks into: Washington Operations, International Representation, Civil/Regulatory Government Representation, Defense Systems Representation, International/Government Planning, Government Market Analysis and Development. The activities of the last office covered a wide range of Government relations functions:

> The Director of this section is responsible for developing and recommending long-range Government marketing plans and analyses. As such, he maintains liaison with high-level Government personnel to obtain marketing intelligence information, i.e., current status of major program decisions, policy and key personnel changes, and the general attitude of the Department of Defense relating to the Government market. Another employee conducts technical investigations, surveys and analyses of technology

needs, objectives, and priorities within selected areas of the market place. He also attends hearings on "Capitol Hill," contacts legislative representatives to determine their position on R&D programs, and participates on industry and Government committees, boards, etc., dealing with legislative, regulatory, trade, and similar aspects of the domestic and international business environment. Another staff member spends essentially all of his time in direct lobbying (drafting legislation for discussion and/or review with Government personnel, etc.) and lobbying support activities. He coordinates his activities with a registered lobbyist of the Rockwell International Corporation. Another employee participates and exercises leadership in committees that influence national and international regulations of the telecommunications industry. The remaining staff member gathers, analyzes and evaluates budgetary data of all Government offices that affect the Collins Radio Group. All these employees, except the latter, provide entertainment and lobbying support activities as required.[77]

In the preliminary audit, DCAA questioned over $2 million in Rockwell and Collins costs, some 31.5 percent of the total claimed. This figure dropped to 13.7 percent for the Rockwell final audit (no final Collins audit has been released by DCAA).[78] The basis for DCAA's evaluation lay in their conclusion that "some individuals were engaged in unallowable lobbying (influencing legislation) and entertaining."[79] Rockwell asserted that entertainment costs were not being charged to contracts.[80] Several items of lobbying costs were questioned, however, including the costs of preparing films and outside technical help which, in DCAA's opinion, represented "lobbying-type costs designed to influence legislation."[81]

In the case of Collins' office, DCAA noted:

None of the employees of Collins' Washington office are registered lobyists. However, Mr. E.J. LaFleur, Manager, Government Relations and Contract Policy, spends essentially all of his time on direct lobbying and lobbying support. He coordinates his work with Mr. R.J. (Doc) Watson, a registered lobbyist of the Rockwell International Corporation.[82]

United Technologies

United Technologies maintains one of the larger offices in Washington, though a smaller number of staff work on defense issues, perhaps because UT is the least defense-dependent firm in the study. At least two members of the staff have good access to the Washington scene. Office Director and corporate Senior Vice President Clark MacGregor has a law degree from the University of Minnesota (1948).

After several years of legal practice, he became a Congressman from Minnesota, serving for 10 years as a member of the Judiciary and the Banking and Currency Committees. From 1971 to 1972, MacGregor was counsel to President Nixon and campaign director of the Committee to Reelect the President. In November 1972, he became a vice president for United Technologies, working in Washington where he is considered an influential aerospace representative.[83] MacGregor acknowledges that his experience gives him special access on the Hill. "Having been an activist Republican who is still respected by the Democrats is very important to me—it gives me the credibility I need."[84]

In 1977, Hugh Witt joined the UT office staff as manager of Government liaison. Witt is a former Air Force official who was the first director of the Office of Federal Procurement Policy in the OMB. OFPP drafted and implemented a major revision of Federal procurement regulatons, giving Witt special knowledge of, and access to, the procurement process of the Executive branch.

United Technologies retains three outside firms as lobbyists— Fred Slatinshek; Cederberg & Associates; and Alcarde, Henderson, O'Bannon & Bracy. UT also employs the law firm of Covington and Burling as counsel, though again it is not registered as a company lobbyist.

The DCAA did not audit UT's Washington office. Since its defense-related staff is small and its registered lobbyists few, the company appears to have a lean but efficient Government relations effort.

FOOTNOTES

1. Mark Green and Andrew Buchsbaum, *The Corporate Lobbies: Political Profiles of the Business Roundtable and the Chamber of Commerce,* A Public Citizen/Big Business Day Report (Washington D.C.: Public Citizen, copyright, 1980), p. 7.
2. "New Ways to Lobby a Recalcitrant Congress," *Business Week,* 3 Sept. 1979.
3. Phyllis S. McGrath, *Redefining Corporate-Federal Relations,* A Report from the Conference Board's Division of Management Research (New York: The Conference Board, Inc., 1979), p. 58.

4. "Carter Fund-Raiser Backs 2 Jet-Fighters," *The New York Times,* 7 Dec. 1977; "Effort to Override Cut in F-14 Orders is Urged by Downey," *The New York Times,* 10 Jan. 1978; "Moynihan Asks Expansion of Plane Lobbying Study," *The New York Times,* 16 Feb. 1978; Weisman, Steven R., "Carey Aide Accuses O'Neill on Grumman Cutback," *The New York Times,* 17 Feb. 1978; Rachelle Patterson, "Carter to Decide in 2 Weeks on F-18's Future," *Boston Globe,* 6 Dec. 1977; A. Harris and George C. Wilson, "Aircraft Contracts Stir Dogfight Here," *The Washington Post,* 5 Dec. 1977.
5. McGrath, *Redefining Corporate-Federal Relations,* p. 15.
6. Kenneth H. Bacon, "Pentagon Studies How Boeing Got Secret Information," *The Wall Street Journal,* 29 Feb. 1979.
7. "How the weapons lobby works in Washington," Business Week, 12 Feb. 1979.
8. Michael J. Malbin, *Unelected Representatives* (New York: Basic Books, Inc., 1980), p. 10.
9. Ibid., p. 5.
10. See, for example, U.S. Congress, Joint Committee on Defense Production, *DoD-Industry Relations: Conflicts of Interest and Standards of Conduct,* 94th Congress, 2nd Session, 2 and 3 Feb. 1976.
11. Defense Contract Audit Agency, *Audit Report on Review of Washington, D.C. Office Operations, The Boeing Company, Seattle, Washington,* Report No. 7381-99-6-0417, 16 March 1976, pp. 5-6 (Appendix); hereafter referred to as DCAA, *Boeing Audit* (preliminary).
12. Ibid., p. 7 (Appendix).
13. Ibid., pp. 7-9 (Appendix). In addition to these departments, the Boeing office had, in 1975, a vice president's office, departments of International Affairs and of National Affairs, and departments for other areas of production: Boeing Vertol, Boeing Commercial Airplane, and Boeing Computer Services.
14. McGrath, *Redefining Corporate Federal Relations,* p. 35.
15. James Barron, "How Grumman Spends Its Campaign Fund," *The New York Times,* 26 Oct. 1980.
16. Paul W. Cherington and Ralph L. Gillen, *The Business Representative in Washington* (Washington: The Brookings Institution, 1962), p. 95.
17. Green and Buchsbaum, *The Corporate Lobbies,* p. 14.
18. U.S., 1946 Legislative Reorganization Act, Title III, Section 30F. This law was aimed at correcting excesses and abuses which abounded in pre-war lobbying. Congressional Investigations of defense industry practices in the 20th century have included 1919 hearings on World War I defense industry profit-taking, a 1929 investigation of a Naval lobbying program on behalf of the N.Y. Shipbuilding Co., Sen. Gerald Nye's hearings in 1935, investigating the munitions industry, as well as later hearings on personnel transfers between the industry and the Pentagon (see Congressional Quarterly, *The Washington Lobby,* 3rd ed.).
19. There is also no official enforcement agency for the registration requirement.
20. Lester Milbrath, *The Washington Lobbyists* (Chicago: Rand-McNally Inc., 1963), pp. 8-9.
21. Ibid., p. 8.
22. *Business Week,* 12 Feb. 1979.
23. Data on office size and defense personnel is drawn from *Armed Forces Journal International,* June and July 1980.
24. See *Armed Forces Journal International,* June and July 1980 and DCAA audit material below.
25. "Receipts" are amounts a registered lobbyist discloses having received from the employing company, including salary; "expenditures" are amounts a registered lobbyist discloses as having spent on lobbying activity, not including salary or fee, and usually reimbursed. Because the regis-

tration requirement is limited and lobbyists are able to define the amounts disclosed, these amounts probably understate the level of lobbying and Government relations activity.
26. The other companies whose Washington offices were audited for those years were Hughes, LTV, Martin Marietta, Raytheon and Sperry. Audits of all 10 companies' Washington expenditures were carried out only for 1974 and 1975. There have been no subsequent DCAA audits of the Washington offices of defense contractors.
27. The released texts also included audits of Hughes Aircraft, Martin Marietta, Raytheon and Sperry.
28. Two Rockwell audits had been conducted, one of the corporate office in Washington and the other of the firm's Collins Radio division's office. Only the final audit of the corporate office was released by the Air Force.
29. General Dynamics and Boeing figures are for 1974 and the first nine months of 1975, while Lockheed and Rockwell's figures cover all of 1974 and 1975. Rockwell's expenditures also include $1.5 m. spent in 1973 by the Collins Radio office.
30. Confidential interviews. The full text of the preliminary audit for Grumman has not been released.
31. DCAA, *Boeing Audit* (preliminary), p. ii.
32. Ibid., p. A/4.
33. Ibid.
34. In the preliminary audit of Rockwell's corporate office, nearly 50% — $1.26 m.— in claimed costs were questioned by DCAA. See Defense Contract Audit Agency, *Audit Review of Washington, D.C. Office Operations and Other Expenses, Rockwell International Corporation, Pittsburgh, Pennsylvania,* Report No. 3191-99-6-0318, 6 April 1976, p. iii; hereafter referred to as DCAA, *Rockwell Audit* (preliminary).
35. No sanitized versions of General Dynamics or Rockwell/Collins final audits have been released.
36. DCAA, *Rockwell Audit,* final version, dated 19 Aug 1977, p. 3; hereafter referred to as DCAA, *Rockwell Audit* (final).
37. DCAA, *Boeing Audit,* final version, dated 12 July 1977; hereafter referred to as DCAA, *Boeing Audit* (final).
38. Deborah G. Meyer, "Industry's Top Ten Defense Contractors and Their Washington Executives," *Armed Forces Journal International,* June 1980.
39. DCAA, *Boeing Audit* (preliminary), p. iii.
40. Ibid. Boeing, in the final audit, noted, "It is the policy of the company not to seek reimbursement of entertainment as defined in the ASPR" [DCAA, *Boeing Audit* (final), p. iii]. DCAA noted that, "Implementation of Defense Department guidelines and additional information provided by the contractor enabled some refinement of the amounts questioned" (Ibid., p. A/3-4).
41. DCAA, *Boeing Audit* (preliminary), p. A/4.
42. 29 Feb. 1979.
43. After a period of time, these clearances were reinstated by DoD. Interview with DoD Directorate of Industrial Personnel Security Clearance Review, 2 Feb. 1981.
44. *The Wall Street Journal,* 29 Feb. 1979.
45. *Business Week,* 12 Feb. 1979.
46. Ibid.
47. Defense Contract Audit Agency, *Audit Review of the Operations of the Washington, D.C. Office of the General Dynamics Corporation, St. Louis, Missouri,* Audit No. 7241-99-6-0169, 31 March 1976, p. 2 (Appendix); hereafter referred to as DCAA, *General Dynamics Audit* (preliminary). General Dynamics noted in the audit that its Washington office averaged $1.6 m. per year in costs. Ibid., p. 1 (Appendix).
48. Ibid., p. 4 (Appendix).
49. Ibid., p. iv.

50. Ibid., p. A/3
51. Ibid., p. A/4. General Dynamics agreed to delete nearly $70,000 claimed under this heading.
52. Ibid., p. A/5. Since no final audit has been released, there is no information on whether this item was withdrawn.
53. *Armed Forces Journal International*, June 1980. In 1981 Grumman board vice chairman and former Navy pilot John Carr was moved to the Washington office. According to Carr, "We want to make a statement that we consider Washington a very, very important part of our business." See *The New York Times*, 13 Jan. 1981 and *Aerospace Daily*, 14 Jan. 1981.
54. Confidential interviews.
55. Defense Contract Audit Agency, *Audit Report on Review of Washington Office Grumman Aerospace Corporation, Bethpage, New York*, Audit No. 241-19-T-0450, 21 Sept. 1977, p. iii; hereafter referred to as DCAA, *Grumman Audit* (final). The 1976 sanitized audit of Grumman reported over $81,000 in questioned costs. Grumman stated that in its view the costs were allowable. DCAA, *Grumman Audit*, preliminary version, dated 19 Aug. 1976, p. iii; and DCAA, *Grumman Audit* (final), p. 4.
56. DCAA, *Grumman Audit* (final), p. 3.
57. *Business Week*, 12 Feb. 1979
58. Defense Contract Audit Agency, *Audit Report on Review of Contractor's Washington, D.C. Area Office, Lockheed Aircraft Corporation, Burbank, California*, Audit No. 4601-99-6-0159, 5 May 1976, p. iii; hereafter referred to as DCAA, *Lockheed Audit* (preliminary).
59. Ibid., p. 1 (Appendix).
60. Ibid., p. iv.
61. Ibid.
62. Ibid., p. A/2. Lockheed's response to DCAA's opinion was that "the contractor can find no justification in ASPR or law for considering that the costs of lobbying are unallowable" (DCAA, *Lockheed Audit*, final version dated 9 Sept. 1977, p. 4).
63. *Armed Forces Journal International*, June 1980.
64. *Business Week*, 12 Feb. 1979.
65. Mark Green, *The Other Government: The Unseen Power of Washington Lawyers* (New York: Grossman Publishers/Viking, 1975), p. 18.
66. *Business Week*, 12 Feb. 1979.
67. Deborah Meyer, "DoD Announces New Top 100 Contractors," *Armed Forces Journal International*, July 1980.
68. *Business Week*, 12 Feb. 1979. •
69. In 1980, Timmons became Presidential candidate Ronald Reagan's deputy director of campaign operations (see *The New York Times*, 30 June 1980).
70. *Business Week*, 12 Feb. 1979.
71. Joint Committee on Defense Production, *DoD-Industry Relations*, p. 67.
72. Mark Green, *The Other Government*, pp. 45-46.
73. Ibid., p. 45.
74. *Armed Forces Journal International*, July 1980.
75. DCAA, *Rockwell Audit* (preliminary), p. iii; and Defense Contract Audit Agency, *Audit Report on Review of Washington, D.C. Office Operations, Collins Radio Group (CRG), A Division of the Electronics Operation, Rockwell International Corporation, Richardson, Texas, for Fiscal Years 1973, 1974 and 1975*, Audit No. 1161-05-6-0371, 26 April 1976, p. 1; hereafter referred to as DCAA, *Collins Audit* (preliminary).
76. DCAA, *Rockwell Audit* (preliminary), pp. 3-4 (Appendix).
77. DCAA, *Collins Audit* (preliminary), p. 3 (Appendix).
78. DCAA, *Rockwell Audit* (final), p. 4.
79. Ibid.
80. Ibid., p. 5.

81. Ibid., p. A/9.
82. DCAA, *Collins Audit* (preliminary), p. A/2
83. *Business Week*, 12. Feb. 1979 and *Armed Forces Journal International*, June 1980.
84. *Business Week*, 12 Feb. 1979.

10
Strength in Unity: Trade Associations

Trade associations have for many years been an important channel for corporate Government relations in Washington. Created to promote industry-wide coordination on such items as common standards, their development was encouraged by the Federal Government. Herbert Hoover, for instance, while Secretary of Commerce stimulated a number of industries to form trade associations in order to create a network of advisory groups to the Department of Commerce.[1] As the associations became more effective, most business firms felt less need for direct Washington representation. Instead they relied on the trade groups for regular information on Executive and Legislative activities via newsletters and representation of the industry's position in Congressional testimony and on advisory committees to the Executive branch. Some trade association staffs also lobbied in Congress. In addition, several broader business groups, like the National Association of Manufacturers and the U.S. Chamber of Commerce, hired registered lobbyists to work on behalf of their members' interests.

Trade associations are uniquely suited for such purposes—they carry the weight of the industry without speaking on behalf of the specific interests of any one company. Many firms still prefer to have their interests represented in this more general, apparently disinterested framework and forego the visibility and cost of a corporate Washington base.

A growing number of firms, however, have decided that they need to supplement trade association efforts with direct corporate representation. As one lobbyist for a chemical firm put it, "The associations represent the lowest common denominator of their membership on any subject. That's just not good enough for us."[2] In this view, trade associations cannot supply the cohesion and clarity of purpose that a firm needs to protect and assert its interests.[3]

Despite the growth in representation by individual firms, trade associations have continued to expand, playing an increasingly active role in the "iron triangle." By 1978 there were 1,500 trade association offices in Washington.[4] These continued to provide the traditional services: training programs, standard-setting, research, and the generation and dissemination of information. Associations also maintain regular working groups, representing their corporate members and working closely with corporate Washington office staffs. Association staffers along with corporate representatives serve regularly on Federal advisory committees.[5] Many association activities are seen as especially valuable at the technical level:

> Smaller trade associations... are most active and effective in articulating specific material demands to political decision-makers. Often the values they hold are shared by government authorities and result in a favorable bias. The material resources they command, coupled with the technical information at their disposal, render them uniquely suited for exchanges in which issues are construed to be technical problems of implementing goals shared by the organization and the authorities.[6]

Trade associations constitute a critical link between industry and Federal officials. Their views appear neutral, since they speak for no company. Sometimes an association in coordination with agency officials can become a *de facto* policy-maker. This specialized, regular access increases the influence of the corporations they represent, while it effectively excludes non-specialists and proponents of policy alternatives.

Many associations have expanded the range of their political activity into direct lobbying and, recently, campaign contributions by Political Action Committees. By 1977-78, 547 trade association PACs had been created.[7] Trade association, along with trade union, PACs are the largest PAC contributors in the country. The single largest in the U.S. in 1977-78 was the American Medical Association PAC, the chief political arm of the nation's doctors, which made over $1.6 million in campaign contributions. The Realtors PAC (National Association of Realtors) came second with $1.1 million in contributions, followed by the Automobile and Truck Dealers Election Action Committee (National Automobile Dealers Association) with over $964,000.[8]

Defense Industry Trade Associations

In strengthening their side of the "iron triangle," defense contractors have made the most of the common purpose of the defense trade association.

> Contractors—and their industry associations—are divided by economic self-interest in acquiring the largest possible

slice of the defense dollar, but the same contractors are unified in common motivation to influence defense procurement and policy.[9]

While individual contractors need their own channels of influence, many common interests unite them: a need for a regular flow of information, especially on forthcoming research and development; general maintenance of the level of defense and space spending; the right to exploit patents developed through contract work; a regular distribution of defense dollars among different types of weapons systems; access to Defense Department and NASA officials in social settings; an influence over defense procurement policy issues in DoD, the White House (OMB) and the Congress.

Many defense industry trade associations have been created to fill these needs. To assess the general level of activity of these groups, we surveyed 20 such associations (see Appendix). Most replied with basic information. Some had clearly technical missions. From others, whose activities were tied to political and policy-making processes, we sought more information.

Because their activity seemed most important, we focused on three service associations and nine industry associations. The Association of the U.S. Army, the Navy League and Air Force Association have active and retired service members, but only the Air Force Association with roughly 200 corporate members can be linked to trade association activity.

The industry groups include the Aerospace Industries Association (AIA), the American Defense Preparedness Association (ADPA), the National Security Industrial Association (NSIA), and the Shipbuilders Council of America (SCA), as well as such specialized groups as the American League for Exports and Security Assistance, the Armed Forces Communication and Electronics Association, the Electronics Industries Association, the National Council of Technical Service Industries, and the National Defense Transportation Association. All provide services which help knit the industry and the Executive branch together.

Conventions: Most associations sponsor at least one convention per year. Widely attended by military and civilian DoD personnel, it presents a variety of panels and classified briefings; it also distributes information on forthcoming programs, weapons, and policy development. It would be hard to imagine a more efficient setting for gathering information on future R & D trends and becoming acquainted with key procurement and policy-making officials.

Publications: Virtually all of the 12 trade and service organizations publish a newsletter. The SCA puts out a regular intelligence report on Washington policy developments of interest to their industry. The ADPA publishes *National Defense*, a monthly magazine filled with industry advertising and articles on defense procurement policy and weapons development. ADPA also publishes a members' newsletter,

The Common Defense. A typical issue provides information on weapons developments, a listing of new sources for information on DoD plans, relevant international and domestic news, brief discussions of budgetary debates, and advertisement for association publications and coming events.

Policy Representation: Association officials regularly testify before Congress on issues ranging from the general level of defense spending to legislative developments that might affect the industry, to specific procurement policies. AIA head Karl Harr, for example, often testified in the 1970s on Federal efforts to revise Federal procurement policies. Specialized committees also meet with the Executive branch. DoD discussions on changes in cost allowability standards for industry, for example, were held by the Pentagon Defense Acquisition Regulatory Council (formerly the Armed Services Procurement Regulation Committee), industry representatives, and staffs of key trade associations.

Government Contacts and Lobbying: Although almost all associations responding to our survey denied doing any lobbying in the narrow sense, trade association staff are actively involved in Government relations activities aimed at both Congress and the Executive branch. They encourage increased defense spending and specific research and development projects, supply information on the industry to DoD and NASA, and send information received from Federal officials to industry members. Senator Proxmire described defense-related trade associations as a "go-between for ideas and information to flow from defense industry to the Pentagon."[10]

Relations between trade associations and the Congress, traditional lobbying, are less clear. Only three of the associations surveyed — the Aerospace Industries Association, the Shipbuilders Council of America, and the National Council of Technical Service Industries, have registered lobbyists. Some — the Association of the U.S. Army, the National Defense Transportation Association, and the Navy League — claim that they do not lobby.[11] AIA leaves much of the lobbying to individual firms.[12] AIA Director, Karl Haar said, "We don't even dream of buying any influence of any kind."[13] Only one of the associations surveyed, the SCA, had created a Political Action Committee by January 1979, contributing $6,850 to Congressional campaigns in 1977 and 1978.[14]

The lack of registered lobbyists, however, reflects the inadequacy of the existing definition of lobbying rather than any lack of effort on the part of the trade associations. One Pentagon official noted, "As a social unit, they are an incredible force to be reckoned with by Congress."[15] Confidential interviews by Donald Hall with association officials confirm the impression of aggressive action: associations both pressure the Executive branch and lobby in Congress.[16]

The Companies

Individual companies belong to a variety of defense-related trade associations. All eight, however, belong to the three key industry groups and one service organization—the Air Force Association. We have focused on these four associations because they appear to be more comprehensively involved with defense policy issues. In addition, the defense industry is represented in Washington by an "association of associations"—the Council of Defense and Space Industry Associations.

Aerospace Industries Association (AIA): AIA, founded in 1919, is one of the most influential industry trade associations, with 63 corporate members and a mid-1970 budget of over $2 million.[17] AIA's objective is to assist its members with "non-competitive problems affecting financial management and accounting, contract administration and procurement law," and to seek "equitable procurement policies and practices" in DoD and NASA. AIA officials testify in Congress and serve on advisory committees and the Association publishes regular research reports, including a handbook of detailed annual data—*Aerospace Facts and Figures*. The Association President is Karl G. Harr, Jr. and its registered lobbyist is the firm of Mayer, Brown and Plath in Washington. AIA is located at 1725 DeSales St., N.W., Washington, DC 20036.

American Defense Preparedness Association (ADPA): ADPA was founded in 1919 to "achieve peace through industrial preparedness... and national strength as represented by our armed forces." ADPA has 33,000 individual members, both military and civilian, and 400 corporate members. Although the Association claims that "from the very beginning (it) has avoided politics and has never lobbied," it fosters close Government-industry relations. It was founded in World War I as the Army Ordnance Association with the encouragement of Army General John J. Pershing and with the help of Newton D. Baker, Secretary of War, and Bernard Baruch, head of the War Industries Board. It brought together engineers, bankers, industrialists and defense officials concerned with maintaining defense production capabilities in the U.S. The Association was organized around the procurement districts of the Office of Army Ordnance with local chapters relating directly to each Army office. After World War II the Association expanded to cover the entire defense industry, developing technical divisions and specialized sections for a wide variety of weapons systems. In the ADPA's own words, "The Association freely admits that it supports the so called military industrial complex." It takes pride in the fact that of the 60 largest defense contractors, 48 are ADPA members.[18]

ADPA's president is Henry A. Miley, Jr. and its officers include Ralph E. Hawes, Jr. and George E. Blackshaw of General Dynamics, Ira Hedrick of Grumman, Jack Catton and Robert Fuhrman of Lockheed, and Herman Hicks and Thomas Campobasso of Rockwell. It has no registered lobbyist. Its office is located at 740 15th St., N.W., Washington, DC, 20005.

National Security Industrial Association (NSIA): NSIA, founded in 1944, has 275 corporate members. It represents companies and research organizations that work with national security agencies of the Government and, like ADPA, is dedicated to "a close working relationship between industrial concerns and national security." NSIA publishes a bi-monthly newsletter and maintains eight advisory groups to provide advice to DoD and NASA. At its annual James Forrestal Memorial Dinner, it presents an award to a figure who has done the most to improve industry-government relationships. NSIA's president is W.H. Robinson, Jr. and its officers include H.W. Neffner, Boeing vice president for contract negotiations and pricing; James Beggs, General Dynamics executive vice president; Michael Pelehach, Grumman senior vice president; W.R. Wilson, Lockheed senior vice president; A.H. Smith, McDonnell Douglas vice president for contracts and pricing; and Clark MacGregor, United Technologies vice president and head of their Washington office. It lists no registered lobbyists and is located at 750 15th St., N.W., Washington, DC, 20005.

Air Force Association (AFA): The Air Force Association, with approximately 90,000 individual members, is the only service association with corporate members—200 of them. Its members "share a concern for military might in the air," and meet regularly with DoD. AFA publishes a magazine and the Air Force encourages membership. The Association has no registered lobbyists and is located at 1750 Pennsylvania Ave., N.W., Washington, DC, 20006.

Council of Defense and Space Industry Associations (CODSIA): CODSIA includes two groups discussed above—AIA and NSIA—as well as the Motor Vehicle Manufacturers Association, Electronics Industries Association, Shipbuilders Council of America and the Western Electronic Manufacturers Association. CODSIA ties these associations more closely to the DoD, who encouraged its foundation as "a vehicle for obtaining broad industry reactions to new or revised regulations and similar matters." According to CODSIA's statement of purpose:

> It provides a central channel of communication in order to simplify, expedite and improve industry-wide consideration of the many policies, regulations, problems and questions of broad application involved in procurement actions by the DoD, NASA, AEC, GSA, HEW, DOT and other procurement activities of the government.[19]

CODSIA's policy committee, composed of two members from each association, considers "cases" brought by any three members of the Association and provides, on average, 70 letters of comment and recommendation to Government agencies every year. Its objective is to minimize duplication of effort, to obtain Government information for its members and to simplify Government contact with the defense industry. It helps organize regular meetings between the defense industry and the Defense Procurement Regulations Council of DoD. CODSIA helps focus even more sharply the industry's influence with the Defense Department.

Several companies in our study also participate actively in two of the most influential general business lobbying organizations in Washington: the Business Council and the Business Roundtable. The Business Council was created in 1933 as a vehicle of communication between the new Roosevelt Administration and the business community, many of whom saw Roosevelt as a threat. According to the Council's own description it is

> dedicated to service in the national interest with the primary objective of developing a constructive point of view on matters of public policy affecting the business interests of the country; and to provide a medium for a better understanding of government problems by business.[20]

The Council has a number of program committees, holds annual meetings and regularly consults with the Executive branch. Its members consist of individuals "actively identified with private enterprise in the field of industry and commerce, chosen to be broadly representative from a geographic as well as functional and product point of view." The membership roster numbers over 200. Council officers in 1979 included Reginald Jones, CEO of General Electric as chairman, and as vice presidents top corporate officials from Bechtel, Bethlehem Steel, Exxon and Sperry Rand. Directors of five companies in our study serve on the Business Council:

Boeing:
William Allen, Chairman Emeritus, member, since 1959.
William Batten, Chairman, NY Stock Exchange, since 1961.
H.J. Haynes, Chairman, Standard Oil of Calif., since 1975.
David Packard, Chairman, Hewlett-Packard, since 1963.
Charles Piggott, Chairman, PACCAR, since 1975
George Weyerhaeuser, Chairman, Wyerhaeuser Co., since 1970.
T.A. Wilson, Chairman, Boeing, since 1974.

Grumman:
James A. Linen, III, Consultant, TIME, Inc., since 1969.

Lockheed:
Edward W. Carter, Chairman, Carter, Hawley, Hale Stores, since 1964.
Courtland Gross, retired founder and retired Board member, Lockheed, since 1964.
Jack K. Horton, Chairman, Southern California Edison, since 1967.

Rockwell:
W.F. Rockwell, Jr., Chairman Emeritus, Rockwell, since 1973.
William Sneath, Chairman, Union Carbide Corp., since 1978.

United Technologies:
Harry Gray, Chairman, U. Tech., since 1976.

In addition, five companies are members of the Business Roundtable: Boeing, General Dynamics, McDonnell Douglas, Rockwell and United Technologies. The Roundtable has been described by Mark Green and Andrew Buchsbaum as "the voice of big business in Washington."[21] Of its 153 members, 148 come from the top 500 companies on *Fortune*'s list. The Roundtable, through its policy committee, influences public policy by bringing together corporate chief executive officers with officials of the Executive branch. Chairman of the Roundtable is Clifton C. Garvin, Jr. of Exxon. Other officers include Theodore Brophy of GTE, James Evans of Union Pacific and Walter Wriston of Citicorp.

FOOTNOTES

1. Grant McConnell, *Private Power and American Democracy* (New York: Knopf, Inc., 1967), pp. 65-66, 161.
2. "Why the corporate lobbyist is necessary," *Business Week*, 18 March 1972.
3. Paul W. Cherington and Ralph L. Gillen, *The Business Representative in Washington* (Washington, DC: The Brookings Institution, 1962); and "New Ways to Lobby a Recalcitrant Congress," *Business Week*, 3 Sept. 1979.
4. "For trade associations, politics is the new focus," *Business Week*, 17 April 1978.
5. Cherington and Gillen, *The Business Representative in Washington*, p. 62.
6. Harmon Zeigler and Wayne G. Peak, *Interest Groups in American Society*, 2nd ed. (New Jersey: Prentice Hall, 1972).
7. *Business Week*, 17 April 1978; and U.S. Federal Election Commission, *Reports on Financial Activity, 1977-78, Final Report Party Political Committees;* Vol. IV - Non-party detailed tables (no connected organization, trade/membership/health, cooperative, corporation without stock), April 1980.
8. Congressional Quarterly, *The Washington Lobby*, 3rd ed. (Washington, DC: The Congressional Quarterly, 1979); and *FEC Reports on Financial Activity*, 4 April 1980.
9. Donald R. Hall, *Cooperative Lobbying: The Power Of Pressure* (Tuscon, AZ: University of Arizona Press, 1969), p. 54.
10. U.S. Congress, Senate, "The Power and Influence of the Professional Military Associations," Testimony of Sen. William Proxmire, *Congressional Record*, 93rd Congress, 2nd Session, 21 Feb. 1974, S2049.

11. Ibid., S.2050.
12. *Business Week,* 17 April 1978.
13. Hall, p. 53.
14. *FEC Reports on Financial Activity,* 4 April 1980.
15. Lucian K. Truscott, IV, "Inside the Air Force Association's Annual Bacchanalia," *Rolling Stone,* 26 Feb. 1976.
16. Hall, p. 53.
17. Proxmire testimony.
18. "History of Partners in Preparedness," *National Defense,* No. 347, March-April, 1978. pp. 393, 394, 496.
19. CODSIA, "Organizations and Functions" (Washington, DC: Council of Defense and Space Industry Associations, 1977).
20. *The Business Council, 1979* (Washington, DC: The Business Council, 1979), p. 128.
21. Mark Green and Andrew Buchsbaum, *The Corporate Lobbies: Political Profiles of the Business Roundtable and the Chamber of Commerce,* A Public Citizen/Big Business Day Report (Washington, DC: Public Citizen (c), 1980).

11
A Voice in Policy-Making: Advisory Committees

Advisory committees can be one of the most significant channels of communication between the industrial and the Executive side of the "iron triangle." As of December 1979, there were 820 committees with 20,460 members.[1] These bodies, composed of Government and private sector representatives to every Federal agency, provide advice on virtually every national policy issue. Members are usually selected by the committee itself or named by the Executive agency, and terms of office range from ad hoc to indefinite, depending on the committee. They may discuss technical issues or broader policy problems, as some sample names suggest: the Moab District Grazing Advisory Board to the Department of the Interior, the National Archives Advisory Council to the General Services Administration, the Navy Resale Advisory Committee to the Department of Defense, the Stratospheric Research Advisory Committee to the National Aeronautics and Space Administration, and the National Commission on Civil Disorders.

The work of these committees is often crucial to the formation of Government policy. Issues like atomic weapons development, the Three Mile Island nuclear near-disaster, and the future of national forest lands have all been debated by advisory committees. "Outsiders holding advisory positions within bureaucracy have been at the center of some of the most celebrated policy disputes that have arisen within the national government since World War II."[2]

Committee Membership

Even on less earth-shaking matters, these committees offer an arena in which its members present and argue for the public—and all too often the private—interest. Federal policies that have an effect on an industry are commonly discussed and sometimes formulated. Committee members have early input, carrying back from meetings information on policy developments of interest to the institutions and firms they represent; they become acquainted with Government officials and meet other influential members in their field.

Whether members of such committees "represent" the industry or are representatives of it is a moot point. They are ordinarily men with a very clear interest in what Government decides to do. By their attendance at meetings and other agency relationships, they become privy to the major issues and also to the men who must address them.

This can, and does, result in significant "advantages" to the member of the committee. He, of course, is always hopeful of having influence with the Government official. The point he would like to make may not be a large one in the order of national affairs, but that does not make it less meaningful either to his industry, to his company, or to himself. The member also hopes to learn what the Government is likely to do. Even when he is not able to influence such action, the mere learning about it—or even suspecting what will happen—can be vitally important.[3]

The major problem that results from this special early access is one of bias. Because advisory committees are concerned with a specific issue or policy area and select their own membership, they tend to reinforce a closed, interacting network of policy-makers, all of whom have expertise in the area, but who share a similar interest in the preservation of the industry-Government relationship, through closed meetings and selective membership. Wider views are not represented.

The bias that results is institutional. Alternative or public perspectives are absent; only a limited range of technical disagreements survives. Inside a committee, Government and industry representatives often become convinced that they are by definition working in the public interest—while their work tends to preserve and further agency and/or industry interests.

> This expansion of the administrative machinery represents an institutionalization of the symbiotic relationship between groups and government, whereby exchange relationships become legal, fluid channels of communication are proscribed and confrontations are removed from the public arena into closed chambers.[4]

The problems of the "closed door" deliberations led in the 1970s to demands for fuller disclosure of committee membership and activities. The Federal Advisory Committees Act of 1972 (PL 92-463; U.S.C. App. I, ELR 41019) required all committees to make minutes of their meetings available to the public. They were also required to hold open meetings except when certain questions were being considered, file regular annual reports including membership lists, and in general be more accessible. The Office of Management and Budget (OMB) was designated to oversee this process and the Library of Congress was to make regular data available. An important stipulation required advisory committees to seek to obtain "balance" in their membership "in terms of the points of view represented and the functions to be performed by the advisory committee" (Sec. 10 (a) 1).

A subsequent evaluation of compliance, however, found that many advisory committees have fallen seriously short in several respects.[5] Many committees claimed they were excused from filing reports for a variety of reasons. Those reports that were filed were often found to be thin and misleading, or irregularly available. Most important, roughly half of all committee meetings continued to take place behind closed doors, using various exclusions from the Freedom of Information Act as justification: national security, foreign policy, personnel matters, trade secrets, confidential financial information, or the discussion of inter-agency and intra-agency memoranda.

Even more seriously, few committees made an effort to achieve a balanced representation. Committees and agencies often interpreted "balance" to mean the representation of women, minorities, or different geographical regions. Different interests and points of view, however, were not used as criteria. Members were still being drawn largely from the "old boy" networks with the Government arguing that anyone not a Government employee constituted a representative of the "public."

Defense-Related Advisory Committees

Our examination of defense-related advisory committees confirms their importance in providing the industrial side of the "iron triangle" with early access to defense information. Members are cleared for security and much of the material they handle is classified. Despite the decline in the number of such committees,[6] their membership remains high and their tasks significant.

DoD advisory committee membership at the end of 1979 was 777, while NASA committees had 483 members, drawn from Federal agencies, research institutions and defense contractors. These figures underestimate the total number of committees that deal with defense issues since they do not include committees like the Defense Acquisition Regulation Council that are incorporated into DoD policy-making and do not report to the public. Finally, the members of some advisory groups are not counted, since their groups function as task-forces and subcommittees of other groups, e.g., the Defense Science Board.[7]

In 1979 The Department of Defense ranked sixth among Federal agencies in terms of number of advisory committees, 11th in number of advisory committee members (777), and fourth in terms of the annual cost of operating such committees.[8]

DoD advisory groups deal with a wide agenda of issues of importance to both the agency and the industry. Most critical for early access to decisions in the "iron triangle" is the network of scientific advisory bodies, especially the Defense Science Board. The DSB has 24 at-large members, an unnamed number of associate members, plus the chairmen of the three service-related scientific advisory groups. The chairman of the DSB is chosen by the Under Secretary of Defense for Research and Engineering. The at-large members are chosen for "their preeminence in the fields of research and engineering," and a large number are drawn from defense industry companies and defense research institutions. The DSB charter indicates the range of the group's responsibility: to advise the Secretary of Defense, the Under Secretary of Defense for Research and Engineering, and the DSB's counterparts in the services—the Army Science Board, Naval Research Advisory Committee and Air Force Scientific Advisory Board. Members of these groups are generally selected by the agency and by the group members themselves. These key committees provide company members with access to decisions about new weapons at the earliest possible stage, well before Congress or the general public are aware of them.

The DoD science advisory network, moreover, is much more extensive than it appears. Each of these committees is broken down into a myriad of task forces, ad hoc groups and working subcommittees, which parallel the R & D and procurement structure of the Defense Department. This large network draws even more scientific and industry representatives into the early stage of DoD policy-making.

It is difficult for the public to determine whether industry representatives acquire preferential access through such committees, for the committees provide limited public information. Though almost all such committees contain substantial industry representation, few require disclosure of affiliation. Only the initial annual report filed with the Library of Congress provides a listing by place of employment. No committee reports indicate the extent of a firm's interest and contracting involvement with the agency or the weapons systems about which the committee is giving advice.

In addition, DoD committees are especially reluctant to divulge information on their deliberations. In 1979, we calculated, DoD groups held the highest proportion of closed or partly closed meetings (80.8 percent) with the exception of a few temporary commissions, the advisory groups of the National Endowment for the Arts (85.8 percent), and the Veterans Administration (84.1 percent).[9]

Despite these limitations on information, publicly available charters and minutes shed some light on the sweeping range of discussion. The DSB, for instance, states: "The Board shall concern itself with policy matters in the area of long-range planning," and it shall advise the Secretary of Defense and the Deputy Director for Research and Engineering "as to specific systems and weapons only down to such details as fulfill the requirements of these offices."

Specific advice will be given on:

— desirable scope, internal balance and, where appropriate, the substance of research, development, engineering, test and evaluation effort that should be pressed by the Dept. of Defense. . . .
— the effectiveness of research and development in providing combat-worthy weapons systems, with attention to prompt and effective utilization of new knowledge; the rapid evaluation of the effectiveness of the projected weapons systems in meeting military requirements.
— preferred management practices and policies for the effective prosecution of these programs.[10]

The variety of work performed and the possibilities for early and exclusive access to critical information for contractors can be seen in a sample of one year of minutes of subcommittee meetings of the Air Force Scientific Advisory Board. Its Space and Missile Systems Organization Advisory Group (SAMSO), for instance, held a closed meeting in January 1975 and focused on several significant policy issues:

This briefing provided a program for a near term demonstration which would prove the viability of lasers in space.

A summary of the impact of recent SAL (Strategic Arms Limitations) agreements on numbers of delivery systems was presented. This agreement will have a significant impact on future programs. If all planned efforts were added to current U.S. force structures, the U.S. would possess more deliverable warheads than permitted. There was discussion on the apparent advantage in numbers of ballistic missiles and submarines which the Soviets have. If the U.S. relies on submarine ballistic missile forces in the future, the future vulnerability of these forces must be considered.

Status of NASA sponsored shuttle program and interface with related Air Force sponsored programs was presented. Discussion included development schedules and program funding.[11]

Attending this meeting were representatives of several universities and research firms involved with contracts for the programs in question: Dr. Gerald Dineen, the chairman of Lincoln Labs and in 1980 Assistant Secretary of Defense for Command, Control and Communications, Professor John McCarthy of MIT, Dr. Willis Ware of the Rand Corporation and Dr. Ivan Getting of the Aerospace Corporation. The Aerospace Corporation was described in a later meeting of the Command, Control and Communications Group as the "principal Federal Contract Research Center supporting SAMSO."[12]

The Aeronautical Systems Division Advisory Group met at Wright Patterson Air Force Base on January 16, 1975 to examine the "approach being used on the Advanced Strategic Air Launched Missile." They recommended its continuation. They also looked at "the current Remotely Piloted Vehicle programs," which were "endorsed and some recommendations made for follow-on work."[13]

The Study Group on Management and Support of Command, Control and Communications met several times in 1975, discussing significant hardware items and inviting comments and discussion by manufacturers of the systems in question. Among the membership was Dr. Michael Yarymovych, former Air Force Chief Scientist, and vice president for North American Aerospace Operations of Rockwell International (see Profile). This group discussed security assistance programs as well as World-Wide Military Command and Control Systems. Both subjects were of special interest to Rockwell, which had a major communications operation in Iran at the time and was a prime contractor for NAVSTAR work on missile guidance and communication. Industry participation was invited at various meetings from the Federal Contract Research Labs (Lincoln Labs, MITRE Corp., Aerospace Corp.), as well as from major contracting firms—Raytheon, GTE Sylvania, RCA, Hughes Aircraft, Systems Development Corp., Boeing and Rockwell (Collins Radio). Minutes of the meetings, though brief, note the group's concern about missile communications and current research capabilities.

The Aerospace Vehicles Panels Committee on Gas Turbine Technology also met and discussed funding problems: "The competition for R & D funds was a primary concern since programs will require a strong justification for continued funding."[14] At a June 1975 meeting this group heard Pratt and Whitney/United Technologies representatives discuss development programs and future propulsion requirements and in November had reports on panel visits in UT's Florida and Hartford, CT. plants.

The Companies

Our data base for reviewing advisory committees and the membership of personnel from our eight companies includes data disclosed to the OMB and the Library of Congress. For three years this data was printed in annual reports prepared by the Metcalfe subcommittee and the Glenn subcommittee of the Senate Governmental Affairs Committee.[15] These indexes are the only attempt to aggregate membership by committee, by institution, and by individual. Because this source is unique, it is regrettable that Sen. Glenn's subcommittee decided in 1978 to discontinue publication of the index. In addition, we reviewed committee reports filed with the Library of Congress and the annual reports of the General Services Administration, *Federal Advisory Committees* (GPO Annual), which contains aggregations by agency.

The companies in this study are well-represented in these closed-circuit channels of policy influence and communications in the Department of Defense and NASA.

Boeing is the most actively represented on advisory committees (16 company personnel with 23 memberships on defense-related Federal advisory committees between 1976 and the end of 1978). These committees covered a number of areas of interest to Boeing's work: future scientific and R & D requirements (11 memberships on the four key committees—far above any other company in the study), strategic target planning (Boeing was a prime contractor on the Minuteman ICBM), military airlift (the 747 can be used for such purposes and the company was building a YC-14 in the years covered). Two of Boeing's advisory committee members, Ben Plymale and Hua Lin, were involved in the 1978 MX incident when classified data was telexed to Seattle.

Lockheed ranked second in the study with 15 company personnel holding 20 committee memberships. Five of Lockheed's representatives, including Willis Hawkins who held four different advisory committee memberships, sat on the key scientific advisory panels during this period. The subjects with which the committees dealt were also tied to Lockheed's work: space programs (Lockheed is a prime contractor for satellites, including reconnaissance and LANDSAT programs), intelligence (Lockheed is a prime NSA contractor), aviation safety (the L-1011 is Lockheed's entry in the wide-bodied commercial transport market), and military airlift (Lockheed is the principal DoD contractor

TABLE XIV

FEDERAL ADVISORY COMMITTEE MEMBERSHIPS

(1976-78)

Company	Company Personnel on Committees	Committee Memberships Held	Memberships on R & D Committees
Boeing	16	23	12
General Dynamics	7	7	5
Grumman	7	7	4
Lockheed	15	20	5
McDonnell Douglas	11	11	3
Northrop	9	10	1
Rockwell	7	7	4
United Technologies	11	13	1

Source: *Federal Advisory Committees: Index* (1976, 1977) and Annual Reports filed with the Library of Congress.

for airlift with C-130, C-141, and C-5 programs). Many of Lockheed's committee members advise NASA, for which the company is a major contractor.

United Technologies ranked third with 11 company representatives holding 11 advisory committee memberships. Only one of these was involved with scientific advisory group activity, but a number are connected to groups working on aircraft propulsion questions of major interest to Pratt and Whitney: fuel conservation technology, space propulsion and power, jet engine hydro-carbon fuels, aviation safety and operating systems, materials and structures.

McDonnell Douglas ranked fourth with 11 people and 11 memberships, two of them scientific advisory. Robert L. Johnson, corporate vice president, served on both the DSB and the Army Science Board, while Robert Weiser served on the DSB as an associate member in 1978 (see Profile). Most of the remainder of McDonnell Douglas memberships are on NASA committees, with whom MDC is a major contractor. One member sits on the military airlift committee—MDC's DC-10 has been added to the Air Force's airlift capabilities.

Northrop had nine people and 10 memberships. Donald Hicks, Sr., vice president for marketing and technology, has been on the DSB (personnel transfer). Kent Kresa, general manager of the Ventura Division (transfer) is on the Executive Panel advising the Chief of Naval Operations as well as the Army Science Board. Others are linked to important areas of Northrop work: exports, intelligence, electronics, aerodynamics, communications (two from the Northrop Page Communications subsidiary).

General Dynamics had seven people holding seven committee memberships in this period, including five on the key scientific committees: Leonard Buchanan, the general manager of its Pomona Division, and Robert Smith sat on the DSB; Grant Hansen, head of the Convair Division, and William Dietz sat on the Air Force Board, while Edward Heiniman sat on the Navy group.

Grumman had seven representatives with eight memberships. Four of these are involved with defense scientific advice: Thomas Guarino of the Aerospace Division; Ira Hedrick of Aerospace on the Air Force Board; Offenhartz and Sandler, both on the DSB in 1976. Others are involved with space work (Grumman is an important NASA contractor) and general aviation (at the time Grumman owned general aviation manufacturing facilities in Savannah, GA).

Rockwell International had seven members and seven committee memberships. Jack Bell, John Fosness (general manager at Columbus), and Herman Hicks all sat on the DSB. Others were involved with space (NAVSTAR), guidance (Rockwell's Autonetics Division work is significant here), and general aviation (Rockwell manufactures general aviation aircraft).

FOOTNOTES

1. In 1977 there were 1,159 advisory committees with a total membership of 24,678. The drop in numbers reflects the Carter Administration's efforts to establish a zero-based review for such committees.
2. Francis Rourke, *Bureaucracy, Politics and Public Policy* (Boston: Little Brown, 1969), p. 100.
3. U.S. Congress, Senate Committee on Government Operations, Subcommittee on Intergovernmental Relations, *Hearings on S. 3067, Advisory Committees*, Part 2, 91st Congress, 2d Session, 8-9 Oct. 1970.
4. Itzhak Galnoor, "Government Secrecy: Exchanges, Intermediaries and Middlemen," *Public Administration Review*, 35:1, Jan. 1975, p. 36.
5. Kit Gage and Samuel S. Epstein, "The Federal Advisory Committee System: An Assessment," *Environmental Law Reporter*, 7:2, Feb. 1977, pp. 5001-12.
6. The number of advisory committees to the DoD dropped from 78 in 1975 to 37 in 1979, while NASA advisory committees dropped from 37 to 12.
7. There are also other advisory committees which are important to the companies in our study, but advise other agencies, such as the Department of Transportation's Technical Advisory Committee and Radio Technical Commission for Aeronautics, on which company representatives participate.

    The Department of Commerce, which has had industry advisory committees since the 1920s, maintained a large industry advisory structure for the multilateral trade negotiations, including an aircraft industry advisory group. That group had members from seven of our companies (all but Northrop), plus six other aircraft exporting companies and two organizations (the Aerospace Industries Association and the General Aviation Manufacturer's Association). The Chairman of the group was Lockheed's director of marketing development George Prill, and the group concerned itself with issues of major interest to the industry: Government-directed procurement overseas, coproduction as a requirement for overseas sales contracts, industry offsets as a way of obtaining overseas contracts, foreign government subsidies and financial support for industry experts. ("Aircraft Issues Buried in Stalled Talks," *Aviation Week and Space Technology*, 14 Aug. 1978, p. 22).
8. HEW ranked first in all three categories with 258 committees with 3,978 members costing $26.84 m. to operate. In terms of number of committees, Commerce (93), Interior (65), Agriculture (61), and the U.S. Commission on Civil Liberties (51), ranked ahead of DoD. As for members, HEW, Commerce (2306), State (1689), Small Business Administration (1446), National Endowment for the Humanities (968), Agriculture (873), National Science Foundation (845), the Commission on Civil Liberties (834), Interior (816), and Labor (779) ranked ahead of DoD. On expenditures, HEW, Labor ($12.99 m.), and Commerce ($9.22 m.) cost more to operate than DoD (General Services Administration, *Federal Advisory Committees*).
9. Ibid.
10. *Charter of the Defense Science Board*, Washington, DC.
11. U.S. Department of Defense, U.S.A.F. Scientific Advisory Board Headquarters, United States Air Force, *1975 Report of Closed Meetings under Section 10 (d) of the Federal Advisory Committee Act*, 1975.
12. Ibid.
13. Ibid.
14. Ibid.
15. U.S. Senate, Committee on Governmental Affairs, Subcommittee on Reports, Accounting and Management, *Federal Advisory Committees*, Index to the Membership of Federal Advisory Committees, 1976 and 1977; and Senate Committee on Governmental Affairs, *Federal Advisory Committees*, 1978.

12
Getting Together: Entertainment

An ingredient in the cement that holds the "iron triangle" together is social. Defense policy-makers and personnel from the industry spend a fair amount of time together. Their social relations have raised controversial issues about the risk of favoritism, improper influence, and possible corruption. A Government employee who accepts hospitality from a Government contractor could either be, or appear to be, in conflict with the neutrality and distance his/her official duties required. For contractors, providing and accepting such hospitality facilitates an atmosphere of good working relations. As Chairman Robert Anderson of Rockwell International put it in 1976:

> Entertainment is certainly not essential to successful accomplishment of Government business. Yet I think it is fair to note that it affords a benefit just as it does in connection with commercial business.
>
> It provides an opportunity to get to know better the people with whom we are working and to achieve a better understanding of mutual problems.
>
> In short, it is one means of approaching what we are all striving for in our complex society, improved communications.[1]

Contractors have in the past provided regular entertainment for customer personnel in the Defense Department and NASA, consisting of casual business lunches and golf dates, banquets, free air travel, and tickets to sporting and cultural events. In addition, they maintained hospitality suites at annual conventions of trade associations and guest facilities for hunting and fishing weekends. Most of these expenses were borne by the contractor, though some may have been charged to defense contracts. Questions were raised in Congressional hearings in the 1970s about whether such entertainment might have violated DoD standards of conduct. Since then, several steps have been taken to narrow the scope for and probability of impropriety but the DoD standard of conduct still contains massive loopholes.

It is an exaggeration to assume that social interaction exerts much influence on any one contract decision. A free lunch or a weekend on Wye Island has doubtless not been enough to buy a government employee. Grumman lobbyist Gordon Ochenrider was probably correct when he argued, "You trust an admiral or a general with a one billion dollar project and yet you think he can be bought for a $20 dinner. It's ridiculous."[2]

The major problem with contractor entertainment is that it reinforces the closed-circuit of policy-making in the "iron triangle." It contributes to shared perceptions of the present and expectations about the future, to the view that outsiders and critics are the enemy of both industry and Government. Weapons systems may become desirable because they are in the interests of both participants in the social system. In addition, the social relations established between contractor and DoD personnel make the company's task of gathering and transmitting information less complex. If a phone call is answered, not by a distant voice but by a friend, material becomes more available and agreement more likely. Access is a major reward of close social ties. Entertainment, then, is not so much a question of corruption or bribery as of policy bias, access to information, and an imbalance of power that favors the private "insiders'" interest.

Directives and Practices

The Federal Government and the Department of Defense have long-standing directives designed to limit the impact of contractor entertainment. Defense Department Directive 5500.7, which is part of the DoD Standards of Conduct, is explicit in prohibiting DoD employees from accepting entertainment.

> Except as provided in paragraph B of this section, DoD personnel will not solicit or accept any gift, gratuity, favor, entertainment, loan, or any other thing of monetary value either directly or indirectly from any person, firm, corporation, or other entity which:
> 1) Is engaged or is endeavoring to engage in procurement activities or business or financial transactions of any sort with any agency of the DoD;
> 2) Conducts operations or activities that are regulated by any agency of the DoD; or
> 3) Has interests that may be substantially affected by the performance or nonperformance of the official duty of the DoD personnel concerned.

The DoD explained that the prohibition is intended to ensure public confidence in the integrity of policy-makers and administrators:

> Acceptance of gifts, gratuities, favors, entertainment, etc., no matter how innocently tendered and received, from those who have or seek business with the Department of Defense may be a source of embarrassment to the department and the personnel involved, may affect the objective judgment of the recipient and impair public confidence in the integrity of the business relations between the department and industry.[3]

It seems clear that the directive has in mind precisely the gratuities that had been regularly provided by the contracting industry:

> a gift, gratuity, favor, entertainment, etc., includes any tangible item, intangible benefits, discounts, tickets, passes, transportation, and accommodation or hospitality given or extended to or on behalf of the recipient.[4]

The discrepancy between directives and contractor practice through the mid-1970s can be explained both by inconsistent DoD enforcement and the existence of many gaping loopholes in the directive, which shortcircuited its effectiveness. Excluded from the prohibition on accepting entertainment are cases where "the interests of the Government are served by participation of DoD personnel in widely attended luncheons, dinners and similar gatherings sponsored by industrial, technical, and professional associations for the discussion of matters of mutual interest to Government and industry." It need not apply where "the invitation is addressed to and approved by the employing agency of DoD," or in the plant when "the conduct of official business within the plant will be facilitated and when no provision can be made for individual payment" or, to quote one of the widest exclusions, in "situations in which, in the judgment of the individual concerned, the Government's interest will be served by participation by DoD personnel in activities at the expense of a defense contractor."[5]

Opening the gates still wider, the Directive permits gratuities when they are a part of a "customary exchange of social amenities between personal friends and relatives when motivated by such relationships and extended on a personal basis."[6]

In 1974 and 1975 it was revealed that Northrop had been providing generous entertainment to substantial numbers of DoD and NASA personnel. The Northrop revelations were followed by reports that Rockwell International, Martin Marietta and Raytheon had all entertained Government employees at guest facilities for hunting and fishing, on Maryland's Eastern Shore. The number of guests disclosed by Northrop reached nearly 100 and included a broad range of officials whose jobs could link them to procurement decisions affecting Northrop's involvement in aircraft, electronics, logistics and overseas sales, among them:

Lt. Gen. Dale S. Sweat, Vice-Commander, Tactical Air Command, Langley AFB, Virginia.

Maj. Gen. Homer K. Hansen, Vice-Commander, Aeronautical Systems Division, Air Force Systems Command, Wright Patterson AFB, Ohio.

Maj. Gen. Harold L. Price, Director, Military Assistance and Sales, Deputy Chief of Staff - Systems and Logistics, USAF, Washington.

David R.S. McColl, Deputy for Research, Office of the Assistant Secretary of the Air Force (Research and Development), Washington.

Col. Delbert H. Jacobs, Office of the Deputy Chief of Staff - Research and Development, USAF, Washington.

Maj. Gen. John J. Pesch, Deputy Director, Air National Guard, Washington.

Eric von Marbod, Comptroller, Defense Security Assistant Agency, Washington.

Adm. John P. Weinel, Director J-5, Plans and Policy, Office of the Joint Chiefs of Staff, Washington.

Rear Adm. George C. Halvorson, Deputy Commander for Systems Acquisitions, Ordnance Systems Command, U.S. Navy, Washington.

Vice Adm. William D. Houser, Deputy Chief of Naval Operations for Air Warfare, Washington.

Capt. Wynn V. Whidden, Deputy Director, Aviation Plans and Requirements Division, Office of the Chief of Naval Operations, Washington.

Vice Adm. Joseph P. Moorer, Director, Strategic Plans and Policy Division, Office of the Chief of Naval Operations, Washington.[7]

Efforts at Reform

Not surprisingly, there was a strong, public reaction. In 1975 Deputy Secretary of Defense William Clements, Jr., addressed specific cases of possible violation by sending letters of admonition to all known guests of contractors at weekend hotels and lodges.

> Even in cases in which a technical violation of the regulations does not exist, such practices create the appearance of a conflict of interest which tends to undermine public confidence in the very high standards all Dept. of Defense personnel are expected to uphold.
>
> To maintain the public trust, our relationships with Defense contractors must be above reproach, and we must demonstrate impartiality and objectivity in all dealings with contractors. In particular, acceptance of gratuities creates an image which is inconsistent with this standard.[8]

Clements also wrote trade associations, industry chief executives and DoD offices urging strict adherence to DoD Directive 5500.7. To some

47 associations he pointed out that Defense Department employees could attend meetings only when the association itself was host. "Acceptance of gratuities or hospitality from private companies in connection with such association activities is prohibited." He also pointed out that seating at any banquet or dinner must be random, in order to avoid any appearance of conflict.

In another letter to nearly 100 leading defense contractors and the membership of the Council of Defense and Space Industry Association (CODSIA), Clements noted:

> The Department of Defense and representatives of private industry have a mutual responsibility in meeting the Defense requirement of our nation. In the accomplishment of this purpose, it is necessary that Defense personnel demonstrate absolute integrity in their dealing with contractors. Defense personnel must not under any circumstance violate or give the appearance of violation of the Standards of Conduct Directive.
>
> Industry must stop tendering that which the recipient is prohibited from receiving.[9]

A third letter went to 75 DoD system program offices and commands, urging compliance with the Standards of Conduct and asking for assessments of the degree of compliance.

Continuing efforts to clean its own house, the DoD reviewed auditing standards to ensure that the Government was not being charged for the costs of entertainment and requested DCCA audits of eight company Washington offices. In addition to supplying the data which we have examined in chapter 10, the audits show that a small number of expenditures for entertainment had indeed been claimed as contract-related costs, which, in the opinion of the DCAA should have been unallowable.

Outside the Department, the Congressional Joint Committee on Defense Production (JCDP) under the leadership of Chairman William Proxmire, conducted its own investigation, sending a survey to 41 contractors in October 1975. From the results the Committee estimated that the companies had spent several million dollars annually on such practices as part of their efforts to "develop and maintain useful contacts."[10] Hospitality suites, sports tickets, meals, and transportation for defense officials were all provided, though DoD regulations prohibited the latter except locally or where commercial and Government alternatives were not available. In general, companies deducted such entertainment and gratuities from income tax as business expenses.

Public disclosure and stronger enforcement apparently has had a somewhat dampening effect on corporate practices. *The Wall Street Journal* reported that the Association of Old Crows, which promotes Government spending for electronic warfare equipment, had cancelled its annual golf tournament.[11] According to the *Journal* the nature of DoD industry contacts was changing and expense accounts for meals, tickets, and trips to lodges were a thing of the past. General Dynamics

Getting Together: Entertainment 179

lobbyist Edward LeFevre said, "We've got directives out to everybody in the company saying no lunches, no dinners for military people. Everybody's taking this thing seriously, so we're eating in our offices these days. We're brown-bagging it."

More significantly, the Standards of Conduct have been revised (1976) and strengthened. Employees must obtain interpretations of the regulations before accepting gratuities. They can no longer waive the prohibition of gratuities by claiming that the offer comes from close personal friends or relatives who happen to be employed by a contractor.[12]

The Companies

The JCDP survey provides the bulk of information for the companies in this study. Wider data is almost impossible to obtain, because both corporate disclosure and the dissemination of Government audits are unsatisfactory. It is, therefore, impossible to estimate systematically the corporate funds spent on entertainment.

From existing data, however, we can conclude that defense contractors have in the past probably understated the amount of entertainment they provided DoD and NASA personnel. Lockheed, for example, disclosed minimal entertainment in response to the Committee survey but elsewhere disclosed a level of spending which suggested a major corporate effort. Only Rockwell and Northrop—albeit inadvertently, and under pressure—provided minimally adequate data. One company, General Dynamics, refused to disclose any entertainment efforts, asking that the JCDP figures be kept confidential.

Boeing appears to have provided relatively little entertainment. President M.T. Stamper reported to the Joint Committee in February 1976 that the company complied with the Standards of Conduct directive and charged none of its entertainment to Government contracts. Stamper also stated that Boeing maintains no facilities for entertaining and does not provide travel to Government officials. However, Boeing provided a fair number of sporting and cultural tickets from 1973 to 1975 and operated hospitality suites at trade and service association functions.

General Dynamics replied to the Joint Committee Survey, but requested that its disclosure be kept confidential, thus denying Congress and the public information on its entertainment practices. In 1976, however, General Dynamics' chief lobbyist, Edward LeFevre stated: "We never had any boats, hunting lodges or places in the Bahamas. I used to regret that, but now I'm glad we don't. You don't have to do that. Everybody had a good time, but I don't think you benefit."[13]

Grumman also reported a comparatively low level of entertainment activities. Chairman John C. Bierwirth reported to the Joint Committee in February 1976 that the company operated no facilities for entertainment and spent little on overnight stays and golf events. He also claimed that no entertainment costs were charged to contracts.

Grumman reported providing little air travel, a good number of tickets to cultural and sporting events, and hospitality suites at trade and service association events.

Lockheed reported a relatively low level of activity to the Joint Committee, claiming that it maintained no facilities for entertainment, although Government personnel were provided with travel on company flights if seats were available. It also gave away a fair number of tickets to cultural and sporting events and maintained hospitality suites at key meetings.

In Lockheed's report to the SEC (*8K* of May 1977), however, the company disclosed that it spent between $372,000 and $432,000 each year between 1970 and 1975 for the entertainment of Government officials, a sizeable sum of money for reportedly minimal activity.

McDonnell Douglas President Sanford McDonnell denied any major entertainment expenditures in his December 1975 response to the committee, noting that the company has "a reputation built on the quality and performance of our products and entertainment of customers has never been the leading nor a central focus of the marketing effort." The activities disclosed—no entertainment facilities, hospitality suites discontinued in 1975, a small number of season tickets and little air travel—suggest low expenditures, but the company's minimal disclosure makes any full evaluation impossible.

Northrop became a household word in the 1970s, not only for its technical achievements with the F-5, but also for its questionable political contributions and controversial entertainment practices as it moved rapidly up the list of the DoD's top 100 contractors. The disclosure of Northrop's entertainment of nearly 100 DoD officials between 1972 and 1974 at its facilities on Maryland's Eastern Shore provoked the Joint Committee on Defense Production's investigation and Secretary Clement's administrative actions. In 1975 Northrop revised its entertainment policies. According to memos from F.W. Lynch, Sr. vice president for administration:

> There will be no action in the form of entertainment or hospitality for public officials taken by any Northrop employee which could cause embarrassment to the company by its public disclosure or which exceed that generally regarded as accepted practice.[14]

A later memo was even stronger:

> There will be no entertainment or hospitality of any type extended by a Northrop employee to a DoD official nor will there be any action taken by any Northrop employee which would place either the company or a DoD official in a position that might be construed as providing or accepting improper contractor hospitality.[15]

In his response to the Joint Committee in March 1976, Lynch disclosed that Northrop spent $214,000 from 1973 to 1975 providing meals for DoD officials, as well as a fair number (356) of season tickets to sporting and cultural events, and regular hospitality suites at association meetings.[16] Lynch, and company Chairman, T.V. Jones, also noted Northrop's use of Maryland, Georgia, and North Carolina facilities:

> Our belief in open and informal communication was such that we felt this was not essential—it was not even important, but it was a small thing that could move in the direction of bringing our people in closer, informal communication with the people and the customer that understood the problems of the DoD so that we could understand better how to solve them.[17]

Rockwell's entertainment of Government officials at a variety of company facilities was another target of the Joint Committee hearings and investigations. According to company disclosures and Joint Committee research, the company maintained four facilities: Nemcolin, the estate of company Chairman Willard F. Rockwell, Jr. at Farmington, PA; Wye Island, MD; Pinebloom Lodge in Albany, GA; and Bimini in the Bahamas. Rockwell entertained frequently at Wye Island and, in the Joint Committee's view, had maintained inadequate records.[18] Robert Anderson, then company president, testified:

> It has been the company's long-standing policy that such activities will be kept to a minimum and within the bounds of common courtesies consistent with ethical business conduct and with applicable laws and regulations, including DoD and NASA regulations.[19]

Anderson did note, however, that food and refreshments were normally provided in meetings, hospitality suites were maintained (the largest number of any company in the study), some air travel and a fair number of sporting and cultural tickets were given to "agency personnel"—hardly a "relatively minor activity."[20] Anderson argued that such practices bore little or no relationship to procurement policies and decisions.

> I want to emphasize that it is not the company's purpose in proffering entertainment to influence any agency official or employee with respect to the manner in which he discharges his duties on behalf of the Government. It is inconceivable to me that any such official or employee would be influenced by a luncheon or dinner or by an invitation to attend a football game or by a visit to a hunting facility.[21]

Rockwell's entertainment of high level officials in DoD has also been controversial. In 1975 Rockwell President Robert Anderson invited Dr. Malcolm Currie, Director of Defense Research and Engineering, on a fishing weekend in the Bahamas. Currie was centrally involved in weapons decisions affecting Rockwell, including the B-1 and the Condor missile and was reprimanded by Secretary of Defense Donald Rumsfeld in March 1976 for accepting Rockwell's hospitality. Rumsfeld exhonorated Currie of any conflict of interest.[22]

United Technologies indicated a low level of entertainment activity in a letter to the Joint Committee (February 26, 1976). The company reported no entertainment facilities, air travel that conformed to DoD regulations, a small number of sports and cultural tickets, and a relatively low number of hospitality suites at trade and service association meetings.

FOOTNOTES

1. U.S. Congress, Joint Committee on Defense Production, *DoD-Industry Relations: Conflicts of Interest and Standards of Conduct,* 94th Congress, 2nd Session, 2 and 3 Feb. 1976, p. 26.
2. Kenneth H. Bacon, "Pentagon and Contractors Grow Cautious After Disclosures of Wining and Dining," *The Wall Street Journal,* 8 April 1976, p. 40.
3. U.S. Department of Defense, Directive 5500.7, *Standards of Conduct,* 8 Aug. 1967.
4. Statute 10 U.S.C. 2207 provides a penalty for contractors who use entertainment deliberately to win contracts. It states that a contract can be cancelled:
    > ... if the Secretary or his designee finds after notice and hearing, that the contractor, or his agent or other representatives, offered or gave any gratuity, such as entertainment or a gift, to an officer, official, or employee of the United States to obtain a contract or favorable treatment in the awarding, amending or making of determinations concerning the performance of a contract.
5. Dept. of Defense Directive 5500.7.
6. Ibid.
7. Joint Committee on Defense Production, *DoD-Industry Relations,* pp. 234-240.
8. Ibid., p. 241.
9. Ibid., letter of Deputy Secretary of Defense to contractors, 2 Dec. 1975, p. 314.
10. Ibid., p. 4.
11. *The Wall Street Journal,* 8 April 1976.
12. Council on Economic Priorities, "Military Maneuvers/Update 1977," *Council on Economic Priorities Newsletter,* CEP Publication N7-1, 22 Feb. 1977.

13. *The Wall Street Journal,* 8 April 1976.
14. Memo of 7 Aug. 1975, reprinted in Joint Committee on Defense Production, *DoD-Industry Relations,* p. 192.
15. Memo of 27 Oct. 1975, Ibid., p. 193.
16. Lynch's Oct. 1975 memo excluded further hospitality suites at events "with a primary DoD orientation."
17. Joint Committee on Defense Production, *DoD-Industry Relations,* p. 59.
18. Ibid., pp. 31-35; *The New York Times,* 18 March 1976.
19. Ibid., p. 25.
20. Ibid., p. 26.
21. Ibid.
22. John W. Finney, "Furor Over Missile Decision Reflects Pitfalls of Policy-Making Jobs in the Pentagon," *The New York Times,* 5 April 1976; and John W. Finney, "Rumsfeld Clears Pentagon Aide of Conflict of Interest in Missile Program; Eagleton Charges a 'Whitewash,'" *The New York Times,* 9 June 1976. CEP joined the Federation of American Scientists, Americans for Democratic Action and the Environmental Defense Fund in urging in October 1976 that Dr. Currie be excluded from the decision to proceed with the production of the B-1 bomber. He was not excluded.

13
Moving The Public: Advertising and the Grass Roots

Contractors, along with other corporations, have begun to put the public to work on their behalf. They spend large sums appealing to a huge constituency: employees, stockholders, suppliers and subcontractors, as well as citizens of communities where plants are located, for help in putting pressure on Executive and Congressional policy-makers. They place advertisements in trade magazines, urge their constituents to write letters to Congressmen and encourage local delegations to carry the corporation's message to Capitol Hill and the White House.

Such expenditures, along with lobbying expenditures aimed at Congress directly, are clearly legal and consistent with individual and corporate rights to freedom of speech. A business has a right to market its wares in defense, as with soap or automobiles. Yet, clearly, expenditures aimed at influencing public and Congressional attitudes towards defense spending and weapons procurement have a different character from general commercial advertising. Because they aim at the policy and legislative process, such spending is political as well as commercial. Advertising and grass-roots expenditures become part of a lobbying effort and Government relations, as well as a commercial strategy.

While the expenditures of corporations for direct lobbying have been tax-deductible since 1962, the Internal Revenue Code does not allow taxpayers to deduct expenditures made "in connection with any attempt to influence the general public or segments thereof, with respect to legislative matters, elections, or referendums" (Sec 162(e)(2)(B).[1] Advertising expenditures may be deducted from income, as long as they are "institutional or 'good will' advertising which keeps the taxpayer's name before the public."[2] Advertising with respect to legislation, however, is treated as non-deductible by the Internal Revenue Service.[3]

In addition, the Department of Defense does not have a clear standard with respect to the allowability of grass-roots spending as a cost to be reimbursed by defense contracts (see Conclusions and Recommendations). Because it is difficult to define and apply the IRS standard, and because DoD may allow contract reimbursement of defense contractor grass-roots lobbying expenditures, the taxpayer may well be subsidizing these costs.

In fact, all defense-related advertising carries political weight. The readers of ads, the respondents to grass-roots efforts include contractors, military officers, even Government officials, as well as the general public. Such ads and campaigns are aimed, directly or indirectly at influencing legislators, legislation and appropriations. Contractors tend to identify corporate goals with Government needs, turning the "iron triangle" into a hall of mirrors. The corporate interest becomes synonymous with "national security," a justification that contractors use, with great effect, at the grass-roots level. In the effort to promote the F-14, Grumman Aerospace's George M. Skurla notes that cutting the production run of the plane was "quite simply reducing the defense of the United States."[4] P.E. Vassallo, Grumman vice president for corporate procurement operations, asked the "Grumman Industrial Team Members" to "assist the Navy and Grumman in getting these much needed F-14s reinstated through the legislative process."[5]

Advertising and the Grass Roots

Advertising plays a major role in the selling of weapons. Four of the companies in our study use advertising and public relations agencies that rank among the largest in the country: Hill and Knowlton (Grumman), McCann-Erickson (Lockheed), J. Walter Thompson (McDonnell Douglas), and Marsteller (United Technologies). Contractors bombard their constituents with advertising, much of it in the military press—*Aviation Week, National Defense, Armed Forces Journal International, U.S. Naval Institute Proceedings, Army,* and *Air Force Magazine.*

These publications are read by many influential policy-makers in the triangle: active and retired military personnel, Government officials and industry employees. *Aviation Week* occupies a special position.

> Packed with full-page color advertisements showing off new aircraft, missiles, and electronics systems, and with regular columns and features on job changes, forthcoming professional meetings, and air-traffic records. McGraw Hill's

> *Aviation Week* arrives every Monday morning on the desks of most of its 102,000 subscribers in 132 countries. For its frequent advance disclosures of technology that may change the balance of power, the magazine is read at the highest levels of government throughout the world. As a trade journal, it is indispensable to the aerospace and defense industries it serves, keeping them abreast of technical developments, funding, and trends in policy, and not infrequetly acting as the industry's spokesman to influence policy changes. As a primary source of military information for the general press, it is more influential than some reporters will readily admit. Most important of all, because it identifies solidly with the defense community and has built a reputation as a guardian of the national interest, as this community defines it, *Aviation Week* has privileged access to defense information and plays a pivotal role in the capital's public-information wars. This means that it can publish sensitive information with a degree of impunity that can only remind such men as Daniel Ellsberg, Daniel Schorr, and Howard Morland that the government has always employed more than a single standard in defining national security interests for the press.[6]

Publisher James Pierce boasts of the power of advertising in *Aviation Week* and its influence on decision-makers.

> Within the highly structured governmental organizations there are individuals like you and me. There are differences of opinion. There are uncertainties. There are factions and, yes, there are conflicts. Advertising is the force that reaches into the minds of the people who, together make the decision.
>
> Advertising is the way—virtually the only way—you can cover all the individuals from top to bottom, with influence on the decision.... Advertising can be the *tie-breaker*. Advertising supplies the information and impressions that give the company the edge that matters...
>
> Employees in the government are estimated to change jobs every two or three years. With advertising, you can keep making the same basic selling points to buyers as they play musical chairs.[7]

Some corporate officials make only modest claims for advertising. Deane Aylesworth, director of advertising for Lockheed notes: "There is no way to alter a buying decision through any marketing or sales technique... but good marketing can contribute to a positive image for your company and that certainly helps."[8] Peter Bush at Boeing made a similar point: "The concept of military advertising is much the same as that in trade advertising. It's informational, image service. It is not designed to singlehandedly alter buying decisions."[9]

John Bickers at McDonnell Douglas, however, pointed out that "there are a lot of people who have the chance to make comments about products to the decision-makers. When you figure there are 30,000 mail drops in the Pentagon alone, you're talking to a lot of people."[10] A General Dynamics spokesman, Larry Channave, defended ads in specialist publications as in the interest of the taxpayers and the firm alike.

> It is well-founded that advertising produces real benefits, some of which accrue to the Government. It serves to generate public interest in and support of important defense programs, attracts potential employees with needed technological skills, and more directly to the point, generates additional sales which increase the contractor's business base for absorption of costs thus resulting in a cost reduction on Government contracts.[11]

Corporate confidence in advertising often appears boundless. During the development of a new short take-off and landing cargo plane, Boeing and McDonnell Douglas ran seemingly endless campaigns touting their rival versions of the plane, while at the same time Lockheed's campaign told the reader that a new plane was unnecessary: the Defense Department could fill its cargo needs with Lockheed's C-130. Aggressive advertising campaigns also accompanied the competition of United Technologies and Boeing (Vertol) for the Army's UTTAS helicopter contract and the Navy's LAMPS helicopter contract in the late 1970s.

It is difficult, if not impossible, to estimate the total amount spent on the advertising of defense hardware. According to *Advertising Age*, military ads are generally only a small portion of overall corporate advertising. Fairchild, they point out, received 60 percent of its sales income from DoD but spent only roughly 25 percent of its advertising budget on such products.[12] Standard sources on advertising do not break down data by product line.

Politics and Plant Locations

Geography is central to the grass-roots politics of the "iron triangle." Struggles over weapons systems choices in Washington are played out in local communities. Grumman and the New York Congressional delegation lobbied hard to retain the F-14, contending with politicians from Massachusetts (Senator Edward Kennedy, House Speaker Tip O'Neill) who were promoting the F-18 (McDonnell Douglas and General Electric) as beneficial to the economy of Massachusetts. The C-5A contract award to Lockheed in Georgia and the F-111 to General Dynamics in Texas have been associated with the political power of the Georgia delegation (Senator Richard Russell) and the Presidency of Texan Lyndon Johnson. It has also been suggested that NASA's award of the space shuttle orbiter contract to Rockwell in California over Grumman was related to the Presidential campaign of Richard Nixon.

Corporations target their geographic constituencies as a grass roots element in their Government relations planning. ITT's Washington office reportedly followed local officials closely. "Every Senator, Congressman, Governor and important state official was assigned to a senior ITT manager for 'cognizance' on a geographical basis."[13] The intention is to link the company with the district's interests. As one Washington business representative put it, "We try to pull it right down to the district and we think if we do that we make him stand still and listen, whether he is a Republican or a Democrat."[14] Congressional members from areas with defense plants are particularly sensitive to arguments that stress the economic prosperity derived from Federal contracts.

The eight companies cast a wide net. Boeing, based in Seattle, does substantial contract work in Wichita, Kansas and Pennsylvania. General Dynamics has plants in Connecticut, Missouri, Texas and California; Grumman in New York, Florida and Georgia; Lockheed in Georgia and California; McDonnell Douglas in Missouri and California; Northrop in California and Illinois. Rockwell's production facilities are widely distributed while United Technologies, by contrast, is concentrated in Connecticut.[15]

In addition to the general advertising that reaches all of their constituents, the corporations reach local communities through the media and through a direct appeal, mobilizing workers and their families to take the corporation's message to Washington.

The Companies: Three Campaigns

It is increasingly clear that a wide variety of American social institutions are using grass-roots mobilization as a central part of their political strategy. According to Representative Benjamin Rosenthal (D-NY):

> There is little doubt that over the past several years, private sector interest groups—corporate taxpayers and tax-exempt entities, such as trade groups, unions, and even public charities—have turned increasingly to grass-roots efforts as the most effective mechanism for influencing public policy decision-making.[16]

Hard information on the level of corporate grass-roots efforts and the magnitude of corporate expenditures is difficult to come by. Few companies openly discuss their grass-roots efforts, and virtually none offer systematic data about the corporate funds spent for this purpose. Corporate reluctance is matched by Federal indifference. According to Representative Rosenthal:

> No data are available from any single source, or even a combination of sources, on the amount of money presently being expended for direct and grassroots lobbying activities at the Federal, State, and local levels.
>
> For example, the Internal Revenue Service, which is responsible for assuring compliance with our tax laws, main-

tains no statistical information on lobbying expenditures...
IRS has advised the subcommittee that it is "not in a position to furnish... statistical information as to the lobbying expenditures of corporations, since we do not keep such data for either statistics of income purposes or as part of our taxpayers compliance measurement program corporation studies."[17]

By searching available hearings, news coverage and fragmentary Federal data gathered for other purposes, we have obtained some information on grass-roots campaigns mounted by three of the companies during the 1970s. An examination of these campaigns sheds some light on the techniques, the level of effort, and the constituencies brought into play.

Lockheed and Rockwell

In 1971 Lockheed faced a serious financial crisis. According to William Wilson, vice president for advertising, Lockheed attempted to obtain Congressional approval of a Federal loan guarantee, mounting "a total effort involving all of our employees, the unions, the contractors, the airline customers, our bankers, our supporters in government." The grass roots were to play a major part.

We have plants and offices in many states and we naturally asked people in those areas to talk to those members of Congress that they were acquainted with. In all this, we were helped considerably by our subcontractors and suppliers.[18]

In addition, Lockheed sent letters to shareholders and managers, "truth squads" to media in "big cities and small hamlets throughout the country," and urged employees to write Congress. Wilson notes, also, that Lockheed's ad agency, Hill and Knowlton, "gave us special and effective assistance." This campaign met with success when Lockheed won the vote for the guarantee in the summer of 1971.

Starting in 1973 Rockwell International undertook a major effort to persuade the Federal Government to support the B-1 program. "Operation Common Sense" (OCS) planned a lobbying campaign in support of the bomber, the space shuttle and the Minuteman guidance system. Working documents named members of the House and Senate Armed Services Committees and Defense Appropriations subcommittees, along with a list of companies in their districts or states that had received Rockwell subcontracts for the programs. Company officers, convinced of the importance of lobbying and early action, determined to rebut opposing views. In the December meeting, Rockwell's John Rane, Jr. discussed the American Friends Service Committee, a group opposed to the B-1, stating that he would "be responsible for ascertaining more about the leadership of AFSC and (would) recommend at the next meeting a program to confront this organization."[19] In January Mr. Rane "commented on the activities of Mr. Dale Grubb as the Committee's representative in Washington and Los Angeles to work with associations such as the American Legion." The minutes describe the role that these groups might play:

> Comments from members of the Committee ensued regarding the use of speakers at meetings of organizations such as the legion, the inviting of key subcontractors and others using public relations personnel. This discussion resulted in a decision to formulate a program to start in California, at Palmdale, and submit plans for a Veterans or American Legion Day in Palmdale to see if this proposal has merit. Earl Blount has the responsibility to handle this assignment, with the understanding that we must be careful to avoid obvious friction or jealousies that might arise between organizations such as the American Legion and the Veterans of Foreign Wars.[20]

Only partial data are available to document the funds expended by Rockwell in the early years of campaign to support the B-1 and its other military programs. Data supplied by the House Subcommittee on Commerce, Consumer and Monetary Affairs indicate, however, that Rockwell spent roughly $700,000.00 for such efforts between 1974 and 1975. According to the opinion of the Defense Contract Audit Agency, which reviewed the expenditures of Rockwell's B-1 Division in 1976, most of these expenses were claimed as contract costs by the firm. Some were questioned by DCAA as possibly not allowable.[21]

According to the DCAA examination, these sums were spent for a variety of grass-roots activities:

— Rockwell employees speaking with editors, writers, publishers, and Government and contractor personnel throughout the country.
— Paid media advertising (unstated amount not claimed on contracts).
— A film on their chief test pilot and his first flight in the B-1 ($35,000 not claimed on contracts).
— Several films which, in our opinion, were made and shown in attempts to develop positive support for the B-1 and other defense programs.
— Motion picture expenses . . . much of the footage has been shown on television news programs, commentaries, etc.
— An economic impact study . . . the results of the study appear to have been used in preparing papers designed to influence public opinion on the B-1 program.
— Costs for "Operation Common Sense" and "Keep the B-1 Sold" . . . It is possible that unclaimed amounts include additional costs related to these and similar projects.
— Administrative expenses for a Director of Program Relations, whose time appeared to be spent on efforts to influence B-1 legislation.
— Briefings and presentations at or to Air Force Association sym-

posiums, Strategic Air Command conferences, Thunderbird reunion, the Society of Experimental Test Pilots, Air Force Association Convention, Strategic Air Command Bomb/Navigation Competition, etc.
— A speaker's bureau activity which provides to Rockwell employees a basic speaker's package that appears to attempt to influence public opinion for the B-1 program.
— Special projects, and economic/government analyses functions.
— Presentations, decals, pictures, displays, handouts, etc.[22]

As the debate in Congress became more heated and a decision on the B-1 program drew near, Rockwell increased its pressure. From evidence supplied by Rockwell to the House Subcommittee on Commerce, Consumer and Monetary Affairs, we have calculated that the company spent some $1.35 million on grass-roots and informational activities from 1975 to 1977 in connection with the B-1, the space shuttle and California referenda, over $900,000 of which was deducted from pretax income as a cost of doing business. In 1976 alone, $770,000 was spent for this purpose.[23]

Faced with a number of amendments to the Defense Authorization and Appropriations acts that would have either delayed or eliminated the program, Rockwell turned to its employees. In a special issue of its internal newspaper, *Rockwell International News*, entitled "Special B-1 Edition," readers were asked by company President Robert Anderson "to support a program that is vital to the nation." Noting the need to promote the B-1 against active opposition and supplying supportive quotes from "experts," Anderson stated:

> If you agree with the experts, write, wire or telephone your congressman today and urge him to support national defense and the B-1 bomber which the experts say is needed for the security of our country. Also, I hope you will urge your family, neighbors and friends to take similar action.

The newspaper also contained details on how to contact a Congressman, information to be used in letters, and the names of the Congressional conferees meeting on the Appropriations bill.

This newsletter went to all plant locations and was accompanied by instructions to managerial personnel on how to organize the employee letter-writing campaign. A covering letter from President Anderson to "B-1 team leaders" told them that they had been "selected to carry out a most important assignment." Noting the "well-disciplined and highly vocal" opposition to the B-1, Anderson stated: "We have to match their messages with facts on the B-1. That is your assignment." Another cover sheet from Richard Goode, personnel director, listed distribution points for information. "If any of your employees desire to write letters, there will be stationery, envelopes and stamps available at the above locations. Please provide these for employees who want them." A sample public address system was also included. "Every

Rockwell plant across the country is doing the same thing," it said. "Let's do our share."

These frenetic activities were soon rewarded. In an August 1976 *Report to Management* Rockwell noted that "employees in record numbers have expressed their feelings on the B-1 bomber" and circulated a "Thank You" that referred to 80,000 messages sent to members of Congress. Warren Nelson, of Representative Les Aspin's office, commented on the effectiveness of Rockwell's campaign. He observed that Rockwell:

> got all the employees of the plant just outside our district that makes Admiral televisions to send letters to their congressmen. A couple of letters we got made reference to how their jobs would be lost if they didn't get the B-1 bomber. . . . They also went around here with a chart which impressed a lot of congressmen, showing how much money from Rockwell would go into every district in the country.[24]

Rockwell also turned to its stockholders. Chairman Willard F. Rockwell, Jr. wrote to stockholders of 35,000,000 outstanding shares on August 13, 1976, enclosing a reprint of a statement by Air Force Secretary Thomas Reed and noting that many people "have not been heard from by members of Congress." Claiming that the "well-organized opposition" was "bombarding" Congress with mail, he urged those who agreed with him to make their "views known immediately to the U.S. representatives and senators of your state."

At the same time the company enlisted support through advertising that was placed in both the specialist and general press: *Air Force Magazine, Aviation Week, Armed Forces Journal, National Defense, U.S. Naval Institute Proceedings*; as well as *Fortune, Business Week, Time* and *Newsweek*. In the daily press[25] ads invited the reader to write to Chief Test Pilot C.D. Brock, Jr. in Los Angeles. Brock responded with a pamphlet, "Why We Need the B-1." Noting a series of critical votes in Congress, which would begin on August 23, he urged readers to write their member of Congress.

Support came also from a Washington newsletter, *Washington Alert*, published by Presbrey Associates, which devoted two issues and two special reports to the B-1 Program. The April 1976 report, edited by Martha Rountree, urged readers not only to "wire or write themselves but to organize members in their community to personally express their views to their Representatives and Senators at this time." The July 1976 report targeted the upcoming Senate Appropriations vote, listing key senators and noting that "inputs from constituents can make the big difference." The DCAA audit of the Washington office expenditures of Rockwell between 1974 and 1975 disclosed that the firm had paid Presbrey Associates $39,350 in 1974 and 1975 for purposes the audit did not describe.[26]

Grumman

Because of an increase in the unit costs of the F-14 and the introduction of a new, less expensive fighter, the F-18, the DoD sought to slow production of the F-14 in 1977 over Navy objections.

In the past Grumman had maintained a low level Congressional lobbying effort. Now, however, they recognized the need to develop such a strategy. Dave Walsh, Grumman's marketing director said:

> Our job is not only to convince the user, but we also have a responsibility to the Congress. We're witnessing a rather dramatic increase in our acceptance of the fact that the Congress plays an important role.[27]

Like Lockheed and Rockwell, Grumman appealed to employees and stockholders, sought support from subcontractors, and approached local officials and groups with arguments about the contribution of Grumman and the F-14 to the local, state, and regional economy. An advertising campaign described the advantages of the F-14 to the defense specialist, the business community and the public. It pointed out that the F-14 was available for future needs and linked the plane with the taxpayer. "The F-14 Tomcat. It belongs to you." An "Owner's Manual" touted the capabilities of the F-14, its radar tracking range and its ability to fire on six targets while tracking 24. Although the pamphlet made no request that readers pressure Congress, responses, which reportedly totalled more than 20,000, were put to political use. They were broken down by Congressional district and the relevant member of Congress was informed of her/his constituent's interest in the program.[28]

Grumman ads in Long Island's *Newsday* urged direct contacts with Congress. They described the cut-backs as "a most serious crisis for the entire Long Island community." Reducing the production rate and buying the F-18 meant spending "billions of dollars to develop a substitute aircraft that will provide the nation with far less capability at about the same unit cost." Subcontracting on Long Island alone involved about 1,100 firms, with another 2,000 across the state. "The business fortunes of Grumman Aerospace—the island's largest single employer—directly or indirectly affect most everyone who lives here,"[29] said George M. Skurla, chairman of the board.

Grumman also encouraged its employees to write Congress. In April 1978, a visitor to Gruman's Calverton, Long Island plant noted posters on the wall appealing to employees for donations to support the F-14 campaign.[30]

At the May 18, 1978 Annual Meeting, Chairman John C. Bierwirth and Aerospace President George Skurla encouraged stockholder support. Noting the atmosphere of "strong debate" in Congress and warning of the costs of delay, he praised his company's grass-roots efforts.

> In connection with this critical decision, let me assure you that we have marshalled the political clout of our total Long

> Island and New York State congressional delegation, along with congressmen and senators from other states who support a minimum production rate of 36 aircraft per year. We have taken our message to taxpayers throughout the United States, asking for their support for the best defense of our country in terms of cost and battle effectiveness.[31]

Chairman Bierwirth also took up the refrain, pointedly noting the stockholders' stake in the outcome.

> Perhaps you've read about the debate in Washington over the future role of the Navy in our national military strategy. At issue is how many carriers and carrier aircraft the country needs. That debate obviously can affect the business outlook of the company that has produced the finest carrier aircraft for over 40 years.[32]

Grumman then turned to its subcontractors, numbering at least 35 (including Bendix, Teledyne, Garrett AiResearch, Fairchild, Sunstrand, United Technologies, Honeywell, Curtiss Wright, Kaman, Rohr, Hughes, General Electric, Goodrich, Brunswick, Uniroyal, and Sperry). On February 1, 1978, P.E. Vassalo, vice president for corporate procurement operations, sent a letter to the "Grumman Industrial Team Members" pointing out the pending cut and asking the members "to assist the Navy and Grumman in getting these much needed F-14s reinstated through the Legislative process."

The company also held briefings for the state's Congressional delegation, Governor Hugh Carey, and State Commerce Commissioner John Dyson on Grumman's importance to Long Island and the economy of the entire state.[33] Commissioner Dyson reportedly asked for broader Grumman data in order to mobilize the "entire Northeast" on behalf of the program.

In the spring and summer of 1978 Congress restored the original production rate for the F-14. Grumman's grass-roots campaign was sufficiently visible for Defense Secretary Harold Brown to announce an audit of Grumman to determine whether contract funds had been used to finance the effort.[34] Although such an audit may have been carried out, no results have been made public.

FOOTNOTES

1. See Sec. 162 (e) of the Internal Revenue Code allowing deductions for "ordinary and necessary expenses" associated with "appearances before, submission of statements to, or sending communications to, the committees, or individual members, of Congress or of any legislative body . . . with respect to legislation or proposed legislation of direct interest to the taxpayer."
2. Internal Revenue Service Regulations on Section 162 (e) of IRC of 1954, as cited in U.S. Senate, Committee on the Judiciary, Subcommittee on Administrative Practice and Procedure, *Sourcebook on Corporate Image and Corporate Advocacy Advertising*, (1978), p. 2129.
3. Ibid., p. 2130.
4. Advertisement in *Newsday*, 3 Feb. 1978.
5. Letter to Grumman Industrial Team Members, 1 Feb. 1978.
6. Tom Gervasi, "The Doomsday Beat," *Columbia Journalism Review*, May/June 1979, p. 34.
7. *Aviation Week and Space Technology*, 27 October 1980.
8. *Advertising Age*, 14 July 1980, p. S4.
9. Ibid., pp. S4-S5.
10. Ibid., p. S5.
11. Text of talk to Federal Bar Association, Western Briefing Conference on Government Contracts, San Francisco, CA, 13 Oct. 1976, p. 6.
12. *Advertising Age*, 14 July 1980, p. S6.
13. Thomas S. Burns, "Inside ITT's Washington Office," *Business and Society Review*, Autumn 1974, p. 24.
14. Quoted in Paul W. Cherington and Ralph L. Gillen, *The Business Representative in Washington* (Washington: The Brookings Institution, 1962), p. 118.
15. The quality of company-disclosed data varies from Grumman's fairly clear disclosure of plant location and floor space, to virtually no detailed plant location information from United Technologies. No company provided complete information on what defense work was being done in specific locations. Neither the Defense Department nor the firms disclose the value and termination dates of DoD contracts by specific company location; nor do they disclose information on subcontracts. Data on the labor force are equally elusive. Accordingly, we have had to assemble our information through a painstaking review of company *10K*s, Annual Reports, and press accounts.
16. U.S. House of Representatives, Committee on Government Operations, Subcommittee on Commerce, Consumer and Monetary Affairs, *Hearings: IRS Administration of Tax Laws Related to Lobbying* (Part I), May 22, 23, 25 and July 18, 1978, p. 2.
17. Ibid., p. 2. See also the testimony of Harvey J. Shulman on the inadequacies of Federal reporting and enforcement, pp. 41-117.
18. Senate Committee on the Judiciary, *Sourcebook on Corporate Image*, p. 187.
19. Minutes of meeting of OCS Executive Committee, 5 December 1973, p. 1.
20. Minutes of meeting of OCS Executive Committee, 15-16 January 1974, p. 2.
21. DCAA pointed out that the results of this audit were preliminary and had "not been settled with the contractor." The DCAA also noted, however, that these costs probably understated the actual level of effort by Rockwell in grass-roots mobilization, since "the contractor has recorded significant costs for 1974 and 1975 which have not been claimed on Government contracts." Rockwell, the evaluation noted, did not claim media or some film costs. Memorandum from Richard Ratia, Resident Auditor, through the

Regional Manager, DCAA, to the Director, "Public Relations and Lobbying Expense—Rockwell International Corporation, B-1 Division" (No. 4641/6C179211/RR/mm, 22 April 1977).
22. Ibid.
23. Letter from Robert A. DePalma, V.P. for Finance, Rockwell International, to Rep. Benjamin S. Rosenthal, 30 June 1978.
24. "The Politics of Producing a Plane," *Newsday*, 17 May 1977.
25. *Seattle Post-Intelligencer*, 20 July 1976; *The Wall Street Journal*, 21 July 1976.
26. Defense Contract Audit Agency, *Audit Review of Washington, D.C. Office Operations and other Expenses, Rockwell International Corporation, Pittsburgh, PA*, Audit Report No. 3191-99-6-0318, 6 April 1976, pp. A-4-5. The audit, which was preliminary, noted that Rockwell voluntarily deleted these costs as claims against defense contracts.
27. "The Politics of Producing a Plane," *Newsday*, 17 May 1977.
28. Confidential interview, July 1979.
29. Advertisement in *Newsday*, 3 Feb. 1978.
30. Confidential interview, July 1979.
31. *Grumman Overview*, 3:3, June 1978.
32. Ibid.
33. *Newsday*, 17 May, 1978.
34. Bernard Weinraub, "Inquiry Set on Grumman Lobbying," *The New York Times*, 15 Feb. 1978.

14
Greasing the Machinery: Questionable Payments

The Contractors, the Defense Department, and Overseas Sales

With the decline of defense spending that followed the Vietnam war, many contractors, including those in this study, saw a decrease in their sales to the U.S. Government. Foreign markets became an attractive, and even necessary, supplement. In the last decade overseas sales have come to represent a sizable percentage of company business, ranging from 10 percent to 50 percent of total sales from 1970 to 1979 (see Table I).

The benefit to the contractors is obvious. Less obvious is the benefit to the Defense Department and the degree to which Federal agencies have encouraged and facilitated these sales. Overseas "add-ons" to a production run reduce the unit cost; overseas purchases and use provide additional information on the effectiveness of equipment. Foreign sales enable the DoD, when it cuts back on domestic contracts, to do so without damaging the U.S. defense-production capability—the facilities and work force that the DoD might want to call on at some future time. Finally, sales of military equipment to foreign governments are frequently seen as furthering U.S. **defense** and foreign policy objectives.

The Defense Department, accordingly, has gone out of its way to help contractors. In the 1970s, major military sales overseas were coordinated through the DoD's Defense Security Assistance Agency, with the advice and assistance of overseas military attachés and military advisory groups. These agencies had a hand in the sales strategies of the companies and the actual procurement of the weapons.

Enthusiasm for foreign sales has not, to our knowledge, led to questionable sales practices by Government officials. Many corporations, however, overstepped the mark. According to disclosures filed with the Securities and Exchange Commission, roughly 400 U.S. companies engaged in "questionable sales practices" or made "questionable payments" overseas in the late 1960s and 1970s, totalling hundreds of millions of dollars.[1] These practices and payments were engaged in as part of a strategy for developing overseas commercial and military markets.

For the purposes of this study, we use the terms "questionable sales practices" and "questionable payments" in the widest sense.[2] Some companies reported having created off-the-books accounts, or "slush funds," to handle commissions and payments to foreign government officials. Some paid large sales commissions to agents overseas and later found that some of these had gone to foreign officials. Others have acknowledged making direct payments to foreign officials, both as "grease" to minor functionaries and gifts to high-level policy-makers. Still others have admitted engaging in commercial transactions that involved "kickbacks" and foreign bank accounts. Such practices were often concealed from outside auditors, shareholders, the Internal Revenue Service, and even from many officials inside the company.

Federal Response

Federal agencies were sufficiently concerned to move to inhibit further concealment and questionable practices. The SEC developed a disclosure program which, though voluntary, placed corporations under pressure to disclose their activities or risk further action. At the start, some companies were enjoined from concealment and obliged to conduct a review of sales practices to be followed by a full public report. Five of the eight companies in this study—Boeing, Grumman, Lockheed, McDonnell Douglas, and Northrop—carried out such a review.

The Internal Revenue Service also reviewed corporate tax returns for evidence that questionable payments might have been concealed and deducted as a cost of doing business. The Federal Trade Commission examined company disclosures for evidence that foreign sales practices might have resulted in a restraint of trade. The Department of Justice created a joint task force with the SEC to examine possible violations of mail and wire fraud, banking secrecy and perjury statutes.[3] The Congress also reacted sharply to the disclosures by corporations, with demands for stronger prohibitions. After hearings in 1977, the Senate and House passed the Foreign Corrupt Practices Act, which made payments to foreign government officials illegal and set out penalties for corporations and executives who had made such payments in order to obtain sales, channel business or alter the carrying out of local legislation or regulations.

Senate harings and disclosures to the SEC were followed closely by the American and foreign press. The governments of Japan, the Netherlands and Italy, among others, undertook their own investigations of the practices, and in some cases brought suit against alleged recipients of bribes.

Many corporations were responsive to the SEC disclosure program and the various enforcement and investigative actions. Some executives, however, resented Federal activity. Corporate personnel argued that the Federal Corrupt Practices Act would be ineffective, because it would be unenforceable overseas. They argued that tying the hands of American business with such legislation would put them at a competitive disadvantage with their foreign competitors, who were not so restrained. It was also suggested that setting such standards constituted an attempt to impose U.S. standards of doing business on other countries, where practices were substantially different. Charles Bowen, chairman of Booz, Allen & Hamilton expressed scorn for attempts to restrain corporate behavior overseas, describing the reformers as "a bunch of pip-squeak moralists running around trying to apply United States puritanical standards to other countries." Asked if he would fire an employee who paid a bribe overseas, he replied: "Hell, no! Why fire him for something he was paid to do?"[4]

Although there appears to have been some retreat from these practices, many analysts feel that most companies continue to make "facilitating payments" though they conceal them more carefully. According to Barry Richman of the UCLA Graduate School of Management:

> Some companies have hidden their payments so well they haven't even been disclosed. Others are still making payments, but they've become more sophisticated. They are simply changing distribution channels and using third parties to make the payments so that their own books are clean.[5]

The Companies

The overseas sales practices of the eight companies in this study (see Table XV) include some of the more newsworthy and colorful examples of "questionable payments." The SEC questioned Boeing on its sales commissions of at least $52 million paid between 1971 and 1978, including $27 million in payments to officials of seven foreign governments.[6] Lockheed's special board committee noted in 1977 that the company might have made as much as $38 million in questionable payments.[7] A similar committee of the McDonnell Douglas board reported that between 1969 and 1978 the company might have made $21.6 million in questionable payments in 18 countries.[8] These three companies dominate the international market for commercial air transport and were engaged in a sharp competition for sales in the 1970s. In addition, they ranked among the five companies most dependent on overseas sales during that period (see Table III). All three companies have negotiated settlements with the SEC according to which each

TABLE XV

QUESTIONABLE PAYMENTS OVERSEAS
(1970-79)

Company	Overseas Sales* ($billions)	/of Total Co. Sales	Questionable Payments Overseas** ($millions)
Boeing	$17.301	41.79%	$52.0
General Dynamics	N.D.	10%	N.D.
Grumman	.774	17.14%	10.0
Lockheed	6.991	22.04%	38.0
McDonnell Douglas	9.861	34.53%	21.6
Northrop	4.379	52.04%	1.85
Rockwell	7.426	21.55%	.67
United Technologies	13.423	32.0%	10.15

Source: Company Disclosures, 10K's, Annual Reports.

* See Table I for years covered.
** See Chapter 15 for definition of term.

agreed, without admitting any earlier guilt, to refrain from future violations of the securities laws.

The other companies, with the exception of General Dynamics, have acknowledged making overseas payments, though of smaller amounts. United Technologies has disclosed that some of its corporate entities, particularly Otis, made over $10 million in overseas payments, "some of which were questionable," between 1971 and 1976.[9] Grumman's Gulfstream Aircraft subsidiary, sold by the company in 1978, admitted it had inadequately disclosed commission payments in 17 countries connected to sales of Gulfstream aircraft. Gulfstream pleaded guilty to concealing $5 million in commissions, though they and the parent company stated that they did not consider the payments questionable.[10] Northrop revealed a total of roughly $1.85 million in questionable payments, some of which "may have been paid to employees of foreign governments."[11] Rockwell's total was smaller—$666,000," which were or may have been made to foreign governmental officials or employees."[12] General Dynamics has made no disclosure on this issue and did very little overseas business before the F-16 program in the latter part of the 1970s.[13]

FOOTNOTES

1. See Gordon Adams and Sherri Zann Rosenthal, *The Invisible Hand: Questionable Corporate Payments Overseas* (New York: Council on Economic Priorities, 1976); and Tom Kennedy and Charles E. Simon, *An Examination of Questionable Payments and Practices* (New York: Praeger Special Studies, 1978).
2. This definition of questionable payments also applies to the discussion of such payments in the company profiles.
3. Adams and Rosenthal, p. 10.
4. *The Wall Street Journal*, 9 July 1976.
5. Deborah Rankin, "Accounting Ruses Used in Disguising Dubious Payments," *The New York Times*, 27 Feb. 1978.
6. Judith Miller, "Boeing Charged by SEC," *The New York Times*, 29 July 1978.
7. *Report of the Special Review Committee of the Board of Directors of Lockheed Aircraft Corporation*, 16 May 1977.
8. David Garino, "McDonnell Douglas Is Said to Have Made More Foreign Payments than Disclosed," *The Wall Street Journal*, 20 July 1980.
9. Company 8K, 20 April 1977.
10. Nicholas M. Horrock, "Former Grumman Unit Fined," *The New York Times*, 4 Jan. 1979; John F. Berry, "Iran Payoff is Charged to Grumman," *The Washington Post*, 5 Jan. 1979; John F. Berry, "Audit Shows Foreign Payoff by Grumman," *The Washington Post*, 9 Feb. 1979; William M. Carley, "Grumman Panel Finds Payoffs Continued Despite Board's Policy," *The Wall Street Journal*, 28 Feb. 1979; letter to CEP from Weyman B. Jones, V.P. for Public Affairs, Grumman Corp., 13 October 1980.
11. Comany 8K, April 1977.
12. Company S7, 1976.
13. For further details on payments, see the company profiles.

PART IV
CONCLUSIONS AND
RECOMMENDATIONS

15
PENETRATING THE IRON TRIANGLE

This study has examined the Government relations practices of military contractors, a key element in the closed network or "iron triangle" of defense policy. Although defense procurement and national security policy are of crucial importance to all Americans, decisions on defense policy and weapons procurement rest almost entirely in the hands of insiders and policy experts, walled off from outsiders and alternative perspectives. The policy-makers, whose expertise is real and necessary, are also people and organizations with interests to protect and promote: 1) defense contractors whose success is measured by weapons sales, 2) the defense department, with positions and a future to protect and, 3) members of Congress who share in making military policy and are prime targets of industry-Government relations.

While the shared high degree of expertise inside the triangle has clear advantages, the closed nature of the policy process has an offsetting disadvantage. It encourages a narrowing of views and shared expectations that another generation of weapons is both desirable and inevitable and that defense spending must rise. The problem posed in this study is how to pry open the "iron triangle" of defense policy and weapons procurement in order to insure greater public awareness of policy alternatives, more effective restraint on the Government relations activities of the contracting industry, and broader public involvement in the policy process itself.

Wider Disclosure

The ability of the public to play a more effective role in the policy process depends, first, on a more extensive flow of information about defense contracting and the Government relations practices of defense contractors. Current disclosure requirements in these areas are inadequate and available information, as this study has suggested, is often inconsistently reported and poorly aggregated and analyzed. We have noted a number of areas where disclosure, reporting and aggregation could be improved, often with little additional effort or cost to either the contractors or the Federal Government.

1. **Contracting Data.** Defense contracts, the primary resource sustaining the "iron triangle," are of significant importance to most of the companies in this study. Research and development contracts are the opening wedge in developing a continuous, working relationship between contractors and the Federal Government. Contract dollars are used by the contractors as part of their Government relations strategy through the award of subcontracts and through reminders to members of Congress of the impact those subcontracts have on their districts. Yet, it is exceedingly difficult to obtain a clear picture of a company's involvement with DoD contracts, the current status of their R&D funding, and their policies and practices for awarding subcontracts. In our view, the following constitute minimal, non-onerous changes needed in disclosure requirements:

    a. Currently all income from the Government is lumped together in a company's reporting. Defense contractors could easily identify annual revenues from Government contracts by Federal agency. Requiring such disclosure would involve a change in SEC disclosure regulations but no significant change in current accounting practices.

    b. Current disclosures on R&D are difficult to compare because they use different terms and measures. SEC requirements could be revised to elicit uniform disclosure and to allow stockholders and the public to distinguish between corporate investment in R&D and corporate R&D investments which have been reimbursed by the DoD programs for Independent Research and Development and Bids and Proposals (IR&D/B&P). This requirement is not likely to impose new calculations or record-keeping for the companies. At least one company in the study (Grumman) was willing to disclose such information. The DoD, too, should disclose annually the funds it provides individual contractors under the IR&D/B&P programs.[1]

    c. Because contracts are the glue that binds defense contractors to their political constituencies, the local impact of contracts should be public knowledge. Some of the responsibility of disclosure lies with the Federal Government. It would involve no great addition to DoD's current data for the Department to maintain a publicly-available data base on contract awards, indicating the work location of prime contract awards and the anticipated date of contract termination. In addition, on the basis of data supplied by contractors, DoD could maintain a data base on the size of the work force involved on each major weapon system. Of even greater import, DoD should maintain and make public data on the network of first- and second-tier subcontracting companies for major prime contracts, including dollar value of subcontracts and the work force involved. This requirement was partly in effect for one year, FY1979, but was changed in subsequent years to indicate only aggregate subcontracting data on a geographic basis, making it virtually impossible to identify the subcontracting companies and communities in question.[2]

2. **Transfer of Personnel.** This study reports a high rate of movement of personnel between the eight defense contractors, the Defense Department and NASA. Such personnel movements are critical to the development of shared perceptions and closed networks between contractors and the procuring agencies. Initial reforms in reporting and data aggregation in the early 1970s improved available information in this area significantly. Yet current requirements, which oblige a transferee to report to DoD for three years after a shift, are weakly enforced, and the data provided makes it difficult to determine the exact range of responsibilities the individual had on the two sides of the "iron triangle." DoD aggregation and analysis of the data are also inadequate.

The public would be served by an upgrading of the reporting requirement to ask for a detailed description of the individual's duties, both in the Government and with the contractor. Enforcement of the requirement would be facilitated by transferees providing, as well, a description of specific steps he/she and the contractor have taken to minimize the risk of placing that individual in a conflict of interest situation. This reform would require minimal change in the reporting form currently used.

In addition, the DoD does an inadequate job of maintaining and analyzing the data it now receives. Currently, the reports are collated and a summary account of numbers and transfers is filed with Congress. DoD could expand its analysis to focus on situations where a conflict of interest appears possible and bring relevant cases to the attention of the General Counsel's office for review. DoD should also enforce the reporting requirement more strictly, reminding those transferees who have failed to comply.

3. **Advisory Committee.** Contractors obtain unique access to, and influence in, the definition of future weapons and aerospace systems through membership in advisory committees to DoD and NASA. Yet, there is now no public report on individual membership on such committees which specifies the members' employers.[3] Current annual reports from the General Services Administration provide aggregate data by agency on committee memberships and budgets but no

individual committee details. Committee reports filed with the Library of Congress are neither aggregated nor analyzed.

The General Services Administration or the Library of Congress, where committee reports are filed, could pull available data together and prepare a more comprehensive report on committee membership, analyzing data by committee, individual members, and employers. In addition, each committee member can, without significant additional work, disclose to GSA or the Library any personal (grant or contract) or employer interest in the subject matter discussed by the committee.[4]

4. Board of Directors. Although this study did not find much indication of extensive board involvement in Government relations activities, board members can provide a valuable network of information and contacts for a firm, through membership on the boards of other defense contractors and previous employment or advisory involvement with the Federal Government. In the board biographies generally prepared by defense contractors for distribution to the public and the press, care could be paid to complete disclosure of membership on the boards of other defense contracting and subcontracting companies, as well as past and current ties with the Federal Government.

5. Lobbying. Defense contractors, like other corporations, trade unions and interest groups, lobby actively to protect their interests and obtain advantages in Washington. This study has found, unfortunately, that current definitions of lobbying and reporting requirements make it virtually impossible to estimate the size of these efforts. Current lobbying legislation, written in 1946, defines a lobbyist as someone whose "principle purpose" is to engage in direct contact with members of Congress in order to influence legislation. Only individuals and organizations fitting this description need register and report. This narrow definition contrasts with a more realistic meaning of lobbying as a wide range of individual and group contacts seeking to influence policy and legislation. These may be directed at either the Congressional or the Executive branch. The current statute leaves some wide gaps:

    a. Contacts with staff employees of Congressional members are not considered lobbying.

    b. Individuals who do not solicit funds for lobbying, but use their own funds, need not register as lobbyists.

    c. If lobbying is not considered the "principal purpose," the individual need not register.

    d. Contacts with Congress which can be described as gathering information, testifying or monitoring hearings do not constitute lobbying.

    e. Contacts with Congress stimulated from the grass roots are not considered lobbying and need not be reported.

    f. The law does not define clearly what expenditures need to be disclosed as lobbying expenditures.

g. The law contains no enforcement mechanism for failure to register or report.

Because of these gaps, the data on lobbying in this study clearly underestimate the actual level of activity of the eight companies. Provisions for fuller disclosure, however, have been difficult to formulate. They must tread carefully between the need for a broader definition and greater disclosure, on the one hand, and burdensome reporting requirements and First Amendment rights, on the other.

Common Cause and other supporters of reform efforts in the 1970s[5] argue that greater public disclosure is the most effective form of restraint. As Sen. Abraham Ribicoff (D-CN) put it:

> To protect the democratic process itself, and assure public confidence in it, the lobbyist must work in the open. His work must not be cloaked in secrecy. Secrecy inevitably spreads suspicion. Secrecy helps disguise the voice of a single special interest as the voice of the general public. . . . The stream of leters or mailgrams we all receive may be a spontaneous reflection of the public view, or it may only represent a secretly-generated campaign by just one special interest. Congress and the public have a right to know which it is.[6]

Opponents of reform legislation, however, argue that an extensive disclosure requirement would impose unacceptable burdens on lobbyists and would have a "chilling effect" on the willingness of many to exercise their First Amendment rights. Andrew Feinstein of Public Citizen warned of the risks involved in a "poorly designed and drafted" bill which would risk "freezing some organizations out of the legislative process."[7]

While finding the balance between excessive reporting and walk-through loopholes poses stubborn problems, a solution needs to be found. An easily measurable threshold of activity, metered in time or funds, can be found to replace the "principal purpose" test; all lobbyists meeting this test would file quarterly reports, disclosing full expenditures for lobbying purposes. In addition, such reports can cover expenditures both for direct lobbying in Washington, aimed at members and staff of Congress, and expenditures for "indirect" or grass-roots mobilizations aimed, ultimately, at Congress.[8]

6. **Political Action Committees.** PACs have emerged as a major Government relations technique for corporations in the 1970s. The eight contractors in this study have spent over $2 million since their PACs were created, $1.2 million of which went to Federal campaigns. Current disclosures of Federal campaign contributions to the Federal Election Commission appear generally adequate. The capabilities of the FEC to gather, computerize and analyze PAC data, however, need

strengthening. PAC contributions to party campaign committees, for instance, are not computerized, and require time-consuming efforts to aggregate.[9]

As this study suggests, however, PAC expenditures and activities range far more broadly than contributions to Federal campaigns. Future PAC legislation should consider ways to widen reporting requirements to cover PAC contributions to state and local candidates and party campaign committees, and to other types of PAC spending such as political education within the firm and grass-roots campaigns.

In addition, the Institute for Public Representation (IPR) of Georgetown University Law School has filed a petition before the SEC requesting a ruling that would require management to report to stockholders on their PAC activities. Since corporate treasury funds are used for PAC administration, we consider IPR's petition to be in the stockholders' interest.

Greater Restraint on Government Relations

Disclosure is one route toward greater understanding of corporate Government relations practices. Public information can serve as a restraint on corporate power in the "iron triangle." More is required, however. This study suggests some areas where legislation and regulations may be necessary to restrain corporate behavior and to ensure an arms-length relationship between contractors and the Executive branch.

1. **Personnel Transfers.** This study concludes that current conflict of interest legislation and selling laws are inadequate to keep contractors and the DoD at arms length. While the benefits of expertise are real, Federal employees should not immediately upon leaving Government service work for a firm with which they dealt while in office. The recent Proxmire-Bennett bill suggests a way to guard against conflicts of interest while retaining the expertise of Federal employees. The bill would prohibit Federal procurement officials for two years from accepting employment with a contractor affected by their actions while in an official capacity.[10] The bill covers a wider scope of official actions than do current statutes, ranging from design decisions to the definition of program requirements and the administration of contracts. Passage of the bill would reduce temptation for Federal employees, since it would distance them from specific companies with which they must work.

2. **Board of Directors.** In order to loosen the ties binding the defense contracting companies, Congress might consider legislation prohibiting or limiting interlocking directorates among defense contractors.

3. **Lobbying.** Our review of audits conducted by the Defense Contract Audit Agency (DCAA) and internal Government documents on the effort to define a cost allowability principle for lobbying have revealed that many of the costs of defense contractor lobbying (both

direct and indirect) are charged to defense contracts. Taxpayers thus bear the cost of these expensive lobbying campaigns, in addition to any costs imposed by the success of the campaigns. In the opinion of DCAA, there was no justification for such a practice:

> We found no recognizable benefit to Government contracts [in contract or lobbying efforts] since the Department of Defense and other executive agencies make determinations of policy and program needs, and justify their own requirements for appropriations. Attempts by contractors to influence legislation favoring procurement of their products can can be inimical to DoD policies as well as program determinations.[11]

However, DCAA's recommendation that such costs not be covered by defense contract dollars met strong resistance from contractors and some DoD officials. After further guidance to DCAA from the counsels of the uniformed services, many of these costs were allowed, because the counsels argued, it was virtually impossible to distinguish between lobbying and legitimate, allowable "legislative liaison."[12]

Subsequent DoD and Executive branch efforts to define a cost principle covering lobbying took two years and failed in the end. DoD's first effort to define such a principle appeared clear:

> Lobbying is defined as any activity or communication which is intended or designed to directly influence members, their staffs or committee staffs of any federal, state, local or foreign Government legislative body to favor or oppose pending, proposed or existing legislation. Lobbying activity includes but is not limited to personal discussions or conferences, advertisements, telegrams, telephonic communications, letters and the like, and the directly associated costs related thereto.[13]

Criticism of this principle, however, came from Government officials, contractors and citizens. Many felt the distinction between lobbying and liaison was still unclear and would be hard to enforce. Contractor representatives objected to maintaining documentation that would help make such a distinction possible, seeing this as an additional and onerous requirement.[14] *Industry objected to any such cost principle* arguing that it would inhibit their exercise of their First Amendment rights. As United Technologies put it:

> In our view all persons and institutions have a right, if not an obligation, to participate in public dialogue on public issues affecting its customers, employees, products and business. We believe that reasonable communications and contracts whether individual or institutional are normal and customary and are in the public interest. Thus, the proposed ASPR, while not expressly forbidding a corporation's exercise of a constitutional right, would have a prostrating impact on the exercise of that right.[15]

Penetrating the Iron Triangle

Under this concerted attack, the DoD retreated. With the failure of their effort, portions of defense contractor lobbying costs continued to be reimbursed by the taxpayer, through defense contracts, as long as DoD considers such costs "reasonable." The documentation establishing their "reasonable" character is in the hands of the contractors and is not supplied to DoD.

The issue, however, is far from resolved. Critics of this practice continue to reflect the views of a Government official who commented on the DoD draft.

> We can see no benefit to the Government from this type of effort and do not believe it to be in the public interest for contractors to enjoy reimbursement of expenses for lobbying while such reimbursement is not available to the general public.[16]

Senator William Proxmire has protested the abandonment of the effort to define a cost principle.[17] The head of the Office of Federal Procurement Policy replied by suggesting that Congress could step into the breach and legislate a prohibition.[18] Either the Executive branch or Congress could undertake a renewed effort to define an adequate cost principle which would reduce or eliminate such reimbursement, now inappropriately borne by taxpayers. Less complex is the question of the deducation of grass-roots lobbying: the legislation is there but it has been frequently disregarded. While direct lobbying costs are tax deductible, Section 162e.2.B of the code prohibits the deduction from income of grass-roots lobbying costs; however, 1978 hearings in the House Subcommittee on Commerce, Consumer and Monetary Affairs indicated that such expenditures were routinely deducted. Reportedly, IRS enforcement of this prohibition has improved since the hearings, but strict attention to this problem remains necessary as corporate grass-roots efforts expand.

4. **Political Action Committees.** Corporate, trade association, membership and trade union PACs have become significant sources of campaign funds in the past six years, topping political parties as providers of support for Federal candidates. Moreover, PACs are a particularly useful instrument for certain groups in American society — but not for others.

> They do not work as well for groups that do not have substantial organizational or financial resources, or that have not had a history of involvement in the political process....
> PACs have also been a boon to ideological (particularly conservative) and single-issue constituencies that have felt unrepresented by parties and interest groups.[19]

PACs, then represent "interested" money; their sponsors have particular agendas to advance. This combination of special interest and growing importance as sources of funds suggests the need for considering some restraints over PAC activities, in the defense sector as elsewhere. A Congressional effort in 1977 sought to pass legislation providing for public financing of Congressional campaigns, as now exists for presidential general elections, in order to reduce the impact of PAC funding on candidates' positions. Faced with industry and Congressional opposition, this effort died. In 1978 and 1979, a scaled down effort, sponsored by Reps. David Obey (D-WI) and Tom Railsback (R-IL), sought to limit the funds House candidates could receive from one PAC to $2,500 (down from $5,000) and $50,000 overall from all PACs (as against no current ceiling). Opponents of the Obey/Railsback bill argued that it would reduce PAC effectiveness. Wilbur Jones, Manager of Public Affairs of the Chamber of Commerce noted that "the effectiveness of PACs would be seriously reduced by the bill at a time when business has finally begun to realize its potential."[20]

Subsequent amendments to the bill raised the individual PAC ceiling to $3,500 and the overall PAC total of $70,000, but the bill, which passed the House in Fall 1979 was bottled up in the Senate.[21] Full Congressional consideration and passage of this bill might help restrain the impact of PACs on the legislative side of the iron triangle.

Wider Perspectives and Public Participation

Wide disclosure of contracting and Government relations data should stimualte more active public discussion of the policies and weapons choices made within the "iron triangle.' A widened debate on defense issues would go far in informing the public about current defense policies and practices.[22] Restraints on contractor Government relations practices should help limit the dominance of the defense industry's point of view in defining these policies and weapons. New mechanisms could ensure that new participants, wider perspectives, and alternative policies become involved in the policy process. One vehicle would be to pry open the self-contained isolation of the Congressional committees that currently consider the defense budget and defense policies. The creation of Budget Committees in each house of Congress in 1974 was a helpful step in this direction, permitting one committee for the first time to review all segments of the Federal budget in relation to each other.

Beyond this step, other Congressional committees need to be encouraged to review aspects of defense policy and spending over which they have jurisdiction. The Banking committees, for instance, can review procurement policies; Commerce committees can review local and regional impacts of defense spending; Science and Technology committees can review aerospace policies and the nation's investment of research and development funds; Governmental Operations committees can examine general areas of national security policy, procurement policies and the management of the defense department. The Foreign Relations committees can examine the relationship between foreign policy objectives, national security issues, military missions and military capabilities.

There may be other ways of directly introducing alternative perspectives into the "iron triangle" itself. Such a change would be critically important at the research and development state of policy-making. The R&D process, as this study has noted, is the starting point for building the "iron triangle," yet one of its least visible aspects. Some 65 percent of the nation's total public investment in R&D goes into weapons and space systems,[23] employing a substantial proportion of the nation's technical talent. Federal advisory committees responsible for the definition of defense and aerospace R&D could include public representatives. When an *ad hoc* advisory committee is created to review a major system such as the B-1 or the MX missile[24] its membership should not be restricted to individuals drawn from the defense triangle. There is ample precedent for participation of non-specialists on Federal advisory bodies.[25]

Over the years the "iron triangle" of defense has become a closed and inbred community, monopolizing the debate on national security and the weapons systems needed to provide that security. National security cannot be debated wisely in military terms alone. The claims for military spending must be weighed against those of economic renovation, energy independence, full employment, a healthy and educated citizenry and national economic prosperity. Greater disclosure and restraints on the arms industry's political power can help lead to a wider debate on national needs and a definition of national security that is set in a wider context.

FOOTNOTES

1. CEP obtained disclosure of the top 25 corporate recipients of IR&D/B&P funds for 1973, 1974 and 1975 and published that data in "Contingency Costs: The Impact of Federal Expenditures for Military Research and Development, 1975-76," CEP Newsletter N6-7, 30 Aug. 1976).
2. CEP has received the FY1979 subcontracting data, disclosing first- and second-tier subcontractors, for sixteen companies: Bendix, Boeing, General Dynamics, General Electric, Grumman, Hughes Aircraft, Litton Systems, Lockheed, Martin Marietta, McDonnell Douglas, Tenneco's Newport News Shipbuilding and Dry Dock Co., Northrop, Rockwell International, TRW, United Technologies and Westinghouse Electric. These print-outs do not, however, include labor force data. See Department of Defense, Directorate for Information Operations and Reports, *Subcontracts by Contractor and Location for FY1979.*
3. Between 1976 and 1978, a subcommittee of the Senate Government Affairs Committee oversaw the preparation of a detailed index of advisory committee members, broken down by individual, committee and employer. For 1976 and 1977, see U.S. Senate, Committee on Governmental Affairs, Subcommittee on Reports, Accounting and Management, *Federal Advisory Committees: Index to Membership* (Washington, DC: GPO, 1976 and 1977). For 1978, see U.S. Senate, Committee on Governmental Affairs, Subcommittee on Energy, Nuclear Proliferation and Federal Services, *Federal Advisory Committees: Index to the Membership* (Washington, DC: GOP, 1978). The index was discontinued after the death of subcommittee Chairman Sen. Lee Metcalfe (D-MT) in 1978.
4. The review of Federal advisory committees by Gage and Epstein also recommends closer attention to sources of employment, grants and contracting relationships of committee members. See Kit Gage and Samuel S. Epstein, "The Federal Advisory Committee System: An Assessment," *Environmental Law Reporter,* 7, no. 2 (Feb. 1977), p. 50004.
5. See Congressional Quarterly, *The Washington Lobbyists,* 3rd. ed. (Washington, DC: *Congressional Quarterly,* 1979) and Hope Eastman, *Lobbying: A Constitutionally Protected Right* (Washington, DC: American Enterprise Institute, 1977).
6. Testimony before the Senate Committee on Government Operations, 22 April 1975, quoted in Eastman, *Lobbying,* pp. 16-17.
7. Testimony before the Subcommittee on Administrative Law and Governmental Relations of the House Committee on the Judiciary, 29 April 1977, cited in Eastman, *Lobbying,* p. 19.
8. The issue of lobbying the Executive branch is complex, involving necessary interactions between citizens, groups and the Federal government. Some reform efforts have sought to include such lobbying, though this was opposed by the Carter Administration. See "Testimony of Peter F. Flaherty, Deputy Attorney General, on Lobbying Reform: before the Subcommittee on Administrative Law and Governmental Relations of the House Committee on the Judiciary, 21 April 1977, supplied by the Department of Justice.

9. Companies may also increase the impact of corporate PAC contributions by encouraging employees to make individual contributions to the same candidates. Current candidate disclosures to the FEC, however, make it virtually impossible to identify the corporate employers of individual contributors.
10. See "Military Maneuvers/Update—1977," CEP Newsletter N7-1 (22 Feb. 1977).
11. Defense Contract Audit Agency, *Audit Review of Washington, D.C. Office Operations and Other Expenses, Rockwell International Corporation, Pittsburgh, Pennsylvania,* Audit Report No. 3191-99-6-0318 (6 April 1976) p. A2.
12. The counsels' memorandum defined such liaison as "attendance at committee hearings, exchange of information with Congressional sources and similar activities." See "Summary of Conclusions Reached *re* Allowability of Costs of Lobbying Under Existing Government Contracts," Memorandum of 16 Dec. 1976, p. 2. This document, along with others noted below, was supplied by Common Cause, which obtained them under a Freedom of Information Act Request.
13. This proposed principle explicitly excluded costs for "legislative liaison," defined as

    attendance at committee hearings, appearance before committee hearings at the request of the committee, gathering information regarding pending legislation and the like, provided, however, that the contractor did not initiate the request or his attendance is not part of a lobbying plan or campaign.

    See "ASPR Case 76-190, Lobbying Costs" Memorandum from George H. Strouse, Chairman, ASPR Section XV, Part 2 Subcommittee, to ASPR Committee Chairman, 12 Sept. 1977, Tab A, p. 1.
14. See, for example, the comments on the draft principle submitted by the Council of Defense and Space Industries Associations, quoted and summarized in "ASPR Case 76-190, Lobbying Costs," Memorandum from George H. Strouse, Chairman, ASPR Section XV, Part 2 Subcommittee to ASPR Committee Chairman, 4 April 1978, p. 7.
15. Letter from C.W. Schick, Asst. Controller, Government Contract Accounting, United Technologies, to T.G. Cassidy, Chairman, ASPR Committee, Office of the Undersecretary of Defense, Research and Engineering, 26 Jan. 1978, p. 1.
16. Letter from William E. Mathis, Director, Procurement and Contracts Management Division, Environmental Protection Agency, to Philip G. Read, Director, Federal Procurement Regulations Directorate, General Services Administration, 19 Jan. 1979, p. 1.
17. Letter to Karen Hastie Williams, Director, Office of Federal Procurement Policy, 22 Oct. 1980.
18. Letter to Sen. William Proxmire, 8 Dec. 1980.
19. Edwin Epstein, "The PAC Phenomenon: An Overview," *Arizona Law Review,* 22, no. 2 (Fall 1980), p. 1617.
20. Steven V. Roberts, "House Members Pressing to Curb Special-Interest Gifts," *The New York Times,* 26 Sept. 1979.
21. See Steven V. Roberts, "Problem with Campaign Funds," *The New York Times,* 19 Oct. 1979; *Congressional Quarterly,* 5 Jan. 1980, p. 33; Warren Weaver, Jr., "Senate Bottles Up a Bill to Limit Contributions in Races for the House," *The New York Times,* 15 Feb. 1980.
22. See Gordon M. Adams, "Disarming the Military Subgovernment," *Harvard Journal on Legislation,* 14, no. 3 (April 1977), pp. 497-503.
23. This figure represents the share of total Federal R&D spending composed of DoD, NASA and Dept. of Energy nuclear weapons programs, according to a 1980 study by the Battelle Memorial Institute. See *Aerospace Daily,* 29 Dec. 1980, p. 277.

24. See "Weinberger Picks Panel to Study Where to Put MX Missile System," *The New York Times*, 17 March 1981.
25. See, for example, "Response of the Public Interest Subcommittee to the Draft Report of the Subcommittee on Industrial Innovation, Dept. of Commerce," Prepared and Delivered by Alice Tepper Marlin, CEP Occasional Paper, 2 Oct. 1979.

PART V
PROFILES

KEY TO READING THE PROFILES

See text for full description of each data category

Symbols:
nd - no date
NA - not available

BASIC CORPORATE AND CONTRACTING DATA

A. Corporate Data

Company name and address; dates of company fiscal year; 1979 Fortune 500 rank; executive titles and salaries; auditor; outside legal counsel; advertising and/or public relations agencies; banking data, including transfer agents, registrars, credit banks and pension plan trustees, where available.

Table I: A ten-year review of sales and income figures, Defense Department and NASA contract awards, company disclosure of sales to the U.S. Government and overseas sales; Government figures on foreign military sales contracts; number of employees. (Note: NASA figures and rank aggregate NASA data on the parent company and subsidiaries where necessary.)

B. Principal Defense/Space Contracting Operations

Name and address of each company division or group involved with defense contracting; name of executive officer and defense products made at the plant, as available.

C. **Contracting History**
Summary of corporate production and notable Government relations activities in the 1970s.

D. **U.S. Government-Owned, Company-Operated Plants and Equipment (GOCO)**
Facilities owned by the U.S. Government and leased to the company, including total company floor space; plant space leased from the Government; lease cost; location; size and use, as available.

RESEARCH AND DEVELOPMENT

The company's major R&D projects in the 1970s, Table II—DoD and NASA contract awards by year, company-sponsored R&D spending, and the amount of company R&D reimbursed by the Defense Department under the R&D program for 1973-78, as disclosed by DoD under the Freedom of Information Act. (Note: Grumman Corporation's figures for R&D were disclosed to CEP by the company. Some contract figures aggregate Government data on the parent company and subsidiaries where necessary.)

BOARD OF DIRECTORS

Biographical data on each director, including the date named on the board, current position (inside the company), education and military background where relevant, past corporate employment, Government positions, and other corporate directorships (dollar figures in parentheses, DoD cover contracts awarded to these companies in FY1979), trade association memberships relevant to defense contracting and shares of company stock owned.

PERSONNEL TRANSFERS

Table III counts employees that moved to jobs in the company from the Defense Department or NASA, or moved from the company to NASA or the Defense Department between 1970 and 1979 as disclosed by DoD and NASA. Data are broken down by military branch and direction of transfer (Government to company, or company to Government).

Appearances of Potential Conflict of Interest
For definition of this term as used in this study, see Chapter 6. Individuals fitting this definition are listed with a description of jobs transferred from and to, and the starting date of the second position. Data are drawn from individual reports filed with DoD.

Comments and Policy Statement
Comments on notable categories of transfers, some of whom may not fit the definition in Chapter 6. Policy Statements are taken from letters by company officials to Sen. William Proxmire, published in

U.S. Congress, Joint Committee on Defense Production, **Defense Contractor Entertainment Practices**. 95th Congress, 1st Session, September 1977.

POLITICAL ACTION COMMITTEES

Total expenditures as disclosed by the Federal Election Commission, includes *all* expenditures by the PAC, including contributions to state and local candidates and miscellaneous expenses.

Total contributions to Federal campaigns aggregated by CEP on the basis of the Federal Election Commission's index of contributions to individual candidates and FEC listings of contributions to local party committees who may have contributed to Federal candidates.

The time span covered by the data varies depending on when the PAC was registered with the FEC.

Contributions to Federal Candidates in States with (company) Production Facilities (Key Geographic Locations)

A break-down of Federal candidates from areas with company plant locations who received contributions from the company PAC (with party affiliations).

Contributions to Members of Key Congressional Committees

Contributions to members of defense-related Congressional committees, including candidates who also represent a key geographic location. Some committee members may have served on a given committee for the 94th-96th Congresses, the full period covered by the data, while others may have served for shorter periods of time. Members listed may subsequently have changed committees.

Contributions to Other Federal Candidates

Name, party, state, district (where available) and contributions given to other Federal candidates who do not fit into any of the above categories.

Contributions to Other Campaign Committees

Contributions to Federal-level committees contributing to individual candidates, e.g., the Republican National Committee. Also includes contributions to state and local committees that may, in turn, have contributed to Federal candidates, e.g., the Suffolk County Democratic Committee.

Contributions to Presidential Campaign Committees

Contributions to 1976 and 1980 Presidential campaigns, where available.

WASHINGTON OPERATIONS

Address of the company's Washington office, names of director and staff; activities of the office, as available. Registered lobbyists includes the names and addresses of lobbyists employed by the company and funds paid to and expended by the lobbyists as disclosed in the *Congressional Record*.

ADVISORY COMMITTEE MEMBERSHIPS
Company employees serving on defense and NASA-related Federal advisory committees, with years of service.

DEFENSE-RELATED TRADE ASSOCIATION MEMBERSHIPS
Company memberships in trade associations related to defense procurement and policy-making.

ENTERTAINMENT
Statement of company policy regarding entertainment of DoD officials and other influential personnel; data on the provision of tickets, hospitality suites, air travel, meals and entertainment facilities, as disclosed to Joint Committee on Defense Production in 1976.

QUESTIONABLE PAYMENTS
A summary of questionable payments issues and disclosures in the 1970s.

BOEING

BASIC CORPORATE AND CONTRACTING DATA

A. Corporate Data

Boeing Company
7755 East Marginal Way South
Seattle, WA 98108

Fortune 500 (1979): 29
Fiscal Year: Jan. 1—Dec. 31

Chairman:
T. A. Wilson (1979 salary: $522,000)

President:
M. T. Stamper (1979 salary: $339,000)

Auditor:
Touche, Ross & Co.
Financial Center
Seattle, WA

Outside Legal Counsel:
Perkins, Coie, Stone, Olsen & Williams
1900 Washington Bldg.
1325 4th Ave.
Seattle, WA

TABLE I
Corporate Data
($ in M.)

	1970	1971	1972	1973	1974	1975	1976	1977	1978	1979
Sales	$3,677.1	3,039.8	2,369.6	3,335.2	3,730.7	3,718.9	3,918.5	4,018.8	5,463.0	8,131.0
Net Income	$ 22.1	42.2	30.4	51.2	72.4	76.3	102.9	180.3	322.9	505.4
Dept. of Defense Contracts	$ 474.7	731.9	1,170.9	1,229.2	1,076.4	1,560.8	1,176.3	1,579.9	1,524.5	1,514.5
Rank	12	9	5	3	6	2	6	4	7	7
NASA Contracts	$ 158.0	114.4	94.2	75.5	60.0	46.2	60.3	69.1	85.7	101.5
Rank	4	5	5	7	7	9	8	7	6	6
DoD/NASA Contracts as % of Sales	17.2%	27.8	53.4	39.1	30.5	43.2	31.6	41.0	29.5	19.9
Government Sales	$ 756.0	706.0	894.0	1,434.1	1,511.2	1,432.5	1,356.5	1,525.0	1,584.3	1,544.9
Government Sales as % of Sales	20.6%	23.2	37.7	43.0	40.5	38.5	34.6	38.0	29.0	19.0
Foreign Military Sales Contracts	0	$ .4	18.2	94.8	30.5	129.1	17.5	1.6	1.6	44.2
Rank	NA	NA	12	6	17	10	NA	NA	NA	NA
FMS Contracts as % of Sales		.01%	.8	2.8	.8	3.5	.4	.04	.03	.5
Overseas and Export Sales	$ 882.5	1,428.7	1,066.3	1,167.3	1,641.5	1,524.7	1,880.9	1,430.7	2,294.5	3,984.2
Overseas and Export Sales as % of Sales	24.0%	47.0	45.0	35.0	44.0	41.0	48.0	35.6	42.0	49.0
Employees	79,100	56,300	58,600	68,200	74,400	72,600	65,400	66,900	81,200	98,300

Advertising/Public Relations Agency:
Cole & Weber, Inc.
Seattle, WA

Banking:

Transfer Agent and Registrar:
First National Bank of Boston

Lenders:
Citibank (agent for the banks)
Bank of America
Chase Manhattan
Morgan Guaranty
Chemical Bank
Manufacturers Hanover
Bank of Montreal
Bankers Trust
Continental Illinois
First National Bank of Chicago
Security Pacific National Bank, Los Angeles
Irving Trust
Wells Fargo Bank
Marine Midland Bank
Mellon Bank
Crocker National Bank
   (see Board of Directors: Stanley Hiller)
Seattle First National Bank (see Board of Directors:
   Charles Piggot, William Reed and T.A. Wilson)
Pacific National Bank of Washington
   (see Board of Directors: Harold Haynes)
(and 20 other banks)

Trustee:
Employee Savings Plan and Pension Fund, First National
   Bank of Chicago

B. Principal Defense/Space Contracting Operations

Boeing Aerospace Co.
Kent, WA
H.K. Hebeler, President

E-3A—Airborne-Warning and Control System (based on 707),
   U.S. Air Force
ALCM-B—Air-launched Cruise Missile, U.S. Air Force
Minuteman ICBM—strategic missile, U.S. Air Force
Roland Air-defense Missile System, U.S. Army
Inertial Upper Stage Rocket Booster for Space Shuttle Payloads,
   U.S. Air Force, NASA

E-4B—Airborne Command Post (based on 747), U.S. Air Force
YC-14—Short Takeoff and Landing Transport, U.S. Air Force (cancelled 1979)
MX—transportable launcher for ICBM, U.S. Air Force
General Support Rocket System, ground-to-ground weapon, U.S. Army

Boeing Vertol Co.
Philadelphia, PA
Joseph Mallen, President

CH-47 Chinook Helicopter, U.S. Army and foreign contractors
CH-46 Helicopter Update, U.S. Army

Boeing Military Airplane Co.
Wichita, KS
Lionel D. Alford, President

B-52—offensive avionics update, U.S. Air Force
B-52—cruise missile carrier installation, U.S. Air Force
B-1 bomber avionics, U.S. Air Force
CX long-range jet transport design, U.S. Air Force

Boeing Marine Systems
Renton, WA
R.E. Bateman, President

Pegasus patrol hydrofoil missileships, U.S. Navy

C. Contracting History

Boeing has long been a major DoD contractor as well as the dominant commercial air transport manufacturer in the U.S. and abroad. Its principal defense contracts have involved transport aircraft, missiles, aircraft avionics, and helicopters. The company's defense and commercial work have always been closely linked. The 707 Jetliner, for instance, also serves as the airframe for the Air Force's KC-135 tanker and for the E-3A Airborne Warning and Control Plane (AWACS). Boeing competed unsuccessfully for the Air Force's Giant C-5A Transport and developed a wide-bodied 747 as a commercial plane, which is also the airframe (E-4B) for the Airborne Command Post. Aside from the KC-135 and the E-3A, Boeing has not won a major military airframe contract in the past decade.

Following a build-up of staff in the previous decade, Boeing, like other aerospace contractors, ran into market changes in the early 1970s. According to *Aviation Week* (20 June 1970), "Then the long slide began, greased by a softening of the commercial aircraft market, the phase-down of such government efforts as the Saturn booster program and the loss of such sought-after programs as the Navy's

Advanced Surface Missile System and—most recently—the USAF strategic bomber." In addition, the space shuttle fuel tank contract went to Martin-Marietta, and funding for Boeing's supersonic transport work was cancelled by Congress. Boeing responded by reducing its Seattle area employment by 56,000 jobs and attempting to diversify into such areas as mass transit and community development (*The Christian Science Monitor*, 16 Sept. 1971).

New defense contracts and overseas commercial sales were vital to Boeing's business growth (*The Wall Street Journal*, 6 June 1972). In the early 1970s Boeing was awarded new DoD contracts in a variety of areas: SRAM missiles for B-52 bombers, Minuteman III ICBM work, development of the E-3A AWACS, avionics integration on the B-1 bomber, the inertial upper stage of NASA's space shuttle, modifications to the CH-46 and CH-47 helicopters, and the development of a STOL cargo plane, the YC-14.

The E-3A contract was seen as an important element in Boeing's recovery. The justification for this program shifted continually from a warning system based in the U.S., to tactical air control in Europe, to radar jamming. According to *The New York Times* (7 Jan. 1975), "In a way, the AWACS has been a plane in search of a mission ever since it was conceived several years ago when the Boeing company was in serious financial difficulty on its transport program. To some in the Pentagon, the plane was flippantly known as the 'B.B.O.' for 'Boeing bail out'." Air Force efforts to obtain AWACS funds from Congress were backed by Washington Senators Jackson and Magnuson (*The New York Times*, 29 Oct. 1975; *The Washington Post*, 23 Feb. 1975).

Helicopter contracts to Boeing's Vertol Division were also a source of problems in 1970s. Vertol lost two major awards, the UTTAS (Army) and the LAMPS (Navy), to United Technologies in 1976 and 1977. The Army, however, awarded CH-46 and CH-47 work to the company. The General Accounting Office (GAO) suggested that the CH-47 program would constitute virtually the only military work at Vertol, implying that "the Army's decision to upgrade the CH-47 fleet was partly aimed at keeping Boeing Vertol in the helicopter business, though it notes that the Army denies any such aim" (*The Wall Street Journal*, 27 Feb. 1978).

Overseas commercial aircraft sales were the other key element in Boeing's recovery. Such sales accounted for over 70% of all Boeing's commercial business in the early 1970s.

In the late 1970s Boeing continued an active effort in both commercial and defense markets. Corporate fortunes have soared on the strength of renewed commercial aircraft orders for the 727, 737, and 747. In addition, Boeing has virtually no U.S. competition for the next generation of commercial air transport and is actively marketing its 757 and 767. The latter program, on which the company has spent sizeable development funds, has attracted a large volume of orders.

By 1979 Boeing had over $12 billion in backlog orders for commercial aircraft and was expanding company production facilities and employment.

Further efforts in the defense market are being made. Boeing received awards for engineering and development work on the MX missile system. In 1979, it became known that the company's Washington office personnel had telexed classified information on the Air Force strategic missile plans to Seattle, "in such a way that it was probably intercepted by the Soviet Union" (*The New York Times*, 2 March 1979). As a result several Boeing and DoD employees had their security clearances suspended for a time (*The Wall Street Journal*, 29 Feb. 1979).

In late 1979, the company further enhanced its capabilities for competing for defense contracts by creating a new operating division: the Boeing Military Airplane Company, which combines Seattle research and development operations with corporate activity in Wichita. Boeing also competed with General Dynamics for the Air Force's air-launched cruise missile contract for which it was awarded a major contract in 1980. It has also received continued contract awards for updating the B-52 (in Kansas), for the AWACS, and for helicopter modifications.

D. U.S. Government-Owned, Company-Operated Plants

Total company floor space: 37,829,000 sq. ft.
Leased from U.S. Government: 424,000 sq. ft. (1.1%)
Total Lease Cost: Not disclosed
Location: Air Force Plant 77
　　　　　　Ogden, UT
　　　　　　424,000 sq. ft.
Use: Missiles
Other GOCO equipment: Office space, installations and equipment at various government bases
Cost: Not disclosed

RESEARCH AND DEVELOPMENT

Major Defense/Space R&D Projects

Air-launched cruise missile, U.S. Air Force
MX transportable launcher, U.S. Air Force
General support rocket system, U.S. Army
AMST-YC-14 transport, U.S. Air Force
Inertial upper stage-space shuttle, U.S. Air Force/NASA

TABLE II
Research and Development
($ in M.)

	1970	1971	1972	1973	1974	1975	1976	1977	1978	1979
I. U.S. Government Contracts										
DoD	$180.1	285.8	298.6	401.5	428.2	833.9	438.0	524.6	669.6	697.6
NASA	$158.0	114.4	94.2	75.5	60.0	46.2	60.3	69.1	85.7	101.5
Total	$338.1	400.2	392.8	477.0	488.2	880.1	498.3	593.7	755.3	799.1
II. Company-sponsored R&D	$ 66.1	57.8	51.6	128.7	-78.5	188.1	190.6	221.6	276.1	525.0
III. IR&D	NA	NA	NA	$ 27.4	31.6	34.6	35.6	37.5	39.9	NA

I. From DoD yearly publication "500 Contractors Receiving the Largest Dollar Volume of Military Prime Contract Awards for RDT&E" and NASA Annual Procurement Reports.

II. Prior to 1973 disclosed as "independent research and development." From 1973 on: "Company sponsored research and development . . . not recoverable under contracts and charged directly to earnings as incurred amounted to approximately . . ." (10K, 1979)

III. Company-sponsored R&D costs charged to DoD as disclosed by DoD.

BOARD OF DIRECTORS

William M. Batten (1968)
Chairman of the Board and Chief Executive Officer, New York Stock Exchange
Past Corporate Employment:
J.C. Penney (1935-74); (Chairman of the Board-1964).
Corporate Directorships:
American Telephone and Telegraph ($244,878,000); Citicorp; Texas Instruments ($373,631,000).
Key Association Memberships:
Business Council (Chairman, 1971-72); Committee for Economic Development (Trustee).
Shares owned:
3,750

Harold J. Haynes (1974)
Chairman of the Board and Chief Executive Officer, Standard Oil Company of California ($241,451,000)
Past Corporate Employment:
Standard Oil Company of California (1947-present) (Chairman-1974).
Corporate Directorships:
Citicorp
Key Association Memberships:
Business Council; Committee for Economic Development, National Petroleum Council.
Key Educational and Research Ties:
California Institute of Technology (Trustee); Stanford Research Institute (Director)
Shares owned:
600

Harold Walter Haynes (1966)
Executive Vice President and Chief Financial Officer, Boeing
Past Corporate Employment:
Boeing Company (1954-present)
Corporate Directorships:
Pacific National Bank, WA (see Basic Data, Lending Banks); The Bank of Investment and Credit, Berne, Switzerland.
Shares owned:
17,950

Stanley Hiller, Jr. (1976)
Chairman of the Board, Baker International Corp. (mining and oil equipment).

Past Corporate Employment:
Founder, President and General Manager, Hiller Aircraft Corp.; Partner, Hiller Investment Company (1965-present); Chairman of the Board, Baker International Corp.
Corporate Directorships:
Benicia Industries; Crocker National Corp. (see Basic Data: Banking); Arcata National Corp.; ELTRA Corp. ($30,000).
Key Association Memberships:
American Institute for Aeronautics and Astronautics; National Defense Transportation Society (Distinguished Service Award, 1958); American Helicopter Society (Honorary Fellow).
Shares owned:
2,100

Rene McPherson (1980)
Chairman and Chief Executive Officer, Dana Corp
Corporate Directorships:
Brown Brothers Corp., Ltd.; Gulf United Corp.; Manufacturers Hanover Corp.; Standard Oil Co. (Ohio)
Shares owned:
100

Lee L. Morgan (1980)
Chairman and Chief Executive Officer, Caterpillar Tractor Co.
Corporate Directorships:
Commercial National Bank; First Chicago Corp.; Minnesota Mining & Mfg. Co.
Shares owned:
500

David Packard (1978)
Chairman of the Board, Hewlett-Packard Co. ($85,830,000)
Past Corporate Employment:
Co-founder and Partner, Hewlett-Packard Co. (1939-present); (President-1947; Chief Executive Officer-1965).
Government Positions:
Deputy Secretary of Defense (1969-71); Member of President's Commission on Personnel Interchange (1972-74).
Corporate Directorships:
Hewlett-Packard Co.; Caterpillar Tractor Co. ($16,781,000); Standard Oil Co. of California ($241,451,000).
Key Association Memberships:
Business Roundtable; Business Council; Institute of Electrical & Electronics Engineers; Trilateral Commission.
Key Educational and Research Positions:
Stanford Research Institute ($26,296,000) (Director 1958-69).
Shares owned:
1,500

Charles M. Piggott (1972)
President and Chief Executive Officer, PACCAR, Inc. ($12,897,000) (transportation equipment)
Past Corporate Employment:
PACCAR, Inc. (1959-present); (President-1965).
Corporate Directorships:
SAFECO Corp.; Citicorp; Seattle First National Bank (see Basic Data: Lending Banks); Standard Oil Company of California ($241,451,000).
Key Association Memberships:
Business Council.
Key Educational and Research Positions:
Stanford Research Institute (Director) ($26,296,000).
Shares owned:
1,500

William Reed (1951) retired 1979
Managing Partner, Simpson Reed and Co. (capital management)
Past Corporate Employment:
Chairman (ret.), Crown Simpson Pulp Co., Simpson Timber Co., Simpson Lee Paper Co.; President, Lumbermen's Mercury Co.; President, State Bank Shelton; President, Malahat Logging Company; Executive V.P., Rayonier, Inc.
Government Positions:
Head, U.S. Delegation Economic Committee for Europe (1960); Member, Washington Representative National Committee (1940-44).
Corporate Directorships:
Simlog Corp.; Simpson Timber Co.; Crown Simpson Co.; Burlington Northern Railway; Seattle First National Bank (see Basic Data: Lending Banks).
Key Educational and Research Positions:
California Institute of Technology (1957-70) ($2,218,000) (Director 1957-65, Member, President's Council).
Shares owned:
6,508

David Skinner (1962)
President, Skinner Corp. (diversified investments)
Corporate Directorships:
Skinner Corp.; BanCal Tri-State Corp.; Pacific Marine Schwabacker, Inc.; SAFECO Corp.; Pacific Northwest Bell Telephone Co. (subs. AT&T, See Batten) ($296,000).
Shares owned:
1,500

Malcolm T. Stamper (1972)
President, Boeing Co.
Past Corporate Employment:
General Motors Corp. (1949-62); Boeing Co. (1962-present).
Corporate Directorships:
Federal Reserve Bank of San Francisco; Nordstrom Co.
Key Association Memberships:
National Alliance of Businessmen.
Shares owned:
1,458

George H. Weyerhaeuser (1962)
President and Chief Executive Officer, Weyerhaeuser Co.
Past Corporate Employment:
Weyerhaeuser Company (1949-present).
Corporate Directorships:
Puget Sound National Bank; Equitable Life Assurance Society of U.S.; SAFECO Corp.; Standard Oil Co. of California ($241,451,000).
Key Association Memberships:
Business Council.
Key Educational and Research Positions:
Rand Corp. (Director); Stanford Research Institute (Advisory Council).
Shares owned:
1,800

T.A. Wilson (1966)
Chairman of the Board and Chief Executive Officer, Boeing Co.
Past Corporate Employment:
Boeing Company (1943-present).
Corporate Directorships:
Seattle First National Bank (see Basic Data: Lending Banks); PACCAR, Inc. ($12,897,000).
Key Association Memberships:
Business Council; American Institute of Aeronautics and Astronautics (Fellow).
Shares owned:
49,500

PERSONNEL TRANSFERS

Table III
(DoD   1970-79)
(NASA 1974-79)

	Total	Air Force	Army	Navy	Office of Secretary of Defense	Other
DoD Military to Boeing	316	240	40	29	6	1
DoD Civilian to Boeing	35	16	2	5	10	2
NASA to Boeing	3					
Boeing to DoD	37	15	8	3	9	2
Boeing to NASA	7					
Total	398	271	50	37	25	5

Appearances of Potential Conflict of Interest (see Chapter 6): 16

1. DoD to Boeing

Babione, Dale R.
  DoD:
    Deputy Asst. Secretary of Defense for Procurement.
  Boeing:
    August 1979, Director of Government Business Relations.

Ball, Edward L., Jr.
  DoD:
    Deputy Director, Office of Undersecretary of Defense for Research & Engineering.
  Boeing:
    November 1972, Director of Planning (Long Range and Operational).

Fowler, Richard
  DoD:
    Program Analyst working on execution of specific systems and programs, Air Force Headquarters.
  Boeing:
    April 1978, Market Analyst, providing guidance between Boeing's management and DoD weapons system acquisitions.

Hargis, Calvin
  DoD:
    Deputy to Undersecretary of the Air Force for Research & Development, for advice on all aircraft development programs.
  Boeing:
    July 1974, Deputy Director, Compass Cope Program.

Harwood, Elliot B.
  DoD:
    Acting Asst. Director for Engineering Management, developing DoD policy for research and development, in the Office of Undersecretary of Defense for Research & Engineering.
  Boeing:
    July 1973, Manager of corporate Independent Research & Development (IR&D) activities, administering and documenting in-house research and development.

Plymale, Benjamin T. (see Advisory Committees)
  DoD:
    Deputy to Director of Defense Research and Engineering for Strategic and Space Systems research and development on strategic offensive and defensive systems.
  Boeing:
    July 1972, V.P. product development, for management of new business activities, General Manager, space and ballistic groups.

Quinn, Gary
  DoD:
    Program Manager, overseas defense research, Defense Advanced Research Projects Agency.
  Boeing:
    June 1973, Analyst of corporate international business development.

Sullivan, Leonard
  DoD:
    Asst. Secretary of Defense for Program Analysis and Evaluation.
  Boeing:
    April 1976, Independent consultant on defense and transportation policy.

Taylor, James
  DoD:
    Aerospace engineer on flight simulators, Air Force.
  Boeing:
    July 1978, Consultant on customer relations and management.

2. Boeing to NASA

Hauler, Elliot B.
Boeing:
   Director of Marketing, international sales, Boeing Aerospace.
NASA:
   December 1975, Director, industry affairs.

3. "Revolving Door"

Jones, Thomas K. (see Advisory Committees)
Boeing:
   Design and supervisory engineer and Deputy program manager.
DoD:
   August 1971, Staff asst. in SALT Group to Deputy Director of Defense for Research and Engineering
Boeing:
   September 1974, Program and products evaluation manager.

Lin, Hua (see Advisory Committees)
Boeing:
   Chief of missile technology, Minuteman program; Program manager, site defense; Production development manager, strategic systems.
DoD:
   June 1975, Asst. Director of Offensive Systems, reviewing and evaluating programs and proposals for research and development for offensive strategic deterrent weapons, in the office of the Deputy Director of Defense for Research and Engineering (Space Systems).
Boeing:
   May 1978, Chief scientist, engineering technology and applied research.

McDougal, James
Boeing:
   Specialist, engineering microwave area.
DoD:
   November 1973, Engineer, Air Force Avionics Laboratory.
Boeing:
   January 1978, senior specialist engineer, Independent Research and Development, for lethal defense of manned bomber.

Nagel, Adelbert
Boeing:
   Research engineer and supervisor.

NASA:
August 1970, Head, Hypersonic Aircraft Systems Research Branch; then Chief of Aeronautical Systems Division, technical and administrative supervision, Langley Research Center.

Boeing:
September 1978, Supervision, product development, manager of solar power satellite Independent Research and Development.

Shrontz, Frank
DoD:
Asst. Secretary of of the Air Force for Installations and Logistics; Asst. Secretary of Defense for Installations and Logistics (Procurement, Logistics and Management Production).

Boeing:
January 1977, V.P., contract administration and planning; V.P. and General Manager, Boeing Commercial Airplane Division.

DoD:
No date, Policy advisor for procurement, production, logistics, installations, Office of Asst. Secretary of Defense for Installations and Logistics.

Tiffany, Charles
Boeing:
Chief, structures and materials research and development.

DoD:
June 1971, Engineering advisor on aircraft structures problems, U.S. Air Force Systems Command, Wright-Patterson Air Force Base.

Boeing:
January 1979, Director of engineering, directing government-contracted and company-funded engineering efforts.

Comments

1. Three Boeing transfers have had ties to the SALT talks: T.K. Jones, John A. Blaylock and Gordon Frew all served in the SALT task force in the Office of Secretary of Defense. Boeing has multiple interests in strategic weaponry discussed in such talks, including the Minuteman and cruise missiles.

2. Five transfers have taken place between Boeing's Vertol division and Army offices involved with helicopter work: Valentin Berger, Ronald Gormont, Wilbur Hogan, Joseph Moro and Robert Oehrli. Vertol is doing major helicopter overhaul work for the Army.
3. Policy Statement—"It has been our policy for a number of years to make no post-retirement offers to either military or government personnel prior to their resignation or announced retirement." (M.T. Stamper, President)

POLITICAL ACTION COMMITTEE

Name: Boeing Civic Pledge Program
Total Expenditures (10/76-5/80): $260,850
Total Contributions to Federal Campaigns (10/76-5/80): $85,655
(Boeing's PAC was formed in 1971. This data, which begins with 1976, is incomplete for the years given because of the unusual structure of Boeing's PAC. See Chapter 8)

Key
(D) = Democrat
(R) = Republican
(C) = Recipient was a candidate and not elected to that office.
 + = Candidate is also a member of a key Congressional committee.
 * = Candidate is a member of two committees, but contribution s/he received is only listed once to avoid being double-counted in the total for this section.

A. Contributions to Federal Candidates in States with Boeing Production Facilities (Key Geographic Locations)

WASHINGTON
Boeing plants located in Seattle (dist. 1, 7), Kent (dist. 6, 7) and Renton (dist. 7)

Senate

Slade Gorton (R) (C)	$ 25
+Sen. Warren Magnuson (D)	$3,900

House

Rep. Don Bonker (D-3)	$ 600
+Rep. Norman Dicks (D-6)	$1,175
Ron Dunlap (R-7) (C)	$ 225
Rep. Thomas S. Foley (D-5)	$ 200
Rep. Michael E. Lowry (D-7)	$ 800
+Rep. Mike McCormack (D-4)	$ 800
Rep. Joel Pritchard (R-1)	$ 50
Rep. Allan B. Swift (D-2)	$ 400

Total Washington: $8,175
% Total Federal Contributions: 9.5%

KANSAS

Boeing plants located in Wichita (dist. 4, 5)

Senate

Sen. Robert Dole (R)	$ 0
(received contributions as presidential cand. See F)	
+Sen. Nancy Kassebaum (R)	$ 325

House

+Rep. Dan Glickman (D-4)	$ 509
Rep. James E. Jeffries (R-2)	$ 225
Rep. Robert E. Whittaker (R-5)	$ 575
+Rep. Larry Winn (R-3)	$ 450

Total Kansas: $2,084
% Total Federal Contributions: 2.4%

PENNSYLVANIA

Boeing plants located in Philadelphia (dist. 1, 2, 3, 4, 13)

Senate

no contributions

House

Rep. Donald Bailey (D-21)	$ 100
Rep. Robert W. Edgar (D-7)	$ 220

Jim Nelligan (R-11) (C) $ 50
Rep. Gus Yatron (D-6) $ 100

Total Pennsylvania: $470
% Total Federal Contributions: .5%

Total to Key Geographic Locations: $10,729
% Total Federal Contributions: 12.53%

B. Contributions to Members of Key Congressional Committees

Senate Armed Services Committee

Cohen	$ 200	Morgan	$ 500
Helms	$ 50	Stennis	$ 200
Humphrey, Gordon	$ 300	Thurmond	$ 500
Jepsen	$ 250	Warner	$ 250
McIntyre	$ 325		

House Armed Services Committee

Bailey	$ 100	Ichord	$ 525
Byron	$ 500	Lloyd, James	$ 300
Courter	$ 150	Mavroules	$ 200
Daniel, Robert	$ 300	McDonald	$ 200
Davis	$ 500	Mitchell	$ 300
Dickinson	$ 500	Spence	$ 700
Downey	$ 100	Stump	$ 400
Hillis	$ 455	Trible	$ 300
Holt	$ 400	White	$ 400

Senate Defense Appropriations Subcommittee

Garn	$ 525	Magnuson (Chairman)	$3,900
Hollings	$1,000	Stennis	*
Inouye	$ 600		

House Defense Appropriations Subcommittee

Addabbo	$ 200	Giaimo	$ 400
Dicks	$1,175	Whitten	$ 500
Edwards	$ 800		

Senate Committee on Commerce, Science and Transportation
Subcommittee on Aviation

Kassebaum	$ 325	Pressler	$ 100
Inouye	*		

Subcommittee on Science, Technology and Space

Ford	$ 500	Long	$ 500
Kassebaum	*	Schmitt	$ 500

House Committee on Science and Technology

Blanchard	$ 200	Lloyd, James		*
Carney	$ 200	Lujan	$	350
Davis, Robert	$ 225	Mavroules		*
Dornan	$ 325	McCormack	$	800
Downey	*	Pursell	$	100
Flippo	$ 500	Rudd	$	420
Gammage	$ 170	White		*
Glickman	$ 509	Winn	$	450
Goldwater, Jr.	$ 500	Wydler	$	200
Harkin	$ 200	Young, Robert	$	150
Kramer	$ 200			

Senate Committee on Environment and Public Works
Subcommittee on Transportation

Pressler	*	Randolph	$ 300

House Committee on Public Works and Transportation
Subcommittee on Aviation

Abdnor	$ 120	Johnson, Harold	$ 325
Anderson, Glenn	$ 300	Mineta	$ 200
Boner	$ 200	Rahall	$ 100
Flippo	*	Snyder	$ 205
Goldwater, Jr.	*	Stump	*
Hefner	$ 250	Taylor	$ 200
		Young, Robert	*

Total to Key Committees: $27,629
% Total Federal Contributions: 33.3%

C. Contributions to Other Influential Members of Congress

Rep. John Rhodes (R-AZ) (Minority Leader)	$ 800
Rep. James Wright (D-TX) (Majority Leader)	$1,000

Total to Other Influentials: 1,800
% Total Federal Contributions: 2.1%

D. Contributions to Other Federal Candidates

Senate

Bayh (D-IN)	$ 275	Obenshain (R-VA) (C)	$ 225
Boschwitz (R-MN)	$ 200	Sasser (D-TN)	$ 300
Chafee (R-RI)	$ 200	Simpson (R-WY)	$ 500
Church (D-ID)	$ 500	Stewart (D-AL)	$ 500
Durenberger (R-MN)	$ 300	Stone (D-FL)	$1,000
Mathias (R-MD)	$ 405	Symms (R-ID)	$ 25
Matsunaga (D-HI)	$ 500		

House

Alexander (D-AR)	$ 400	Kelly (R-FL)	$ 300
Ashbrook (R-OH)	$ 220	Lent (R-NY)	$ 300
Bevill (D-AL)	$ 300	Livingston (R-LA)	$ 250
Biaggi (D-NY)	$ 300	Long (D-LA)	$ 250
Bolling (D-MO)	$ 250	Marriot (R-UT)	$ 500
Breaux (D-LA)	$ 300	McEwen (R-NY)	$ 200
Campbell, Jr. (R-SC)	$ 200	McKay (D-UT)	$ 300
Clausen (R-CA)	$ 300	Meyner (D-NJ)	$ 100
Deckard (R-IN)	$ 200	Moorhead (R-CA)	$ 325
Derrick (D-SC)	$ 450	Murphy (D-NY)	$ 275
Derwinski (R-IL)	$ 300	Neal (D-NC)	$ 300
Devine (R-OH)	$ 300	Okver (R-VA) (C)	$ 25
Duncan (D-OR)	$ 250	Pepper (D-FL)	$ 250
Evans (D-IN)	$ 200	Shelby (D-AL)	$ 100
Florio (D-NJ)	$ 250	Slack (D-WV)	$ 200
Grassley (R-IA)	$ 550	Smith (R-OR) (C)	$ 25
Hansen (R-ID)	$ 315	Staggers (D-WV)	$ 250
Hubbard (D-KY)	$ 200	Ullman (D-OR)	$ 500
Hyde (R-IL)	$ 200	Vento (DFL-MN)	$ 225
Ireland (D-FL)	$ 250	Vander Jagt (R-MI)	$ 300
Jenrette (D-SC)	$ 250	Whittaker (R-KS)	$ 50
Jones (D-TN)	$ 225	Young (R-AK)	$ 250

Total to Other Federal Candidates: $16,415
% Total Federal Contributions: 19.2%

E. Contributions to Party Campaign Committees

Republican federal-level committees: $21,716
Democratic federal-level committees: $10,700

Total to Party Committees: $32,416
% Total Federal Contributions: 37.8%

F. Contributions to Presidential Candidates

John Anderson (I)	$ 25
Howard Baker (R)	$ 110
George Bush (R)	$ 305
Jimmy Carter (D)	$1,075
Philip Crane (R)	$ 50
Robert Dole (R)	$2,130
Lyndon La Rouche (D)	$ 10
Ronald Reagan (R)	$ 220

Total to Presidential Candidates: $3,925
% Total Federal Contributions: 4.6%

WASHINGTON OPERATIONS

Washington Office:
1700 N. Moore St., 20th Floor, Rosslyn, VA 22209

Director:
Russell B. Light, Executive V.P., Washington office

Staff:
Dale R. Babione, Director, Gov't. Business Relations
(see Personnel Transfers)
Gene M. Bradley, Director, Congressional Affairs
Joan L. Huntley, Manager, Congressional Affairs

Activities:
1. International: Gathering information on international matters and U.S. policy; assisting foreign customers in Washington to make contact with diplomats; reporting to Boeing management.
2. National Affairs and Strategic Planning: Gathering information on national economic, political and social issues; handling public relations; reporting to company management; coordinating company-Government contacts on national issues and trends.
3. Government Relations: Preparing fact sheets for members of Congress on Boeing programs; following legislation affecting company interests; arranging company management testimony; preparing bills and amendments; gathering data on members for political contributions; arranging visits to Boeing facilities.
4. Boeing Aerospace, Boeing Vertol, Boeing Commercial Airplane all maintain staff to monitor specific programs and products in Executive branch, gather information on new business possibilities and government plans, and maintain Executive branch contacts.

Registered Lobbyists:

	Receipts	Expenditures	Years
Dale R. Babione 1700 North Moore St. Rosslyn, VA	*	*	79
Edward M. Bond 1700 North Moore St. Rosslyn, VA	$ 2,100.00	$ 633.90	79

Name & Address		
Gene M. Bradley 1700 North Moore St. Rosslyn, VA	$ 7,487.00	$ 7,714.25 76-79
Thomas H. Brownell 23830 30th Ave. South Kent, WA	$ 405.80	$ 1,183.93 79
E. Keith Cooper 1700 North Moore St. Rosslyn, VA	$ 5,796.00	$ 3,076.35 76-77
Nancy Fussell 1700 North Moore St. Rosslyn, VA	$ 30.44	* 79
Joan L. Huntley 1700 North Moore St. Rosslyn, VA	$ 2,143.67	$ 1,014.89 76-79
Gilbert W. Keyes PO Box 3999 Seattle, WA	$ 2,283.60	$ 3,000.00 77-79
Clifford C. LaPlante 1700 North Moore St. Rosslyn, VA	$11,385.00	$ 1,914.03 76-78
Russell B. Light 1700 North Moore St. Rosslyn, VA	$14,671.44	$10,507.40 76-79
W. Thomas MacNew PO Box 1658 Philadelphia, PA (for Boeing Vertol)	*	$ 1,600.00 78
Ronald E. McWilliams 1700 North Moore St. Rosslyn, VA	$ 1,155.77	$ 6,695.60 77-79
Garry C. Porter 11356 Southeast Black Rd. Olalla, WA	$ 1,640.00	$ 781.00 78-79
Robert P. St. Louis 1700 North Moore St. Rosslyn, VA	$ 3,000.00	$ 2,287.49 79
Clyde Summerville 1700 North Moore St. Rosslyn, VA	$ 130.00	$ 72.00 79
TOTAL	**$52,228.72**	**$40,481.47**

*No figures reported; quarterly report was filed.

DEFENSE-RELATED TRADE ASSOCIATION MEMBERSHIPS

Aerospace Industries Association
Air Force Association
American Defense Preparedness Association
American Institute of Aeronautics and Astronautics
American League for Exports and Security Assistance
Armed Forces Communication and Electronics Association
National Association for Remotely-Piloted Vehicles
National Council of Technical Service Industries
National Security Industrial Association

ADVISORY COMMITTEE MEMBERSHIPS

1976-78: 23

Bateman, Robert E.
  (V.P. and General Manager, Boeing Marine
   DoD—Defense Science Board, 1978

Boileau, Oliver C.
  (President, Boeing Aerospace) (moved to General Dynamics, 1980)
    DoD—Financial Management Advisory Committee, 1976
    DoD—Defense Science Board, 1976, 1977
    DoD—Joint Strategic Target Planning Staff, Scientific Advisory Group, 1976, 1977, 1978

Boullion, E.H.
  (President, Boeing Commercial Airplane)
    DoD—Military Aircraft Committee, 1976, 1977, 1978

Brock, Robert
  (V.P. and General Manager, Boeing Aerospace)
    DoD—Army Scientific Advisory Panel, 1976

Cosgrove, Benjamin
    NASA—Research and Technology Advisory Council, Panel on Aviation Safety and Operating Systems, 1977

Hamilton, William L.
(V.P., Planning and International Business)
    NASA—Research and Technology Advisory Council, Committee on Aerodynamics and Configurations, 1977-78
    DoD—Defense Intelligence Agency, Scientific Advisory Council, 1976, 1977
    DoD—Defense Science Board, 1976, 1977

James, Russell
    DoD—Board of Advisors to the Superintendent, Naval Post Graduate School, 1976

Jones, Thomas
(Program and Product Evaluation Manager) (see Personnel Transfers)
    DoD—Defense Science Board, 1976, 1977

Lin, Hua
(Chief Scientist, Engineering Technology and Applied Research and Chief of Missile Technology) (see Personnel Transfers)
    DoD—Army Science Board, 1978

Plymale, Benjamin T.
(V.P., Product Development and General Manager, Space and Ballistics Groups) (see Personnel Transfers)
    DoD—Defense Nuclear Agency, Scientific Advisory Group on Effects, 1976, 1977, 1978
    DoD—Defense Science Board, 1977, 1978

Sebestyn, George S.
(V.P. and General Manager, Navy Systems and Advanced Products Division) (see Personnel Transfers)
    DoD—Defense Science Board, 1976, 1977
    DoD—Naval Research Advisory Committee, 1976

Selby, William L.
    DoD—Defense Science Board, 1976

Sellers, Robert
    DoD—Defense Science Board, 1976

Swan, Walter C.
    NASA—Research and Technology Advisory Council, Committee on Aeronautical Propulsion, 1976, 1977
    DoD—U.S. Air Force Scientific Advisory Board, 1976, 1977, 1978

Thornton, Dean
(V.P., Finance, Contracts and International Operations, Boeing Commercial Airplane Company)
DoD—Financial Management Advisory Committee, 1976

Turner, Jonathan
NASA—Research and Technology Advisory Council, Committee on Materials and Structures, 1976, 1977

Comment:
Boeing also had members on five advisory boards to the Department of Transportation concerned with aeronautical communications and three to the Department of Commerce concerned with the multilateral trade negotiations.

ENTERTAINMENT

President M.T. Stamper informed the Joint Committee on Defense Production that Boeing complies with government regulations on favors, gratuities and entertainment; and costs for entertainment are not charged to contracts.

Entertaining:
Nothing disclosed over $100 per guest; no facilities disclosed.

Hospitality Suites:
1973: 16, 1974: 27, 1975: 23
Including National Security Industrial Association, Air Force Association, Association of the U.S. Army, Navy League and Marine Corps Anniversary functions.

Tickets:
1973-75: 192 season tickets, some made available to Government officials.

Air Travel:
Leased jet transports five or six times for business travel to officers, directors and employees; not made available to Government officials.

Disclosure:
Good

QUESTIONABLE PAYMENTS

Boeing was under investigation by the SEC from 1975 to 1978 concerning sales practices surrounding overseas commercial aircraft sales between 1971 and 1977. Boeing denied that it had made any illegal political contributions or maintained any off-the-books funds for questionable payments (*The Wall Street Journal*, 13 Feb. 1976).

In 1976, however, Boeing disclosed that it had paid $70 m. in sales commissions in connection with the sale of commercial aircraft in the early 1970s (Ibid., 5 March 1976). A large proportion of such payments had gone to consultants, several of whom were foreign Government officials, but none of whom "had authority to purchase or approve the purchase of the Company's products or services" (Company *8K*, Feb. 1976).

Boeing also disclosed that it had entertained foreign and domestic airline officials, but denied any questionable payment or bribes. In addition, Boeing sales representatives overseas suggested that sales had been lost in Japan and Pakistan, because the company had refused to pay bribes (*The Wall Street Journal*, 14 May 1976).

Boeing was reluctant to supply the SEC with documentation on its sales practices and commissions and resisted public disclosure of information supplied the SEC containing the names of 18 consultants involved in Boeing's overseas aircraft sales. Boeing asked the Federal Government to protect this information as proprietary (Ibid., 16 Dec. 1976).

Gradually, instances of other possibly questionable sales activities have come to light. According to *The Wall Street Journal* (17 Jan. 1977), payments were allegedly made in Venezuela in connection with the sale of a 737 for the use of Venezuelan President Carlos Andres Perez. In another case, rebates from a Boeing sale of the 747 may have been paid by Japan Air Lines to Japanese politicians. Boeing denied any such payments (*The New York Times*, 16 Feb. 1977).

In July 1978, the SEC accused Boeing of failing to disclose $52 m. in questionable foreign payments between 1971 and 1978, including $27 m. to officials of seven foreign governments. These included officials in Kuwait, Saudi Arabia, the United Arab Emirates, Iran, Nepal, Japan and Egypt (Ibid., 29 July 1978). Boeing neither admitted nor denied the allegations in the complaint, nor were the payments described as bribes or illegal. Boeing consented to an injunction prohibiting the company from failing to disclose the conduct described in the complaint and from any false or misleading statements (Company *10K* for 1978). A special committee of the board (David Packard, William Batten and Harold J. Haynes) was appointed to examine Boeing's disclosure and policy. The committee completed its internal investigation in February 1979, finding Boeing's internal investigation "reasonably complete" and its disclosures in 1978 "reasonably adequate and accurate" (Company *10K* for 1978). In its 10K for 1979, Boeing noted that the I.R.S. was "continuing to review the company's income tax returns" for 1973-78, including an investigation of "the company's practices relative to commissions and consulting fees paid by the company in connection with its sales to foreign customers." The company pointed out that it felt the payments were "properly deductible." Boeing also noted that it was cooperating with a Justice Department investigation of "foreign sales and marketing activities."

DISCLOSURE

Poor.

GENERAL DYNAMICS

BASIC CORPORATE AND CONTRACTING DATA

A. Corporate Data

General Dynamics Corporation
Pierre Laclede Center
St.Louis, MO 63105

Fortune 500 (1979): 83
Fiscal Year: Jan. 1—Dec. 31

Chairman:
David S. Lewis (1979 salary: $688,000)

President:
Oliver C. Boileau (1979 salary: NA)

Auditor:
Arthur Andersen & Co.
One South Memorial Dr.
St. Louis, MO

Outside Legal Counsel:
Busby, Rehm & Leonard
900 17th Street, N.W.
Washington, DC

TABLE I
Corporate Data
($ in M.)

	1970	1971	1972	1973	1974	1975	1976	1977	1978	1979
Sales	$2,223.6	1,868.8	1,539.4	1,641.8	1,968.4	2,160.0	2,553.5	2,901.2	3,205.2	4,059.6
Net Income	$ (6.9)	21.6	24.6	39.3	52.2	84.5'	99.6	103.4	(48.1)	185.2
Dept. of Defense Contracts	$1,183.2	1,489.0	1,289.2	707.2	1,853.2	1,288.8	1,073.0	1,371.5	4,153.6	3,492.1
Rank	2	2	3	9	1	6	7	8	1	1
NASA Contracts	$ 38.0	50.8	66.6	80.4	79.5	85.3	76.3	78.7	64.4	46.9
Rank	14	13	8	5	5	4	4	6	12	14
DoD/NASA Contracts as % of Sales	54.9%	82.4	88.7	48.0	98.2	63.6	45.0	50.0	131.6	87.2
Government Sales	NA	NA	NA	$1,001.5	1,082.6	1,317.6	1,685.3	1,972.8	2,115.4	2,679.3
Government Sales as % of Sales	..	..	..	61.0%	55.0	61.0	66.0	68.0	66.0	68.0
Foreign Military Sales Contracts	$ 28.0	11.3	16.9	14.3	13.5	73.1	45.8	303.3	1,475.5	518.0
Rank	4	9	14	14	24	15	18	4	1	2
FMS Contracts as % of Sales	1.3%	0.6	1.1	0.9	0.7	3.4	1.8	10.5	46.0	12.8
Overseas and Export Sales	NA	NA	NA	NA	NA	NA	NA	NA	NA	NA
Overseas and Export Sales as % of Sales	min.**	min.	min.	min.	min.	min.	min.	min.	min.	min.
Employees	80,900	66,900	60,900	62,400	63,600	63,800	71,600	73,300	77,100	81,600

'General Dynamics states that "export sales were less than 10% of total sales." (10K, 1978)
**Minimal

C. Stanley Dees, Sellers, Conner & Cunio
1625 K St., N.W.
Washington, DC

Jackson, Walker, Winstead, Cantwell & Miller
4300 First National Bank Building
Dallas, TX
   (security counsel)

Jenner & Block
One IBM Plaza
Chicago, IL
   (see Board of Directors: Albert Jenner)

Advertising/Public Relations Agencies:

Dymic Ads
7733 Forsyth
St. Louis, MO

Deutsch, Shea & Evans
49 East 53rd St.
New York, NY

Knoth & Meads
426 Pennsylvania Ave.
San Diego, CA

Banking:

Transfer Agents and Registrars:
Bradford Trust Co., New York
First Jersey National Bank
First National Bank of Chicago
Bank of America
Montreal Trust Co.
American National Bank and Trust Co., San Francisco
Royal Trust Co., Montreal
Mercantile Trust Co., St. Louis

Investment Bank:
Lazard Freres
   (see Board of Directors: Donald C. Cook)

Trustee:
Savings and Stock Investment Plan and Hourly Employees Savings and Stock Investment Plan (11.2% of outstanding stock), Bankers Trust Co.

B. Principal Defense/Space Contracting Operations

Ft. Worth Division
North Grants Lane
Fort Worth, TX
Richard E. Adams, V.P. and Gen. Mgr.

F-16—fighter, U.S. Air Force
F-16/79—export fighter
F-111—spare parts modification, U.S. Air Force, Australia
Advanced fighter technology integration research, U.S. Air Force

Convair Division
5001 Kearny Villa Road
San Diego, CA
Leonard F. Buchanan, V.P. and Gen. Mgr.

Tomahawk—sea and ground launched cruise missiles, U.S. Navy, U.S. Air Force
Atlas/Centaur—space launch vehicles and boosters, DoD, NASA
Space Shuttle—mid-fuselage cargo section space shuttle, Rockwell, NASA
Large space structure assembly, NASA

Pomona Division
1675 West Mission Boulevard
Pomona, CA
Ralph E. Hawes, V.P. and Gen. Mgr.

Standard 1 and 2—surface-to-air shipboard missile, U.S. Navy
Phalanx—radar-controlled gun system, U.S. Navy, Saudi Navy
Division Air Defense gun system, U.S. Army
RAM—anti-missile ship defense missile, U.S. Navy, West Germany, Denmark
AIM-7F Sparrow—air-to-air missile, U.S. Air Force, U.S. Navy
Stinger—surface-to-air shoulder-fired missile, U.S. Army
Viper—anti-tank weapon, U.S. Army
MX—Reentry advanced impact fuse, U.S. Air Force

Electronics Division
5011 Kearny Road
San Diego, CA
Frank O. Chesus, V.P. and Gen. Mgr.

F-16—avionics testing, U.S. Air Force
Standoff target acquisition system, U.S. Army
Missile tracking systems, U.S. Army, U.S. Navy, U.S. Air Force
Trident submarine weapons system monitoring equipment, U.S. Navy
NAVSTAR—global positioning system, ground station equipment, U.S. Navy
PPS-15—lightweight surveillance radar, U.S. Army, Spain

Electric Boat Division
Eastern Point Road
Groton, CT
P. Takis Veliotis, V.P. and Gen. Mgr.
F.G. Tovar, Gen. Mgr., Quonset Point, RI

SSN 668—attack submarines, U.S. Navy
Trident ballistic missile submarine, U.S. Navy

C. Contracting History

After a difficult decade General Dynamics emerged in the 1970s as a leading defense contractor with a wide range of defense programs. In the 1960s, General Dynamics' last commercial air transports, the Convair 880 and 990 jets, had incurred a $450 m. loss (*Forbes*, 1 July 1974). In addition, its Quincy, MA shipyard, purchased from Bethlehem Steel in 1964, ran up over $200 m. in losses by the early 1970s (*The Wall Street Journal*, 1 Aug. 1972). In the defense arena, the Pomona Division's Standard missile for the Navy lost money. The Fort Worth Division designed and built the Air Force's F-111 fighter-bomber but ran into "embarrassing political squabbling and highly publicized cost overruns" on the program (*Business Week*, 3 May 1976). The F-111 contract was profitable to General Dynamics, but was "a public relations catastrophe" (Ibid.). These problems led *Business Week* (Ibid.) to conclude that by 1970 "the company was a prime candidate for extinction."

In the late 1960s Chicago investor Henry Crown became the leading stockholder and named David Lewis as chairman and chief executive officer. Lewis had been with McDonnell Douglas for 24 years and had the reputation of having pushed through McDonnell Douglas Corporation's profitable F-4 Phantom program, salvaged troubled DC-8 and DC-9 production, and carried off the DC-10 design and marketing effort (Ibid.).

Lewis brought with him a number of aerospace managers: Hilliard Paige (former head of General Electric aerospace), Gordon E. MacDonald (financial officer at Hughes Aircraft), James M. Beggs (Westinghouse and the Department of Transportation), and Gene K. Beare (General Telephone and Electronics). Lewis centralized management in his hands and stopped the practice of bidding on every possible contract, which had resulted in losses (Ibid.). On the Standard missile, for instance, he said, "They couldn't stand the thought of not building it, so they bid lower than anyone in sight" (*The Wall Street Journal*, 1 Aug. 1972).

Lewis set as his goal raising commercial sales to 50% of General Dynamics' business. In the early 1970s, however, it became clear that this goal would not be reached quickly. Lewis noted, "You couldn't find a better time to have high priority government contracts. For the stability of the company, you can't beat government business in hard times" (*Business Week*, 3 Feb. 1975). As a result, General Dynamics kept a high volume of DoD business in the early 1970s and continued to grow.

During the late 1970s General Dynamics' defense business soared. According to *Business Week* (3 May 1976), "Lewis has turned General Dynamics from a sure-fire casualty into a consistently profitable growth company." The company operates in a wide range of markets—missiles, aircraft, electronics and shipbuilding. Missile contracts have climbed, with the Tomahawk cruise missile prototypes the most recent success story. Although the Tomahawk lost the competition for the ALCM contract to Boeing, its design will be used in several versions. The company's fortunes mainly have focused on two contracting areas: fighter aircraft and shipbuilding.

General Dynamics stands to become the leading Air Force contractor of the 1980s on the strength of its F-16 fighter program. Lewis eked out annual production rates of the F-111 from the company's Government-owned Forth Worth plant, buying the time to compete with Northrop for the Air Force's future light inexpensive fighter (Ibid., 3 Feb. 1975; *Fortune*, 3 Feb. 1977). The two companies each built a prototype of the fighter and flew off in 1974 and 1975. The F-16 contract priced each plane at $4.6 m. in 1976 dollars with a total order expected to go over $1.6 b.

California Democrat Charles Wilson suggested at the time that, merit aside, the contract award was helped by the influence of the Texas Congressional delegation: "I knew what the Texans were doing—they've got a lot of clout we haven't got." *The Washington Star* (25 Jan. 1975) suggested that California Congressmen Robert Leggett and Bob Wilson wouldn't support Northrop because General Dynamics had plants in their districts.

General Dynamics' success with the F-16 made the Air Force the firm's best salesman in the emerging European competition over a fighter to replace Lockheed's F-104s. In June 1975, the Belgian, Dutch, Norwegian and Danish governments all chose the F-16 over Swedish and French competitors for a total order of 350 planes. In addition, General Dynamics has undertaken a far-reaching program of co-production with firms in those countries which will produce 40% of the NATO version of the plane, 10% of the U.S. Air Force versions, and 15% of export versions. Lewis refers to the F-16 program as follows: "It could be another (F-4) Phantom." The company is also working hard to live down its F-111 cost experience. "We're out to lose our reputation for large cost overruns," stated one executive (*The Wall Street Journal*, 6 Feb. 1976). As the problems of managing a multinational consortium grow, General Dynamics has its work cut out: "the most complex and frustrating managerial task that any defense contractor has ever grappled with" (*Fortune*, March 1977). According to David Lewis, "If we don't maintain the costs of this thing, we could lose it" (Ibid.).

General Dynamics hopes to extend the market for the F-16 beyond its European partners. Although it lost the competition for the Canadian fighter order to McDonnell Douglas/Northrop's F-18, the F-16 remains in competition for Spanish and Australian orders and is being redesigned as a lighter-weight fighter for export sales under the Air Force's FX program.

General Dynamics' shipbuilding activity produced problems in the 1970s. In 1974 GD's Electric Boat shipyards in Groton, CT and Quonset Point, RI began two significant contracts: SSN 688 attack submarines and Trident missile submarines for the U.S. Navy. Navy shipbuilding, under the Nixon-Ford administration, looked as if it were going to grow, and Electric Boat, as the principal submarine shipyard, stood to benefit. *Barrons* (31 Dec. 1973) suggested General Dynamics' shipyards would be profitable for years to come.

By 1976 "the Boat" was in trouble, principally on the SSN 668 program, and asked the Navy for revisions in the contract to increase the price. The company had booked no profits on this program by 1976 and was running well over cost, due to inflation and changes in specifications (*Business Week*, 3 May 1976). In April 1976, General Dynamics filed a claim for $400 m. in additional payments on attack submarine work as part of over $1.5 b. in claims from the Navy's three leading shipyards.

In 1976 Congress rejected a supplemental budget request to settle these disputes. The courts, pending a negotiated or court-ordered settlement, ordered the Litton and Tenneco shipyards to stay open with the Navy footing the bill for operating costs. By 1977 Electric Boat calculated it was losing over $300 m. on the 688s and shuffled management. The new manager, T.P. Veliotis, laid off 4,000 workers on his arrival in October 1977 (*The New York Times*, 26 Oct. 1977; see also *Business Week*, 31 Oct. 1977).

Disagreements on the submarine program came to a head in March 1978 when General Dynamics threatened to close the Groton yard unless the claims were settled (*The Washington Post*, 14 March 1978). The Navy suggested it might take over the yard or seek an injunction to prevent the closing. After further discussion General Dynamics agreed to continue work for two months, pending a settlement, provided the Navy covered all current costs of production. An agreement was reached on June 9, 1978. The Navy absorbed $484 m. of the overrun, while General Dynamics absorbed $359 m. (*The New York Times*, 10 June 1978; *Fortune*, 31 July 1978; *Forbes*, 24 Dec. 1979).

The SSN 668 turned out not to be a financial disaster for General Dynamics. The company's Trident program, which is behind schedule and over cost will not affect the company's position since the contract contains clauses for cost escalation (*The New York Times*, 25 Nov. 1980). It was possible for *The New York Times* (4 April 1979) to describe the April 7th launch of the Trident SS Ohio as sign of "a remarkable turnaround at the vulnerable shipyards."

General Dynamics' healthy contracting situation explains why Smith Barney's *Research from Washington* newsletter (15 March 1979) said the firm "will almost certainly be the dominant defense contractor in terms of DoD orders during the 1980s." As of 1980 the company had its highest backlog in history—$11.5 b.—and anticipated increasing business in all areas of military production. There was some discussion of developing the company's FB-111 B/C for use as an interim strategic penetrating bomber. In a sagging commercial economy, Chairman David Lewis saw the company's defense business as the key to its survival: "We believe that the strong base provided by our large backlog of very high priority government programs will enable the company to continue to grow during these uncertain times" (*Aerospace Daily*, 5 May 1980).

D. U.S. Government-Owned, Company-Operated Plants

Total company floor space: 13,323,000 sq. ft. (partial disclosure)
Leased from U.S. Government: 9,500,000 sq. ft. (54.9%)
Total Lease Cost: Not disclosed

Location: Air Force Plant 4/ACJF
Fort Worth, TX
6.5 m. sq. ft.
Use: F-16

Location: Navy Plant 451
Pomona, CA
1.4 m. sq. ft.
Use: Pomona Division missile

Location: Air Force Plant 19
San Diego, CA
1.6 m. sq. ft.
Use: Convair Division—space systems

RESEARCH AND DEVELOPMENT

Major Defense/Space R&D Projects

Tomahawk—air-launched cruise missile, U.S. Navy
Large space structures assembly, NASA
Air defense system, U.S. Army
Viper—anti-tank weapon, U.S. Army
RAM—anti-missile missile, U.S. Navy

TABLE II
Research and Development
($ in M.)

	1970	1971	1972	1973	1974	1975	1976	1977	1978	1979
I. U.S. Government Contracts										
DoD	$131.9	149.5	131.9	226.5	214.4	175.2	446.5	497.5	482.6	491.5
NASA	$ 38.0	50.8	66.6	80.4	79.5	85.3	76.3	78.7	64.4	46.9
Total	$169.9	200.3	198.5	306.9	293.9	260.5	522.8	576.2	547.0	538.4
II. Company-sponsored R&D	NA	NA	NA	$ 19.1	20.6	20.9	24.0	34.2	41.0	48.0
III. IR&D	NA	NA	NA	$ 7.8	7.4	8.9	10.5	13.7	21.8	NA

I. From DoD yearly publication "500 Contractors Receiving the Largest Dollar Volume of Military Prime Contract Awards for RDT&E" and NASA Annual Procurement Reports.

II. "Research and development expenditures for company-sponsored projects are expensed as incurred." (10K, 1978)

III. Company-sponsored R&D costs charged to DoD as disclosed by DoD.

BOARD OF DIRECTORS:

Thomas G. Ayers (1980)
Chairman of Executive Committee and Director, Commonwealth Edison.
Past Corporate Employment:
Chairman, Commonwealth Edison (retired 1980).
Corporate Directorships:
First Chicago Corp.; Northwest Industries, Inc.; G.D. Searle Co.; Tribune Co.; Zenith Radio Corp. ($357,000); Breeder Reactor Corp.; Dearborn Park Corp.
Shares owned:
100

James M. Beggs (1974)
Executive V.P. of Aerospace, General Dynamics (Convair, Electronics, Fort Worth and Pomona Divisions).
Education:
Design engineering, U.S. Naval Academy (1947).
Military:
Submarine duty, U.S. Navy (1947-54).
Past Corporate Employment:
Westinghouse Electric Corp. (1955-68); V.P. Defense and Space Center, Managing Director for Operations, Summa Corp. (1973-74).
Government Positions:
Associate Administrator, Office of Advanced Research Technology, NASA (1968-69); Under Secretary of Transportation (1969-74).
Corporate Directorships:
EMC, Inc. ($632,000); Consolidated Rail Corp.
Key Association Memberships:
National Space Club, Board of Governors; American Institute of Aeronautics and Astronautics; American Society of Engineers.
Shares owned:
9,353

Oliver C. Boileau (1980)
President, General Dynamics.
Past Corporate Employment:
Design engineer, RCA Corp. (1951-52); Boeing Co. (1953-80) (Minuteman Missile Program Manager, V.P. and General Manager, Boeing Missile Division-1969); V.P. aerospace group-1970; President-1973).
Corporate Directorships:
Pacific Northwest Bell Telephone Co. ($296,000); Washington Mutual Savings Bank.

Key Association Memberships:
Institute of Electrical and Electronic Engineers; National Academy of Engineers; American Institute of Aeronautics and Astronautics; Air Force Association; Navy League; American Defense Preparedness Association; National Space Club; Defense Science Board.
Shares owned:
NA

Donald C. Cook (1976)
General Partner, Lazard Freres and Co. (see Basic Data: Banking)
Past Corporate Employment:
Partner, Cook & Berger (attorneys) (1947-49); American Electric Power Services Corp. (1953-76) (President-1961, retired as Chairman and Chief Executive Officer 1972).
Government Positions:
Special Counsel, House Committee on Naval Affairs (1943-45); Commissioner SEC (1949-53) (Chairman-1952; Chief Counsel, Preparedness Investigating Subcommittee, Senate Armed Services Committee 1950-52).
Corporate Directorships:
American Broadcasting Co.; Lincoln National Corp./Lincoln Life Insurance Co.; Amerada-Hess Corp. ($236,510,000).
Shares owned:
1,250

Henry Crown (1960-66, 1970-present)
Chairman, Henry Crown & Co. (real estate)
Past Corporate Employment:
President, Material Service Corp. (1921-41), (Chairman of the Board-1941; merged with General Dynamics-1959).
Shares owned:
1,318,250

Lester Crown (1974)
Executive V.P., General Dynamics; President and CEO, Material Service Corp.
Past Corporate Employment:
Material Service Corp. (1950-present), (President-1970).
Corporate Directorships:
Esmark, Inc.; Trans World Airlines, Inc.
Shares owned:
3,878,292

Nathan Cummings (1970)
Founder and Honorable Chairman of the Board, Consolidated Foods.

General Dynamics

Past Corporate Employment:
  Consolidated Foods Corp. and predecessors (1938-present).
Corporate Directorships:
  Magnatex, Ltd. (London).
Shares owned:
  1,068,129

Milton Falkoff (1970)
Financial Consultant, Chicago, IL
Past Corporate Employment:
  V.P., Henry Crown & Co. (1948-76).
Corporate Directorships:
  Farmers Investment Co.
Shares owned:
  350

Guy W. Fiske (1977)
Executive V.P., General Dynamics
Past Corporate Employment:
  Staff Specialist in Administration, General Electric Co. (1948-68); ITT (1968-77) (Corporate Product Line Manager for Controls, Instruments and Electronics-1968; Product Line Manager for Automotive Products-nd; Corporate V.P. and Group General Manager for the Company's Automotive Products Group, North America-1972).
Shares owned:
  16,657

Albert E. Jenner, Jr. (1970)
Senior Partner, Jenner & Block (attorneys)
Government Positions:
  Chairman, Advisory Committee on Federal Rules of Evidence, U.S. Supreme Court (1965-75); Chairman, Illinois Committee on Uniform State Laws; Sr. Counsel, Warren Commission (1963-64); Chief Special Counsel to House of Representatives, Judicial Committee (Nixon Impeachment Inquiry).
Corporate Directorships:
  Walter E. Heller Int'l.; United Bank of America.
Shares owned:
  31,750

Earl Dallam Johnson (1955-63; 1971-present)
Business and Financial Consultant, Greenwich, CT
Past Corporate Employment:
  General Dynamics (1955-63) (Senior V.P.-1958; President-1959; Vice Chairman of the Board-1962); Executive V.P. and Director, Delta Airlines (1963-65).

Government Positions:
Assistant Secretary of the Army for Manpower and Reserve Forces (1950-52); Under Secretary of the Army, responsible for Army procurement, research and development, fiscal and budgetary matters and the Mutual Defense Assistance Program abroad (1952-55).
Corporate Directorships:
Damson Oil Corp.; Menasco Manufacturing Co., Ltd. ($6,610,000).
Key Association Memberships:
National Security Industrial Association; Air Force Association; Navy League; National Defense Transportation Association; Air Transport Association of America (President, 1954).
Shares owned:
2,500

David Lewis, Jr. (1970)
Chairman of the Board and Chief Executive Officer, General Dynamics
Education:
B.S., Aeronautical Engineering, Georgia Institute of Technology (1939).
Past Corporate Employment:
Aerodynamicist, Glenn L. Martin Co. (1939-46); McDonnell Aircraft (1946-70) (Senior V.P.-1959; Executive V.P.-1961; President-1962-70).
Corporate Directorships:
Bankamerica Corp.; Ralston Purina ($5,830,000).
Key Association Memberships:
American Institute of Aeronautics and Astronautics (fellow); Aerospace Industries Association (Board of Governors); National Academy of Engineering.
Shares owned:
98,971

Edward E. Lynn (1976)
Vice President and General Counsel, General Dynamics Corp.
Past Corporate Employment:
Jenner & Block (attorneys) (1947-57); V.P., Fairbanks, Morese & Co. (1957-61); General Counsel, V.P. and Chief Legal Officer, Youngstown Sheet and Tube Co. (later Lykes Youngstown Corp.).
Shares owned:
7,093

Gordon MacDonald (1971)
Executive V.P. Finance and Chief Financial Officer, General Dynamics Corp.

Past Corporate Employment:
V.P. and Comptroller, Hughes Aircraft Co. (1946-71).
Corporate Directorships:
Bank of Ladue.
Shares owned:
39,303

Robert W. Reneker (1970)

Former Chairman, Esmark, Inc. (chemicals, energy and financial services) (retired 1977).
Past Corporate Employment:
Swift & Co. (1934-77) (reorganized into Esmark & Co., 1973).
Corporate Directorships:
Continental Illinois; Morton-Norwich Products, Inc. ($1,279,000).
Shares owned:
15,000

Elliot H. Stein (1978)

President, Scherck, Stein & Franc, Inc. (investment brokerage)
Past Corporate Employment:
Mark C. Steinberg & Co. (1939-41, 1946-51).
Corporate Directorships:
Alvey, Inc.; Moog Automotive Co.; General American Life Insurance Co.; Ralston Purina Co. ($5,830,000); City Investing Co.; General Steel Industries.
Shares owned:
1,250

P. Takis Veliotis (1980)

Executive V.P., Marine, General Dynamics.
Past Corporate Employment:
General Dynamics (1973-80); (President and General Manager, Quincy Shipbuilding-1973; General Manager, Electric Boat Division-1977-80).
Corporate Directorships:
Multibank Financial Corp.
Key Association Memberships:
Society of Naval Architects and Marine Engineers; American Bureau of Shipping; Shipbuilders Council of America.
Shares owned:
1,498

PERSONNEL TRANSFERS

Table III
(DoD 1970-79)
(NASA 1974-79)

	Total	Air Force	Army	Navy	Office of Secretary of Defense	Other
DoD Military to General Dynamics	189	106	20	55	0	8
DoD Civilian to General Dynamics	17	4	1	6	6	0
NASA to General Dynamics	1					
General Dynamics to DoD	32	1	2	24	4	1
General Dynamics to NASA	0					
Total	239	111	23	85	10	9

Appearances of Potential Conflict of Interest (see Chapter 6): 16

I. DoD to GD

Blackshaw, George
DoD:
> Director, air warfare and tactical missiles, Office of Under Secretary of Defense.

GD:
> October 1978, V.P. research and engineering, Convair Division (missiles).

Hansen, Grant
DoD:
> Asst. Secretary of the Air Force for Research and Development.

GD:
> June 1973, V.P. and General Manager, Convair Division.

Hubbard, Ronald
DoD:
> Supervisory electronics engineer, development of advanced electro-optical systems, Air Force Avionics Lab.

GD:
> March 1978, Senior engineering specialist, development of advanced electro-optical systems.

General Dynamics 269

Jay, William W.
  DoD:
    Legal counsel to supevisor of shipbuilding, Navy Sea Systems Command, Office of Regional Counsel, Pascagoula, MS.
  GD:
    January 1979, associate division counsel, contract negotiations for supplies and Navy contracts, Electric Boat.

Simon, Allan D.
  DoD:
    Asst. Director for Air Warfare, Office of Director of Defense Research and Engineering.
  GD:
    March 1973, consultant, technical and planning matters.

2. NASA To GD

Straeter, Terry
  NASA:
    Manager, Head of Programming Techniques Branch, advanced software technology.
  GD:
    March 1979, Director, technical software, software development methodology.

3. GD to DoD

Ball, Edward
  GD:
    Director, general engineering and administration.
  DoD:
    August 1969, Assistant Director, Office of Director of Defense Research and Engineering.

Buckberg, Morton
  GD:
    Design studies for ship contract definition phase.
  DoD:
    May 1970, Section head, Ship Development and Design Center, Naval Ship Engineering Center.

Cauldwell, Frederic
  GD:
    Head, submarine hydrodynamics section.
  DoD:
    November 1967, Navy Bureau Head, Hull Form and Fluid Dynamics.

Drake, Edward
  GD:
    Asst. General Counsel, Contracts, Claims and Litigation, Quincy Division.
  DoD:
    July 1973, Asst. Counsel, legal review of shipbuilder claims, Naval Sea Systems Command.

Erickson, Floyd
  GD:
    Head of cost analysis.
  DoD:
    July 1975, Head, Weapons System Cost Analysis Division, Navy.

Marafioti, Frank
  GD:
    Engineering, research specialist on complex hull structures.
  DoD:
    January 1973, Navy Engineer, static and dynamic analysis of complex submarine hull structures.

Paige, Hilliard W.
  GD:
    President.
  DoD:
    September 1973, Consultant, Office of Secretary of Defense.

Steele, George, Jr.
  GD:
    Asst. Division Counsel.
  DoD:
    July 1971, Attorney, Naval Electronics Systems Command. February 1973, Trial Attorney, Office of General Counsel, Contract Appeals Division.

Sylvester, Gordon E.
  GD:
    V.P. for operations, Fort Worth Division.
  DoD:
    July 1977, Consultant to Directorate of Manufacturing, Air Force Systems Command, Wright-Patterson.

4. "Revolving Door"

Hinman, Kenneth Ray
  GD:
    Senior Project Engineer; Manager, Design Integration Group on cruise missile; Chief Engineer, fighter-attack aircraft programs (including V/STOL).

DoD:
April 1976, Staff specialist on air warfare, monitoring R&D on advanced weapons systems and interdiction programs, Office of Director of Defense Research and Engineering.
GD:
August 1979, Director, advanced aircraft programs, marketing, evaluation of new aircraft programs.

Comments

1. The company has a large volume of transfers with the U.S. Navy: six of 17 transfers of civilians to the firm and 24 of 32 transfers from the firm to DoD. A large part of the firm's defense business is in naval shipbuilding.
2. General Dynamics has no policy statement on transfers of personnel.

POLITICAL ACTION COMMITTEES

Name: General Dynamics Corporation Voluntary Political Contribution Plan
Total Expenditures (7/77-8/80): $509,978
Total Contributions to Federal Campaigns (2/77-5/80): $109,121

Key
(D) = Democrat
(R) = Republican
(C) = Recipient was a candidate and not elected to that office.
+ = Candidate is also a member of a key Congressional committee.
* = Candidate is a member of two committees, but contributions s/he received is only listed once to avoid being double-counted in the total for this section.

A. Contributors to Federal Candidates in States with General Dynamics Production Facilities (Key Geographic Locations)

MISSOURI

General Dynamics home office located in St. Louis (dist. 1, 3)

<u>Senate</u>

no contributions $ 0

272 General Dynamics

House
+ Rep. Bill Burlison (D-10)	$ 500
+ Rep. Richard Ichord (D-8)	$1,000
McNarry (C)	$5,000

Total Missouri: $6,500
% Total Federal Contributions: 5.8%

TEXAS
General Dynamics plant located in Fort Worth (dist. 6, 12, 24)
Senate
+ Sen. John Tower (R)	$1,125

House
Bob Barnes (C)	$1,000
Rep. Leo Berman (R-24)	$1,000
Rep. Martin Frost (D-24)	$2,300
Rep. W.P. Gramm (D-6)	$ 100
Rep. Tom Loeffler (R-21)	$ 500
Darla Martensen (C)	$ 50
Rep. Jim Mattox (D-5)	$1,025
William Powers (D-6) (C)	$ 25
+ Rep. Richard C. White (D-16)	$ 300
Rep. James Wright (D-12)	$1,039

Total Texas: $8,464
% Total Federal Contributions: 7.8%

CALIFORNIA
General Dynamics plants located in San Diego (dist. 41, 42, 43) and Pomona (dist. 33, 35)
Senate
Sen. Alan Cranston (D)	$ 550

House
+ Rep. Glenn Anderson (D-32)	$ 200
+ Rep. Robert Badham (R-40)	$ 600
Rep. Claire Burgener (R-43)	$1,000
+ Rep. Robert K. Dornan (R-27)	$ 125
Rep. David Drier (R-35) (C)	$ 660
+ Rep. Vic Fazio (D-4)	$ 650
Rep. Wayne Grisham (R-33)	$ 125
+ Rep. Barry Goldwater, Jr. (R-20)	$ 150
+ Rep. James Lloyd (D-35)	$ 150
+ Rep. John J. McFall (D-14)	$ 500

Rep. John H. Rousselot (R-26)	$ 250
Rep. Lionel Van Deerlin (D-42)	$ 100
+ Rep. Bob Wilson (R-41)	$1,700
+ Rep. Charles Wilson (D-31)	$ 500

Total California: $7,260
% Total Federal Contributions: 6.7%

CONNECTICUT

General Dynamics plant located in Groton (dist. 2)

Senate

no contributions	$ 0

House

Rep. Christopher Dodd (D-2)	$3,100
+ Rep. Robert Giaimo (D-3)	$2,000

Total Connecticut: $5,100
% Total Federal Contributions: 4.7%

NOTE: General Dynamics also has production facilities in Quincy, MA (dist. 11) and Quonset Point, RI (dist. 2) involving the following Members of Congress:

Senate

Sen. Claiborne Pell (D-RI)	$1,000
Sen. Paul Tsongas (D-MA)	$2,100
Sen. John Chafee (R-RI)	$ 100

House

Rep. Edward Beard (D-RI-2)	$ 500
Rep. Brian Donnelly (D-MA-11)	$1,640
Rep. Margaret Heckler (R-MA-10)	$ 400

Total Other Facilities: $5,740
% Total Federal Contributions: 5.3%

Total to Key Geographic Locations: $33,064
% Total Federal Contributions: 30.3%

B. Contributions to Members of Key Congressional Committees

Senate Armed Services Committee

Culver	$ 200	McIntyre	$ 500
Goldwater	$ 800	Morgan	$ 250
Hart	$ 400	Thurmond	$2,000
Helms	$ 100	Tower	$1,125

Humphrey, Gordon	$ 200	Warner	$ 400
Jepsen	$ 450		

House Armed Services Committee

Badham	$ 600	Holt	$ 400
Bailey	$ 100	Ichord	$1,000
Byron	$ 400	Lloyd, James	$ 150
Carr	$ 500	Mavroules	$ 400
Courter	$1,150	Nichols	$ 400
Daniel, Dan	$ 100	Price	$ 400
Daniel, Robert	$ 100	Spence	$ 650
Davis, Mendel	$ 500	Stump	$ 100
Dickinson	$2,000	White	$ 300
Dougherty	$ 500	Wilson, Bob	$1,500
Fazio	$ 650	Wilson, Charles	$ 500
Hillis	$ 350		

Senate Defense Appropriations Subcommittee

Brooke	$1,150	Magnuson	$1,000
Garn	$ 25	Stevens	$ 500
Hollings	$2,000		

House Defense Appropriations Subcommittee

Addabbo	$ 700	Giaimo	$2,000
Burlison	$ 500	Kemp	$ 100
Cederberg	$ 100	McFall	$ 500
Chappell	$ 600	Robinson	$ 300
Edwards, Jack	$ 500		

Senate Committee on Commerce, Science and Transportation
Subcommittee on Aviation

Goldwater	*	Stevens	*

Subcommittee on Science, Technology and Space

Hollings	*

House Committee on Science and Technology

Ambro	$ 200	Fuqua	$ 500
Blanchard	$ 100	Goldwater, Jr.	$ 150
Carney	$ 300	Lloyd	*
Davis, Robert	$ 100	Mavroules	*
Dornan	$ 125	Rudd	$ 650
Flowers	$ 500	White	*

Senate Committee on Environment and Public Works
Subcommittee on Transportation

Domenici	$ 200

House Committee on Public Works and Transportation
Subcommittee on Aviation

Abdnor	$500	Goldwater, Jr.	*
Ambro	*	Hefner	$ 125
Anderson	$ 200	Shuster	$ 200

Total to Key Committees: $33,000
% Total Federal Contributions: 30.2%

General Dynamics

C. Contributions to Other Influential Members of Congress

Sen. Howard Baker (R-TN), Minority Leader $ 200
   (also received contributions as a Presidential candidate)
Rep. John Rhodes (R-AZ), Minority Leader $1,450

Total to Other Influentials: $1,650
% Total Federal Contributions: 1.5%

D. Contributions to Other Federal Candidates

Senate

Armstrong (R-CO)	$ 800	Percy (R-IL)	$2,100
Glenn (D-OH)	$2,500	Shasteen (R-NE) (C)	$ 200
McGovern (D-SD)	$ 525	Stone (D-FL)	$ 500
		Swigert (R-CO)	$ 100

House

Alexander (D-AR)	$ 100	Jones (D-NC)	$ 250
Annunzio (D-IL)	$ 500	Kelly (R-FL)	$ 200
Ashley (D-OH)	$ 500	Livingston (R-LA)	$ 15
Bauman (R-MD)	$ 150	Mathis (D-GA)	$ 100
Biaggi (D-NY)	$ 100	McDade (R-PA)	$ 250
Bronson, W. (R-MA) (C)	$1,500	Murphy (D-NY)	$ 500
Broyhill (R-NC)	$ 250	Nelli (NA) (C)	$ 200
Cheney (R-WY)	$ 50	Pauken (TN) (C)	$1,000
Conable (R-NY)	$ 50	Porter (R-IL)	$2,000
Cunningham (R-WA)	$ 100	Quayle (R-IN)	$1,000
Derwinski (R-IL)	$ 450	Rooney (D-PA)	$ 100
Dingell (D-MI)	$ 100	Simpson (R-WY)	$ 200
Grassley (R-IA)	$ 200	Staggers (D-WV)	$ 250
Gilman (R-NY)	$ 100	Symms (R-ID)	$ 250
Hanley (D-NY)	$ 250	Thorsness (R-SD)	$ 700
Hatchelor (NA-FL) (C)	$ 100	Vander Jagt (R-MI)	$ 200
Hubbard (D-KY)	$ 200	Williams (R-NJ)	$ 200
Ireland (D-FL)	$ 750	Winn (R-KS)	$ 150
		Zefferretti (D-NY)	$ 300

Total to Other Federal Candidates: $20,040
% Total Federal Contributions: 18.4%

E. Contributions to Party Campaign Committees

Republican federal-level committees: $13,445.00
Democratic federal-level committees: $ 3,245.00

Total to Party Committees: $16,690.00
% Total Federal Contributions: 15.3%

F. Contributions to Presidential Candidates

John Anderson (I)	$ 150
Howard Baker (R)	$1,131
George Bush (R)	$2,210
Jimmy Carter (D)	$3,449
John Connally (R)	$1,242
Edward Kennedy (D)	$2,000
Ronald Reagan (R)	$3,995

Total to Presidential Candidates: $14,177
% Total Federal Contributions: 13.0%

WASHINGTON OPERATIONS

Washington Office:
1745 Jefferson Davis Highway, Suite 1000, Arlington, VA 22202
1025 Connecticut Ave., N.W., Suite 800, Washington, DC 20006

Director:
E.J. Lefevre, Vice President of Government Relations

Activities:
1. **International:** Liaison with foreign embassies and procurement missions; information gathering and disseminating on foreign business.
2. **National Affairs and Strategic Planning:** Liaison with Washington press corps. The office was upgraded in 1975 to handle F-16 programs and "to strengthen efforts to obtain R&D contracts leading to future advanced aerospace systems programs."

Registered Lobbyists

	Receipts	Expenditures	Years
F. Slatinshek & Associates, 218 N. Lee St., Alexandria, VA (with Grumman, Gould and United Technologies)	$1,637.50	*	77-79

*No figures reported; quarterly report was filed.

General Dynamics 277

DEFENSE-RELATED TRADE ASSOCIATION MEMBERSHIPS

Aerospace Industries Association
Air Force Association
American Defense Preparedness Association
American Institute of Aeronautics and Astronautics
American League for Exports and Security Assistance
Armed Forces Communication and Electronics Association
National Security Industrial Association
Shipbuilders Council of America

ADVISORY COMMITTEE MEMBERSHIPS

1976-78: 7

Buchanan, Leonard
(V.P. and General Manager, Pomona Division, then V.P. and General Manager, Convair Division)
DoD—Defense Science Board, 1976

Dietz, William C.
DoD—Air Force Scientific Advisory Board, 1976, 1977, 1978

Hansen, Grant L.
(V.P. and General Manager, Convair Division)
DoD—Air Force Scientific Advisory Board, 1976, 1977

Heiniman, Edward
DoD—Naval Research Advisory Committee, 1976.

Marshe, Blake
(Convair Division)
NASA—Research and Technology Advisory Council, Committee on Aerodynamics and Configurations, 1976, 1977.

Murphy, James L.
(GD International Corp.)
DoD—Defense Industry Advisory Group, 1976, 1977

Smith, Robert
DoD—Defense Science Board, 1977, 1978

Comment:
General Dynamics also had members on two advisory boards to the Department of Commerce concerned with communications equipment and with multilateral trade negotiations.

ENTERTAINMENT

General Dynamics' response to the Joint Committee of Defense Production survey requested that the data be kept confidential.

Disclosure: Poor.

QUESTIONABLE PAYMENTS

General Dynamics has made no disclosure on this issue, nor has there been any allegation of any questionable corporate payments. Foreign sales were under 10% of the company's business into the 1970s, though the F-16 program should change this proportion.

DISCLOSURE

Very poor.

GRUMMAN

BASIC CORPORATE AND CONTRACTING DATA

A. Corporate Data

Grumman Corporation
Bethpage, NY 11714

Fortune 500 (1979): 216
Fiscal Year: Jan. 1—Dec. 31

Chairman:
   John C. Bierwirth (1979 salary: $263,000)

President:
   Joseph G. Gavin, Jr. (1979 salary: $246,000)

Auditor:
   Arthur Andersen & Co.
   1345 Avenue of the Americas
   New York, NY

Outside Legal Counsel:
   Cahill, Gordon & Reindel
   80 Pine St.
   New York, NY

TABLE I
Corporate Data
($ in M.)

	1970	1971	1972	1973	1974	1975	1976	1977	1978	1979
Sales*	$993.3	799.0	683.5	1,082.6	1,112.9	1,328.6	1,502.1	1,552.7	1,468.2	1,492.9
Net Income	$ 20.3	(18.0)	(70.0)	28.2	32.9	23.5	23.6	32.4	20.0	19.6
Dept. of Defense Contracts	$660.8	1,098.4	1,119.8	909.0	687.0	1,343.3	982.0	1,428.1	1,180.0	1,364.2
Rank	8	4	7	5	12	5	8	7	10	8
NASA Contracts	$284.0	113.7	28.5	12.0	11.1	14.1	13.4	4.8	5.1	5.9
Rank	2	6	17	25	28	21	25	49	48	47
DoD/NASA Contracts as % of Sales	95.1%	151.6	168.0	85.1	62.7	102.2	66.3	92.3	80.7	91.8
Government Sales	NA	$ 719.0	NA	941.8	957.1	1,116.0	1,232.0	1,258.0	1,175.9	1,113.0
Government Sales as % of Sales	NA	90.0%	NA	87.0	86.0	84.0	82.0	81.0	80.1	74.6
Foreign Military Sales Contracts	$ .036	.269	.137	.024	42.5	297.9	303.7	252.8	70.0	41.4
Rank	NA	NA	NA	NA	13	2	3	5	14	NA
FMS Contracts as % of Sales	.004%	.03	.02	.002	3.8	22.4	20.2	16.3	4.8	2.8
Overseas and Export Sales	NA	NA	NA	NA	NA	NA	NA	$ 431.2	316.3	73.2
Overseas and Export Sales as % of Sales	—	—	—	—	—	—	—	27.8%	21.5	4.9
Employees	28,000	25,000	25,000	27,000	30,000	28,000	28,000	27,000	26,000	28,000

*In 1978 Grumman sold Grumman American Aviation and adjusted past sales figures accordingly. Only 1978 figures reflect this change.

Advertising/Public Relations Agency:
Creamer, Inc.
1301 Avenue of the Americas
New York, NY

Hill and Knowlton, Inc.
33 Third Ave.
New York, NY

Banking:

Transfer Agent:
Manufacturers Hanover

Investment Banker:
Dillon Read

Lenders:
Bank of New York
Bankers Trust Co. ($16.4 m. in revolving credit and $4.6 m. in short-term credit; trustee for 24.8% of the outstanding stock)
Chase Manhattan Bank
Citibank
European-American Bank (revolving credit term loans and short-term credit, (see Board of Directors: Joseph G. Gavin, Jr.)
Marine Midland
Mellon Bank
Morgan Guaranty

B. Principal Defense/Space Contracting Operations

Grumman Aerospace
Bethpage, NY
George M. Skurla, Chairman and President

F-14—fighter plane. U.S. Navy, Iran
A-6E—attack plane, U.S. Navy
EA-6B—electronics countermeasure plane, U.S. Navy
E-2C Hawkeye—electronic surveillance plane, U.S. Navy, Japan, Israel
EF-111A—electronic countermeasures, U.S. Air Force
Radar antennae. U.S. Navy
Orbiter wings for space shuttle, NASA
Large space structure assemblies, NASA
V/STOL aircraft—research and development, U.S. Navy
Forward-swept wing fighter design, U.S. Air Force
Avionics for OV-1 Mohawk, U.S. Army

NOTE: Grumman Aerospace also has operations in Milledgeville, GA working on composite materials and subcontracting.

C. Contracting History

Grumman has been a leading Navy aircraft contractor since the 1930s, diversifying its government business into other agencies (Air Force, NASA, Army) in the 1960s and 70s. Throughout the past decade, Grumman has also had some difficulties with its F-14 program for the Navy and faces some uncertainty about future DoD contracts.

At the start of the decade, Grumman's Lunar Excursion Module program for NASA had ended. Previous Navy fighter and surveillance aircraft programs were winding down, as was subcontract work on the Air Force F-111. Grumman had, however, won a Navy contract for the F-14, in 1969. This program has been the company's mainstay through the decade. In addition, the firm has had major contracts for the A-6 fighter, the EA-6B electronic countermeasures version of the A-6, and the E-2C Hawkeye Navy patrol aircraft.

The F-14 was also a headache for the company in the early 1970s. The original Navy contract foresaw a purchase of over 700 planes. In the early 1970s, however, Grumman encountered serious cost problems on the program, due to rapid inflation and a loss of other government business, forcing the firm to allocate more overhead costs to the F-14 program (*Business Week*, 16 Dec. 1972).

By 1972 Grumman reported to the Navy that cost increases would add at least $2.2 million to the price of each plane. In 1971 and 1972 Grumman's own corporate balance sheet recorded losses. In 1972, Grumman began negotiating with the Navy to change the contract to a new, higher price for the plane. According to Grumman, the terms of the existing contract were "such as to seriously threaten Grumman Aerospace Corporation's ability to remain a viable producer of essential defense and space hardware and to meet its responsibilities to shareholders" (Ibid., 16 Dec. 1972). Grumman Chairman John Bierwirth was even more dramatic: "If we are forced to produce the plane under existing conditions, two months later we will have to close the doors of the aerospace division and we will take the government to court" (Ibid.). Grumman's short-term credit line with Bankers Trust was cut off in April 1972 (Ibid., 13 Jan. 1973; *The New York Times*, 21 July 1974). The Navy, however, provided a loan of some $54 m. at 6.8% interest beyond normal progress payments (*Business Week*, 13 Jan. 1973).

As part of the continuing negotiations, the Navy decided to trim the size of the F-14 production run to around 300 planes. When the Navy and Grumman reached an agreement in 1973, according to Chairman Bierwirth, "We took a loss of $220 million on those 134 planes" (*The New York Times*, 21 July 1974). The Navy changed the terms of the contract for subsequent planes, raising the original price of $11.5 m. to $17.9 m. per plane. By the late 1970s the price was closer to $25 m.

Despite the New Navy contract for the plane and the Iranian contract for 80 F-14s, Grumman still had a cash flow problem, reflected in the statement by Vice Admiral Kent Lee that the Navy was "acting as Grumman's banker until Grumman can re-establish commercial credit" (*Electronics News*, 8 July 1974). The DoD proposed to solve the problem with $131 m. in loans for the two orders (*The Wall Street Journal*, 18 July 1974). Congress refused to approve the advance in August, 1974 (*The New York Times*, 14 Aug. 1974).

According to *Fortune* (Feb. 1976), Grumman "was saved from a spectacular bankruptcy by the Shah of Iran." By the fall of 1974, a $200 m. loan had been arranged with nine American banks ($125 m.) and the Melli Bank of Iran ($75 m.). This financial package, including the unprecedented involvement of a foreign bank in defense contract financing, helped the company overcome the problem.

Although the F-14 continued to be a major source of corporate revenue, the future of the company's defense business after the mid-1980s remains unclear. As part of Navy questioning about the size and shape of its fighter arsenal, Defense Secretary Brown began efforts in 1977 to reduce the production rate of the F-14. For the Navy, reducing purchases of the F-14 was tied to the decision to buy a growing number of cheaper F-18s (Northrop/McDonnell Douglas). In 1980 this trade-off became more questionable as F-18 costs rose dramatically. An anticipated Iranian follow-on order for the F-14 collapsed in 1978 and possible Canadian and Australian orders fell through.

In response to the F-14 problems Grumman stepped up its lobbying activities in Congress. In 1977 they added a second registered lobbyist to their Washington operations, F. Slatinshek, former counsel of the House Armed Services Committee. The company also undertook a major campaign to encourage employees, stockholders, and community residents in Long Island to lobby Congress to prevent reductions in the production run of the F-14. Long Island Representatives Otis Pike and Tom Downey supported this effort, as did the Senator from New York Daniel P. Moynihan. Questions were raised in the Defense Department as to whether Federal contract dollars had been used to lobby Congress in this effort. A DCAA audit of this expenditure, ordered by Secretary of Defense Brown, has never been made public (*The New York Times*, 15 Feb. 1978; 17 Feb. 1978).

The F-14 program is due to end in the mid-1980s. In addition, the A-6 and EA-6B programs should terminate in that period and the future of the E-2C is unclear after 1985. New defense spending plans could alter this picture after 1981, however, and Grumman continues an active search for new defense business in advanced fighter and V/STOL fighter design. In addition, the firm continues to seek overseas business for its programs, notably the E-2C Hawkeye, which has recently been ordered by the governments of Japan and Israel. The company also has a contract to modify several Air Force F-111s for electronic warfare.

Grumman is also attempting to diversify into non-defense activities. It is seeking commercial aircraft subcontract work, principally from Boeing. Its Boeing subcontracts now include wing skins for the 727, wing spoilers for the 757, and center wing stubs for the 767. In addition, Grumman's Flexible Bus division is one of the two principal domestic bus manufacturers.

D. U.S. Government-Owned, Company-Operated Plants

Total Company floor space: 10,358,000 sq. ft.
Leased from U.S. Government: 2,521,000 sq. ft. (24.3%)
Total Lease Cost: Not disclosed

Location: Navy Plant 464
Bethpage, NY
1.65 m. sq. ft.
Use: E-2C, A-6, EA-6B, F-14A, NASA orbiter wing
Cost: Not disclosed

Location: Navy Plant 466
Calverton, NY
676,786 sq. ft.
Use: A-6E, EA-6B, F-14A
Cost: $1,655 m. (1979)

RESEARCH AND DEVELOPMENT

Major Defense/Space R&D Projects

Large space structures, NASA
V/STOL fighter, U.S. Navy
Advanced tactical fighter and forward-swept wing designs, U.S. Air Force
Electronic weapons guide system, U.S. Navy
Space operating surveillance systems, DoD

TABLE II
Research and Development
($ in M.)

	1970	1971	1972	1973	1974	1975	1976	1977	1978	1979
I. U.S. Government Contracts										
DoD	$346.1	568.0	200.9	333.1	65.4	74.7	37.3	69.5	63.9	54.5
NASA	$284.0	113.7	28.5	12.0	11.1	14.1	13.4	4.8	5.1	5.9
Total	$630.1	681.7	229.4	345.1	76.5	88.3	50.7	74.3	69.0	60.4
II. Company-sponsored R&D	$ 5.8	4.6	4.4	29.9	36.6	37.3	38.5	43.7	51.7	59.4
III. IR&D	NA	NA	29.7	23.0	26.0	29.5	32.5	35.5	39.0	41.0

I. DoD yearly pubication "500 Contractors Receiving the Largest Dollar Volume of Military Prime Contract Awards for RDT&E" and NASA Annual Procurement Reports.

II. Figures for 1970-72 are from the 10K, figures for 1973-79 are "Total F&D costs including government allowed IR&D/B&P" (letter from Grumman, 4 Nov. 1980).

III. Company-sponsored R&D and B&P costs charged to DoD as disclosed by Grumman.

BOARD OF DIRECTORS

Archie E. Albright (1976)
  Vice Chairman of the Board, Drexel, Burnham, Lambert, Inc.
  Past Corporate Employment:
    Patterson, Belknap & Webb (1948-53); Stauffer Chemical Co. (1953-68); Partner, Kuhn, Loeb & Co. (1968-71); Chairman of the Board and Chief Executive Officer, Drexel, Firestone, Inc. (1972-73); Drexel, Burnham, Lambert, Inc. (1973-present).
  Corporate Directorships:
    P.R. Mallory & Co., Inc. ($5,068,000); Bowmar Instruments Co. ($1,675,000); LaPointe Industries ($413,000); General Vehicle Corp.
  Shares Owned:
    100

Kenneth S. Axelson (1974)
  Senior V.P. and Director, J.C. Penney Co.
  Past Corporate Employment:
    Accountant, Arthur Andersen & Co., Seattle (1946-48); Management consultant, McKinsey & Co. (1950-52); Partner, Peat, Marwick, Mitchell & Co. (1952-63); J.C. Penney Co. (1963-present).
  Government Positions:
    Member, Advisory Committee on Implementation-Central Market System-SEC (1974-75); Deputy Mayor of Finance, N.Y.C. (1975-76); Emergency Financial Control Board, N.Y.C. (1976).
  Corporate Directorships:
    Discount Corp. of N.Y.; Protection Mutual Insurance Co.; Dry Dock Savings Bank (trustee).
  Shares owned:
    220

Lucy Wilson Benson (1980)
  Consultant, U.S. State Department
  Government Positions:
    Secretary of Human Services, Commonwealth of Massachusetts (1975-77); Under-Secretary of State for Science and Technology (1977); numerous Massachusetts State commissions.
  Corporate Directorships:
    Northeast Utilities; Dreyfus 3rd Century Fund; Continental Group.
  Key Educational and Research Positions:
    Brookings Institution, Council on Foreign Relations.
  Shares owned:
    200

John C. Bierwirth (1971)
Chairman of the Board, Grumman Corp.
Past Corporate Employment:
Associate, White & Case, N.Y.C. (1950-53); Assistant V.P., N.Y. Trust Co. (1953); National Distillers and Chemical Corporation (1957-72); Grumman Corp. (1976-present).
Corporate Directorships:
Koppers Co. Inc.; Centenial Insurance Co.; General Reinsurance Co.; Atlantic Mutual Insurance Co. (trustee).
Key Association Memberships:
Committee for Economic Development.
Shares owned:
46,300

John F. Carr (1976)
Vice Chairman of the Board, Grumman Corp.
Past Corporate Employment:
Attorney, Sage, Gray, Todd & Sims, N.Y.C. (1948-50); contract negotiator, Honeywell Regulator Co. (1953-55); Grumman Corp. (1955-present).
Government Positions:
Attorney, Office of General Counsel, Department of Navy (1950-53).
Shares owned:
15,426

Charles E. Dunbar (1972)
Director and retired Chairman of the Board, Discount Corp. of N.Y.
Past Corporate Employment:
Robinson, Miller & Co. (1936-38); Discount Corp. of N.Y. (1938-present).
Corporate Directorships:
Tri-Continental Corp.; East River Savings Bank (trustee).
Shares owned:
550

C. Clyde Ferguson, Jr. (1977)
Professor of Law, Harvard Law School
Past Employment:
Professor of Law, Rutgers Law School (1955-63), Dean and Professor of Law, Howard University Law School (1963-69); Professor of Law, Harvard Law School (1975-present).
Government Positions:
Assistant U.S. Attorney, Southern district N.Y. (1954-55); General Counsel, U.S. Commission on Civil Rights (1961-63);

Special U.S. coordinator of relief to civilian victims of Nigerian Civil War (1969-70); Ambassador to Uganda (1970-72); Deputy Assistant Secretary of State on African Affairs, Washington DC (1972-73); U.S. representative, Economic and Social Council of the U.N. (1973-75).
Shares owned:
391

Robert Freese (1977)
V.P. and Treasurer, Grumman Corp.
Past Corporate Employment:
Grumman Corp. (1956-present).
Corporate Directorships:
Bank of New York, Valley Long Island Region, Advisory Board.
Shares owned:
8,922

Joseph G. Gavin, Jr. (1972)
President, Grumman Corp.
Past Corporate Employment:
Grumman Aerospace (1946-present) (Chief Missile and Space Engineer-1957; V.P. of Grumman Corp.-1962; Director of Space Programs-1968).
Corporate Directorships:
European-American Bancorp.
Key Association Memberships:
American institute of Aeronautics and Astronautics (fellow); American Astronautics Society; Aerospace Industries Association.
Shares owned:
44,875

Ira G. Hedrick (1976)
Senior V.P., Grumman Aerospace (retired 1979)
Government Positions:
Member, Science Advisory Board, U.S. Air Force; Member, Advisory Committee on Materials and Structures, NASA.
Corporate Directorships:
Advanced Systems Technology ($248,000).
Key Association Memberships:
American Defense Preparedness Association.
Shares owned:
12,246

James A. Linen (1978)
Chairman, Linen, Fortenberry & Assoc., Inc.
Past Corporate Employment:
President, Time, Inc. (1960-69).
Corporate Directorships:
Simmons Co. ($880,000).
Key Association Memberships:
Iran-U.S. Business Council (Vice Chairman); Council on Japan-U.S. Economic Relations (Advisor); Asian Institute of Technology (trustee); Business Council; Council on Foreign Relations; International Chamber of Commerce.
Shares owned:
1,000

Ellis L. Phillips, Jr. (1975)
Educational Consultant; President, Action Committee for Long Island.
Past Employment:
Attorney, Burke & Burke, N.Y.C. (1948-53); Assistant Dean, Columbia School of Law (1953-61); Professor, Columbia Law School (1961-70), President, Ithaca College (1970-75).
Government Positions:
Staff Member, President's Committee on International Information Activities (1953); Special Assistant to U.S. Ambassador to England (1957-58).
Shares owned:
19,156

John T. Sargent (1978)
Chairman of the Board, Doubleday, Inc.
Past Corporate Employment:
Editor, Doubleday & Co. (1945-present).
Corporate Directorships:
East River Savings Bank (trustee).
Shares owned:
200

George M. Skurla (1974)
Chairman of the Board and President, Grumman Aerospace Corp.
Past Corporate Employment:
Grumman Corp. (1944-present), Director of Operations, Apollo Lunar Modules (1965-70).
Corporate Directorships:
Litco Corp. of N.Y./Long Island Trust Co.

Key Association Memberships:
American Institute of Aeronautics and Astronautics (fellow); Air Force Association; American Defense Preparedness Association; Association of the U.S. Army.
Shares owned:
21,126

PERSONNEL TRANSFERS

Table III
(DoD 1970-79)
(NASA 1974-79)

	Total	Air Force	Army	Navy	Office of Secretary of Defense	Other
DoD Military to Grumman	67	25	1	37	3	1
DoD Civilian to Grumman	5	0	0	2	3	0
NASA to Grumman	1					
Grumman to DoD	16	1	3	8	1	3
Grumman to NASA	7					
Total	96	26	4	47	6	4

Appearances of Potential Conflict of Interest (see Chapter 6): 10

1. DoD to Grumman

Garafolo, John
  DoD:
    Asst. Branch Head, Anti-submarine and Special Mission Air Support Group, Logistics Fleet, Naval Air Systems Command.
  Grumman:
    August 1969, Planning manager, integrated logistics support.

Luckenbill, William H.
  DoD:
    Program Analyst, Naval Air Systems Command.
  Grumman:
    March 1970, Government Liaison Representative, Washington Office.

Singer, Sidney
   DoD:
      Budget analyst, Office of Secretary of Defense.
   Grumman:
      February 1969, Staff assistant, liaison with government agencies.

2. Grumman to DoD

Coutinho, John
   Grumman:
      Stress analyst.
   DoD:
      May 1975, Director, manufacturing operations, Air Force.

Erickson, James
   Grumman:
      Manufacturing Manager, supervised production of aerospace sytems.
   DoD:
      May 1975, Army Material, Systems Analysis, Acting Chief, Engineering Branch.

McCullough, Hugh
   Grumman:
      Director of Long-Range Planning.
   DoD:
      September 1969, Special Asst. to Asst. Secretary of Defense for Installations and Logistics.

3. Grumman to NASA

Bower, Robert Edward
   Grumman:
      Director of advanced development, Independent Research and Development program and contracts.
   NASA:
      September 1971, Director of Aeronautics, Langley Air Force Base.

Gray, Edward
   Grumman:
      Director, military space program, directing corporate acquisition strategy.
   NASA:
      April 1973, Asst. Administrator for Industry Affairs and Technology Utilization, liaision with contractor managers.

Voris, Roy Marline
 Grumman:
  Special Asst. to Sr. V.P. for Business Development, Director Public Affairs and Special Asst. to Board Chairman.
 NASA:
  October 1973, Chief, Industrial Applications Division, application of technology to non-aerospace industrial sector.

4. "Revolving Door"

Simon, Allan
 DoD:
  Asst. Secretary for Air Warfare, Office of Director of Defense Research and Engineering.
 Grumman:
  No date (filed 1975), Technical consultant.
 DoD:
  June 1978, Associate Member, Army Science Board.

Comments

1. Ten of Grumman's 21 DoD civilian transfers are with the Navy, the principal Grumman customer.
2. Grumman has no policy statement on transfers of personnel.

POLITICAL ACTION COMMITTEE

Name: Grumman Political Action Comittee
Total Expenditures (2/77-5/80): $390,980
Total Contributions to Federal Campaigns (2/77-5/80): $337,990

Key
(D) = Democrat
(R) = Republican
(C) = Recipient was a candidate and not elected to that office.
 + = Candidate is also a member of a key Congressional committee.
 * = Candidate is a member of two committees, but contribution s/he received is only listed once to avoid being double-counted in the total for this section.

A. Contributions to Federal Candidates in States with Grumman Production Facilities (Key Geographic Locations)

NEW YORK
Grumman plant located in Bethpage (dist. 3)

Senate

Sen. Jacob Javits (R)	$5,000
+ Sen. Daniel P. Moynihan (D)	$5,000

House

+ Rep. Joseph P. Addabbo (D-7)	$8,000
Stuart Ain (R-6) (C)	$1,000
+ Rep. Jerome Ambro (D-3)	$7,000
Rep. Mario Biaggi (D-10)	$ 750
Gregory Carman (R-3) (C)	$1,000
+ Rep. William Carney (R-1)	$5,500
Rep. Shirley Chisholm (D-12)	$1,000
+ Rep. Thomas Downey (D-2)	$4,950
Rep. Robert Garcia (D-21)	$ 100
+ Rep. Jack Kemp (RC-38)	$2,000
Rep. Norman Lent (R-4)	$7,000
John Matthews (D-5) (C)	$1,000
Rep. Robert McEwen (RC-30)	$1,000
Rep. Matthew McHugh (D-27)	$1,000
+ Rep. Donald Mitchell (RC-31)	$3,500
John Randolph (D-1) (C)	$1,000
Rep. Charles Rangel (D-19)	$2,000
Everett Rosenblum (D-4) (C)	$1,000
+ Rep. Samuel Stratton (D-28)	$ 500
Harold Withers (R-2) (C)	$1,000
Rep. Lester L. Wolff (D-6)	$6,000
+ Rep. John Wydler (R-5)	$7,000
Rep. Leo Zeferetti (D-15)	$ 500

Total New York: $73,800
% Total Federal Contributions: 21.8%

GEORGIA

Grumman Aerospace operations in Milledgeville (dist. 8)

Senate

+ Sen. Sam Nunn (D))	$5,000

House

+ Rep. Jack Brinkley (D-3)	$1,000
+ Rep. Billy Lee Evans (D-8)	$1,400
Rep. Ronald Ginn (D-1)	$ 500
+ Rep. Lawrence McDonald (D-7)	$1,000

Total Georgia: $8,900
% Total Federal Contributions: 2.6%

Total to Key Geographic Locations: $82,700
% Total Federal Contributions: 24.5%

B. Contributions to Members of Key Congressional Committees

Senate Armed Services Committee

Culver	$2,000	Morgan	$2,000
Goldwater	$5,000	Nunn	$5,000
Hart	$3,000	Thurmond	$5,000
Humphrey, Gordon	$1,000	Tower	$5,000
Jepsen	$1,000	Warner	$3,500

House Armed Services Committee

Badham	$1,000	Lloyd, James	$2,500
Bailey	$ 500	McDonald	$1,000
Brinkley	$1,000	Mitchell, Don	$3,500
Daniel, Dan	$1,500	Nedzi	$1,000
Daniel, Robert	$4,500	Spence	$1,000
Davis, Mendel	$6,000	Stratton	$ 500
Dickinson	$1,000	White, Richard	$2,000
Downey	$4,950	Whitehurst	$1,500
Holt	$1,500	Wilson, Bob	$1,000
Ichord	$ 500	Wilson, Charles	$1,000

Senate Defense Appropriations Subcommittee

Garn	$4,000	Inouye	$2,000
Hollings	$5,000	Magnuson	$2,000

House Defense Appropriations Subcommittee

Addabbo	$8,000	Edwards, Jack	$3,000
Burlison	$ 500	Kemp	$2,000
Chappell	$4,000	McFall	$ 500
Cederberg	$1,000	Robinson	$ 500
Conte	$ 500		

Senate Committee on Commerce, Science and Transportation
Subcommittee on Aviation

Goldwater	*

Subcommittee on Science, Technology and Space

Goldwater	*

House Committee on Science and Technology

Ambro	$7,000	Gammage	$ 500
Carney	$5,500	Harsha	$ 200
Downey	*	Lloyd, Jim	*
Flowers	$1,000	McCormack	$ 500
Fuqua	$1,500	White	*
		Wydler	$7,000

Senate Committee on Environment and Public Works
Subcommittee on Transportation

Moynihan	$5,000

House Committee on Public Works and Transportation
  Subcommittee on Aviation

Ambro	•	Harsha	•
Edgar	$1,000	Mineta	$ 500
Evans	$1,400	Shuster	$ 800

Total to Key Committees: $134,850
% Total Federal Contributions: 39.9%

C. Contributions to Other Influential Members of Congress

Sen. Howard Baker (R-TN), Minority Leader	$5,000
Sen. Alan Cranston (D-CA), Majority Whip	$1,000
Rep. Robert Michel (R-IL), Minority Whip	$1,000
Rep. Thomas P. O'Neill, Jr., (D-MA), Speaker of the House	$5,000
Rep. John Rhodes (R-AZ), Minority Leader	$2,000
Rep. James C. Wright, Jr., (D-TX), Majority Leader	$2,500

Total to Other Influentials: $16,500
% Total Federal Contributions: 4.9%

D. Contributions to Other Federal Candidates

Senate
Church (D-ID)	$1,000	Kruger (D-TX)	$2,000
Dole (R-KS)	$1,000	Mathias (R-MD)	$1,000
Glenn (D-OH)	$3,000		

House
Ashbrook (R-OH)	$ 400	Jenrette (D-SC)	$ 500
Corman (D-CA)	$1,000	Mitchell, Parren (R-MD)	$ 750
Devine (R-OH)	$1,000	Vander Jagt (R-MI)	$1,000
Duncan (D-OR)	$ 500	Wylie (R-OH)	$ 200
Howard (D-NJ)	$1,000	Young (R-AL)	$ 500

Total to Other Federal Candidates: $14,850
% Total Federal Contributions: 4.4%

E. Contributions to Party Campaign Committees

Republican federal-level committees: $39,100
Democratic federal-level committees: $75,340

Total to Party Committees: $114,440
% Total Federal Contributions: 33.9%

F. Contributions to Presidential Candidates

John Anderson (I)	$1,000
Howard Baker (R)	$5,000
George Bush (R)	$2,500
Jimmy Carter (D)	$5,000
John Connally (R)	$5,000
Edward Kennedy (D)	$2,500
Ronald Reagan (R)	$5,000
R. Sargent Shriver (D)	$ 500

Total to Presidential Candidates: $26,500
% Total Federal Contributions: 7.8%

COMMENT:

The International Association of Machinists (IAM) filed a complaint with the Federal Election Commission (FEC) in 1979 against Grumman and nine other corporate PACs. IAM alleged that "Grumman manifests the less than free and voluntary character of employee responses to the company's political solicitations in several salient respects: 1) Grumman solicits unprotected career employees for PAC donations which will buy political support for 'Grumman's plans and projects,' and 2) makes no provision to protect the anonymity of non-contributors or of contribution amounts. 3) 75% of the itemized contributors are mid-level managerial and professional employees (the majority of Grumman PAC's receipts are unitemized), and they contributed 51% of the itemized contributions. 4) There is no known restriction on solicitation by supervisors or superiors. 5) The average annual contribution for mid-level managers and professionals is $116, while executive-level personnel contributed an average of $468. 6) Although most employees are either Democrats or Republicans, as a corporation reliant on Government contracts Grumman attempts to maximize its political influence by splitting the employees' PAC donations evenly between Democrats and Republicans. 7) 98% of the itemized PAC receipts were obtained in California, Florida, New York and Virginia, but only 54% of the PAC money went to candidates in those states. 8) Employees are not permitted to designate, either by party or candidate, the recipients of their money. 9) There is no information available concerning contribution rates for Grumman employees. 10) The PAC reports several clear orchestration (sic) of the amounts of employee PAC contributions: 70% of the annual itemized contributions were exactly $104."

(From *Complaints Against Operations of Corporate Political Action Committees*, filed before the FEC by the International Association of Machinists, October 1979.)

A Grumman spokesman stated that the complaint is "filled with errors. For example, anonymity of contributors is protected, supervisors don't solicit and so on and on." The complaint was dismissed by the FEC in December 1979, stating that there were insufficient grounds for the commission to believe there is a violation of the act, that it did not appear that corporate solicitation systems violated the act and that the complaint raised some issues the FEC was not empowered to decide upon, among other grounds. The Machinists Union has since taken the complaint against the 10 PACs to Federal District Court on the grounds that the Federal Election Law permits PACs to solicit employees in such a way that they cannot make a truly voluntary decision.

WASHINGTON OPERATIONS

Washington Office:
1600 Wilson Blvd., Suite 711, Arlington, VA 22209

Directors:
John F. Carr, Vice Chairman, Grumman Corp.
Gordon H. Ochenrider, Senior V.P., Grumman Aerospace

Activities:
1. International: Supporting foreign marketing and international sales.
2. National Affairs and Stretegic Planning: Gathering information, performing public relations, entertainment and lobbying tasks.
3. Government Relations: Keeping abreast of Congressional activities and their effect on company programs.

Registered Lobbyists

	Receipts	Expenditures	Years
Cederberg & Associates** 7100 Sussex Place Alexandria, VA	$ 400	*	79
G.H. Ochenrider Grumman Aerospace Corp. 1600 Wilson Blvd. Arlington, VA	$25,000	$10,190	77-79
F. Slatinshek & Assoc.*** 218 N. Lee St. Alexandria, VA	$ 6,550	*	77-79
TOTAL	**$31,950**	**$10,190**	

*No figures reported; quarterly reports were filed.

**With Martin Marietta, RCA and United Technologies
***With General Dynamics, Gould and United Technologies

DEFENSE-RELATED TRADE ASSOCIATION MEMBERSHIPS

Aerospace Industries Association
Air Force Association
American Defense Preparedness Association
American Institute of Aeronautics and Astronautics
Armed Forces Communication and Electronics Association
National Security Industrial Association

ADVISORY COMMITTEE MEMBERSHIPS

1976-78: 8

Guarino, Thomas
  (V.P., Aerospace Programs, Grumman Aerospace)
    DoD—Defense Science Board, 1976

Hedrick, Ira J.
  (Senior V.P., Presidential Asst. for corporate technology, Grumman Aerospace) (ret. 1979) (see Board of Directors)
    DoD—U.S. Air Force Science Advisory Board, 1976, 1977, 1978
    NASA—Research and Technology Advisory Council, Committee on Materials and Structures 1976, 1977

Hilgeman, Theodore
    NASA—Ad Hoc Advisory Subcommittee for Scientific Definition of Explorer Class Payloads, Space Science Steering Committee, 1976

Kelley, Thomas J.
  (V.P. Engineering, Grumman Aerospace)
    NASA—Research and Technology Advisory Council, Panel on Space Vehicles, 1976, 1977

Meyer, Corwin
  (President, Grumman American Aviation) (sold in 1978)
    NASA—Research and Technology Advisory Council, Panel on General Aviation Technology, 1977, 1978

Offenhartz, Edward
    DoD—Defense Science Board, 1976

Sandler, Gerald
   DoD—Defense Science Board, 1976

Comment:
In 1977 Grumman also had one member on the Commerce Department's Advisory Committee on Aerospace Equipment for the Multilateral Trade Negotiations.

ENTERTAINMENT

Grumman Chairman John C. Bierwirth informed the Joint Committee on Defense Production that Grumman maintains no facilities for entertainment.

Entertaining:
   Roughly $5,000 per year was spent on overnight travel and golf invitations, none of which was charged to government contracts.

Hospitality Suites:
   1973: 16, 1974: 14, 1975: 14.
   Includes Old Crows, Navy League, Air Force Association, Marine Corps Aviation Association, National Security Industrial Association

Tickets:
   1973-75: 236 season tickets, occasionally used by government officials.

Air Travel:
   Rarely; only for special events.

Disclosure:
   Good.

QUESTIONABLE PAYMENTS

In 1974 Grumman received contracts from the Iranian Air Force for the sale of 80 F-14s. As part of this effort, Grumman retained in February 1972, Eastern International, a Long Island family firm headed by Iranian Houshang Lavi, to act as its sales agent in dealing with the Iranian Government. In May 1974, a restructured Lavi contract was sold to another firm, Shaham S.A., of New Jersey, headed by former Army officer Albert Fuge. The sales commisions in the contracts were estimated by Grumman to be worth $24 m. (letter to shareholders, 24 March 1976).

In 1975, Grumman paid $6 m. of those commissions, divided between the Lavis ($3.1 m.) and Fuge ($2.9 m.). In June 1975, the Iranian Government reportedly protested the use of sales agents for the F-14 and held a complex negotiation with Fuge and Grumman International President Peter Oram. As a result of this negotiation, Fuge signed over to the Government of Iran $24 m. worth of sales commissions (*The New York Times*, 11 Jan. 1978).

Subsequently, the Iranian Government and Grumman engaged in lengthy discussions (a year and a half) leading to an agreement in December 1977 to settle the claim by supplying Iran with $24 m. in free spare parts for the F-14 (cancelled in May 1979) (Company *8K*, Dec. 1977; *The New York Times*, 16 Dec. 1977).

As early as 1976, the SEC and the Department of Justice had begun to examine Grumman's payments to agents involved with overseas sales. Grumman has systematically denied that any of its agents' fees involved in the F-14 sale were passed on to Government officials. In January 1979, Grumman agreed to a consent decree with the SEC "restraining it from violating various provisions of the securities laws" (letter to shareholders, 15 Jan. 1979). Grumman officials described this settlement as a "prudent business decision" (Ibid.). In early May 1979, Grumman also arrived at a settlement with the plantiffs in a suit brought by the Lavis, who had claimed that Fuge and Grumman had conspired to deprive them of commissions. Grumman agreed to pay the agents $11.9 m. over a nine month period and up to an additional $4.4 m., pending any claims from the Iranian Government. Such claims could arise from Grumman's unilateral withdrawal from its spares' shipments ($1.6 m. already sent) to Iran, terminating the firm's business in that country (*The Wall Street Journal*, 3, May 1979).

SEC investigations and Grumman's own reports suggest that Grumman's general aviation subsidiary, Gulfstream Aircraft (sold in 1978) and in some cases Page Airways acting as its intermediary, had inadequately disclosed commission payments in several countries, including: Cameroun, Ivory Coast, Togo, Nigeria, Gabon, Abu Dhabi, Algeria, Saudi Arabia, Morocco, the United Arab Emirates, Jordan, Greece, Malaya, Japan, Korea, Panama and Venezuela. In 1979 Gulfstream pleaded guilty to making false statements to conceal $5 m. in commissions (*The New York Times*, 4 Jan. 1979; *The Washington Post*, 5 Jan. 1979). Grumman claims that "none of the several lengthy investigations of these matters produced evidence of any questionable payment by any Grumman officer or employee anywhere in the world. There were no off-the-books funds. Any questionable payments were made by independent businessmen over whom Grumman had no direct control" (letter to CEP, 13 Oct. 1980). Page denies any such transactions (*The Wall Street Journal*, 28 Feb. 1979).

Grumman's board appointed an audit committee in 1978 to investigate all questionable payments. In 1979 the board committee reported some details on above payments totalling roughly $10 m. (*The Washington Post*, 9 Feb. 1979). It observed that the company's original 1975 policy on proper sales contracts and the disclosure of information in such contracts had not been followed by company personnel. According to *The Wall Street Journal* (28 Feb. 1979), the report stated: "This company-wide lack of response to the policies and directives of the board created an intolerable situation which cannot be condoned and must not continue." Grumman representatives described such problems as "procedural lapses" (letter to CEP, 13 Oct. 1980). According to *The Wall Street Journal* (28 Feb. 1979), the Grumman board "has gotten tougher" about making sure its instructions are followed.

DISCLOSURE

Fair.

LOCKHEED

Basic Corporate and Contracting Data

A. Corporate Data

Lockheed Corporation
2555 North Hollywood Way
Burbank, CA 91520

Fortune 500 (1979): 82
Fiscal Year: Jan. 1—Dec. 31

Chairman:
  Roy A. Anderson (1979 salary: $340,000)

President:
  Lawrence O. Kitchen (1979 salary: $257,000)

Auditor:
  Arthur Young & Co.
  515 S. Flower St.
  Los Angeles, CA

Outside Legal Counsel:
  O'Melveny & Myers
  611 W. 6th St.
  Los Angeles, CA

TABLE I
Corporate Data
($ in M.)

	1970	1971	1972	1973	1974	1975	1976	1977	1978	1979
Sales*	$2,536.0	2,852.0	2,473.0	2,757.0	3,276.0	3,383.0	3,188.0	3,348.0	3,485.0	4,058.0
Net Income	$ (188.0)	(40.0)	(7.0)	18.0	23.0	45.0	39.0	55.0	65.0	57.0
Dept. of Defense Contracts	$1,847.7	1,510.5	1,705.4	1,658.9	1,464.4	2,080.3	1,509.8	1,673.4	2,226.4	1,796.6
Rank	1	1	1	1	2	1	2	2	4	5
NASA Contracts	$ 41.0	51.3	46.6	50.8	51.2	60.2	75.4	96.2	106.0	106.1
Rank	13	12	10	9	8	7	5	4	4	5
DoD/NASA Contracts as % of Sales	74.5%	54.8	70.8	62.0	46.2	63.3	49.7	52.9	67.0	46.9
Government Sales	$2,282.4	2,623.8	1,830.0	1,627.0	2,040.0	2,210.0	2,240.0	2,076.0	1,968.0	2,317.0
Government Sales as % of Sales	90.0%	92.0	74.0	59.0	62.3	65.3	70.3	62.0	56.5	57.1
Foreign Military Sales Contracts	$ 25.3	44.0	28.5	50.8	60.0	171.7	139.1	305.2	297.3	141.8
Rank	6	3	7	8	11	8	9	3	4	7
FMS Contracts as % of Sales	1.0%	1.5	1.2	1.8	1.8	5.1	4.4	9.1	8.5	3.5
Overseas and Export Sales	$ 152.2	142.6	222.6	452.0	650.0	938.0	839.0	1,031.0	1,172.0	1,312.0
Overseas and Export Sales as % of Sales	6.0%	5.0	9.0	16.4	19.8	27.7	26.3	30.8	33.6	32.3
Employees	84,600	74,700	69,600	66,900	62,100	57,600	55,100	55,100	61,500	66,500

*Sales figures for 1970-73 from 1974 10K or previous 10Ks; for 1974-79 from 1979 10K.

Rogovin, Stern & Huge
1730 Rhode Island Ave. NW
Washington, DC

Miller & Chevalier
1700 Pennsylvania Ave. NW
Washington, DC

Advertising/Public Relations Agency:
McCann-Erickson, Inc.
6420 Wilshire Blvd.
Los Angeles, CA

Banking:
   Transfer Agents and Registrars:
      Chemical Bank
      United California Bank (see Board of Directors: Roy A. Anderson, Edward W. Carter, Jack K. Horton)
      Manufacturers Hanover Trust

   Lenders:
      Bank of America (owns 7.5% of senior preferred stock)
      Bankers Trust (owns 7.5% of senior preferred stock; agent for the banks)
      Chase Manhattan (owns 7.5% of senior preferred stock) (see Board of Directors: John Swearingen)
      Citibank (owns 7.5% of senior preferred stock)
      Manufacturers Hanover (owns 7.5% of senior preferred stock)
      Morgan Guaranty (owns 7.5% of senior preferred stock)
      Security Pacific National Bank (owns 7.5% of senior preferred stock)
      Continental Illinois (owns 5.8% of senior preferred stock)
      Mellon Bank (owns 5.8% of senior preferred stock)
      Irving Trust
      Western Bancorp. (see Board of Directors: Edward W. Carter, Jack K. Horton)
      First National Bank of Chicago (see Board of Directors: Gilbert R. Ellis, John Swearingen)
      Bank of California
      Chemical Bank
      Citizens & Southern National Bank
      Crocker National Bank
      First National Bank of Atlanta
      First National Bank of Boston
      Fulton National Bank of Atlanta
      Girard Bank
      Pacific National Bank of Washington
      Philadelphia National Bank
      Trust Company Bank
      United California Bank (see Board of Directors: Roy A. Anderson, Edward W. Carter, Jack K. Horton)
      Wells Fargo Bank

   Investment Banker:
      Goldman Sachs

B. Principal Defense/Space Contracting Operations

Lockheed California Co.
Burbank, CA
Edgar M. Cortright, President

P-3C Orion—anti-submarine patrol plane, U.S. Navy, Netherlands, Australia and Japan
CP-140 Aurora—anti-submarine patrol plane, (based on P-3C and S-3A), Canada
TR-1—reconnaissance aircraft, U.S. Air Force
VTX—advance training aircraft-research, U.S. Navy
Utility and tanker aircraft, U.S. Navy

Lockheed Georgia Co.
Marietta, GA
Robert B. Ormsby, Jr., President

C-130 Hercules—cargo aircraft, U.S. Air Force, foreign orders
C-141 Starlifter—cargo aircraft (stretched version), U.S. Air Force
C-5A Galaxy—cargo aircraft (wing repair), U.S. Air Force
Cruise missile carrier design (based on C-5A) U.S. Air Force

Lockheed Missiles and Space Co.
Sunnyvale, CA
Robert A. Fuhrman, President

Trident I—sub-launched ballistic missile, U.S. Navy
Trident II—second generation missile research, U.S. Navy
Acquila remotely piloted vehicle research, U.S. Army
Precision Location Strike System research, U.S. Air Force
Space Telescope, NASA
Retractable solar wing for space shuttle, NASA
Protective silica tile for space shuttle, NASA

Lockheed Electronics Co.
Plainfield, NJ
Harold L. Brownman, President

MK 86—weapon control system, U.S. Navy

Lockheed Engineering & Management Services Co., Inc.
Houston, TX
Robert B. Young, Jr., President

Space shuttle simulation and testing, NASA
LANDSAT—earth survey satellite data analysis, NASA
Material and component testing for space shuttle orbiter vehicle, NASA
Technical support and missile range instrumentation, U.S. Army

Lockheed Shipbuilding and Construction Co.
Seattle, WA
Lawrence A. Smith, President

Icebreakers, Coast Guard
Submarine tenders, U.S. Navy
Cable repair research, U.S. Navy
Ship repair and overhaul, U.S. Navy
Ship landing docks research, U.S. Navy

Lockheed Aircraft Service Co.
Ontario, CA
Robert L. Vader, President

C-130 maintenance, Saudi Air Force
Air traffic control, Saudi Air Force
Training equipment, U.S. Air Force, U.S. Navy, U.S. Marines, Canada, Egypt, Venezuela, Saudi Arabia
F-104 maintenance, Germany
Aircraft maintenance training, Greece

C. Contracting History

Lockheed's defense contracting and commercial business problems have been the repeated subject of headlines through the 1970s. The company has remained a top ranking Defense Department contractor, though it experienced losses in its commercial business during the decade. It was also one of the first U.S. companies to benefit from sizeable Federal Government loan guarantees, which quite possibly ensured its survival as a firm.

Lockheed began the 1970s in a state of crisis. Its giant C-5A Galaxy transport plane for the Air Force increased nearly 100% in unit costs, from an original price of $3.4 b. (for 120 planes) to $4.5 b. (for 81 planes). Three other Lockheed defense contracts were causing the firm trouble at the same time. Lockheed's motors for Boeing's Short Range Attack Missile were over cost. The experimental Cheyenne helicopter crashed in tests and the Army hastily cancelled the production contract. Lockheed was seeking additional funds for shipbuilding work it was doing for the Navy (*The Wall Street Journal*, 6 March 1970).

According to Lockheed Chairman Dan Haughton, "the cumulative impact of the disagreements on four programs creates a critical financial problem which cannot be supported out of our current and projected assets and income." In Haughton's view, a negative settlement could "*seriously* deplete our corporate resources" (Ibid.). In response to the problems, Lockheed wrote Deputy Secretary of Defense David Packard that without interim financing of $640 m. it would have to halt work on the programs (*The Wall Street Journal*, 6 May 1970). Packard, in turn, testified to the Senate Armed Services Committee that "short of bankruptcy and reorganization" Lockheed's only solution was to seek a merger partner or new financial aid, since the company was "so badly overextended that they have essentially no reserve financial resources available" (*Business Week*, 30 May 1970).

Lockheed was also having difficulty with its commercial aircraft programs. In the mid-1960s the company reentered commercial aircraft, after a ten-year absence, with the jumbo L-1011 Tri-Star. Lockheed borrowed to undertake this program, increasing its bank credit (from a 24 bank consortium headed by Bankers Trust) to $400 million. By 1970 according to the *The Wall Street Journal* (6 March 1970) $300 m. of that line had been used and, with the defense contract squeeze, "the company is considered to be seriously short of cash."

According to Deputy Secretary Packard, the two problems, commercial and military, were linked. Even with a favorable solution of the defense contract problem, he testified, Lockheed needed a "concomitant resolution of the company's commercial problems," since these could "seriously jeopardize production of military hardware over the next two or three years" (*Business Week*, 30 May 1970).

The Federal Government played a major role in pulling Lockheed out of the crisis. According to Packard's December 1970 letter to Congress on the proposed solution, without major assistance "bankruptcy of Lockheed was and is inevitable" (*The Washington Post*, 31 Dec. 1970). The Government's proposed package provided over $1 b. in new federal funding, with Lockheed absorbing a sizeable loss — $480 m. — on the four defense programs (Ibid., 5 April 1971).

This package came apart in February 1971, when Lockheed's engine partner on the L-1011, Britain's Rolls-Royce, collapsed into bankruptcy and was nationalized by the British Government. Rolls had clearly underestimated the technological difficulties, cost, and timing for its engine program and demanded a new agreement with Lockheed.

As the leading defense contractor, Lockheed hoped the Federal Government would help seek ways to preserve its existence as a private firm. As Rep. William Moorehead (D-PA) of the House Banking Committee put it, Lockheed was like "an 80-ton dinosaur who comes to your door and says, 'If you don't feed me I will die and what are you going to do with 80 tons of dead, stinking dinosaur in your yard'" (Ibid., 5 April 1971).

The Treasury and Defense Departments, the banks, trade unions, and customer airlines all went to work for Lockheed. By August 1971, the Senate (by one vote) and the House (by three votes) had passed an emergency Federal loan guarantee, allowing Lockheed to borrow $250 m. in banking credit, increasing the contractor's debt to over $650 million. According to the *The Wall Street Journal* (5 Aug. 1971) a "well-coordinated" lobbying campaign had carried the day for Lockheed.

Even with the loan guarantee, Lockheed's recovery in the 1970s was linked to a two-fold strategy: doing high-volume Defense Department business and pushing overseas commercial and military sales. Merger was another possible strategy. Felix Rohatyn of Lazard Freres negotiated for Textron to purchase 45% of Lockheed and participate in management. The talks collapsed in 1975, however, "ostensibly because of delays necessitated by a government investigation of possible fraud related to Lockheed shipbuilding claims," (*The New York Times*, 14 Feb. 1976. See also Ibid., 8 May 1974; *The Washington Post*, 2 June, 9 June 1974; *Aviation Week*, 10 June 1974; *Electronics News*, 10 March 1975).

The defense/foreign sales strategy paid off for Lockheed. Sales of the L-1011 were gradual through the decade, but substantial contracts were negotiated with All-Nippon Airways, Cathay Pacific, and a variety of Arab customers. Simultaneously, Lockheed expanded foreign sales of its military products, particularly the C-130 Hercules military transport (1,500 delivered to buyers in 43 nations between 1956 and 1976), and the P-3C Orion anti-submarine warfare plane (over 1,000 in sales since 1960). Lockheed acknowledged the importance of overseas sales: "Lockheed's foreign sales generally are more profitable than its domestic sales and generally provide favourable advances which have been a significant factor in Lockheed's total financing program" (Company *8K*, 31 July 1975).

Foreign sales caused some headaches for Lockheed's management however, when the company's questionable payments were disclosed in 1975 (see below). The banks reportedly urged at this time that senior management be replaced before agreeing to renew Lockheed's lines of credit. According to *Fortune*, "The spreading firestorm of publicity over those payments, which most businessmen now euphemistically call questionable, persuaded the bankers that, as one reports, 'Dan and Carl had to go'" (*Fortune*, Oct. 1977). Bankers Trust reportedly resisted this idea, but came under pressure from others in the consortium, notably First National of Chicago (*The Wall Street Journal*, 8 April 1976). According to one banker, "It was evident that when we gave these guys more loan money, we were just giving them a cookie jar full of cash to make payoffs" (Ibid.). Lockheed denied that loan funds were used in this way but Lockheed Chief Executive Officer Dan Haughton and President Carl Kotchian stepped down (Ibid.). Robert Haack, a board member and former president of the New York Stock Exchange, replaced Haughton. Haack was well-placed to aid Lockheed, since, according to *Fortune* (Oct. 1977), "He already knew on a first-name basis all of the players who affected Lockheed's fate."

In the fall of 1976, Lockheed's bank credit was restructured, with the approval of the banks, the Federal Government, and Lockheed's stockholders. Several banks had urged Lockheed to write off its sizeable R&D investment in the L-1011. For years Lockheed had been postponing this decision, arguing that L-1011 orders would eventually recover the R&D costs. Lockheed began writing off these costs in 1976.

Federal Government sales were clearly important to Lockheed's recovery. From fiscal year 1970 through fiscal year 1979, Lockheed received $21.1 b. from Government sales, some 67.3% of company sales for the period. According to Bankers Trust Vice President Frederick Leary in 1976, "the rest of the company is going like gangbusters helping absorb the L-1011 losses, and that way you can carry a sick baby for a long while" (*The Wall Street Journal*, 8 April 1976). As Smith Barney investment firm put it in 1976, "With the money it has coming in on its military operations, Lockheed has a very good chance of rebuilding itself" (*The New York Times*, 17 Oct. 1976). Brian Freeman, Chairman of the Federal Loan Guarantee Board said in 1977, "Its military programs make Lockheed a cash machine" (*Business Week*, 10 Oct. 1977). The new Lockheed Chief Executive Officer, Roy Anderson, who succeeded Haack in 1977, concurred, stating that Lockheed's military programs provided "the sound base and the cash that enabled us to keep going" (*Fortune*, Oct. 1977).

Military sales could help because the firm's leading military programs were steady, tried and true performers, whose development costs had long since been paid, and which continued to turn steady cash flow for the company. DoD depended on Lockheed in several key areas in the 1970s: *airlift* (the C-130, the lengthened version of the C-141, and repairs on the wings of the C-5A fleet—which could bring in over $1 b. to the firm); *ASW planes* (the S-3A carrier-borne ASW plane, and the P-3C Orion sold to the U.S. and many foreign buyers); and *sea-launched ballistic missiles* (Polaris and Poseidon in the early 1970s, followed by a $1.3 b. contract for the new Trident missile in 1974).

Lockheed also remained a critical supplier of surveillance aircraft and satellites for the Air Force and the Central Intelligence Agency. CIA surveillance satellites were said to represent 40% of Lockheed's Missile and Space Division sales in the mid-1970s (*Business Week*, 10 Oct. 1977). In 1978 the Defense Department reopened production of surveillance aircraft with a redesigned U-2, designated the TR-1, of which current plans are to order 25 (worth $550 m.).

Foreign sales continued to play a major role in Lockheed's balance sheet, especially the sale of 45 P-3Cs to Japan (for $141 b.) and of 18 redesigned P-3Cs to Canada (for $697 m.) to be called the CP-140 Aurora. The Federal Government assisted with both sales. Secretary of Defense Donald Rumsfeld lobbied for the Japanese sale, and DoD, the Federal Reserve and Treasury all lobbied to keep the Canadian sale from falling through (*The New York Times*, 27 May 1976; and *The Washington Post*, 5 May 1976). In June 1976, Lockheed also won a $625 m. contract from the Saudi Government for an air traffic control system.

Lockheed's financial picture was much improved by 1980. The Federal loan guarantee had ended in 1977. A new $425 m. credit line was negotiated in 1979, to decline to $275 m. by 1981. L-1011 orders had increased, although the company was facing increased costs for accelerating its production rate (*Forbes*, 10 Dec. 1979). Moreover, L-1011 R&D costs were still being written off, leading one Lockheed executive to state that "TriStar has been bleeding off the profits" (*The New York Times*, 1 July 1979). Defense business continued to pick up. Lockheed was competing to design the Air Force's new CX transport aircraft, and Lockheed Shipbuilding and Construction Co. could benefit from increased spending for the Rapid Deployment Force, which might use its LSD-41 landing ship dock. In addition, Lockheed announced its intention of investing $500 m. in independent R&D funds for work on future military projects in areas where the company already had an advantage: sea-launched missiles, anti-submarine warfare aircraft, and cargo aircraft.

D. U.S. Government-Owned, Company-Operated Plants

Total company floor space: 25,318,000 sq. ft.

Leased from U.S. Government: 8,043,190 sq. ft. (31.77%)

Total leasecost: $358,830 (partial disclosure)

Location: Air Force Plant 42 (site 2 and part of site 5)
Palmdale, CA
412,883 sq. ft.
Use: Classified
Cost: $237,784 (partial, for L-1011 taxiway only)

Location: Air Force Plant 42 (site 4)
Palmdale, CA
501,336 sq. ft.
Use: Warehouse
Cost: $121,046

Location: Air Force Plant 6
Marietta, GA
6,305,741 sq. ft.
Use: C-130 Jetstar, C-141, C-5
Cost: Not disclosed

Location: Navy/DoD Plant 484
Sunnyvale, CA
823,230 sq. ft.
Use: Polaris, Poseidon and Trident I missiles
Cost: Not disclosed

RESEARCH AND DEVELOPMENT

Major Defense/Space R&D Projects

CX—military transport design work, U.S. Air Force
VTX—advanced training aircraft, U.S. Navy
Utility and tanker aircraft, U.S. Navy
Cruise missile carrier, U.S. Air Force
Trident I and II missiles, U.S. Navy
Ground-launched interceptor missile, U.S. Army
Precision Location Strike System, U.S. Air Force
Space telescope, NASA
Shuttle retractable wing, NASA
Ship landing docks, U.S. Navy
Cable repair ship, U.S. Navy

BOARD OF DIRECTORS

Roy A. Anderson (1971)
 Chairman of the Board and Chief Executive Officer, Lockheed Corp.
Past Corporate Employment:
 Westinghouse Electric Co. (1952-56); Lockheed Corp. (1956-present) (Missiles and Space Co.-1956; Lockheed Georgia Co.-1965 (director of finance-1965); Lockheed Corp.-1969 (V.P. and Controller-1969)).
Corporate Directorships:
 United California Bank (see Basic Data: Banking); Avantek; Sutro Mortgage Investment Trust, Los Angeles.
Shares owned:
 12,125

TABLE II
Research and Development
($ in M.)

	1970	1971	1972	1973	1974	1975	1976	1977	1978	1979
I. U.S. Government Contracts										
DoD	$526.3	333.7	372.7	430.5	326.5	508.1	658.7	560.2	349.7	231.6
NASA	$ 41.0	51.3	46.6	50.8	51.2	60.2	75.4	96.2	106.0	106.1
Total	$567.3	385.0	419.3	481.3	377.7	568.3	734.1	656.4	455.7	337.7
II. Company-sponsored R&D	$ 42.0	33.0	33.0	39.0	42.0	45.0	53.0	56.6	64.0	66.0
III. IR&D	NA	NA	NA	19.0	21.8	24.3	28.1	29.0	29.3	NA

I. From DoD yearly publication "500 Contractors Receiving the Largest Dollar Volume of Military Prime Contract Awards for RDT&E" and NASA Annual Procurement Reports.

II. "Company sponsored R&D effort, a portion of which was included in overhead allocable to U.S. government contracts." (Does not include costs for the L-1011 TriStar) (10K, 1979).

III. Company-sponsored R&D costs charged to DoD as disclosed by DoD.

Michael Berberian (1973)
Secretary-Treasurer, Berberian Brothers, Inc. (wholesale distributor of foods)
Shares owned:
145,000

Edward W. Carter (1979)
Chairman of the Board, Carter Hawley Hale Stores, Inc.
Military:
Ensign to rear admiral, U.S. Navy (1945).
Government Positions:
Staff member, Naval Operations (1962-64); Deputy Commander, weapons systems and engineering, Naval Sea Systems Command (1976).
Corporate Directorships:
American Telephone and Telegraph Co. ($244,878,000); Del Monte Corp. ($11,579,000); Pacific Mutual Life Insurance Co.; Southern California Edison Co. ($7,762,000); Western Bancorp. (see Basic Data: Banking).
Shares owned:
100

Joseph P. Downer (1976)
Executive V.P., Atlantic Richfield Co.
Past Corporate Employment:
Continental Oil Co. (1948-52); Wertheim & Co. (1952-59); Sinclair Oil Corp. (1959-69) (merged into Atlantic Richfield Co.-1969).
Corporate Directorships:
Fiduciary Trust Co., N.Y.
Shares owned:
200

Gilbert R. Ellis (1978)
Chairman and Chief Executive Officer, Household Finance Corp.
Past Corporate Employment:
Household Finance Corp. (1935—present).
Corporate Directorships:
First Chicago Corp./First National Bank of Chicago.
Shares owned:
200

Houston I. Flournoy (1976)
V.P. for Government Affairs, University of Southern California (1978-present)
Past Employment:
Dean of the Center for Public Affairs, University of Southern California (1975-78).

Government Positions:
California State Assembly (1961-66); Controller, State of California (1967-74).
Corporate Directorships:
Gilbraltar Financial Corp.; Fremont General Corp.; Tosco Corp. ($104,000).
Shares owned:
100

Robert A. Fuhrman (1980)
President, Lockheed Missiles & Space Co.; Senior V.P., Lockheed Corp.
Past Corporate Employment:
Lockheed Corp. (1959-present) (Manager, Polaris Systems Integration,-1959; Corp. V.P. and General Manager, Lockheed Missiles Systems Division-1969; President, Lockheed Georgia-1970; President, Lockheed California Company-1971; Executive V.P. Lockheed Missiles & Space-1973).
Government Positions:
Production Panel for Navy & Marine Corps Acquisition Review Committee; Alabama Space & Rocket Center Advisory Committee; Defense Science Board.
Key Association Memberships:
American Institute of Aeronautics and Astronautics; American Defense Preparedness Association.
Shares owned:
6,925

John T. Gurash (1977)
Retired Chairman of the Board, INA Corp. (insurance holding co.)
Past Corporate Employment:
American Surety Co., N.Y. (1930-44); Pacific Employers, Inc. (1944-53) (1959-66); Meritplan Insurance Co. (1953-59); INA Corp. (1966-75).
Corporate Directorships:
Lloyds Bank of California; Insurance Co. of North America; Compagnie Financiere de Suez; Purex Corp. ($2,824,000); Household Finance Corp.; MGIC Investment Corp.
Shares owned:
250

Willis M. Hawkins (1972)
Sr. V.P., Lockheed Corp.; President, Lockheed California Co. (retired 1979)
Past Corporate Employment:
Grumman Aircraft Co. (1936-37); Lockheed Corp. (1937-63; 1966-79) (Director of engineering, Missiles and Space Co.-

1953;Asst. General Manager, Missiles and Space Co.-1959;
V.P., science and engineering, Lockheed Corp.-1962-63 and
1966; Senior V.P., science and engineering-1969; President,
California Co.-1976).

Government Positions:
Asst. Secretary of the Army for Research and Development
(1963-66); Member, U.S. Army Scientific Advisory Panel
(1957-73); Member, Industry Advisory Panel, National
Science Foundation (1973-present); Technical consultant to
NASA (1974-present).

Government Awards:
Recipient, Distinguished Public Service Medal for contribution
to Polaris missile program, U.S. Navy (1961); Distinguished
Civilian Service Award, U.S. Army (1965).

Corporate Directorships:
Riverside Research Institute (trustee); Wackenhut Corp.
($344,000); R&D Associates.

Key Association Memberships:
American Institute of Aeronautics and Astronautics (fellow).

Shares owned:
3,200

Jack K. Horton (1966)
Chairman of the Board, Southern California Edison Co.

Past Corporate Employment:
Shell Oil Co. (1937-42); Private law practice (1942-43);
Standard Oil Co. (1943-44); Gas and Electric Co. (1944-51);
Southern California Edison Co. (1951-present).

Corporate Directorships:
United California Bank (see Basic Data: Banking); Pacific
Mutual Life Insurance Co.; Western Bancorp. (see Basic Data:
Banking).

Key Association Memberships:
Business Council.

Shares owned:
200

Lawrence O. Kitchen (1975)
President and Chief Operating Officer, Lockheed Corp.

Past Corporate Employment:
Lockheed Corp. (1958-present) (Lockheed Missiles & Space
Co.-1968; director, financial management controls, Missile
System Division, Lockheed-Georgia-1970; President, Lockheed
Aircraft Corp.-1975).

Government Positions:
Aeronautical engineer and staff asst. to the asst. chief for
Logistics Plan and Policy, Bureau of Aeronautics, U.S. Navy
(1946-58).

Key Association Memberships:
National Defense Transportation Association; American Institute of Aeronautics and Astronautics; Navy League; Air Force Association; Association of the U.S. Army; American Defense Preparedness Association.
Shares owned:
7,975

Vincent Marafino (1980)
Senior V.P. Finance, Lockheed Corp.
Past Corporate Employment:
Chief accountant, American Standard Advance Technology Laboratories (until 1959); Lockheed Corp. (1959-present) (Accounting and Finance Executive, Lockheed Missiles and Space Co.-1969; Controller, Lockheed Corp.-1971).
Shares owned:
5,875

Joseph R. Rensch (1978)
President, Pacific Lighting Corp.
Past Corporate Employment:
Pacific Lighting Corp. (1947-present).
Corporate Directorships:
Union Bancorp, Inc./Union Bank; Bekins Co.; Kaiser Steel Corp. ($1,509,000); Olga Corp.
Shares owned:
200

Leslie N. Shaw (1973)
V.P., Great Western Financial Corp. (savings and loan holding co.)
Past Corporate Employment:
Chairman of the Board and President, First City Savings and Loan Association (1969-74); V.P., Great Western Financial Corp. (1969-present).
Shares owned:
100

John Swearingen (1978)
Chairman of the Board and Chief Executive Officer, Standard Oil Co. of Indiana
Past Corporate Employment:
Standard Oil (1939-present).
Corporate Directorships:
Chase Manhattan Corp. (see Basic Data: Banking); American National Bank and Trust Co., Chicago.
Shares owned:
2,000

Fred Vinson, Jr. (1971)
Partner, Reasoner, Davis & Vinson (law firm)
Past Corporate Employment:
Partner, Reasoner, Davis & Vinson (1963-64, 1969-present):
Government Positions:
Asst. Attorney General, Criminal Division, Department of Justice (1965-69).
Shares owned:
200

PERSONNEL TRANSFERS

Table III
(DoD 1970-79)
(NASA 1974-79)

	Total	Air Force	Army	Navy	Office of Secretary of Defense	Other
DoD Military to Lockheed	240	162	15	56	2	5
DoD Civilian to Lockheed	30	5	10	8	3	4
NASA to Lockheed	6					
Lockheed to DoD	34	8	5	7	4	10
Lockheed to NASA	11					
Total	321	175	30	71	9	19

Appearances of Potential Conflict of Interest
(see Chapter 6): 13

1. DoD to Lockheed
Alne, Leonard
DoD:
Director, Sales Negotiations, Defense Security Assistance Agency (left June 1974).
Lockheed:
January 1977, Consultant on sale of military aircraft to foreign buyers.

Brownman, Harold
   DoD:
      Asst. Secretary of the Army for Installations and Logistics, Army.
   Lockheed:
      January 1977, V.P. for Operations, staff coordination of facilities, capital equipment, manufacturing and procurement, Missiles and Space Co.

Carlson, Herbert
   DoD:
      Contract administrator and Contracting officer, Army Purchasing directorate.
   Lockheed:
      April 1975, Procurement representative, Electronics division.

Kelland, Arthur
   DoD:
      Chief, National Security Agency (details classified).
   Lockheed:
      March 1969, Program manager, Missiles and Space Co.

Wilson, Lloyd
   DoD:
      Deputy Director for Strategic and Space Systems, Office of Director for Research and Engineering.
   Lockheed:
      Filed 1971, Consultant to Missiles and Space Co.

2. Lockheed to DoD

Aurand, Henry
   Lockheed:
      Asst. to Director of Engineering, Research and Development division, Missiles and Space Co.
   DoD:
      August 1969, Head, Ocean Acoustics Division and Supervisor, Underwater Acoustic Research and Development, Naval Undersea Center.

Green, Leon, Jr.
   Lockheed:
      Director of Planning, Washington area.
   DoD:
      August 1970, Executive Secretary, Defense Science Board, Directorate of Defense Research & Engineering.

Schwartz, Martin
   Lockheed:
      Consultant, Strategic Aircraft Operations, Analyses and Development.

DoD:
> Filed 1980, Air Force Systems Command, ASD/ENO, Wright-Patterson Air Force Base.

3. Lockheed to NASA
Hallom, Cecil
  Lockheed:
> Senior scientist, large area crop inventory experiment, Electronics division.

  NASA:
> October 1976, Aerospace systems technician, inventory of crops on a global basis using satellites, Earth Observations Division, Johnson Space Center.

4. "Revolving Door"
Hawkins, Willis M. (see Board of Directors)
  Lockheed:
> Sr. V.P., Science and Engineering, Lockheed Corp. (1962-63).

  DoD:
> 1963, Asst. Secretary of the Army for Research and Development.

  Lockheed:
> 1966, Senior V.P., Science and Engineering.

Newman, Edward H.
  DoD:
> Staff Officer, Systems Acquisition Management, Space and Missile Systems Organization, Air Force Systems Command.

  Lockheed:
> July 1966, Staff Officer, configuration management, prepared regulations, managed proposal group, managed procedures group, Missiles and Space Co.

  DoD:
> September 1974, Chief, Configuration and Standardization Branch and Training Chief, Acquisition Management Support Division (policy, procedures and dissemination), Space and Missile Systems Organization, Air Force Systems Command.

Osborne, Bartley P., Jr.
  Lockheed:
> Senior R&D engineering advisor and program manager, tactical aircraft for Navy and Air Force.

  DoD:
> September 1974, Staff specialist for aeronautics, coordination and oversight of aeronautics technology base activities by military departments, Engineering Technology Office,

Research and Advanced Technology section, Office of Secretary of Defense for Research and Engineering.
Lockheed:
September 1978, Engineering Manager, advanced programs management of contract and company sponsored conceptual studies of new military aircraft.

Plummer, James W.
Lockheed:
V.P. and general manager, space systems division, Missiles and Space Co.
DoD:
December 1973, Under Secretary of the Air Force.
Lockheed:
November 1976, Executive V.P., general business management, Missiles and Space Co.

Comments

1. Several transfers occurred with Naval Undersea Center: Henry Westfall, Henry Aurand and David Edilbrute. Lockheed is centrally involved in anti-submarine work.
2. Twenty-four transfers involved Lockheed's Missiles and Space Co.
3. Lockheed has no policy statement on transfers of personnel.

POLITICAL ACTION COMMITTEE

Name: Lockheed Good Government Program
Total Expenditures (4/77-6/80): $172,805
Total Contributions to Federal Campaigns (4/77-6/80): $126,510

Key
- (D) = Democrat;
- (R) = Republican
- (C) = Recipient was a candidate and not elected to that office.
- \+ = Candidate is also a member of a key Congressional committee.
- * = Candidate is a member of a two committees, but contribution s/he received is only listed once to avoid being double-counted in the total for this section.

A. Contributions to Federal Candidates in States with Lockheed Production Facilities (Key Geographic Locations)

CALIFORNIA

Lockheed plants located in Burbank (dist. 22) and Sunnyvale (dist. 12 & 13)

Senate

Sen. Alan Cranston (D)	$1,500
Sen. S.I. Hayakawa (R)	$ 600

House

Cecil Alexander (D-32) (C)	$ 200
+ Rep. Glenn Anderson (D-32)	$ 400
Henry Ares (R-30) (C)	$ 200
+ Rep. Robert Badham (R-40)	$ 150
Rep. Clair Burgener (R-43)	$ 250
Rep. Donald Clausen (R-2)	$ 335
Rep. Tony Coelho (D-15)	$ 200
Rep. James Corman (D-21)	$2,450
Rep. George E. Danielson (D-30)	$ 225
Rep. William Dannemyer (R-39)	$ 200
+ Rep. Robert Dornan (R-27)	$ 250
+ Rep. Vic Fazio (D-4)	$ 350
+ Rep. Barry Goldwater, Jr. (R-20)	$2,000
Rep. Wayne Grisham (R-33)	$ 300
Rep. Mark Hannaford (D-34)	$ 700
+ Rep. Harold Johnson (D-1)	$ 200
Rep. Robert Lagomarsino (R-19)	$ 150
Rep. Robert Legget (D-4)	$ 600
Rep. Jerry Lewis (R-37)	$ 200
+ Rep. Jim Lloyd (D-35)	$1,700
Rep. Paul McCloskey, Jr. (R-12)	$ 500
+ Rep. John McFall (D-14)	$ 800
+ Rep. Norman Mineta (D-13)	$2,050
Rep. Carlos J. Moorehead (R-22)	$ 750
Rep. Leon Panetta (D-16)	$ 200
Rep. Jerry Patterson (D-38)	$ 325
+ Rep. William Royer (R-11)	$ 750
Rep. John Rousselot (R-26)	$2,500
Eric Seastrand (R-16) (C)	$ 100
Rep. William Thomas (R-18)	$ 700
Rep. Lionel Van Deerlin (D-42)	$ 250
+ Rep. Bob Wilson (R-41)	$ 700
+ Rep. Charles H. Wilson (D-31)	$2,350

Total California: $25,135
% Total Federal Contributions: 19.9%

GEORGIA

Lockheed plant located in Marietta (dist. 7)

Senate

+ Sen. Sam Nunn (D)	$2,000
Sen. Herman Talmadge (D)	$3,000

House

Rep. Douglas Barnard (D-10)	$ 800
+ Rep. Jack Brinkley (D-3)	$1,400
+ Rep. Billy Lee Evans (D-8)	$ 700
+ Rep. John Flynt (D-6)	$ 500
Rep. Wyche Fowler (D-5)	$ 500
+ Rep. Newton Gingrich (D-6)	$ 700
Rep. Ronald Ginn (D-1)	$ 450
+ Rep. Elliot Levitas (D-4)	$ 500
Rep. Dawson Mathis (D-2)	$ 850
+ Rep. Lawrence McDonald (D-7)	$1,500
Virginia Shapard (D-6) (C)	$ 350

Total Georgia: $13,250
% Total Federal Contributions: 10.47%

NEW JERSEY

Lockheed plant located in Plainfield (dist. 12)

Senate

Sen. Bill Bradley (D)	$1,000

House

+ Rep. James Courter (R-13)	$ 375
+ Rep. Harold Hollenbeck (R-9)	$ 275
Rep. Matthew Rinaldo (R-12)	$1,500
+ Rep. Robert Roe (D-8)	$ 100

Total New Jersey: $3,250
% Total Federal Contributions: 2.56%

TEXAS

Lockheed plants located in Houston (dist. 7, 8, 9, 18, 22)

Senate

+ Sen. John Tower (R)	$2,500

House

Rep. Robert Gammage (D-22)	$ 550
Rep. Tom Loeffler (R-21)	$ 200
Rep. Jim Mattox (D-5)	$ 100

+ Rep. Dale Milford (D-24)		$ 500	
Tom Pauken (R-5) (C)		$ 100	
Sam Taylor (D-1) (C)		$ 200	
+ Rep. Charles Wilson (D-2)		$ 250	
+ Rep. Joe Wyatt (D-14)		$ 425	

Total Texas: $4,825
% Total Federal Contributions: 3.8%

WASHINGTON

Lockheed plants located in Seattle (dist. 1, 7)

Senate

+ Sen. Warren Magnuson (D)	$2,000

House

Brian Corcoran (D-2) (C)	$ 400
Rep. John Cunningham (R-7)	$ 500
+ Rep. Norman Dicks (D-6)	$1,800
Rep. Thomas S. Foley (D-5)	$ 400
+ Rep. Mike McCormack (D-4)	$ 350

Total Washington: $5,450
% Total Federal Contributions: 4.3%

Total to Key Geographic Locations: $51,910
% Total Federal Contributions: 41.03%

B. Contributions to Members of Key Congressional Committees

Senate Armed Services Committee

Cohen	$ 500	McIntyre	$ 500
Culver	$ 500	Morgan	$ 500
Hart	$ 200	Nunn	$2,000
Helms	$ 500	Stennis	$ 200
Humphrey, Gordon	$ 400	Thurmond	$2,100
Jepsen	$ 500	Tower	$2,500
		Warner	$ 500

House Armed Services Committee

Badham	$ 150	Leggett	$ 600
Bailey	$ 100	Lloyd, James	$1,700
Brinkley	$1,400	McDonald	$1,500
Byron, Beverly	$ 300	Mavroules	$ 100
Byron, Goodloe	$ 200	Mitchell, Donald	$ 200
Carr	$ 150	Mollohan	$ 250
Courter	$ 375	Montgomery	$ 250
Davis, Mendel	$1,100	Runnels	$ 250

Dickinson	$ 800	Spence	$1,000
Dougherty	$ 500	Stratton	$ 400
Evans	$ 700	Stump	$ 200
Fazio	$ 350	Trible	$ 200
Hillis	$ 500	Wilson, Bob	$ 750
Holt	$ 300	Wilson, Charles H.	$2,350
Ichord	$ 800	Wyatt	$ 425

Senate Defense Appropriations Subcommittee

Brooke	$ 950	Johnston	$ 500
Garn	$1,000	Magnuson	$2,000
Hollings	$2,000	Stennis	*
Inouye	$1,000	Stevens	$1,000

House Defense Appropriations Subcommittee

Addabbo	$ 500	Edwards	$ 300
Burlison	$ 100	Flynt	$ 500
Cederberg	$ 800	Giamo	$ 200
Chappell	$ 200	McFall	$ 800
Conte	$ 100	Wilson, Charles N.	$ 250
Dicks	$1,800		

Senate Committee on Commerce, Science and Transportation
Subcommittee on Aviation

Kassebaum	$1,000	Pressler	$ 500
Inouye	*		

Subcommittee on Science, Technology and Space

Griffin	$1,000	Hollings	*
Heflin	$ 250	Kassebaum	$*

House Committee on Science and Technology

Blanchard	$ 50	Kramer	$ 100
Brown	$ 500	Lloyd, James	*
Davis, Robert	$1,000	Lujan	$ 150
Dornan	$ 250	Mavroules	*
Ertel	$ 400	McCormack	$ 350
Flippo	$ 900	Milford	$ 500
Flowers	$ 100	Neal	$ 200
Fuqua	$ 300	Pursell	$ 400
Gammage	$ 550	Roe	$ 100
Goldwater, Jr.	$2,000	Royer	$ 750
Harkin	$ 200	Volkmer	$ 100
Hollenbeck	$ 275	Wydler	$ 550

Senate Committee on Environment and Public Works
Subcommittee on Transportation

Domenici	$ 500	Pressler	*

House Committee on Public Works and Transportation
Subcommittee on Aviation

Abdnor	$ 400	Levitas	$ 500
Anderson, Glenn	$ 400	Milford	*
Ertel	*	Mineta	$2,050
Evans	*	Rahall	$ 100
Flippo	*	Shuster	$ 200

Gingrich	$ 700	Snyder	$ 400
Goldwater, Jr.	*	Stump	*
Harsha	$ 200	Taylor	$ 100
Johnson	$ 200		

Total to Key Committees: $60,975
% Total Federal Contributions: 48.2%

C. Contributions to Other Influential Members of Congress

Sen. Howard Baker (R-TN), Minority Leader $ 500
   (also received contributions as a presidential candidate)
Rep. John Rhodes (R-AZ), Minority Whip $ 700

Total to Other Influentials: $1,200
% Total Federal Contributions: .95%

D. Contributions to Other Candidates

Senate
Armstrong (R-CO)	$ 500	Mathias (R-MD)	$ 250
Boschwitz (R-MN)	$1,000	Matsunaga (D-HI)	$ 200
Bush (R-TX) (C)	$ 150	Moore (R-WV)	$ 500
Cochran (R-MS)	$ 500	Moynihan (D-NY)	$ 200
DeConcini (D-AZ)	$ 750	Percy (D-IL)	$1,000
Durenberger (R-MI)	$ 500	Stewart (D-AL)	$ 500
Heinz (R-PA)	$ 100	Swigert (R-CO)	$ 200
Leahy (D-UT) (C)	$ 500		

House
Alexander (D-AR)	$ 100	Lent (RC-NY)	$ 100
Anderson, John (R-IL)	$ 300	Livingston (R-LA)	$ 125
Ashley (D-OH)	$ 450	Long (D-LA)	$ 100
Aucoin (D-OR)	$ 100	Lott (R-MS)	$ 500
Bauman (R-MD)	$ 150	Madigan (R-IL)	$ 250
Bevill (D-AL)	$ 100	Marriot (R-UT)	$ 500
Bolling (D-MO)	$ 750	McClory (R-IL)	$ 100
Bonior (D-MI)	$ 100	McEwen (R-NY)	$ 100
Breaux (D-CA)	$ 200	McQuaid (R-CA)	$ 500
Brown (R-OH)	$ 300	Moore (R-LA)	$ 200
Buchan (R-AL)	$ 200	Moorhead, W. (D-PA)	$ 500
Campbell (R-SC)	$ 225	Murphy (D-NY)	$ 200
Cheney (R-WY)	$ 500	Murray (R-IA)	$ 100
Coughlin (R-PA)	$ 200	Neal (D-NC)	$ 200
Derrick (D-SC)	$ 700	Petri (R-WI)	$ 250
Derwinski (R-IL)	$ 125	Porter (R-IL)	$ 200
Duncan (D-OR)	$ 200	Pursell (R-MI)	$ 400

Findley (R-IL)	$ 150	Richardson (D-NM) (C)	$ 50
Fithian (D-IN)	$ 200	Rostenkowski (D-IL)	$ 300
Frenzil (R-MN)	$ 200	Rumsfeld (NA) (C)	$2,000
Gilman (R-NY)	$ 100	Ruppe (R-MI)	$ 100
Gurney (R-FL)	$ 200	Shasteen (R-NE) (C)	$ 200
Hansen (R-ID)	$ 300	Symms (R-ID)	$2,000
Herrity (R-VA) (C)	$ 200	Traxler (D-MI)	$ 300
Jeffries (R-KS)	$ 300	Vander Jagt (R-MI)	$ 800
Jenrette (D-SC)	$ 550	Yatron (D-PA)	$ 100
Jones, James (D-OK)	$ 200	Young, Don (R-AK)	$ 350

Total to Other Federal Candidates: $24,075
% Total Federal Contributions: 19.03%

E. Contributions to Party Campaign Committees

Republican federal-level committees: $1,000
Democratic federal-level committees: $5,900

Total to Party Committees: $6,900
% Total Federal Contributions 5.5%

F. Contributions to Presidential Candidates

Howard Baker (R)	$ 625
George Bush (R)	$ 500
Jimmy Carter (D)	$1,900
John Connally (R)	$3,000
Ronald Reagan (R)	$3,500

Total to Presidential Candidates: $9,525
% Total Federal Contributions: 7.5%

WASHINGTON OPERATIONS

Washington Offices:

Lockheed Corp.
900 17th St. NW
Washington, DC 20006

Lockheed California Co.
1745 Jefferson Davis Highway
Arlington, VA 22202

Lockheed

Lockheed Missiles and Space Co.
1911 Jefferson Davis Highway
Arlington, VA 22202

Lockheed Electronics Co., Inc.
1911 North Fort Meyer Drive
Arlington, VA 22209

Activities:
1. Technical liaison and customer coordination.
2. Market intelligence gathering.
3. Lobbying and answering Congressional inquiries.
4. Entertainment.
5. Foreign Sales liaison.

Registered Lobbyists:

	Receipts	Expenditures	Years
Ricardo R. Alvarado 6108 Fort Hunt Rd. Alexandria, VA	$28,495.00	$11,772.00	76-79
James E. Kneale 2335 South Meade St. Arlington, VA	*	*	79
Miller & Chevalier 1700 Pennsylvania Ave. NW Washington, DC	$129,960.00	*	76-79
TOTAL	**$158,455.00**	**$11,772.00**	

*No figures reported; quarterly report was filed.

DEFENSE-RELATED TRADE ASSOCIATION MEMBERSHIPS

Aerospace Industries Association
Air Force Association
American Defense Preparedness Association
American Institute of Aeronautics and Astronautics
American League for Exports and Security Assistance

Armed Forces Communication and Electronics Association
National Association for Remotely-Piloted Vehicles
National Council of Technical Service Industries
National Security Industrial Association
Shipbuilders Council of America

ADVISORY COMMITTEE MEMBERSHIPS

1976-78: 20

Araki, Minoru Sam
    DoD—Defense Science Board, 1976

Brownman, Harold J.
    DoD—Defense Intelligence Agency Advisory Committee (formerly Scientific Advisory Committee), 1977, 1978

Frisbee, Lloyd E.
(V.P. and General Manager, Engineering and Operations, Lockheed-California)
    NASA—Research and Technology Advisory Council, Panel on Aviation Safety Operating Systems, 1976, 1977, 1978

Hawkins, Willis M.
(President, Lockheed-California, Corporate V.P.) (see Board of Directors)
    DoD—Defense Science Board, 1976
    DoD—Army Scientific Advisory Panel, 1976
    DoD—Army Science Board, 1977, 1978
    NASA—Aerospace Safety Advisory Panel, 1976, 1977, 1978
    NASA—Space Program Advisory Council, 1976, 1977

Hopps, Russell H.
>NASA—Research and Technology Advisory Council, Committee on Aerodynamics and Configurations, 1976, 1977

Jenkins, Lawrence E.
>NASA—Research and Technology Advisory Council, Panel on Space Vehicles, 1976, 1977

Kitchen, Lawrence O.
>(President and Chief Operating Officer) (see Board of Directors)
>DoD—Military Airlift Committee, 1976, 1977, 1978

Martin, Walt
>(Lockheed Palo Alto Research Labs)
>NASA—Out of Elliptic, Mission Ad Hoc Committee of Space Science Steering Committee, 1977, 1978

Oder, Frederick C.
>(V.P. and general manager, Space Systems Division)
>DoD—Defense Intelligence Agency, Scientific Advisory Committee 1976, 1977

Orwat, Norman
>DoD—Defense Industry Advisory Group Europe, 1977

Quinlivan, William J.
>NASA—Research and Technology Advisory Council, Panel on Aviation, Safety Operating Systems, 1976, 1977

Sheperd, William
>DoD—Defense Science Board, 1978

Smelt, Ronald
>(V.P. and Chief Scientist)
>NASA—Advisory Board on Fuel Conservation Technology, 1976
>NASA—Research and Technology Advisory Council, 1976, 1977

Stuart, Derald
>(V.P. and general manager, Missile Systems division)
>DoD—Defense Science Board, 1976

Wright, Frank
>NASA—Research and Technology Advisory Council, Panel on Aviation Safety Operation Systems, 1976, 1977

ENTERTAINMENT

Lockheed President Lawrence O. Kitchen informed the Joint Committee on Defense Production that Lockheed's personnel follow Government regulations regarding entertainment of DoD personnel and "costs incurred for this purpose are relatively small in amount per occasion."

In May 1977, Lockheed disclosed that it had spent sums ranging from $372,000 to $432,000 in each of the years between 1970 and 1975 for the entertainment of Government officials, including armed forces personnel. None of this amount, Lockheed stated, was tax deducted or reimbursed by contract income. (Source: Lockheed 8K, May, 1977)

Entertaining:
Only on four occasions were costs of more than $100 per guest incurred; no facilities disclosed.

Hospitality Suites:
1973:14, 1974:22, 1975:24.
Including National Security Industrial Association, American Institute of Aeronautics and Astronautics, Navy League, Air Force Association and American Defense Preparedness Association.

Tickets:
1973-75: 289 season tickets, some made available to Government officials.

Air Travel:
Government officials were offered available seats on Lockheed company jets only on flights already scheduled for company personnel.

Disclosure:
Good.

QUESTIONABLE PAYMENTS

On this issue, Lockheed has attracted more public discussion than almost any other defense contracting company. In July 1975 in the wake of investigations by the SEC and the Multinationals Subcommittee of the Senate Foreign Relations Committee, Lockheed disclosed that it had paid out something in the neighborhood of $200 m. in commissions and agents' fees, roughly $22 m. of which was "known or thought to have flowed to foreign officials and to foreign political organizations in a number of countries abroad" (*Lockheed Starletter*, 6 Aug. 1975, p. 3; see also *The Wall Street Journal*, 4 Aug. 1975). Lockheed defended its payments as "consistent with practices engaged in by numerous other companies abroad" (*Starletter*, 6 Aug. 1975). The company also disclosed that it had maintained a fund of roughly $750,000, some of which was used "outside the normal channels of financial accountability," on some of the commissions and payments in question (Ibid., p. 4).

Further company disclosure indicated that Lockheed's payments covered a number of countries and involved both commercial (L-1011) and military (C-130, P-3C) sales overseas.

By September 1975, this issue had become tied to discussions on Lockheed's business fortunes and the continuation of its top management in office (see "Contracting History"). Company Chairman, Dan Haughton, stated that Federal and loan-guaranteed monies were not used for the commissions or payments and that the payments were necessary to doing business (Haughton testimony, Senate Banking Committee, 25 Aug. 1975, Lockheed reprint). Haughton and President A. Carl Kotchian gave repeated testimony to the Senate Committee and the SEC, disclosing details of payments but declining to name recipients or to admit wrongdoing (e.g., *The New York Times*, 13 Sept. 1975; Ibid., 10 Oct. 1975).

By December 1975, Lockheed and the SEC were in serious disagreement about whether or not the SEC should be allowed to disclose any names of payment recipients. The SEC had subpoenaed documents, which Lockheed had withheld. The Court ordered Lockheed to turn over the documents but agreed to keep them in Court in order to prevent their disclosure under Freedom of Information Act requests (Ibid., 16 Dec. 1975).

In February 1976, Lockheed, while still in negotiation with the SEC, appointed a special review committee of the board (Jack Horton, Robert Haack, Dwight Cochran, and Fred M. Vinson, Jr.) to investigate the payments (*The Wall Street Journal*, 2 Feb. 1976). Meanwhile, it was alleged in Senate hearings that Lockheed payments were linked to major political figures in the Netherlands, Japan, and Italy. The payments issue caused political turmoil in those countries (Ibid., 9 Feb. 1976). Later others joined the list: South Africa, Nigeria, Spain; and still later, Taiwan, Malaysia, Mexico, Kuwait, Argentina, Colombia, Peru, Venezuela, Saudi Arabia, and Turkey.

Some specifics emerged from hearings overseas: the Netherlands' payments involved the F-104 (*The New York Times*, 8 Feb. 1976). In Japan the sales of the F-104 and the L-1011 were particularly involved, while the Italian controversy surrounded C-130 sales (*TheWashington Post*, 13 Feb. 1976). Total payments in Japan alone might have been as high as $12 m., according to *TheWashington Post* (14 Feb. 1976). By February Lockheed's banks and the Federal Government were suggesting a change in management. In February Lockheed's board replaced both officers, asking outside member Robert Haack to assume the chairmanship. Lawrence Kitchen was asked to take the post of president and chief operating officer (*The Wall Street Journal*, 8 April 1976; *The New York Times*, 14 Feb. 1976).

Haack and Lockheed completed negotiation on a consent decree with the SEC by April 1976. Lockheed agreet to avoid "certain business practices with respect to overseas business transactions," according to Chairman Haack, (*The New York Times*, 14 April 1976), and also agreed to undertake an expanded review of its sales practices, auditing, and management. The expanded special review committee included outside board members Joseph Downer, Houston Flournoy, Ellison Hazard, and J. Wilson Newman (Ibid.).

After a year of investigation, the special committee reported in May, 1977 that Lockheed's questionable payments overseas may have totaled as much as $38 m., some of them directly to foreign government officials. Haughton and Kotchian, "appear to the committee to have been willing to distort such a primary principle as integrity for short term expediency, in order to aid, in their mind, the Company's financial survival. It is obvious to the Committee that they were responsible for the questionable payments and practices" (*Report*, 6 June 1977, p. 17). The committee recommended that two-thirds of the board be outside directors, that the company's auditing be strengthened, and that management be regularly reviewed for performance. No names of countries or recipients were given, and it was concluded that no questionable domestic payments had been made.

Two years later, in February 1979, the Justice Department announced that it was dropping any plans to prosecute Kotchian in connection with the payments. An investigation of Haughton had been dropped nine months earlier. *The Wall Street Journal* (16 Feb. 1979), citing Kotchian's lawyer Mitchell Rogovin, said that Kotchian "was prepared to show at trial that the federal government was 'aware' of some Lockheed payments at the time they were made." The *Journal* went on to note: "It's understood that Mr. Kotchian was prepared to argue in his defense that the Central Intelligence Agency knew about some

Lockheed payoffs because it had placed a 'deep cover' agent inside the company" (Ibid.). In February 1979, Lockheed and the SEC also reached a final agreement on disclosure, permitting countries of payment to be named, but sealing the names of individual recipients. (Ibid., 20 Feb. 1979). In June 1979, Lockheed pleaded guilty to having concealed $2.6 m. in payments in Japan in connection with the All-Nippon Airlines purchase of the L-1011. The Department of Justice alleged that $1.8 m. of this sum went to the office of former Prime Minister Tanaka (*The New York Times*, 2 June 1979; *The Wall Street Journal*, 4 June 1979). The company was fined $647,000 (*The New York Times*, 2 June 1979).

DISCLOSURE

Very poor.

McDONNELL DOUGLAS

BASIC CORPORATE AND CONTRACTING DATA

A. Corporate Data

McDonnell Douglas Corporation
P.O. Box 516
St. Louis, MO 63166

Fortune 500 (1979): 54
Fiscal Year: Jan. 1—Dec. 31

Chairman:
Sanford N. McDonnell (1979 salary: $364,622)

President:
John F. McDonnell (1979 salary: NA)

Auditor:
Ernst & Whinney
10 South Broadway
St. Louis, MO

Outside Legal Counsel:
Bryan, Cave, McPheeters & McRoberts
500 North Broadway
St. Louis

TABLE I
Corporate Data
($ in M.)

	1970	1971	1972	1973	1974	1975	1976	1977	1978	1979
Sales	$2,088.2	2,069.1	2,725.7	3,002.6	3,075.0	3,255.7	3,543.7	3,544.8	4,130.3	5,278.5
Net Income	$ 5.5	20.4	97.6	133.3	106.7	85.6	108.9	123.0	161.1	199.1
Dept. of Defense Contracts	$ 882.7	896.6	1,700.2	1,143.3	1,309.3	1,397.9	2,464.6	2,574.0	2,863.3	3,229.2
Rank	5	7	2	4	3	4	1	1	2	2
NASA Contracts	$ 236.0	302.9	343.1	272.4	156.0	125.5	124.8	138.5	139.7	113.7
Rank	3	1	1	2	3	3	2	2	3	4
DoD/NASA Contracts as % of Sales	53.6%	58.0	75.0	47.2	47.6	46.8	73.1	76.5	72.7	63.3
Government Sales	$1,412.0	1,386.0	1,517.0	1,604.0	1,586.0	1,831.0	2,376.0	2,659.0	2,864.0	3,002.0
Government Sales as % of Sales	67.6%	67.0	55.7	53.4	51.6	56.2	67.0	75.0	69.3	56.9
Foreign Military Sales Contracts	$ 261.1	52.4	802.8	223.9	119.7	419.0	480.5	446.1	273.9	638.9
Rank	1	2	1	2	8	1	2	2	5	1
FMS Contracts as % of Sales	12.5%	2.5	29.5	7.5	3.9	12.9	13.6	12.6	6.6	12.1
Overseas and Export Sales	NA	NA	545.1	1,075.0	1,367.0	1,291.5	1,521.2	1,128.6	1,143.8	1,788.4
Overseas and Export Sales as % of Sales	—	—	20.0%	35.8	44.5	39.7	42.9	31.8	27.7	33.9
Employees	92,552	92,105	86,713	78,799	70,739	62,830	57,867	61,577	70,547	82,736

McCarthy & McCarthy
Toronto Dominion Centre
P.O. Box 48
Toronto, Canada (see Board of Directors: Donald S. MacDonald)

Banking:

Transfer Agents and Registrars:
St. Louis Union Trust Co., St. Louis (See Board of Directors: James S. McDonnell III)
Chase Manhattan Bank
Chemical Bank

Lenders:
First National Bank, St. Louis (revolving credit and term loans up to $2 m.) (see Board of Directors: Edwin S. Jones and James S. McDonnell III)
Fifteen other banks, names undisclosed

Trustee:
Salaried Employees Savings Plan (24% of outstanding common stock), Bankers Trust Co.

Investment Banker:
Morgan Stanley

B. Principal Defense/Space Contracting Operations

McDonnell Aircraft Company
St. Louis, MO
George S. Graff, President

F-4 Phantom—fighter, U.S. Air Force and foreign orders (ended Oct. 1979)
F-15 Eagle—fighter, U.S. Air Force and foreign orders
F-18 Hornet—fighter, U.S. Navy and foreign orders
AV-8B—V/STOL attack aircraft, U.S. Marine Corps.
YC-15—STOL cargo jet, U.S. Air Force

McDonnell Douglas Electronics Company
St. Louis, MO
David C. Arnold, President

Visual simulation systems, U.S. Air Force and foreign orders
Data display sets, U.S. Air Force

McDonnell Douglas Astronautics Company
Huntington Beach, CA
Robert L. Johnson, Head of West Coast aerospace activities and Corporate V.P.

Harpoon—anti-ship missile, U.S. Navy and foreign orders
Guidance system, cruise missile, U.S. Navy, U.S. Air Force

Ballistic missile defense systems technology, U.S. Army
Advanced maneuverable re-entry vehicle for ballistic missiles, U.S. Air Force
Payload assist module for Delta missile or space shuttle, Hughes Aircraft, Ford, NASA
Delta launch vehicle, U.S. Air Force, NASA
Aft propulsion system and rocket boosters for space shuttle, NASA
Military space systems, U.S. Department of Defense
ALWT—advanced lightweight torpedo, U.S. Navy
IWDM—intermediate water depth mine, U.S. Navy

McDonnell Douglas-Tulsa
Tulsa, OK
James B. Miller, V.P., Manufacturing

F-4C Phantom—modification program

C. Contracting History

McDonnell Douglas has had an extremely successful decade in the 1970s. From 1970-79 the firm recorded total Government sales of over $20 b., nearly 62% of total corporate sales. McDonnell Douglas has consistently ranked as a leading contractor for both DoD and NASA.

The company entered the decade as a strong contractor. In 1967, McDonnell had absorbed the Douglas Aircraft Company in Long Beach, CA. The objective was to improve Douglas' management and to add a commercial business base to McDonnell's defense contracting (*The New York Times*, 31 May 1979; 3 June 1979). Douglas had run into cost problems with its DC-9 commercial jet and was about to undertake an expensive development program for its jumbo DC-10.

In the 1970s, McDonnell Douglas, unlike other defense firms, did not experience a sharp decline in DoD procurement. Instead, it was remarkably successful in beating out other contractors. In 1971, McDonnell Douglas was selected over Rockwell and Fairchild to build the next U.S. Air Force fighter, the F-15. In 1972 McDonnell was selected over Raytheon and Hughes to develop a site defense system for the Minuteman missile and has continued to be the Army's leading ballistic missile defense (BMD) contractor. In 1975 McDonnell was selected over E-Systems as the contractor for guidance systems for the forthcoming cruise missile, a contract which will generate substantial income for the 1980s. In 1976 McDonnell was selected with RCA and Raytheon to develop a system for Shipboard Intermediate Range Combat. The company also received a contract to develop a second generation vertical/short take-off and landing aircraft for the Marine Corps and Navy, the AV-8B Harrier. McDonnell Douglas also entered into cooperation with Northrop to develop a lightweight fighter, the F-18, for the Navy, based on Northrop's losing design for the Air Force fighter competition. The Navy plans to order a large number of F-18s, which are expected to produce further income for McDonnell Douglas in the 1980s. In 1977, the DC-10, which had yet to be profitable for Douglas (*The New York Times*, 31 May 1979; 3 June 1979), was selected over Boeing's 747 as the air frame for the Air Force's Advanced Tanker/Cargo Aircraft. At least 20 KC-10s will be ordered to supplement the C5A cargo and KC-135 tanker fleets. California members of Congress reportedly lobbied hard for this contract which would "provide a significant boost for DC-10 production," and "stability and continuity" for the Long Beach labor force. (*Los Angeles Times*, 20 Dec. 1977). The first KC-10 was rolled out in 1980.

While there had been some controversies over MDC's contracting in the early 1970s, they were short-lived. In 1971, Congress took a brief look at the possibility of trading off the F-15 against Grumman's F-14, buying only one expensive fighter. Although the House Appropriations Committee suggested that the F-14 be chosen, the idea never came to fruition (*DMS Market Intelligence Report*, August 1971). Cost increases for the F-15 were generally explained by inflation, the Air Force's decision to reduce the production rate from 12 to nine per month, and problems encountered with the Pratt & Whitney F-100 engines—clearly not a McDonnell Douglas problem (Ibid.).

In 1974, a brief controversy erupted over the Renegotiation Board's decision on McDonnell Douglas' 1967-69 profits, which combined higher profit rates in St. Louis with the lower profit rate of Douglas Aircraft's operations. One board member, Goodwin Chase, and Senator William Proxmire protested this decision, suggesting a need for higher recovery from McDonnell Douglas. The board majority stood by its finding, however, and McDonnell Douglas was not asked for a higher rebate (*Aviation Week*, 19 August 1974).

By the late 1970s McDonnell Douglas' contracting future looked bright. The F-4 Phantom sold well, through 1979 both in the U.S. and abroad. The F-15 won an order from Israel and others were in the offing. The F-18 looked secure, though increasingly expensive, as did cruise missile guidance, ballistic missiles defense, Harpoon anti-ship missiles and NASA contracts. Cargo aircraft programs were also moving along well.

The only major problem for the firm came on the commercial side: the Chicago crash of the DC-10 in 1979. It was unclear how this accident might affect the firm. Some analysts saw the impact as short-lived, while one McDonnell Douglas employee noted: "The most devastating result would be that customers become suspicious of our technology and engineering" (*The New York Times*, 3 June 1979). In July 1979, McDonnell Douglas retained J. Walter Thompson and began an advertising campaign to restore public confidence in the plane (*The New York Times*, 22 July 1979).

D. U.S. Government-Owned, Company-Operated Plants

Total company floor space: 26,766,914 sq. ft.
Leased from U.S. Government: 3,580,409 sq. ft. (13.4%)
Total lease cost: $1,177,375

Location: Air Force Plant 84
St. Louis, MO
738,910 sq. ft.
Use: F-4 Spares, F-15, F-18, Harpoon, space shuttle, AV-8B
Cost: $960,375

Location: Air Force Plant 3
(with Rockwell International)
Tulsa, OK
2,841,499 sq. ft.
Use: Aircraft components
Cost: $217,000

RESEARCH AND DEVELOPMENT
Major Defense/Space R&D Projects

CX—military transport design work, U.S. Air Force
AV-8B—V/STOL attack aircraft, U.S. Marine Corps
YC-15—STOL cargo jet, U.S. Air Force
Cruise missile guidance, U.S. Navy, U.S. Air Force
Advanced maneuverable re-entry vehicle, U.S. Army
Ballistic Missile Defense, U.S. Air Force
Shuttle propulsion and rocket boosters, NASA
Military space systems, DoD

BOARD OF DIRECTORS

John C. Brizendine (1973)
President, Douglas Aircraft Co., McDonnell Douglas Corp.
Military:
Lieutenant, U.S. Navy Reserve (1946-61).
Past Corporate Employment:
Douglas Aircraft Co. and McDonnell Douglas Corp. (1950-present) (President, Douglas Aircraft-1973).
Key Association Memberships:
American Institute of Aeronautics and Astronautics (fellow); Air Force Association; Navy League; National Defense Transportation Association.
Shares owned:
19,150

TABLE II
Research and Development
($ in M.)

	1970	1971	1972	1973	1974	1975	1976	1977	1978	1979
I. U.S. Government Contracts										
DoD	$263.8	385.8	441.0	497.7	340.9	283.6	346.9	492.0	796.5	770.6
NASA	$236.0	302.9	343.1	272.4	56.0	125.6	124.8	138.5	139.7	113.7
Total	$499.8	688.7	784.1	770.1	496.9	409.	471.7	630.5	936.2	884.3
II. Company-sponsored R&D	$275.8	204.2	147.5	142.8	39.5	132.2	105.6	123.9	168.8	194.0
III. IR&D	NA	NA	NA	$ 14.4	18.9	22.3	19.6	23.2	24.8	NA

I. From DoD yearly pubication "500 Contractors Receiving the Largest Dollar Volume of Military Prime Contract Awards for RDT&E" and NASA Annual Procurement Reports.

II. "Company-initiated independent research and development and bid and proposal work" (10K, 1978).

III. Company-sponsored R&D costs charged to DoD as disclosed by DoD.

McDonnell Douglas   345

George H. Capps (1970)
President, Capital Coal and Coke Co., St. Louis, MO
Past Corporate Employment:
President, Capital Coal and Coke Co. (1950-present);
President, Volkswagen Mid-America, Inc. (1961-present).
Government Positions:
Special Agent, FBI (1941-50).
Corporate Directorships:
Mallinckrodt, Inc. ($527,000); Boatmen's National Bank; General American Life Insurance Co.; Petrolite Corp.; VICO Insurance Co.; Southern Bell Telephone ($4,010,000).
Shares owned:
663

Michael N. Chetkovich (1980)
Lecturer and director of external affairs, School of Business Administration, University of California at Berkeley.
Past Corporate Employment:
Managing Partner, Deloitte, Haskins & Sells (1952-78).
Corporate Directorships:
Phillips Petroleum Company; American International Group, Inc.
Shares owned:
NA

William Danforth, M.D. (1976)
Chancellor, Washington University, St. Louis, MO (1971-present).
Past Employment:
Fellow, Washington University Medical School (1957-64); President, Washington University Medical Center (1965-71).
Corporate Directorships:
Mallinckrodt, Inc. ($527,000); Ralston Purina Co. ($5,830,000).
Shares owned:
600

Donald W. Douglas, Jr. (1953) (deceased, 1981)
Business consultant, Santa Monica, CA
Past Corporate Employment:
Douglas Aircraft Co. and McDonnell Douglas Corp. (1939-81); Vice-Chairman of the Board, AUI Manufacturing (1971-81).
Corporate Directorships:
Hilton Corp.; Capistrano National Bank; Biphase Engines.
Key Association Memberships:
Aerospace Industries Association; Air Force Association; American Ordnance Association; Conquistadores del Cielo; National Defense Transportation Association; American Institute of Aeronautics and Astronautics; National Security

Industrial Association; Navy League; Transportation
Association of America.
Shares owned:
2,223
George S. Graff (1973)
Corporate V.P., McDonnell Douglas Corp.; President,
McDonnell Aircraft.
Past Corporate Employment:
Continental Aviation-Engineering Corp. (1940-42); McDonnell
Aircraft Corp. and McDonnell Douglas Corp. (1942-present).
Government Positions:
NACA/NASA Advisory Committees on Stability and Control,
Missile and Spacecraft Dynamics, Aircraft Aerodynamics,
Aeronautics (1951-present).
Key Association Memberships:
American Institute of Aeronautics and Astronautics; Air Force
Association; American Defense Preparedness Association;
American Rocket Society; Armed Forces Management
Association; National Defense Transportation Association;
Navy League.
Shares owned:
21,077*
Robert L. Johnson (1978) (see Personnel Transfers)
Corporate V.P., McDonnell Douglas; President, McDonnell
Douglas Astronautics Co.
Past Corporate Employment:
Douglas Aircraft Co. and McDonnell Douglas Corp. (1946-69;
1973-present) (Corp. V.P., Engineering and Research-1973;
President, McDonnell Douglas Astronautics-1975; Head of
West Coast aerospace activities-1980).
Government Positions:
Asst. Secretary of the Army (1969-73); Consultant, Research
and Development Board, Department of Defense (1969-73);
Army Scientific Advisory Panel.
Key Association Memberships:
American Defense Preparedness Association (director);
American Institute of Aeronautics and Astronautics; National
Space Club; Navy League.
Shares owned:
4,077
Edwin S. Jones (1971)
Chairman of the Executive Committee, First Union Bancorporation, St. Louis, MO and Chairman of the Executive Committee,
First National Bank in St. Louis.
Past Corporate Employment:
First National Bank in St. Louis (1946-present) (V.P. and
Director, First Union Bancorporation-1969).

Corporate Directorships:
Angelica Corp. ($308,000); Anheuser-Busch, Inc.; General American life Insurance Co.; General Steel Industries; INTERCO, Inc. ($2,173,000); St. Louis Union Trust Co.; Union Electric Co. ($730,000); Southwestern Bell Telephone Co. ($4,930,000).
Key Association Memberships:
Business Roundtable.
Shares owned:
643

Robert C. Little (1973)
Corporate V.P., Engineering and Marketing, McDonnell Douglas Corp.
Past Corporate Employment:
McDonnell Aircraft Corp. and McDonnell Douglas Corp. (1948-present) (Program Manager, F-4, 1960-64).
Key Association Memberships:
American Institute of Aeronautics and Astronautics.
Shares owned:
20,712

Hon. Donald S. MacDonald (1978)
Partner, McCarthy & McCarthy (see Basic Data: Outside Legal Counsel)
Past Corporate Employment:
McCarthy & McCarthy (1957-62).
Government Positions:
Member of Canadian Parliament (1962-77); Parliamentary Secretary to Minister of Justice (1963); Parliamentary Secretary to Minister of Finance (1965); Parliamentary Secretary to Secretary of State for External Affairs (1966); Parliamentary Secretary to Minister of Industry (1968); Minister of National Defense (1970-72); Minister of Energy, Mines and Resources (1972-74); Minister of Finance (1975-77).
Corporate Directorships:
Boise Cascade Corp. ($758,000); Shell Canada Limited; DuPont of Canada Limited.
Shares owned:
100

James S. McDonnell III (1975)
Corporate V.P., Marketing, McDonnell Douglas Corp.
Military:
Special Weapons Center, New Mexico, U.S. Air Force (1959-62).
Past Corporate Employment:
McDonnell Aircraft Corp. and McDonnell Douglas Corp. (1963-present).

Corporate Directorships:
Advisory Director, St. Louis Union Trust Co.
Shares owned:
1,610,624†

James S. McDonnell (1939) (deceased, 1980)
Chairman of the Board, McDonnell Douglas Corp.
Past Corporate Employment:
Aeronautical Engineer (1924-38); Founder, President and Director, McDonnell Aircraft Corp. (1939-67); Chairman and Chief Executive Officer, McDonnell Douglas (1967-1980).
Government Positions:
Member, Aviation Advisory Commission, White House (1970-73); Member, Industry Advisory Council, Department of Defense (1972-74).
Corporate Directorships:
Commercial National Bank of Little Rock.
Key Association Memberships:
Aerospace Industries Association.
Shares owned:
1,821,572*†

John Finney McDonnell (1973)
President, McDonnell Douglas Corp.
Past Corporate Employment:
McDonnell Aircraft Corp. and McDonnell Douglas Corp. (1957-present) (V.P., McDonnell Douglas Finance Corp.-1968; President, McDonnell Douglas Corp.-1980).
Shares owned:
1,306,355*†

Sanford N. McDonnell (1962)
Chairman and Chief Executive Officer, McDonnell-Douglas Corp.
Past Corporate Employment:
McDonnell Aircraft Corp. and McDonnell Douglas Corp. (1951-present) (President-1971; Chief Executive Officer-1972).
Corporate Directorships:
First Union Bancorporation, St. Louis.
Key Association Memberships:
Aerospace Industries Association; Air Force Association; American Institute of Aeronautics and Astronautics; American Defense Preparedness Association; American Security Council; Armed Forces Management Association; Association of U.S. Army; Navy League; National Defense Transportation Association; National Aeronautic Association.
Shares owned:
97,620*

James T. McMillan (1978)
President, McDonnell Douglas Finance Corp.; Corporate V.P., McDonnell Douglas Corp.
Past Corporate Employment:
Douglas Aircraft Corp. and McDonnell Douglas Corp. (1954-present); (Asst. Gen. Counsel-1959; McDonnell Douglas Finance Corp.-1967).
Corporate Directorships:
California Life Corp.
Key Association Memberships:
National Defense Transportation Association.
Shares owned:
10,541

William R. Orthwein, Jr. (1951)
Corporate V.P., McDonnell Douglas Corp.; President, McDonnell Douglas Automation Co.
Past Corporate Employment:
General American Life Insurance Co. (1938-42); McDonnell Aircraft Corp. and McDonnell Douglas Corp. (1942-present) (V.P., Personnel and Public Relations-1952 and Chief Executive Officer, McDonnell Automation Center-1963).
Corporate Directorships:
Mercantile Bancorporation, Inc./Mercantile Trust Co.
Key Association Memberships:
The Business Roundtable.
Shares owned:
244,361*

John T. Sant (1978)
Corporate V.P., General Counsel, McDonnell Douglas Corp.
Past Corporate Employment:
McDonnell Aircraft Corp. and McDonnell Douglas Corp. (1960-present).
Shares owned:
7,519

*Board member is voting trustee for 9,065,722 shares (24%) held by McDonnell Douglas's three Employee Savings Plans. The shares are in trust with Bankers Trust.

†Board member is a trustee of the McDonnell Foundation and holds voting power over the foundation's 814,549 shares (2%).

PERSONNEL TRANSFERS

Table III
(DoD 1970-79)
(NASA 1974-79)

	Total	Air Force	Army	Navy	Office of Secretary of Defense	Other
DoD Military to McDonnell Douglas	159	121	5	28	1	5
DoD Civilian to McDonnell Douglas	12	2	3	2	3	2
NASA to McDonnell Douglas	2					
McDonnell Douglas to DoD	29	4	13	3	4	4
McDonnell Douglas to NASA	9					
Total	211	127	21	33	8	11

Appearances of Potential Conflict of Interest (see Chapter 6): 15

1. DoD to MDC

Branch, William H.
DoD:
> Associate Member, Defense Science Board, Task Force on Anti-Ballistic Missile System Technology, Office of Secretary of Defense.

MDC:
> September 1973, Director, Advanced Defense Systems.

Gaylor, Noel
DoD:
> Commander in Chief, Pacific (retired), Navy.

MDC:
> November 1976, Consultant, Actron Division.

Sloan, George
DoD:
> Staff, Defense Security Assistance Agency.

MDC:
> No date, Corporate advisor on future planning.

Weiser, Charles R.
DoD:
> Staff Office of Director of Defense Research and Engineering.

MDC:
> August 1971, Deputy General Manager, Director, Advanced Defense Systems.

2. MDC to DoD

James, Bruce
  MDC:
    Program Manager, research and development programs, McDonnell Douglas Astronautics.
  DoD:
    December 1974, research and development program management in Office of Deputy Director of Tactical Technology, Defense Advanced Research Projects Agency.

Kozkowski, Donald
  MDC:
    Section Chief, managing advanced fighter aircraft team.
  DoD:
    December 1975, Consultant to Deputy for Development Planning, Wright-Patterson Air Force Base, Air Force.

Marver, Gene R.
  MDC:
    V.P., Engineering, Douglas Electronics Corp.
  DoD:
    June 1974, Consultant, RPV System, MGS Office Chief, Avionics and Weaponization Directorate, Army Aviation System Command.

Mittino, John A.
  MDC:
    Manager, system requirements (to June 1971).
  DoD:
    No date, Industrial specialist, electronics, Office of Asst. Secretary of Defense for Installations and Logistics.

Momyer, William
  MDC:
    Consultant, planning technology and strategy.
  DoD:
    To March 1979, Consultant, Army/Air Force NATO Fire Support Requirments.

Thomas, Arthur N., Jr.
  MDC:
    Senior Project Engineer, Astronautics Co. (to March 1976).
  DoD:
    No date, Deputy for Air and Missile Defense, Office of Asst. Secretary of the Army for Research and Development.

Winten, Wayne R.
  MDC:
    Manager of Advanced Ballistic Missile Defense Systems Engineering, Managing R&D contracts on BMD systems, Astronautics Co.

DoD:
February 1974, Planning Director, Army Ballistic Missile Defense Program Office.

3. MDC to NASA
Yardley, John F.
MDC:
V.P. and General Manager, Skylab Program.
NASA:
May 1974, Associate Administrator for Space Flight.

4. "Revolving Door"
Johnson, Robert L.
MDC:
V.P., Research and Engineering.
DoD:
October 1969, Asst. Secretary of the Army for Research and Development.
MDC:
January 1973, Corporate V.P., Engineering and Research; President, McDonnell Douglas Astronautics Co. (1975).

Rose, James T.
MDC:
Manager, Space Shuttle Program support.
NASA:
July 1974, Director of Engineering, Space Shuttle Program.
MDC:
July 1976, Manager, Space Processing Programs, Payload Development for Research and Commercial Applications in space.

Shearer, Richard
DoD:
Policy planning, Office of Asst. Secretary of Defense for International Security Affairs.
MDC:
December 1965, Manager, planning, long-range environmental projections.
DoD:
February 1972, Director of Nuclear Planning, Office of Asst. Secretary of Defense for International Security Affairs.

Comments

1. Several McDonnell Douglas transfers involve BMD work, where McDonnell Douglas is the prime systems contractor. See Robert L. Johnson, William H. Branch (advisor to Defense Science Board on ABM Systems), Arthur N. Thomas, Jr. (Army air and missile defense), and Wayne R. Winten (Army-BMD program office).

2. Policy Statement—"While McDonnell Douglas employs ex-government personnel without discrimination, company policy requires that no solicitation nor discussions will be held until the individual involved has notified the government of his intention to resign or retire. We adhere to the spirit as well as the letter of all laws and regulations with respect to employment of former government personnel while not discriminating against use of individual professional and management talents a former government employee may possess."

POLITICAL ACTION COMMITTEE

Name: McDonnell Douglas Good Government Fund
Total Expenditures (4/76-7/80): $125,526
Total Contributions to Federal Campaigns (4/76-7/80): $115,200

Key
(D) = Democrat
(R) = Republican
(C) = Recipient was a candidate and not elected to that office.
 + = Candidate is also a member of a key Congressional committee.
 * = Candidate is a member of two committees, but contribution s/he received is only listed once to avoid being double-counted in the total for this section.

A. Contributions to Federal Candidates in States with McDonnell Douglas Production Facilities (Key Geographic Locations)

MISSOURI
McDonnell Douglas plants located in St. Louis (dist. 1, 3)

Senate

Sen. John Danforth (R)	$ 500
+Sen. Stuart Symington (D)	$ 500

House

Joseph Badaracco (R-3) (C)	$ 200
Rep. Richard Bolling (D-5)	$ 800
+Rep. Bill Burlison (D-10)	$5,000
Rep. William Clay (D-1)	$ 400
Rep. Thomas E. Coleman (R-6)	$1,300
Joe Frappier (R-9) (C)	$ 400
Rep. Richard Gephardt (D-3)	$1,150
+Rep. Richard Ichord (D-8)	$5,000
Rep. Ike Skelton (D-4)	$1,000
*Rep. Robert O. Snyder (R-2)	$ 200

+ Rep. Gene Taylor (R-7)	$1,700
+ Rep. Harold L. Volkmer (D-9)	$1,775
+ Rep. Robert A. Young (D-2)	$2,900

Total Missouri: $22,825
% Total Federal Contributions: 19.8%

NOTE: A large part of the McDonnell Douglas labor force in St. Louis lives in East St. Louis, IL. Funds to Members of Congress from that area went to:

+ Rep. Melvin Price (D-IL-23)	$5,120

/ **Total Federal Contributions:** 4.4%

CALIFORNIA

McDonnell Douglas plants located in Huntington Beach (dist. 3, 4, 38, 40) and Long Beach (dist. 32, 24)

Senate

Sen. Alan Cranston (D)	$1,000
Sen. S.I. Hayakawa (R)	$ 200
Sen. John V. Tunney (D)	$ 650

House

Cecil Alexander (D-32) (C)	$ 600
+ Rep. Glenn Anderson (D-32)	$1,900
+ Rep. Robert Badham (R-40)	$1,300
Rep. Clair Burgener (R-43)	$ 600
Rep. Yvonne Burke (D-28)	$ 200
Rep. James Corman (D-21)	$3,280
+ Rep. Vic Fazio (D-4)	$ 100
+ Rep. Barry Goldwater, Jr. (R-20)	$ 500
Rep. Wayne R. Grisham (R-33)	$ 225
Rep. Mark W. Hannaford (D-34)	$1,850
+ Rep. Harold T. Johnson (D-1)	$ 500
Rep. Robert J. Lagomarsino (R-19)	$1,000
+ Rep. James Lloyd (D-35)	$3,300
Rep. Daniel E. Lungren (R-34)	$ 950
+ Rep. John J. McFall (D-14)	$2,700
+ Rep. Norman Mineta (D-13)	$1,150
Rep. Jerry Patterson (D-38)	$1,650
Rep. Shirley Pettis (R-37)	$ 200
Rep. John Rousselot (R-26)	$ 250
+ Rep. William Royer (R-11)	$ 500
Burt Talcott (R-16) (C)	$ 200
Rep. Lionel Van Deerlin (D-42)	$ 400
+ Rep. Bob Wilson (R-41)	$2,500
+ Rep. Charles H. Wilson (D-31)	$5,075

Total California: $32,780
% Total Federal Contributions: 28.5%

McDonnell Douglas

OKLAHOMA
McDonnell Douglas plant located in Tulsa (dist. 1)
Senate
    No contributions $ 0
House
Rep. Mickey H. Edwards (R-5)	$ 100
Rep. Glenn English (D-6)	$ 300
James Inhofe (R-1) (C)	$ 200
Rep. James Jones (D-1)	$1,400
Rep. Theodore Risenhoover (D-2)	$ 100
Rep. Tom Steed (D-4)	$ 700

Total Oklahoma: $2,800
% Total Federal Contributions: 2.4%

Total to Key Geographic Locations: $63,525
% Total Federal Contributions: 55.1%

B. Contributions to Members of Key Congressional Committees

Senate Armed Services Committee

Cannon	$ 400	Symington	$ 500
Helms	$ 300	Taft	$ 200
Humphrey, Gordon	$ 400	Thurmond	$ 500
Jepsen	$ 500	Tower	$ 500
Nunn	$ 500		

House Armed Services Committee

Badham	$1,300	Mitchell	$ 300
Bailey	$ 250	Mollahan	$ 200
Brinkley	$ 200	Montgomery	$ 200
Byron, Beverly	$ 400	Nichols	$ 500
Byron, Goodloe	$ 100	Price	$5,120
Daniel, Dan	$ 500	Runnels	$ 200
Daniel, Robert	$ 500	Spence	$ 900
Davis, Mendel	$ 200	Stump	$ 300
Dickinson	$1,600	Treen	$ 200
Fazio	$ 100	Trible	$ 300
Hillis	$ 400	Whitehurst	$ 700
Holt	$ 500	Whitley	$ 200
Ichord	$5,000	Wilson, Bob	$2,500
Lloyd, James	$3,300	Wilson, Charles	$5,075
Mavroules	$ 200		

Senate Defense Appropriations Subcommittee

Brooke	$ 400	Johnston	$ 200
Hollings	$ 500	Magnuson	$ 500
Huddleston	$ 200	McClure	$ 100
Inouye	$ 500	Stevens	$ 500

House Defense Appropriations Subcommittee

Addabbo	$ 400	Edwards, Jack	$ 600
Burlison	$5,000	Giamo	$ 400
Cederberg	$1,400	McFall	$2,700
Dicks	$ 125	Sikes	$ 200

Senate Committee on Commerce, Science and Transportation
Subcommittee on Aviation

Cannon		Inouye	*

Subcommittee on Science, Technology and Space

Griffin	$ 200	Hollings	*
Heflin	$ 100		

House Committee on Science and Technology

Blanchard	$ 100	Lloyd, James	*
Brown	$ 100	McCormack	$ 400
Flippo	$ 700	Nelson	$ 500
Flowers	$ 200	Pursell	$ 100
Frey	$ 500	Royer	$ 500
Fuqua	$1,200	Rudd	$ 500
Gammage	$ 100	Teague	$ 600
Goldwater, Jr.	$ 500	Volkmer	$1,775
Harkin	$ 350	Winn	$ 600
Hollenbeck	$ 100	Young, Robert	$2,900
Kramer	$ 100		

Senate Committee on Environment and Public Works
Subcommittee on Transportation

Domenici	$ 500

House Committee on Public Works and Transportation
Subcommittee on Aviation

Abdnor	$ 100	Johnson	$ 500
Anderson, Glenn	$1,900	Mineta	$1,150
Flippo	*	Rahall	$ 100
Goldwater, Jr.	*	Shuster	$ 200
Hammerschmidt	$ 400	Stump	*
Harsha	$ 100	Taylor	$1,700
Hefner	$ 250	Young, Robert	*

Total to Key Committees: $67,795
% Total Federal Contributions: 58.8%

McDonnell Douglas

C. Contributions to Other Influential Members of Congress

Sen. Howard Baker (R-TN), Minority Leader	$ 500
Rep. Robert Byrd (D-WV), Majority Leader	$ 400
Rep. Robert H. Michel, (R-IL), Minority Whip	$ 700
Rep. Thomas P. O'Neill (D-MA), Speaker of the House	$ 700
Rep. John Rhodes (R-AZ), Minority Leader	$2,100

Total to Other Influentials: $4,400
% Total Federal Contributions: 3.8%

D. Contributions to Other Federal Candidates

Senate

Bradley (D-NJ)	$ 200	Moss (D-UT)	$ 300
Chafee (R-RI)	$ 100	Percy (R-IL)	$1,600
Cochran (R-MS)	$ 100	Sasser (D-TN)	$ 300
Glenn (D-OH)	$ 300	Stewart (D-AL)	$ 100
Mathias (R-MD)	$ 250		

House

Alexander, Bill (D-AK)	$ 700	McDade (R-PA)	$ 125
Ashbrook (R-OH)	$ 100	McEwen (RC-NY)	$ 100
Bevill (D-AL)	$ 200	McKay (D-UT)	$ 200
Buchanon (R-AL)	$ 200	O'Brien (R-IL)	$ 600
Burke (R-FL)	$ 100	Petri (R-WI)	$ 500
Derwinski (R-FL)	$ 100	Rostenkowski (D-IL)	$ 300
Devine (R-OH)	$ 200	Schulze (R-PA)	$ 100
Evans, David (D-IN)	$ 300	Slack (D-WV)	$2,000
Evans, Thomas (R-DE)	$1,000	Vander Jagt (R-MI)	$ 300
Findly (R-IL)	$ 100	Wolf (R-VA)	$ 100
Guyer (R-OH)	$ 100	Young, Bill (R-FL)	$ 500
Hansen (R-ID)	$200		

Total to Other Federal Candidates: $11,375
% Total Federal Contributions: 9.9%

E. Contributions to Party Campaign Committees

Republican federal-level committees: $1,625
Democratic federal-level committees: $7,200

Total to Party Committees: $8,825
% Total Federal Contributions: 7.7%

F. Contributions to Presidential Candidates

Jimmy Carter (D)	$ 500

% Total Federal Contributions: 0.4%

McDonnell Douglas

WASHINGTON OPERATIONS

Washington Office:
1150 17th Street NW, Washington, DC 20036

Director:
Albert James Redway, V.P., Eastern Region
Gordon M. Graham, V.P., Washington office

Staff:
John R. Dierker, Administrative Asst. to V.P.
Earl J. Morgan, Director, Legislative Liaison
Frank Tomlinson, Public Relations Representative
G.P. Vrias, Sr., Washington Representative, Action Industries

Activities:
No information

Registered Lobbyists:

	Receipts	Expenditures	Years
John R. Dierker 1150 17th St. NW Washington, DC	$ 4,500.00	$2,106.95	76-79
Thomas R. Gunn P.O. Box 516 St. Louis, MO	$ 975.00	$ 595.00	77-79
R.J. Maglione 1911 North Fort Meyer Dr. Arlington, VA	$ 6,900.00	$3,475.00	77
Earl J. Morgan 1150 17th St. NW Washington, DC	$ 3,330.00	$1,422.50	76-79
James W. Wilson, Jr. 1150 17th St. NW Washington, DC	*	*	79
TOTAL	$15,705.00	$7,599.45	

*No figures reported; quarterly reports were filed.

McDonnell Douglas

DEFENSE-RELATED TRADE ASSOCIATION MEMBERSHIPS

Aerospace Industries Association
Air Force Association
American Defense Preparedness Association
American Institute of Aeronautics and Astronautics
Armed Forces Communication and Electronics Association
National Association for Remotely-Piloted Vehicles
National Security Industrial Association

ADVISORY COMMITTEE MEMBERSHIPS

1976-78: 11

Black, Richard
    NASA—Research and Technical Advisory Council, Panel on Aviation, Safety and Operating systems, 1976

Conrad, Charles
    (V.P. Commercial Sales, International).
    NASA—Space Programs Advisory Council, 1976, 1977

Dubin, Eugene
    (V.P. Engineering)
    NASA—Advisory Committee on Aeronautical Propulsion, 1976

Gunkel, James R.
    NASA—Research and Technology Advisory Council, Committee on Aerodynamics and Configurations, 1976

Hage, Robert E.
    (Executive V.P., Marketing)
    DoD-Military Airlift Committee, 1976, 1977, 1978

Jarrett, Alfred L.
>   NASA—Research and Technology Advisory Council, Committee on Aerodynamics and Configurations, 1976, 1977

Johnson, Robert L.
>   (Corp. V.P., President, McDonnell Douglas Astronautics Co.)
>   DoD—Army Science Board, 1978

Patten, Paul
>   NASA—Research and Technology Advisory Council, Panel on Aeronautical Operating Systems, Ad Hoc Panel on Terminal Configured Vehicles, 1976, 1977

Siegal, Howard
>   NASA—Committee on Materials and Structures, 1976, 1977

Trent, Warren C.
>   NASA—Research and Technology Advisory Committee, Committee on Aeronautical Propulsion, 1976, 1977

Weiser, Robert C.
>   (Deputy General Manager, Director, Advanced Defense Systems)
>   DoD—Defense Science Board (Associate Member), 1978

Comment:
McDonnell Douglas also had members on advisory boards to the Departments of Commerce and Transportation and to the FCC concerned with multilateral trade negotiations and aeronautical communications.

ENTERTAINMENT

S.N. McDonnell, Chief Executive Officer, informed the Joint Committee on Defense Production that MDC had "a reputation built on the quality and performance of our products, and entertainment of customers has never been the leading edge nor a central focus of the marketing effort."

Entertaining:
Nothing disclosed over $100, no facilities maintained.

Hospitality Suites:
Suites in hotels for Air Force Association, Navy League, Association of the U.S. Army. Discontinued in 1975.

Tickets:
1975: 134 season tickets.

Air Travel:
Only when linked to government business.

Disclosure:
Good.

QUESTIONABLE PAYMENTS

McDonnell Douglas, like other contractors, relied in part on overseas sales in the 1970s to compensate for uncertain post-Vietman defense contracting and the slow-down in domestic commercial sales.

The first suggestion of questionable payments by McDonnell Douglas in connection with such sales came in the 1975 Annual Report stating that approximately $2.5 m. "appeared to have gone to foreign government officials or officials of government-owned airlines." The company added that there was no violation of U.S. Law and the payments were properly accounted for but might involve further tax liabilities. McDonnell Douglas denied having any overseas slush funds or making any illegal political contributions and noted it was cooperating with I.R.S. and SEC investigations into foreign commissions.

In 1978 the company's 10K, filed with the SEC, disclosed that other McDonnell Douglas commission payments were also under investigation and that negotiations were underway with the SEC on the need for further disclosure. McDonnell Douglas also reported that Federal Trade Commission and Department of Justice investigations were underway.

In December 1978, the SEC filed a suit against the company, charging violations of anti-fraud, reporting and proxy provisions of the securities laws, involving some $15.6 m. in payments since 1969. Of this sum $4.6 m. were said to have gone to officials of Government- and state-owned airlines, another $3.7 m. were "other payments to airline officials," and $7.3 m. were commissions paid without using accounting controls to insure the purposes for which they were used (*The Wall Street Journal*, 15 Dec. 1978).

Without admitting to the charges, McDonnell Douglas agreed to settle the suit. The firm was enjoined against any future violations of the securities laws and appointed a special committee to investigate corporate policy, consisting of board members William Danforth and Donald S. MacDonald, and Harold C. Stuart of Tulsa, a former Assistant Secretary of the Air Force, special counsel (*The Wall Street Journal*, 18 Dec. 1978; *The New York Times*, 16 Dec. 1978).

McDonnell Douglas' settlement disclosed some names of countries and amounts paid though no individual recipients were specified. Payments involved 17 foreign countries: Korea ($3.3 m.), the Philippines, Japan, Pakistan, Iran, Kuwait, Kenya, Uganda, Tanzania, Zaire, Argentina, Venezuela, Mexico, W. Germany, Netherlands, Austria, and Italy. It was not clear from the company's report how much of the commissions were passed on in questionable payments or bribes, and the company defended its practice as one which "simply conformed to local custom or to demands which under United States law could be regarded as extortion" (*The New York Times*, 16 Dec. 1978; *The Wall Street Journal*, 18 Dec. 1978).

The company also reported that over $7 m. of the payments in question were under investigation for possible violation of the Foreign Corrupt Practices Act of 1977, including $4.5 m. in Kuwait, $1.8 m. in Japan and $930,000 in Iran. The company stated that it believed "such payments were entirely proper" (*The Wall Street Journal*, 18 Dec. 1978). The disclosures also noted that the Federal Trade Commission investigation was settled with a Consent Order in December 1978 (Ibid.).

McDonnell Douglas' 1978 10K stated that, despite the disclosures, company controls were adequate to deal with the problem:

> McDonnell Douglas will continue to use consultants and representatives in connection with foreign sales where this is deemed to be in the best interests of McDonnell Douglas and its shareholders, provided that the transactions fully comply with all applicable laws and corporate policy. McDonnell Douglas believes that its current policies and procedures, which absolutely prohibit any improper payments to foreign airline or government officials, are providing the highest practicable degree of assurance that applicable laws are being fully observed.

In November 1979, McDonnell Douglas was indicted by a grand jury, following the Department of Justice/U.S. Customs Bureau investigation "for fraud and conspiracy regarding secret payments to private or government officials in Pakistan, Korea, the Philippines, Venezuela and Zaire from 1972 to 1977" (*The New York Times*, 10 Nov. 1979). The Justice Department charge concerned $6 m. of questionable payments to Government and airlines officials in Venezuela ($2.1 m.), Korea ($3.3 m.), Zaire ($625,000), the Philippines ($400,000), as well as $1 m. in payments to Pakistani sales agents concealed from Pakistani International Airlines between 1972 and 1977 (*The Wall Street Journal*, 12 Nov. 1979). Trial on the indictment is scheduled to begin in January 1981.

In July 1980, the special board committee reported that McDonnell Douglas had made $21.6 m. in payments between 1969 and 1978 in 18 countries, including Iran, Kuwait, Trinidad and Tobago. The committee urged tighter controls and proposed that the company's board of directors be restructured to include a majority of outside directors.

DISCLOSURE

Very poor.

NORTHROP

BASIC CORPORATE AND CONTRACTING DATA

A. Corporate Data

Northrop Corporation
1800 Century Park East
Los Angeles, CA 90067

Fortune 500 (1979): 204
Fiscal Year: Jan. 1—Dec. 31

Chairman:
  Thomas V. Jones (1979 salary: $1,245,038)

President:
  Thomas O. Paine (1979 salary: $478,494)

Auditor:
  Touche, Ross & Co.
  Los Angeles, CA

Outside Legal Counsel:
  O'Melveny & Meyers
  611 W. 6th St.
  Los Angeles, CA

  Wilmer, Cutler and Pickering
  1666 K St. NW
  Washington, DC

TABLE I
Corporate Data
($ in M.)

	1970	1971	1972	1973	1974	1975	1976	1977	1978	1979
Sales	$ 626.9	573.9	573.7	698.9	853.3	988.1	1,265.0	1,601.4	1,829.8	1,582.8
Net Income*	$ 19.9	11.0	11.1	11.6	18.1	24.7	35.9	66.2	88.4	90.3
Dept. of Defense Contracts	$ 184.2	150.9	369.6	446.4	490.8	620.3	1,480.2	1,046.7	586.0	800.3
Rank	33	34	17	15	13	12	3	10	15	13
NASA Contracts	$ 9.4	19.0	14.9	16.5	16.3	16.9	18.0	18.8	21.2	26.1
Rank	31	22	24	22	22	19	20	22	25	23
DoD/NASA Contracts as % of Sales	30.9%	29.6	67.0	66.2	59.4	64.5	118.0	66.6	33.2	52.2
Government Sales	NA	NA	$333.3	423.5	552.4	612.5	943.4	1,306.9	1,450.5	1,119.0
Government Sales as % of Sales			58.1%	60.6	64.7	62.0	74.6	81.6	79.3	61.2
Foreign Military Sales Contracts	$ 18.4	3.2	109.5	171.2	220.7	293.4	1,292.5	853.0	267.0	472.3
Rank	8	NA	2	4	2	3	1	1	7	3
FMS Contracts as % of Sales	2.9%	.6	19.1	24.5	25.9	29.7	102.2	53.3	14.6	29.8
Overseas and Export Sales	NA	$ 76.1	172.1	NA	NA	523.7	746.4	1,020.2	1,138.8	701.6
Overseas and Export Sales as % of Sales		13.3%	30.0			53.0	59.0	63.7	62.2	44.3
Employees	16,200	15,400	22,000	24,900	26,200	23,300	24,000	26,200	31,200	28,800

*1970 figure based on July 31 fiscal year.

Advertising/Public Relations Agency:
Needham, Harper & Steers, Inc.
10889 Wilshire Blvd.
Los Angeles, CA

Banking:

Transfer Agent and Registrar:
United California Bank

Lenders:
Security Pacific National Bank, Los Angeles (revolving credit up to $4.5 m.) (see Board of Directors: Richard Flamson)
Manufacturers Hanover (revolving credit up to $3.44 m.)
Wells Fargo Bank (revolving credit up to $2.5 m.)
Chase Manhattan Bank and seven others unnamed (loan and credit agreement, $50 m. revolving credit line)

Trustee:
Salaried and Hourly Employees Rated Savings Plan (10% of company stock, 1979), Manufacturers Hanover

B. Principal Defense/Space Contracting Operations

1. Aircraft Group
Ross F. Miller, Senior V.P. and group executive
Joe C. Jones, V.P. and Asst. to the Chief Executive Officer for Aeronautical Systems

Aircraft Division
Hawthorne, CA
Ross F. Miller, V.P. and Gen. Mgr.

F-5E/F—tactical fighter, U.S. Air Force and foreign orders
F/A-18—carrier strike fighter, U.S. Navy and U.S. Marine Corps
F-18L—land strike fighter, possible foreign orders
F-5G—possible foreign orders

Aircraft Services Division
Hawthorne, CA
F.J. Manzella, V.P. and Gen. Mgr.

Services, construction, maintenance support and training, Peace Hawk program, Saudi Arabia

Northrop Worldwide Aircraft Services
Lawton, OK

Maintenance, management training, base supplies and fire protection; U.S. Navy, Army and Air Force, NASA and civil agencies

Northrop Services, Inc.
Anaheim, CA
Donald A. McInnis, Corp. V.P. and President

> Technical, scientific and managerial support services; U.S. Navy, NASA, civil agencies

2. Tactical and Electronics Systems Group
Frank W. Lynch, Senior V.P. and Group Executive

Electronics Division
Hawthorne, CA
David N. Ferguson, V.P. and Gen. Mgr.

> E-3A (AWACS)—navigation system, Boeing
> MX—inertial measurement unit, U.S. Air Force

Ventura Division
Newbury Park, CA
Kent Kresa, V.P. and Gen. Mgr.

> BQM-74C—remotely piloted air launchable target vehicle, U.S. Navy
> MQM-74C Chukar II—earlier version of BQM-74C; U.S. Navy, NATO
> Basic Training Targets, U.S. Army, foreign orders

Defense Systems Division
Rolling Meadows, IL
Wallace C. Solberg, V.P. and Gen. Mgr.

> Compact jamming system—U.S. Navy, U.S. Marine Corps.
> B-52, F-15 and F/A-18—electronic countermeasures, U.S. Air Force, U.S. Navy

Electro-Mechanical Division
Anaheim, CA
George H. Hage, V.P. and Gen. Mgr.

> Television Sight Unit—electrical optical system for F-14, U.S. Navy
> Hawk missile components—ground-to-air missile; U.S. Army, U.S. Marine Corps, foreign orders

3. Other

Precision Products Division
Norwood, MA
Joseph Yamron, V.P. and Gen. Mgr.

> Gyroscopes, U.S. Navy, Army, Air Force, NASA, and foreign orders
> Strapdown inertial guidance and navigation systems for Harpoon, Phoenix and AMRAAM missiles, U.S. Navy, U.S. Air Force

**Northrop Research and Technology Center
Palos Verdes Peninsula, CA
William J. Chalmers, V.P. and manager**
Advanced technology research projects; U.S. military

C. Contracting History

Northrop emerged in the 1970s as a major Pentagon contractor for several systems: fighter aircraft, navigation and guidance, electronic countermeasures, communications, remotely-piloted vehicles, electro-optical systems and aircraft services. The company also developed a reputation for efficient production and cost control.

Northrop made $150,000 in contributions to Nixon's 1972 Presidential campaign. The company and its then president and chairman, Thomas V. Jones, pleaded guilty to charges brought by the Watergate Special Prosecutor and were fined $5,000 for these contributions, which "violated a law banning contributions by government contractors" (*Commercial and Financial Chronicle*, 10 June 1974; *Fortune*, 10 April 1978). At this time Northrop was emerging as a major defense contractor with its F-5 aircraft series manufactured for, and sold widely to, overseas markets. Northrop was also competing with General Dynamics for an Air Force fighter order, using its F-17 design. In January 1975, however, the F-17 lost this competition and later a pending European order for fighter aircraft.

Northrop effectively used its Government relations practices to further corporate goals. A special Ernst and Ernst audit, and a Senate investigation disclosed in 1975 that Northrop employed a number of retired U.S. military officers for sensitive work such as overseas sales and intelligence community liaison (*The New York Times*, 26 June 1975). In September 1975, questions were raised about Northrop's entertainment of Pentagon and Congressional personnel at company facilities in Maryland. A number of the Pentagon officials so entertained were in a position to be useful to Northrop. In 1976 the Defense Department admonished 38 employees for having accepted Northrop's hospitality, contrary to the DoD code of conduct (*The New York Times*, 24 Jan. 1976). Northrop President Jones later told Congress that such practices had ended and the company reimbursed DoD for those costs that had been charged to contracts.

Company sales continued to rise through this period. The F-5 continued its overseas success while Northrop, along with McDonnell Douglas, made progress in selling the F-18 to the Navy as a new, low-cost fighter plane. Jones had resigned as chairman in 1975 in the wake of the campaign contributions and payments revelations but remained as president. He was later reinstated, the board arguing that he had been doing an excellent job as company manager (*The New York Times*, 19 Sept. 1976). That same year Northrop received a

$1.5 b. Saudi contract for Air Force support, training, and construction; and the Swiss ordered 72 F-5s.

Contracting success continued into 1977. The F-18 program moved along and new contracts were won for F-15 ECM and the Saudi Peace Hawk program. In its April 10, 1978 issue, *Fortune* praised the firm for superb overseas salesmanship, for using its own plant and equipment for defense work, for meeting cost goals and setting realizable performance goals for its products. The F-5 series had sold over 2,200 planes and all other programs were in superb shape, according to *Fortune*. It was also noted, in the July 17, 1978 *Washington Post*, that Northrop had increased its Government relations effort: new lobbyists had been hired, including Wallace Timmons, former Nixon staffer, and Stanley Sommer, former staffer of the Senate Appropriations Committee; and the company continued to hire a large number of retired military personnel. The General Accounting Office pointed out that Northrop had become so central to overseas defense efforts that they had been made responsible for the actual management of some of the Pentagon's overseas effort—developing specifications, schedules and contracts for sales to Saudi Arabia, in particular. The GAO suggested that the company might have a "potential organization conflict of interest," receiving information "not normally made available to contractors." At that point, Northrop was monitoring virtually all Saudi and Iranian foreign military sales programs, with a "major input into the decision-making process." To carry out this work Northrop was using 61 former DoD employees, according to the GAO.

By 1980 Northrop was in the process of developing significant new military business. As sales of the current F-5 tapered off, the company received permission from the Department of Defense to design a new version of the aircraft for future overseas sales. In addition, the company received a major additional contract in its Peace Hawk program to upgrade the Saudi Arabian Air Force. Northrop is also a major corporate beneficiary of the Air Force's MX program, receiving a $235 m. contract for development on its Advanced Inertial Reference Sphere (AIRS) for the program. As coproducer of the F-18, Northrop benefited from the Canadian decision in April 1980 to add that airplane to its inventory. The F-18 program also has a cost increase problem, however, with unit costs rising to between $20 and $25 m. by the summer of 1980 (*Aviation Week*, 30 June 1980; *Armed Forces Journal*, 19 July 1980).

D. U.S. Government-Owned, Company-Operated Plants

Total company floor space: Not disclosed
Leased from U.S. Government: 399,597 sq. ft.
Total lease cost: Not disclosed

Location: Air Force Plant 42
Palmdale, CA
266,684 sq. ft.
Use: F-5E and F-5F
Cost: Not disclosed

Location: Palmdale, CA
35,420 sq. ft.
Use: Not disclosed
Cost: Not disclosed

Location: Fort Irwin, CA
6,400 acres
Use: Not disclosed
Cost: Not disclosed

RESEARCH AND DEVELOPMENT

Major Defense/Space R&D Projects

F-5G—export fighter development, foreign orders
F-18L—land-based fighter, foreign orders
Unmanned target aircraft, U.S. Navy
Electronic counter-measures, U.S. Navy, U.S. Air Force
Electro-optical systems, U.S. Navy, U.S. Air Force
Guidance systems, U.S. Air Force

TABLE II
Research and Development
($ in M.)

		1970	1971	1972	1973	1974	1975	1976	1977	1978	1979
I.	U.S. Government Contracts										
	DoD	$41.4	29.8	46.6	40.6	74.9	58.6	133.9	89.9	63.9	65.0
	NASA	$ 9.4	19.0	14.9	16.5	16.3	16.9	18.0	18.8	21.2	26.1
	Total	$50.8	48.8	61.5	57.1	91.2	75.5	151.9	108.7	85.1	91.1
II.	Company-sponsored R&D	NA	$ 9.9	NA	17.7	20.4	22.1	25.8	31.5	55.6	46.3
III.	IR&D	NA	NA	NA	$12.6	16.0	17.5	19.8	22.3	24.4	NA

I. From DoD yearly pubication "500 Contractors Receiving the Largest Dollar Volume of Military Prime Contract Awards for RDT&E" and NASA Annual Procurement Reports.

II. "Company sponsored research and development costs, those costs not recoverable under contract arrangements, are charged against income as incurred." (Annual Report, 1978)

III. Company-sponsored R&D costs as disclosed by DoD.

BOARD OF DIRECTORS

William F. Ballhaus (1975)
President and director, Beckman Instruments, Inc.
Past Corporate Employment:
Northrop Corp. (1953-65); Beckman Instruments, Inc. (1965-present).
Government Positions:
Technical Advisory Panel on Aerospace, Office Secretary of Defense (1954-60); National Advisory Committee on Aeronautics (1954-57).
Corporate Directorships:
Amerace Corp. ($1,553,000); Pacific Indemnity Co.; Union Oli Co. of California ($1,193,000).
Key Association Memberships:
American Institute Aeronautics and Astronautics (fellow), Association of the U.S. Army.
Shares owned:
22,650

Thomas C. Barger (1975)
Oil consultant
Past Corporate Employment:
Arabian American Oil Co. (1937-69) (Chairman, 1968-69).
Corporate Directorships:
California First Bank; Kratos Corp. ($376,000); Offshore Technology Corp.; WD-40 Corp.; Kaufman & Broad, Inc.
Shares owned:
2,475

Richard Flamson III, (1976)
President and Chief Executive Officer, Security Pacific Corp. and Security Pacific National Bank.
Past Corporate Employment:
Security Pacific National Bank, (1955-present) (see Basic Data: Banking).
Corporate Directorships:
Kaufman & Broad, Inc.
Shares owned:
0

Ivan A. Getting (1977)
Consultant to and director of Institute of Electrical and Electronics Engineers.
Past Corporate Employment:
Radiation Lab, Mass. Institute of Technology (1940-51); V.P., Research and Engineering, Raytheon (1951-60); President, Aerospace Corp., El Segundo, CA (1960-retired before 1977).

Government Positions:
   Asst. for development planning to Deputy Chief of Staff for Development, U.S. Air Force (1950-51).
Corporate Directorships:
   Northern Energy Corp.; Medtronic, Inc. ($33,000); First National Bank of Waseca, MN.
Key Association Memberships:
   American Institute Aeronautics and Astronautics.
Shares owned:
   600

Richard E. Horner (1977)
President, Chief Executive Officer and Director, E.F. Johnson Co. (mobile communications equipment).
Military:
   Director, flight testing engineering, Wright Field (1944-45, 1947-49).
Past Corporate Employment:
   Senior V.P., technology, Northrop Corp., Beverly Hills, CA (1960-70); President, E.F. Johnson Co. (1970-present).
Government Positions:
   Technical Director, Air Force Flight Test Center (1950-55); Deputy Asst. Secretary, Air Force (1955-57); Asst. Secretary, Air Force, for Research and Development (1957-59); Associate Administrator, NASA (1959-60).
Corporate Directorships:
   First National Bank of Waseca, MN; Medtronic, Inc. ($33,000); Northwestern National Bank, Minneapolis (member, trust committee).
Key Association Memberships:
   American Institute of Aeronautics and Astronautics (fellow and past President); American Astronautical Society; Electronic Industries Association.
Shares owned:
   500

Thomas V. Jones (1959)
Chairman of the Board and Chief Executive Officer, Northrop Corp.
Past Corporate Employment:
   Engineer, Douglas Aircraft Co. (1941-47); Technical Advisor, Brazilian Air Ministry and Professor, Brazilian Institute of Technology (1947-51); Staff Consultant, Air Staff of Rand Corporation (1951-53); Northrup Corp. (1953-present).
Key Association Memberships:
   American Institute of Aeronautics and Astronautics (fellow); Navy League; Aerospace Industries Association.
Shares owned:
   240,278

Earle M. Jorgensen (1954)
Chairman of the Board and Chief Executive Officer, Earle M. Jorgensen Co. (steel and aluminum products).
Past Corporate Employment:
Earle M. Jorgensen Co. (1923-present).
Corporate Directorships:
Kerr-McGee Corp. ($63,311,000); City Investing Co. (advisory committee).
Shares owned:
3,600

Thomas M. McDaniel, Jr. (1968)
Consultant, director and retired President, Southern California Edison Co.
Past Corporate Employment:
Salesman, IBM (no date); Asst. to V.P., Bethelehem Steel Co. (no date); Principal, Arthur Anderson & Co. (no date).
Corporate Directorships:
Bankamericorp.; Dillingham Corp. ($11,462,000); Pacific Indemnity Co.; Southern California Edison Co. ($71,762,000); Associated South Investment Co.
Shares owned:
1,116

Richard W. Millar (1946)
Vice Chairman of the Board, Northrop Corp.
Past Corporate Employment:
Blair & Co. (1922-30); Bankam Co. (1930-32); Vultee Aircraft (1939-43); Northrop Corp. (1946-present); Consultant, Kuhn, Loeb & Co. (to 1975).
Corporate Directorships:
Quotron Systems; Pegasus Income and Capital Fund; Agman, Inc.
Shares owned:
2,000

Thomas O. Paine (1976)
President and Chief Operating Officer, Northrop Corp.
Past Corporate Employment:
General Electric (1949-68, 1970-76); Northrop Corp. (1976-present).
Government Positions:
Administrator, NASA (1968-70).
Key Association Memberships:
American Institute of Aeronautics and Astronautics.
Shares owned:
22,532

Charles W. Robinson (1978)
Chairman, Energy Transition Corp.
Past Corporate Employment:
Vice Chairman, Blyth, Eastman, Dillon & Co. (no date).
Government Positions:
Undersecretary for Economic Affairs, State Dept. (1974-76).
Corporate Directorships:
Arthur D. Little, Inc.; Nike, Inc.
Shares owned:
0

PERSONNEL TRANSFERS

Table III
(DoD 1970-79)
(NASA 1974-79)

	Total	Air Force	Army	Navy	Office of Secretary of Defense	Other
DoD Military to Northrop	284	197	16	54	2	15
DoD Civilian to Northrop	50	24	4	9	8	5
NASA to Northrop	9					
Northrop to DoD	16	3	2	5	4	2
Northrop to NASA	1					
Total	360	224	22	68	14	22

Appearances of Potential Conflict of Interest (see Chapter 6): 20

1. DoD to Northrop

Ashby, Donald
  DoD:
   Chief, Material Support Branch, Division of International Logistics, San Antonio Air Logistics Center, Kelly AFB, Texas, providing worldwide logistic support; then Deputy Chief, Peace Hawk Division, San Antonio Air Logistics Center.

Northrop:
> July 1979, Logistics specialist, collect and present logistic data to USAF planning, programming and management personnel, Northrop Worldwide Aircraft Services.

Alexander, Robert
DoD:
> Deputy Director, Directorate of Mission and Management support, Air Force Logistics Command.

Northrop:
> June 1976, Field manager, Northrop Dayton Support Group, analyzing information on foreign military sales, Northrop Worldwide Aircraft Services.

Alne, Leonard A.
DoD:
> Director, sales negotiations, Defense Security Assistance Agency (left 1974).

Northrop:
> September 1974, Consultant and advisor, sale of military aircraft to foreign buyers.

Bernstein, Charles
DoD:
> Reviewing and evaluating all strategic programs, Office of Asst. Secretary of Defense for Systems Analysis/Strategic Programs.

Northrop:
> September 1970, Director, technical planning—review, evaluating and coordinating all R&D plans. Later V.P. and Asst. to the Chief Executive Officer for analysis.

Crocket, Rufus
DoD:
> Deputy Asst. Secretary of the Air Force, Office of Secretary of the Air Force.

Northrop:
> September 1975, Program Director, Technical facilities and construction, Peace Hawk III and V, Saudi Arabia, George Fuller Construction Co.

James, Larry B.
DoD:
> Director, Tactical Technical Office, Defense Advanced Research Projects Agency.

Northrop:
> May 1978, V.P. for Engineering, Ventura Division.

Jones, Joe
DoD:
> Deputy Asst. Secretary of Air Force for Research and Development and Acting Asst. Secretary of Air Force for R&D.

Northrop:
September 1974, Asst. to Chairman for Aeronautical Systems (see Basic Data: Sect. B).

Kresa, Kent
DoD:
Deputy Director, Strategic Technology Office and Special Asst. for Undersea Warfare Technology and Director, Tactical Technology Office, Defense Advanced Research Projects Agency.
Northrop:
March 1975, V.P. and Manager, Ventura Division.

Lukasik, Stephen J.
DoD:
Director, Defense Advanced Research Projects Agency.
Northrop:
July 1976, Consultant (to 1977).

Nelson, Ivan H.
DoD:
Supervisory Logistics Management Specialist, Air Force Logistics Command, Tinker AFB, OK.
Northrop:
December 1978, Senior Logistics Specialist, establish, operate and maintain support group to track status of Imperial Iranian Air Force.

Simecka, William
DoD:
Chief Scientist, Eglin Air Force Base, Air Force.
Northrop:
July 1968, V.P., Technical and Marketing, Electro-Mechanical Division.

Taylor, Robert Q.
DoD:
Deputy Project Manager, TOW Missile System, Redstone Arsenal, U.S. Army (left Sept. 1977).
Northrop:
(No date), Engineer, coordinated engineering tasks with Army, Northrop Services.

Wenninger, George
DoD:
Asst. Director for Tactical Systems, Planning and Analysis, Office of Director of Defense Research and Engineering.
Northrop:
October 1972, Manager, Laser Systems Laboratories; Asst. to V.P., Research and Technology;

Zankowsky, Charles
  DoD:
    Logistics management specialist and supply systems analyst, U.S. Air Force, Washington, D.C.
  Northrop:
    March 1979, Northrop Worldwide Aircraft Services, no details.

2. NASA to Northrop
Farley, Clare F.
  NASA:
    Deputy Asst. Administrator for Technology Utilization, Headquarters.
  Northrop:
    July 1976, Executive Asst. to the President.
Jackson, Roy P.
  NASA:
    Office of Aeronautics and Space Technology, Associate Administrator for Aeronautics and Space Technology.
  Northrop:
    October 1973, Corporate V.P. and Program Manager, F-17.

3. Northrop to DoD
Kuo, Franklin
  Northrop:
    Consultant, computer/communications.
  DoD:
    December 1975, Asst. Director for Tele-processing, Office of Secretary of Defense.
La Vier, Eugene
  Northrop:
    Principal Scientist, Nuclear vulnerabilities of weapons systems and information systems, Corporate Lab.
  DoD:
    April 1971, Director of Vulnerability, Defense Nuclear Agency.

4. "Revolving Door"
Silverstein, Robert L.
  DoD:
    Not stated.
  Northrop:
    December 1976, Director, Northrop Corporate Analysis Center, foreign and defense policy studies.

DoD:
July 1977, Consultant to Undersecretary of Defense for intelligence, surveillance, command and control, Office of Secretary of Defense.

Thyberg, Robert
DoD:
Chief of Naval Material, air weapons technical administration, Navy.
Northrop:
September 1970, Senior Engineer, Trident programs, Northrop Services.
DoD:
February 1972, Director, tactical electromagnetic programs, Plans and Program Office, Navy.

Comments

1. Numerous transfers took place in 1976 from the San Antonio Logistics Center to Northrop, many of them involved with foreign military sales: Donald Ashby, John Bernardoni, Willis Clay, Thomas Hill, Herbert Holzmann, Ronald Morris, Leland Schneider.
2. There were numerous transfers from Wright-Patterson Logistics to Northrop: 1976—Ray Brooks, Lawrence Coyle, Donald Sharp; 1978—Edward Thornhill, Dorothy Tucker.
3. Worldwide Services, which handles Northrop's overseas programs, especially the Peace Hawk (Saudi Arabia), hired a large number of transferees.
4. There were several transfers of individuals with high positions in Northrop or in DoD or NASA: Charles Bernstein, Joe Jones, Kent Kresa, George Wenninger, Clare Farley, Roy Jackson.
5. There were transfers from Defense Advanced Research Projects Agency to Northrop: Kent Kresa, Joe Jones, and Stephen Lukasik. DARPA plays a central role in the definition of future defense technology.
6. Northrop has no policy statement on transfers of personnel.

POLITICAL ACTION COMMITTEE

Name: Northrop Employees Political Action Committee
Total Expenditures (2/78-7/80): $110,416
Total Contributions to Federal Campaigns (2/78-7/80): $88,039

Key
- (D) = Democrat
- (R) = Republican
- (C) = Recipient was a candidate and not elected to that office.
- + = Candidate is also a member of a key Congressional committee.
- * = Candidate is a member of two committees, but contribution s/he received is only listed once to avoid being double-counted in the total for this section.

A. Contributions to Federal Candidates in States with Northrop Production Facilities (Key Geographic Locations)

CALIFORNIA

Northrop plant locations in Anaheim (dist. 38, 39), Hawthorne (dist. 28, 31) and Newbury Park (dist. 20)

Senate

Sen. Alan Cranston (D)	$1,500
Sen. S.I. Hayakawa (R)	$ 100

House

+ Rep. Glenn Anderson (D-32)	$ 200
+ Rep. Robert E. Badham (R-40)	$ 850
Rep. Anthony Coelho (D-15)	$ 400
Rep. James C. Corman (D-21)	$1,325
Rep. George E. Danielson (D-30)	$ 200
Rep. William Dannemeyer (R-39)	$ 300
Rep. Julian Dixon (D-28)	$ 500
+ Rep. Robert Dornan (R-27)	$ 550
+ Rep. Vic Fazio (D-40)	$ 600
+ Rep. Barry Goldwater, Jr. (R-20)	$ 345
Rep. Wayne Grisham (R-33)	$ 100
Nate Holden (D-28) (C)	$ 250
+ Rep. Harold T. Johnson (D-1)	$ 250
Rep. Jerry Lewis (R-37)	$ 100
+ Rep. James Lloyd (D-35)	$2,500
Rep. Daniel Lungren (R-34)	$ 100
Rep. Robert Matsui (D-3)	$ 300
Lawrence Mattera (R-42) (C)	$ 200
+ Rep. John J. McFall (D-14)	$ 800
Rep. Carlos Moorehead (R-22)	$ 125
Rep. Charles Pashayan (R-17)	$ 550
Rep. Jerry Patterson (D-38)	$ 150
Rep. John H. Rousselot (R-26)	$ 200
Rep. William Thomas (R-18)	$ 100
+ Rep. Bob Wilson (R-41)	$1,500
+ Rep. Charles Wilson (D-31)	$4,000

Total California: $18,095
% Total Federal Contributions: 20.6%

ILLINOIS
Northrop plant located in Rolling Meadows (dist. 12)
Senate
    Charles Percy (R) $ 500
House
    Rep. Thomas Corcoran (R-15) $ 300
    Rep. Paul Findley (R-20) $ 150
+ Rep. Melvin Price (D-23) $ 500
    Rep. Dan Rostenkowki (D-8) $ 200

Total Illinois: $1,650
% Total Federal Contributions: 1.9%

MASSACHUSETTS
Northrop plant located in Norwood (dist. 9)
Senate
+ Sen. Edward Brooke (R) $ 800
    Sen. Paul Tsongas (D) $ 500
House
    Rep. Margaret Heckler (R-10) $ 200
+ Rep. Nicholas Mavroules (D-6) $ 250
    Rep. John Moakley (D-9) $ 200

Total Massachusetts: $1,950
% Total Federal Contributions: 2.2%

OKLAHOMA
Northrop plant located in Lawton (dist. 4)
    No contributions

Total to Key Geographic Locations: $21,695
% Total Federal Contributions: 24.6%

B. Contributions to Members of Key Congressional Committees

Senate Armed Services Committee

Anderson, Wendell	$ 300	McIntyre	$1,000
Goldwater	$1,000	Morgan	$ 500
Helms	$ 300	Stennis	$ 500
Jepsen	$ 700	Thurmond	$1,000
Leahy	$ 500	Tower	$1,000
Nunn	$1,000	Warner	$5,000

House Armed Services Committee

Badham	$ 850	Mavroules	$ 250
Bailey	$ 200	McDonald	$ 300
Brinkley	$ 200	Mitchell, Donald	$ 300
Byron	$ 400	Montgomery	$ 200
Courter	$ 250	Nedzi	$ 300
Davis	$ 500	Nichols	$ 500
Dickinson	$ 600	Price	$ 500
Dougherty	$ 200	Spence	$ 450
Fazio	$ 600	Stratton	$ 200
Hillis	$ 300	Stump	$ 300
Holt	$ 600	Trible	$ 400
Ichord	$ 400	Wilson, Bob	$1,500
Lloyd, James	$2,500	Wilson, Charles H.	$4,000

Senate Defense Appropriations Subcommittee

Brooke	$ 800	Magnuson	$ 500
Hollings	$1,000	McClure	$ 300
Huddleston	$ 300	Stennis	*
Inouye	$1,000	Stevens	$ 300
Johnston	$ 500		

House Defense Appropriations Subcommittee

Burlison	$ 800	Edwards	$ 500
Cederberg	$ 300	Giamo	$ 500
Chappell	$ 300	McFall	$ 800
Dicks	$ 300	Robinson	$ 500
		Wilson, Charles, N.	$ 250

Senate Committee on Commerce, Science and Transportation
Subcommittee on Aviation

Goldwater	*	Inouye	*
Hollings	*	Stevens	*

Subcommittee on Science, Technology and Space

Goldwater	*	Griffin	$ 500

House Committee on Science and Technology

Ambro	$ 200	Lloyd, James	*
Davis, Robert	*	Mavroules	*
Dornan	$ 550	Rudd	$ 400
Gammage	$ 200	Winn	$ 550
Goldwater Jr.	$ 345		

Senate Committee on Environment and Public Works
Subcommittee on Transportation

Domenici	$ 300

House Committee on Public Works and Transportation
Subcommittee on Aviation

Ambro	*	Johnson, Harold	*
Goldwater	*	Stump	*

Total Contributions to Key Committees: $41,595
% Total Federal Contributions: 47.2%

C. Contributions to Other Influential Members of Congress

Sen. Howard Baker (R-TN), Minority Leader $1,000
(also received contributions as a Presidential candidate)
Rep. James Wright (D-TX), Majority Leader $ 500

Total to Other Influentials: $1,500
% Total Federal Contributions: 1.7%

D. Contributions to Other Federal Candidates

Senate

Anaya (R-NM)	$ 500	DeConcini (D-AZ)	$ 500
Armstrong (R-CO)	$ 500	Glenn (D-OH)	$1,000
Baxter (R-DE)	$ 300	Hatfield, P. (D-MT) (C)	$ 500
Biden (D-DE)	$ 500	Mathias (R-MD)	$ 250
Clark (D-IA)	$ 500	McGovern (D-SD)	$ 250
Church (D-ID)	$ 500	Saba (D-ND) (C)	$ 250
Dantin (D-MS)	$ 500	Simpson (R-WY)	$ 300
		Stewart (D-AL)	$ 500

House

Alexander (D-AR)	$ 200	Hamilton (D-IN)	$ 450
Andrews (R-ND)	$ 200	Ireland (D-FL)	$ 500
Bauman (R-MD)	$ 150	Loeffler (R-TX)	$ 200
Bolling (D-MO)	$ 700	Lott (R-MS)	$ 200
Briggs (R-FL) (C)	$ 200	Mattox (D-TX)	$ 250
Burke (R-FL)	$ 200	McCormick (D-AZ)	$ 200
Crane (R-IL)	$ 200	McEwen (R-NY)	$ 200
Coughlin (R-PA)	$ 100	McKay (D-UT)	$ 500
Cunningham (R-WA)	$ 200	Pepper (D-FL)	$ 200
Derrick (D-SC)	$ 200	Petri (R-WI)	$ 200
Devine (R-OH)	$ 200	Quillen (R-TN)	$ 200
Duncan, John (R-TN)	$ 200	Rodino (D-NJ)	$ 500
Duncan, Robert (D-OR)	$ 250	Santini (D-NE)	$ 200
Fascell (D-FL)	$ 200	Vander Jagt (R-MI)	$ 400
Fisher (D-VA)	$ 200	Withers (R-NY)	$ 200
Guyer (R-OH)	$ 200	Witzenburger (R-WY)	$ 300
Hadley (D-SC)	$ 500	Zablocki (D-NY)	$1,000

Total to Other Federal Candidates: $16,650
% Total Federal Contributions: 18.9%

E. Contributions to Party Campaign Committees

Republican federal-level committees: $4,542
Democratic federal-level committees: $6,500

Total to Party Committees: $11,042
% Total Federal Contributions: 12.5%

F. Contributions to Presidential Candidates

John Anderson (R)	$ 100
Howard Baker (R)	$ 100
George Bush (R)	$ 100
Jimmy Carter (D)	$4,250
Philip Crane (R)	$ 10
Edward Kennedy (D)	$1,000
Ronald Reagan (R)	$3,142

Total to Presidential Candidates: $8,702
% Total Federal Contributions: 9.9%

WASHINGTON OPERATIONS

Washington Office:
1701 N. Fort Meyer Dr., Arlington, VA 22209

Director:
Stanley Ebner, Corporate V.P., Manager, Eastern Regional Office.

James V. Holcombe, Senior V.P. and Asst. to Chief Executive Officer for Government Relations.

Staff:
John Pesch, legislative liaison
Stanley Sommer, legislative affairs

Activities:
No information.

Registered Lobbyists:

	Receipts	Expenditures	Years
James R. Calloway 1101 Connecticut Ave. Washington, DC	$ 39,500.00	$ 150.00	78-79

Timothy P. Furlong
  Manatt, Phelps,
    Rothenbert & Tunney
  1888 Century Park East
  Los Angeles, CA
    and
  1875 I St. NW
  Washington, DC
	*	*	79

Ed Hartung
  3707 Moss Dr.
  Annadale, VA
	$ 1,000.00	*	79

Jack McDonald & Assoc., Inc.
  6845 Elm St., No. 512
  McLean, VA
	$ 50,999.94	$ 26,950.00	77-79

James McDonald
  (Jack McDonald Assoc.)
  6845 Elm St., No. 512
  McLean, VA
	$ 24,750.00	*	77-79

William E. Minshall
  1730 M St. NW
  Washington, DC
	$ 3,300.00	*	77

Joel B. Paris III
  Georgia International
    Services Inc.
  25 Pine Island Court
  Roswell, GA
	$ 1,000.00	$ 210.00	77-79

John Joseph Pesch
  1701 N. Fort Meyer Dr.
  Arlington, VA
	$ 47,514.00	$ 28,000.48	77-79

S.L. Sommer & Assoc., Inc.
  1701 N. Fort Meyer Dr.
  Arlington, VA
	$ 92,300.00	$102,388.19	76-79

Timmons & Co.
  1776 F St. NW
  Washington, DC
	$ 4,226.00	*	78-79

Williams & Jensen
  1130 17th St. NW
  Washington, DC
	$ 2,250.00	$ 170.00	77-78

Winston P. Wilson
  523 North Forrest St.
  Forrest City, AK
	$ 73,130.00	$ 25,242.20	77-79

TOTAL	**$339,969.94**	**$183,110.87**	

*No figures reported; quarterly reports were filed.

DEFENSE-RELATED TRADE ASSOCIATION MEMBERSHIPS

Aerospace Industries Association
Air Force Association
American Defense Preparedness Association
American Institute of Aeronautics and Astronautics
American League for Exports and Security Assistance
Armed Forces Communication and Electronics Association
National Association for Remotely-Piloted Vehicles
National Council of Technical Service Industries
National Security Industrial Association

ADVISORY COMMITTEE MEMBERSHIPS

1976-78: 10

Burchinal, David
(V.P. and Sr. Corp. Executive, Europe, Middle East, Near East and Africa)
>DoD—Defense Industry Advisory Group, Europe 1976, 1977

Chalmers, William J.
(V.P. and Manager, Northrop Research and Technology Center) (see Basic Data)
>DoD—Defense Intelligence Agency, Scientific Advisory Council, 1977, 1978

Espinosa, Robert
(Defense Systems Division)
>DoD—Advisory Group on Electron Devices, 1977, 1978

Fellers, Walter E.
(Aircraft Division)
>NASA—Research and Technology Advisory Committee, Committee on Aerodynamics and Configurations, 1976, 1977

Gasich, Walko E.
(Sr. V.P. and Executive, Aircraft Group)
DoD—Joint Strategic Target Planning Staff, Scientific Advisory Group, 1976

Hicks, Donald A.
(Sr. V.P. for Marketing and Technology)
DoD—Defense Science Board, 1976, 1977, 1978.

III, Charles
(Page Communications)
DoD—Chief of Naval Operations, Command, Control and Communications Advisory Committee, 1976, 1977

Kresa, Kent
(V.P. and General Manager, Ventura Division) (see Personnel Transfers)
DoD—Chief of Naval Operations, Executive Panel Advisory Committee, 1976, 1977, 1978
DoD—Army Science Board, 1976, 1978

McLead, James
(Page Communications)
DoD—Chief of Naval Operations, Command, Control and Communications Advisory Committee, 1976, 1977

ENTERTAINMENT

Northrop made no general policy statement with regard to the Joint Committee on Defense Production with regard to entertainment, but did disclose some specific items.

Entertaining:
Some activities at Eastern Shore hunting lodge, North Carolina fishing trips and Augusta, GA house (see also Contracting History); no dollar data.

Hospitality Suites:
1973: 19, 1974: 26, 1975: 24
Including Navy League, Air Force Association, Association of the U.S. Army, American Defense Preparedness Association, National Security Industrial Association, Old Crows

Tickets:
  1973-75: 356 season tickets.
Meals:
  1973-75: $214,000
Disclosure:
  Good.

QUESTIONABLE PAYMENTS

Northrop's questionable payments abroad were revealed in the wake of investigations of illegal domestic campaign contributions.

The SEC and Northrop's outside auditors, Ernst and Ernst, questioned $30 m. in company sales commissions paid overseas between 1971 and 1973. Northrop board members Ballhaus, Barger, McDaniel, Millar and Wilson undertook a special investigation of these payments in 1975. Their special report, *Executive Committee's Report*, released in July 1975, reviewed 19 instances and found two items totalling $454,400, which it found questionable: a single payment ($4,400) to a tax assessor in Iran, and a large sum ($450,000) which it found had probably passed from sales agent Adnan Kashoggi to two Saudi generals. Northrop also announced a new, tougher policy on questionable payments stating: "Northrop does not authorize or condone unlawful payments to government officials whether made directly by corporate personnel or individually by third parties on Northrop's behalf, with or without the knowledge or acquiescence of company officials."

In February 1976, however, Northrop revealed another $861,000 in "improper payments," involving activity of Northrop's Page-Europa subsidiary in Greece, Italy, Portugal, Somalia and Turkey (Company 8K, Feb. 1976). This figure grew on further company investigation to $1.016 m. by March 1977, plus an additional $383,103 in commissions and fee payments by other divisions "in circumstances that would now be contrary to Northrop's new policies and procedures," of which $215,000 "may have been paid to employees of foreign governments," (Company *8K*, April 1977). Northrop's total disclosure of questionable payments, eliminating duplicate reports, covers $1,853.5 m.

DISCLOSURE

Very Poor.

ROCKWELL INTERNATIONAL

BASIC CORPORATE AND CONTRACTING DATA

A. Corporate Data

Rockwell International
  Corporation
600 Grant Street
Pittsburgh, PA 15219

Fortune 500 (1979): 45
Fiscal Year: Oct. 1—Sept. 30

Chairman:
  Robert Anderson (1979 salary: $967,000)
President:
  Donald R. Beall (1979 salary: $568,000)
Auditor:
  Deloitte, Haskins and Sells
  Two Gateway Center
  Pittsburgh, PA

Outside Legal Counsel:
  Kirkpatrick, Lockhart, Johnson and Hutchinson
  Oliver Building
  Pittsburgh, PA
    Counsel, Thomas P. Johnson (see Board of Directors)

TABLE I
Corporate Data
($ in M.)

	1970	1971	1972	1973	1974	1975	1976	1977	1978	1979
Sales	$2,583.4	2,394.6	2,570.3	3,047.9	4,178.4	4,653.6	5,042.7	5,744.2	5,668.8	6,176.4
Net Income	$ 72.2	80.0	103.8	131.8	130.4	104.3	122.2	144.1	176.6	261.1
Dept. of Defense Contracts	$ 707.1	549.1	703.9	790.3	819.2	732.3	966.0	1,480.0	890.2	683.9
Rank	7	13	9	10	9	10	10	6	11	15
NASA Contracts	$ 531.0	172.5	175.1	317.7	486.5	681.6	906.3	1,011.4	890.3	1,071.8
Rank	1	2	3	1	1	1	1	1	1	1
DoD/NASA Contracts as % of Sales	48.0%	30.1	34.2	36.4	31.2	30.4	37.1	43.4	31.4	28.4
Government Sales	$1,343.0	1,149.0	1,157.0	1,219.0	1,504.0	1,768.0	1,967.0	2,527.0	1,927.0	2,224.0
Government Sales as % of Sales	52.0%	48.0	45.0	40.0	36.0	38.0	39.0	44.0	34.0	36.0
Foreign Military Sales Contracts	$ 17.6	6.7	19.5	10.7	17.1	50.2	56.2	13.6	19.9	9.0
Rank	9	14	11	21	21	18	16	NA	NA	NA
FMS Contracts as % of Sales	.7%	.3	.8	.4	.4	1.0	1.1	.2	.4	.1
Overseas and Export Sales	NA	NA	NA	$ 517.0	887.0	1,044.0	1,127.0	1,153.0	1,252.0	1,303.0
Overseas and Export Sales as % of Sales	—	—	—	17.0%	21.2	22.4	22.3	20.1	22.0	21.1
Employees	94,385	84,766	92,192	100,341	137,523	122,789	119,117	115,162	114,208	114,452

NOTE: In 1979 Rockwell adjusted 1970-79 sales figures to reflect the sale of Admiral business and the Industrial Components group. Only 1979 figures here reflect this change.

Reed, Smith, Shaw and McClay
Union Trust Bldg.
Pittsburgh, PA
> Counsel, William A. Siefert, Jr. (see Board of Directors)

Chadbourne, Parke, Whiteside and Wolff
30 Rockefeller Plaza
New York, NY

Banking:
Transfer Agents:
First National Bank of Boston
Mellon Bank, Pittsburgh
National Trust Co., Ltd., Toronto
First National Bank of Chicago
National Bank of Detroit
United California Bank
Royal Trust Co., Toronto

Bond Offerers:
Paine-Webber, Inc.
Lehman Brothers, Kuhn, Loeb
Smith, Barney, Harris, Upham & Co.
Merrill, Lynch, Pierce, Fenner & Smith

Lenders:
Security Pacific National Bank ($200 m. revolving credit line)
> (see Board of Directors: Frederick G. Larkin, Robert Anderson).

Other short-term lenders:
names undisclosed

Investment Bankers:
Lehman Brothers
Kuhn Loeb
Merrill Lynch White Weld

Trustee:
Employee Savings Plan (23.3% of outstanding common stock), United California Bank.

B. Principal Defense/Space Contracting Operations

1. Aerospace Operations
George W. Jeffs, President, North American Space Operations
Bastian Hello, President, North American Aircraft Group (Los Angeles, Columbus, Tulsa)

Los Angeles Division
El Segundo, CA
C.E. Blalock, V.P. and Gen. Mgr.

B-1—manned bomber testing program, U.S. Air Force
Advanced aircraft research, Department of Defense
Composites and metallic structures, U.S. Air Force

Space Division
Downey, CA
George Merrick, President
Space shuttle orbiter, NASA
Space shuttle systems integration, NASA
NAVSTAR satellite—global positioning system, U.S. Air Force
Surveillance satellites, U.S. Air Force
Satellite-borne sensor systems, U.S. Air Force

Rocketdyne Division
Canoga Park, CA
Norman Ryker, V.P. and Gen. Mgr.
Space shuttle main engine, NASA
Liquid propellant rocket engines, U.S. Air Force
High energy laser research, U.S. Air Force
Water jet propulsion—surface effects ship, U.S. Navy
MX—Fourth-Stage engine and propellant, U.S. Air Force

Columbus Division
Columbus, OH
J.P. Fasnes, V.P. and Gen. Mgr.
T-2—jet trainer aircraft, U.S. Navy
Advanced strategic air-launched missile research, U.S. Air Force
Hellfire—anti-tank missile, U.S. Army
Highly-maneuverable aircraft technology (HiMAT)—Remotely-piloted research aircraft, NASA and U.S. Air Force
XFV-12A—V/STOL prototype, U.S. Navy
OV-10—observation, counterinsurgency aircraft, U.S. Air Force

Tulsa Division
Tulsa, OK
William J. Cecka, Jr., V.P. and Gen. Mgr.
Work on F-15, B-1 and YC-14, U.S. Air Force
Boeing 747—commercial leading wing edges and fuselage components
Boeing 757—major fuselage sections
Payload bay doors—space shuttle, NASA
MX—Fourth Stage work, U.S. Air Force
Nose Cones—Tomahawk cruise missile, General Dynamics

2. **Electronics Operations**
   Donald J. Yockey, Corp. V.P. and President
   a. **Electronics Systems Group**

Autonetics Division
Anaheim, CA
Newport Beach, CA
  Minuteman—guidance and control, U.S. Air Force
  Airborne navigation systems, U.S. Department of Defense
  Microprocessors, filters and circuits, U.S. Department of Defense
  Ship navigation systems for Trident ballistic missile firing
    attack subs, U.S. Navy
  Command, control and communications systems,
    U.S. Navy
  MX—flight computer and guidance and control integration,
    U.S. Air Force
  UHF—terminals for U.S. Air Force Satellite communications systems

  b. Avionics and Missile Group
Collins Radio
Dallas, TX
Cedar Rapids, IA
Newport Beach, CA
Seal Beach, CA
  Numerous communications devices and radios, U.S. Navy and
    Air Force
  Satellite communications equipment, U.S. Air Force
  TACAN—navigation system, U.S. Air Force
  GBU-15 (Pavestrike)—cruciform wing guided bomb, U.S. Air Force
  Hellfire—anti-tank missile, U.S. Army
  Avionics equipment for F-15, U.S. Air Force
  NAVSTAR satellite—global positioning system, U.S. Air Force

Energy Systems Group
S.F. Iacobellis, President
C. James Meechan, V.P.
  Chemical processing waste management site support, Hanford
    Project, Hanford, WA, nuclear warheads, U.S. Department
    of Energy
  Components manufacturing for nuclear warheads, management,
    Rocky Flats, CO, U.S. Department of Energy

C. Contracting History

Rockwell International (so named since 1973) resulted from the 1967 merger between Rockwell Standard and North American Aviation. North American Aviation, long a prime defense contractor, needed to make a new start; its work on the B-70 bomber had been cancelled, one of its Apollo program space capsules had burned, killing three astronauts, and it had lost a fighter competition to McDonnell Douglas' F-15. Rockwell hoped to diversify from auto parts and axles and was seeking a defense market merger partner.

North American had a potentially major defense effort under way to acquire a contract for the next manned bomber, the B-1. As company chairman Willard Rockwell put it, "We knew that as a company we had just one more chance, the B-1" (*Fortune*, July 1970).

Rockwell was awarded the B-1 contract in 1970 but the program was the focus of growing controversy up to 1977. By 1971, cost estimates were rising rapidly from the original $29.2 m. per-plane estimate of 1969. The plane's weight was rising, the spacecraft type crew capsule was in doubt, avionics were proving more costly, range was down and the B-1 supersonic capability had been reduced (see G. Adams, *The B-1 Bomber*, CEP, 1976).

The Pentagon worked to save the program. In 1971, the R & D program was reduced from seven to three planes. In 1973, the Air Force appointed a new director of the B-1 Program Office, while GAO and Pentagon reviews showed continuing cost, management and performance problems (see the "Bisplinghoff Report," *Report of Ad Hoc Management Review Committee on the B-1 to the Air Force Secretary, Congressional Record*, 7 Feb. 1974, pp. S1487-1490). The Pentagon also began a classified Joint Strategic Bomber Survey to evaluate the need for the B-1 as part of the nation's strategic arsenal (see G. Adams, *The B-1 Bomber*).

Rockwell, meanwhile, undertook its own operation to support the B-1 in the face of growing opposition. In 1972, company personnel made significant contributions to the Nixon reelection campaign through the "Voices of Politics" program. Rockwell also created an internal political planning operation, "Operation Common Sense," a company committee which followed and planned Washington and grass-roots activities in support of the company's defense programs. "Operation Common Sense" tracked company subcontracts in the states and districts of key Congressional authorization and Appropriations Committee members, and planned local displays, talks and promotional activity for Rockwell programs.

The effort on behalf of the B-1 accelerated as the Air Force neared a production decision. CEP's analysis of data supplied by Rockwell to a House subcommittee reveals that Rockwell may have spent over $1.3 m. between 1975 and 1977 to finance grass-roots activity promoting the B-1. In addition, public hearings and documents from 1975 and 1976 indicate that Rockwell supplied entertainment in Eastern Shore facilities to over 90 Defense Department employees, placing "considerable emphasis upon entertaining military officers who were responsible for the procurement of aircraft and missiles within their services" (*The New York Times*, 18 March 1976; see also Joint Committee on Defense Production, *DoD—Industry Relations—Conflict of Interest and Standards of Conduct Hearings*, Feb. 2 and 3, 1976, pp. 24-55). Rockwell President Robert Anderson also invited Dr. Malcolm Currie, Director of Defense Research and Engineering, for a fishing weekend in the Bahamas in September 1975. Currie, who was centrally involved in Rockwell weapons decisions, including the B-1 and the Condor missile, was reprimanded for accepting this hospitality by Secretary of Defense Donald Rumsfeld in March 1976 though he was exonerated by Rumsfeld of any conflict of interest (*The New York Times*, 5 April 1976; 9 June 1976; see also, U.S. Congress, Joint Committee on Defense Production, Subcommittee on Investigations, *Conflict of Interest and the Condor Missile Program*, Report, together with Minority Views, Sept. 1976, pp. 108, 113-14, 121-22, A2-A4). Rockwell also hired a number of former Pentagon employees, some of whom played key B-1 roles: the chief of the Air Force B-1 Configuration Identification Division; the comptroller of the Los Angeles Office of the Air Force Contract Management Division; the director of Procurement Policy in the Office of the Air Force (CEP, *Military Maneuvers*, 1975). Rockwell also mustered economic arguments for the B-1, contracting with Chase Econometric Associates for econometric and input/output analysis of the program's impact, from which it prepared presentations for many members of Congress. The B-1 network was widespread with over 3,000 subcontractors, suppliers and vendors in 48 states. Rockwell's final appeal, in 1976, included employee and stockholder letters to Congress, advertising efforts, and expanded Washington lobbying activity to prevent passage of a Congressional amendment that would delay the B-1 production decision into 1977.

Despite Rockwell's effort, President Carter cancelled the B-1 production program in June 1977. Although this decision was a major setback for the anticipated future sales of Rockwell's aerospace operations, other efforts continued. It had been awarded NASA's space shuttle after spending three years and $40 m. preparing its bid. The Rocketdyne Division received a 1971 contract for the shuttle's main engine, and in 1972 the company was awarded the major contract to manufacture five orbiters—the main air frame of the shuttle itself.

The shuttle, too, had been a focus of "Operation Common Sense" and Rockwell lobbying. It had encountered cost and scheduling problems, leading to a cost increase of $965 m. after inflation (*Aerospace Daily*, 11 Feb. 1980, p. 217), a delay of nearly two years, and Air Force concern about maintaining its own schedule of surveillance satellite launches. Performance problems have been encountered with heat resistant tiles on the orbiter and in tests of Rocketdyne's main engine.

In 1974 Rockwell received a major DoD contract for satellites for the NAVSTAR Global Positioning System, a key part of the defense communications network. In 1976 the company won a large Army contract for the Hellfire missile, a battlefield weapon to be used with the Advanced Attack Helicopter. In 1971 the company bought control of Collins Radio and subsequently incorporated Collins into its defense business. Collins has proven to be a major contributor to company profits with a wide variety of military communications and electronics contracts. Rockwell also continues to manufacture and sell the OV-10 counter-insurgency plane, most recently to Morocco.

Rockwell's recent successes are with the MX missile and aircraft programs. As the largest single corporate beneficiary of MX contract work in fiscal year 1980, it will develop the MX missile's engine, Fourth Stage and guidance systems. Should the MX enter production, the company's defense business would benefit substantially. In addition, Rockwell continues to test the four B-1 prototypes and is actively marketing the design for future Air Force use as a bomber and/or cruise missile carrier. Discussions about producing a new manned bomber became more active in 1980 and a development decision is due in 1981. The company also has ongoing work in forward-swept wing aircraft for the Air Force, V/STOL aircraft for the Navy, and laser weaponry.

D. U.S. Government-Owned, Company-Operated Plants

Total company floor space: 50,100,000 sq. ft.
Leased from U.S. Government: 6,488,035 sq. ft. (13%)
Total Lease Cost: $217,000 (partial disclosure)

Location: Naval Weapons Industrial Reserve Plant 303
Columbus, OH
3,359,349 sq. ft.
Use: Aircraft (T-2, OV-10, XFV-12A, B-1, space shuttle), Missiles (HOBO, Hellfire, Minuteman, MX engineering)
Cost: Not disclosed

Location: Air Force Plant 3
Tulsa, OK
(with McDonnell Douglas)
2,352,951 sq. ft.
Use: Aircraft Components (F-15 Aft Section), Modification and Overhaul of F-4
Cost: $217,000

Location: Air Force Plant 42 (Site 1)
East Palmdale, CA
111,360 sq. ft.
Use: Spacecraft, space shuttle
Cost: Not disclosed

Location: Air Force Plant 42 (Sites 1 and 3)
Palmdale, CA
664,375 sq. ft.
Use: B-1
Cost: Not disclosed

TABLE II
Research and Development
($ in M.)

	1970	1971	1972	1973	1974	1975	1976	1977	1978	1979
I. U.S. Government Contracts										
DoD	$139.9	180.9	397.6	405.4	421.1	431.9	606.1	513.6	473.3	328.1
NASA	$531.0	172.5	175.1	317.7	486.5	631.6	906.3	1,011.4	890.3	1,071.8
Total	$670.9	353.4	572.7	723.1	907.6	1,063.5	1,512.4	1,525.0	1,363.6	1,399.9
II. Company-sponsored R&D	NA	NA	NA	$ 40.8	60.0	77.8	86.3	97.0	124.4	152.6
III. IR&D	NA	NA	NA	$ 23.0	20.7	22.4	26.0	32.2	30.0	NA

I. From DoD yearly pubication "500 Contractors Receiving the Largest Dollar Volume of Military Prime Contract Awards for RDT&E" and NASA Annual Procurement Reports.

II. "Company-initiated research and development" (10K, 1979)

III. Company-sponsored R&D costs charged to DoD, as disclosed by DoD.

RESEARCH AND DEVELOPMENT

Major Defense/Space R&D Projects

Space shuttle—orbiter, main engine and system integration, NASA
Military satellites, U.S. Air Force
MX—Fourth Stage engine, propellant, flight computer, guidance and control, U.S. Air Force
High Energy lasers, U.S. Air Force
HiMAT—remotely piloted research aircraft, U.S. Air Force, NASA
B-1—testing program, U.S. Air Force
XFV-12A—V/STOL prototype, U.S. Navy
Composites and metal structures, U.S. Air Force
GBU-15 (Pavestrike)—cruciform wing guided bomb, U.S. Air Force
Communications systems, U.S. Navy, U.S. Air Force, U.S. Army
Electronic defense systems, DoD

BOARD OF DIRECTORS

Robert Anderson (1968)
Chairman and Chief Executive Officer, Rockwell International
Past Corporate Employment:
Chrysler Corp. (1946-68); Rockwell (1968-present) (President, Chief Executive Officer-1974).
Corporate Directorships:
Security Pacific Corp.(see Basic Data: Banking); Ducommun, Inc. ($328,000); Celanese Corp. ($1,278.000).
Key Association Memberships:
Aerospace Industries Association.
Shares owned:
82,088

Donald R. Beall (1978)
President and Chief Operating Officer, Rockwell International
Past Corporate Employment:
Philco Ford Corp. (1961-68); Collins Radio Group (Rockwell subsidiary) President (1974-76).
Key Association Memberships:
Air Force Communications and Electronics Association; Electronic Industries Association.
Shares owned:
26,111

Robert De Palma (1979)
V.P. Finance and Chief Financial Officer, Rockwell International

Past Corporate Employment:
Director, Wheeling-Pittsburgh Steel Corp. (no date); Davison Sand & Gravel Company (no date); Rockwell International (1970-present).
Corporate Directorships:
European-American Bancorp.
Shares owned:
6,119

Robin Chandler Duke (1977)
Chairman, Draper World Population Fund, International Family Planning
Corporate Directorships:
East River Savings Bank.
Shares owned:
315

Fred L. Hartley (1966)
Chairman and President, Union Oil Co. of California
Past Corporate Employment:
Union Oil Co. of California (1939-present).
Corporate Directorships:
Union Bancorp, Inc.
Key Association Memberships:
Committee on Economic Development.
Shares owned:
140

Thomas Phillips Johnson (1943)
Partner, Kirkpatrick, Lockhart, Johnson and Hutchison (attorneys)
Past Corporate Employment:
Associate, Reed, Smith, Shaw and McClay (1937-42); partner, Kirkpatrick, Lockhart, Johnson and Hutchison (1943-present).
Corporate Directorships:
AVM Corp.; Trion, Inc. ($323,000); T.W. Phillips Gas & Oil Co.; Cyclops Corp. ($350,000); Blair Strip Steel Co.; Seneca Bank and Trust Co.
Shares owned:
95,247

George F. Karch (1966)
Chairman, Cleveland Trust Co. (retired 1973)
Past Corporate Employment:
Cleveland Trust Co. (1926-73) (Chairman of the Board-1966).
Corporate Directorships:
Brush-Wellman ($960,000); Medusa Corp.; Oglebay-Norton Co.; RPM, Inc. ($33,000); Standard Brands ($6,864,000).
Shares owned:
100

Frederick G. Larkin, Jr. (1969)
Chairman of the Executive Committee, Security Pacific National Bank
Past Corporate Employment:
Security Pacific National Bank (1936-present).
Corporate Directorships:
Carnation Co. ($12,591,000); Getty Oil Co.; Southern California Edison Co. ($7,762,000); Western American Bank, Ltd. Europe.
Shares owned:
100

William H. Muchnic (1956)
President, Valley Co., Inc. (investments)
Past Corporate Employment:
Locomotive Finished Material Co. (Rockwell subsidiary) (1948-67); Valley Co., Inc. (1967-present).
Corporate Directorships:
Rice-Hall Association (investment counselors).
Shares owned:
205,108

Henry T. Mudd (1961)
Chairman of the Board and Chief Executive Officer, Cyprus Mines Corp.
Past Corporate Employment:
Cyprus Mines Corp. (1946-present).
Corporate Directorships:
United California Bank; Western Bancorp; Southern Pacific Co.; Envirodyne, Inc. ($334,000).
Shares owned:
280

Bruce M. Rockwell (1969)
V.P., First of Michigan Corp. (investment banking)
Past Corporate Employment:
First of Michigan Corp. (1961-present).
Shares owned:
42,537

S. Kent Rockwell (1978)
President, Utility Products Group, Rockwell International
Past Corporate Employment:
President, Milrock, Inc. (1969); Chairman and President, Keystone Aircraft Sales (1975); Rockwell International (1976-present).
Shares owned:
829,849

W.F. Rockwell, Jr. (1942)
Chairman of the Executive Committee, Rockwell International (retired 1979).
Past Corporate Employment:
President, Rockwell Manufacturing Co. (1947); Chief Executive Officer, Rockwell International (1970-74).
Corporate Directorships:
El Paso Co.; Mellon Bank N.A./Mellon National Corp.; Allegheny-Ludlum Industries ($154,000); Lone Star Industries, Inc. ($54,000); Cross & Trecker Corp. ($3,746,000).
Key Association Memberships:
Business Council; Business Roundtable.
Shares owned:
1,035,639

William Roesch (1980)
President and Chief Executive Officer, United States Steel Corp.
Past Corporate Employment:
Jones & Laughlin Steel Corp. (to 1974); Director and Chief Executive Officer, Kaiser Industries (1974-78); Executive V.P., U.S. Steel Corp. (1978-79), President and Chief Executive Officer (1979-present).
Corporate Directorships:
Hilton Hotels
Shares owned:
400

William A. Siefert, Jr. (1952)
Partner, Reed, Smith, Shaw & McClay (attorneys)
Corporate Directorships:
Old Republic International Corp./Old Republic Insurance Co./Old Republic Life Insurance Co. of Illinois and N.Y.
Shares owned:
22,844

Robert E. Seymour (1972)
Chairman of the Board, Consolidated Natural Gas Co.
Past Corporate Employment:
President, People's Natural Gas Co., Pittsburgh (1963-68); Consolidated Natural Gas Co. (1968-present).
Corporate Directorships:
Pittsburgh National Bank/Pittsburgh National Corp., Wheeling-Pittsburgh Steel Corp. ($30,000); Pittsburgh Brewing Co.
Shares owned:
899

Ross Siragusa, Jr. (1964)
President, Game Time, Inc. (park and playground equipment)
Past Corporate Employment:
Admiral Corp. (1953-75); Vice President, Rockwell International and President, Admiral Group (1969-75).
Shares owned:
163,304

William Sneath (1979)
Chairman of the Board and Chief Executive Officer, Union Carbide Corp.
Past Corporate Employment:
Union Carbide (1950-present).
Corporate Directorships:
Metropolitan Life Insurance Co.
Key Association Memberships:
Business Council; Business Roundtable.
Shares owned:
200

Joseph F. Toot, Jr. (1977)
Executive V.P., Timken Co. (bearings and specialty steel)
Past Corporate Employment:
Timken Co. (1962-present).
Corporate Directorships:
Clevetrust.
Shares owned:
176,000

Martin Walker (1979)
Senior V.P., President of Automotive Operations, Rockwell International
Past Corporate Employment:
General Motors Corp. (1954-70); Rockwell International (1972-present).
Shares owned:
8,751

PERSONNEL TRANSFERS

Table III
(DoD   1970-79)
(NASA 1974-79)

	Total	Air Force	Army	Navy	Office of Secretary of Defense	Other
DoD Military to Rockwell	150	103	11	26	5	5
DoD Civilian to Rockwell	26	8	0	10	5	3
NASA to Rockwell	6					
Rockwell to DoD	47	6	8	23	6	6
Rockwell to NASA	5					
Total	234	117	19	59	15	13

Appearances of Potential Conflict of Interest (see Chapter 6): 18

1. DoD to Rockwell

Branigan, John E.
DoD:
>Engineer, rocket propulsion, propellant development, Air Force Systems Command.

Rockwell:
>September 1978, Technical Director for development of positive expulsion propellant storage assemblies.

Donohue, John T.
DoD:
>Systems engineering for NIMITZ carriers, Naval Sea Systems Command.

Rockwell:
>August 1979, Naval systems engineering.

Fulfrost, Jack
DoD:
>Superintendent, Advanced Navigation Projects Division, Navigation Lab, Naval Air Development Center.

Rockwell:
>October 1976, Member, technical staff, studies for naval applications, Autonetics.

Hadley, Steven G.
DoD:
>Research chemist and supervisory physical scientist for high

energy lasers, Weapons Lab, Kirtland Air Force Base, NM, Air Force.
Rockwell:
August 1977, Manager, Advanced Laser Concepts (DoD and DoE applications), Rocketdyne Division.

Laidlaw, William
DoD:
Special Assistant to Director of Defense Research and Engineering.
Rockwell:
November 1967, V.P., Research and Engineering.

Larson, Harold V.
DoD:
Deputy Director, Administration of Security Assistance Program, Defense Security Assistance Agency.
Rockwell:
August 1973, Manager, International Marketing, Collins Radio.

Simon, Allan D.
DoD:
Asst. Director for Air Warfare, Directorate of Defense Research and Engineering.
Rockwell:
March 1973, Consultant, technical and planning matters.

Yarymovych, Michael I.
DoD:
Chief Scientist and Director NATO, Advisory Group for Aerospace R & D, Air Force.
Rockwell:
May 1977, V.P., Engineering, North American Aerospace Operations.

2. NASA to Rockwell

Myers, Dale D.
NASA:
Associate Administrator for Manned Space Flight.
Rockwell:
April 1974, President, North American Aircraft Operations (1977: Under Secretary, Department of Energy).

3. Rockwell to DoD

Brinkman, John
Rockwell:
Director, R & D, Autonetics Div.; Director, Science Center.
DoD:
March 1971, Army Weapons Command, and Deputy Director, Directorate of Defense Research and Engineering.

Clapp, Spencer D.
  Rockwell:
    Manager, Navy/Air Force Laser Program.
  DoD:
    August 1976, General Engineer associated with high energy laser project office, Army Missile Command.

Cruden, Joseph C.
  Rockwell:
    Planning Director.
  DoD:
    February 1971, Deputy Director, Naval Material Command.

Erers, William H.
  Rockwell:
    Project Manager, chemical and transfer laser programs.
  DoD:
    May 1975, Chief, Applied Technology Division, High Energy Laser Systems Project Office, Army.

Parker, Robert
  Rockwell:
    Engineer.
  DoD:
    August 1973, Principal Deputy Director, Directorate of Defense Research and Engineering.

Staney, William
  Rockwell:
    Research Engineer, R & D on electronic equipment.
  DoD:
    October 1975, Deputy Director for Tactical Warfare Program, Directorate of Defense Research and Engineering.

Walsh, Thomas
  Rockwell:
    Manager, Device Development and Applications, Collins.
  DoD:
    February 1976, staff specialist for electronic R & D efforts, Directorate of Defense Research and Engineering.

4. "Revolving Door"

Anderson, David
  DoD:
    Operations Research Analyst, Air Force
  Rockwell:
    August 1970, Executive Advisor, B-1 Division.
  DoD:
    January 1972, Staff Specialist, Directorate of Defense Research and Engineering.

Braunstein, David
   DoD:
      Training advisor, Air Force Security Service.
   Rockwell:
      August 1974, Associate Program Manager, Marine Systems Div.
   DoD:
      August 1975, Naval National Command, program administration for materials technology; Program Manager, Defense Advanced Research Projects Agency.

Comments

1. There were substantial transfers with the Defense Communications Agency; 5 people. To DoD: 1969—Jerry Lebo; 1970—Robert Choisser, Thomas Austin; 1971—Ronald Mitchell; 1974—Kenneth Nichols. To Rockwell: 1978—James Aldrich. Rockwell's Collins Radio Division is a major DoD communications contractor.
2. Policy Statement—"There are, of course, statutory provisions relating to the hiring of former Government officials and our personnel people are mindful of them in implementing our employment policy." Source: Anderson's testimony to U.S. Congress Joint Committee on Defense Production (94th Congress, 2nd Session) (*DoD Industry Relations: Conflict of Interest and Standards of Conduct,* Feb. 2 and 3, 1978, p. 27).

POLITICAL ACTION COMMITTEES

Name: Rockwell International Corp.
              Good Government Committee
Total Expenditures (5/76-5/80): $162,805
Total Contributions to Federal Campaigns (5/76-5/80): $104,270

   Key
   (D) = Democrat
   (R) = Republican
   (C) = Recipient was a candidate and not elected to that office.
    + = Candidate is also a member of a key Congressional committee.
    * = Candidate is a member of two committees, but contribution s/he received is only listed once to avoid being double-counted in the total for this section.

A. Contributions to Federal Candidates in States with Rockwell Production Facilities (Key Geographic Locations).

CALIFORNIA

Rockwell plants located in Anaheim (dist. 38, 39), Canoga Park (dist. 20), Downey (dist. 30, 33), El Segundo (dist. 27) and Newport Beach (dist. 40).

Senate

Sen. Alan Cranston (D)	$1,100
Sen. S.I. Hayakawa (R)	$1,000
Sen. John V. Tunney (D)	$ 600

House

+Rep. Glenn Anderson (D-32)	$ 500
+Rep. Robert Badham (R-40)	$ 200
Rep. Yvonne Burke (D-28)	$ 200
Rep. George Danielson (D-30)	$ 100
Rep. William Dannemeyer (R-39)	$ 425
+Rep. Robert Dornan (R-27)	$ 900
+Rep. Vic Fazio (D-4)	$ 200
Rep. Wayne Grisham (R-33)	$ 770
+Rep. Barry Goldwater Jr. (R-20)	$1,200
Rep. Mark Hannaford (D-34)	$ 400
Rep. Robert Leggett (D-4)	$ 100
Rep. Daniel Lungren (R-34)	$ 100
+Rep. James Lloyd (D-35)	$1,200
+Rep. John McFall (D-14)	$ 800
+Rep. Norman Mineta (D-13)	$ 300
Rep. Jerry Patterson (D-38)	$ 600
Rep. Shirley Pettis (R-37)	$ 200
Rep. John Rousselot (D-26)	$ 250
+Rep. Bob Wilson (R-41)	$ 500

Total California: $11,645
%Total Federal Contributions: 11.2%

IOWA

Rockwell plant located in Cedar Rapids (dist. 2)

Senate

+Sen. Roger Jepsen (R)	$ 900

House

+Rep. Thomas Harkin (D-5)	$ 100
Rep. Thomas Tauke (R-2)	$ 600

Total Iowa: $1,600
%Total Federal Contributions: 1.5%

OHIO
Rockwell plant located in Columbus (dist. 10, 12, 15)
Senate
    Sen. John Glenn (D) $ 500
    + Sen. Robert Taft, Jr. (R) $1,000
House
    Rep. John Ashbrook (R-17) $ 500
    Rep. Samuel L. Devine (R-12) $ 500
    Rep. Tennyson Guyer (R-4) $ 500
    Dudley Kirscher (D-3) (C) $ 200

Total Ohio: $3,200
% Total Federal Contributions: 3.1%

OKLAHOMA
Rockwell plant located in Tulsa (dist. 1, 2)
Senate
    No contributions $ 0
House
    Rep. Mickey Edwards (R-5) $ 200
    Rep. Glenn L. English (D-6) $ 200
    Rep. James Jones (D-1) $ 300
    Rep. Ted Risenhoover (D-2) $ 100

Total Oklahoma: $800
% Total Federal Contributions: 0.8%

PENNSYLVANIA
Rockwell plant located in Pittsburgh (dist. 14, 18, 20)
Senate
    Sen. H. John Heinz III (R) $ 750
House
    + Rep. Donald Bailey (D-21) $ 500
    Robert Casey (R-18) (C) $ 200
    Rep. Lawrence Coughlin (R-13) $ 700
    + Rep. Charles Dougherty $ 250
    H. Joseph Hepford (R-17) (C) $ 100
    Ted Humes (R-12) (C) $ 200
    Rep. Joseph McDade (R-10) $ 200
    + Rep. Bud Shuster (R-9) $ 400
    Stan Thomas (R-14) (C) $ 500

Total Pennsylvania: $3,800
% Total Federal Contributions: 3.6%

TEXAS
Rockwell plant located in Dallas (dist. 3, 4, 5, 6, 24)

Senate
+Sen. John Tower (R)	$1,000

House
Leo Berman (R-24) (C)	$ 250
Rep. James Collins (R-3)	$2,500
Rep. Marvin Leath (D-11)	$ 250
Rep. Jim Mattox (D-5)	$ 250
+Rep. Dale Milford (D-24)	$ 500
Thomas W. Pauken (R-5) (C)	$ 500
+Rep. Olin Teague (D-6)	$ 600
+Rep. Richard C. White (D-16)	$ 200
Rep. James Wright (D-12)	$ 200
+Rep. Charles Wilson (D-2)	$1,100

Total Texas: $7,350
% Total Federal Contributions: 7.0%

Total to Key Geographic Locations: $28,395
% Total Federal Contributions: 27.2%

B. Contributions to Members of Key Congressional Committees

Senate Armed Services Committee
Cannon	$ 300	Taft	$1,000
Helms	$3,200	Thurmond	$ 500
Jepsen	$ 900	Tower	$1,000
Morgan	$ 250	Warner	$ 100
Nunn	$ 500		

House Armed Services Committee
Badham	$ 200	Holt	$ 300
Bailey	$ 500	Ichord	$ 800
Brinkley	$ 200	Lloyd, James	$1,200
Davis, Mendel	$ 500	Mavroules	$ 100
Dickinson	$ 400	McDonald	$ 200
Dougherty	$ 250	Mitchell, Donald	$ 300
Fazio	$ 200	White	$ 200
Hillis	$ 300	Wilson, Bob	$ 500

Senate Defense Appropriations Subcommittee
Hollings	$ 500	Montoya	$ 300
Magnuson	$2,500	Weicker	$ 200

Rockwell International

House Defense Appropriations Subcommittee

Cederberg	$ 200	Flynt	$ 200
Chappell	$ 500	Giaimo	$ 200
Conte	$ 300	McFall	$ 800
Dicks	$ 250	Whitten	$ 800
Edwards, Jack	$ 450	Wilson, Charles N.	$1,100

Senate Committee on Commerce, Science and Transportation
Subcommittee on Aviation

Cannon	*	Pressler	$ 250

Subcommittee on Science, Technology and Space

Ford	$ 500	Schmitt	$ 500
Griffin	$1,000		

House Committee on Science and Technology

Blanchard	$ 550	Lujan	$ 300
Dornan	$ 900	McCormack	$1,100
Flippo	$ 600	Milford	$ 500
Flowers	$3,000	Nelson	$ 525
Fuqua	$1,300	Ottinger	$ 300
Goldwater, Jr.	$1,200	Rudd	$ 300
Harkin	$ 100	Teague	$ 600
Harsha	$ 200	Winn	$ 500
Lloyd, James	*	White	
Lloyd, Marilyn	$ 100	Wydler	$ 100

Senate Committee on Environment and Public Works
Subcommittee on Transportation

Buckley	$ 500	Pressler	*
Montoya	*	Randolph	$ 500

House Committee on Public Works and Transportation
Subcommittee on Aviation

Abdnor	$ 100	Milford	*
Anderson, Glenn	$ 500	Mineta	$ 300
Flippo	*	Shuster	$ 300
Goldwater, Jr.	*	Snyder	$ 300
Harsha	*	Taylor	$ 200
McCormack	*		

Total to Key Committees: $39,025
% Total Federal Contributions: 37.4%

C. Contributions to Other Influential Members of Congress

Rep. Robert Michel (R-IL), Minority Whip $ 200

% Total Federal Contributions: 0.2%

Rockwell International

D. Contributions to Other Federal Candidates

Senate

Allen (D-AL)	$ 200	McCollister (R-NE) (C)	$ 300
Beall (R-MD)	$ 400	Moss (D-UT)	$1,000
Boschwitz (IR-MN)	$1,000	Roth (R-DE)	$ 300
Durenberger (R-MN)	$1,000	Swigert (R-CO)	$ 500
Esch (R-MI) (C)	$ 500	Talmadge (D-GA)	$ 150
Lugar (R-IN)	$ 500		

House

Alexander, Bill (D-AR)	$ 500	Hubbard (D-KY)	$ 100
Annunzio (D-IL)	$ 200	Jeffries (R-KS)	$ 750
Balletta (R-NY)	$ 100	Jenrette (D-SC)	$ 600
Broomfield (R-MI)	$1,000	Johnson (R-PA)	$ 100
Brown (R-MI)	$ 500	Maxfield (D-MO)	$ 100
Cohalon (RC-NY)	$ 200	Quillen (R-TN)	$ 200
Coleman (R-MO)	$ 100	Riley (R-IA)	$ 100
Corcoran, Brian (R-WA)	$ 300	Russell (NA) (C)	$ 200
Corcoran, Thomas (R-IL)	$ 200	Scott (R-CO) (C)	$ 100
Duncan (R-TN)	$ 100	Steers (R-MD	$ 300
Fithian (D-IN)	$ 200	Steiger (D-WI)	$ 500
Freeman (R-KS)	$ 200	Traxler (D-MI)	$1,150
Friedman (R-CO)	$ 200	Vander Jagt (R-MI)	$ 500
Gephardt (D-MO)	$ 100	Young (R-IL)	$ 200
Holland (D-SC)	$ 400		

Total to Party Federal Candidates: $15,050
% Total Federal Contributions: 14.4%

E. Contributions to Other Candidates

Republican federal-level committees: $24,700
Democratic federal-level committees: $ 100

Total to Party Committees: $24,800
% Total Federal Contributions: 23.8%

F. Contributions to Presidential Campaign Committees

George Bush (R)	$ 675
John Connally (R)	$3,875
Gerald Ford (R)	$1,000
Ronald Reagan (R)	$3,600

Total to Presidential Candidates: $9,150
% Total Federal Contributions: 8.8%

WASHINGTON OPERATIONS

Washington Office:
1745 Jefferson Davis Highway, Arlington, VA 22202

Director:
William L. Clark, Staff V.P., Washington Office

Staff:
Jerome M. Syverson, Director of Public Relations
Susan J. Clark, Legislative Liaison Representative
Ralph J. Watson, Sr., Legislative Liaison Representative

Activities:

1. International: Liaison with foreign customers.
2. National Affairs and Strategic Planning: Gathering intelligence on future long-range plans, government operations, customer requirements; gathering and analyzing budgetary data. Public relations—participating in trade, industry and military associations; preparing and presenting displays, handouts, brochures and films on Rockwell programs.
3. Congressional Relations: Lobbying activity—monitoring Congressional activity related to Rockwell programs; supporting efforts of Mr. Watson, registered lobbyist; drafting legislation for discussion and review with government personnel.
4. Marketing liaison with military and executive departments and commercial customers.

Registered Lobbyists

	Receipts	Expenditures	Years
Anne Genevieve Allen Rockwell International 2230 E. Imperial Highway El Segundo, CA (formerly with B-1 Division)	$ 4,538.16	$ 9,454.73	76-79
Theodore M. Letterman 2600 Chinook Dr. Placentia, CA	*	*	79

416   Rockwell International

Potter International 　1140 Connecticut Ave. NW 　Washington, DC	$65,750.00	*	77-79
John M. Torbet 　3117 14th St. 　South Arlington, VA	$ 450.83	$ 2,155.74	76-79
Ralph J. Watson* 　1745 Jefferson Davis Hwy. 　Arlington, VA	$ 7,161.20	$ 1,778.92	76-79
Winner/Wagner Assoc., Inc. 　6535 Wilshire Blvd. 　Los Angeles, CA	$ 2,500.00	$ 165.72	79
TOTAL	**$80,400.19**	**$13,555.11**	

*No figures reported; quarterly reports were filed.

DEFENSE-RELATED TRADE ASSOCIATION MEMBERSHIPS

Aerospace Industries Association
Air Force Association
American Defense Preparedness Association
American Institute of Aeronautics and Astronautics
American League for Exports and Security Assistance
Armed Forces Communication and Electronics Association
National Association for Remotely-Piloted Vehicles
National Security Industrial Association

ADVISORY COMMITTEE MEMBERSHIPS

1976-78: 7

Bell, Jack
　DoD—Defense Science Board, 1976

Feltz, Charles H.
  NASA—Research and Technology Advisory Council, Panel on Space Vehicles, 1976, 1977

Fosness, John P.
  (V.P., General Manager, Columbus Division)
  DoD—Defense Science Board, 1976

Hicks, Herman
  DoD—Defense Science Board, 1976, 1977

Holladay, William L.
  NASA—Research and Technology Advisory Council, Committee on Guidance Control and Information Systems, 1976, 1977

Langley, Charles
  DoD—Army Ad Hoc Tank Production Facility Advisory Group, 1976

Olcott, John W.
  NASA—Research and Technology Advisory Council, Panel on General Aviation Technology, 1976

Comment:
Rockwell International also had members on an advisory board to the Department of Commerce concerned with multilateral trade negotiations, to the FCC concerned with aeronautic communications and to the Executive Office of the President concerned with Maritime Satellites.

ENTERTAINMENT

Rockwell President Robert Anderson stated: "Our company, like every company that I have ever heard of, engages to some extent in activities that may be regarded as falling in this category (entertainment and gratuities), but is has been the company's longstanding policy that such activities will be kept to a minimum and within the bounds of common courtesies consistent with ethical business conduct and with applicable laws and regulations, including DoD and NASA regulations."

"I think that some entertainment is a normal and usual concomitant of commercial business practices and that it serves useful purposes." (Source: Anderson's testimony before U.S. Congress, Joint Committee on Defense Production in *DoD Industry Relations: Conflict of Interest and Standards of Conduct*, Feb. 2 and 3, 1978, p. 25.)

Entertaining:
Facilities maintained in Wye Island, MD. (1968-75); Nemacolin Inn, Farmington, PA (no date); Pinebloom Lodge, Albany, GA (1971-74); Bimini (sold in 1975).

Hospitality Suites:
1973: 43, 1974: 44, 1975: 34.
Including Air Force Association, Association of the U.S. Army, Navy League, National Security Industrial Association, American Defense Preparedness Association, Old Crows.

Tickets:
Average of 190 season tickets per year, including use by "agency personnel."

Air Travel:
Limited air travel provided to agency personnel.

Disclosure:
Good

QUESTIONABLE PAYMENTS

Rockwell conducted an investigation of its overseas sales practices in 1975, covering the years 1971 to 1975, and followed up with a 1976 disclosure as well. These reviews disclosed possible "improper conduct" involving total payments of $666,000 in five countries, none of which was named. These payments "were or may have been made to foreign governmental officials or employees" (Company S7, 1976). Rockwell also cooperated with a Federal Trade Commission investigation in 1976 on the restraint of trade implications of its payments. The company settled a stockholder derivative suit on the issue in 1977 by agreeing to work to prevent any illegal or improper disbursements (Company *10K*, 1977). As of December, 1980, an investigation of Rockwell continued in the Justice Department (phone interview with company, Dec. 1980).

Corporate policy states that "illegal or otherwise improper payments are not to be made directly or indirectly to officials or employees of foreign governments or agencies thereof" (Company *8K* Amendment 1, 22 Dec. 1975).

DISCLOSURE

Very poor.

UNITED TECHNOLOGIES

BASIC CORPORATE AND CONTRACTING DATA

A. Corporate Data

United Technologies Corporation
United Technologies Building
Hartford, CT 06101

Fortune 500 (1979): 26
Fiscal Year: Jan. 1—Dec. 31

President and Chairman:
Harry J. Gray (1979 salary: $804,000)

Auditor:
Price, Waterhouse & Co.
One Financial Plaza
Hartford, CT

Outside Legal Counsel:
Day, Berry & Howard
1 Constitution Plaza
Hartford, CT

Wachtel, Lipton Rosen & Katz
299 Park Avenue
New York, N.Y.

TABLE I
Corporate Data
($ in M.)

	1970	1971	1972	1973	1974	1975	1976	1977	1978	1979
Sales	$2,426.7	2,028.7	2,023.7	2,288.9	3,321.1	3,877.7	5,166.2	5,550.6	6,265.3	9,053.3
Net Income	$ 45.5	(43.9)	50.6	58.1	104.7	117.5	157.4	196.0	234.1	325.6
Dept. of Defense Contracts	$ 873.8	732.9	995.6	741.3	1,212.0	1,407.4	1,233.1	1,584.7	2,399.8	2,553.6
Rank	6	8	8	8	4	3	5	3	3	3
NASA Contracts	$ 27.0	28.4	15.9	25.0	39.7	36.2	17.5	33.8	50.8	73.3
Rank	17	16	23	19	10	11	21	14	15	11
DoD/NASA Contracts as % of Sales	37.1%	37.5	50.0	33.5	37.7	37.2	24.2	29.1	39.1	29.0
Government Sales	$1,286.1	977.8	1,038.1	1,062.5	1,084.9	1,285.1	1,522.7	1,645.5	1,712.6	2,075.4
Government Sales as % of Sales	53.0%	48.2	51.3	46.4	32.7	33.1	29.5	29.6	27.3	23.0
Foreign Military Sales Contracts	$ 2.7	13.4	27.9	68.3	126.0	192.0	104.2	87.1	115.3	249.1
Rank	NA	8	8	7	6	6	11	12	11	5
FMS Contracts as % of Sales	0.1%	0.7	1.4	3.0	3.8	5.0	2.0	1.6	1.8	2.8
Overseas and Export Sales	$ 381.0	519.0	471.0	497.0	743.0	1,408.0	2,105.7	2,042.9	2,306.3	3,509.4
Overseas and Export Sales as % of Sales	15.7%	25.6	23.3	21.7	22.4	36.3	40.8	36.8	36.8	32.6
Employees	73,274	62,046	63,849	64,942	95,031	138,072	133,383	138,587	152,213	197,700

Covington & Burling
888 16th Street, NW
Washington, DC

Advertising/Public Relations Agency:
Marsteller, Inc.
866 Third Ave.
New York, NY

Banking:

Transfer Agents and Registrars:
Citibank (see Board of Directors: Harry J. Gray, William E. Simon, Darwin Smith and William Spencer)
Chase Manhattan Bank
(see Board of Directors: Alexander Haig)
Irving Trust Co.
Chemical Bank

Lenders:
Citibank (credit line up to $115 m.) (see Board of Directors: William Spencer, Harry J. Gray, William E. Simon and Darwin Smith)
Chase Manhattan (credit line up to $85 m.) (see Board of Directors: Alexander M. Haig, Jr.)
Morgan Guaranty Trust (credit line up to $46.5 m.)
Hartford National Bank (credit line up to $10 m.)
(see Board of Directors: T. Mitchell Ford)

Investment Bankers:
Goldman Sachs
Lazard Freres
Merrill Lynch White Weld

Trustee:
Pension Fund, Citibank

B. Principal Defense/Space Contracting Operations

1. Power Group
Robert J. Carlson, Executive V.P.

Pratt & Whitney Aircraft Group
East Hartford, CT
Frank McAbee, Executive V.P.

TF-33—engine for E-3A, U.S. Air Force
J 52—engine for A-6, A-4,EA-6B, U.S. Navy
F-100—engine for F-15, F-16, U.S. Air Force
TF-30—engine for F-111, F-14, U.S. Air Force and Navy
T74—engine for U-21A, U.S. Army

Power Systems Division
Farmington, CT
Rolf D. Bibow, V.P.

Fuel cell power plant—space shuttle, NASA

Chemical Systems Division
Sunnyvale, CA
Barnet R. Adelman, President

Propulsion and control equipment—inertial upper stage, space shuttle launch vehicle, U.S. Air Force
Booster Rockets—Titan III, U.S. Air Force
Ram-jet propulsion engine research—for advanced strategic air launched missile, U.S. Army, Navy and Air Force

Sikorsky Aircraft Division
Stratford, CT
Robert F. Daniell, President

UH-60A Black Hawk—helicopter, U.S. Army
CH-53E Super Stallion—heavy-lift helicopter, U.S. Navy and Marine Corps
SH-60B Seahawk—helicopter, U.S. Navy

Hamilton Standard Division
Windsor Locks, CT
Anthony D. Autorino, President

Helicopter engine controls—F-15 and F-16, U.S. Dept. of Defense and Air Force
Data System—KC-10 tanker plane, U.S. Air Force
Guidance—inertial upper stage, space shuttle launch vehicle, U.S. Air Force
Guidance—Titan III, U.S. Air Force
Space suit and life support back pack—shuttle program, NASA
Environmental controls—shuttle orbiter, NASA
Environmental equipment—F-15, F-16, U.S. Air Force
Air inlet controls—F-15, U.S. Air Force
Flight Controls—UH-60A, U.S. Army

2. **Electronics Group**
   Peter L. Scott, Executive V.P.

Norden Systems, Inc.
Norwalk, CT
Herman A. Michelson, President

Electronic systems—U.S. Air Force, Navy and Marine Corps
Surveillance radar—U.S. Navy
Radar systems—A-6, B-52, U.S. Navy, U.S. Air Force
Display units—space shuttle, NASA
Marine Integrated Fire and Air Support System, U.S. Marine Corps
Surface Surveillance Radar System—Trident submarine, U.S. Navy

3. Research

**United Technologies Research Center
East Hartford, CT
Russell G. Meyerand, Jr., V.P., R&D**

Nuclear fusion
Solar and wind energy
Laser technology
Advanced materials
Computer-aided design and manufacturing

C. Contracting History

Since 1971 United Technologies has been a consistently successful military contractor. Its military products range across a multiplicity of markets—fuels, control devices, electronics, helicopters and, above all, aircraft engines. In addition, United Technologies has made a series of acquisitions that have reduced its dependency on Government contracting from 53% of sales in 1970 to 23% in 1979.

United Technologies acquired, among other companies: Otis Corporation, Essex International, Ambac Corporation, Dynell Electronics, Carrier Corporation, and Mostek Corporation, all doing primarily non-defense business. In addition, United Technologies tried to buy Babcock and Wilcox in 1977, losing out to J. Ray McDermott. Harry J. Gray, recruited as chairman from Litton Corporation, in 1971 has won a considerable reputation for this diversification. According to *Business Week* (10 Dec. 1979), "He has... transformed an ailing, inbred corporation highly vulnerable to the vagaries of a single market into a vital and diversified growth company."

United Technologies' military business has continued to grow. The Pratt & Whitney Division dominated the military aircraft engine market, providing the engines for the F-14, F-15, F-16, A-6, A-4, and E-3A. In the late 1970s, the F-100 engine for the F-15 and F-16 developed "production shortfalls and mechanical problems" leading the Air Force to award GE a contract to develop a possible back-up engine. (*Business Week*, 10 Dec. 1979). United Technologies had received $700 m. by 1980 to fix the F-100 engine, but is facing a strong GE challenge in this market in both the civilian and military areas, including the AV-8B and FX export fighter.

Another significant military development for United Technologies in the 1970s has been the dominance it has established over the market for heavy-lift helicopters. United Technologies and Boeing's Vertol Division both produced for this market in the Vietnam War. After the war, United Technologies' Sikorsky Division won the two most significant competitions for future heavy-lift helicopters. The Army awarded its UTTAS contract, eventually to be worth over $3 b., to Sikorsky in December 1976. The Navy followed with its LAMPS award, based on the same design, eventually valued at over $3.5 b., to Sikorsky in September 1977. Lobbying by Connecticut's Congressional delegation was said to be important in these contract decisions (*The New York Times*, 26 March 1978).

United Technologies' other divisions—especially Norden, Electronics, and Chemicals—have also maintained significant military business. Norden, in particular, moved up from the status of a subcontractor to a prime contractor when it won the Marine Corps contract for a computer-based fire and air control system in October 1979. Hamilton Standard Division holds a major subcontract for compressors on Boeing's cruise missile.

Few questions have been raised about United Technologies' Government relations practices during the decade. The head of the firm's Washington office, Clark MacGregor, was once a Nixon campaign manager, while Hugh E. Witt, vice president for Government liaison, was employed both in DoD and as director of the OMB's Office of Federal Procurement Policy. In early 1980, the company further strengthened its possibilities for close Federal and overseas ties. Although Gray was quoted as saying "in this system, we don't need a No. 2 man" (*Business Week*, 10 Dec. 1979), he hired former Nixon advisor and NATO Supreme Allied Commander Gen. Alexander M. Haig, Jr. as president and chief operating officer. (Haig became Secretary of State in 1981.)

D. U.S. Government-Owned, Company-Operated Plants

Total company floor space: 70.6 sq. ft.
Leased from U.S. Government: None disclosed

RESEARCH AND DEVELOPMENT

Major Defense/Space R&D Projects

LAMPS—Helicopter, U.S. Navy
Inertial Upper Stage, Space Shuttle launch vehicle, U.S. Air Force
Ram-jet propulsion, U.S. Army, U.S. Navy, U.S. Air Force
Laser technology, U.S. Department of Defense
Advanced materials, U.S. Department of Defense

TABLE II
Research and Development
($ in M.)

	1970	1971	1972	1973	1974	1975	1976	1977	1978	1979
I. U.S. Government Contracts										
DoD	$180.5	155.7	378.9	175.9	166.8	251.1	113.2	157.7	156.9	173.4
NASA	$ 27.0	28.4	15.9	25.0	39.7	36.2	17.5	33.9	50.8	73.3
Total	$207.5	184.1	394.8	200.9	206.5	287.3	130.7	191.6	207.7	241.7
II. Company-sponsored R&D	NA	NA	$205.0	243.0	298.0	324.0	358.4	368.3	438.9	545.5
III. IR&D	NA	NA	NA	$ 43.9	44.5	46.4	52.3	54.7	52.9	NA

I. From DoD yearly publication "500 Contractors Receiving the Largest Dollar Volume of Military Prime Contract Awards for RDT&E" and NASA Annual Procurement Reports.

II. "The company spends substantial amounts on research and development which are charged against income as incurred" (10K, 1976). "The Corporation spends substantial amounts of its own funds on research and development. Such expenditures... are charged against income as incurred and relate principally to the power business and, to a lesser extent, to the flights systems business" (10K, 1978).

III. Company-sponsored R&D costs charged to DoD, as disclosed by DoD

United Technologies 427

BOARD OF DIRECTORS

Robert J. Carlson (1979)
Executive V.P., Power Group, United Technologies
Past Corporate Employment:
Deere and Co. (1952-79) (V.P.-1970, Senior V.P.-1972); President, Pratt & Whitney Aircraft Group, United Technologies (1979-present).
Corporate Directorships:
Connecticut Natural Gas Corp., Hartford National Bank/Hartford National Corp.
Key Association Memberships:
Committee on Economic Development (trustee).
Shares owned:
100

Hubert Faure (1976)
Group V.P., United Technologies
Past Corporate Employment:
President, Otis Elevator International (1972-75).
Government Positions:
Attache, French Embassy, Bogota, Colombia (1947).
Corporate Directorships:
S.A. Imetal; Societe des Grands Magasins Jones; Banque Rothschild (supervisory board).
Shares owned:
157 preferred

T. Mitchell Ford (1970)
President and Chairman, Emhart Corp. (hardware and machinery)
Past Corporate Employment:
Becket & Wagner (attorneys) (1948-52); Emhart Corp. (1958-present).
Government Positions:
Assistant general counsel, CIA (1952-55).
Corporate Directorships:
Hartford National Corp. (see Basic Data: Banking); Travelers Corp.; Bliss & Laughlin Ind., Inc. ($484,000).
Shares owned:
1,000

Harry J. Gray (1971)
President and Chairman, United Technologies
Past Corporate Employment:
Litton Industries (1956-71); United Technologies (1971-present).

Corporate Directorships:
Aetna Life and Casualty Co.; Citicorp/Citibank (see Basic Data: Banking); Exxon Corp. ($341,462,000).
Key Association Memberships:
Business Council; Aerospace Industries Association; Navy League.
Shares owned:
132,000

Alexander M. Haig, Jr. (1980)
President and Chief Operating Officer, United Technologies (resigned 1981)
Military:
U.S. Army (1947-73, 1974-78) (Staff Officer and Military Asst. to Secretary of the Army-1962; Staff Officer and Asst. to Secretary of Defense-1964; Brigade Commander, 1st Infantry Division, Vietnam-1966; Regimental Commander, U.S. Military Academy-1967; Vice-Chief of Staff, U.S. Army-1973; Commander in Chief, U.S. European Command-1974; Supreme Allied Commander in Europe-1974).
Government Positions:
Deputy Asst. to the President for National Security Affairs (1969-73); Asst. to the President, White House Chief of Staff (1973-74).
Corporate Directorships:
Crown Cork & Seal; Chase Manhattan Bank (see Basic Data: Banking)
Shares owned:
100

Melvin Holm (1979)
Chairman and Chief Executive Officer, Carrier Corp., United Technologies
Past Corporate Employment:
Carrier Corp. (1937-78) (Chairman of the Board and Chief Executive Officer-1968-78).
Corporate Directorships:
Warner & Swasey Co. ($773,000); New York Telephone Co. ($730,000); SKF Industries ($4,177,000); Lincoln First Banks, Inc.; Mutual of New York (trustee).
Shares owned:
20,250 preferred

Paul W. O'Malley (1974)
Group V.P., United Technologies.
Past Corporate Employment:
Essex International, Inc. (1952-74).

Corporate Directorships:
Detroit Bank and Trust Co./Detroit Bank Corp.; Lincoln National Bank and Trust Co.; Tecumseh Products Co. ($13,000).
Shares owned:
332,283

Walter F. Probst (1974)
Former Chairman of the Board and Chief Executive Officer, Essex Group, Inc.
Past Corporate Employment:
Attorney, Cook, Smith, Jacobs & Beane (1937-42); Essex Corp. (1942-74).
Corporate Directorships:
American Fletcher Corp.; Lincoln National Bank and Trust Co.
Shares owned:
474,744

Peter L. Scott (1979)
Executive V.P., Electronics Group, United Technologies
Past Corporate Employment:
NCR, United Technologies (1975-present).
Shares owned:
18,000

William E. Simon (1979)
Senior Consultant on Economic and Financial Matters, Blyth, Eastman, Paine, Webber
Past Corporate Employment:
Weeden & Co. (1952-57); Salomon Bros. (1964-70).
Government Positions:
Deputy Secretary of the Treasury (1973-74); Administrator, Federal Energy Office (1973-74); Secretary of the Treasury (1974-77).
Corporate Directorships:
Citicorp (see Basic Data: Banking); Xerox; Dart Ind.; Power Corp.
Shares owned:
NA

Darwin Smith (1980)
Executive, Kimberly Clark Corp.
Past Corporate Employment:
Kimberly Clark Corp. (1958-71).
Corporate Directorships:
American Natural Resources Co.; Citicorp (see Basic Data: Banking).
Shares owned:
NA

Richard S. Smith (1972)
Senior V.P., National Steel
Past Corporate Employment:
Northwestern Mutual Life Insurance (1949-52); First National City Bank, N.Y. (1952-62); V.P., Hanna Mining Co. (1963-64); National Steel Corp. (1964-present).
Corporate Directorships:
National Aluminum Corp.; Advance Investors Corp.; St. John D'el Rey Mining Co.
Shares owned:
200

William Spencer (1970)
President and Director, Citicorp/Citibank
Past Corporate Employment:
Chemical Bank and Trust Co. (1939-51); Citibank (1951-present).
Corporate Directorships:
Asia Pacific Capital Corp.; Bedford Stuyvesant Development and Service Corp.; Sears, Roebuck & Co. ($1,126,000).
Shares owned:
600

Robert Sproull (1972)
President, University of Rochester
Past Employment:
Research physicist, RCA Labs (1943-46); Cornell University (1946-63); President, University of Rochester (1970-present).
Government Positions:
Advanced Research Projects Agency, Department of Defense (1953-65); Chairman, Defense Science Board (1968-70).
Corporate Directorships:
Security Trust Co.; Xerox Corp.; Sybron Corp. ($1,052,000).
Shares owned:
2,000

Alfred Van Sinderen (1969)
President and Director, Southern New England Telephone Co.
Past Corporate Employment:
Southern New England Telephone (1947-present).
Corporate Directorships:
Stanley Works ($2,419,000); Federal Reserve Bank, Boston.
Shares owned:
3,000

Jacqueline G. Wexler (1978)
President, Academic Consulting Association
Past Employment:
Professor and President, Webster College (1956-60);
President, Hunter College (1970-79).
Corporate Directorships:
Interpublic Group.
Shares owned:
200

PERSONNEL TRANSFERS

Table III
(DoD 1970-79)
(NASA 1974-79)

	Total	Air Force	Army	Navy	Office of Secretary of Defense	Other
DoD Military to United Technologies	50	31	6	8	1	4
DoD Civilian to United Technologies	11	5	1		4	1
NASA to United Technologies	3					
United Technologies to DoD	12	2	8		2	
United Technologies to NASA	7					
Total	83	38	15	8	7	5

Appearances of Potential Conflict of Interest (see Chapter 6): 8

1. DoD to UT

Cantus, Howard H.
  DoD:
    Deputy Asst. for House Legislative Affairs, Office of Asst. Secretary of Defense for Legislative Affairs.
  UT:
    November 1977, Manager, Energy Programs, Washington office, Power Systems Division.

Witt, Hugh E.
DoD:
> Senior Civilian Asst., Office of Asst. Secretary of Defense for Installations and Logistics (subsequently 1974-77, Director, Office of Federal Procurement Policy, Executive Office of the President).

UT:
> March 1977, Director of Government Liaison, Washington office.

2. NASA to UT

Carter, James
NASA:
> Aerospace technologist, theoretical aerodynamics.

UT:
> December 1979, Supervisor, Computational Fluid Dynamics Group, aerodynamics analysis.

Newby, David
NASA:
> Director, Administration and Program Support, Marshall Space Flight Center.

UT:
> April 1976, management consultant.

3. UT to DoD

Curtiss, Howard C.
UT:
> Engineering consultant, Sikorsky.

DoD:
> July 1978, Consultant, Army Science Board.

Long, Richard Lewis
UT:
> Chief Advanced Research, R&D Planning; Senior Project Engineer, Advanced Projects, Sikorsky.

DoD:
> January 1972, Deputy Director, Directorate for Research, Development and Engineering, U.S. Army Aviation Systems Command.

4. "Revolving Door"

Velkoff, Henry
DoD:
> Consultant on helicopter research, U.S. Army Aviation Systems Command.

UT:
December 1971, Engineering consultant, helicopter rotors, Sikorsky.
DoD:
(until September 1963), Research scientist, advanced propulsion, U.S. Air Force.

Zimmerman, Charles
DoD:
Army Special Asst., Chief engineer, advise on engineering matters and conduct engineering studies.
UT:
October 1967, Consultant on engineering and policy, Sikorsky.
DoD:
(until May 1972), Member, Scientific Advisory Group for Aviation Systems.

Comments

United Technologies has no policy statement on transfer of personnel.

POLITICAL ACTION COMMITTEES

Name: United Technologies Corporation PAC
Total Expenditures (4/76-5/80): $341,978
Total Contributions to Federal Campaigns (4/76-5/80): $289,225

Key
(D) = Democrat
(R) = Republican
(C) = Recipient was a candidate and not elected to that office.
 + = Candidate is also a member of a key Congressional committee.
 * = Candidate is a member of two committees, but contribution s/he received is only listed once to avoid being double-counted in the total for this section.

A. Contributions to Federal Candidates in States with United Technologies Production Facilities (Key Geographic Locations)

CONNECTICUT

United Technologies plants located in East Hartford (dist. 1), Farmington (dist. 6), Norwalk (dist. 4), Stratford (dist. 3), and Windsor Locks (dist. 6)

Senate

Gloria Schaffer (D) (C)	$ 500
+ Sen. Lowell Weicker	$3,500

House

Rep. William Cotter (D-1)	$4,100
Rep. Christopher J. Dodd (D-2) (Sen. candidate in 1980)	$2,400
+ Rep. Robert Giamo (D-3)	$4,000
George Guidera (R-5) (C)	$1,500
Rep. Stewart McKinney (R-4)	$ 200
Daniel F. Mackinnon (R-6) (C)	$ 500
Rep. Toby Moffet (D-6)	$ 200
Geoffrey Peterson (D-4) (C)	$ 500
Rep. Ronald Sarasin (R-5)	$2,500
Thomas Upson (R-6) (C)	$ 700

Total Connecticut: $20,600
% Total Federal Contributions: 0.7%

CALIFORNIA

United Technologies plants located in Sunnyvale (dist. 12, 13)

Senate

Sen. S.I. Hayakawa (R)	$4,000

House

+ Rep. Robert E. Badham (R-40)	$ 300
Rep. Clair Burgener (R-43)	$ 200
Rep. William E. Dannemeyer (R-39)	$ 500
+ Rep. Robert Dornan (R-27)	$ 100
Rep. Wayne Grisham (R-33)	$ 400
+ Rep. Barry Goldwater, Jr. (R-20)	$1,500
Rep. Mark Hannaford (D-34)	$ 200
+ Rep. Robert Leggett (D-4)	$ 100
Rep. James Lloyd (D-35)	$ 400
Rep. Jerry Lewis (R-37)	$ 500
Rep. Paul McCloskey (R-12)	$ 300
+ Rep. John McFall (D-14)	$ 600
+ Rep. Norman Mineta (D-13)	$2,100
Rep. John Rousselot (R-26)	$ 250

United Technologies

+ Rep. William Royer (R-11)			$ 300
Burt Talcott (R-16) (C)			$ 500
+ Rep. Bob Wilson (R-41)			$2,000

Total California: $14,250
% Total Federal Contributions: 4.9%

Total to Key Geographic Locations: $34,850
% Total Federal Contributions: 12.0%

B. Contributions to Members of Key Congressional Committees

Senate Armed Services Committee

Byrd, Harry	$1,200	McIntyre	$1,500
Cannon	$1,000	Morgan	$ 250
Cohen	$ 500	Stennis	$ 500
Goldwater	$1,000	Taft	$4,000
Helms	$ 500	Thurmond	$2,700
Humphrey, Gordon	$ 500	Tower	$2,000
Jepsen	$ 250	Warner	$1,250

House Armed Services Committee

Badham	$ 300	Holt	$ 800
Bailey	$ 600	Ichord	$ 900
Beard, Robin	$ 750	Leggett	$ 100
Byron, B.	$ 300	Lloyd	$ 400
Byron G.	$ 200	McDonald	$ 500
Courter	$1,250	Mitchell, Donald	$ 300
Daniel, Robert	$ 800	Mollohan	$1,700
Davis, Mendel	$ 800	Spence	$1,100
Dickinson	$1,600	Stump	$ 600
Dougherty	$1,100	Trible	$ 700
Hillis	$ 500	Wilson, Bob	$2,000

Senate Defense Appropriations Subcommittee

Brooke	$2,000	McClure	$ 200
Hollings	$1,000	Stennis	•
Huddleston	$ 400	Stevens	$1,000
Johnston	$ 500	Weicker	$3,500

House Defense Appropriations Subcommittee

Addabbo	$1,000	Edwards, Jack	$1,100
Burlison	$ 300	Flynt	$ 500
Cederberg	$2,000	Giamo	$4,000
Chappell	$ 800	McFall	$ 600
Conte	$ 100	Robinson	$ 400
Dicks	$ 125	Sikes	$1,000

Senate Committee on Commerce, Science and Transportation Subcommittee on Aviation

Cannon	•	Packwood	$ 250
Goldwater	•	Pressler	$ 500
Kassebaum	$1,150	Stevens	•
		Stump	•

Subcommittee on Science, Technology and Space

Goldwater	*	Kassebaum	*
Griffin	$4,500	Long	$ 500
Hollings	*	Schmitt	$1,500

House Committee on Science and Technology

Ambro	$ 350	Hollenbeck	$ 700
Carney	$ 800	Lloyd, James	*
Davis, Robert	$ 600	Lujan	$ 150
Dornan	$ 100	McCormack	$ 750
Ertel	$ 200	Milford	$2,100
Fish	$ 100	Myers	$ 200
Flippo	$ 400	Neal	$ 300
Flowers	$1,600	Pursell	$1,200
Forsythe	$ 200	Roe	$ 300
Frey	$ 500	Royer	$ 300
Fuqua	$1,100	Roth	$ 300
Gammage	$ 100	Rudd	$1,200
Goldwater, Jr.	$1,500	Teague	$1,600
Harsha	$ 200	Walker	$ 200
		Wydler	$1,000

Senate Committee on Environment and Public Works
Subcommittee on Transportation

Buckley	$1,400	Moynihan	$ 850
Domenici	$ 600	Stafford	$1,000

House Committee on Public Works and Transportation
Subcommittee on Aviation

Abdnor	$ 800	Harsha	*
Ambro	*	Hefner	$ 225
Anderson, Glenn	$ 300	Milford	*
Cochran	$ 300	Mineta	$1,600
Edgar	$ 100	Rahall	$ 200
Ertel	*	Royer	*
Evans, Billy	$ 200	Schuster	$ 200
Flippo	*	Snyder, Gene	$600
Goldwater, Jr.	*	Stump	*

Total to Key Committees: $89,800
% Total Federal Contributions: 31.0%

C. Contributions to Other Influential Members of Congress

Sen. Robert C. Byrd (D WV), Majority Leader	$1,000
Sen. Howard Baker (R-TN), Minority Leader	$2,200
Rep. John Rhodes (R-AZ), Minority Leader	$2,000
Rep. James Wright, Jr., (D-TX), Majority Leader	$ 600

Total to Other Influentials: $5,800
% Total Federal Contributions: 2.0%

D. Contributions to Other Federal Candidates

Senate

Armstrong, Wm. (R-CO)	$3,000	Heinz (R-PA)	$ 200
Bell (R-NJ) (C)	$1,000	Holton (R-VA) (C)	$ 200
Boschwitz (R-MN)	$1,000	Humphrey, H. (D-MN)	$ 150
Brock (D-TN)	$4,500	Lugar (R-IN)	$3,500
Callaway (R-CO) (C)	$1,000	Martin (R-AL)	$ 500
Chafee (R-RI)	$2,000	Mathias (R-MD)	$ 500
Cochran (R-MS)	$2,000	McCollister (R-NE) (C)	$1,200
Danforth (R-MO)	$ 200	Moss (D-UT)	$ 500
Dole (R-KS)	$ 500	Moore (R-WV) (C)	$1,000
Durenberger (IR-MN)	$3,000	Quayle (R-IN)	$2,150
Esch (R-MI) (C)	$5,000	(also a House cand.)	
Glenn (D-OH)	$ 150	Percy (R-IL)	$1,300
Green (D-PA) (C)	$ 200	Simpson (R-WY)	$ 200
		Wallop (R-WY)	$ 600

House

Alexander (D-AK)	$ 100	Jenrette (D-SC)	$ 900
Ashbrook (R-OH)	$ 100	Kane (R-PA)	$ 500
Ashley (D-OH)	$ 250	Kelly (R-FL)	$1,000
Aucoin (R-OR)	$ 200	Kircher (R-OH) (C)	$ 550
Bell (R-IN) (C)	$ 250	Lee, Gary (R-NY)	$ 700
Bereuter (R-NE)	$ 200	Lent (RC-NY)	$ 100
Bethune (R-AR)	$ 300	Livingston (R-LA)	$1,375
Breux (D-LA)	$ 100	Loeffler (R-TX)	$ 600
Briggs (R-FL) (C)	$ 500	Long (D-LA)	$ 250
Bronson (R-MA) (C)	$ 500	Lott (R-MS)	$1,700
Brooks (D-TX)	$ 250	Madigan (R-IL)	$ 100
Brown, Clarence (R-OH)	$ 500	Martin, L. (R-IL) (C)	$ 400
Brown (R-MI)	$ 750	Martin, James (R-NC)	$ 600
Buchanan (R-AL)	$ 500	Martinelli (R-NY)	$ 500
Buikema (R-IL) (C)	$ 500	Mason (R-MA) (C)	$ 500
Burgess (R-TX) (C)	$ 250	McClory (R-IL)	$ 950
Burke, Herbert (R-FL)	$ 200	McDade (R-PA)	$1,250
Bush, G. (R-TX) (C)	$ 300	McEwen (RC-NY)	$ 200
Campbell (R-SC)	$ 950	McKay (D-UT)	$1,000
Caputo (RC-NY)	$ 500	Mica (D-FL)	$ 600
Casey (R-PA) (C)	$ 500	Mizell (R-NC)	$ 250
Chase (R-MO) (C)	$ 500	Moore (R-LA)	$ 300
Cheney (R-WY)	$ 200	Murtha (D-PA)	$ 300
Clinger (R-PA)	$ 700	Nelligan (R-PA) (C)	$ 300
Coleman (R-MO)	$ 500	Oberstar (D-MN)	$ 200
Cohalen (RC-NY)	$ 500	Petri (R-WI)	$ 300
Conable (R-NY)	$ 50	Pursell (R-MI)	$ 200
Conlin (R-MI)	$ 750	Quayle (R-IN)	$2,150
Corcoran (R-IL)	$ 200	(also a Sen. cand.)	
Cornwell (D-IN)	$ 100	Richardson (D-SC)	$ 500
Coughlin (R-PA)	$ 500	Rodino (D-NJ)	$ 400
Cunningham (R-WA)	$ 500	Rogers (D-FL)	$ 300
Deckard (R-IN)	$ 750	Roukema (R-NJ) (C)	$ 500

Subcommittee on Science, Technology and Space

Goldwater	*	Kassebaum	*
Griffin	$4,500	Long	$ 500
Hollings	*	Schmitt	$1,500

House Committee on Science and Technology

Ambro	$ 350	Hollenbeck	$ 700
Carney	$ 800	Lloyd, James	*
Davis, Robert	$ 600	Lujan	$ 150
Dornan	$ 100	McCormack	$ 750
Ertel	$ 200	Milford	$2,100
Fish	$ 100	Myers	$ 200
Flippo	$ 400	Neal	$ 300
Flowers	$1,600	Pursell	$1,200
Forsythe	$ 200	Roe	$ 300
Frey	$ 500	Royer	$ 300
Fuqua	$1,100	Roth	$ 300
Gammage	$ 100	Rudd	$1,200
Goldwater, Jr.	$1,500	Teague	$1,600
Harsha	$ 200	Walker	$ 200
		Wydler	$1,000

Senate Committee on Environment and Public Works
Subcommittee on Transportation

Buckley	$1,400	Moynihan	$ 850
Domenici	$ 600	Stafford	$1,000

House Committee on Public Works and Transportation
Subcommittee on Aviation

Abdnor	$ 800	Harsha	*
Ambro	*	Hefner	$ 225
Anderson, Glenn	$ 300	Milford	*
Cochran	$ 300	Mineta	$1,600
Edgar	$ 100	Rahall	$ 200
Ertel	*	Royer	*
Evans, Billy	$ 200	Schuster	$ 200
Flippo	*	Snyder, Gene	$600
Goldwater, Jr.	*	Stump	*

Total to Key Committees: $89,800
% Total Federal Contributions: 31.0%

C. Contributions to Other Influential Members of Congress

Sen. Robert C. Byrd (D WV), Majority Leader	$1,000
Sen. Howard Baker (R-TN), Minority Leader	$2,200
Rep. John Rhodes (R-AZ), Minority Leader	$2,000
Rep. James Wright, Jr., (D-TX), Majority Leader	$ 600

Total to Other Influentials: $5,800
% Total Federal Contributions: 2.0%

D. Contributions to Other Federal Candidates

Senate

Armstrong, Wm. (R-CO)	$3,000	Heinz (R-PA)	$ 200
Bell (R-NJ) (C)	$1,000	Holton (R-VA) (C)	$ 200
Boschwitz (R-MN)	$1,000	Humphrey, H. (D-MN)	$ 150
Brock (D-TN)	$4,500	Lugar (R-IN)	$3,500
Callaway (R-CO) (C)	$1,000	Martin (R-AL)	$ 500
Chafee (R-RI)	$2,000	Mathias (R-MD)	$ 500
Cochran (R-MS)	$2,000	McCollister (R-NE) (C)	$1,200
Danforth (R-MO)	$ 200	Moss (D-UT)	$ 500
Dole (R-KS)	$ 500	Moore (R-WV) (C)	$1,000
Durenberger (IR-MN)	$3,000	Quayle (R-IN)	$2,150
Esch (R-MI) (C)	$5,000	(also a House cand.)	
Glenn (D-OH)	$ 150	Percy (R-IL)	$1,300
Green (D-PA) (C)	$ 200	Simpson (R-WY)	$ 200
		Wallop (R-WY)	$ 600

House

Alexander (D-AK)	$ 100	Jenrette (D-SC)	$ 900
Ashbrook (R-OH)	$ 100	Kane (R-PA)	$ 500
Ashley (D-OH)	$ 250	Kelly (R-FL)	$1,000
Aucoin (R-OR)	$ 200	Kircher (R-OH) (C)	$ 550
Bell (R-IN) (C)	$ 250	Lee, Gary (R-NY)	$ 700
Bereuter (R-NE)	$ 200	Lent (RC-NY)	$ 100
Bethune (R-AR)	$ 300	Livingston (R-LA)	$1,375
Breux (D-LA)	$ 100	Loeffler (R-TX)	$ 600
Briggs (R-FL) (C)	$ 500	Long (D-LA)	$ 250
Bronson (R-MA) (C)	$ 500	Lott (R-MS)	$1,700
Brooks (D-TX)	$ 250	Madigan (R-IL)	$ 100
Brown, Clarence (R-OH)	$ 500	Martin, L. (R-IL) (C)	$ 400
Brown (R-MI)	$ 750	Martin, James (R-NC)	$ 600
Buchanan (R-AL)	$ 500	Martinelli (R-NY)	$ 500
Buikema (R-IL) (C)	$ 500	Mason (R-MA) (C)	$ 500
Burgess (R-TX) (C)	$ 250	McClory (R-IL)	$ 950
Burke, Herbert (R-FL)	$ 200	McDade (R-PA)	$1,250
Bush, G. (R-TX) (C)	$ 300	McEwen (RC-NY)	$ 200
Campbell (R-SC)	$ 950	McKay (D-UT)	$1,000
Caputo (RC-NY)	$ 500	Mica (D-FL)	$ 600
Casey (R-PA) (C)	$ 500	Mizell (R-NC)	$ 250
Chase (R-MO) (C)	$ 500	Moore (R-LA)	$ 300
Cheney (R-WY)	$ 200	Murtha (D-PA)	$ 300
Clinger (R-PA)	$ 700	Nelligan (R-PA) (C)	$ 300
Coleman (R-MO)	$ 500	Oberstar (D-MN)	$ 200
Cohalen (RC-NY)	$ 500	Petri (R-WI)	$ 300
Conable (R-NY)	$ 50	Pursell (R-MI)	$ 200
Conlin (R-MI)	$ 750	Quayle (R-IN)	$2,150
Corcoran (R-IL)	$ 200	(also a Sen. cand.)	
Cornwell (D-IN)	$ 100	Richardson (D-SC)	$ 500
Coughlin (R-PA)	$ 500	Rodino (D-NJ)	$ 400
Cunningham (R-WA)	$ 500	Rogers (D-FL)	$ 300
Deckard (R-IN)	$ 750	Roukema (R-NJ) (C)	$ 500

Dellibovi (R-NY)	$ 250	Roush (D-IN)	$ 250
Derrick (D-SC)	$ 650	Ruppe (R-MI)	$ 700
Devine (R-OH)	$1,000	Schulze (R-PA)	$ 200
Donelon (R-LA) (C)	$ 500	Scott (R-CO) (C)	$1,000
Duncan, John (R-TN)	$1,550	Sensenbrenner (R-WI)	$ 300
Duncan, Robert (D-OR)	$ 500	Serotkin (R-MI) (C)	$ 500
Dunne (R-IL)	$ 500	Sharp (R-MI)	$ 400
Erdahl (IR-MN)	$ 500	Shriver (R-KS)	$1,000
Erlenborn (R-IL)	$ 500	Skelton (D-MO)	$ 100
Evans (D-IN)	$ 100	Skubitz (D-KS)	$ 500
Evans (R-DE)	$ 700	Slack (D-WV)	$ 200
Fithian (D-IN)	$ 600	Snyder, Robert (R-MO)	$ 500
Foley (D-WA)	$ 100	Snowe (R-ME)	$ 375
Frappier (R-MO) (C)	$ 500	Solomon (R-NY)	$ 250
Frenzel (R-MN)	$ 300	Spooner (R-LA) (C)	$ 500
Garner (R-WA) (C)	$ 500	Stangeland (IR-MN)	$ 500
Gibbons (D-FL)	$ 200	Steers (R-MD)	$ 200
Gilman (R-NY)	$ 300	Steiger (R-WI)	$ 300
Gudger (D-NC)	$ 200	Stokes (D-OH)	$ 100
Gurney (R-FL)	$ 500	Stockman (R-MI)	$ 500
Guyer (R-OH)	$ 100	Tauke (R-IN)	$ 250
Hall (D-TX)	$ 100	Thorsness (R-SD)	$ 500
Hamilton (D-IN)	$ 350	Tsongas (D-MA)	$ 250
Herrity (R-VA) (C)	$ 300	Vander Jagt (R-MI)	$ 500
Holland (D-SC)	$ 300	Wallace (R-NY) (C)	$ 200
Hopkins (R-KY)	$ 750	Williams (R-OH)	$ 500
Hubbard (D-KY)	$ 450	Wilson, J. (R-LA) (C)	$ 500
Huckaby (D-LA)	$ 500	Wolf (R-VA) (C)	$ 150
Ireland (D-FL)	$1,300	Young, Andrew (D-GA)	$ 250
Jeffries (R-KS)	$ 400	Young, Don (R-AK)	$ 200

Total to Other Federal Candidates: $92,000
% Total Federal Contributions: 31.8%

E. Contributions to Party Campaign Committees

Republican federal-level committees: $38,375
Democratic federal-level committees: $30,700

Total to Party Committees: $69,075
% Total Federal Contributions: 23.9%

F. Contributions to Presidential Candidates

Jimmy Carter (D)	$ 1,500
John Connally (R)	$ 1,000
Gerald Ford (R)	$10,100

Total to Presidential Candidates: $12,600
% Total Federal Contributions: 4.4%

Comments

The International Association of Machinists (IAM) filed a complaint with the Federal Election Commission in 1979 against United Technologies and nine other corporate PACs. Specifically, IAM alleged that "United Technologies manifests the less than free and voluntary character of employee responses to the company's political solicitations in several salient respects: 1) United Technologies operates a PAC to support candidates helpful to the industry in which the company operates and for that purpose it solicits unprotected career employees and 2) makes no provision for protecting the anonymity of non-contributors or of contribution amounts. 3) Some 61% of the itemized contributors are mid-level managers and professionals. 4) United Technologies does not restrict solicitation by supervisors or other employees. 5) The average annual contribution for mid-level managerial and professional employees is $241, while the publicly identified officers and vice presidents made contributions averaging $1,071. 6) Though the employees include both Democrats and Republicans, 78% of the PAC contributions were given to Republicans. 7) 89% of the itemized PAC receipts were obtained from employees in California, Connecticut, Indiana and Washington, D.C., but only 13% was contributed by the PAC to candidates in those states. 8) Contributing employees are not permitted to designate, either by party or candidate, the recipients of their money. 9) The overall participation rate for United Technologies' employees is 11%, but the largest single bloc of contributors—publicly identified executives and corporate officers—responded to the PAC solicitation with a 95% participation rate. 10) There is company orchestration: most of the contributors give in similar amounts, or within a narrow range of amounts" (from *Complaint Against Operations of Corporate Political Action Committees* filed before the FEC by the International Association of Machinists, October 1979.)

The complaint was dismissed by the FEC in December 1979, stating that there were insufficient grounds for the Commission to believe there was a violation of the Federal Election Campaigns Act, that it did not appear that corporate solicitation systems violated the act, and that the complaint raised some issues the FEC was not empowered to decide upon, among other grounds. The Machinists Union has since taken the complaint against the 10 corporate PACs to Federal District Court on grounds that the Federal Election Law permits PACs to solicit employees in such a way that they cannot make a truly voluntary decision.

WASHINGTON OPERATIONS

Washington Office:
1125 15th Street, NW, Washington, DC 20005

Director:
Clark MacGregor, Senior V.P.

Staff:
Christian J. Lund, Director of Government Relations
Hugh E. Witt, Manager of Government Liaison (see Personnel Transfers)
Eugene J. Tallia, V.P., Government Relations, Sikorsky Aircraft
James A. Shinkoff, V.P., Hamilton-Standard Division
Howard H. Cantus, Manager, Washington office, Energy Programs (see Personnel Transfers)

Activities:
Not available.

Registered Lobbyists:

	Receipts	Expenditures	Years
Cederberg & Associates, Inc. 7100 Sussex Place Alexandria, VA (with Grumman, Martin Marietta and RCA)	$ 400.00	*	79
Christian J. Lund 1125 15th St. NW Washington, DC	$140,639.00	$10,749.38	76-79
F. Slatinshek & Associates, Inc. 218 N. Lee St. Alexandria, VA (with General Dynamics, Grumman and Gould)	$ 1,637.50	*	77-79
TOTAL	$142,676.50	$10,749.38	

*No figures reported; quarterly report was filed.

United Technologies

DEFENSE-RELATED TRADE ASSOCIATION MEMBERSHIPS

Aerospace Industries Association
Air Force Association
American Defense Preparedness Association
American Institute of Aeronautics and Astronautics
National Association for Remotely-Piloted Vehicles
National Security Industrial Association

ADVISORY COMMITTEE MEMBERSHIPS

1976-78: 13

Altman, David
(Chemical Systems Division)
NASA—Space Program Advisory Council, 1976, 1977

Carter, Edward
(Sikorsky Aircraft)
NASA—Research and Technology Advisory Council, Committee on Aerodynamics and Configurations, 1976, 1977

Coar, Richard
(Pratt & Whitney)
NASA—Advisory Board on Aircraft Fuel Conservation Technology, 1976

Corcoran, William J.
NASA—Committee on Space Propulsion and Power, 1976
NASA—Research and Technology Council, 1976, 1977

DeMaria, Anthony J.
DoD—Advisory Group on Electron Devices, 1977, 1978

Jolly, Harvey P.
DoD—Defense Industry Advisory Group, Europe, 1976, 1977

Leopold, Dr. Rueven
DoD—Defense Science Board, Associate Member, 1978

Marsh, Allyn
(Pratt & Whitney)
NASA—Research and Technology Advisory Council, Committee on Aeronautical Propulsion, Ad Hoc Panel on Jet Engine Hydrocarbon Fuels, 1976

Sallee, Philip
(Pratt & Whitney)
NASA—Research and Technology Advisory Council, Panel on Aviation Safety and Operating Systems, 1976, 1977

Shank, Maurice
(Pratt & Whitney)
NASA—Research and Technology Advisory Council, Committee on Aerodynamics and Configurations, 1976
NASA—Research and Technology Advisory Council, Committee on Aeronautical Propulsion, 1976, 1977

Versnyder, Francis L.
(Pratt & Whitney)
NASA—Committee on Materials and Structures, 1976, 1977

ENTERTAINMENT

United Technologies made no general policy statement in regard to entertainment, but did disclose some specific items (source: letter to the Joint Committee on Defense Production, 26 Feb. 1976, from T.D. Chambers, United Technologies Asst. Corporation Counsel).

Entertainment:
No facilities maintained.

Hospitality Suites:
1973-75: 43
Includes Air Force Association, Association of the U.S. Army, Marine Corps Aviation Association, Navy Helicopter Association, American Defense Preparedness Association, National Security Industrial Association.

Tickets:
1973-75: 147

Air Travel:
As permitted under DoD regulations.

QUESTIONABLE PAYMENTS

United Technologies disclosed in 1976 that it had undertaken its own review of the years 1970 to 1975 and found payments of $1,950,000 some of which may have gone to foreign government officials. United Technologies also disclosed that Otis Elevator, heavily involved in overseas construction and 70% owned by United Technologies as of November 1975, was conducting an investigation (Company *8K*, March 1976).

In June 1976, Otis disclosed that preliminary results indicated an estimated $5-6 m. in "questionable foreign payments," $1.2 m. coming "to some extent from an off-book fund" (Company *8K*, 8 June 1976).

In April 1977, final reports by United Technologies and Otis provided additional data. United Technologies disclosed another $960,000 in payments in 1976 similar to those noted earlier, making a total of $2.91 m. (Company *8K*, 20 April 1977). Otis indicated a final total of $7.235 m. in payments, "some parts of which were questionable" between 1971 and 1976 (Company *8K*, 20 April 1977). Combining the two, United Technologies thus disclosed some $10.145 m. in payments. The disclosere did not indicate the countries or recipients of the payments.

United Technologies also made a statement of company policy on this issue:

> "The Corporation has taken action to assure that no illegal or improper political contributions or foreign payment commitments are made in the future. This action has included the issuance of a comprehensive policy statement and the adoption of procedures to implement that policy. The procedures include a requirement that all sales representative agreements with foreign persons that have the potential of obligating United or its subsidiaries to payment of commissions or fees of $100,000 or more be approved by the chief executive officer, the chief financial officer and the corporate legal office. In addition, all agreements with foreign sales representatives are required to include a certification by the representative that no payment in violation of the policy will be made from any commission or fees paid by the Corporation" (Company *8K*, March 1976).

DISCLOSURE

Poor.

Appendix A

MAY 1979 Questionnaire on Contractor Government Relations

Government/Defense/NASA sales

1. What were company sales to the federal government, the Department of Defense and the National Aeronautics and Space Administration for each of the years from 1974-1978?

   ($ millions)

	1974	1975	1976	1977	1978
Sales to federal government					
Sales to Department of Defense					
Sales to NASA					

2. What were your total exports of military equipment for the same years (including commercial, Foreign Military Sales, and Military Assistance Program sales)?

   ($000)

	1974	1975	1976	1977	1978
Total exports of military equipment					

3. How much was the company reimbursed by the Department of Defense for company-sponsored (Independent) Research and Development and Bid and Proposal expenses from 1974 to 1978?

   ($000)

	1974	1975	1976	1977	1978
Reimbursements for Independent Research & Development and Bid & Proposal					

4. How much did your company spend on Research and Development from 1974-1978 and how was that expenditure divided between defense/NASA related R&D and commercial/civilian R&D?

	1974	1975	($000) 1976	1977	1978

Company R&D investment (defense/NASA)

Company R&D investment (commercial/civilian)

5. What are your major current Research & Development projects in the defense/NASA area? At which company locations are these under way? (Use addended sheets if necessary.)

    PROJECT   LOCATION

6. Government-Owned, Contractor-Operated (GOCO) plant and equipment.
   a. How many square feet of GOCO plant do you use in your defense R&D and production work?

   b. What dollar value of GOCO equipment do you use in your defense R&D and production work?

   c. What are your total annual lease costs for GOCO plant and equipment?

7. Defense-related employment.
   a. How many company employees are currently employed on contract work for the Department of Defense?

   b. How many are currently employed on contract work for NASA?

   c. How many are employed on contract work for other federal agencies?

8. a. Who is the lead underwriter for the company?

   b. Which banks are the leading lenders to the company?

9. a. Who is the company's outside legal counsel? Address?

   b. What legal counsel does the company retain in Washington, DC?

10. Transfer of Personnel.
    a. Do you have any policy concerning the employment of retired military and civilian employees of the Department of Defense or NASA? (You may append an answer.)

    b. How many such personnel do you currently employ?

c. How many such personnel do you retain as consultants?

d. What is company policy on permitting any such employees to engage in selling relationships with the Department of Defense or NASA?

e. What are company procedures regarding compliance by such personnel with the reporting requirement of the Department of Defense and NASA with regard to former DoD/NASA employees? (DoD Directive 7700.15 "Reporting Procedures on Defense Related Employment")

11. Trade Associations.
   a. To which of the appended list of industry trade asociations does the company belong? (Please check beside relevant names on list at end of questionnaire.)

   b. How much has your company paid in dues to these associations between 1974 and 1978?

   ($000)
   1974   1975   1976   1977   1978

   Dues paid

12. Washington Office.
   a. Do you maintain corporate offices in or near Washington, DC?

   b. Addresses:

   c. Dates established:

13. Who are the permanent professional-level employees in your Washington office and what are their responsibilities? (Exclude clerical staff.)

   NAME   RESPONSIBILITIES

14. What were the total expenditures of your Washington offices from 1974 to 1978? How much of this expenditure was reimbursed by the Department of Defense as contract-related costs?

   ($000)
   1974   1975   1976   1977   1978

   Total expenditures

   Reimbursed by Department
   of Defense

15. Roughly how many visits per month (on average) did ranking corporate personnel whose job responsibilities encompass Department of Defense and NASA work pay to Washington, DC during 1977 and 1978? (Ranking personnel include the Chief Executive and Operating officers, company

members of the Board, Vice-Presidents, Divisional and Group heads and the chief administrators of operating defense and aerospace programs.)

0-5 _____
5-10 _____
10-20 _____
20-50 _____
over 50 _____

16. How much did you spend for defense and NASA-related public relations from 1974 to 1978?

	1974	1975	($000) 1976	1977	1978
Public relations expenditures for DoD and NASA work					

17. How much did you spend for advertising on defense and NASA-related projects from 1974 to 1978?

	1974	1975	($000) 1976	1977	1978
Advertising for DoD and NASA-related projects					

18. What outside public relations and advertising firms do you use to handle defense and NASA-related advertising?

Name _____ Name _____
Address _____ Address _____

Name _____ Name _____
Address _____ Address _____

Name _____ Name _____
Address _____ Address _____

19. How much did the company spend for the purposes of lobbying Congress with regard to defense issues and on behalf of defense and NASA-related business from 1974 to 1978?

	1974	1975	($000) 1976	1977	1978
Lobbying expenditures related to DoD and NASA work					

20. How much did you spend for all government marketing including activities related to proposal preparation and contract negotiation with the Department of Defense and NASA from 1974 to 1978?

($000)

	1974	1975	1976	1977	1978
Government marketing expenditures					

21. How much did you spend for defense and NASA-related grass roots lobbying from 1970 to 1978? (According to Section 162(e)(2)(B) of the Internal Revenue Code, grass roots lobbying is defined as representational activities "in connection with any atempt to influence the general public, or segments thereof, with respect to legislative matters, elections or referendums.")

($000)

	1974	1975	1976	1977	1978
Grass roots lobbying expenditures linked to defense issues and DoD & NASA sales					

22. What office(s) within the company coordinates Congressional lobbying efforts?

23. What office(s) within the company coordinates Goverment marketing efforts?

24. Political Action Committees.
    a. Does the company have a Political Action Committee(s)? (Please provide name(s) of committee(s) and or corporate employee(s) responsible for it (them).)

    b. When was (were) the committee(s) created?

    c. How much has the committee(s) spent since 1974?

    ($000)

	1974	1975	1976	1977	1978
Committee expenditures					

25. Has the company disclosed to the Securities and Exchange Commission any questionable foreign or domestic payments made over the past 10 years? Does the company have a formal policy statement with respect to questionable payments? (Please enclose relevant statements.)

Appendix B

TRADE ASSOCIATIONS—Buying Power

_____ Aerospace Electrical Society
_____ Aerospace Industries Association of America
_____ Air Force Association
_____ American Defense Preparedness Association
_____ American Institute of Aeronautics and Astronautics
_____ American League for International Security Assistance
_____ American Security Council
_____ Armed Forces Communications and Electronics Association
_____ Army Aviation Association of America
_____ Association of Old Crows
_____ Association of the US Army
_____ Electronic Industries Association
_____ Laser Institute of America
_____ National Aeronautic Association
_____ National Aerospace Services Association

_____ National Association for Remotely Piloted Vehicles
_____ National Contract Management Association
_____ National Council of Technical Service Industries
_____ National Defense Transportation Association
_____ National Electronic Manufacturers
_____ National Security Industrial Association
_____ National Space Club
_____ Navy League of the US
_____ Shipbuilders Council of America
_____ Society of American Military Engineers
_____ US Naval Institute

BIBLIOGRAPHY

Books

Adamany, David. *Campaign Finance in America.* N. Scituate, Massachusetts: Duxbury Press, 1972.

Adams, Gordon. *The B-1 Bomber: An Analysis of Its Strategic Utility, Cost, Constituency and Economic Impact.* New York: Council on Economic Priorities report, 1976.

Adams, Gordon and Sherri Zann Rosenthal. *The Invisible Hand: Questionable Corporate Payments Overseas.* New York: Council on Economic Priorities, 1976.

Alexander, Herbert. *Financing Politics: Money Elections and Political Reform.* 2nd ed. Washington DC: Congressional Quarterly Press, 1980.

_____. *Money in Politics*, Washington DC: Public Affairs Press, 1972.

Armacost, Michael H. *The Politics of Weapons Innovation: the Thor-Jupiter Controversy.* New York: Columbia University Press, 1969.

Art, Robert J. *The TFX Decision.* Boston: Little Brown and Co., 1968.

Bailey, Stephen. *Congress in the Seventies.* 2nd ed. New York: St. Martin's Press, 1970.

Baran, Paul and Paul M. Sweezey. *Monopoly Capital.* New York: Monthly Review Press, 1968.
Barone, Michael, Grant Ujifusa and Douglas Matthews. *The Almanac of American Politics, 1978.* New York: E.P. Dutton, 1977.
_____. *The Almanac of American Politics, 1980.* New York: E.P. Dutton, 1979.
Bentley, Arthur. *The Process of Government: A Study of Social Pressure.* 2nd ed. Evanston, Illinois: Principia Press of Illinois, 1945.
Bernstein, Marver. *Regulating Business by Independent Commission.* Princeton, New Jersey: Princeton University Press, 1955.
Block, Fred. *The Origins of International Economic Disorder.* California: University of California Press, Ltd., 1977.
The Boston Study Group. *The Price of Defense.* New York: New York Times Books, 1979.
Brownson, Charles B. *Congressional Staff Directory.* Virginia: Congressional Staff Directory, Ltd., 1978, 1979, 1980.
Burt, Richard. *New Weapons Technologies, Debates and Directions,* Adelphi Paper No. 126. London: International Institute for Strategic Studies, 1976.
Cater, Douglass. *Power in Washington.* New York: Random House, 1964.
Cherington, Paul W., and Ralph L. Gillen. *The Business Representative in Washington.* Washington: The Brookings Institution, 1962.
Close, Arthur C. Ed. *Washington Representatives: 1979.* Washington DC: Columbia Books, Inc., 1979.
Collins, John. *U.S.-Soviet Military Balance: Concepts and Capabilities, 1960-1980.* New York: McGraw-Hill, 1980.
Common Cause. *Serving Two Masters, A Common Cause Study of Conflicts of Interest in the Executive Branch.* Washington DC: Common Cause, 1976.
Congressional Quarterly. The Washington Lobby. 3rd ed. Washington DC: The Congressional Quarterly, 1979.
Corporate Data Exchange. *CDE Handbook: Banking and Finance: The Hidden Cost.* New York: Corporate Data Exchange, 1980.
Council on Economic Priorities, "Advertising to the Military," *Economic Priorities Report.* New York: Council on Economic Priorities, Nov./Dec. 1972.
Dahl, Robert. *Who Governs: Democracy and Power in North America.* New Haven: Yale University Press, 1961.
Dexter, Lewis Anthony. *How Organizations Are Represented in Washington.* Indianapolis: Bobbs-Merrill, 1969.
Directory of Corporate Affiliations. Skokie, Illinois: National Register Publishing Co., Inc./Macmillan Inc., 1980.
Eastman, Hope. *Lobbying: A Constitutionally Protected Right.* Washington DC: American Enterprise Institute, 1977.

Edelstein, Michael. *The Economic Impact of Military Spending*. New York: Council on Economic Priorities, 1977.

Fitzgerald, A.E. *The High Priests of Waste*. New York: Norton, 1972.

Flash, Edward S. *Economic Advice and Presidential Leadership*. New York: Columbia University Press, 1965.

Fox, Ronald J. *Arming America: How the U.S. Buys Weapons*. Boston: Harvard Graduate School of Business Administration, 1974.

Freeman, John Lieper. *The Political Process*. Garden City, New York: Doubleday, 1955.

Galbraith, John Kenneth. *How to Control the Military*. New York: The New American Library, 1969.

Gansler, Jacques S. *The Defense Industry*. Cambridge: MIT Press, 1980.

Green, Mark. *The Other Government: The Unseen Power of Washington Lawyers*. New York: Grossman Publisher/Viking, 1975.

Green, Mark and Andrew Buchsbaum. *The Corporate Lobbies: Political Profiles of the Business Roundtable and the Chamber of Commerce*. Washington DC: Public Citizen, 1980.

Hall, Donald R. *Cooperative Lobbying: The Power of Pressure*. Tucson, Arizona: University of Arizona Press, 1969.

Harris, Spencer Phelps, Ed. *The Legal Connection: A Directory of Publicly-Held Corporations and Their Law Firms*. 1st ed. Menlo Park, California: Spencer Phelps Harris, 1979.

Heard, Alexander. *The Costs of Democracy*. Chapel Hill, North Carolina: University of North Carolina Press, 1960.

Herring, Pendleton. *Group Representation before Congress*. Baltimore, Maryland: Johns Hopkins Press, 1929.

Hunter, Floyd. *Community Power Structure*. Chapel Hill, North Carolina: University of North Carolina Press, 1953.

Inside Director: The Directory of Lawyers on the Boards of American Industry. New York: Law Journal Seminars Press, 1979.

Jones, Charles. *Introduction to the Study of Public Policy*. New York: St. Martin's Press, 1970.

Kaufman, Richard F. *The War Profiteers*. Garden City, New York: Doubleday, Anchor Books, 1972.

Kennedy, Tom and Charles E. Simon. *An Examination of Questionable Payments and Practices*. New York: Praeger Special Studies, 1978.

Malbin, Michael J. *Unelected Representatives*. New York: Basic Books Inc., 1980.

McConnell, Grant. *Private Power and American Democracy*. New York: Knopf, Inc., 1967.

McGrath, Phyllis S. *Redefining Corporate-Federal Relations*. New York: The Conference Board, Inc., 1979.

Melman, Seymour. *Pentagon Capitalism*. New York: McGraw-Hill Book Company, 1970.

———. *The Permanent War Economy*. New York: Simon and Schuster, Touchstone Books, 1974.

Milbrath, Lester. *The Washington Lobbyists*. Chicago: Rand-McNally Inc., 1963.

O'Connor, James. *The Fiscal Crisis of the State*. New York: St. Martin's Press, 1973.

Peck, Morton J. and Frederic M. Scherer. *The Weapons Acquisition Process: An Economic Analysis*. Boston: Harvard Graduate School of Business Administration, 1962.

Proxmire, Sen. William. *Report From Wasteland*. New York: Praeger Publishers, 1970.

Reed, Leon S. *Military Maneuvers: An Analysis of the Interchange of Personnel Between Defense Contractors and the Department of Defense*. New York: Council on Economic Priorities, 1975.

Rice, Berkeley. *The C-5A Scandal*. Boston: Houghton Mifflin Co., 1971.

Rourke, Francis. *Bureaucracy, Politics and Public Policy*. Boston: Little Brown, 1969.

Sampson, Anthony. *The Arms Bazaar*. New York: Viking Press, 1977.

Sapolsky, Harvey M. *The Polaris System Development; Bureaucratic and Programmatic Success in Government*. Massachusetts: Harvard University Press, 1972.

Schattschneider, E.E. *The Semi-Sovereign People*. 2nd ed. Hinsdale, Illinois: Dryden Press, 1975.

Standard & Poor's Register of Corporations, Directors and Executives. New York: Standard and Poor's Corp., 1980.

Stekler, Herman O. *The Structure and Performance of the Aerospace Industry*. Berkeley: University of California Press, 1965.

Tri-Association Ad Hoc Committee on IR&D and B&P, *Technical Papers on Independent Research and Development and Bid and Proposal Efforts*. March 1974.

Truman, David. *The Governmental Process: Political Interests and Public Opinion*. New York: Knopf Inc., 1975.

United Nations, Centre for Disarmament. *Economic and Social Consequences of the Arms Race and Military Expenditures, Updated Report of the Secretary-General*. New York: United Nations, 1978.

Yarmolinsky, Adam. *The Military Establishment*. New York: Harper & Row, 1971.

Zeigler, Harmon and Wayne G. Peak. *Interest Groups in American Society*. 2nd ed. Englewood Cliffs, New Jersey: Prentice Hall, 1972.

ARTICLES

"A Financing Loophole Helps Reagan," *Business Week*, 23 June 1980.

"A New High for Pay at the Top," *Business Week*, 14 May 1979.

"A Threat to Crime-Code Reform," *Business Week*, 28 January 1980.

Adams, Gordon. "Disarming the Military Subgovernment," *Harvard Journal on Legislation*, Vol. 14, No. 3, April 1977.

"Aircraft Issues Buried in Stalled Talks," *Aviation Week and Space Technology*, 14 August 1978. p. 22.

Aspin, Les. "Judge Not by Numbers Alone," *The Bulletin of Atomic Scientists*, June 1980.

Auerbach, Joel D. and Rockman, Burt. "Bureaucrats and Clientele Groups: A View from Capital Hill," *American Journal of Political Science*, Vol. 22, No. 4, November 1978.

Bacon, Kenneth H. "The Congressional-Industrial Complex," *The Wall Street Journal*, 14 February 1978.

_____. "Pentagon and Contractors Grow Cautious After Disclosures of Wining and Dining," *The Wall Street Journal*, 8 April 1976.

_____. "Pentagon Studies How Boeing Got Secret Information," *The Wall Street Journal*, 29 February 1979.

"Banks' Influence in Capital Called Strongest of Any Regulated Industry," *The New York Times*, 23 December 1977.

Barron, James. "How Grumman Spends Its Campaign Fund," *The New York Times*, 26 October 1980.

Bennetts, Leslie. "Conservative and Antiabortion Groups Press Attack Against McGovern," *The New York Times*, 2 June 1980.

Berry, John F. "Iran Payoff is Charged to Grumman," *The Washington Post*, 9 February 1979.

Burns, Thomas S. "Inside ITT's Washington Office," *Business and Society Review*, Autumn 1974.

Burt, Richard. "Brown Says Radar-Evading Planes Shift Military Balance Toward U.S.," *The New York Times*, 23 August 1980.

"Business is Learning How to Win in Washington," *Fortune*, 27 March 1978.

Carley, William H. "Grumman Panel Finds Payoffs Continued Despite Board's Policy," *The Wall Street Journal*, 28 February 1979.

"Carter Fund-Raiser Backs 2 Jet Fighters," *The New York Times*, 7 December 1977.

Clymer, Adam. "'Independent' Groups Aim to Give Reagan Financial Edge," *The New York Times*, 23 June 1980.

_____. "Lobbyist Gets Top Political Post in Reagan Presidential Campaign," *The New York Times*, 30 June 1980.

The Common Defense. American Defense Preparedness Association, 15 October 1976.

"Corporate Chiefs Donate to Parties," *The New York Times*, 20 September 1967.

Bibliography   457

Council on Economic Priorities. "Contingency Costs," *Council on Economic Priorities Newsletter*, 30 August 1976.

———. "The Defense Department's Top 100, 1977," *Council on Economic Priorities Newsletter*, August 1977.

———. "Military Maneuvers/Update, 1977," *Council on Economic Priorities Newsletter*, 22 February 1977.

Crittenden, Ann. "Study Finds Corporations in Broader Political Role," *The New York Times*, 31 May 1979.

Dumas, Lloyd. "Economic Conversion, Productive Efficiency and Social Welfare," *Journal of Sociology and Social Welfare*, Vol. IV, No. 3-4, January-March 1977.

Ehrbar, A.F. "United Technologies' Master Plan," *Fortune*, 22 September 1980.

"Effort to Override Cut in F-14 Orders is Urged by Downey," *The New York Times*, 10 January 1978.

Epstein, Edwin M. "Business and Labor Under the Federal Election Campaign Act of 1971," in *Parties, Interest Groups and Campaign Finance Laws*. Ed. Martin A. Malbin. Washington DC: American Enterprise Institute, 1980.

———. "Corporations and Labor Unions in Electoral Politics," *Annals of the American Academy of Political and Social Science*, Vol. 425, May 1976.

———. "The Emergence of Political Action Committees," in *Political Finance*, Ed. Herbert E. Alexander. Beverly Hills: Sage Publications, 1979.

Evans, Roland and Robert Novack, column in *The Washington Post*, 9 January 1981.

Finney, John W. "Aid to Contractor by Currie Reported," *The New York Times*, 15 October 1976.

———. "Furor Over Missile Decision Reflects Pitfalls of Policy-Making Jobs in the Pentagon," *The New York Times*, 5 April 1976.

———. "Rumsfeld Clears Pentagon Aide of Conflict of Interest in Missile Program; Eagleton Charges a 'Whitewash'," *The New York Times*, 9 June 1976.

———. "The Military Industrial Complex Grows More So," *The New York Times*, 11 April 1976.

"For Trade Associations, Politics is the New Focus," *Business Week*, 17 April 1978.

"Directory of the 500 Largest Industrial Corporations," *Fortune*, 5 May 1980.

Gage, Kit and Epstein, Samuel S. "The Federal Advisory Committee System: An Assessment," *Environmental Law Reporter*, Vol. VII, No. 2, February 1977.

Galnoor, Itzhak. "Government Secrecy: Exchanges, Intermediaries and Middlemen," *Public Administration Review*, Vol. 35, No. 1, January 1975.

Gardner, John W. "Forward," in *Campaign Money: Reform and Reality in the States*. Ed. Herbert E. Alexander. New York: The Free Press/Macmillan, 1976.

Garrino, David. "McDonnell Douglas is Said to Have Made More Foreign Payments than Disclosed," *The Wall Street Journal*, 20 July 1980.

Gold, David and Gordon Adams. "The Military Budget, Politics and the American Economy," *URPE Newsletter*. The Union for Radical Political Economists, Vol. 12, No. 4, July/August, 1980.

Goldwasser, Thomas. "The Official Flow to Private Industry," *The New York Times*, 3 April 1977.

Goure, Daniel and Gordon McCormick. "PGM: No Panacea," *Survival* (International Institute for Strategic Studies) Vol. XXII, No. 1, January/February.

Griffin, Richard T. "Taking Account of Henry Crown," *The New York Times*, 12 December 1976.

Harris, A., and Wilson, George C. "Aircraft Contracts Stir Dogfight Here," *The Washington Post*, 5 December 1977.

Hayes, Michael T. "The Semi-Sovereign Pressure Groups: a Critique of Current Theory and an Alternative Typology," *The Journal of Politics*, Vol. 40, 1978.

"History of Partners in Preparedness," *National Defense*, No. 347, March-April 1978.

Holzman, Franklyn D. "Are the Soviets Really Outspending the U.S. on Defense?" *International Security*, Spring 1980.

Horrock, Nicholas M. "Former Grumman Unit is Fined," *The New York Times*, 4 January 1979.

"How the Weapons Lobby Works in Washington," *Business Week*, 12 February 1979, p. 128.

Keller, Bill and Irwin B. Arieff. "As Campaign Costs Skyrocket, Lobbyists Take Growing Role in Washington Fund-Raisers," *Congressional Quarterly*, 17 May 1980.

Kinsley, Michael. "The Conflict of Interest Craze," *Washington Monthly*, November 1978.

Kurth, James R. "The Political Economy of Weapons Procurement: The Follow-On Imperative," *American Economic Review*, Vol. LXII No. 2, May 1972.

Lanouette, William J. "Complex Financing Laws Shape Presidential Campaign Strategies," *National Journal*, 4 August 1979.

Light, Larry. "Surge in Independent Campaign Spending," *Congressional Quarterly*, 14 June 1980.

"Lobbyists Join Forces Against Federal Disclosure Law," *The New York Times*, 15 March 1979.

Malbin, Michael. "The Business PAC Phenomenon: Neither a Mountain Nor a Molehill," *Regulation*, Vol. 3, No. 3, May-June 1979.

Mann, Michael. "Rockwell's B-1 Promotion Blitz," *Business and Society Review*, Fall 1976.

Membrino, John O. "The MX Contract: It Was a Case of Square Shooting," *The Boston Globe*, 17 February 1980.

Merry, Robert W. "Firms' Action Groups are Seen Transforming the Country's Politics," *The Wall Street Journal*, 11 September 1978.

Meyer, Deborah. "Industry's Top Ten Defense Contractors and Their Washington Executives," *Armed Forces Journal International*, June 1980.

_____. "DoD Announces New Top 100 Contractors," *Armed Forces Journal International*, July 1980.

Miller, Judith. "Boeing Charged by SEC," *The New York Times*, 29 July 1978.

Mintz, Morton. "3.2 Million in Election Gifts Laid to Defense Contractors," *The Washington Post*, 10 December 1973.

Moore, John L. "Weapons Builders Aid GOP," *The Washington Post*, 13 October 1974.

"Moynihan Asks Expansion of Plane Lobbying Study," *The New York Times*, 16 February 1978.

"New Chairman for EIA Requirements Committee," *Defense/Space Daily*, 4 January 1980.

"New Ways to Lobby a Recalcitrant Congress," *Business Week*, 3 September 1979, p. 148.

"Options on F-18 Cancellation Weighed," *Aviation Week and Space Technology*, 30 June 1980.

Paine, Christopher and Gordon Adams. "The R&D Slush Fund," *The Nation*, 26 January 1980.

Patterson, Rachelle. "Carter to Decide in 2 Weeks on F-18's Future," *Boston Globe*, 6 December 1977.

Perry, James. "Congress Unlikely to 'Reform' Campaign Finances," *The Wall Street Journal*, 21 December 1978.

_____. "Liberal Incumbents Are Main Target of TV Ads as Political-Action Groups Exploit Court Ruling," *The Wall Street Journal*, 25 January 1980.

Political Practices Report, 19 February 1980.

"Problem of Campaign Funds," *The New York Times*, 19 October 1979.

Rankin, Deborah. "Accounting Ruses Used in Disguising Dubious Payments," *The New York Times*, 27 February 1978.

Rattner, Steven. "Big Industry Gun Aims at the Hill," *The New York Times*, 7 March 1979.

Roberts, Steven V. "Business is Crying Havoc Over New Lobbying Bill," *The New York Times*, 7 May 1978.

_____. "House, 259 to 140, Approves Bill Requiring Disclosure by Lobbyists," *The New York Times*, 27 April 1978.

_____. "House Members Pressing to Curb Special Interest Gifts," *The New York Times*, 26 September 1979.

_____. "House Toughens Bill on Lobby Disclosure," *The New York Times*, 20 April 1978.

Rundquist, Barry S. "On Testing a Military Industrial Complex Theory," *American Politics Quarterly*, Vol. 6, No. 1, January 1978.

Salamon, Lester M. and John J. Siegfried. "Economic Power and Political Influence: The Impact of Industry Structure on Public Policy," *American Political Science Review*, Vol. 71, No. 3, September 1977.

Shabecoff, Philip. "Big Business is On the Offensive," *The New York Times Magazine*, 9 December 1979.

Sims, David. "Spoon-Feeding the Military - How New Weapons Come to Be," in *The Pentagon Watchers*. Ed. Leonard Rodberg and Derek Shearer. Garden City, New York: Doubleday, 1970.

"Stock Appreciation Rights Come Into Their Own," *Business Week*, 15 May 1978.

"Stocks Sweeten Pay At The Top," *Business Week*, 12 May 1980.

"The Swarming Lobbyists," *Time*, 7 August 1978.

Truscott, Lucian K., IV. "Inside the Air Force Association's Annual Bacchanalia," *Rolling Stone*, 26 February 1976.

"U.S. Builds Plane that Foils Radar," *The New York Times*, 21 August 1980.

Weidenbaum, Murray. "Arms and the American Economy: A Domestic Convergence Hypothesis," Papers and Proceedings of the 80th Annual Meeting of the American Economic Association, *American Economic Review*, Vol. LVIII, No. 2, May 1968.

"Why the Corporate Lobbyist is Necessary," *Business Week*, 18 March 1972.

Weinraub, Bernard. "Million-Dollar Drive Aims to Oust 5 Liberal Senators," *The New York Times*, 23 March 1980.

Weisman, Steven R. "Carey Aide Accuses O'Neill on Grumman Cutback," *The New York Times*, 17 February 1978.

Government Documents

U.S. Central Intelligence Agency. *A Dollar Cost Comparison of Soviet and U.S. Defense Activities, 1968-78*, January 1979.

U.S. Congress, Testimony of Sen. William Proxmire. "The Power and Influence of the Professional Military Associations," *The Congressional Record*. 93rd Congress, 2nd Session, 21 February 1974.

U.S. Congress, Joint Committee on Defense Production. *Defense Contractor Entertainment Practices*, 95th Congress, 1st Session, September 1977.

U.S. Congress, Joint Committee on Defense Production. *DoD-Industry Relations: Conflict of Interest and Standards of Conduct*, 94th Congress, 2nd Session, 2-3 February 1976.

U.S. Congress, Joint Committee on Defense Production, Report by the Subcommittee on Investigations. *Conflict of Interest and the Condor Missile Program*, 94th Congress, 2nd Session, September 1976.

U.S. Congress, Joint Economic Committee, Subcommittee on Priorities and Economy in Government of the Joint Economic Committee, L. Fisher. "Senate Procedures for Authorizing Military Research and Development," *Priorities and Efficiency in Federal Research and Development: A Compendium of Papers*, 94th Congress, 2nd Session, 1976.

U.S. Congress, Senate, Committee on Foreign Relations. *U.S. Military Sales to Iran*, A Staff Report to the Subcommittee on Foreign Assistance, 94th Congress, 2d Session, July 1976.

U.S. Congress, Senate, Committee on Governmental Affairs, Subcommittee on Energy, Nuclear Proliferation and Federal Services. *Federal Advisory Committee Index*, December 1978.

U.S. Congress, Senate, Committee on Governmental Affairs, Subcommittee on Reports, Accounting and Management. *Corporate Ownership and Control*, November 1975.

U.S. Congress, Senate, Committee on Governmental Affairs, Subcommittee on Reports, Accounting and Management. *The Accounting Establishment: A Staff Study*, Washington DC, 1976.

U.S. Congress, Senate, Committee on Governmental Affairs, Subcommittee on Reports, Accounting and Management. *Institutional Investors: Common Stock Holdings and Voting Rights*, May 1976.

U.S. Congress, Senate, Committee on Governmental Affairs, Subcommittee on Reports, Accounting and Management. *Federal Advisory Committees*, Index to the Membership of Federal Advisory Committees, 1976 and 1977.

U.S. Congress, Senate, Committee on Governmental Affairs, Subcommittee on Reports, Accounting and Management. *Interlocking Directorates Among the Major U.S. Corporations*, 95th Congress, 2d Session, January 1978.

U.S. Congress, Senate, Committee on Governmental Affairs, Subcommittee on Reports, Accounting and Management. *Voting Rights in Major Corporations*, January 1978.

U.S. Congress, Senate, Committee on Government Operations, Subcommittee on Intergovernmental Relations, Budgeting, Management and Expenditures. *Disclosure of Corporate Ownership*, March 1974.

U.S. Congress, Senate, Committee on Government Operations, Subcommittee on Intergovernmental Relations. Testimony of David Brown, *Hearings on S. 3067, Advisory Committees*, Part 1, 91st Congress, 2nd Session, 6-7 October 1970.

U.S. Congress, Senate, Committee on the Judiciary, Subcomittee on Administrative Practice and Procedure. *Sourcebook on Corporate Image and Corporate Advocacy Advertising*, 95th Congress, 2nd Session, 1978.

U.S. Department of Defense, Air Force Contract Management Division Directorate, Contracting & Acquisition Policy. *Departmental Industrial Reserve Plant Report*, 1979.

U.S. Department of Defense, Air Force Scientific Advisory Board Headquarters. *1975 Report of Closed Meetings Under Section 10(d) of the Federal Advisory Committee Act*, 1975.

U.S. Department of Defense, Army Production Readiness Office, Office of Development Research and Engineering in the Material Command. *Departmental Industrial Reserve Plant Report*, 1979.

U.S. Department of Defense, Defense Contract Audit Agency. *Audit Report on Review of Washington D.C. Office Operations, The Boeing Company, Seattle, Washington, Audit Report 7381-99-6-0417*, 16 March 1976 (preliminary). Final version 12 July 1977.

U.S. Department of Defense, Defense Contract Audit Agency. *Audit Report on Review of Washington, D.C. Office Operations, Collins Radio Group, (CRG), A Division of the Electronics Operation, Rockwell International Corporation, Richardson, Texas, for Fiscal Years 1973, 1974 and 1975, Audit Report 1161-05-6-0371*, 26 April 1976.

U.S. Department of Defense, Defense Contract Audit Agency. *Audit Report on Review of Washington Office, Grumman Aerospace Corporation, Bethpage, New York, Audit Report 2441-19-T-0450*, 18 August 1976 (preliminary). Final version 21 September 1977.

U.S. Department of Defense, Defense Contract Audit Agency. *Audit Report on Review of Contractor's Washington, DC Area Offices, Lockheed Aircraft Corporation, Burbank California, Audit Report 4601-99-6-0159*, 5 May 1976 (preliminary). Final version 9 September 1977.

U.S. Department of Defense, Defense Contract Audit Agency. *Audit Review of the Operation of the Washington D.C. Office of the General Dynamics Corporation, St. Louis, Missouri, Audit Report 7241-99-6-0169*, 31 March 1976.

U.S. Department of Defense, Defense Contract Audit Agency. *Audit Review of Washington, DC Office Operations and Other Expenses, Rockwell International Corporation, Pittsburgh, Pennsylvania, Audit Report 3191-99-6-0318*, 6 April 1976 (preliminary). Final version 19 August 1977.

U.S. Department of Defense. *Foreign Military Sales, Top 25 Companies and Their Subsidiaries Ranked According to Net Value of Military Prime Contract Awards*, Fiscal Years 1970-79.

U.S. Department of Defense. *Geographic Distribution of Subcontract Awards*, Washington Headquarters Services, Directorate for Information Operations and Reports, 1980.

U.S. Department of Defense, Naval Material Command Industrial Resources Detachment. *Departmental Industrial Plant Reserve Report*, Philadelphia, Pennsylvania, 1979.

U.S. Department of Defense, Washington Headquarters Services, Directorate for Information Operations and Reports. *100 Companies Receiving the Largest Dollar Volume of Military Prime Contract Awards.* Issued annually, fiscal years 1970-79.

U.S. Department of Defense, Washington Headquarters Service, Directorate for Information Operations and Reports. *500 Contractors Receiving the Largest Dollar Volume of Military Prime Contract Awards for RDT&E.* Issued annually, fiscal years 1970-79.

U.S. Department of Defense, Directive 5500.7. *Standards of Conduct*, 8 August 1967.

U.S. Department of Defense and Office of Management and Budget. *Aircraft Industry Capacity Study*, January 1977.

U.S. Federal Election Commission. *Committee Index of Disclosure Document (C)*, 1977-78; 1979-80.

U.S. Federal Election Commission. *Committee Index of Candidates Supported (D)*, 1977-78; 1979-80.

U.S. Federal Election Commission. *FEC Reports on Financial Activity, 1977-78. Final Report, Party and Non-Party Political Committees*, Vol. IV - Non-party detailed tables, (non-connected organizations, trade/membership/health, cooperative, corporations without stock), April 1980.

U.S. General Services Administration. *Employee Standards of Conduct: Improvements Needed in the Army and Air Force Exchange Service and the Navy Resale Systems Office*, FPCD-79-15, 24 April 1979.

U.S. General Services Administration. *Federal Advisory Committees: Eighth Annual Report to the President*, March 1980.

U.S. NASA. *Annual Procurement Report*, Issued annually, fiscal years 1970-79.

U.S. NASA. Personnel Analysis and Planning Office. *Report of NASA and Aerospace Related Employment*, Compiled annually, 1970-79.

U.S. Office of Secretary of Defense, Manpower Division. *Report of DoD and Defense Related Employment as Required by Public Law 91-121.* Compiled annually, 1970-79.

Other

Adams, Gordon. "State-Industry Relations in Advanced Capitalism: The American Aviation Industry, 1916-1926," Paper delivered at the Annual Meeting of the American Political Science Association, Chicago, Illinois, September 1976.

Burch, Philip. "An Analysis of the Business Roundtable," unpublished manuscript, New Brunswick, New Jersey: Rutgers University, 1978.

The Business Council, 1979. Washington, DC: The Business Council, 1979.

Charter of the Defense Science Board. Washington, DC.

CODSIA Organizations and Functions. Washington, DC: Council of Defense and Space Industry Associations, 1977.

Correspondence to CEP from Weyman B. Jones, Vice President for Public Affairs, Grumman Corporation, 13 October 1980.

Epstein, Edwin M. "Business Corporations and Labor Unions in the American Electoral Process: A Policy Analysis of Public Regulation; The Rise of Political Action Committees," Colloquium Paper, Woodrow Wilson Center, Washington, DC, 15 June 1978.

Report of the Special Review Committee of the Board of Directors of Lockheed Aircraft Corporation, 16 May 1977.

United Nations Centre for Disarmament, Research reports commissioned by United Nations Group of Governmental Experts on the relation between disarmament and development, submitted to the UN Secretariat, 1980.

T4-AAN-730

MADE
FOR
LOVE

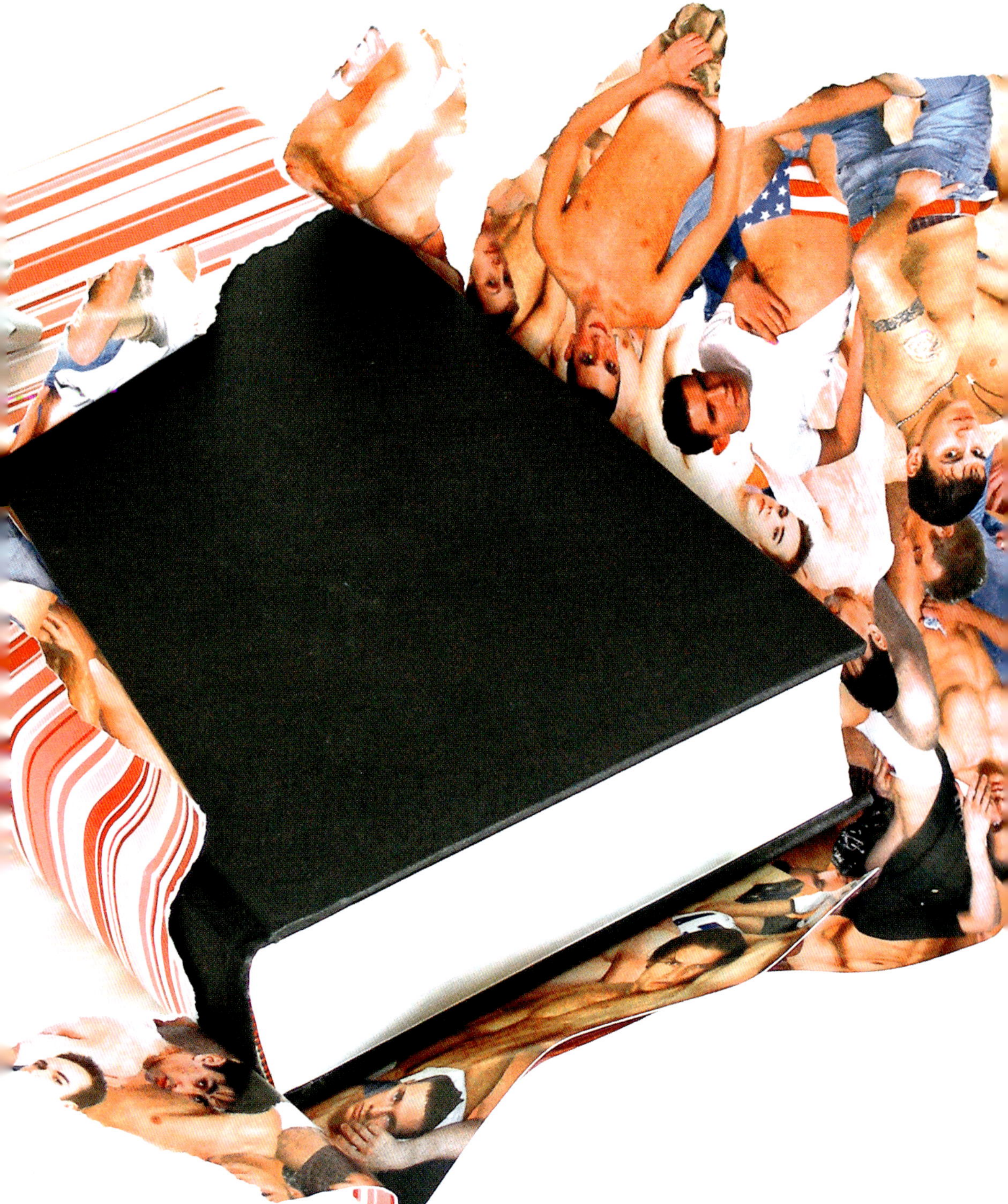

MADE FOR LOVE

AMÉLIE O

stichting
kunstboek

Dear Readers,

I often hear moral crusaders spluttering with holy fervour that society is on the road to ruin, what with rampant nudity and explicit sex. And that the temptations of all that skin, smack dab in the centrefold of daily life can only lead to perversion and addiction. And that this will lead to a breakdown between the sheets, the pornification of our world. Gentle reader, at such times I can only sadly shake my head as I adjust my suspender buckles. What on earth are they talking about? Just because every day I pass a luxury chocolatier, an ice cream parlour, and three pastry shops, and what's more, am confronted with a barrage of advertisements for sweets as I peruse the daily papers, does that mean that I'm suddenly going to start stuffing my face until I burst my bedsprings like a bloated Goldilocks? Come on! Isn't it absurd to imagine that mere overt expressions of sexual phenomena can send an upstanding citizen skidding off the straight and narrow? Anyway, sexuality is part of being human, and if

Beste lezer,

Meermaals hoor ik de heren fatsoenrukkers met schuim op de lippen prediken dat de maatschappij naar de verdoemenis gaat, en wel door het tentoonspreiden van zoveel naakt en seksualiteit. Dat de verzoeking van al dat bloot, opengesmeerd op de bladzijden van het dagelijkse leven, slechts aanleiding kan geven tot perversiteiten en verslavingen. Dat het derhalve de verkeerde kant zal opgaan tussen de lakens, omwille van de pornificatie van de samenleving. Lieve lezer, op die momenten kan ik niet anders dan meewarig het hoofd schudden terwijl ik mijn jarretellenbandjes ajusteer. Waar hebben ze het in godsnaam over? Is het omdat ik elke dag een luxechocolatier, een crèmerie en drie patissiers voorbijwandel en daarenboven in het doorbladeren van mijn dagelijkse kranten en tijdschriften vierentwintig advertenties voor zoetigheden in mijn maag gesplitst krijg dat ik mij plotseling onophoudelijk zal volproppen tot ik moddervet door mijn ledikantje zak? Mais non! Is het niet absurd te denken dat de medemens

it wasn't, there would be no human race in the first place. And furthermore: it sometimes takes nothing but a suggestive turn of phrase or a sudden glimpse of nipple to throw the average brain into a temporary meltdown of varying degrees Centigrade, so the addiction is all in the mind of the beholder, and not in the image or the object arousing lust.

I'll tell you what else. Lucky are those who are born with a dirty mind and a fertile imagination, because for them, hope is alive and kicking. They don't just get a charge out of seeing a lithe body in chunky white briefs, but likewise, passing the grocer's in the morning and glimpsing the firm zucchini gleaming enticingly. They smile secretly in a daydream when they spy a majestic tower rising out of a construction site. They cast their eyes rapturously heavenwards when they light a shiny, smooth Easter candle, or blush unexpectedly when the butcher handles the raw flesh

gederailleerd raakt door de luttele veruiterlijking van seksuele verschijnselen? Seksualiteit is des mensen, zoniet zou er van onze soort niets over blijven. En bovendien: een pikante zinsnede of een plots opduikende tepel kunnen een gemiddeld brein heel even of iets langer op hol doen slaan, maar de verslaving zit nog altijd in de mens, niet in het plaatje of in het object dat lust opwekt.

Ik zal u nog meer zeggen. Fortuinlijk zijn zij die geboren werden met een verdorven geest en een rijke verbeelding, want voor hen is er altijd hoop. Zij worden niet alleen goedgeluimd als zij een lenig lijf in een witte potige onderbroek zien prijken, maar ook als zij 's ochtends langs de groentenboer flaneren en er de stevige courgettes uitnodigend zien blinken. Zij dromen glimlachend weg als zij een majestueuze toren in aanbouw zien. Zij slaan de ogen vreugdevol ten hemel bij het aansteken van een gladde, blinkende

on the scales (for them it's always certified Prime). The curve of the detergent bottle becomes an undulating woman's back, stretching and curling in the hand. Caught in traffic, the gearshift becomes an impatient member, responding with satisfying friction to the slightest touch. They find quiet diversion in the little knob on the sugar bowl lid, while their mother in law hammers on about her stock portfolio. And then there's their barely audible little groan as a disc slips into the laptop drive, and they are in ecstasy when fat flakes of snow splatter their cheeks. They, gentle reader, are happier than most, because every moment when boredom or routine threatens to gain the upper hand is met with the most delicious sensual reveries straight out of their private mental Walhalla, sending them on their merry way through life with a little more spring in their step than other mortals.

So I say to you, moral crusaders, shut your mouths, wash them out with soap and go squawk somewhere else. Don't try to restrict the freedom to imagine, and

paaskaars, of krijgen een bijzondere blos op de wangen wanneer de slager zijn lillend vlees op de weegschaal werpt. Voor hen mag het altijd iets meer zijn. De kromming in de fles afwasmiddel is een glooiende vrouwenrug die zich krols rekt en strekt onder een paar gretige handen. De versnellingspook wordt in de file een trotse fiere eikel die instemmend weerwerk geeft bij de minste beroering. Zij amuseren zich in stilte met het nopje op het deksel van de suikerpot, terwijl hun schoonmoeder het rondborstig over haar beleggingen heeft. Voorts kreunen zij zacht als er een schijfje in hun laptop glijdt en genieten zij met volle teugen als de sneeuw in dikke vlokken op hun wangen spat. Zij, liefste lezer, zijn gelukkiger dan anderen, omdat elk sluipend moment van routine of verveling meteen wordt opgeluisterd door de verrukkelijkste vleselijke gedachten uit het Walhallah van hun hersenpan, waardoor zij doorgaans opgewekter en lankmoediger door het leven stappen dan de rest van de stervelingen.
Heren fatsoenrukkers, hou uw mond, spoel hem met zeep en ga elders snateren. Zet geen beperking op de vrijheid van gedachte, en zeker niet op

certainly not the creative drive. Because even more blessed than those who dream are those who channel their passions into the creation of objects of beauty, be they erect, pliant or invigorating. They are willing to follow their drifting thoughts to create what – you never know – could be the greatest masterpiece of their oeuvre, whether consciously or by accident. Perhaps they were commissioned to design a hand mixer, and got sidetracked in creamy thoughts. In any case, these fruits of their aesthetic fantasy and corrupt genius can bring genuine pleasure to others. Pleasure to look at, in any case. In the absence of direct physical contact, *Made for Love* is visually stimulating in itself. Any time the mood strikes you, day or night, you can find nourishment for your hungry soul and greedy imagination. Uninhibited, unlimited. Take your time.
Free your mind.

Yours,
Amélie O.

de scheppingsdrang. Want zaliger nog dan zij die denken, zijn zij die hun bronstigheid kanaliseren in de schepping van het schone, het erecte, het welwillende of het doortastende. Zij hebben met hun meanderende geest wellicht het meesterwerk uit hun carrière gecreëerd, soms intentioneel, soms per ongeluk. Misschien hadden zij de opdracht om een staafmixer te ontwerpen en kwamen zij op andere vochtige gedachten. Hoe dan ook: de vrucht van hun esthetische verbeelding en van hun gewiekste verdorvenheid is in staat om anderen onvervalst plezier te verschaffen. Genot om naar te kijken. Bij gebrek aan onmiddellijke streling van het vlees, is *Made for Love* tenminste een streling voor het oog. U kunt er elk moment van de dag en van de nacht uw hunkerende ziel en uw broeierige geest aan laven. Zonder gêne, uitgebreid en schaamteloos.

Uw
Amélie O.

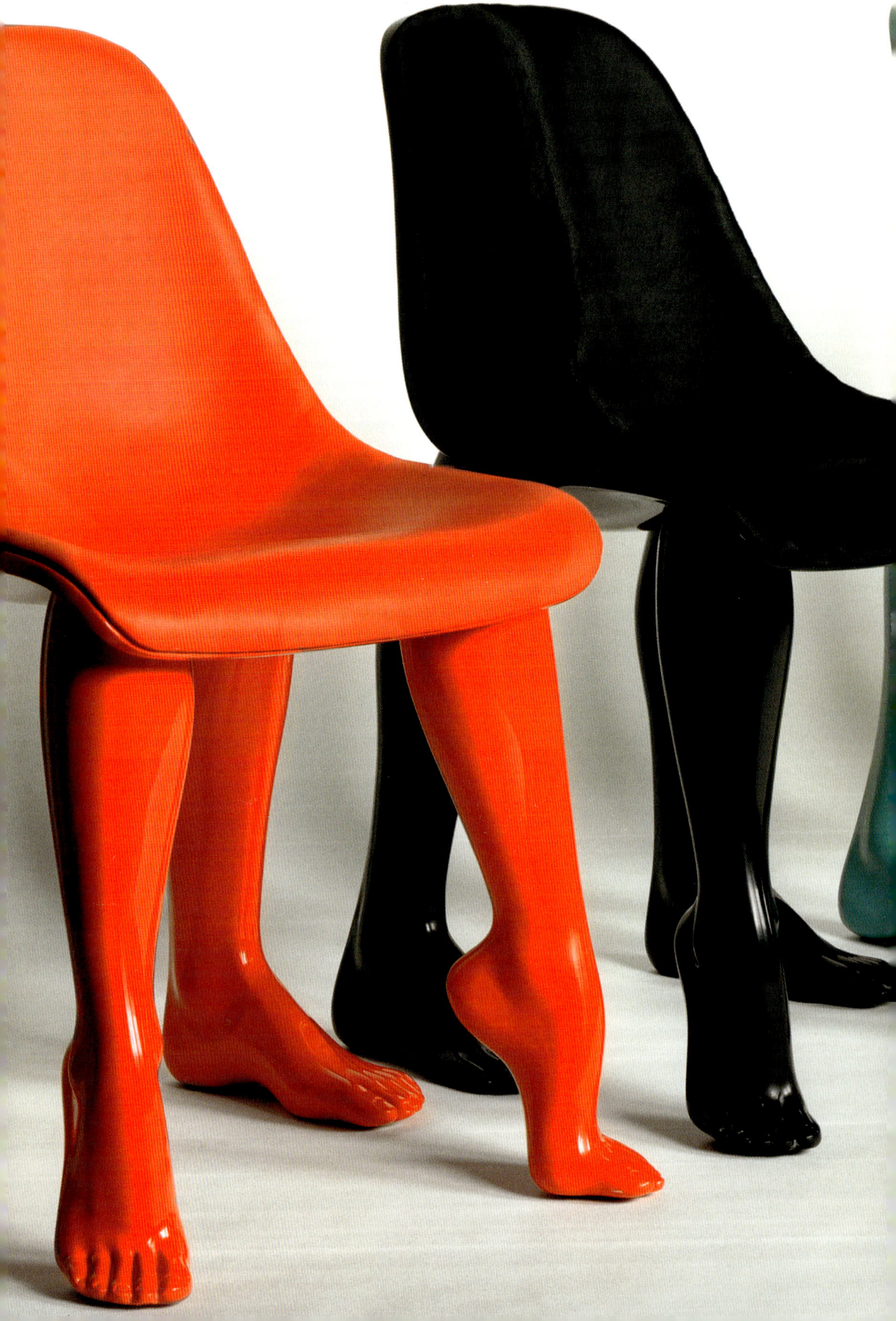

PERSPECTIVE CHAIR | 2008
by Domeau & Pérès (FR) and Pharrel Williams (US)

Naughty chair, the seat supported by feet in a position that needs no further explanation. Body and feet in tinted resin, seat cover in leather.
www.domeauperes.com

HIM & HER | 2008
By Fabio Novembre (IT)

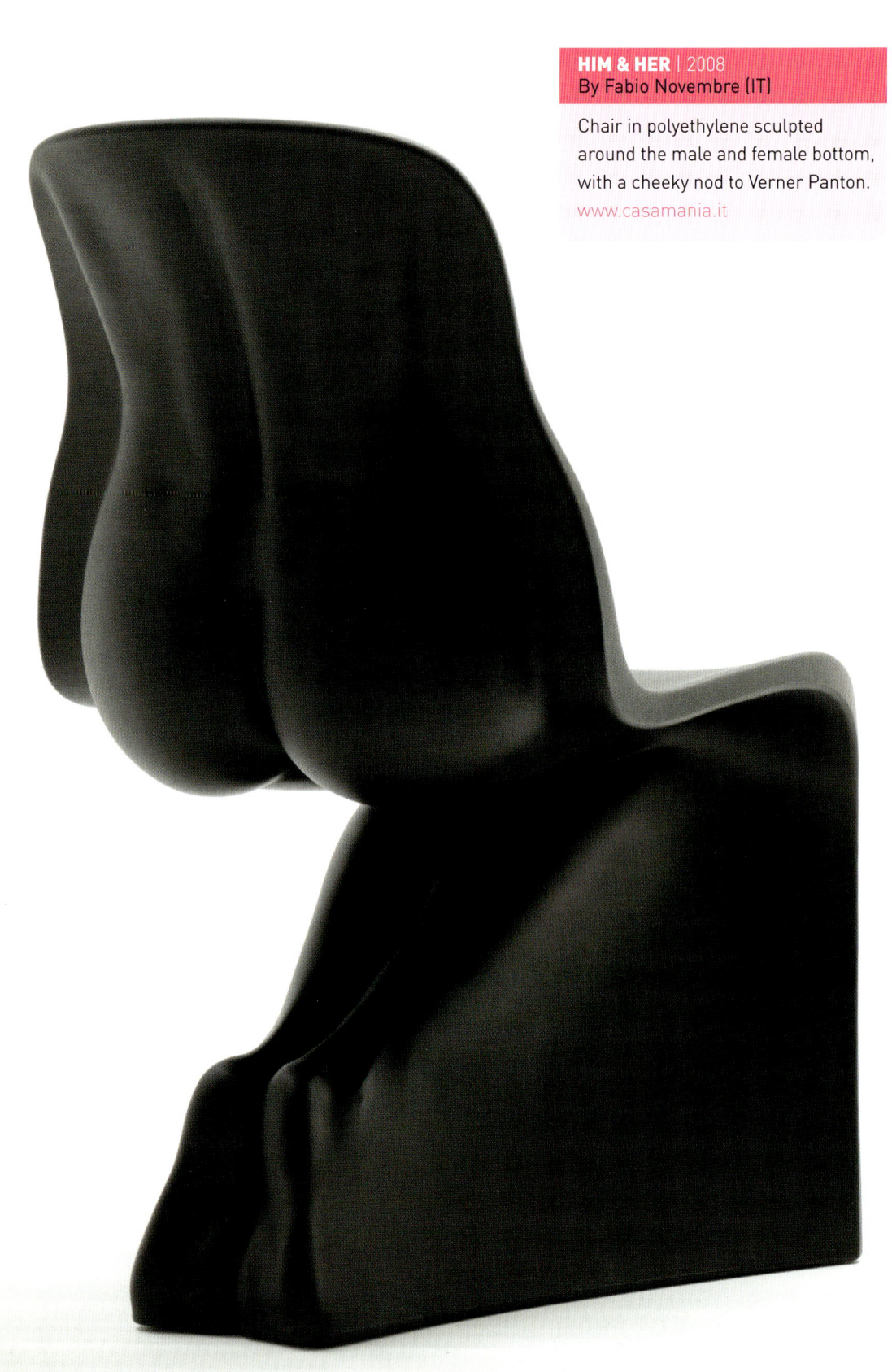

Chair in polyethylene sculpted around the male and female bottom, with a cheeky nod to Verner Panton.
www.casamania.it

A FIRM, COMPACT ASS

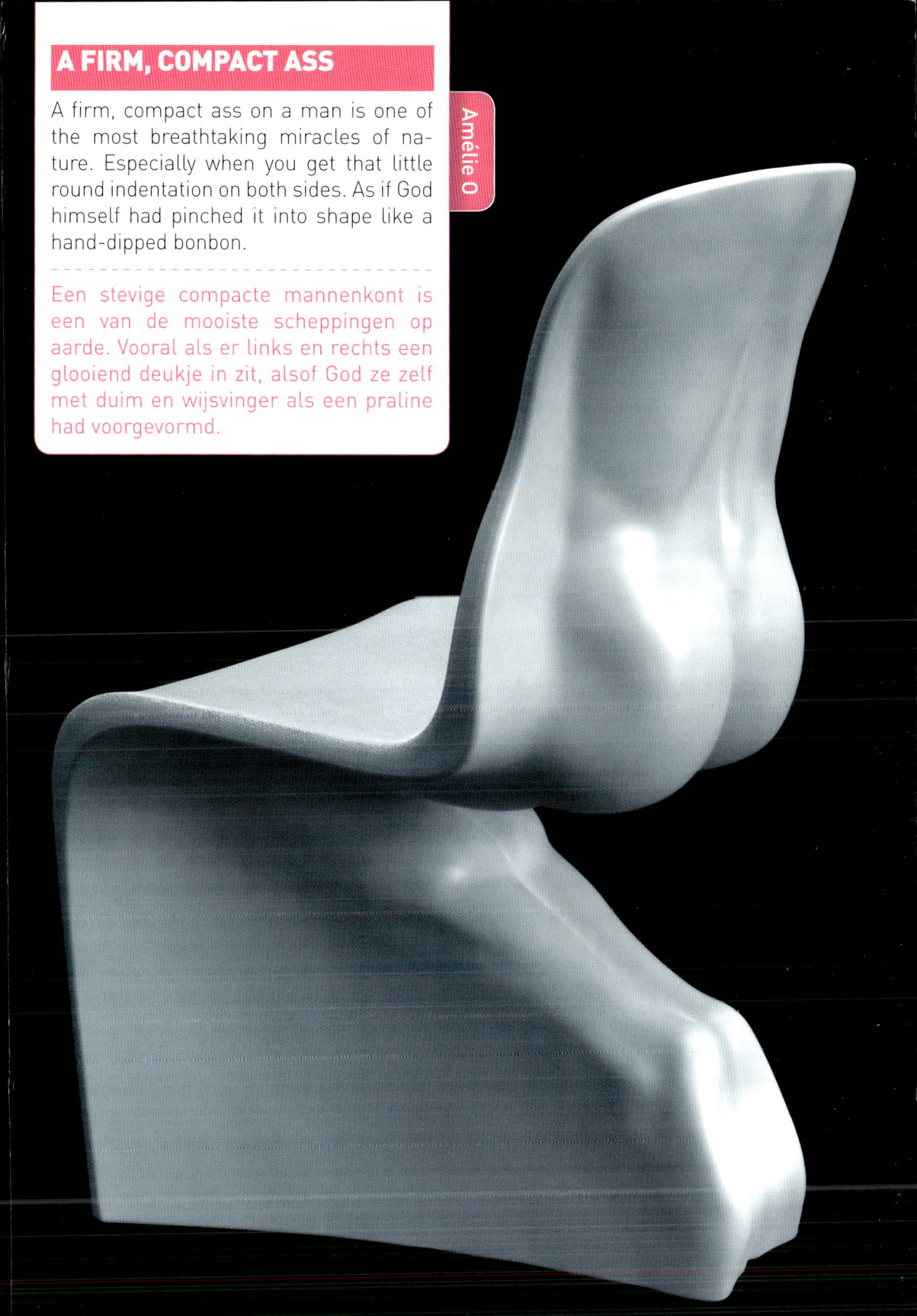

A firm, compact ass on a man is one of the most breathtaking miracles of nature. Especially when you get that little round indentation on both sides. As if God himself had pinched it into shape like a hand-dipped bonbon.

Een stevige compacte mannenkont is een van de mooiste scheppingen op aarde. Vooral als er links en rechts een glooiend deukje in zit, alsof God ze zelf met duim en wijsvinger als een praline had voorgevormd.

Amélie 0

MAID CHAIR | 2008
By Nika Zupanc (SI)

Sexy chair following the sensual curves of the ideal hourglass figure. If you don't have it, at least you can sit on it.
www.nikazupanc.com

SEXY RELAXY | 2004
By Richard Hutten (NL)

Hutten's Sexy Relaxy of 2000, in a moulded LDPE version, with integrated light. Inspired by the film Basic Instinct.
www.richardhutten.nl

CUL IS COOL | 2007
By Ramon Ubeda &
Otto Canalda (ES)

A seat of expanded polypropylene in the form of shapely buttocks.
www.abrproduccion.com

LIBERTINE | 2007
By Peter Jakubik (SK)

Perspex mirror wreathed with wriggling human limbs.
www.comunistar.com

MANOMORTA | 2008
By Enzo Berti (IT)

Handy seating support.
www.bross-italy.com

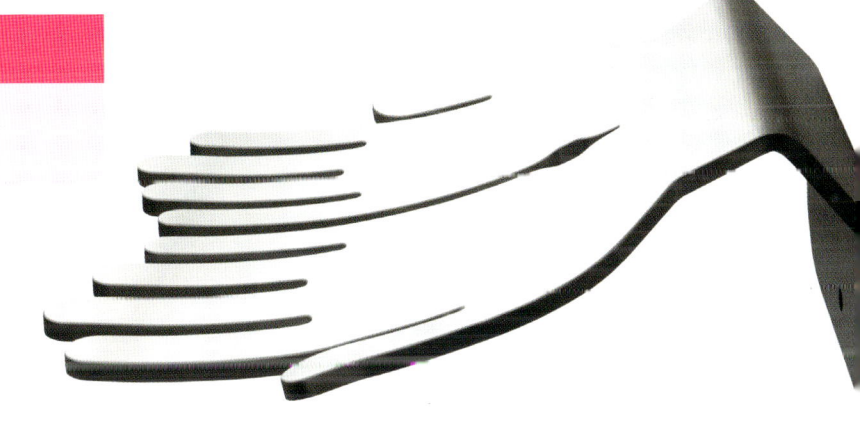

VEUVE CLICQUOT LOVESEAT | 2006
By Karim Rashid (EG)

Opposite facing chairs joined in the centre by a chrome-plated pedestal with an ice bucket. A most intimate place to share your bubbly.
www.veuve-clicquot.com, www.karimrashid.com

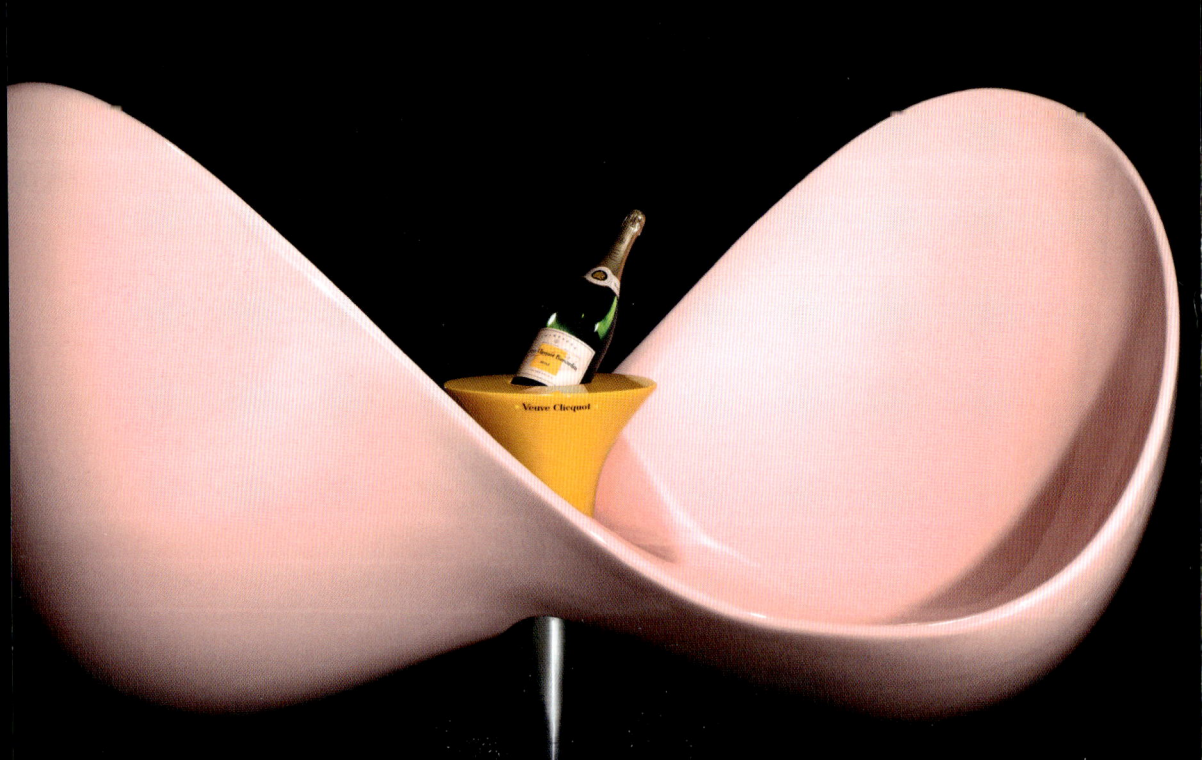

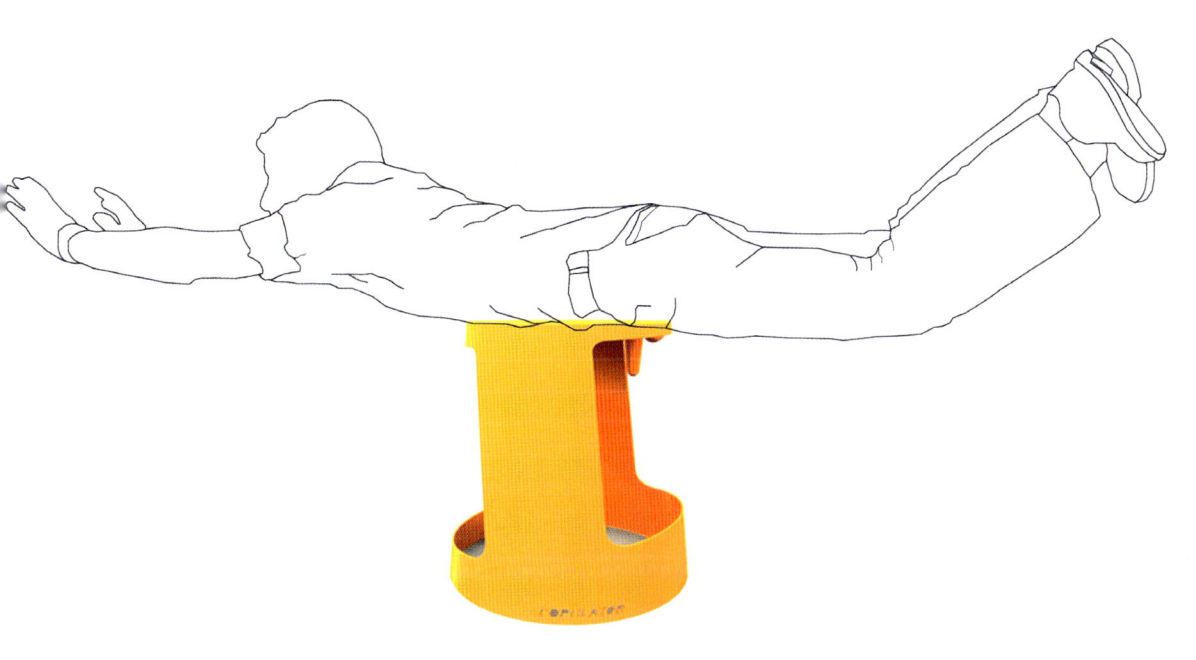

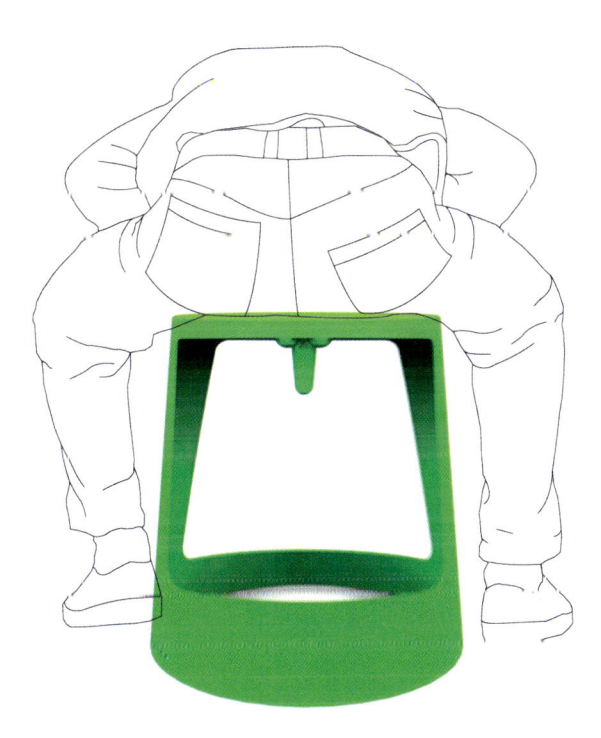

COPULATOR STOOL | 2005
By Agustin Otegui Saiz (MX)

Polypropylene stools. If you leave them stacked long enough, you will end up with a whole bunch of little new ones.

www.agustin-oteguy.com

LOVE | 2008
By Sandro Santantonio (IT)

For the true romantic: a heart-shaped seat. Reinforced fibreglass, with a padding of polyurethane.
www.giovannetticollezioni.it

BOCCA DARK LADY | 2008
By Studio 65 (IT)

Funky limited edition, of the iconic tribute to Salvador Dali (1971), with piercing. Polyurethane covered in elasticized fabric. Dimensions: 212 x 85 cm.
www.gufram.com

MUM | 2007
By Simone Micheli (IT)

Comfortable pouf that succeeds in being both sensual and maternal. Filled with polystyrene micro-balls and feathers and topped with a silicone nipple. Or is it a dildo? Dimensions: Ø130 x H75 cm.
www.adrenalina.it

DIVINA | 2008
By Fabio Novembre (IT)

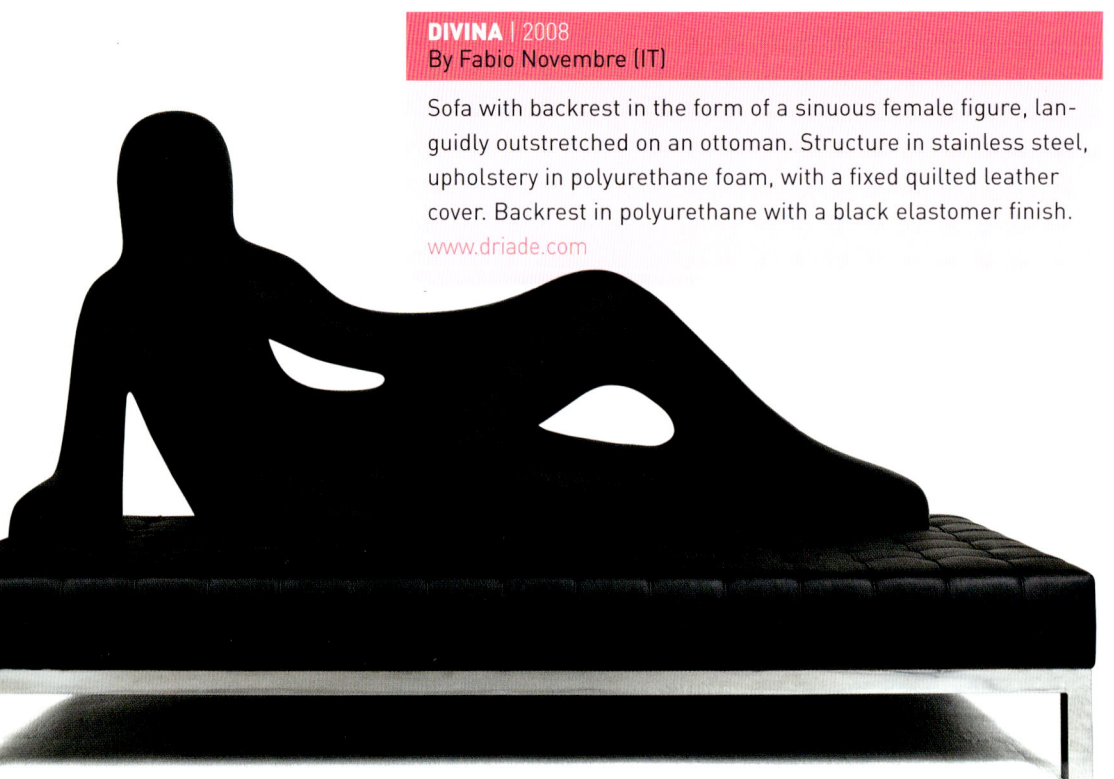

Sofa with backrest in the form of a sinuous female figure, languidly outstretched on an ottoman. Structure in stainless steel, upholstery in polyurethane foam, with a fixed quilted leather cover. Backrest in polyurethane with a black elastomer finish.
www.driade.com

DICKIE | 2005
By Anthony Kleinepier (NL)

Let yourself nod off in the comfortable embrace of a giant male member. Polypropylene with Styrofoam filling. Dimensions: 120 x 110 x 105 cm.
www.moooi.nl

LOUIS KISSING BENCH | 2008
By John Reeves (GB)

Zinc bench, with legs reminiscent of a graceful ballerina rising en pointe, hard-edged external lines juxtaposed with feminine, soft inner curves.
www.reevesd.com

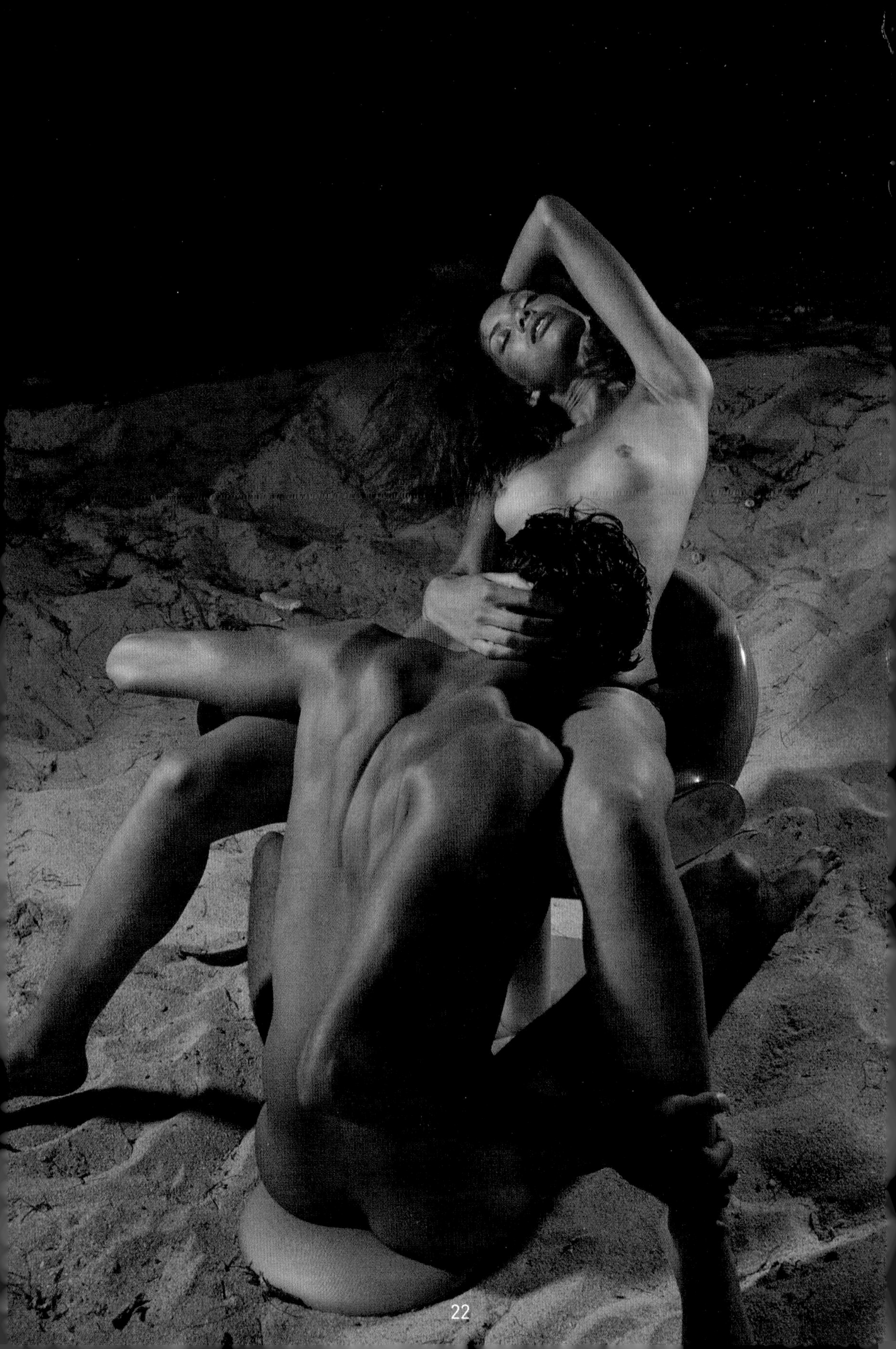

SERIAL ORAL STIMULATION

It is completely beyond me why people will insist on trying to give one another synchronous oral satisfaction. How can one lose oneself in rapture at the epicentre of one's being at the same time as worrying about concentrating on slobbering just-so over one's partner's respective parts? And manage to do a halfway decent job of it? Serial oral stimulation is far more effective, certainly if the throbbing genitalia in question can be presented as an amuse-bouche in a comfortably upholstered, purpose-built chair.

Het is nog steeds de vraag waarom mensen het in hun hoofd halen om elkaar gelijktijdig oraal te willen plezieren. Hoe kan men zich ooit laten gaan in de algehele beroering van het eigen epicentrum als men zich moet concentreren op het aflebberen van de andere? Met een beetje finesse dan toch? Seriele orale activiteiten brengen veel meer schot in de zaak, zeker wanneer het hunkerende geslacht als een amuse-bouche aangeboden wordt op een comfortabel zeteltje.

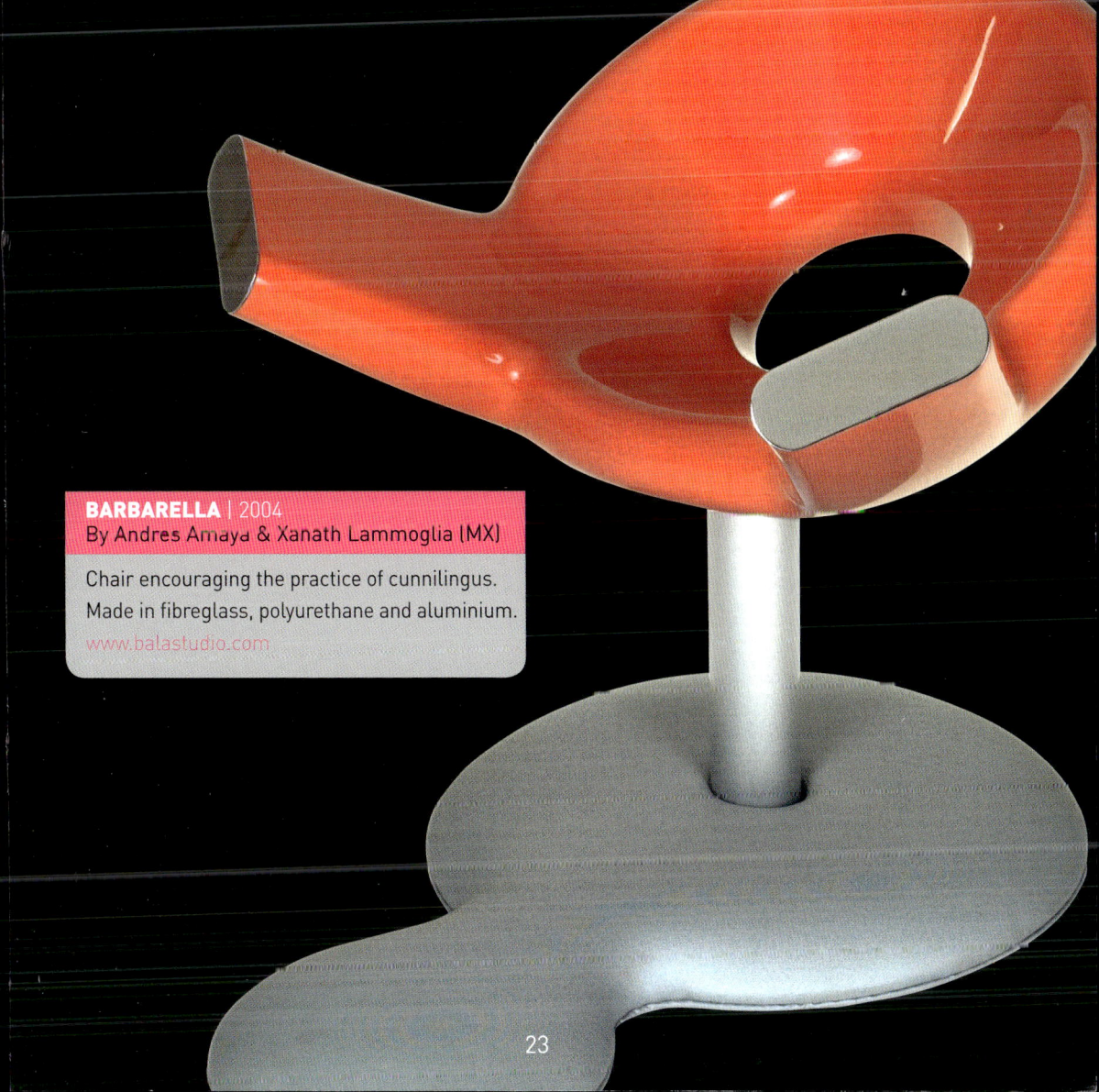

Amélie O

BARBARELLA | 2004
By Andres Amaya & Xanath Lammoglia (MX)

Chair encouraging the practice of cunnilingus. Made in fibreglass, polyurethane and aluminium.
www.balastudio.com

KARIMSUTRA | 2004
By Karim Rashid (EG)

Interactive sex furniture, allowing for a variety of sexual positions, for the Museum of Sex in New York.
www.karimrashid.com

MONTAO | 2004
By Andres Amaya & Xanath Lammoglia (MX)

A change from the missionary position: erotic chair in fibreglass and polyurethane, inspired by a beetle.
www.balastudio.com

ADELA | 2008
By Andres Amaya &
Xanath Lammoglia (MX)

Another alternative for the missionary position: erotic chair in fibreglass and polyurethane.
www.balastudio.com

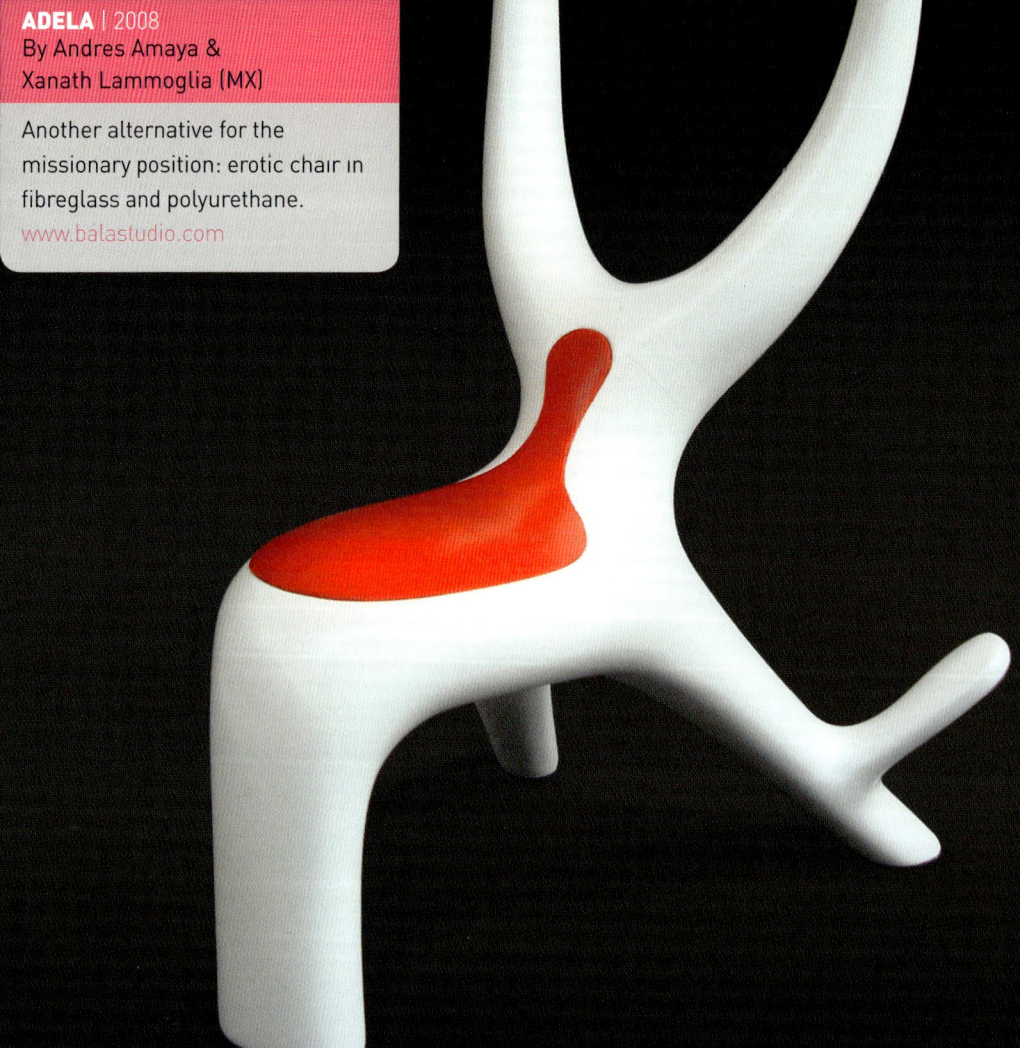

BEDS ARE BORING

A comfy mattress is the nemesis of good sex, because after a while, every act is doomed to devolve into a monotonous daily, er, grind. Beds are boring. The romp on the floor is probably preferable to the standing engagement, though not without hazards of its own. A heedless hump on a carpet that turns out to be made of trendy coconut fibre is bound to end in remorse. An intriguing copulation chair, on the other hand, invitingly positioned in the corner of your candlelit bedroom is sure to be worth a lifetime of enjoyment. That is, as long as you don't end up using it as a handy clothes horse on which to drape your next day's suit for work.

Een gezellige matras is de meest nefaste plek om de liefde te bedrijven omdat seks er na een tijd gedoemd is om in akelige sleur ten onder te gaan. *Le lit, c'est l'ennui total.* De gevloerde wip valt te verkiezen boven de staande, maar ongevallen zijn ook daar onoverkomelijk. Wie zich bij het vossen bijvoorbeeld onverhoeds op een sisallapijl neerwerpt, zal daar zeker spijt van krijgen. De aanschaf van een intrigerend copulatiestoeltje, dat u uitnodigend in een hoek van uw met kaarsen verlichte slaapkamer kunt plaatsen, zal u daarentegen een leven lang plezier bezorgen. Op voorwaarde dat u het niet gebruikt om er uw kostuum, hemd en das voor de volgende dag over te draperen.

Amélie O

BONNIECLYDE | 2005
By Kabiljo Dejana (AT)

Bed made of soft warm pine, bearing no screws or other metal parts and coming with a mallet, to carve both your initials in it. Bearing in mind that, when you engrave something in wood, it changes your attitude and becomes a commitment.

www.kabiljo.com

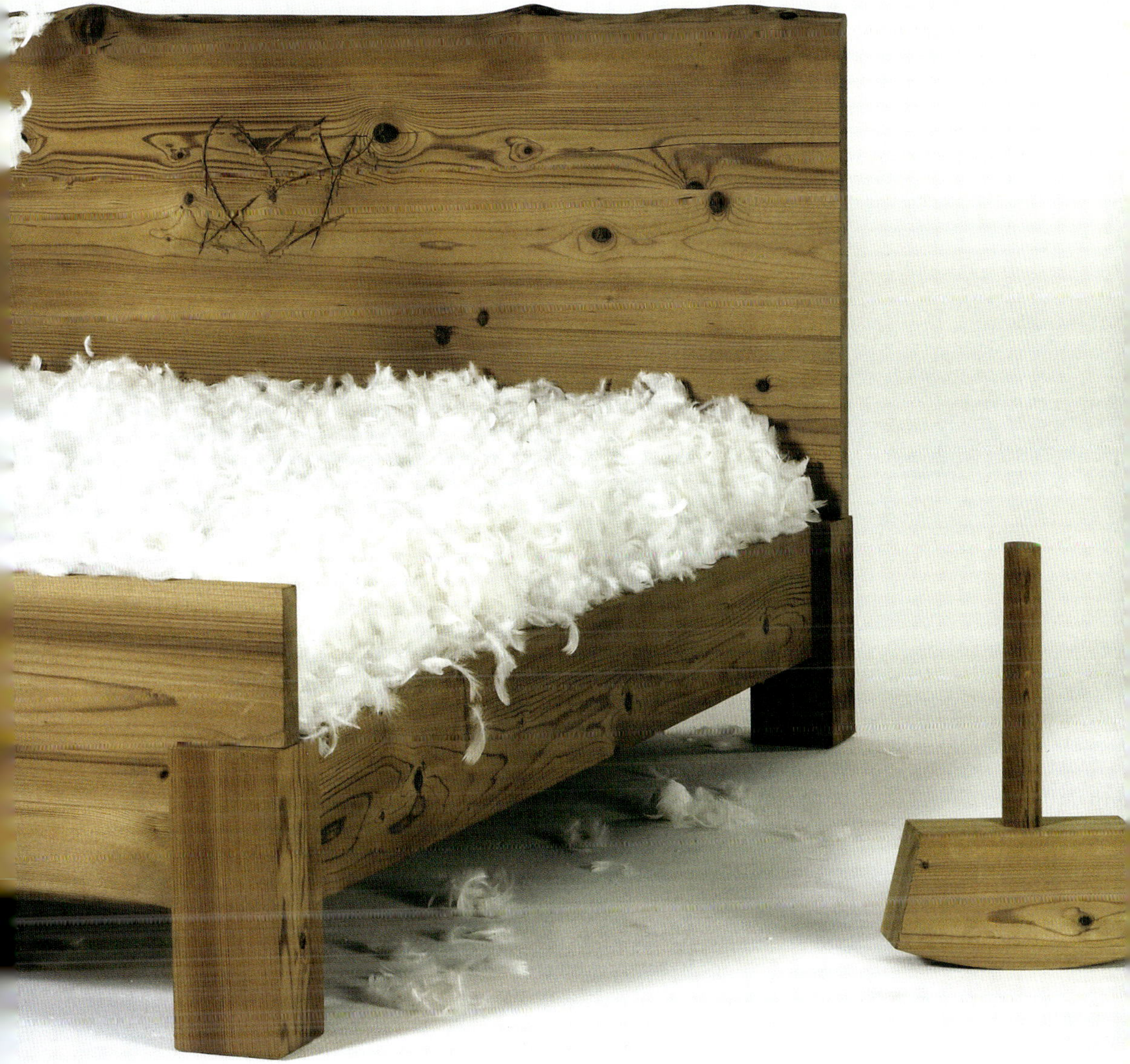

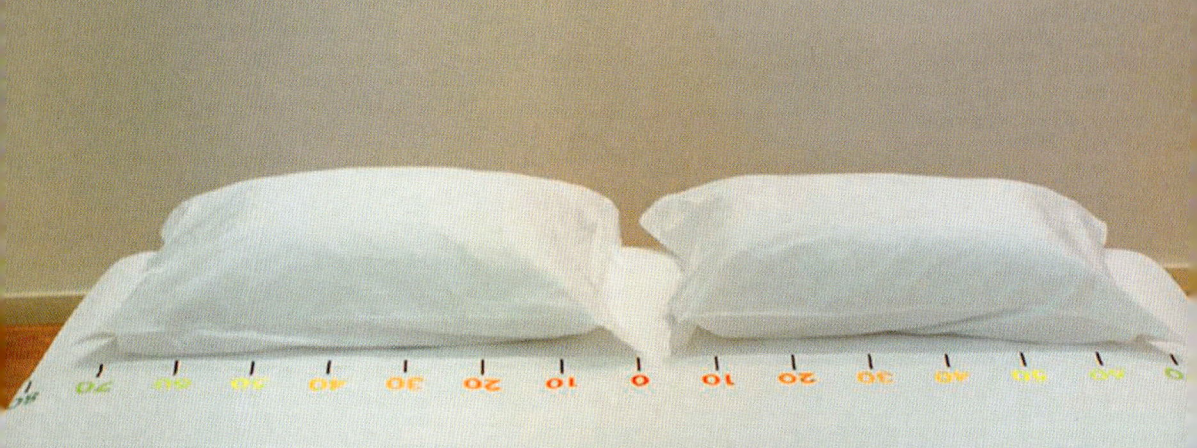

COUPLE | 2002
By Isabel Machado & Filipe Pinto (PT)

Cotton sheet with monitoring system. The numbering rises outwards and from warm to cold colours. Each person knows how much he or she can pull and how far apart the couple rests.
www.experimentadesign.pt

MASCULINE FOIBLES

Amélie O

The notion that men should develop more female emotions has got to be one of the great misconceptions of our age. Just look at all the charming effects: sperm counts are down, and the numbers of desperate alcoholics are up, as are the numbers of macho men aimlessly adrift. Why should we not learn to overlook those old masculine foibles instead? Just roll them off you post-orgasm, pop in your earplugs to block out their snoring and above all, give up expecting the moment to be marked by cuddles and tenderness. Face it, they're just not wired that way.

Dat mannen meer vrouwelijke emoties zouden moeten ontwikkelen, is de grootste misvatting van deze moderne tijden. Voyons, die gedwongen hippe feminisatie werpt nu al behoorlijk wat schone vruchten af: de kwaliteit van het sperma gaat achteruit, het aantal desperate alcoholici neemt toe, evenals het aantal doelloos rondwarende macho's. Laat mannen toch die kleine onhebbelijkheden. Rol ze gewoon van u af na het orgasme, plug uw oordoppen in tegen hun gesnurk en verwacht vooral op dat moment geen tederheid meer. Het zit gewoonweg niet in hun genen.

MAKE LOVE NOT WAR | 2006
By Astrid Schildkopf (DE) and
Olga Bielawska (PL)

Flocked cotton bed linen. There is no room for aggression as long as one is properly equipped.
www.missandlady.de

VESSEL ONE | 2009
By Adam Farlie (NL)

Can an object be a substitute for a person? This bed replaces absent people by their sound. It constantly records the noises made by those who lay on it and when it detects silence, it plays back these 'memories' at random. Made of Corian. Prototype for Exquise Design.
www.exquisedesign.com, www.adamfarlie.com

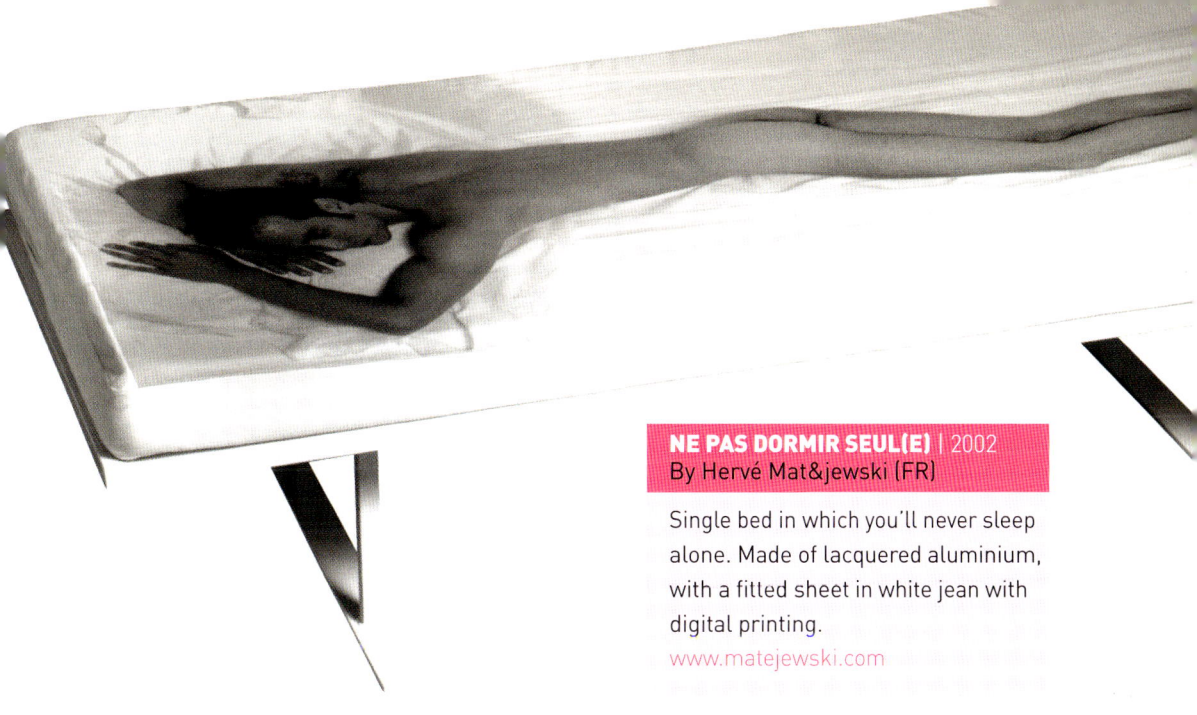

NE PAS DORMIR SEUL(E) | 2002
By Hervé Mat&jewski (FR)

Single bed in which you'll never sleep alone. Made of lacquered aluminium, with a fitted sheet in white jean with digital printing.
www.matejewski.com

PRENDS-MOI DANS TES BRAS | 2003
By Hervé Mat&jewski (FR)

Duvet cover (220 x 200 cm) with digital printing on both sides. Cuddling up becomes a completely new experience.
www.matejewski.com

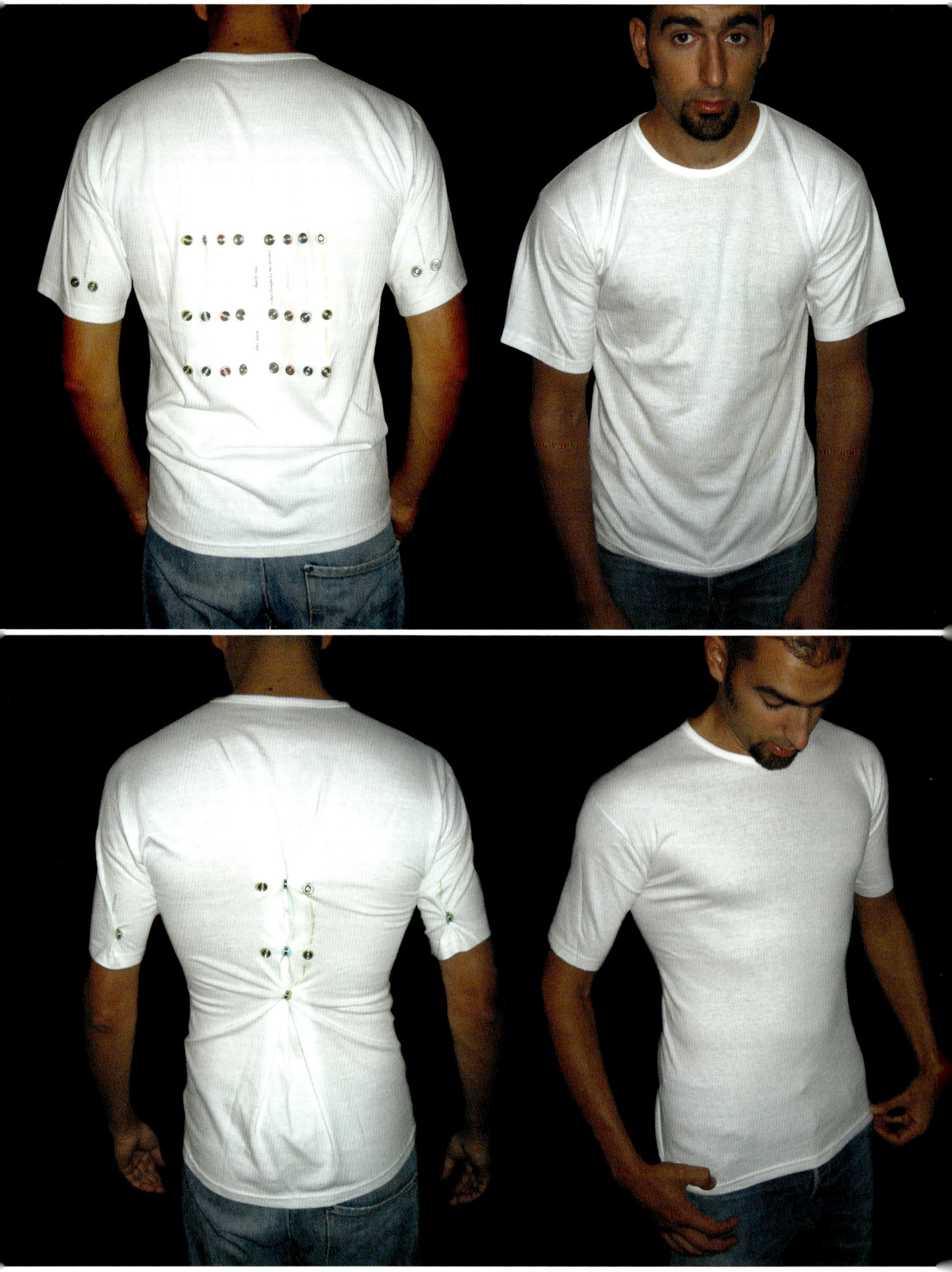

APRETTING | 2003
By Ernest Perera (ES)

Cotton T-shirt, adjustable to how you feel or what you are up to.
www.amordemadre.com

36

1 + 1 | 2003
By Frédérique Daubal (FR)

Pyjamas 'LoveMe Before' and 'LoveMe After', with digital prints. Images are stronger than words.
www.daubal.com

UPSKIRT | 2007
By Peter Jakubik (SK)

Wall hangers with a view, made in wood and plastic.
www.peter-jakubik.com

MAIDSTAND | 2007
By Peter Jakubik (SK)

Fetishist nightstand in MDF with black varnish beech veneering.
www.comunistar.com

BRIEFS | 2007
By Peter Jakubik (SK)

Stool wearing white curly knickers from plastic, inspired by burlesque lingerie.
www.peter-jakubik.com

LEONARDO | 2006
By Olivier Grégoire &
Bertrand Clerc (FR)

Dining table and chairs in Corian, fossilizing a moment of intimacy in a couple. Looking at it, one can still perceive the movements and feelings in the immobility of the furniture.
www.oliviergregoire.com
www.bertrandclerc.com

41

LAPJUICER | 2004
By Theo Humphries & Phil Worthington (GB)

Redesign of a food processor: a barstool with a juice squeezer in the centre of the seat. The juice is collected in a glass under the seat. Perfect for lap dancers who want to treat their spectators to a bit of a squeeze.
www.3eyes.co.uk

PILLORY DINETTE | 2004
By James Piatt (US)

Casual dinner table with holes for head and hands. Ideal for locking in sinners, to be exposed to public scorn and informal meals as punishment. Custom laminate gives it an exaggerated, cartoon like feel.
www.jamespiatt.com

LOLITA LAMP | 2008
By Nika Zupanc (SI)

Table lamp with witty, feminine lampshade.
www.moooi.nl.

VAGINAL MIRROR | 2008
By Christin Johansson (DK), as part of the Danish Crafts exhibition 'Mindcraft'

Mirror in clay, painted with car enamel. A slight modification and it could have accommodated testicles too.
www.danishcrafts.dk

UP YOURS HAND JOB | 2004
by Yve Thelermont &
David Hupton (GB)

Coat hanger with unambiguous message. Resin composite and metal.
www.hiddenart.co.uk

HIS & HERS KEY HOLDER | 2007
By J-Me (UK)

Key holders clearly identifying whose keys are whose. Attach your unique J-me key to your own set of keys and insert it in the lock, to keep it safe until you next need it.
www.j-me.co.uk

MR P – ONE MAN SHY | 2003
By Chaiyut Plypetch (TH)

Plastic lamp, striking a proud, poised and proper attitude, but blushing when you turn it on.
www.propagandaonline.com

LOLA | 2007
By William Brand and
Annet van Egmond (NL)

Hanging lamp in the form of
a lacy black corset.
www.brandvanegmond.nl

SIAMESE LAMP | 1999
By James Piatt (US)

Able lamps, inseparable like
a pair of breasts.
www.jamespiatt.com

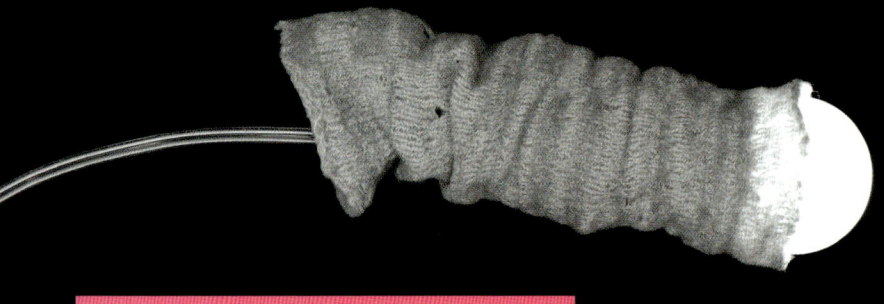

LIGHTSOCK | 2008
By Line Dyrholm (DK)

Cotton knitted sock for protecting small electrical devices. Shapes itself according to its content, hence fits all sorts of equipment. Measurement: 7 x 30 cm.
www.danishcrafts.dk

DREAM | 2005
By Aziz Sariyer (TK)

Table lamp bound to impress male and female visitors alike. Dimensions: Ø16 x H29 cm.
www.derindesign.com

DICK | 2002
By Aziz Sariyer (TK)

Bohemian crystal chandelier in the form of a weighty penis with an impressive length of 150 cm.
www.enterthemothership.nl,
www.rockandroyal.com

HEAVY CALIBRE ARTILLERY

Heavy calibre artillery is hardly as much fun as it's made out to be. When a poor IUD is hanging on for dear life in utero, the overly well-endowed guest is bound to get the thing bent out of shape. Men with large penises rarely take into consideration the proper drilling depth. And a woman whose vocal response is to call out 'harder' has either got a peculiar condition of the cervix or maybe just a brain tumour.

Ferme slagwapens doen soms lang niet zoveel deugd als men zou willen doen geloven. Wanneer er zich ergens diep in de baarmoeder een spiraal schuilhoudt, dan zal de bezoekende partij, indien stevig geschapen, bovendien herhaaldelijk met z'n kop tegen het traliewerk aanlopen. Mannen met een grote penis houden er zelden rekening mee tot welke diepte ze kunnen drillen. Een vrouw die bij penetratie door een exemplaar boven de twintig centimeter nog steeds *'Plus fort!'* schreeuwt, zit wellicht geplaagd met een fluks rekbare baarmoederhalsspier of gewoonweg met een hersentumor.

Amélie 0

50

ERECT1 | 2007
By Ben Oostrum (NL)

Cast iron candleholder in the form of a penis, for lofty candles.
www.boontwerpt.nl

BEDSIDE LAMP | 2009
By Matteo Cibic (IT)

Silicon dildo cunningly incorporated in a lamp. When the dildo is retrieved from the lamp, the light turns red. Ceramic and platinum finish.
www.exquisedesign.com

COQUETTE | 2007
By Peter Jakubik (SK)

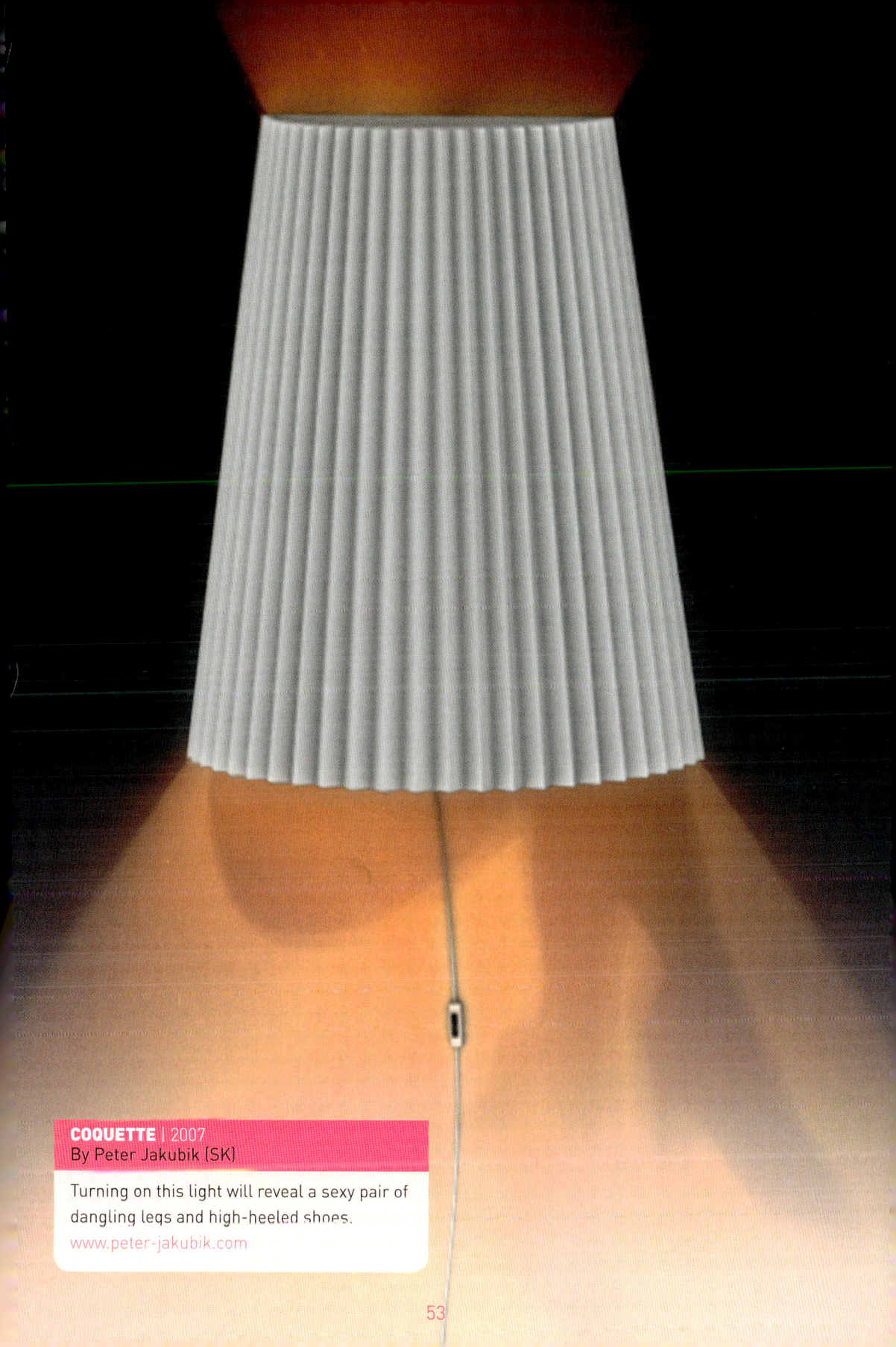

Turning on this light will reveal a sexy pair of dangling legs and high-heeled shoes.
www.peter-jakubik.com

CERAM X | 2003-5
By Pierre Charpin (FR)

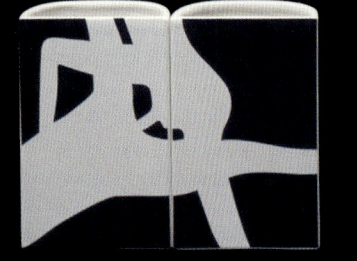

Stackable ceramic boxes, canisters and double vases with lid. Seen from the non-decorated side, they are merely useful objects. Seen from the decorated side, the function becomes secondary and the objects become a source of fantasy and imagination.

www.craft-limoges.org

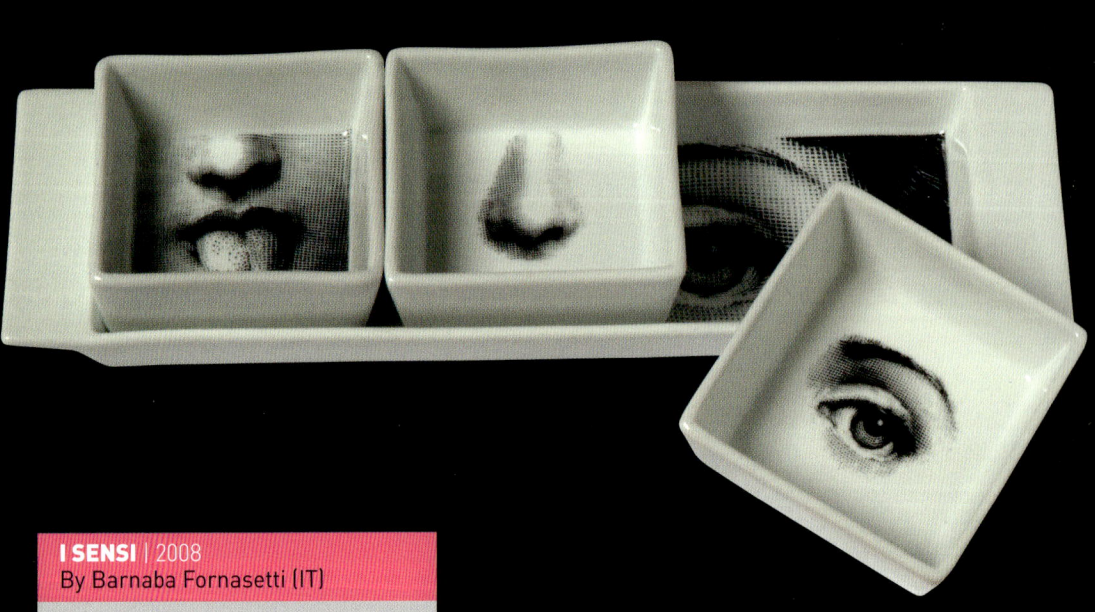

I SENSI | 2008
By Barnaba Fornasetti (IT)

Porcelain appetizer set depicting our senses.

www.fornasetti.com

RECKLESSLY TIGHT JEANS

Amélie O

In the current state of affairs, it has become ever so difficult to assess how hung a guy is. In the glorious heyday of recklessly tight jeans, women assumably had an easier time of it. A sidelong glance across the dance floor was all it took to obtain full disclosure on matters of measurements and for that matter, whether the gentleman 'dressed' left or right. Those were simpler times, unencumbered by awkward attempts to tamper with the packaging in order to surreptitiously size up the merchandise.

Het is in deze moderne tijden zeer moeilijk om van tevoren in te schatten of een man fatsoenlijk geschapen is of niet. In de gloriedagen van de strakke spijkerbroek hadden vrouwen wellicht minder problemen met het keuren van zijn broekinhoud. Men kon van de overkant van de dansvloer onmiddellijk opmaken of hij links droeg of rechts. Er was in die tijd bijgevolg ook minder omstandig zoek- of tastwerk nodig om de afmetingen van zijn marchandise te bepalen.

EMBRIO | 2005
By Olivier Grégoire (FR)

Corian lamp, distractingly remindful of tight swimming trunks.

www.oliviergregoire.com

HORN | 2007-8
By Ingrid Ruegemer (DE)

Crystal champagne flutes.
www.absolute-appetite.com

OFF-CENTRE ERECTION

Good gracious, what on earth is one supposed to do with an off-centre erection? Mount it obliquely? Practise your backhand? Awaken the erogenous potential of your spleen? Admittedly, it's hard to regard with a straight face. A penis that coyly looks away when you try to confront it head on. You're going to have to get out your old geometry textbook to work out this angle.

Hoe moet men in godsnaam met een scheve penis aan de slag? Zijdelings beklimmen? Een rondedans mee wagen? Zich in de milt laten schieten? Het blijft een zielig gezicht, een penis die culpabel wegkijkt als men er een harde confrontatie mee wil aangaan. Alleen als u zich een kwartslag draait, krijgt u nog enig effect.

LIP TEASE TEACUP AND SAUCER | 2008
By Reiko Kaneko (GB/JP)

Teacup of bone China, with 24 carat gold traces of lipstick and a gold tea stain on the saucer.
www.hiddenart.co.uk

BLAUE BLUME TEACUP 'GOLD SHOES' | 2008
By Tina Tsang (GB/SG)

Earthenware teacup with flirty, waving legs instead of the usual ear.
www.hiddenart.co.uk

BLAUE BLUME CAKE STAND 'GOLD SHOES' | 2008
By Tina Tsang (GB/SG)

Earthenware dessert stand with leggy decoration.
www.hiddenart.co.uk

BELLY BUTTON | 2009
By Romain Gnidzaz (FR) &
Marie Lambert (FR)

The belly button as a theme for a curvy, sexy piece of tableware.
www.gnidzaz.net
www.exquisedesign.com

LLADRO RE-CYCLOS: LOVE I (BLOSSOMS), LOVE II (BLOSSOMS) AND LOVE III (BLOSSOMS) | 2006
By Committee (GB)

Re-Cyclos is a reinterpretation by contemporary designers of some of Lladro's classics. These figurines in glazed porcelain pay tribute to the various phases of love. Increasingly covered with delicate flowers, the couples symbolize the evolution of feelings: blinding love, growing intimacy, mature love.
www.lladro.com

COMMUNICATING CUPS | 2006
By Olivier Grégoire & Bertrand Clerc (FR)

Mugs inspired by a children's phone, allowing for extra means of communication at the table.
www.oliviergregoire.com, www.bertrandclerc.com

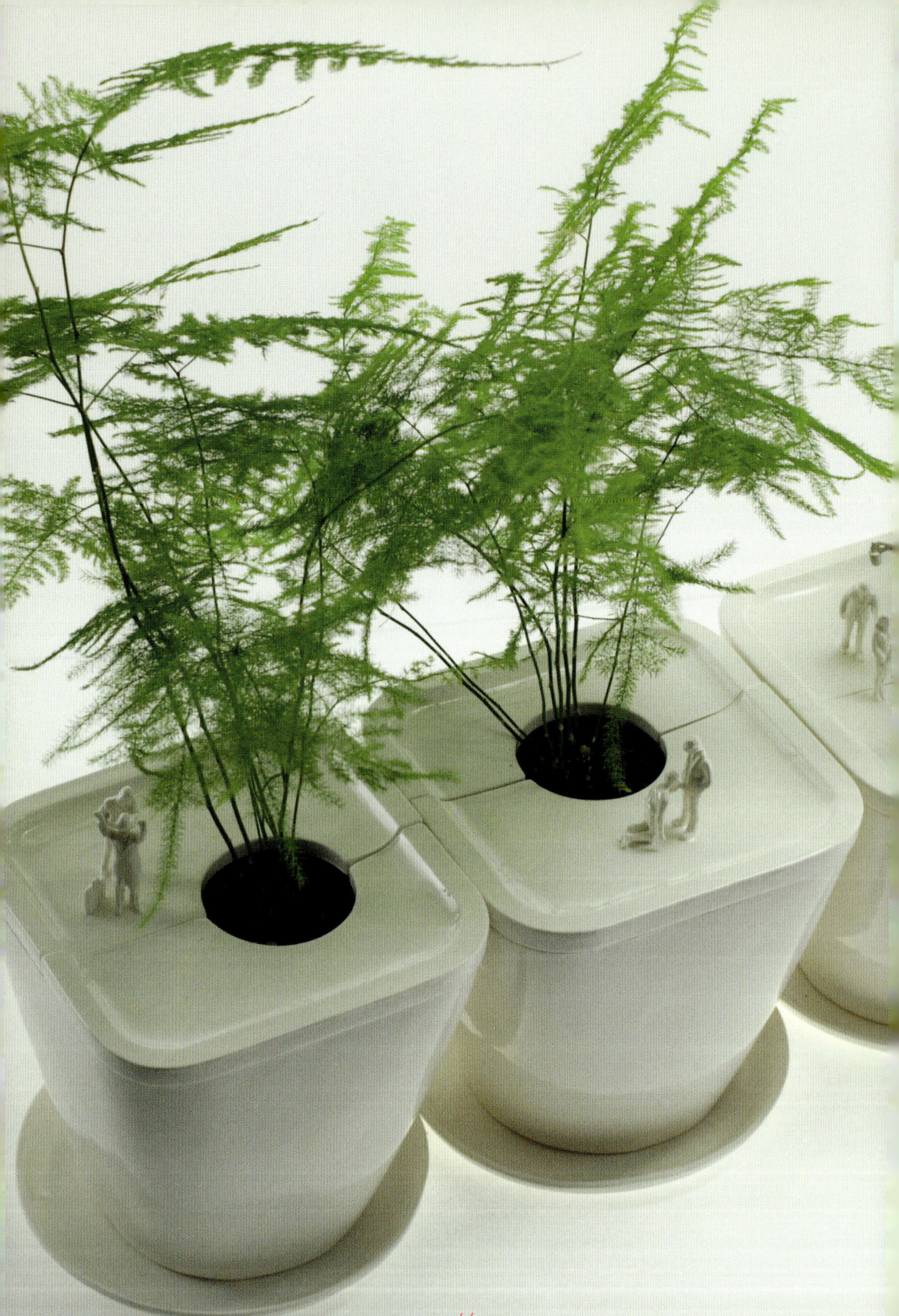

PARK PLANTERS | 2007
By Tristan Zimmerman (GB)

Mischievous plant pots of glazed earthenware ceramic. The Park Planters want to elevate the common household plant to the status of full grown tree, by making it the backdrop for an urban park scene.
www.scienceandsons.com

KISSING SALT AND PEPPER | 1995
By Karim Rashid (EG)

Metal pepper and salt shakers with flat planes at the top and bottom where they seem to melt into one, for Nambe.

www.karimrashid.com

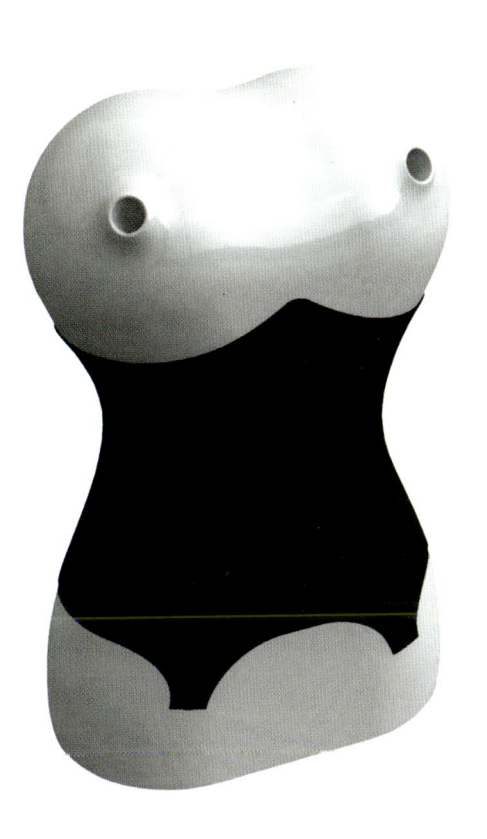

SUGAR BABE | 2007
By Peter Jakubik (SK)

Ceramic sugar dispenser in the form of a buxom female torso.
www.comunistar.com

COOKIE CUTTERS | 2007
By Susanne Burelo (SE)

Hot cutters for teasing appetizers, lustful desserts or lovesick cookies.
www.pipparkakan.se

UN SET PARTOUT | 2007
By Thierry d'Istria (FR)

Dirty minds at breakfast.
www.lateteaucube.com

JUICY BOOBS | 2002
By Dasein (PT)

Double-boobed juicer in white-glazed ceramics, enabling you to squeeze a whole orange in one go.
www.experimentadesign.pt

LEMONSQUEEZER | 2001
By Conor Wilson (GB)

Ceramic lemon squeezer/
lust object
www.conwilson.com

A MAN'S NOSE ...

A man's nose is a far more reliable gauge of the content of his trousers than the size of his feet. Besides, on a date, it's just that little bit easier to get away with staring intently at it. Long, narrow noses may promise a generous length, but alas, little to hold onto. Absurdly small noses are best kept for the strictly utilitarian occasions. Particularly, straight, medium-sized noses with a nice balanced bridge and shapely nostrils offer the best prospects. Men with big, fat bulbous noses generally tend to have a lovely big head on their pricks but the only drawback is that you have to spend the evening gazing at that awful schnozz first.

De neus is bij een man een betrouwbaarder uithangbord voor de inhoud van zijn broek dan zijn schoenmaat. Men kan er bij een afspraakje ook net iets ongegeneerder naar zitten kijken. Lange smalle neuzen garanderen wel een zekere lengte, maar bieden helemaal geen houvast. Bespottelijk kleine neuzen bewaart men beter voor het gewone huishoudelijke werk. Vooral rechte middelmatige neuzen met een mooie egale top en kordate neusvleugels bieden de beste vooruitzichten. Mannen met een grote dikke neustop blijken meestal ook een lekkere dikke eikel op stal te hebben staan. Jammer dat men dan eerst een hele avond moet zitten kijken op een spuuglelijke neus.

Amélie O

SWAN ACT | 2004
By Chaiyut Plypetch (Thai)

Plastic, elegant dust sweeper, that will most gracefully remove dirt with a flick of her ballet skirt.
www.propagandaonline.com

SPIRITOSONA | 2008
By Massimo Giacon (IT)

Bottle stopper in thermoplastic resin, in the form of a female devil temptress with a barrel-shaped torso, looking like a serious case of androgyny. Dimensions: 4 x 3,8 x 12 cm.
www.alessi.com

ROCKET, CUDGEL, CACTUS, PROTECTION | 2007
By Raffaele Iannello (IT)

Squeezer, pepper mill, kitchen paper holder, pot holders and dish brush in silicon, with sleek and sensual forms, suggesting more creative uses for domestic appliances.
www.rafzdesign.com,
www.xxxitchen.com

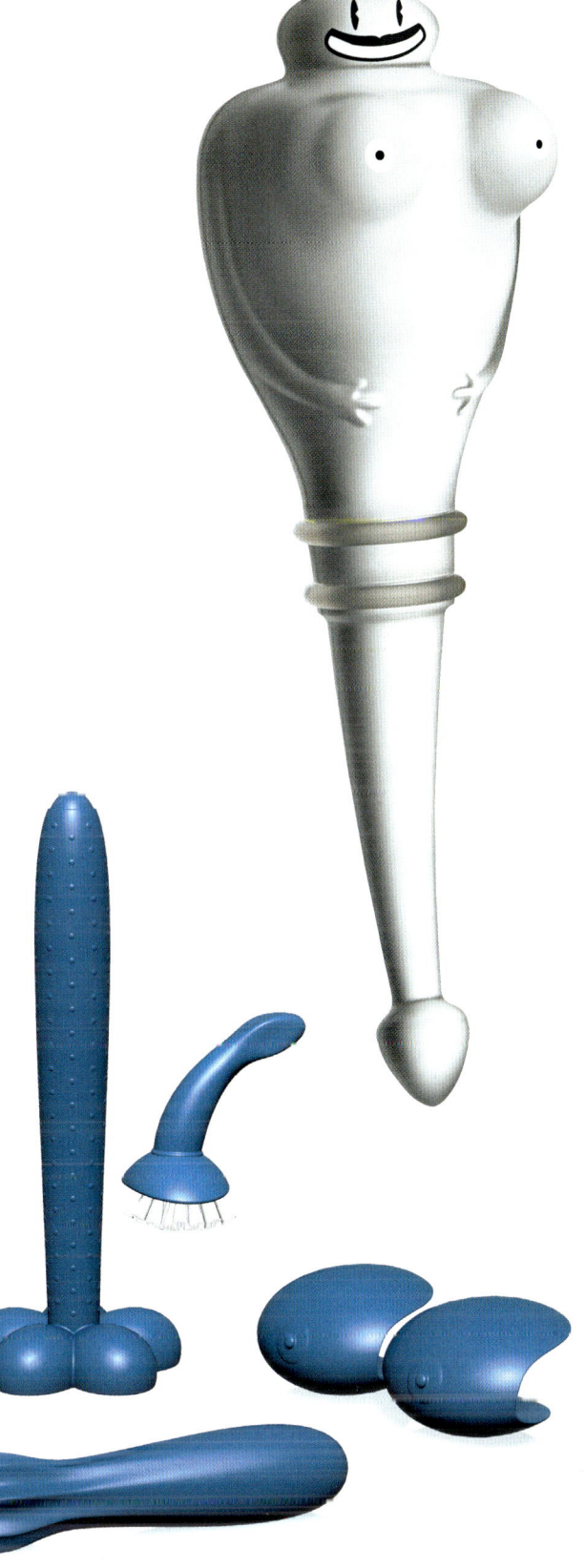

ALOE | 2008
By Kiko Gaspar & Miguel Abarca (ES)

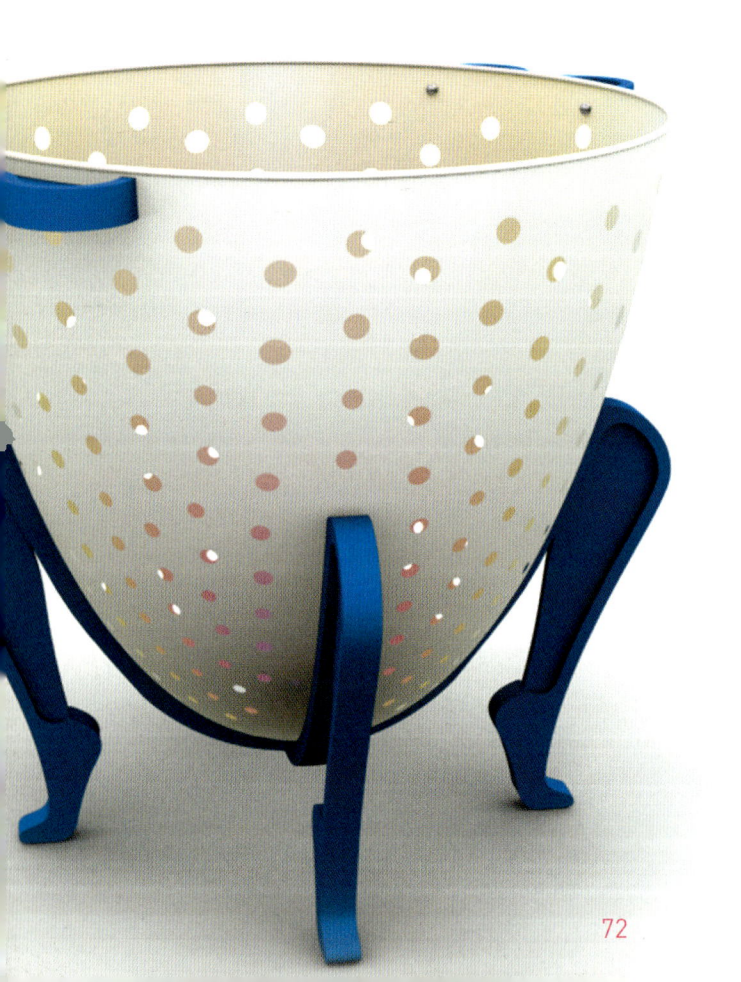

Dildo in high gloss rigid polymer, inspired by the aloe vera plant. 'Aloe' comes packaged in a pot and the function only becomes obvious when plant and pot are separated. The creators want you to have the choice: use it as a dildo or put it on the sill as a plant. Mind you, it won't grow. Dimensions: length: 208 mm, thickness: min. 8 and max. 36 mm.

www.discoh.com, www.ivaginarte.com

PASTA SIEVE | 2006
By Peter Jakubik (SK)

No spaghetti legs for this pasta sieve, but shapely specimens on tiptoe. Steel and plastic.

www.peter-jakubik.com

BIG BOMBS | 2007
By Raffaele Iannello (IT)

Jars of shatterproof glass, with plastic lids with a top knob in soft silicon, that grows when you grab it.
www.rafzdesign.com,
www.xxxitchen.com

JOLLY BIG TITS

Some men hardly even bother concealing their hell-bent fixation on jolly big tits. When an Alpine cleavage comes along in a vertiginously plunging neckline, they are liable to step, mesmerised, into oncoming traffic. Take pity upon these hapless cases, their development got arrested somewhere in their breast-fed infancy and their mouths hanging open is an unconscious reflex.

Sommige mannen generen zich hoegenaamd niet om publiekelijk uit te pakken met hun nijpende voorkeur voor stevige toeters. Wanneer er een riante vleeskloof in een gapende halsuitsnijding te zien valt, dan zullen zij zelfs domweg met hun blik van de klippen duiken, recht de malsheid in. Heb medelijden. Het zijn mannen die in hun zoogtijd zijn blijven steken. Zij willen gewoon af en toe een melkklier vastgrabbelen om hun primaire behoeften te bevredigen.

Amélie O

KISSES URINAL | 2000
By Meike Van Schijndel (NL)

Sexy urinal, turning a daily ritual into an extravagant happening.
www.bathroom-mania.com

75

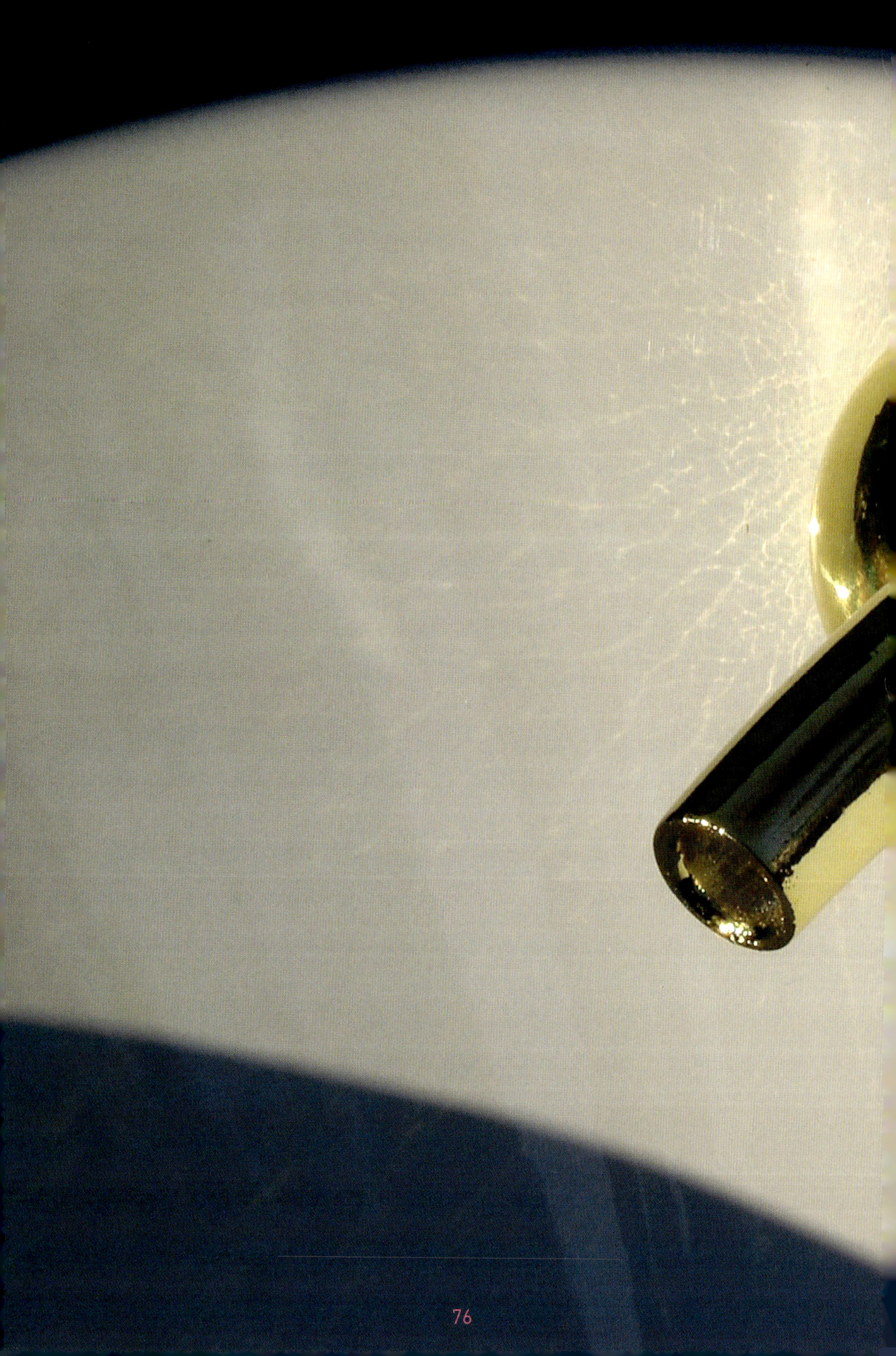

'MY LITTLE FOUNTAIN 2' | 2009
Jan Puylaert (NL) for Wet

A design that turns pouring a glass of tap water into an exciting experience.
www.wet.co.it

CUCOON | 2008
By Susanne Hanggaard, in collaboration with Line Depping and Royal Copenhagen (DK)

Porcelain condom dispenser. Nice persiflage on the cuckoo clock: pull the string and out pops the bird with a condom.

www.danishcrafts.dk

TAKE POSITIONS | 2007
By Atypyk (FR)

Collection of condoms, the wrappings illustrated with 64 kamasutra positions.
www.atypyk.com

PROPHOPOT | 2000
By Dominic Bromley (GB)

Teat ended bedside storage vessel for condoms. Made from rubber and ceramic.
www.scabetti.co.uk

QUISÀZ-QUISÀZ | 2004
By PUPSAM (FR)

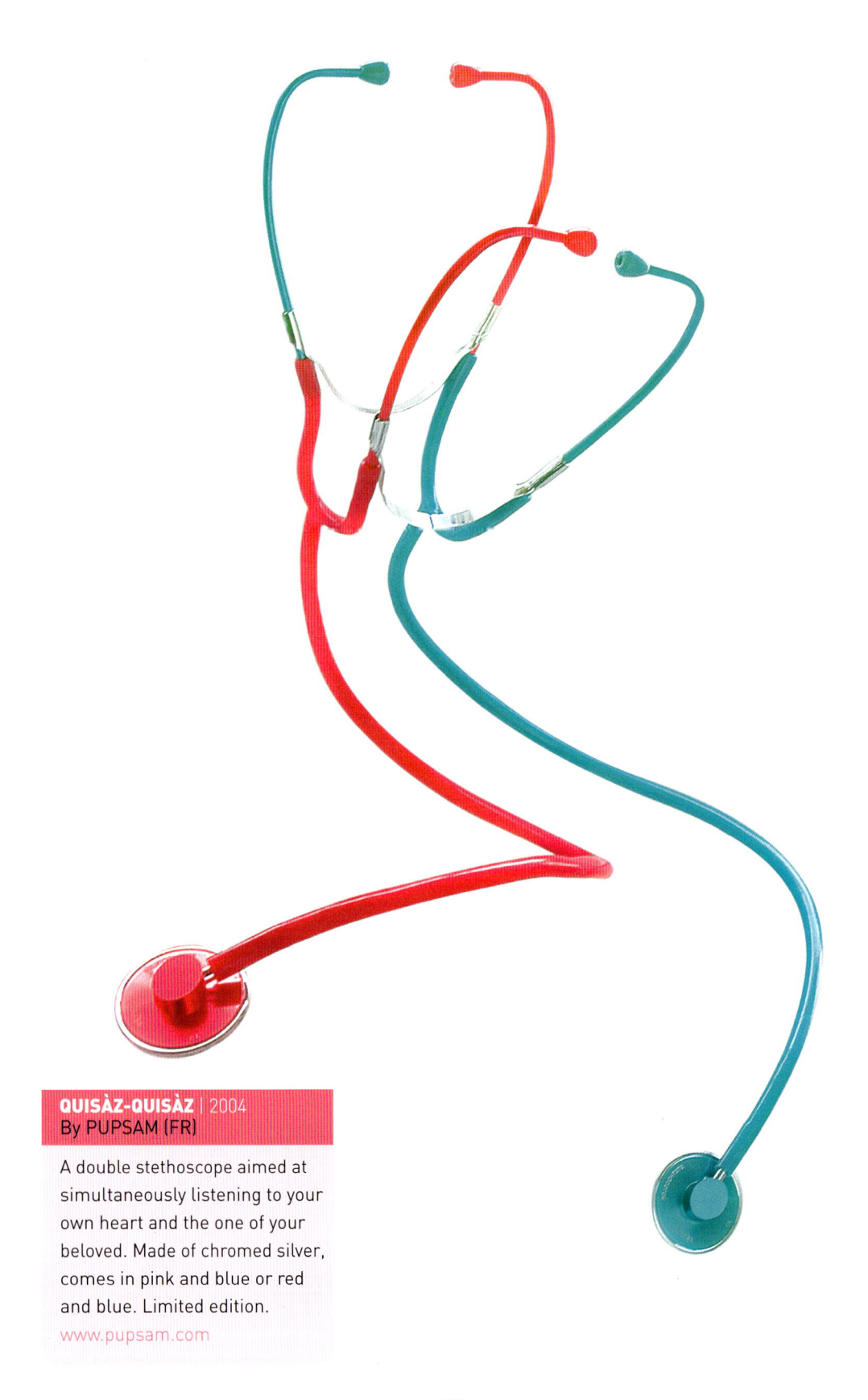

A double stethoscope aimed at simultaneously listening to your own heart and the one of your beloved. Made of chromed silver, comes in pink and blue or red and blue. Limited edition.
www.pupsam.com

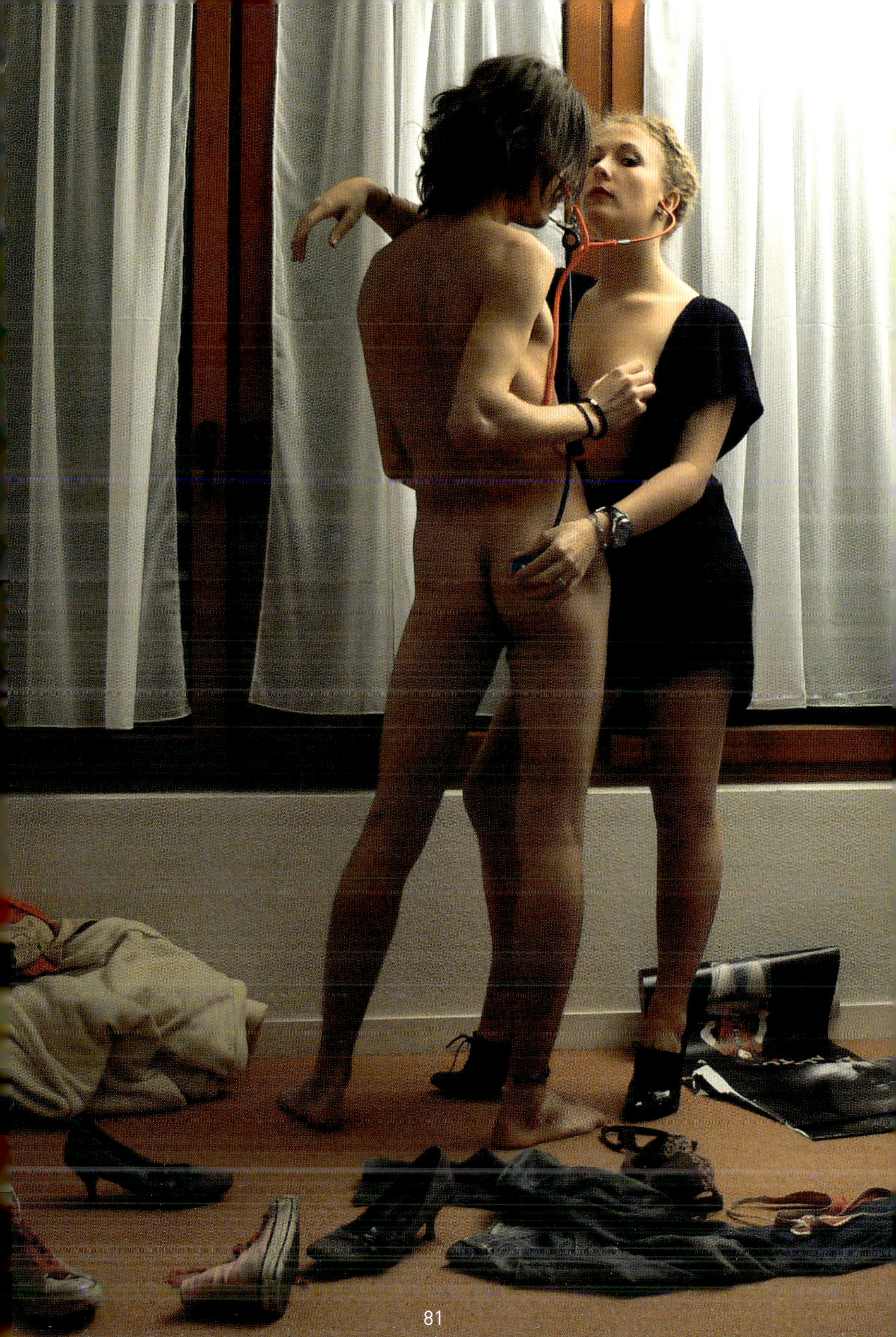

EROTIKAID | 2006
By Alexia Vella (MT)

Conceptual rendezvous kit containing: rendezvous log book, miniature perfume, condoms, feather stick, edible knickers, passion potion, testosterone reconstruction cigarettes, aches and pains soothers, bondage tapes, 2 miniature alcoholic drinks, 2 shot glasses, body oil, sex toy.
www.alexiavilla.com

CONDOM HOLDER | 1992
By Nedda El-Asmar (BE)

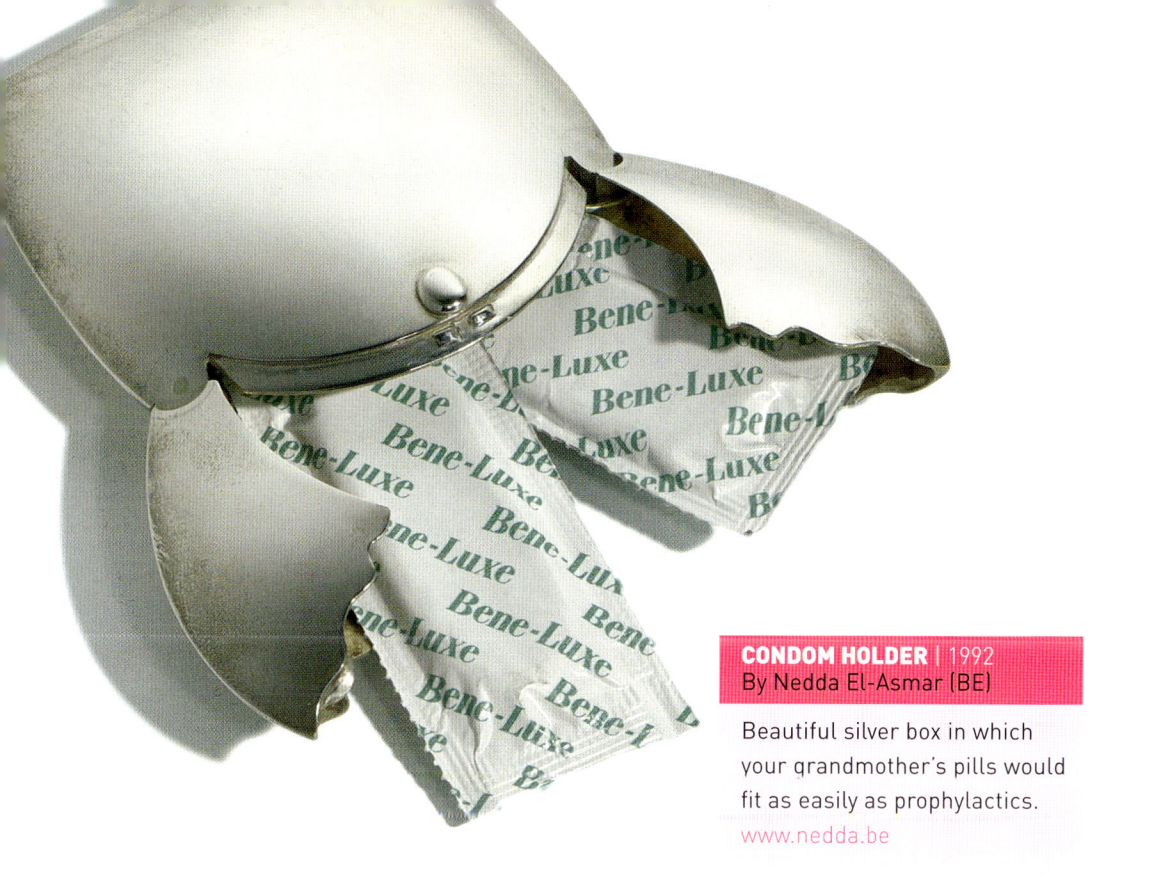

Beautiful silver box in which your grandmother's pills would fit as easily as prophylactics.
www.nedda.be

COHNDOM BOX | 1999
By Susan Cohn (AU)

Condom box named after its designer, made in mirror polished steel. Can contain only one condom, so an economical management is called for.
www.alessi.com

MVS7019U & MVS7013U | 2009
By Madame V (GB)

Heart-shaped nipple covers and bikini bottom
www.madamev.co.uk

DEVILISH NEW PAIR OF UNDIES

There's nothing better than a devilish new pair of undies to brighten up the daily routine with a torrent of sex-mad thoughts. Even if the extravagant detail is concealed beneath a flannel nightie, or a high-necked dress chastely buttoned under a woolly cardigan. No matter, thanks to the lingerie, erotomania is all in the mind.

Niets beters dan de aanschaf van nieuw prikkelend ondergoed om een doordeweekse dag op te fleuren met een eindeloze stroom van sopgeile gedachten. Ook al begraaft men de tierlantijnen onder een flanellen jupon, een tot boven dichtgeknoopte karmelietessenjurk en een wollen cardigan – de geilheid zit, dankzij de lingerie, toch nog het meest tussen de oren.

Amélie O

MVVS09034 & MVVS09026 | 2009
By Madame V (GB)

Slave suit and cuffs.
www.madamev.co.uk

GEORGIA | 2009
By Andrea Knecht (CH-BR)

Lovetoy for women, imagined as an extension of the finger.
www.exquisedesign.com

NIPPLE TASSEL TWIRLING

Nipple Tassel Twirling is an increasingly popular Burlesque dance. The perfect twirl is all in the knees: raise your arms for stability, bend your knees, bounce gently and twirl away.

Tepelkwastjes draaien is een burleske dans die aan populariteit aan het winnen is. De truc zit 'm in de knieën: strek je armen boven het hoofd voor meer evenwicht, buig je knieën, veer zachtjes op en neer en laat de kwastjes lustig draaien.

Amélie O

MVA6135U | 2008
By Madame V (GB)

Rhinestone nipple tassels with crystal finish. For effective twirling or just showing off.
www.madamev.co.uk

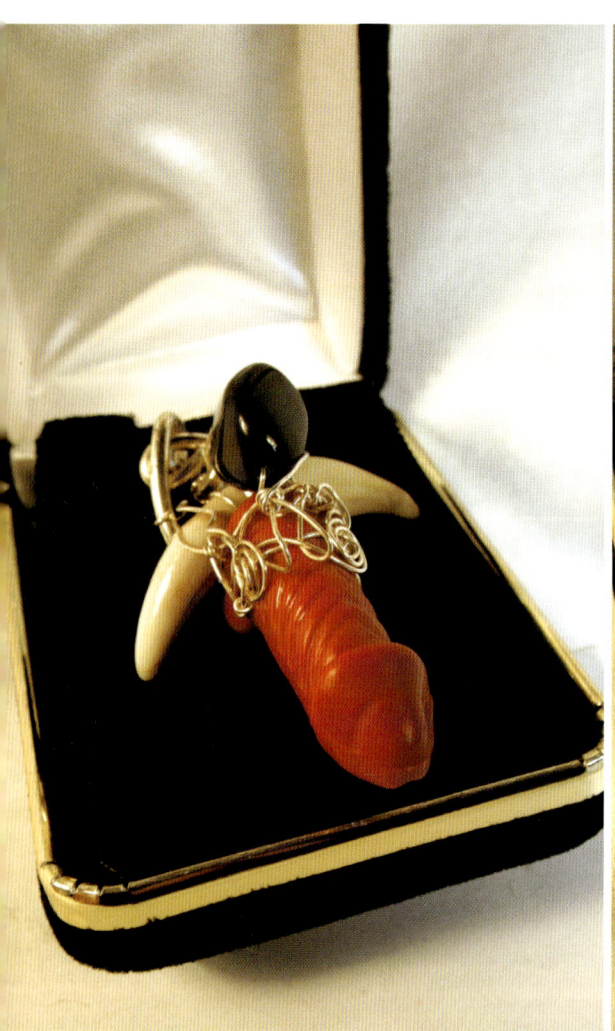

EVIL DICK | 2007
By Chris Gideon (US)

Evil eye pendant in sterling silver, equipped with coyote tooth and black stone and topped up with a red rubber, penis-shaped pencil eraser.
www.blindfaithart.com
www.gideonssilverdesigns.com

HOLY DICK | 2007
By Chris Gideon (US)

Talismanic pendant in sterling silver, topped with a pink rubber penis-shaped pencil eraser.
www.blindfaithart.com,
www.gideonssilverdesigns.com

PINK ORNATE STRAP-ON | 2008
By Shiri Zinn (GB)

Pink jewelled burlesque strap-on in nappa lamb skin, with pink ceramic dildo and 9 carat gold decorative flower print. It has an ornate Chinese satin back hanging elegantly over a leather sash for added support.
www.shirizinn.com

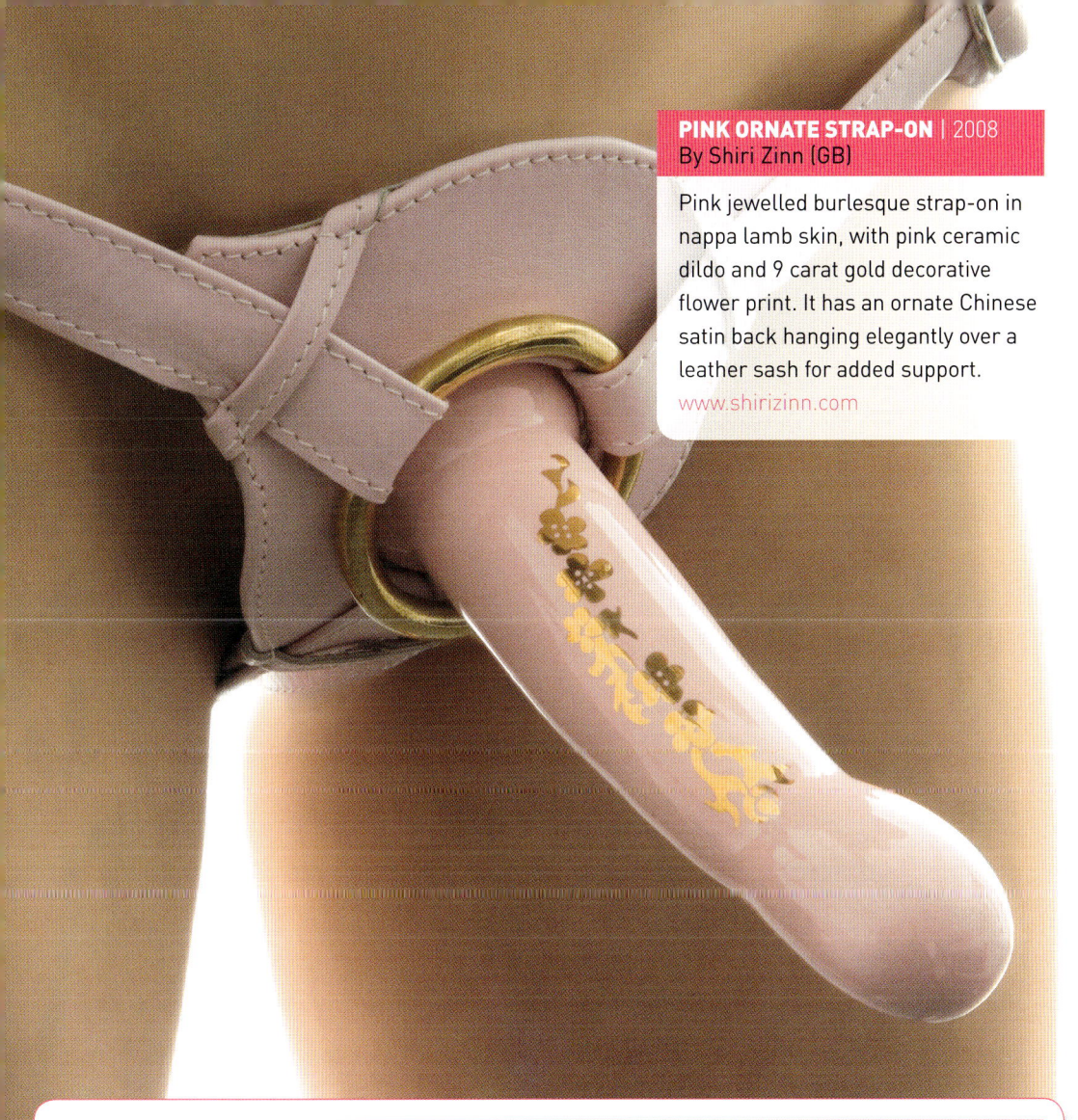

BACKDOOR VISIT

For the sake of one's own sphincter, if nothing else, an unannounced backdoor visit is best gently deflected without further ado, like by calling him a cab, for example. If a man harbours an interest in anal sex, he'd better broach the subject well in advance lest his partner feel overly put on the spot. Women should only consent to anal sex with a dildo ready at hand, a matter of sharing the love, after all. Apply liberally, with lubricant, massaging vigorously. Rinse and repeat.

Onaangekondigd anaal bezoek kan men, uit respect voor eigen sluitspier, toch maar beter in een vroeg stadium kordaat een andere richting uitwijzen. De deur, bijvoorbeeld. Als een man zin heeft in anale seks, boort hij het onderwerp beter vroeg genoeg verbaal aan, voor zijn bedgenoot zich een aangeboord onderwerp voelt. Vrouwen zouden alleen maar mogen toestemmen in anale seks met een dildo binnen handbereik, kwestie van het aarsplezier wat wederzijds te maken. Te gebruiken met omzichtigheid en glijmiddel, maar niettemin flink doortastend.

Amélie O

WINTERCOAT | 2006
By Astrid Schildkopf (DE) and Olga Bielawska (PL)

Cotton slip challenging the bikini wax.
www.missandlady.de

NATURAL MINK | 2006
By Astrid Schildkopf (DE) and Olga Bielawska (PL)

Cotton T-shirt raising the delicate topic of body hair.
www.missandlady.de

AN AFRO DOWN TO MID-THIGH

The full Brazilian approach to intimate grooming is far too radical a stance that can result in serious harm to the aesthetic wellbeing of the beholder. A frozen turkey has got to be a more enchanting sight than a hairless cunt. On the other hand, a half a bale of hay under each arm and an Afro down to mid-thigh might be just a bit too much of a good thing. Of course there are always those intrepid naturalists who are at their best when blazing a trail through the steamy undergrowth of the tropical rainforest.

De volledige ontharing van de schaamstreek is een veel te radicale aanpak die het esthetische welzijn van de medemens volstrekt niet ten goede komt. Een bevroren kalkoen lijkt appetijtelijker dan een kale kut. Anderzijds is een flinke bussel halfzware shag onder de armen en een kroeskop tot midden de dijen dan ook weer van het goede te veel. Hoewel er natuurlijk altijd natuurliefhebbers te vinden zijn die het liefst van al in een dichtbegroeid muf regenwoud gaan vogelen.

Amélie O

EBONY WHIP | 2007
By Shiri Zinn (GB)

Limited edition leather whip with ebony wood handle and pink hair braids.

www.shirizinn.com

LEATHER TASSEL WHIP | 2007
By Shiri Zinn (GB)

Beautiful, original pattern, fine leather print tassel whip, with gold handle and turquoise snake skin. Has a high decorative value even if you're not a fan of actually using it.

www.shirizinn.com

BUNNY'S CAROTTE | 2006
By Pascal Koch (DE)

Sex toy of polished aluminium.
www.pascalkoch.com

8TH HEAVEN | 2007
By Mattali Crasset (FR)

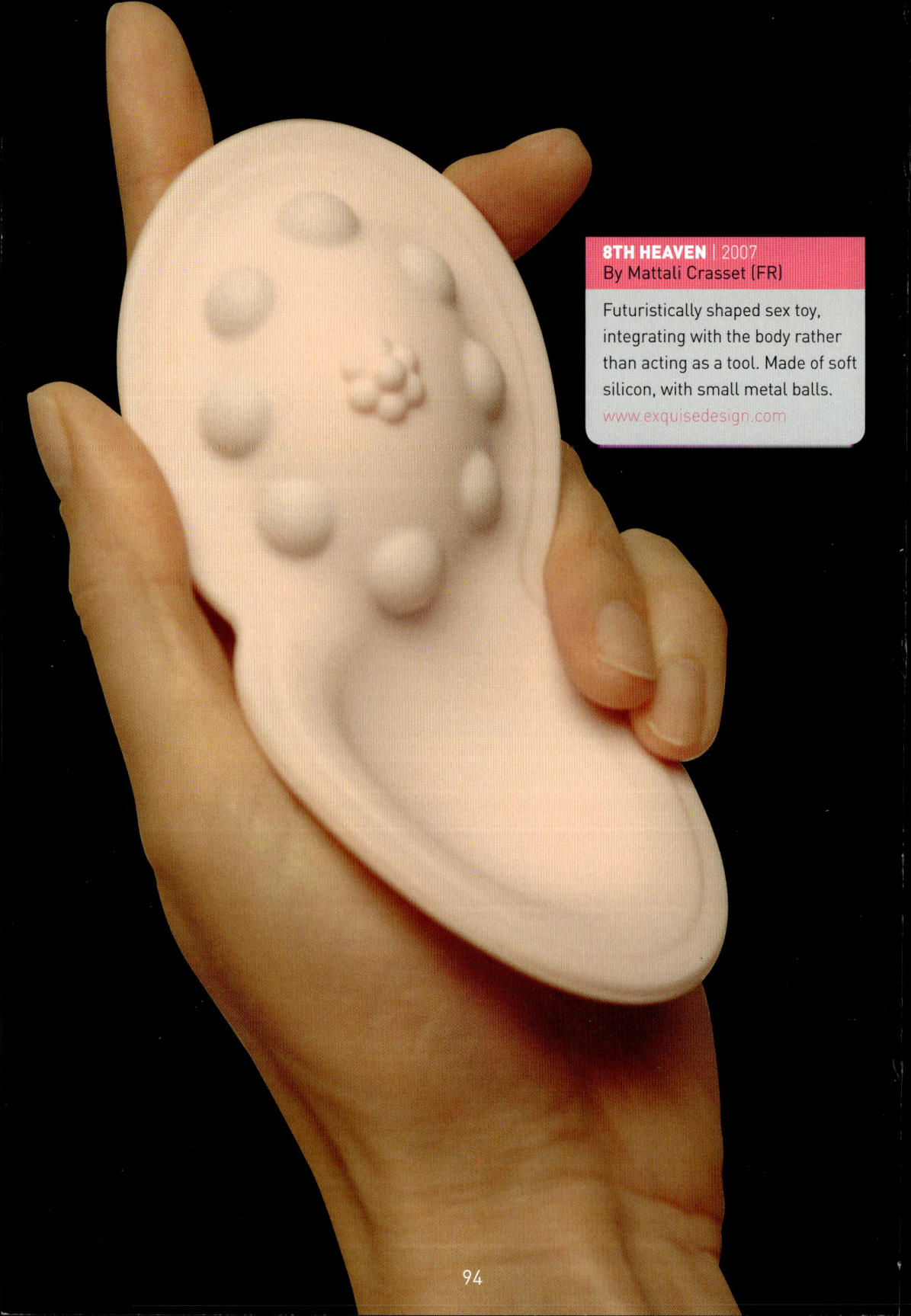

Futuristically shaped sex toy, integrating with the body rather than acting as a tool. Made of soft silicon, with small metal balls.
www.exquisedesign.com

OVERSIZED PHALLUSES

Why is it that most men design vibrators in the form of oversized phalluses and most women come up with more ingenious and discreet instruments? Because men are generally programmed to think in invasive terms between the sheets. The biggest fools immediately commence the joyride with full-throttle ramming, without bothering about the more complicated, decentralized business of breasts, belly, anus or clitoris. And then there's a second type who seem to think that the little button functions something like a choke, remembering to jiggle it at the last minute, hoping the engine will turn over. They pass a few hurried fingers across the general whereabouts before tearing off at top speed in the vaginal express lane. What an effect: you might as well try to give a woman an orgasm with a quilted oven mitt. Well the same goes for those gigantic silicone cattle prods, which are equally useless for directing the good vibes towards either the G-spot or the clitoris because they're just too damned big. And because women prefer finesse and precision.

Waarom ontwerpen de meeste mannen opvallende kloeke falussen als vibrator en de meeste vrouwen ingenieuzere, discretere genotstuigjes? Omdat mannen in bed ook meestal invasief geprogrammeerd zijn. De grootste idioten beginnen bij het minnespel al meteen met het ram- en dramwerk zonder zich te vermoeien met ingewikkelder en omzichtiger bezigheden rond borsten, buik, anus of clitoris. Een tweede soort vermoedt dat het knopje een soort van choque moet zijn en herinnert zich net voor het starten van de rit dat het mechanisme daar ergens wel warm van zal lopen. Net voor zij gezwind in de vagina hun entrée willen maken, schurken zij vlug nog even met een paar vingers over de zone waar de arme stakker zich diep verscholen houdt. Wat een effect: men kan even goed een vrouw een orgasme proberen te bezorgen met een gemoltoneerde ovenwant. Net zo is het met de uit de kluiten gewassen siliconen trilroede, waarmee men noch de G-plek, noch de clitoris op een handige manier al trillend kan bereiken wegens te groot, simpelweg omdat vrouwen meer gebaat zijn bij het fijne millimeterwerk.

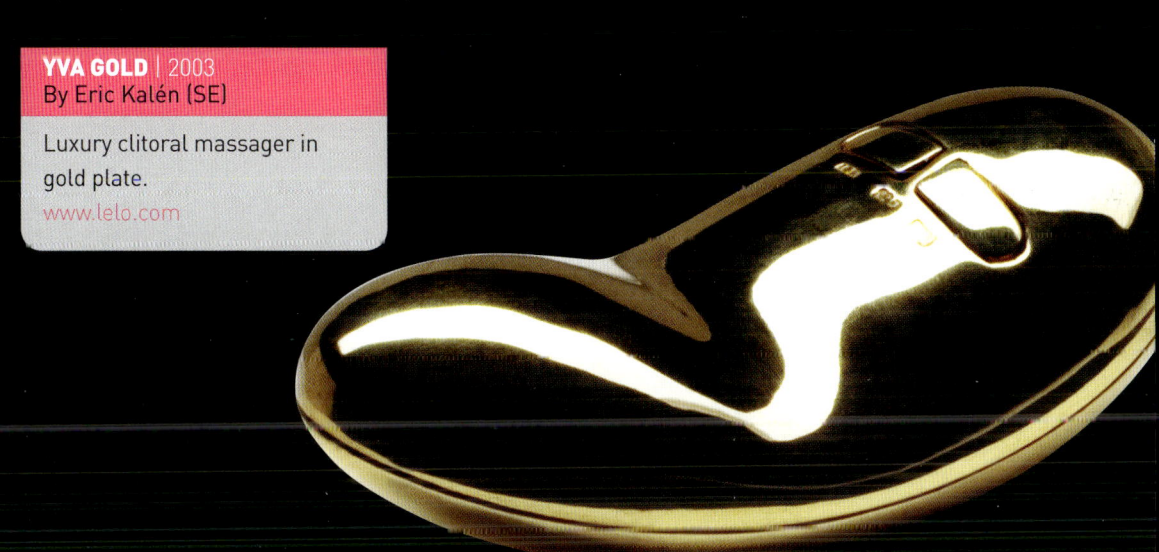

Amélie O

YVA GOLD | 2003
By Eric Kalén (SE)

Luxury clitoral massager in gold plate.
www.lelo.com

APERITIVO | 2008
By Richard Hutten (NL)

Glass dildo looking deceivingly like a champagne flute so you can stand it proudly in your glass-fronted living room cabinet without anybody noticing the difference. Produced by Royal Leerdam.
www.richardhutten.nl

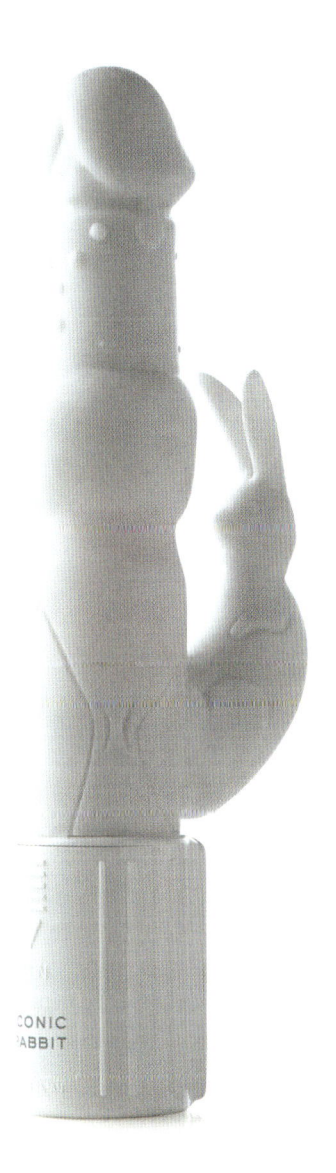

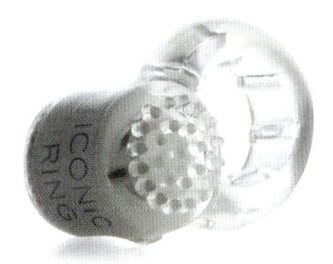

THE USUAL SUSPECTS | 2008
By Vibratex (US) and Jimmyjane (US)

Some vibrators are so familiar they have become household names, particularly 'the rabbit', the 'pocket vibrator', and the 'vibrating ring'. As a result of this popularity, you find them in all – garish – variations. Jimmy Jane distilled them to pure white, in ABS plastic, and gathered them into a single collection.
www.jimmyjane.com

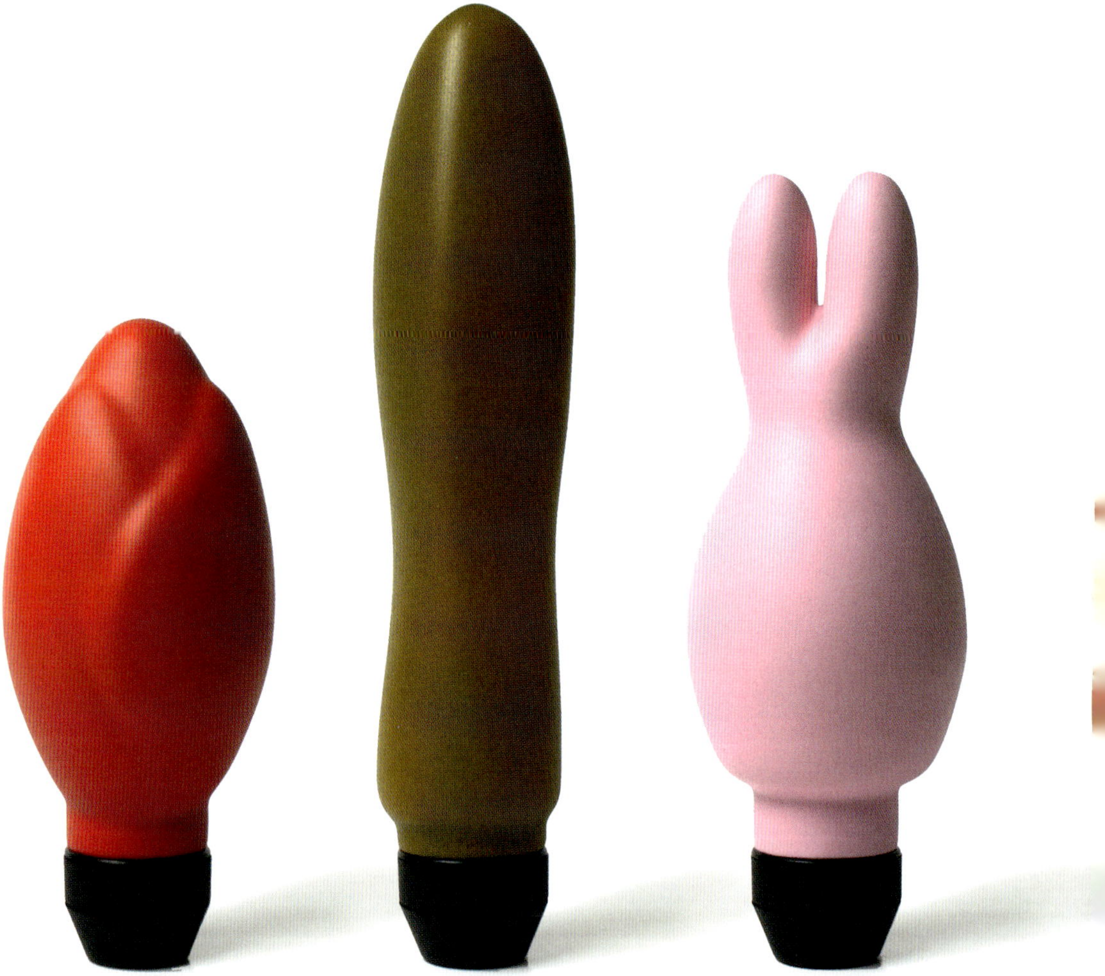

BRRR | 2009
By Studio Oooms (NL)

Complete line of erotic toys acting like the seven dwarfs.
www.oooms.nl

HANDCONTROLLER | 2000
By Conor Wilson (GB)

Ceramic tool inspired by primitive erotic art.
www.conwilson.com

MISS PINK & MISS SAIGON | 2006
By Judith Glover (AU)

Ceramic dildo's. Can easily be warmed to body temperature by holding them under hot water. Combined with the firm and smooth feel of the porcelain, they feel like skin.
www.goldfrau.net

PLEASURE STRING | 2009
By Sara Szyber (SE)

Wearable silicon love toy, micro-perforated in patterns like fine lace, for subtle stimulation. For the modern woman seeking pleasure on the run.
www.exquisedesign.com,
www.indashop.com

FRUIT CONDOM | 2009
By Morgane & Quentin (FR)

A response to the over-design of sex toys today and a useful way to recycle your fruit and veg, once past their prime.
www.exquisedesign.com

I RUB MY DUCKIE BONDAGE | 2007
By BigTeazeToys (US)

Famous waterproof personal massager Duckie, dressed for the occasion in shiny black corset, spiked collar and sporting a tattoo.

www.bigteazetoys.com

SEX TOYS

Amélie O

The point of cute, supposedly witty but revoltingly ugly sex toys for onanism or otherwise, is entirely lost on me. It's almost like you're supposed to complete the scene by imitating a child's voice while you're at it. Maybe the combination is a real turn-on for a few twisted souls out there, but I don't want to hear about it.

Het nut van liefelijke, grappig bedoelde maar uiterst lelijke speeltjes voor onanie of gedeelde stimulatie ontgaat mij volledig. Men heeft al haast de neiging om er een kinderstemmetje bij te imiteren om er zijn gang mee te gaan. Daar zullen dan wel een aantal ziekelijke geesten warm van lopen, maar ik in ieder geval niet.

I RUB MY FISHIE | 2003
By BigTeazeToys (US)

Waterproof personal massager in the form of a fish with manic, bulging eyes, for shower, pool or bath.
www.bigteazetoys.com

FLEXY FELIX | 2004
By Fun Factory (DE)

Anal chain for butt lovers.
www.funfactory.de

RAIN | 2007
By Fun Factory (DE)

Cock ring, easy to handle and fit for all sizes.
www.funfactory.de

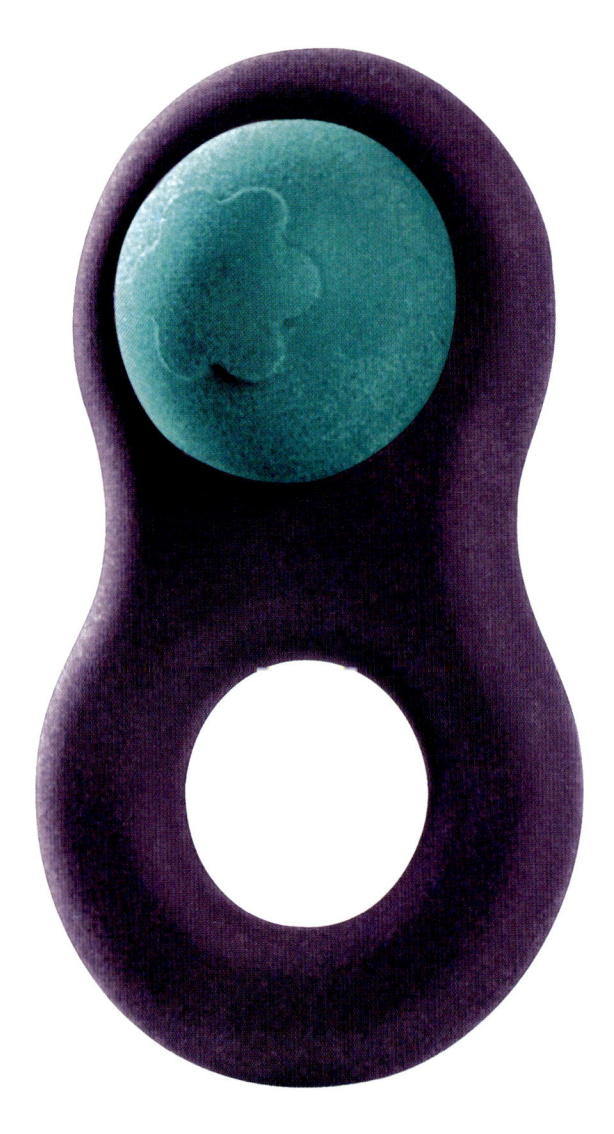

8IGHT | 2007
By Fun Factory (DE)

Multifunctional cock ring with love bud. Use ring according to size.
www.funfactory.de

MARY MERMAID | 2002
By Anja Schnaars (DE)

Vibrator with two powerful motors for rotation and vibration.
www.funfactory.de

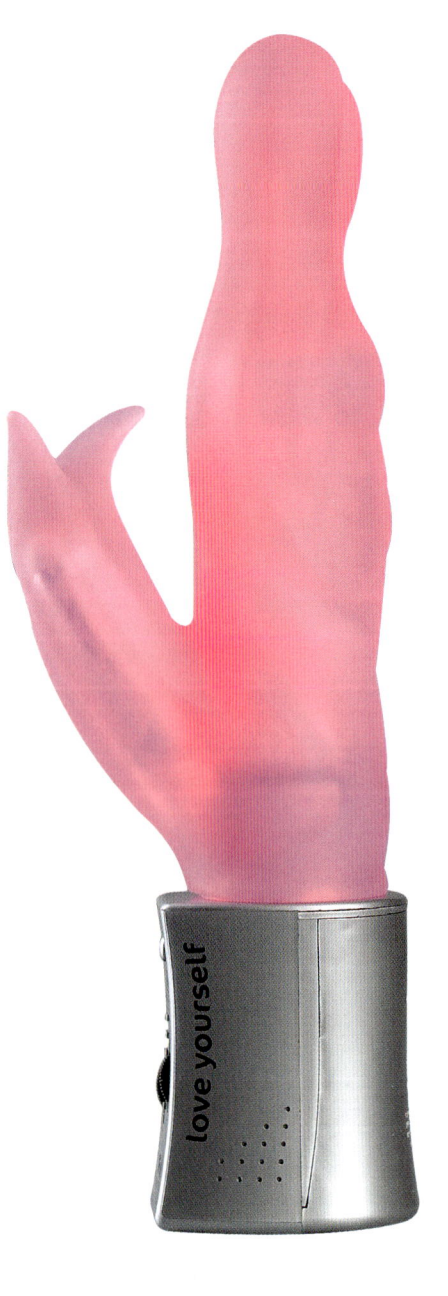

RECKLESSLY TIGHT JEANS

Amélie O

The covert transport of vibrators in public places requires certain precautions. I can remember once blushing furiously when my electric toothbrush unexpectedly started buzzing in my purse in the checkout line. In this light, a vibrator keychain seems just a tad risky to me. Besides, think of the trouble you'd have trying to keep it in your panties.

Met vibrators moet men in publieke ruimten toch enige voorzorgsmaatregelen treffen. Ik heb het al meegemaakt dat ik een rood hoofd kreeg bij de bakker omdat mijn elektrische tandenborstel in mijn handtas per abuus begon te spinnen. Een vibratorsleutelhanger lijkt mij daarom net iets te risicovol. Bovendien ook zeer onhandig om te verstoppen tussen slip en panty.

FLOWER POWER | 2005
By BigTeazeToys (US)

Waterproof personal massager with textured centre and a soft, flexible petal ring that can be removed and used as a cock ring.

www.bigteazetoys.com

LUNA | 2007
By Eric Kalén (SE)

Pleasure and fitness bead system for the vaginal and pelvic floor muscles.
www.lelo.com

THE MILKMAID | 2006
By Studio Ooooms (NL) in cooperation with Davy Grosemans (BE)

Delft blue ceramic dildo, inspired by Johannes Vermeer's painting 'Het Melkmeisje'.
www.ooooms.nl

INTIMATE MASSAGER | 2009
By Philips Design (NL)

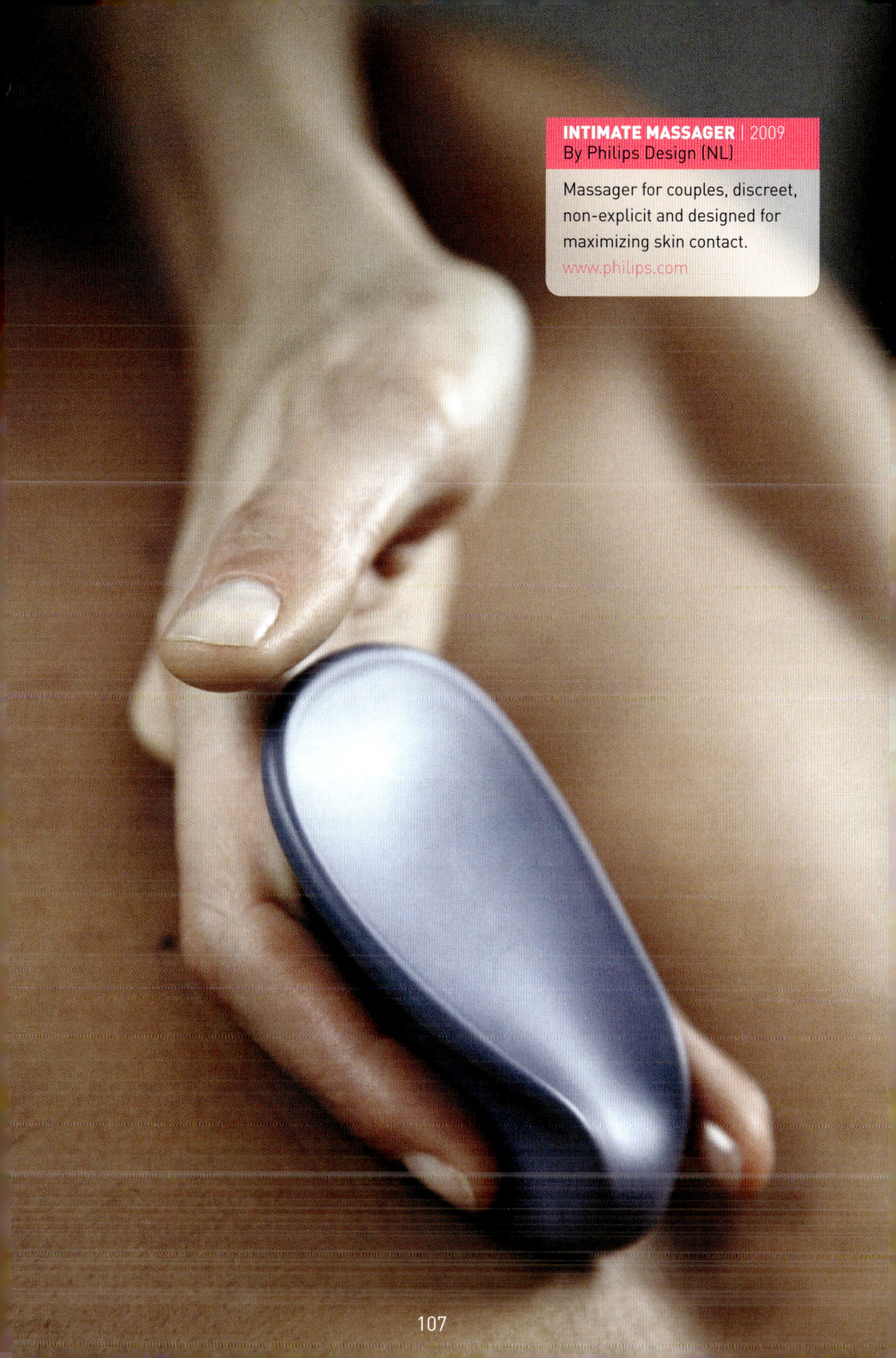

Massager for couples, discreet, non-explicit and designed for maximizing skin contact.
www.philips.com

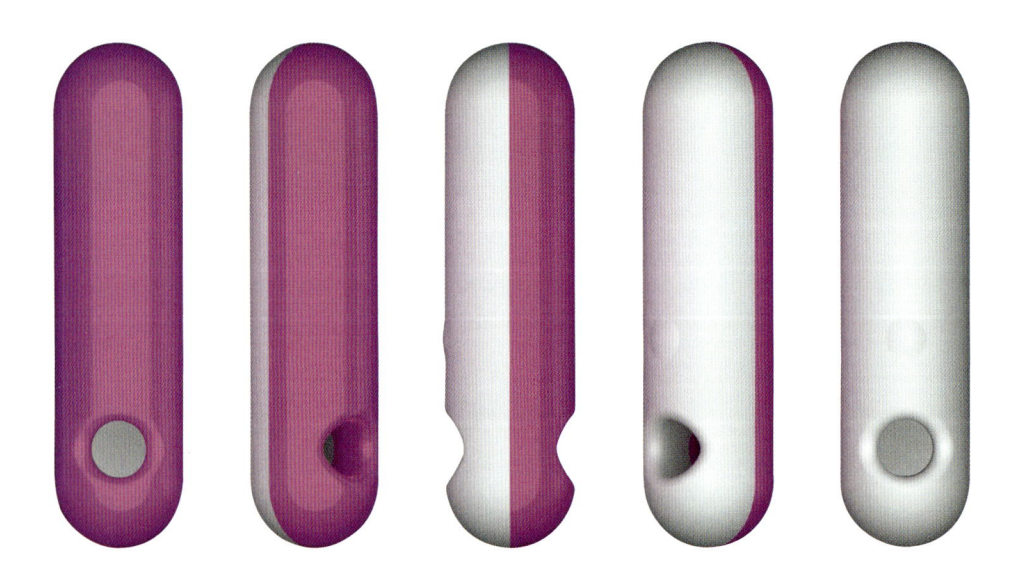

BUZZLET | 2008
By Miuzu (US)

Discreet but powerful vibrator.
Dimensions: 10 cm, Ø 2,5 cm.
www.miuzu.com

OHMIBOD | 2006
By OhMiBod (US)

Vibrator to plug into your iPod, iPhone or any other music player and it automatically vibrates to the rhythm and intensity of your favourite tunes.
www.ohmibod.com

POWERED BY JIMMYJANE | 2009
By Arik Levy (IL)

Wooden jar with an extractable vibrator. Easy storage, making a change from the habitual bedside drawer.

www.jimmyjane.com

LARGE BLACK STOPPER | 2008
By Shiri Zinn (GB)

Solid glass stopper, hand made from molten organic glass.
www.shirizinn.com

OH MY GOD | 2007
By Eric Berthes (FR)

Pewter sex toy for Sonia Rykiel.
www.ericberthes.com

ISCREAM | 2004
By Murielle Scherre (BE)

Ice cream shaped dildo made of silicone, in an innocent pink colour.
www.lafilledo.com

iscream

GLASS VAGINAL EGG SET | 2008
By Shiri Zinn (GB)

Solid glass eggs, the perfect tool for strengthening the pelvic floor muscles.
www.shirizinn.com

TONE THE VAGINAL MUSCLES

Underwear is a must should one choose, whilst going about one's daily tasks, to tone the vaginal muscles with Geisha balls. That is why it is highly unadvisable to go to the office without putting on a pair. Just imagine you're gliding airily down the stairs in your stiletto pumps, when, whoopsie, a nasty fall lands you upturned at the foot of the stairs, spread-legged like a starfish with your dress over your head, massage balls skittering across the parquet floor, coming to a halt just in front of your baffled boss who responds instinctively by grabbing a golf club from the corner of his office and deftly driving those suckers back in their hole. Think about it. A word to the wise: wear underpants. The ass you save could be your own.

Ondergoed is levensnoodzakelijk wanneer men overdag de vagina met geishaballen wil trainen. Ga daarom nooit, nee nooit, uit werken zonder slip. Stelt u zich even voor dat u ten kantore, de trap afschrijdend op uw nieuwe naaldhakken, ongelukkig ten val komt, helemaal tot aan de voet van de trap, de benen gespreid, met een opwaaierend rokje, uw steranijs in de lucht, massageballen stuiterend over het parket, tot vlak voor de voeten van uw baas die daarop geheel verward een golfstick uit de hoek grist om de krengen terug in hun hole te krijgen. Voilà. Eén advies: draag altijd een onderbroek.

Amélie O

DELIGHT | 2005-2007
By Heinrich Brüggemann (DE)

Vibrator combining external stimulation with a simultaneous insertable function.
www.funfactory.de

BAUHAUS BLACK
By Beate Uhse (DE)

Vibrator for the historically conscious.
www.beate-uhse.org

ORGASMATRON 3000 | 2006
By Dominic Wilcox (GB)

Leather-clad washing machine endowed with a saddle, bringing the fun back to housework. Instructions: dial to the required setting, press the 'on' button and climb into the saddle.

www.dominicwilcox.com

LITTLE DEVIL | 2004
By Peter Jakubik (SK)

Silicone butt plug.
www.peter-jakubik.com

SABAR | 2006
By Michael Young (GB)

Vibrator with sensuous curves, scooped out side panels for maximum vibration and a light switch for speed change.
www.michael-young.com

SABAR LOVE HEART | 2006
By Michael Young (GB)

350 vibrating sex toys in the form of a love heart. A woman's Walhalla. Or nightmare?
www.michael-young.com

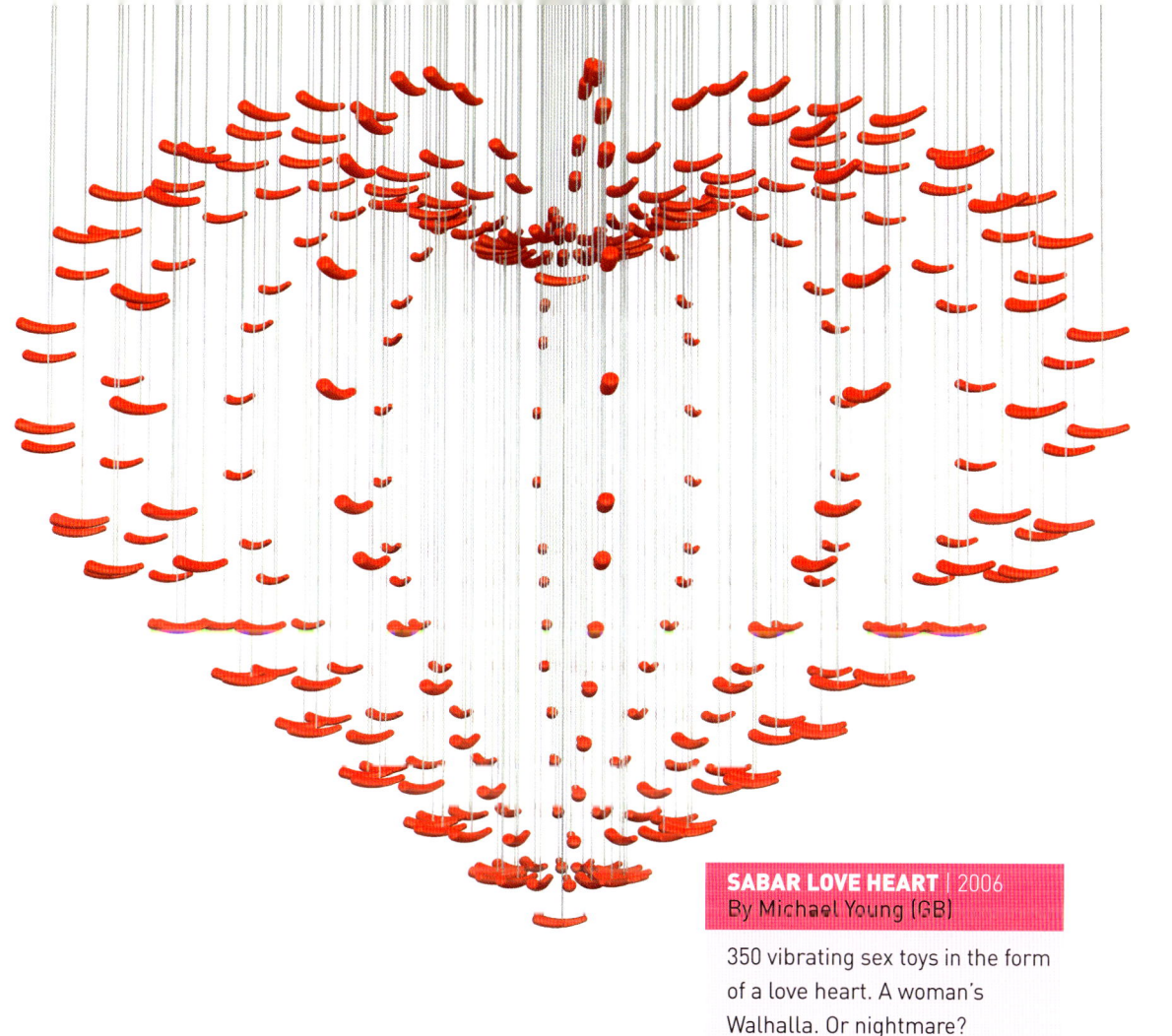

THE GOLDEN PIECE

The quest for the golden piece can be a punishing, epic adventure. One seldom finds a competent penis able to sustain serial orgasms that can withstand the harsh light of day. Even the most heroic of members, regardless of age, will never send me to Olympic heights if it's not at least a bit decent to look at. Namely: smegma-free, of a reasonable length, not too small, not too big, comfortable in girth and attractive in colour. Yes, I'm a bit choosy. What did you expect?

De zoektocht naar de gulden roede is soms een penibel avontuur. Zelden vindt men namelijk een bekwame penis die tot seriële orgasmen in staat blijkt en die bovendien nog eens het daglicht mag aanschouwen. Zelfs het meest montere edele deel, van om het even welke ouderdom, zal er nooit in slagen mij hemelwaarts te neuken als hij er ook niet een béétje ordentelijk uitziet. Te weten: smegmaloos, van een billijke lengte, niet te klein, niet te groot, van behoorlijke dikte en van een aangename kleur. Ik ben niet snel tevreden, neen. Wat had u gedacht?

Amélie O

BLOBB TILES | 2005
By Analia Segal (AT)

Ceramic tiles with discrete anatomical details that make them seem alive.
www.blobb.us

STINKING SWAMP CREATURES

I hate to say it but we are all still just a bunch of godforsaken, stinking swamp creatures with an aversion to soap and water. Our reputation regarding the body's nether regions could hardly be worse. And don't get me started on people who don't wash at least once a day or finish off their toilet time with a perfunctory dry wipe: lack of personal hygiene totally pisses me off, I shit you not. And smelliness really gets my misanthropic tendencies on a roll.

Ik vrees dat wij nog steeds een godgeklaagd stinkend moerasvolk zijn dat water en zeep schuwt. Onze reputatie in de lagere regionen van het lichaam is misschien zelfs lamentabel. Wee degene die zich niet minstens één maal per dag wast en het toiletbezoek met één velletje droog papier afrondt: van vieze mensen word ik echt verschrikkelijk pissig. Mijn misantropische neigingen vallen niet meer te stuiten wanneer iemand mij met stank confronteert.

Amélie O

RENOVA BLACK | 2005
By José Pinheiro (PT)

Black cellulose toilet tissue. Not very practical, but no doubt the finishing touch for your sophisticated bathroom.
www.myrenova.com

MVA4131U | 2000
By Madame V (GB)

Heart-shaped spanker, for a heartfelt beating.
www.madamev.co.uk

HANDCUFFS | 2007
By Beate Uhse (DE)

Handcuffs of chromed steel with red strass stones and a strong Christmassy feel, ideal to tie your lover to the tree by way of an extra.

www.beate-uhse.ag

HUMILIATOR GAG | 2003
By Scott Paul (US)

Comfortable gag with a gag receiver tube for all sorts of accessories.

www.scottpauldesigns.com

GET-A-GRIP BALL | 2005
By Scott Paul (US)

Gag with a 100 % rubber ball with flexible fins, for the teeth to fit into, preventing jaw fatigue.
www.scottpauldesigns.com

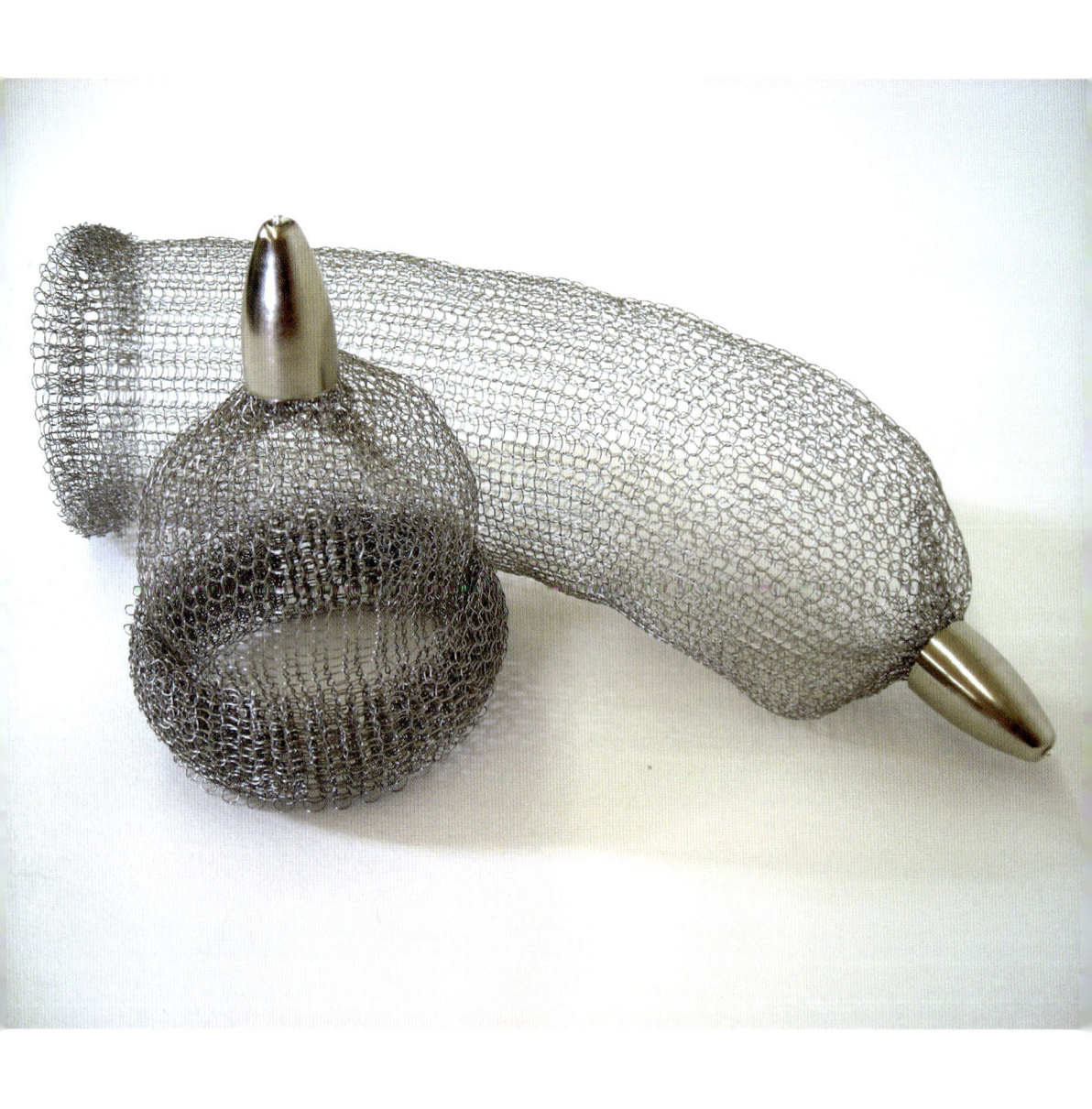

CRUEL CONDOM | 2007
By Scott Paul (US)

Metal mesh condom with hundreds of tiny, prickly metal loops. Not a reliable prophylactic.
www.scottpauldesigns.com

SEATTLE SCREAM | 2008
By Scott Paul (US)

Erotic pin wheel with 24 very sharp points. Dimensions: 18 cm.
www.scottpauldesigns.com

KISS ON THE HAND | 2003
By Nicole Benz (CH)

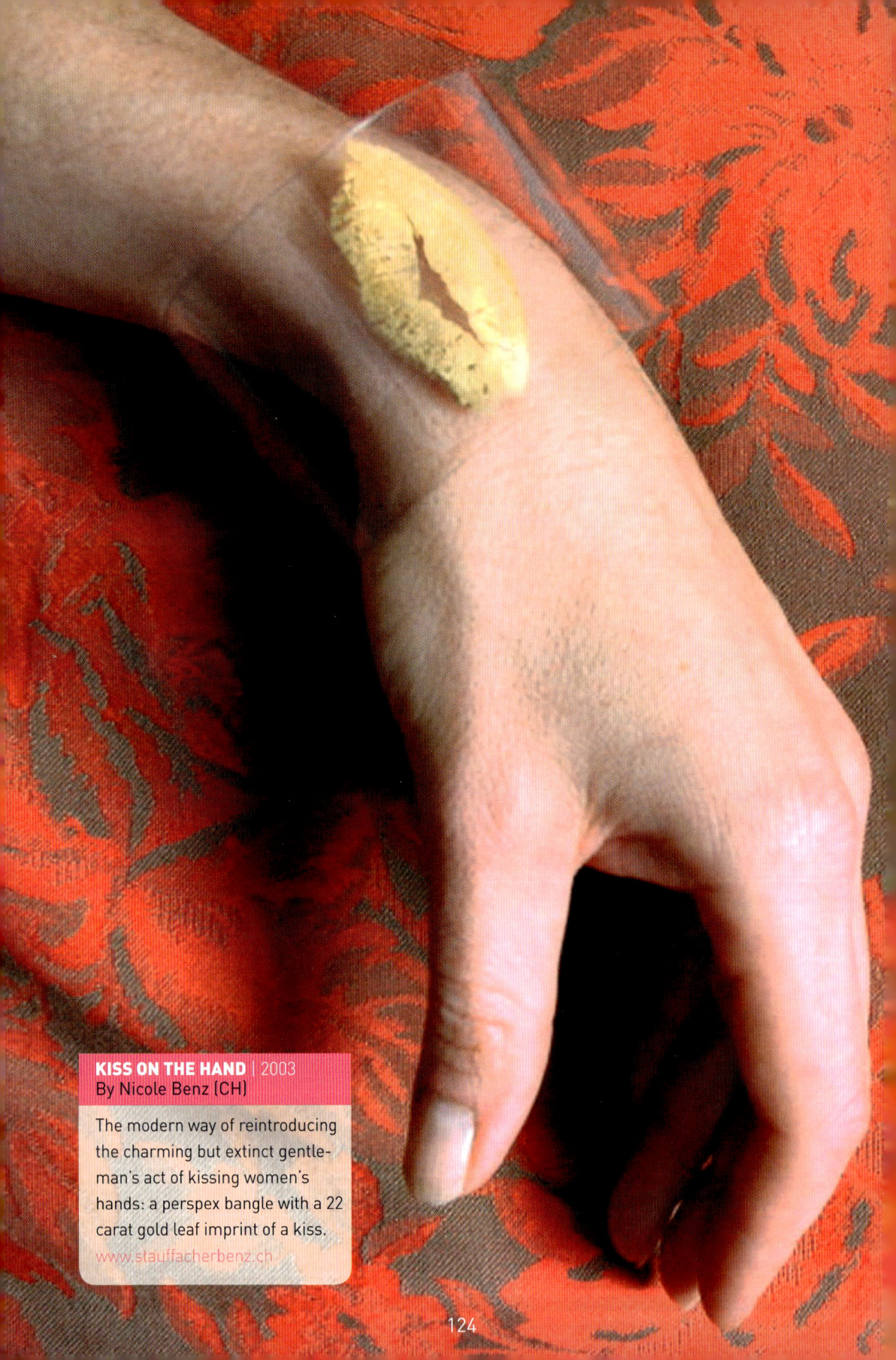

The modern way of reintroducing the charming but extinct gentleman's act of kissing women's hands: a perspex bangle with a 22 carat gold leaf imprint of a kiss.

www.stauffacherbenz.ch

LE POUFFE BASIC | 2006
By Yvan Berthels (BE)

Pouf made of synthetic fabric and foam. Strange meeting of baroque and minimalism.
www.lecouchon.com

GIANT HIGH HEEL SHOE SCULPTURE | 2002
By Bruce Gray (US)

Hand-sculpted, painted steel.
Dimensions: 178 x 152 x 66 cm.

www.brucegray.com

ULTRA-HIGH SPIKES

Stiletto heels can instantly make a woman tall, thin and deliciously sexy. Men really dig ultra-high spikes. Unfortunately, they're kidding themselves. Turns out that, while a heel of average height can significantly tighten the muscles of the vagina and pelvic floor (according to a scientific experiment anyway), those 4-inch-plus jobs are actually going to have the opposite effect. That elegant swivel-hipped stride comes at a cost: it takes so much effort that pretty well all the muscles south of the bellybutton are going to become hopelessly cramped. Pity the man who becomes entangled in those knots.

Stiletto's zijn in staat om een vrouw groot, slank en uitnodigend sexy te maken. Mannen geilen op fijne, ultrahoge hakken. Helaas, ze ijlen. Want waar een hak van gemiddelde hoogte de bekkenbodem- en vaginaspieren aanzienlijk kan doen verstrakken (zo beweert een wetenschappelijk experiment toch), lijkt het met een hak vanaf 11 cm eerder de foute richting uit te gaan. Een elegant loopje kost daarmee namelijk zoveel moeite dat alle spieren vanaf het middenrif onherroepelijk verkrampt zullen raken. Wee de man die daarin blijft vastzitten.

Amélie O

SHOE FETISH #2 | 2008
By Bruce Gray (US)

Painted steel wall sculpture.
Dimensions: 66 x 122 x 5 cm
www.brucegray.com

PRIVATE DANCER | 2009
By Jan Puylaert (NL)

Multifunctional lamp, inspired by the upcoming trend in pole-dancing. Produced by Metal Spot.
www.metalspot.com

SEX WITH A SUPERIOR

If you have never ventured to get it on with your boss, then there will surely come a day when you will lament, wheezing through your dentures, that you let the chance slip by in your younger days. And here's the reason why: sex with a superior may entail certain complications, but if you can factor those in ahead of time, then you're in for a fornicatory feast of rare distinction. The potent mixture of multi-layered power games will leave you with an insatiable fever to fuck, plus an extra motivation to be a happy and productive member of the workforce. But it's always a good idea to do a little strategic planning in advance. And some stone cold hosiery can't hurt either.

Als u het nog nooit heeft aangedurfd om het eens aan te leggen met uw superieur, dan zal u zichzelf toch binnen afzienbare tijd moeten verwijten, rochelend en rammelend met uw looprek, dat u die kans heeft laten liggen in uw goede dagen. En wel hierom: seks met een meerdere brengt weliswaar complicaties met zich mee, maar als men die bij voorbaat kan incalculeren, wordt het copuleren een feest waar men de grandeur niet van mag onderschatten. Twee vormen van macht vermengen levert u terdege een onstilbare neukdrang op, plus een extra motivatie om goedgezind naar het werk te trekken. Het vergt natuurlijk allemaal wel enig lucide voorbereidingswerk. En af en toe een ravissant paar kousen.

Amélie 0

SPIN ME | 2008
By Jimmyjane (US)

Elegant custom bottle, containing provocative adventure strips for fun and play. Instructions: spin – read – obey – repeat.

www.jimmyjane.com

PRETTYPRETTY | 2006
By Kabiljo Dejana (AT)

Stools topped with coiffed horsehair. The hair needs careful daily grooming if you want to avoid your seats suffering from a 'bed head'.
www.kabiljo.com

PLUMERO | 2007
By Elsa Viegas (ES)

Plumy tickler made of Marabu feathers.
www.bijouxindiscrets.com

PARADISE FOUND FINE EROTIC JEWEL TOOLS | 2009
By Betony Vernon (GB-US)

Handcrafted body ornament, glorifying the innate human instinct to attract.
www.paradisefound.it

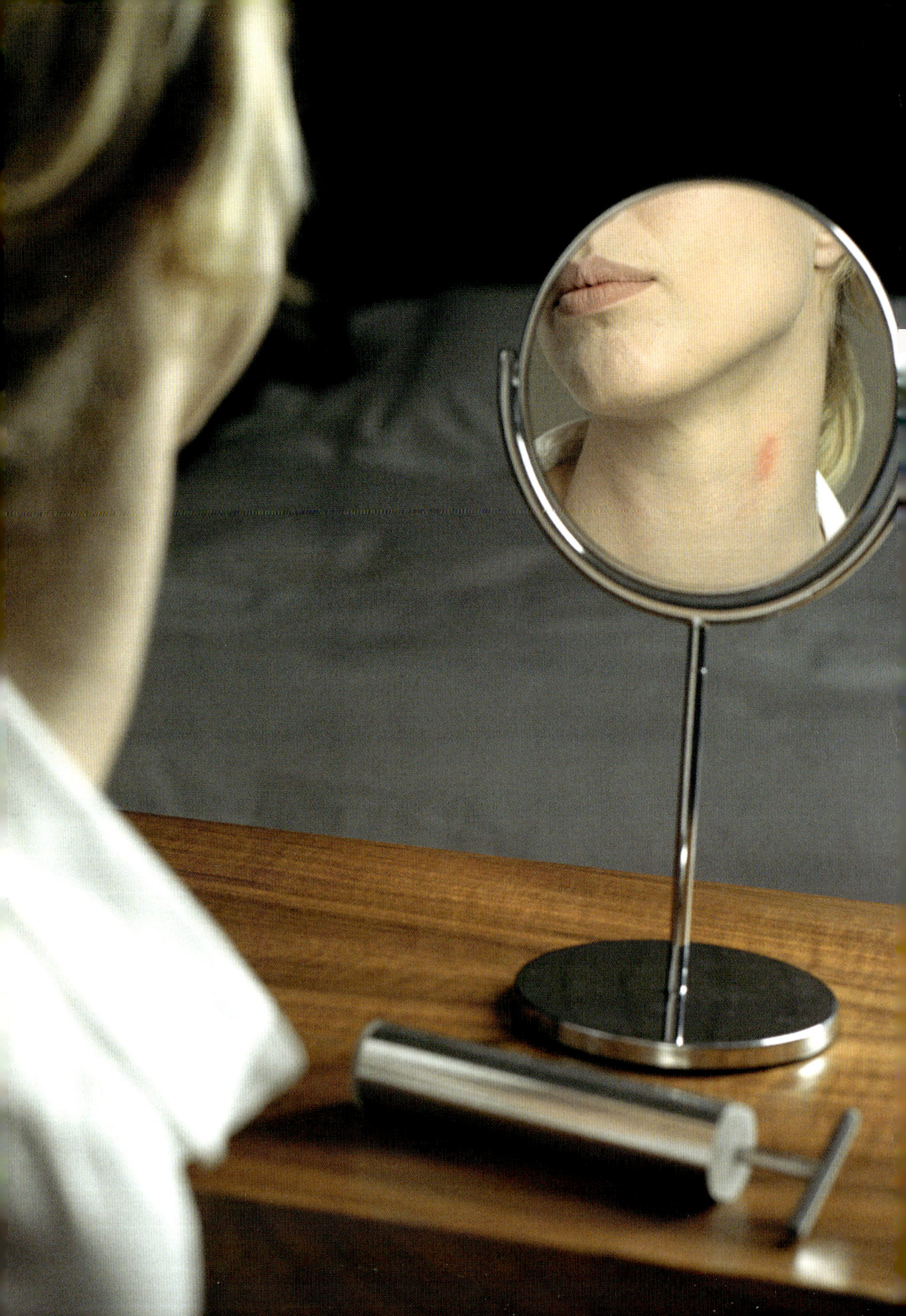

TRACES OF AN IMAGINARY AFFAIR | 2006
By Björn Franke (GB)

Jealousy kit, containing tools to create an imaginary affair. With these tools, you can misleadingly make bite marks, carpet burns and whatever, on your body. The kit also contains probes of perfume, lipstick and hair to apply to body or clothes. To keep your partner on their toes.

www.bjornfranke.com

GREEN-EYED INSECURITY

In overcivilised countries, jealousy is regarded as one of the baser emotions to which intelligent, reasonable and cultivated creatures should not lower themselves. This causes many women to suppress their natural instincts upon the suspicion that their partner's thoughts are straying. But never fear: this modern form of quiet revenge is just the solution. With a few clever aids, nowadays it's child's play to reduce a man to a snivelling heap of green-eyed insecurity, so that he can see what it's like for himself. What can we say, civilisation works in mysterious ways.

Jaloezie lijkt in overgeciviliseerde landen een hoogst verderfelijke gemoedstoestand waartoe verstandige, mentaal ontvoogde wezens zich niet mogen verlagen. Veel vrouwen weigeren daarom te handelen naar hun instincten bij het vermoeden dat hun man van sappiger weiden droomt. Maar zie: een moderne vorm van stille vergelding biedt het juiste alternatief. Met een paar slimme hulpmiddelen wordt het tegenwoodig zowaar een peulenschil om de man op zijn beurt in blinde jaloezie de gordijnen in te jagen, zodat hij de hete adem van het groene monster ook eens voelt. Mais oui, de wegen van de beschaving zijn immer ondoorgrondelijk.

Amélie O

EARL | 2008
By Eric Kalén (SE)

Luxury gentleman's plug, crafted in 18K gold plate, accessorised with matching cufflinks. For the man who has everything and thinks he deserves more.
www.lelo.com

POAA | 1999
By Philippe Starck (FR)

Gold finished dumbbells to develop your biceps, deceivingly looking like love toys.
www.xo-design.com

GOLDEN HEART | 2008
By Anouk Jansen (NL)

House jewel photo frame, in metal with gold colour plating, with passe-partout and magnets inside to hold the photos. Also very wearable, though you may end up feeling like a Swiss bovine.
www.jansenco.nl

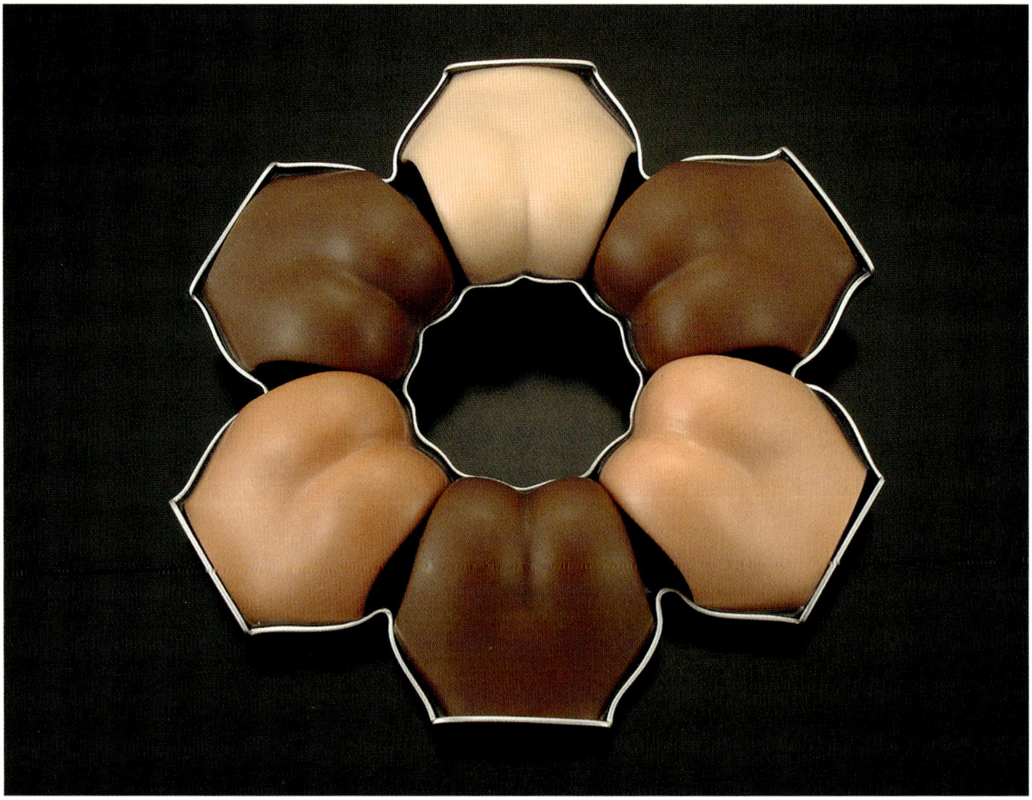

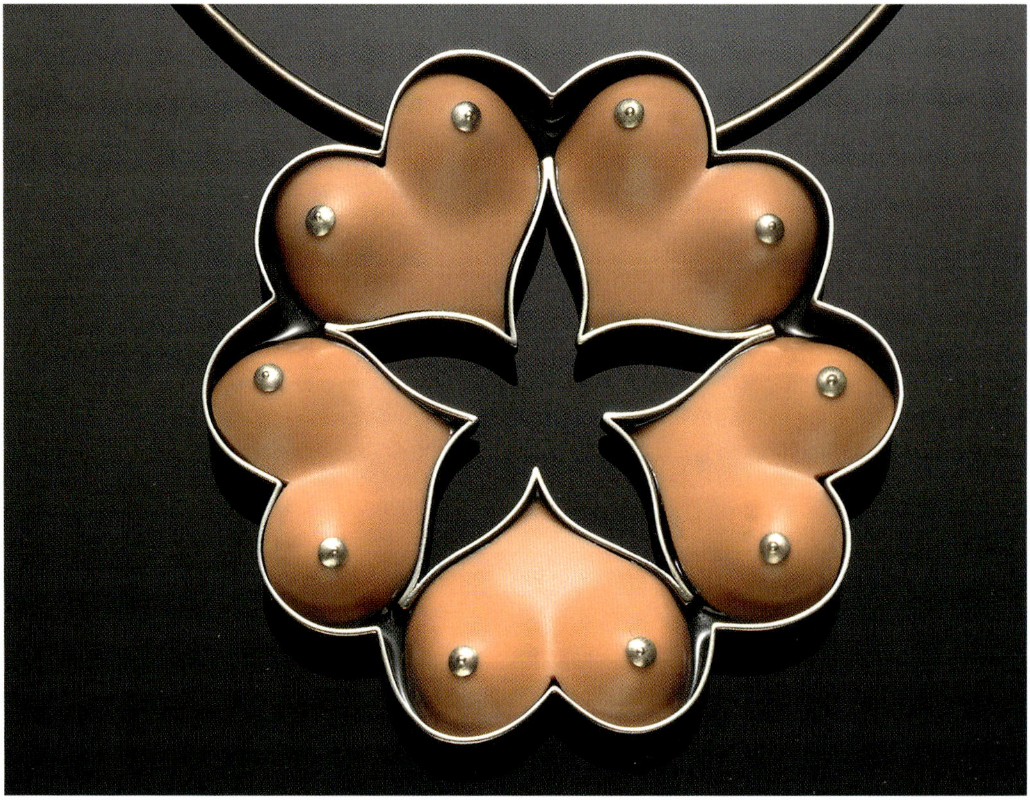

CHEEK TO CHEEK BROOCH | 2004
BUSTED HEART PENDANT | 2005
CHEST NECKPIECE | 2005
By Margaux Lange (US)

Handcrafted brooch and necklaces of sterling silver, plastic Barbie and Ken doll parts and resin.
www.margauxlange.com

BILD LILLI

Barbie was first introduced to the market in 1959. Gossip has it that her body is based on a German doll called Bild Lilli, an erotic gift for gentlemen, sold in tobacco stores and adult oriented toy shops.

Barbie werd op de markt gegooid in 1959. Volgens de roddels is haar lichaam gevormd naar een Duitse pop, Bild Lilli, die als erotisch speeltje voor mannen verkocht werd in tabakswinkels en speelgoedzaken voor de plus 18.

Amélie O

BIG BOY LE BIENHEUREUX | 2006
By Albane Courtière (BE)

Jewellery with penis 'Big Boy' in a leading role: a gold ring with diamond chain attached.

www.albanecourtiere.com

UNPLUGGED | 2009
By Jan Puylaert (NL)

Fun plastic rings that can be joined together. Produced by Pfactor.
www.pfactor.it

AMANTS AIMANTS | 2006
By Stephanie Radenac (FR)

Magnetic bracelets in metallic grey leather for lovers. Can be worn hand in hand or as handcuffs.
www.lateteaucube.com

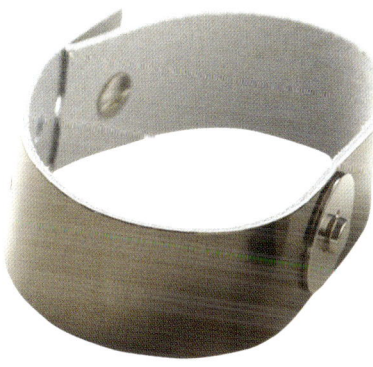

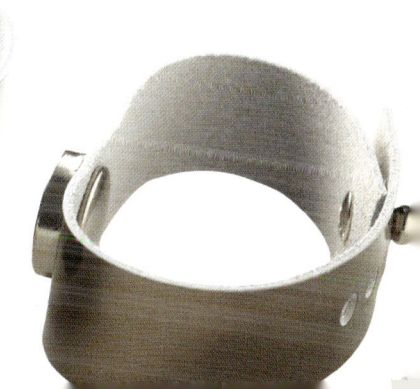

ZEROPOINTZERO | 2008
By Luis Berumen (MX)

The handcuffs of time, symbolised by a digital watch.
www.luisberumen.com

EQUIPPED WITH THE RIGHT TOOLS

Like any sort of hard physical labour, in sex it is important to be equipped with the right tools, however, jewellery should not be worn on the work floor. There is always the chance that one could lose a ring in some particularly slippery and wet manual effort. The process of retrieving it could prove most embarrassing, if not to say inconvenient, requiring you to retrace your steps orifice by orifice – especially if the ring in question happens to be your wedding band and the pipe it's vanished up doesn't belong to your spouse.

Zoals bij elk zwaar labeur is het ook bij het seksen een gulden regel dat men aan de slag gaat met de juiste attributen, maar zonder juwelen. Het is niet ondenkbaar dat men bijvoorbeeld zijn ringen kwijtspeelt in een vreemde omgeving waar het vochtig en glibberig is. De zoektocht zal behoorlijk beschamend zijn als u in lichaamsopeningen moet beginnen te graaien – zeker als het uw trouwring betreft en een gapende afvoer die niet aan uw vrouw of man toebehoort.

Amélie O

PLAISIR NACRÉ | 2008
By Elsa Viegas (ES)

Handcuffs of pearls and steel, chains dressed up like jewellery.
www.bijouxindiscrets.com

RUBBED TRUST | 2008
By Rodrigo Alonso (CL)

Preservative couple jewels: thumb rings that simulate a broken condom and symbolize fidelity and the confidence you have when being part of a couple.
www.musuchouse.com

LIPS BAG | 2007
By Laurence Humier (BE)

Stuff your bag and the prim mouth becomes a full-bodied grin.
www.missdesign.it

SMITTEN MITTENS | 2007
By James Lawrence (GB)

Triplet of mittens for two, with a double mitten at the centre for two hands to fit snugly. So you can hold hands on a cold day and still keep warm.
www.oofcollective.com

SUNGLASSES | 2007
By Beate Uhse (DE)

Sunglasses disclosing discreetly your favourite position.
www.beate-uhse.ag

SEXY | 2001
By NewTree (BE)

Dark chocolate with ginger shavings and guarana extract.

www.newtree.com

APHRODISIAC

Chocolate has always had the reputation of an aphrodisiac, a fact for which we should thank the Aztecs. The emperor Montezuma never entered his harem without having consumed fifty goblets of chocolate. Supposedly, the cocoa bean invigorates men and makes women more willing. No wonder that, when it was first introduced in Europe, chocolate was quickly scooped up by hopeful suitors to present to their languid fiancées. And indeed, scientists today have proved that chocolate contains Phenylethylamin and Seratonin, two substances we produce naturally in the brain when we are happy, in love or in lust. Alas, the amount is too small to sort any effect, so the aphrodisiac qualities of chocolate seem to lie purely in the realm of suggestion.

Chocolade heeft al eeuwen de reputatie een afrodisiacum te zijn, dat hebben we te danken aan de Azteken. Keizer Montezuma ging nooit zijn harem binnen zonder eerst vijftig bekers chocolade naar binnen te hebben gewerkt. De cacaoboon zou mannen potenter en vrouwen gewilliger maken, luidde het. Geen wonder dus dat chocolade, eens in Europa geïntroduceerd, gretig door hoopvolle minnaars in huis werd gehaald om kwijnende verloofdes mee te paaien. Vandaag bewijst de wetenschap dat chocolade inderdaad twee substanties bevat die we van nature in de hersenen aanmaken als we gelukkig, verliefd of opgewonden zijn: phenylethylamine en seratonine. Helaas is de aanwezige hoeveelheid zo klein dat de effecten verwaarloosbaar zijn. Het opwindende effect van chocolade zit dus vooral tussen onze oren.

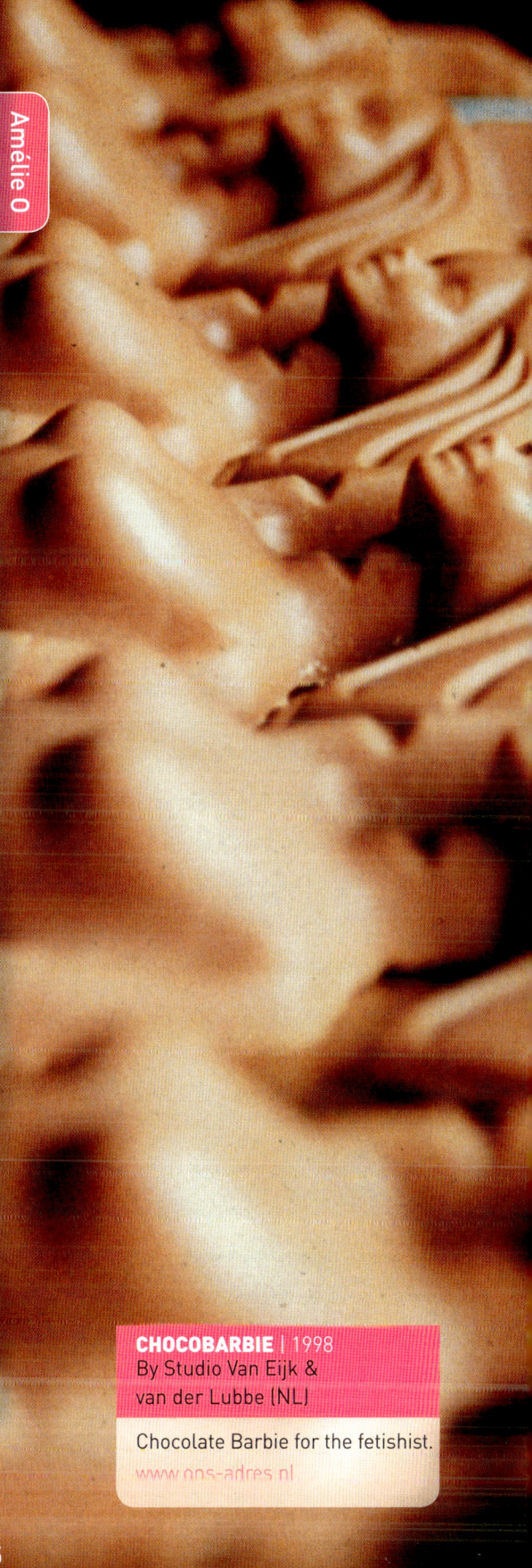

Amélie O

CHOCOBARBIE | 1998
By Studio Van Eijk &
van der Lubbe (NL)

Chocolate Barbie for the fetishist.
www.ons-adres.nl

KISSING COMFORTER | 2006
By Simone Brewster (GB)

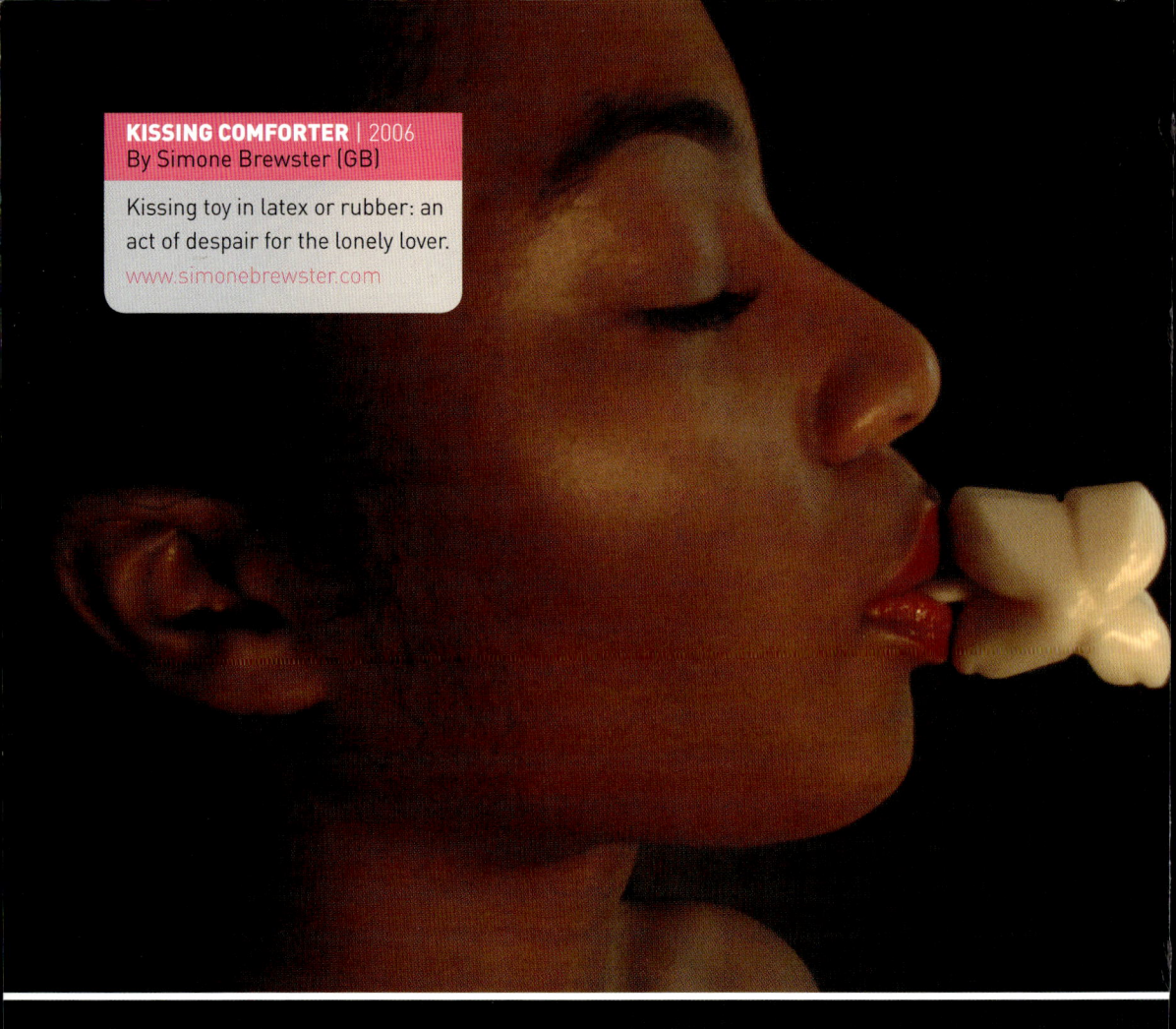

Kissing toy in latex or rubber: an act of despair for the lonely lover.

www.simonebrewster.com

OSO LIBIDINOSO | 2004
By Jordi Garcia (ES)

Fluffy little Wiener bear, hung like a donkey.
www.cha-cha.es

IS A YOUNG PENIS BETTER THAN AN OLD ONE?

Is a young penis better than an old one? Whereas those with a certain patina may lack the endurance to last more than one round, the junior class often lack the moves. What's more, the average younger penis is doggedly fixated on the endlessly delayed orgasm. The first thing a beginner is going to train himself to do, likely with the help of the most dampening of thoughts, is to hold it in, in the expectation that his partner will reach climax if he can just run out the clock. The pleasure, I assure you, is all his own, given how hard he is inwardly concentrating on his own dick. The only thing that the sporting woman can do is promptly fake a whopping big orgasm, before he blurts out 'Look mama, no hands'.

Is een jonge penis beter dan een oude'? Waar het gepatineerde mannen aan veelvoudig doorzettingsvermogen kan ontbreken, missen jongelingen vaak de knepen van het vak. Daarenboven gelooft de gemiddelde jongere penis steevast in het heil van het eindeloos uitgesteld orgasme. Het voornaamste dat een debutant zichzelf vooreerst zal bijbrengen, al dan niet met behulp van allerlei wansmakelijke gedachten, is het binnenhouden van zijn eigen lading, omdat hij verwacht dat de tegenpartij vanzelf binnen een zekere tijdslimiet zal klaarkomen. De voldoening blijft in dit geval geheel de zijne, vermits de lichamelijke dialoog zich van begin tot einde voltrekt tussen hem en zijn jongeheer. Het enige wat de ontvankelijke vrouw kan doen, is dra een flink orgasme veinzen, vóór het nakende 'Kijk, mama, zonder handen!' hem over de lippen schiet.

Amélie O

BAISER PRALINÉ | 2000
By Atelier Blink (SK)

Chocolate shaped as a kissing mouth. Or are we talking about another orbicular muscle? Dimensions: 4 x 3 x 1.5 cm.

www.atelierblink.com

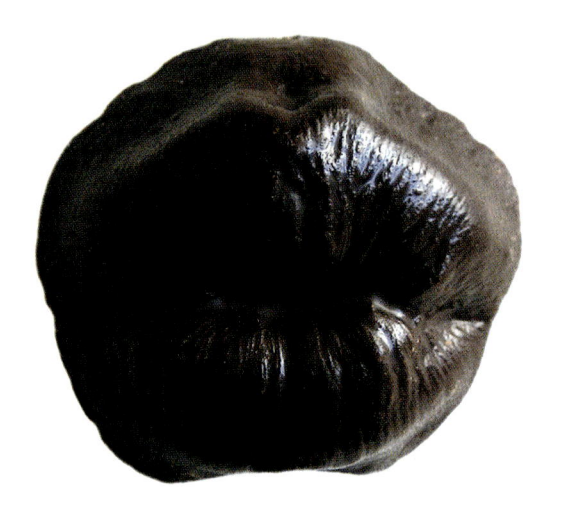

BI | 2007
By Elsa Viegas (ES)

Strawberry and champagne flavoured candy, to be savoured by two. For impatient and/or hungry souls: cracking it will spoil the fun.

www.bijouxindiscrets.com

NUITS COQUINES | 2007
By Elsa Viegas (ES)

Fortune cookies prompting new sensual adventures.

www.bijouxindiscrets.com

POÈME | 2006
By Elsa Viegas (ES)

Jasmine-scented aphrodisiac liquid chocolate and an ostrich pen with silicone tip, to cover your lover with sweet nothings.
www.bijouxindiscrets.com

EVERY DAY IS ITS OWN FEAST DAY FOR LOVE

As St. Valentine was also the patron traditionally called upon in cases of dropsy, plague, rickets and fits, the practitioners of the cult of February 14th can all go and catch one of these diseases as far as I'm concerned. Believe me, anyone who observes this preposterous high holiday of candle-infested love is in for such a shower of derision from me they'll need a beach towel. I mean, how can you devote just a single day of the year, a mere twenty-four hours, to a cellophane-wrapped version of romance that is so stale and mass produced. How can anyone save just one day out of three hundred and sixty-five for overloading the object of one's desire with sanitised, over-the-counter aphrodisiacs? My friends, to me, every day is its own feast day for love.

Aangezien Sint Valentinus ook de heilige was die doorgaans aangeroepen werd voor vallende ziekte, pest, jicht en stuipen, kunnen de praktiserenden van 14 februari van mij gerust voornoemde kwalen krijgen. Al wie op deze dag bij kaarslicht die potsierlijke hoogmis van de liefde bijwoont, zal ik zo hard uitlachen dat het speeksel hen in de haren vliegt. Want hoe kan men zich slechts één keer per jaar, slechts vierentwintig uren lang, te buiten gaan aan een paar opgelegde en afgemeten excessen van de romantiek, verpakt in cellofaan? Hoe kan men slechts één dag op driehonderd vijfenzestig zijn geliefde overladen met gesteriliseerde afrodisiaca? Lieve vrienden, bij mij is het elke dag liefdeskermis!

Amélie 0

MVA7191U | 2008
By Peter Jakubik (SK)

Readymade love letters, handy solutions for the unlettered or for persons suffering from writer's block.

www.madamev.co.uk

ROMEO & JULIETTE | 2007
By Denis Renty (BE)

Champagne, aphrodisiac nectar par excellence.

www.romeojuliette.be

Dear-oh-dear,

Even though saying this
probably hurts me more than it hurts you,
I'll try to say it anyway:
Maybe the spark is gone.
Maybe we've grown apart.
Maybe there's someone else.
Maybe you're not my type at all.
Maybe I'm simply not ready to commit myself.
Maybe it's because I don't love you any more.
Maybe your jus~~t~~ inferiour compared to you.
Maybe I feel inferiour compared to me.
Maybe it's not you, but me.

But whatever the ~~xxxx~~ reason may be,
one thing's for sure:
It's over.

Between the two of us, that is...

~~Her~~ Here's the relieve, at least you g
this handkerchief.

BREAK UP LETTER | 2008
By Jean Sébastien Ides
and Ivan Duval (FR)

Cotton handkerchief cum
break up letter, size A4.
Thoughtful goodbye present.
www.atypyk.com

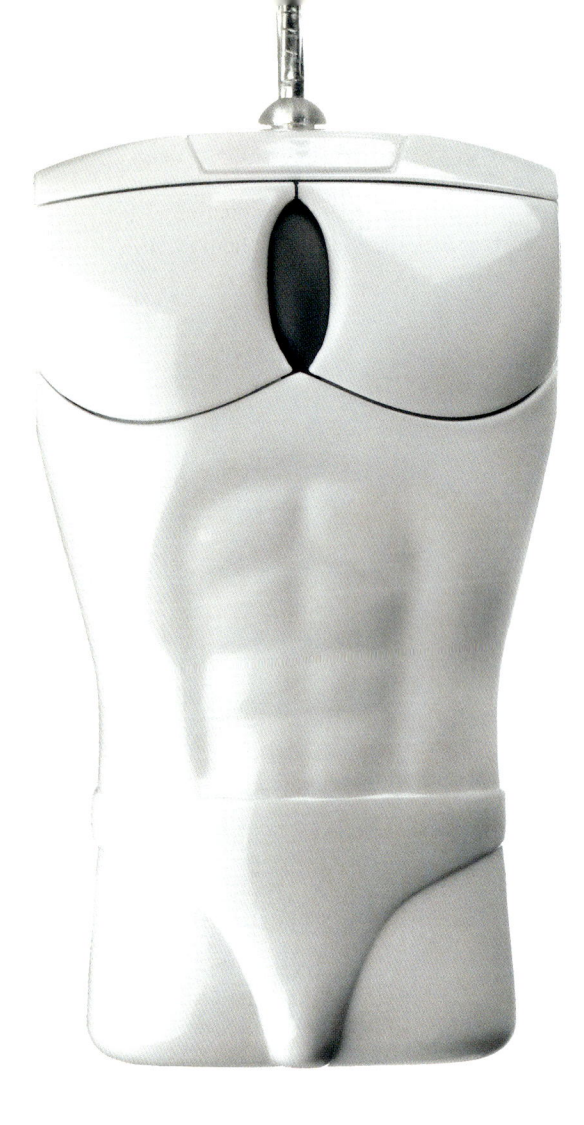

TOY BOY | 2007-8
By Pat Says Now (DE)

Computer mouses in the shape of a perfect male torso or voluptuously dressed in fancy lingerie.
www.pat-says-now.com

STAR | 2007
By Peter Jakubik (SK)

Ceramic pen holder. No need to hammer it home.
www.comunistar.com

PHOTO CREDITS

- Absolute Appetite p 56-57
- Atypyk p 79 t, p 151
- Azad p 137
- Balastudio p 22-23, p 26-27
- Belchevski Kris p 64-65
- Benz Nicole p 124
- Bica Laetitia p 93
- Brewster Christelle p 146
- Burelo Susanne p 67 b
- Calleja Gilbert p 82
- Coles Mike p 88
- Dagen Sean p 110
- Danish Crafts@2008 / www.jeppgudmundsen.com p 44 br
- De Luca Francesco/Heads p 52
- Dufour Pierre p 94
- Foli Mauro – Cervia p 19 b
- Gatti Juan (ABR) p 14
- Grand Hornu Images p 54 t
- Hans Oostrum Fotografie p 50-51
- Hass Sascha & Strasser Laura p 90-91
- Johann Mark p 97, p 129 b
- Karim Rashid Inc. p 66
- Kinet Maarten p 112
- Lelo p 95 b, p 106 tl, p 134 t
- Maricic Christian p 28-29, p 130 t
- Mofo Creative Photography p 79 b
- Mohadjer Nathalie, Schmeier Laurentius, Lembke Alexander p 31
- Morgane & Quentin p 101 b
- Mosso Ale p 131
- Otegui Saiz Agustin p 17
- Plypetch Chayut p 46, p 70
- Quad Graphics p 137
- Rogue Cécile p 101 t
- Romain Gnidzaz p 60-61
- Sablon Frederic p 138
- Studio H2O p 142 l
- Tijou Fabien p 23
- Unger Jonas p 133
- Wells Steve p 111 b
- Wilson Conor p 69 t, p 100 tr
- Young Reed p 52

t = top
b = bottom
r = right
l = left
tl = top left
tr = top right
bl = bottom left
br = bottom right

Co-ordination:
Karolien Van Cauwelaert

Texts & selection:
Els De Pauw
Karolien Van Cauwelaert

Layout & printing:
Group Van Damme,
Oostkamp (B)

Published by:
Stichting Kunstboek bvba
Legeweg 165
B-8020 Oostkamp
T. +32 50 46 19 10
F. +32 50 46 19 18
info@stichtingkunstboek.com
www.stichtingkunstboek.com

ISBN: 978-90-5856-329-3
D/2009/6407/18
NUR 656

All rights reserved. No part of this publication may be reproduced,
stored in a retrieval system, or transmitted in any form,
or by any means, electronic, mechanical, photocopying,
recording or otherwise without prior permission
in writing from the publisher.

© Stichting Kunstboek 2009

PHOTO CREDITS

- Absolute Appetite p 56-57
- Atypyk p 79 t, p 151
- Azad p 137
- Balastudio p 22-23, p 26-27
- Belchevski Kris p 64-65
- Benz Nicole p 124
- Bica Laetitia p 93
- Brewster Christelle p 146
- Burelo Susanne p 67 b
- Calleja Gilbert p 82
- Coles Mike p 88
- Dagen Sean p 110
- Danish Crafts@2008 / www.jeppgudmundsen.com p 44 br
- De Luca Francesco/Heads p 52
- Dufour Pierre p 94
- Foli Mauro – Cervia p 19 b
- Gatti Juan (ABR) p 14
- Grand Hornu Images p 54 t
- Hans Oostrum Fotografie p 50-51
- Hass Sascha & Strasser Laura p 90-91
- Johann Mark p97, p129 b
- Karim Rashid Inc. p 66
- Kinet Maarten p 112
- Lelo p 95 b, p 106 tl, p 134 t
- Maricic Christian p 28-29, p 130 t
- Mofo Creative Photography p 79 b
- Mohadjer Nathalie, Schmeier Laurentius, Lembke Alexander p 31
- Morgane & Quentin p 101 b
- Mosso Ale p 131
- Otegui Saiz Agustin p 17
- Plypetch Chayut p 46, p 70
- Quad Graphics p 137
- Rogue Cécile p 101 t
- Romain Cnidzaz p 60-61
- Sablon Frederic p 138
- Studio H2O p 142 l
- Tijou Fabien p 23
- Unger Jonas p 133
- Wells Steve p 111 b
- Wilson Conor p 69 t, p 100 tr
- Young Reed p 52

t = top
b = bottom
r = right
l = left
tl = top left
tr = top right
bl = bottom left
br = bottom right

Co-ordination:
Karolien Van Cauwelaert

Texts & selection:
Els De Pauw
Karolien Van Cauwelaert

Layout & printing:
Group Van Damme,
Oostkamp (B)

Published by:
Stichting Kunstboek bvba
Legeweg 165
B-8020 Oostkamp
T. +32 50 46 19 10
F. +32 50 46 19 18
info@stichtingkunstboek.com
www.stichtingkunstboek.com

ISBN: 978-90-5856-329-3
D/2009/6407/18
NUR 656

All rights reserved. No part of this publication may be reproduced,
stored in a retrieval system, or transmitted in any form,
or by any means, electronic, mechanical, photocopying,
recording or otherwise without prior permission
in writing from the publisher.

© Stichting Kunstboek 2009